Handbook of Trace Evidence Analysis

Handbook of Trace Evidence Analysis

Edited By

Vincent J. Desiderio
US Postal Inspection Service
USA

Chris E. Taylor
US Army Criminal Investigation Laboratory
USA

Niamh Nic Daéid
University of Dundee
UK

Registered Offices
John Wiley & Sons, Inc., 111 River Street, Hoboken, NJ 07030, USA
John Wiley & Sons Ltd, The Atrium, Southern Gate, Chichester, West Sussex, PO19 8SQ, UK

Editorial Office
The Atrium, Southern Gate, Chichester, West Sussex, PO19 8SQ, UK

For details of our global editorial offices, customer services, and more information about Wiley products visit us at www.wiley.com.

Wiley also publishes its books in a variety of electronic formats and by print-on-demand. Some content that appears in standard print versions of this book may not be available in other formats.

Library of Congress Cataloging-in-Publication Data

Names: Desiderio, Vincent Joseph, Jr., editor. | Taylor, Chris Edward,
    editor. | Nic Daéid, Niamh, editor.
Title: Handbook of trace evidence analysis / edited by Vincent Joseph
    Desiderio Jr., Chris Edward Taylor, Niamh Nic Daéid.
Description: First edition. | Hoboken, NJ : Wiley, [2021] | Includes
    bibliographical references and index.
Identifiers: LCCN 2019058272 (print) | LCCN 2019058273 (ebook) | ISBN
    9781118962114 (hardback) | ISBN 9781118962107 (adobe pdf) | ISBN
    9781118962091 (epub)
Subjects: LCSH: Trace evidence. | Evidence preservation. | Forensic
    sciences. | Evidence, Criminal.
Classification: LCC HV8073.5 .H35 2020 (print) | LCC HV8073.5 (ebook) |
    DDC 363.25/62–dc23
LC record available at https://lccn.loc.gov/2019058272
LC ebook record available at https://lccn.loc.gov/2019058273

Cover Design: Wiley
Cover Images: Human head Courtesy of Sandy Koch, Aftermarket automotive Courtesy of Robyn Weimer, A triangular polypropylene Courtesy of Andy Bowen, An anisotropic crystal Courtesy of Andy Bowen

Set in 9.5/12.5pt STIXTwoText by SPi Global, Chennai, India
Printed and bound in Singapore by Markono Print Media Pte Ltd

10 9 8 7 6 5 4 3 2 1

Vincent "Vinny" Desiderio: Thank you to my wife Sandi and my two boys, Eric and Ryan, for their unyielding support with everything I have ever or will ever accomplish.

Chris E. Taylor: Thank you to my wife, Patricia Caldwell, for her support in my life and professional endeavors. In remembrance of Irving and Joanne Taylor.

Niamh Nic Daéid: Thank you to my wonderful girls, Gill, Emily, Molly, and Smudge, for the constant laughs and the joy that you bring.

To all trace evidence examiners and trace evidence friends that have supported and continue to support the many disciplines of trace evidence and its value to forensic science, the American Society of Trace Evidence Examiners, and the authors that have contributed their time and knowledge to the creation of this book.

Acknowledgments from chapter authors can be found at the end of each chapter.

Contents

List of Contributors

Jason C. Beckert
MicroTrace LCC
Elgin, IL, USA

Andrew M. Bowen
Physical Sciences Unit
United States Postal Inspection Service
Dulles, VA, USA

Patrick Buzzini
Department of Forensic Science
Sam Houston State University
Houston, TX, USA

Brandi L. Clark
Trace Evidence Section
Westchester County Forensic Science
Laboratory
Valhalla, NY, USA

James M. Curran
Department of Statistics
The University of Auckland
Auckland, New Zealand

Tacha Hicks
Faculty of Law
Criminal Justice and Public Administration
School of Criminal Justice and Fondation
pour la formation continue UNIL-EPFL
University of Lausanne
Lausanne, Switzerland

Tamara Hodgins
Royal Canadian Mounted Police National
Forensic Laboratory Service
Edmonton, AB, Canada

Sandra Koch
McCrone Associates
Westmont, IL, USA

Kornelia Nehse
Textiles and Micromorphology Department
Forensic Science Institute (LKA KTI)
Berlin, Germany

Daniel S. Rothenberg
Trace Evidence Section
Westchester County Forensic Science
Laboratory
Valhalla, NY, USA

Ted R. Schwartz
Trace Evidence Section
Westchester County Forensic Science
Laboratory
Valhalla, NY, USA

Tatiana Trejos
Department of Forensic and Investigative
Science
West Virginia University
Morgantown, VA, USA

Robyn B. Weimer
Trace Evidence Section
Virginia Department of Forensic Science
Richmond, VA, USA

Diana M. Wright
Chemistry Unit, Federal Bureau of
Investigation Laboratory
Quantico, VA, USA

Preface

The use and application of trace evidence within the forensic sciences is an important component of criminal investigations. Trace evidence can be helpful when attempting to determine if associations exist between suspects, victims, crime scenes, and/or specific objects that may have been involved in the commission of a crime. In addition, when used in the associative context, this type of evidence can also provide a great deal of investigative information. In this latter context, trace evidence can be used to support or to refute the narratives of witnesses, victims, and suspects, to reconstruct events that may have occurred, and to develop potential leads with respect to specific environments from which objects or individuals may have come or traveled to. Notwithstanding this, trace evidence has continued to see a decrease in its use by forensic science service providers across the United States as well as internationally and it is in part the consequent loss of experience and knowledge that this book aims to address.

The idea of this handbook started with a discussion between Vinny and Chris at an American Academy of Forensic Science (AAFS) meeting several years ago. Vinny and Chris were the first and second presidents, respectively, of the recently created American Society of Trace Evidence Examiners (ASTEE). Both had the passion to continue the path to bolster trace evidence resources to the forensic science community. Besides having a society in the ASTEE to bring practitioners together and support information sharing, training, and social interaction, it was believed that to continue the education and development of the future of trace evidence and its practitioners a reference text could be offered.

The AAFS meetings often allow attendees to see and catch up with colleagues and friends, and during the meeting Chris and Vinney also met up with Niamh Nic Daéid, who was at the time with Strathclyde University (now with the University of Dundee). Niamh had made an unsolicited, but as it turned out well-timed, comment that the trace evidence community really needed a reference book. Within a day Niamh invited a friend and colleague from Wiley to meet with the three of us. The Wiley representative was very interested in our initial pitch and invited us to write a book proposal and so the journey that has resulted in this book properly began.

The concept of the book was developed around the need for updated information in the disciplines of trace evidence. No specific dedicated book has been devoted to trace evidence materials in years, making many existing reference texts out of date, particularly in light of the many changes and challenges that have occurred in regards to forensic science over the past decade. These changes have included the increased awareness of validation, modern methods for addressing and controlling contamination, the shift toward incorporating statistical analyses into the interpretation phase, and cutting edge research into new forensic science methods and their application. Criticism of some areas of trace evidence and court room testimony have also occurred and the need for the creation of standards and the development of regulatory bodies have been stressed and highlighted.

We tasked our authors to address several of these challenges in their opening remarks and answer many of the misunderstandings relating to trace evidence. This volume covers many of the foundational trace evidence and forensic science concepts, including having an approach to the collection of materials from scenes which considers the scientific implications, an in-depth chapter on microscopy, and a "first of its kind" chapter on interpretation. The technical chapters chosen include paint and polymers, glass, fibers, and hair analysis.

We selected our authors so as to reach out to current practitioners and academics who are leaders in the field of trace evidence and forensic science. The reader will also see that for many of the chapters the authors have been paired. By partnering a North American author(s) and international author(s) we believe this has broadened and enriched the concepts discussed. Many of the authors have used their networks to gather information for the text and have acknowledged those individual contributions at the end of their chapters. We feel that the collection of authors and their knowledge of the subject areas make this trace evidence resource extremely valuable.

In addition to updating the information on the current practices in trace evidence, the authors were asked, where practical, to discuss suggested workflows in method and testing selections. With the increase in the criticism of forensic science, several of the chapters address the specific scientific challenges and limitations, including the limitations of our knowledge of the transfer, persistence, and background abundance of trace materials. This open approach is one which our authors readily embraced and is something which has been limited or non-existent in previous texts. Addressing the challenges and limitations is critically important to understanding of how trace evidence can still play a significant role in investigations and legal proceedings.

This reference is designed and planned to serve the purpose of both classroom education and as a comprehensive guidance document for entry level examiners. The information provided may also be of use for attorneys and other criminal justice professionals who may need to gain some insight into the practices within the field. Furthermore, the book provides updated information in several disciplines of trace evidence which have not been offered for years.

The final overarching goal of this reference brings us back to the initial concept discussion between Vinny and Chris. In support for the future of trace evidence, this publication demonstrates how trace evidence continues to provide a valuable contribution within forensic science. The recognition and collection of trace evidence materials, its analysis through many technical disciplines, and the interpretation of the analytical findings within the context of a given case have the potential to make significant impact. The importance of this information cannot be stressed enough. If trace evidence materials are never recognized or are destroyed during handling or are never analyzed, then clearly no additional information can be obtained.

We hope you enjoy the collection of chapters in this book and find them useful in understanding the significance of trace evidence analysis and that you find the book to be a valuable reference for your personal or organization's library.

Finally, we are indebted to each and every one of our authors for their patience, dedication, and willingness to so freely share their knowledge and expertise, and provide an invaluable investment into the future generations of forensic trace examiners. We thank also the fantastic team at Wiley for their invaluable help in getting this book over the line and onto the shelves.

Vincent "Vinny" Desiderio
Chris E. Taylor
Niamh Nic Daéid

1

Trace Evidence Recognition, Collection, and Preservation

Ted R. Schwartz, Daniel S. Rothenberg, and Brandi L. Clark

Westchester County Forensic Science Laboratory, Valhalla, New York, USA

1.1   Introduction

Trace evidence is often not visible to the human eye, therefore it is typically the least understood and, unfortunately, the most overlooked form of evidence at the crime scene, and surprisingly even within the forensic laboratory. Some police officers, scene investigators, and laboratory personnel have a poor understanding of trace evidence. Proper knowledge is essential so that valuable trace evidence does not become lost, contaminated or accidentally transferred to another surface. Such incidents could severely hinder a successful criminal investigation. The goal of this chapter is to provide a foundation of knowledge that will enable successful processing of trace evidence in the forensic field. The following trace evidence principles will be discussed:

- theories of transfer and persistence
- proper trace evidence handling practices
- recognition, collection, and preservation of trace evidence at the crime scene
- recognition, collection, and preservation of trace evidence in the laboratory.

1.2   Theories of Transfer and Persistence

1.2.1   Locard's Exchange Principle

Edmond Locard (1877–1966), an early pioneer of forensic science, developed one of its most fundamental principles. His Exchange Principle theorizes that there will be a transfer of material every time contact is made between two surfaces, therefore during the commission of a crime, where contact is inevitable, it stands to reason that there will normally be some transfer of meaningful evidence. It could be in the form of hairs left by the perpetrator, either at the scene or on the victim. It might be fibers from a carpet at the scene or glass from a broken window that was transferred to the perpetrator's clothes. Crime scene events vary greatly and so will the theoretical transfers; thus explaining the difficulty in finding evidence of these transfers.

Another expression of Locard's Exchange Principle is this: When two surfaces make contact, material from one surface is transferred to the other surface and vice versa. Thus, there

Handbook of Trace Evidence Analysis, First Edition. Edited by Vincent J. Desiderio, Chris E. Taylor, and Niamh Nic Daéid.

is always a potential for a two-way transfer. At a crime scene, there should (in theory) be material transferred *from the perpetrator to the scene*, as well as material *from the scene to the perpetrator*. In reality, one of these types of transfers is more obvious than the other. Intuitively, it is easier to notice items/materials that may have transferred to the scene because they seem foreign or out of place. It is less obvious to consider what items/materials may have been taken away from the scene. A question that crime scene investigators or laboratory analysts often ask themselves is: "What material was transferred onto the surface of the item I am currently examining?" An area rug at a crime scene provides a good example. It is often not too difficult to see transferred material such as possible blood, broken glass or soil.

The more difficult and sometimes forgotten question has to do with the vice versa aspect of the Exchange Principle: "What may have come into contact with this item and caused a transfer *from* this item to another surface?" In the example of the area rug, there may be fibers from the rug that transferred to the shoes or clothing of any individual who came into contact with the rug. If so, then it is necessary to take known exemplar fibers from the rug. These exemplar fibers would be necessary for a comparison should relevant fibers be recovered from other items in the future.

When finding evidence of one item being transferred to another, there is always the question of what other potential items could have transferred that same material. One of the best trace evidence scenarios occurs when there is a two-way transfer. In other words, when there are indications that trace evidence from one surface transferred to the other surface *and* vice versa. A good example of this sometimes develops in pedestrian hit-and-run collisions. Generally, the victim's clothing is searched for paint chips that may have been transferred from the striking vehicle (the vehicle to person transfer). Conversely, when a suspect vehicle is found, it is typically searched for hairs, fibers or other trace evidence that could have originated

from the victim (the person to vehicle transfer). There are many cases in which paint chips are found on the victim's clothing that are similar to the paint on the suspect vehicle and fibers are found on the vehicle that are similar to the victim's clothing. When a two-way transfer such as depicted in Figure 1.1 occurs and there is evidence that each surface/item was involved, the significance of the association is greatly increased.

1.2.2 Primary, Secondary, Tertiary, etc. Transfers

Establishing that a transfer may have occurred is only one aspect of trace evidence examination. The *significance* of this transfer can often be difficult to understand. Finding transferred evidence on an item of evidence does not necessarily mean that there was direct contact between the item and the source of the transferred material. The following section describes ways in which trace evidence can be transferred and an understanding of these concepts will lead to better assessments of any trace evidence found at a scene or in the laboratory.

A *primary transfer* occurs when trace evidence from a particular source is deposited directly onto another surface. For example, assume a woman is wearing a sweater composed of orange acrylic fibers that are easily shed. Her husband, who is wearing a blue sweater, gives her a hug. Numerous orange fibers from the wife's sweater are transferred to the husband's sweater. This is a primary transfer, since the transferred orange fibers on the husband's sweater were a result of direct contact with the wife's sweater.

A *secondary transfer* occurs when previously transferred trace evidence is transferred to yet another surface. Using the same example, assume that the husband now enters his vehicle and drives away. When he reaches his destination, he exits the vehicle, leaving some of the previously transferred orange fibers on the driver seat. Now assume that the orange

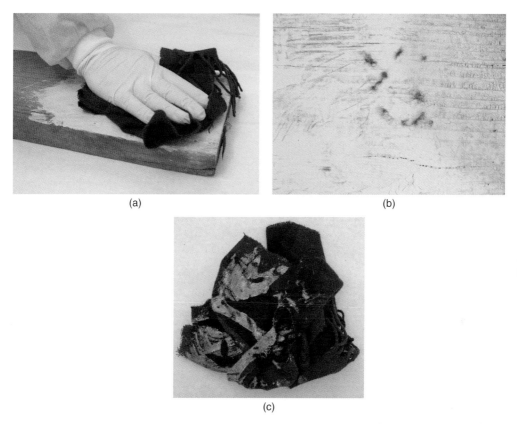

Figure 1.1 An example of a two-way transfer. (a) An article of clothing being slammed into a board with wet paint. (b) Fibers transferred to the board. (c) Paint transferred to the fabric.

fibers on the seat are compared to known fibers from the wife's sweater. What is the significance of a fiber match in this example? If one did not know that the husband was the driver of the vehicle, it might be theorized that the woman herself was in the driver seat due to the matching orange fibers. The orange fibers in the driver seat, however, were not transferred there as a result of direct contact with the source (the orange sweater), but rather as a result of a secondary transfer from the husband's clothing.

Continuing with the scenario, imagine a man breaking into the vehicle and stealing it. As he sits in the car, some of the orange fibers are yet again transferred, this time to his pants. When he gets to his destination, he exits the vehicle. An examination of his pants would likely reveal orange fibers. Again, there may be an assumption that this individual came into direct contact with the woman's sweater, despite knowing that was not the case. This is an example of a *tertiary transfer*, when evidence is transferred three times: an initial transfer and then twice more. If the car thief re-deposits the orange fibers to yet another surface, that would be considered a *quaternary transfer*, and so on. These examples demonstrate that just because a potential source of trace evidence is established, it does not necessarily mean that two items were in *direct* contact with each other. The concept of multiple transfers should be explained to the police, the lawyers, and/or the triers of fact in a particular case so that they are able to arrive at proper conclusions.

Interestingly, the primary, secondary, and tertiary transfers in the presented scenario all followed Locard's Exchange Principle. However, the key point was whether or not the contact was made with the *original source* of the trace evidence. Only the primary transfer involved the original source (the wife's sweater in the example). Subsequent transfers occurred with other objects which happened to have the *already transferred* orange fibers on them.

1.2.3 Non-contact Transfers

While Locard's Exchange Principle deals with contact between two surfaces, not all transfers occur due to direct contact. There are many instances in which trace evidence becomes airborne and then falls onto a surface. Think of breaking a window. Broken glass can travel several feet, potentially landing on any nearby surface (see Figure 1.2). If, for example, there was a jacket on the floor near the window, glass fragments might be deposited. If glass were to be found on the jacket in a subsequent laboratory examination, one might incorrectly conclude that whoever broke the window must have been wearing the jacket at the time.

Numerous types of transfers can occur without direct contact. Shed hairs and fibers,

chipping paint, soil dropped or kicked from shoes, and primer and propellant particles from a discharging firearm are additional examples.

1.2.4 Patterns Due to Contact

The transfer of material that can occur when contact is made between surfaces sometimes results in an impression pattern. Footwear, tires, fabric, and tools are examples of items that have the potential to impart impression patterns. The pattern on the receiving surface corresponds directly to the surface features of the other item. When someone steps onto a floor with a muddy shoe, the mud can transfer to the surface of the floor in a manner that preserves the design of the shoe's outsole (see Figure 1.3). While the mud itself can be useful

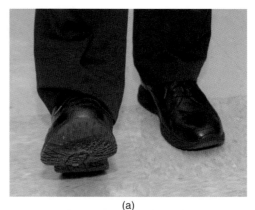

(a)

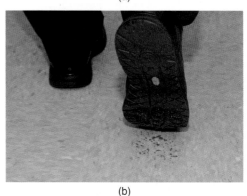

(b)

Figure 1.3 A muddy shoe (a) and a muddy impression (b).

Figure 1.2 A sheet of plate glass being broken by a hammer. The broken glass could potentially land on items several feet away. Source: Courtesy of Keith Mancini, Westchester County Forensic Laboratory.

as soil evidence, the impression pattern of the deposited mud is often of greater importance. If there are indications of deposited material on a piece of evidence, it is important to document it and to determine whether there is an impression pattern present. If so, comparisons can be made between the impression pattern and any item suspected of depositing the material.

Unfortunately, impressions of this type are sometimes missed. For example, an examiner looking for blood on an article of clothing may not realize that the observed reddish material is in the form of a shoe impression. Crime scene investigators and forensic analysts from all disciplines must have an awareness and understanding of impression evidence so that it is not overlooked.

1.2.5 Factors Affecting the Likelihood of a Transfer

If it is presumed that every contact results in a transfer of material, why is it that in many instances, even using microscopy, there is no evidence of a transfer? Well, it is possible that, in some instances, transfers do not occur even when contact is made. There are several factors that can affect the possibility of a transfer. Below is a list of some of them:

- The nature of the material being transferred. A wool fiber, which has a rougher surface due to scales, may attach itself to a surface more readily than a smooth surfaced nylon fiber.
- The degree to which the material will shed. Think of polyurethane foam. If it is relatively new and in good condition, the foam probably will not transfer even if contact with another surface is made. On the other hand, if the foam is old, dry, and brittle, it can break away and easily be transferred. Existing damage to a surface may increase the likelihood of a transfer since broken material is not as securely fixed as intact material.

- The nature of the receiving surface. Material will more likely transfer to a sticky surface as opposed to a non-sticky one. Similarly, a fabric that is composed of clingy fibers, such as a wool sweater, will most likely accept material from another surface better than will a smooth fabric, such as a pair of pants made of microfibers.
- The nature of the contact. If two surfaces rub together, there is a better chance of a transfer as opposed to a mere touching of the surfaces. Also, the more force applied during contact, the more likely transfers will occur.
- The number of times contact is made. It seems fairly straightforward that the more times contact is made between two surfaces, the greater the chances of a transfer. For example, assume that there is broken glass on a floor, and someone steps onto it wearing a pair of boots. One step might result in some glass being wedged into the outsole pattern. However, if several steps are made onto the glass, there will most likely be a greater amount of glass transferred.
- The size of the area where contact is made. If a car tire just barely makes contact with a muddy area, there will probably be some soil transferred to the tire. However, if the tire completes a full rotation in the mud, there should be much more transferred soil. Similarly, if someone is wearing a fuzzy sweater and hugs a person wearing another sweater, there will most likely be more fibers transferred than if the person's elbow alone contacted the other sweater.

1.2.6 Factors Affecting Persistence

Persistence deals with the following types of questions: What happens to materials once they are transferred to another surface? Will transferred material remain on the item indefinitely? What factors affect the chance that transferred material will remain on an item until the time that the item is examined in the laboratory? Theoretically, the transferred material should remain on a surface until it is transferred again. Ideally, the next transfer will take place when it is properly collected in a laboratory setting. However, due to circumstances such as secondary transfer, there is also the possibility that the material will not be present on the item at the time of analysis. Some factors affecting persistence are listed below:

- The nature of the accepting surface. A clingy sweater should retain transferred material longer than a smooth surface, such as nylon wind pants. If the accepting surface is something that solidifies in time, such as wet concrete, the transferred material will typically remain once the substrate has dried.
- The addition of certain foreign material on the surface. Blood, sap, wet paint, and other materials may be involved in the transfer and aid in keeping material on the transferred surface.
- The nature of the transferred material itself. For example, wet, sticky, irregularly shaped or rough surfaced items will tend to adhere better to a surface than a smooth, solid item such as a shard of tempered glass.
- What, if any, activity occurred after the transfer? Consider, for example, gunshot primer residue. If someone fires a gun, primer residue can fall onto that person's hands. If the primer residue is immediately collected from the hands, there is a good chance that the primer residue will be identified in the laboratory. However, if the person washes or wipes his or her hands, or reaches into a pocket, there is a chance that some, if not all, of the material will be removed from the hands prior to collection. Lifesaving attempts made by medical personnel at the scene can affect transferred trace evidence. Additional activities that can affect the persistence of the evidence include laundering, cleaning, and excessive handling.

- The environment surrounding the items in question. If a particle of material is transferred to a surface outdoors on a windy day, there is a good chance that it could be blown off the surface prior to evidence collection. Similarly, rain will most likely remove previously transferred materials.
- Time is another consideration. As more time goes by, the greater the chance that activity, the environment or degradation can adversely affect the transferred material.
- How deeply embedded the material is on the accepting surface. If a piece of glass is sitting on the very top surface of a carpet in a vehicle, it may be subject to loss or secondary transfer. However, if that same particle of glass is embedded deeply enough into the carpet fabric, there is a good chance that it will remain there for a much longer length of time.
- The force involved during the transfer affects persistence. The force of a speeding vehicle striking a pedestrian can leave an indented fabric impression on the vehicle. Such a transfer will tend to persist through rain, wind, and possibly even light wiping. Embedded fibers may persist and be found within these impressions.

1.3 Proper Evidence Handling Practices

When examining or collecting evidence it is important to protect it, prevent its loss, and avoid contamination. Evidence should be handled as little as possible to minimize loss and limit exposure. The most direct and least intrusive techniques should be used. An analyst must be protected from hazardous evidence. In addition, the evidence must be protected from contamination by the analyst. Personal Protective Equipment (PPE) addresses both of these concerns. All evidence has the potential to be hazardous and should always be approached with due diligence and awareness of potential dangers, both physical (sharp edges, dust, debris, pockets concealing weapons) and biological.

1.3.1 Proper Clothing to Wear and Why

PPE in the field of forensic science has come a long way. Recall the stereotypical scene of an investigator using a pencil to lift a piece of evidence at the scene. There were no gloves worn. At the time, fingerprints were the only major evidence investigators knew to protect.

With technological breakthroughs and cutting-edge equipment, information is extracted from smaller and smaller samples. Useable DNA profiles can be obtained from a single hair or from flakes of blood and skin. Comparisons are made using millimeter length fibers. So today, investigators and analysts are faced with growing amounts of useful evidence to protect. Fortunately, PPE exists and this section will explain its usefulness.

In order to protect the evidence from analyst contamination, appropriate PPE must be worn (see Figure 1.4). Clean tools and workspaces are quickly compromised when an analyst does not use gloves, a hairnet, mask, etc. The right PPE and laboratory practices will ensure that no analyst "material" is added to the evidence.

Figure 1.4 An analyst wearing various items of PPE.

Refer to Table 1.1 for additional information regarding PPE.

PPE should be changed as necessary but definitely when: it becomes soiled, a new case is started, and when working with samples that may become involved in a comparison such as victim and suspect items. PPE should be checked prior to use to ensure that it is intact and in good condition. These steps will aid in avoiding contamination or transfer of materials among evidence items.

1.3.2 Other Techniques to Avoid Contamination and Loss

Wet items should be allowed to air dry to avoid mold growth and the inhalation of spores or aerosols. Even when laboratory coats are utilized, wearing garments that shed materials easily should be avoided. If an analyst has a cold or other illness, examination of evidence should be avoided or postponed if possible.

If evidence involves other disciplines besides trace evidence, special consideration of the order of analysis needs to be taken. Analysts from other disciplines should be consulted before any analysis is begun. However, it is ideal for trace evidence to be collected and preserved prior to other analyses.

Questioned evidence should never be brought in contact with known evidence until analysis is completed. For example, questioned fiber evidence should never be brought to a scene to locate potential sources. Instead, photographs and detailed notes should be utilized. Items that can potentially be physically matched to one another should not be brought into contact unless necessary to depict the physical match. Prior to bringing the two items together, the full analysis of the individual items should be completed. Such analysis may include notes, photography, and trace evidence collection.

Appropriate packaging should be used to secure and seal evidence until it can be

Table 1.1 Proper PPE and reasons for using it.

Personal protective equipment	Protecting the evidence	Protecting the analyst
Hair/beard nets	Avoid adding analyst's hair	Avoid materials from evidence getting into analyst's hair
Face masks/face shields/goggles	Avoid analyst's breath/saliva from contacting evidence; biological contamination	Protects analyst's eyes and lungs against materials such as mold spores, dust, blood flakes, etc. that may become loose while examining evidence
Laboratory coats/ sleeves/aprons	Preventing materials from analyst's clothing being deposited on evidence	Protects analyst's clothing from picking up materials from evidence
Disposable gloves	Prevent analyst's skin, sweat, and fingerprints from depositing on evidence	Protect open cuts/wounds and prevent later transfers to eyes, nose, and mouth
Booties	Ensure that no erroneous impressions are left behind	No materials are picked up by footwear

processed to prevent tampering, loss, and/or contamination.

Occasionally, situations of contamination can still arise even when the proper precautions have been taken. Should this happen, document what transpired and communicate with a supervisor or other laboratory advisor. Such actions will help to prevent future occurrences.

1.4 Recognition, Collection, and Preservation of Trace Evidence at the Crime Scene

Generally, as a crime is occurring, many events are unfolding. People are moving. Objects are used, moved, and perhaps broken. Blood may be generated from individuals and deposited on surfaces. Numerous transfers of material are most likely occurring. Ideally, the significant transfers will ultimately be discovered and can be vital to the reconstruction of the crime scene.

The perfect situation occurs when the scene is in the exact condition it was immediately following the incident. Unfortunately, this is not always the case. Certain circumstances may affect the preservation and recognition of evidence at the scene. Sometimes this is not the fault of the investigating police or the crime

scene analysts. People discovering the crime scene, first responding officers, and emergency personnel are examples of people who can significantly alter the scene. Interviews with people present at the scene and reviews of photographs may reveal what has changed. As this is generally the job of the police, it is important that this knowledge is passed on to crime scene investigators and laboratory personnel who will be examining the evidence.

Even within an unadulterated crime scene, evidence may be missed due to a lack of proper training and/or inadequate standard operating procedures. The crime scene investigation is the first step in the scientific analysis. As such, the investigation should be entirely scientific in approach. Too often investigators at the scene process the scene in a rudimentary way. A scientific approach incorporates elements of the scientific method and becomes the basis for hypotheses regarding various actions that may have been taken during the incident. Since most trace evidence is not visible to the naked eye, it is beneficial to the crime scene investigation to use hypotheses to target potentially significant areas for examination and collection. Further complicating trace evidence examination is the typically overwhelming amount of trace materials present at a scene. Typically only a small amount of that material will prove significant to the event in question.

These areas are best determined by offering hypotheses based on observations and facts gathered during the investigation. Entries, exits, and potential paths of movement within the scene would be considered significant areas for examination and collection.

The areas near and around where the incident took place are perhaps the most significant. Unfortunately, these areas are often the most trampled locations at the scene. Each time someone traverses a relevant pathway through the scene, trace evidence is potentially lost due to secondary transfer and/or other mechanisms. It is therefore crucial that these areas be properly documented and that trace evidence is searched for and collected as soon as possible. Personnel should do their best to limit their presence in and around these important locations.

1.4.1 Searching for Relevant Trace Evidence

1.4.1.1 Visible Trace Evidence
Once hypotheses regarding significant areas of interest are made, general searches for evidence can be performed. Grid or quadrant searches can be used to break down a larger area in order to ensure that all areas are searched effectively. If any trace evidence is readily observable at the crime scene, it should be documented thoroughly. Visible items may include paint chips and smears, torn fabric, impressions, broken glass or wood, powders, and other materials. Keep in mind that there may be trace evidence that is not visible. Thus, when documenting and collecting the *visible* evidence, do it in a way that does not disturb the potentially unseen trace evidence. Documentation and collection techniques will be discussed later in this section.

1.4.1.2 Invisible Trace Evidence
Proper lighting is critical to finding evidence at the crime scene. Existing room lights or sunlight are always helpful. A strong flashlight offers versatility as it may be held at various angles while searching. When oblique (side) lighting is required, the flashlight can be held at very low angles, almost parallel to the surface. Impressions, transferred hairs, fibers, and other trace materials are often observed when the light is at a low angle. Turning the room lights off (if indoors) can also be helpful when increased contrast is needed, especially while using oblique lighting.

An alternate light source, which is commonly used by biologists looking for stains, works well for trace evidence illumination. In this technique, strong light of selectable wavelengths can be focused onto a surface. The incident light energy induces fluorescence in some types of samples. Goggles of various colors (generally red, yellow or orange) are worn to help visualize the fluorescence. Certain fibers, fragments of glass, minerals, and other particles fluoresce, thus becoming visible with the use of the alternate light source. Even when materials do not fluoresce, the intense light at discreet wavelengths may develop enough contrast to cause trace evidence not previously seen to become visible. Figure 1.5 shows photographs of a shirt in normal room light (a) and with the alternate light source (b).

Trace evidence is often small, therefore the use of magnification is important when searching for it. Using a magnifying glass at the scene can reveal evidence that is not observable with the naked eye. Magnification is especially useful when combined with some of the lighting techniques described above.

Even using the techniques above, some potentially relevant trace evidence may not be observed. The collection techniques that will be discussed later will assist in securing this unseen evidence from the scene.

1.4.2 Documentation

Notes, sketches, and photographs are all necessary techniques for documentation at the crime scene. Video may be helpful as well. Some important considerations regarding the documentation of trace evidence at the crime scene

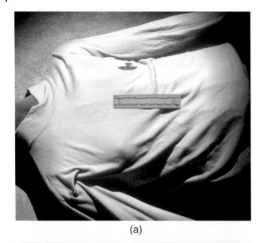

(a)

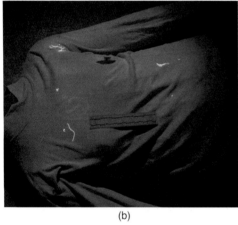

(b)

Figure 1.5 Fibers on an article of clothing. A shirt in normal room light (a). The same shirt with the alternate light source (b). Note the fluorescing fibers. Source: Courtesy of Keith Mancini, Westchester County Forensic Laboratory.

will be presented here. Detailed procedures regarding proper overall scene documentation will not be discussed in this book.

Any observed trace evidence should be fully documented with notes and photography; augment with sketches as needed. Notes should include a description of the item and its location. Be sure to mention any special visualization methods that may have been used, e.g. lighting and/or magnification. Note if the material appears to be part of a pattern or if the material is embedded in a substrate. The location of visible trace evidence items

should be added to the crime scene sketch and location measurements should be included.

Photographs provide optimal documentation of visible trace evidence at the scene. Actually seeing the origin of important evidence in a case can make an impact on jurors during a trial. Photographs should include, at a minimum, a scale, the case number, and the item number. Medium-range photographs should also be taken to show the item's general location and proximity to other items in the scene. Close-up photographs should then be taken. If the material was only observed with oblique lighting, then, ideally, the flash should be taken off the camera and held at the same angle as when it was best visualized. Similarly, if the evidence was only observed with the alternate light source, attempts should be made to photograph the evidence while using the same alternate light source and a barrier filter matching the color of the goggles used.

As previously mentioned, pertinent trace evidence will not always be visible. Bulk (also known as "blind") collection methods should be conducted to ensure that this invisible evidence is properly secured. Collection techniques, such as vacuum sweeping and tape lifting, will be discussed in the next section. Whatever technique is used, it may eventually become important to the case to be able to indicate the general *area* in which a particular piece of evidence was collected. This can be accomplished with photographs, sketches, and notes.

1.4.3 Collection

Remember that no item should be collected without prior documentation.

There are many collection methods for trace evidence. Some methods are mainly used at the crime scene, some mainly in the laboratory, and some can be used in both locations.

Choosing the correct method is not a trivial decision. Some techniques are better in certain situations than others. The collector should be aware of the strengths and limitations of each

Figure 1.6 Some packaging materials for the collection of trace evidence. From left to right: top row: paper fold, sticky note paper, coin envelope, glass vial, plastic box; middle row: white envelope, plastic zip-lock bag, metal container, white, and black gelatin lifters; bottom row: paper bag, specimen cup.

method. Furthermore, it is important to know the proper packaging for use with the various types of trace evidence. Examples are given in Figure 1.6. Even if properly collected, if an item is placed into the wrong type of packaging, there is the potential for the evidence to become lost, damaged or degraded.

The variety of packaging is commensurate with the variety of trace evidence. Which container to use depends upon the type of evidence. In general, a package should not be so large that there is much unused space inside it, but it should be large enough so that it can be properly sealed. Remember that any given package may need to be reopened and resealed several times in different locations. A properly sized package will accommodate reopening and resealing. In addition, some items may be fragile or could potentially be lost, so consider a packaging's support, strength, and rigidity when dealing with fragile evidence.

One of the best initial packages for trace evidence is the paper fold or "druggist fold." Paper folds are relatively cheap. A good quality copy-type paper is all that is needed. Figure 1.7a–m shows photographs of one folding technique. This technique should be practiced many times prior to using it at a

crime scene. Avoid contamination by using gloves, a hair net, and a mask as well as a clean surface when constructing a paper fold. Paper folds can be prepared ahead of time, in a controlled environment, to be used later at a scene.

To use a paper fold, slide out the tucked in flap. Keep the other end folded. Open the pulled-out flap to create a tube-like opening for trace evidence to be deposited. The trace evidence should be contained in the middle third before tucking the flap back in to secure the paper fold. Figure 1.7m shows trace evidence being placed in a paper fold.

1.4.3.1 Collecting the Entire Item Containing Potential Trace Evidence

If trace evidence is visible on an item and it is easy to collect the item, it is acceptable and preferable to collect the entire item. The general rule of thumb is that it is easier to collect trace evidence from an item in a laboratory setting versus collecting the trace evidence from the item at the crime scene. In a laboratory setting, it is also easier for analysts from multiple sections to search for evidence related to their disciplines. As an example, if bedding appears to be important to the case, the

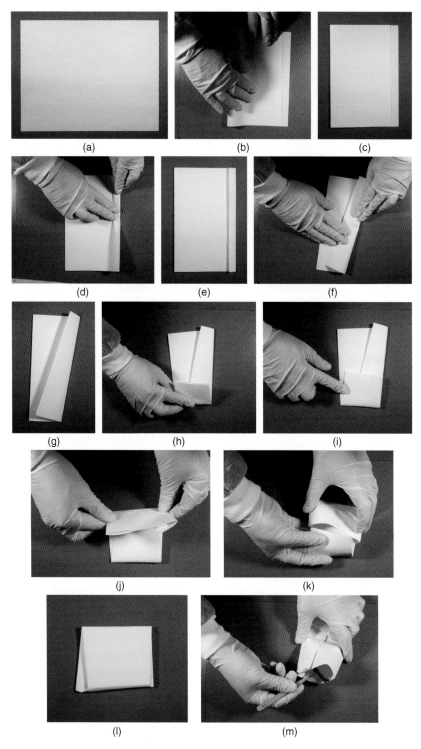

Figure 1.7 The making of a paper fold, also known as a druggist fold. The initial fold may also be made along the long axis of the paper. Note: (m) depicts trace evidence being placed into the paper fold.

bedding itself should be collected rather than collecting individual items of trace evidence from the bedding at the scene.

Since biological evidence may be present on various items, it is generally preferred to package items in paper bags rather than non-breathable plastic bags. If an item is wet, it should be dried before packaging. Items associated with the victim should be dried in a different area from those associated with potential suspects. Unused kraft paper can be used to lay out items. Since material may transfer to the kraft paper or other materials used in the drying process, those items should also be collected. If a bloody impression is present on an article and the blood is still wet, take care not to fold or manipulate the item in a way that will obliterate the impression.

Extra care should be used when dealing with fragile evidence, such as large pieces of broken glass. It may be necessary to wrap the item in paper prior to packaging. Items can also be sandwiched between pieces of clean, unused cardboard or a similar material prior to packaging to prevent further damage.

1.4.3.2 Picking with a Gloved Hand or Tweezers

Pieces of glass, chipped paint, torn pieces of fabric, and visible hairs and fibers are examples of evidence that are visible at a crime scene. Items that are large enough, such as glass pieces, can be picked up with gloved hands (sharp-resistant when necessary) and placed into a proper container such as a pizza-style box. Smaller materials, such as hairs, fibers or paint chips, may require the use of tweezers. Be cautious to not apply too much pressure when using tweezers as this may damage the evidence that is being collected. Remember to change gloves in between items. A paper fold is generally a good primary container for this type of evidence. The paper fold should then be placed into a secondary container, such as an envelope.

Since it is sometimes difficult to ensure that the collected material has been entirely removed from the tweezers, it may be desirable to use containers with an adhesive material. A gelatin lifter is an example of a container with an adhesive material. Gelatin lifters are more commonly used as lifting materials for impression evidence, but can make excellent containers for trace evidence, especially hairs and fibers. The gelatin material on the lifters is mildly sticky, which makes it easy to deposit and secure collected trace evidence. It is also not too sticky so that removal of the trace evidence in the laboratory is possible. The plastic covering of the gelatin lifter is removed. Place the covering, outside surface down, onto a clean surface. The collected trace evidence is placed onto the gelatin surface. The plastic covering is then replaced so that the side originally in contact with the gelatin is again in contact with the gelatin surface. The lifter can then be put in an envelope or another suitable secondary container. Gelatin lifters should not be used, however, if the trace evidence appears wet or if it contains possible biological material. The gelatin is aqueous based and wet and/or bloody materials will diffuse into the gelatin, causing the materials to be difficult to recover.

Sticky notes (such as Post-it$^{®}$ notes) can also be used as a cheaper alternative to gelatin lifters. The adhesive material on these paper products is more sticky than on gelatin lifters, but much less sticky than the adhesive on most tapes. The trace material is placed onto the adhesive portion of the sticky note. The paper can then be folded and placed into a secondary container. Additionally, double-sided tape can be used, where one end is first taped onto the bottom of a container (such as a plastic box or petri dish), and then the trace evidence is stuck to the exposed sticky side. Be aware that a strong adhesive may make it more difficult to remove trace evidence for examination. There is also a chance the adhesive may interact with the sample. If interaction is suspected, the adhesive can be analyzed alongside the evidence.

Other containers, such as some of those shown in Figure 1.6, can also be used.

As previously mentioned, the container chosen should preserve and protect the collected item as much as possible. It is important to remember to properly clean the tweezers in between uses. Alcohol wipes are very useful for this purpose. If any fibrous wipe such as an alcohol pad or laboratory tissue is used, avoid contamination by ensuring that no residual fibers are on the tweezers prior to reuse.

1.4.3.3 Collecting Invisible Trace Evidence

As was previously mentioned, there will most likely be probative trace evidence at the crime scene that is simply not visible. To collect this evidence, different techniques are needed. The two most common methods for collecting bulk samples of trace evidence at the scene are vacuum sweeping and tape lifting. Since there is generally a great deal of microscopic debris at a scene, indiscriminate vacuuming or tape lifting should be avoided. Rather, focus attention on the primary areas that were determined during the assessment of the crime scene. Indiscriminate collection can lead to wasted hours spent in the laboratory searching through debris that is simply irrelevant to the crime.

1.4.3.4 Tape Lifting

In this method, tape is repeatedly pressed onto a surface. It is then placed adhesive side down onto a clean surface. Ideally, both the tape and the clean surface should be clear as this makes it easier to view the collected debris from either side under the stereomicroscope and even with the compound microscope. The backing surface should be slightly larger than the tape used to provide an area suitable for writing the case information. The tape lift can then be inserted into an appropriately sized envelope or bag. If necessary, the tape lift can be rolled or folded if only smaller-sized envelopes or bags are available. Tape lifting may be performed with a variety of different materials. Generally, a good quality clear packing tape works very well. Two-inch-wide or wider tape is preferable in order to make bulk collection more efficient. After use, the tape can then be stuck to various

Figure 1.8 Tape lifting a car seat with 2-in. wide clear tape.

clear surfaces, such as plastic bags or transparency sheets. When using the strip of tape, keep an area on each end free from debris so that the adhesive remains tacky. These sticky ends will help secure the tape to the clear backing, especially if the remainder of the tape picks up much debris. An example of the tape-lifting procedure is shown in Figure 1.8.

If the roll of tape is kept on a dispenser, remember that the exposed portion of tape may have attracted random materials, therefore discard the exposed portion of tape and use "fresh" tape for the tape lifting.

Hinge lifters are a more expensive alternative to tape, but the money buys the convenience of a lifter with both the adhesive and the backing in one package. With these products, the adhesive is peeled back but remains secured to the backing at one side. After tape lifting the area of the scene, the adhesive is pressed back onto the backing and secured. There are usually premade areas for writing the case number and other relevant information. Several crime scene supply companies sell fingerprint hinge lifters (see Figure 1.9). Although lint rollers can also be used, it is better to use clear tape.

Another technique, known as one-to-one (1 : 1) tape lifting, can actually map the location from which a piece of trace evidence was taken. In this technique, the strips of tape can be stuck to the surface and left there while photographs are taken. Numbers can be written on the strips of tape, and a sketch made to

Figure 1.9 An example of trace evidence hinge lifters.

Figure 1.11 Vacuuming for trace evidence using a hand-held vacuum with a reusable trap.

position the exact location of the tape strips. This technique works best on harder, relatively cleaner surfaces. The advantage of 1 : 1 lifting is that trace evidence can be pinpointed to locations at the crime scene with more accuracy than with a bulk collection.

1.4.3.5 Vacuum Sweeping

It is alleged that Albert Schneider, a professor at the University of California and a criminologist for the Berkeley police department, was the first person to employ the use of a vacuum for the collection of trace evidence.

In this technique, a vacuum device with a filter trap is used to collect debris from various surfaces (see Figure 1.10). Generally, a hand-held vacuum cleaner is used

(see Figure 1.11). There are many versions of vacuum-sweeping devices. One method utilizes a reusable chamber that fits one end to the vacuum cleaner and the other end to a nozzle of choice. Clean mesh cloths are placed inside the chamber to trap the debris. The cloth is then removed and packaged, along with the collected debris. A paper fold is a good primary container. Vacuuming with a single, reusable chamber is relatively cheap, since the only consumable portion is the mesh cloth. However, when vacuuming multiple areas, this method can become somewhat labor intensive, since a new mesh filter needs to be put inside the chamber in between vacuumed areas. The chamber and nozzle should also be thoroughly cleaned before moving on to another area of

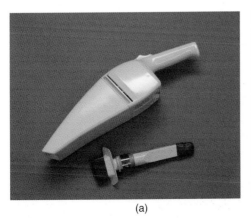

(a)

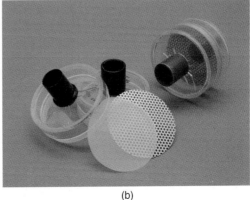

(b)

Figure 1.10 An example of a trace evidence vacuum cleaner with a single-use trap (a) and specialized reusable filter traps (b).

the scene. Cleaning can be accomplished with water or alcohol. Alcohol wipes are a convenient way to clean the chamber and require far less drying time than water. If using fibrous alcohol pads, make sure no residual fibers are present after the cleaning.

Another vacuuming method uses single-use canisters with a built-in nozzle that attaches to the vacuum cleaner. Once the vacuuming of an area is complete, the entire unit is removed from the vacuum cleaner and a plug is put in place to contain the debris. The unit is then packaged and submitted for analysis. This is a more expensive technique, but the canisters ensure that there is no cross-contamination from one area to another. This technique is also less labor intensive, since nothing needs to be cleaned in between the vacuuming of different areas. As with any technique, the vacuum chosen should be evaluated in the laboratory prior to use on cases. Some vacuums are too strong, others perhaps not strong enough. Additionally, some require special tips or techniques when used.

1.4.3.6 Tape Lifting vs. Vacuum Sweeping: Which Method to Use?

There are several considerations when deciding whether to use tape lifting or vacuum sweeping. Tape lifts are generally much easier to scan under the stereomicroscope than the debris collected in vacuum sweeping. For this reason, tape lifting is usually the first choice; it will save time at the analysis stage of the case. Another consideration is the amount of time that has passed since the incident occurred. In general, tape lifting tends to pick up debris that is closer to the surface of the substrate. Vacuum sweeping generally collects materials that are present both at the surface and deeper into the substrate. Hence, if the crime scene investigation is being conducted in a relatively short amount of time after the incident, tape lifting is usually the better choice. It is simply not necessary to sort through debris that may have been deposited weeks or even months prior to the incident. On the other hand, if a

significant amount of time has passed since the incident occurred, then vacuum sweeping may be the preferred method. An example is the processing of a suspect's house in a crime that occurred 6 months prior. Additionally, there may be situations in which it is impossible to reach the desired location with tape lifts. In these circumstances, vacuuming may need to be utilized, especially if a crevice-type tool can be used on the vacuum.

The type of debris present also affects the decision about which technique to use. Larger, heavier items, such as glass fragments, might be harder to pick up on tape. Particularly dirty scenes with much debris might overwhelm the adhesive surface of the tape, making it difficult to efficiently collect material. In these instances, vacuum sweeping may be the better method to employ. Vacuum sweeping is also faster and less labor intensive than tape lifting for collection. However, remember that later, in the laboratory, examining a tape lift will be more efficient than sorting through the combined debris of a vacuum sweeping.

1.4.3.7 Other Techniques

There are other techniques that can be used to remove trace evidence from a scene. They are generally used for other types of evidence, but can collect trace evidence materials as well. Techniques used for lifting impression evidence are good examples. A method that is often used as a "blind search" for impressions is the electrostatic lifting device (see Figure 1.12).

Figure 1.12 An electrostatic lifting device.

Figure 1.13 The dusty impression resulting from the electrostatic lifting device. Note that fibers and other trace evidence are also adhering to the Mylar sheet. Source: Courtesy of Ariel Visci, Westchester County Forensic Laboratory.

In this technique, voltage is applied to a sheet of Mylar that has a metallic backing. Dusty impressions are attracted to the surface of the Mylar and stay fixed onto the Mylar by static electricity (see Figure 1.13). The electrostatic lifts are generally either taped face-up into a box or rolled up and placed into a cardboard tube or paper bag. In addition to impressions, the technique can collect trace evidence. The sheets are examined with oblique lighting for impression evidence, but analysts need to remember that important hairs, fibers, and other debris can be present on the lifts as well, most likely in a 1:1 orientation. Similarly, gelatin lifters and adhesive lifters, when used for lifting impressions, can also remove debris that may or may not be significant to the case.

Gunshot residue (GSR) is often collected from various surfaces with either primer stubs or cloths. Primer stubs are typically aluminum mounts with double-sided carbon tape. In addition to the possible GSR, these collection techniques can pick up other trace evidence. It may become necessary to scan the cloths or stubs under the stereomicroscope. Keep in mind that some laboratories utilize carbon coating techniques on the GSR stubs. If that is the case, the stubs should be scanned prior to coating.

1.4.4 Taking Known Exemplars and Alibi Samples

The collection techniques previously mentioned deal with *questioned* trace evidence. Questioned evidence is generally what was *left at the scene*, the type of evidence that most people think about when conducting a crime scene investigation. Equally important, however, is the evidence that may have been taken away from the scene. Hence, known exemplars need to be considered and potentially collected. These samples are often overlooked because the natural tendency is to look for the questioned evidence.

Another reason that scene exemplars are neglected is because, in many cases, there is no suspect. Without items from the suspect, there are no visual cues indicating what may have been transferred to the suspect from the scene. Thus, it takes a good working hypothesis or two to even begin to think about what to collect for exemplars. Often, they have to be taken in anticipation that a suspect will be developed for without them, comparisons cannot be conducted. For example, if there is a broken window at a scene and blood is observed on some of the glass, the blood is often the only evidence collected. The other important evidence is the glass itself. If a suspect is developed and a search warrant is issued, his or her clothes could be examined for fragments of glass. However, if exemplar glass from the window was never collected, then there would be no known glass to compare any collected glass fragments. Similarly, if a violent crime took place on a shag rug, exemplars of the rug should be taken for comparisons in the event that fibers are collected from a car or someone's clothes.

During the crime scene investigation, it is important to look around and determine what someone might have taken away from the scene. Here are some examples of exemplars to consider collecting from a crime scene:

- paint exemplars from a wall with chipping paint
- fibers from carpets/rugs
- glass exemplars from a broken window (make sure to mark the orientation of the glass, i.e. inside/outside)
- soil from a garden or other location(s) where impressions are observed.

In general, damaged or disturbed areas should be a cue to an investigator to take an exemplar sample.

One of the most important considerations in taking known exemplars is to make sure the exemplars are representative of all the variations in the known sample. For example, if an area rug is composed of three different colored yarns, the exemplar must include all three colors. More specific details and instructions for taking known exemplar samples can be found within the subsequent chapters dealing with each type of trace evidence.

In addition to exemplar specimens, crime scene personnel should consider taking alibi samples. These are somewhat similar to elimination samples, but are taken to include or rule out other potential sources of physical evidence. Often these are collected due to statements made by witnesses or people allegedly associated with an incident. As an example, assume a body is found in a marshy, wooded area. A short time later, police identify a suspect and, when that person is confronted, they notice soil on his shoes and pants. He indicates that he had been in his garden planting flowers. Alibi samples of the soil from the garden should be collected in order to support or disprove the suspect's story.

Elimination samples are generally taken to include or exclude crime scene personnel as potential sources of physical evidence. A classic example is a scene in which shoe impressions are observed. In addition to the questioned impressions, it is a good idea to take test impressions and/or photographs of the footwear of the investigators, medical personnel, and anyone else who may have entered

the scene. If proper PPE is worn, the collection of these samples may not be necessary.

1.4.5 Collection of Trace Evidence from a Body

Victims often use their hands in defense, grabbing and/or scratching at the attacker. In a physical altercation, Locardian transfers may take place. In such situations, the body can become its own crime scene. In some jurisdictions, the body is removed from the scene early in the crime scene investigation. In others, the body remains at the scene until the scene processing is completed. In some jurisdictions, the body is always in the control of the coroner/medical examiner, and in others it is considered part of the scene and is therefore under the control of the scene investigators. Whatever the situation, everyone involved should be aware that there could be important trace evidence on the body and/or the clothing of the deceased.

Removing trace evidence from the body at the scene is not always necessary, especially if proper preservation methods are used. Preservation techniques include bagging the hands and feet (if bare), and placing the body into a brand-new body bag. The bags and body bag eventually can be examined at the laboratory for any valuable evidence that may have fallen off the body during transport. However, if obvious trace evidence is observed while the body is at the scene, proper documentation and collection should be conducted in order to preserve its potential value.

If a search for trace evidence is to be made on the body, it should be done prior to the autopsy. It is ideal if this occurs at the scene, but it can also be done in the morgue itself. Searching the palms of the hands and the soles of bare feet sometimes can yield valuable trace evidence. Looking under fingernails and toenails is always a good idea. In fact, any bare skin should be examined since the body is typically washed prior to autopsy. In some instances it may be advantageous to use specialized lighting such as the alternate light source, ultra-violet (UV), and/or infrared (IR) light to observe additional trace evidence and/or impressions. Magnification is helpful and can be in the form of a magnifying glass or a stereomicroscope. Having the stereomicroscope on a mobile boom stand in the morgue can make it easier to view the various parts of the body. As an example, wounds can be examined for particles that may have originated from a weapon. Any observed trace evidence can be removed with tweezers. If a body is naked, tape lifting might be considered. 1:1 tape lifting can be performed, which allows for a mapping of the trace evidence on the body. Be aware, however, that due to possible prior movements of the body (i.e. rolling it over, removal of clothing, etc.), the location of a particular item of trace evidence might not be the exact location where the item originally was.

1.4.6 Preserving Evidence and Maintaining the Chain of Custody

In general, items should be secured in such a way that they do not sustain damage, degrade or deteriorate. Containers should be marked with the case number, item number, a description of the item, where it was found, the date, and who collected it. The package should be sealed and the person sealing it should place his or her initials across the seal.

Collected items should be properly secured in a vehicle for transportation to the police department or the laboratory. Fragile evidence should be handled carefully so that breakage does not occur during transport. Upon arriving at the destination, the evidence should be placed into a proper storage facility. Depending on a laboratory's standard operating procedure, biological evidence may need to be refrigerated. Most evidence collected solely for trace evidence examination should not be refrigerated. This is mainly because unwanted moisture can form on tape lifts, gelatin lifters, and other packages. This can adversely affect the integrity of those items. Relevant trace evidence should be submitted to the laboratory as soon as possible.

Checklist: Crime Scene Procedures

Searching for Relevant Trace Evidence

☐ Based on observations and gathered information, determine the probable entries, exits, paths of movement within the scene, and the areas where the incident took place.

☐ Examine the above areas for readily observable trace evidence. Do not disturb the potentially unseen trace evidence.

☐ Use proper lighting/light sources to examine for invisible trace evidence.

☐ Use a magnifying glass to reveal evidence that is not observable with the naked eye. Combine with lighting techniques.

Documentation

☐ Document any observed trace evidence with notes and photography, augmenting with sketches when needed.

☐ Describe the item and its location with measurements if necessary.

☐ Document any special visualization methods that may have been used, e.g. lighting and/or magnification.

☐ Note if the material appears to be part of a pattern or if the material is embedded in a substrate.

☐ For invisible trace evidence, indicate the general area in which it will be collected through photographs, sketches, and/or notes.

☐ Remember to take overall, medium-range, and close-up photographs.

Collection

☐ Choose the appropriate collection technique(s).

☐ If trace evidence is visible on an item, it is generally desirable to collect the entire item using proper packaging.

□ If items are wet, dry items associated with the victim in a different area and collect separately from those associated with potential suspects.

□ Choose the proper packaging for collection of the trace evidence.

Taking Known Exemplars and Alibi Samples

□ Take known exemplars, ensuring to represent all the variation in the known sample.

□ Take alibi samples if necessary.

□ If possible/necessary, take elimination samples from crime scene personnel.

Collection of Trace Evidence from a Body

□ Consult with medical examiner/coroner (or other appropriate personnel) prior to examination.

□ Search the palms of the hands, soles of bare feet, and any bare skin.

□ Examine under fingernails and toenails (if bare).

□ Use specialized lighting and/or magnification to observe additional trace evidence and/or impressions.

□ Document any observed trace evidence.

□ Remove any observed trace evidence (tweezers, tape lifting, etc.).

Preserving Evidence and Maintaining the Chain of Custody

□ Secure items so that they do not sustain damage, degrade or deteriorate.

□ Label containers: case number, item number, description of the item, where it was found, date, initials.

□ Seal packages and place initials across the seals.

□ Properly secure items for transportation.

□ Upon arrival, place the evidence into a proper storage facility (i.e. refrigerate biological evidence).

Components of a Crime Scene Kit for Trace Evidence Collection

Note: The contents listed are suggested items to bring to a scene. This is by no means an extensive list and each organization may modify it as needed.

Items for Safety and Avoiding Contamination

- Hair net or hat
- Gloves (i.e. nitrile, vinyl, latex)
- Face mask or face shield
- Safety glasses
- Tyvek suits and/or disposable laboratory coats
- Shoe coverings (i.e. booties)
- Cut-resistant gloves
- Roll of kraft paper
- Alcohol wipes or squirt bottle of ethanol with laboratory wipes

Collection Implements

- Tweezers: sharp tip
- Tweezers: blunt tip
- Tweezers: plastic
- Single-edged razor blades
- Scalpel, scalpel blades
- Tape for tape lifting (i.e. 2-in. wide clear packing tape, large clear hinge-lifters, etc.)
- Tape dispenser (if appropriate)
- Clear material to stick tape lifts onto (i.e. transparency film, clear polyethylene bags, etc.)
- Vacuum sweeping apparatus with appropriate collection supplies
- Needle-nose pliers
- Pair of scissors
- Large spoon or other implement for scooping soil
- Electrostatic lifting device (primarily for dust impressions)
- Gunshot residue stubs

Packaging Supplies

- Clean paper (i.e. white paper, weighing paper) for making paper folds
- Mildly sticky material (i.e. gelatin lifters, sticky notes, etc.)
- Various sized paper bags
- Various sized plastic bags
- Coin envelopes
- Large envelopes
- Small plastic containers (i.e. specimen-type cups, small boxes, Petri dishes, etc.)
- Cardboard boxes for larger items

Items for Searching

- Flashlight
- Alternate light source
- Magnifying glass

Items for Documentation

- Pens/pencils
- Markers
- Appropriate worksheets
- SLR camera with necessary attachments for photo-documentation
- Rulers/Scales
- Labels for photographs
- Numbered placards/cones to put near scene items

1.5 Recognition, Collection, and Preservation of Trace Evidence in the Laboratory

1.5.1 Workspace Preparation

Trace evidence is typically small and often invisible to the naked eye. The same can be said for potential contaminants. It is therefore important to maintain a clean work environment to keep the contaminants away from the evidence. A clean environment also prevents the loss of evidence.

Always begin with proper PPE such as a laboratory coat, gloves, hair net, mask, and sleeves.

Choose a location in the laboratory with minimal foot traffic and no drafts to avoid distraction and loss of trace evidence. Bleach and alcohol are effective cleaners for tools, equipment, and bench tops at the location of choice. In addition to removing dust, these cleaners will kill potential contamination sources of DNA. Cover the cleaned workspace/bench top with a barrier, such as new, clean kraft paper. The paper will act as a containment area for any trace evidence that may stray during examination. If a piece of equipment, such as a microscope, is going to be used, wide tape can be placed on buttons, knobs, and handles to keep the equipment from becoming dirtied or contaminated. The tape will act as a barrier and accumulate the contaminants rather than the equipment. If the tape becomes excessively dirty, it can be replaced with a clean piece.

The workspace chosen should also be comfortable. If using a chair, set the height and back support accordingly. Choose a table, counter or bench top that minimizes reaching and straining. Have all supplies within reach. Make sure the area has sufficient lighting.

Checklist: Preparation of Examination Area in the Laboratory

- ☐ Proper environment: clean, minimal foot traffic, reduced air currents, sufficient lighting.
- ☐ Proper PPE.
- ☐ Clean tools, equipment, and bench top with bleach and/or alcohol.
- ☐ Cover the cleaned workspace/bench top with a barrier such as new, clean kraft paper.

1.5.2 Evidence Examination Considerations

Group items of evidence based upon whether they originated from the victim, scene or suspect. Conduct examinations on items from these groups in designated areas, preferably using a new area when moving on to items from a different group.

Initial examinations of questioned and known items should never be conducted together. The potential for contamination is greatest during the initial examination. Thus, if examined together, evidence transfer could be the result of co-mingling in the laboratory and not from any occurrence at the scene of the crime. Ideally, questioned and known items should be examined on different days, in different locations, and with different PPE. If necessary, questioned and known items can be examined on the same day but they should be examined in different locations with different PPE. If space is limited and the same area must be used, thoroughly clean the area and let enough time pass to ensure confidence in the fact that no previous evidence remains. For a Locardian transfer to have significance there cannot be any suggestion that the transfer occurred due to laboratory processing.

1.5.3 Initial Examination Considerations

An analyst should document the condition of the seals of the evidence packages, the type of packaging used, and any relevant markings from the submitting agency such as the item number and item description. The analyst should also pay attention to the date of the incident and when the item was collected (if noted by the submitting agency). If much time has gone by since the item's collection, it could help to determine which collection technique to use. It can also help in the interpretation of impression evidence, since characteristics such as wear patterns may have changed. Photographs may be used to document packaging, especially when packaging is inappropriate, wet or moldy. When using photographic documentation, use appropriate rulers/scales and include case numbers and analyst initials in the photographs.

A laboratory case number and analyst's initials may be placed on the evidence packaging. The analyst's initials and the date may also be placed on the package to document the opening of the evidence. Do not disturb original seals on evidence unless it is necessary to break those seals to open the package. If breaking the original seals is necessary, this should be documented in the analyst's notes.

A Note Regarding Evidence Handling and Potential DNA Contamination

Consider that the submitter of the evidence may not have been wearing gloves. The evidence package may have been handled by other agency personnel prior to its submission to the lab. DNA profiles can potentially be developed from the outside packages of evidence. Here is a suggested technique to avoid DNA contamination from handlers of the evidence packaging: Initially place evidence packages on separate kraft paper. Open the package and place it on clean, unused paper. Before reaching inside to pull out the item, change gloves, then place the item on another clean sheet of paper. Change gloves between items.

Once the bag is open, shake the bag over the evidence paper to ensure all potential trace evidence is out of the bag. Keep in mind that there may be debris and/or potential contaminants on the outside of the bag. Choose a collection method that avoids co-mingling.

A case number and analyst initials may be placed on the evidence at this time or at the completion of the examination. Such information can be written on a clean area of the evidence, on a clothing label, or on a laboratory-supplied tag or sticker that can be applied to the evidence item. Avoid writing on areas that may be of evidentiary value (i.e. impressions, stains, DNA, etc.)

A trace evidence analyst may often be the first analyst to examine a piece of evidence. Being the initial analyst requires an awareness and recognition that there may be other types of evidence. There may be impression evidence, bloodspatter patterns, GSR, and more that may necessitate special collection techniques or the collaboration of another analyst with expertise in that discipline. A trace evidence analyst must decide at this early stage how to proceed so that the chosen collection techniques protect all types of evidence present.

1.5.4   Evidence Description

Provide an initial, succinct description of the item of evidence, for example "One pair of blue jeans", "A folding knife with reddish brown stains". Since just about anything can appear as evidence, this step of description is often not as easy as it sounds. Items may be damaged, in pieces, heavily soiled or stained or unrecognizable. When faced with such challenges, words such as "like," "style," "type," and "possible" may help with the description. Something dark brown that could be a hair but will need further testing might well be described as "hair-like." Someone not familiar with identifying knives may describe a knife as a "kitchen-style" knife rather than a steak knife or butcher knife.

Additional details can be recorded within the body of the notes. Examples include color, length of sleeves (if the item is a shirt), location and types of logos present, design styles, accessories (belt, pins), and any other agency's markings that may be present.

Document the manufacturer's information if present on the evidence. For clothing, such information may be on tags or printed in the neck area. For tools and weapons, check handles and hilt areas. Compositional information, brand names, part numbers, sizes, and textile manufacturer numbers such as RN and CA are examples of information that can be documented in notes and/or through photography. Overall photographs may be taken at this time in order to document the evidence as it was received.

1.5.5   Macroscopic Evidence Examination

Note any staining present. Document the color(s) and location(s) of the stain(s). If damage is present, document its location. Damage could include suspected bullet holes, stab holes, tears, breaks or burns. If any observable debris (vegetation, clumps of hair, paint chips, etc.) is present, make sure to include that in the notes and/or have it photographed. As mentioned earlier, it's important to be aware of other types of evidence and seek collaboration with another analyst when such evidence is observed.

Light sources can aid in the initial examination of evidence. UV, IR, and alternate light sources can reveal evidence by increasing contrast or inducing fluorescence. The type of lighting used and the settings should be documented in the notes.

Oblique lighting is also an effective means for revealing trace evidence, impressions, and other types of evidence.

If pockets or concealed areas are present on the item, it may be necessary to examine them. Take care when doing such examination as pockets may contain sharp objects. A hemostat clamp is a great tool for reaching into pockets, gripping the fabric and safely pulling out the pocket and its contents.

1.5.6   Stereomicroscopic Examination

For the trace evidence analyst, the stereomicroscope is an invaluable tool. The magnification allows for targeted searches for fibers, paint chips, gunpowder particles, and any other debris of interest. The edges of holes and damaged areas can be examined and characteristics can be observed that help determine what caused the damage.

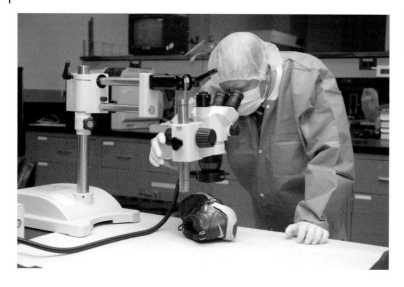

Figure 1.14 Using a stereomicroscope on a benchtop boom.

A benchtop stereomicroscope with a stage is useful for the examination of small items and for the examination of already collected trace evidence.

Figure 1.14 shows an analyst using a stereomicroscope on a benchtop boom. This type of stereomicroscope is very versatile and can be used to scan across larger items such as clothing. A rolling floor-stand boom is shown in Figure 1.15. This type of boom allows for the examination of vehicles, bicycles, and other large or irregular items.

1.5.7 Additional Documentation

Close-up photographs of areas of interest may be necessary. Measurements/locations of holes, areas of damage or patterns may need to be recorded. Premade worksheets with outlines of clothing items can assist with this additional documentation. Sketches and/or tracings of items may also be used to further document items of evidence. If a sketch is a rough drawing and is not to scale, indicate "Sketch not to scale" in the notes.

At the completion of documentation and evidence recognition, all evidence should be collected. The item should be returned to the

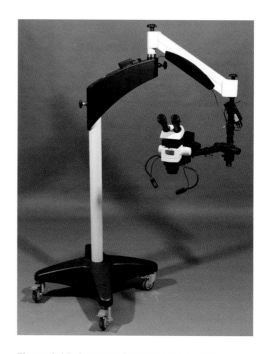

Figure 1.15 A stereomicroscope on a rolling floor-stand boom.

packaging and either resealed or set aside if additional work is necessary.

Gloves and the evidence paper should be changed in preparation for the examination of the next item. Tools used during the examination should be cleaned.

1.5.8 The Collection of Trace Evidence from Items in the Laboratory

The collection of trace evidence at the crime scene has previously been discussed. Why, then, does it need to be discussed again when dealing with collection in the laboratory? The main reason is that since the laboratory is a much more controlled environment, additional methods of collection can be employed. Also, some of the techniques previously discussed can be optimized because of the controlled setting of the laboratory. The laboratory collection methods that will be discussed are:

- picking off observed trace evidence
- shaking/scraping
- tape lifting
- vacuum sweeping.

Since there are additional techniques for trace evidence collection in the laboratory, the analyst has more options to consider. Making the proper decisions can ensure that the maximum benefit is obtained from the trace evidence present on items of evidence. These decisions are generally based on the substrate, the targeted type of trace evidence (based on case information), other types of evidence present on the item, etc. Several studies have been conducted to help assess the proper technique to utilize in various situations (Eyring and Gaudette 2005; Lowrie 1991; Palenik and Palenik 2005; Pounds 1975; Robertson and Roux 1999; Salter 1996; Taupin and Cwiklik 2011). The authors have also conducted studies that involved the use of an alternate light source to visualize fluorescent materials placed onto various fabrics, both before and after various collection methods (Baker et al. 2005; Schwartz et al. 2004).

As will be discussed, it is not always necessary to choose just one of the collection methods described below. Indeed, it is often beneficial to combine two or more of these techniques to ensure collection of as much relevant debris as possible. The various collection methods are presented below.

1.5.9 Collection Techniques

1.5.9.1 Picking off Observed Trace Evidence

This technique generally involves the use of a pair of tweezers or a gloved hand. If required, some form of magnification such as a strong magnifying glass or a stereomicroscope is used. The collected particles can be placed onto/into several different types of packaging materials, such as paper folds, gelatin lifters, coin envelopes, sticky notes, and tape-lifting containers. The use of these containers is described in the section dealing with the collection of trace evidence at the crime scene.

The picking technique is usually the first collection method employed on an item. This technique is best to use when items are to be fingerprinted or swabbed for DNA. Depending on the situation, it will most likely not be the only technique used, since a limited amount of material is collected. Picking targeted particles is always a good idea, primarily for items that could potentially get lost prior to using one of the other collection methods (see Figure 1.16). The tweezers used should be cleaned with ethanol or a bleach solution in between items (see Figure 1.17).

Figure 1.16 Picking trace evidence using tweezers.

Figure 1.17 Cleaning the tweezers with ethanol.

1.5.9.2 Shaking/Scraping

This method was not discussed in the crime scene section because it requires the more controlled environment of the laboratory. The item is held or hung over a large sheet of clean kraft paper and gently shaken. While shaking, a clean, large spatula or a similar tool is scraped across the surface of the item. The combination of shaking and scraping dislodges much of the adhering debris, which then falls onto the paper (see Figures 1.18 and 1.19). The collected trace evidence can then be funneled from the paper into a paper fold or another suitable container (see Figure 1.20). Alternatively, the debris can be tape lifted or vacuumed off the paper.

The shaking/scraping technique is, historically, one of the earliest collection methods used in the laboratory. Other than a clean

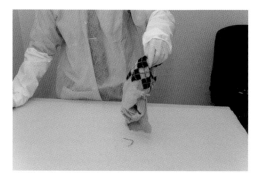

Figure 1.19 The shaking technique in which the article is shaken to dislodge trace evidence onto clean kraft paper.

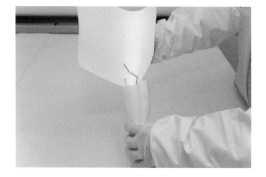

Figure 1.20 Funneling trace evidence into a paper fold after shaking and scraping an article of evidence.

spatula and a good source of kraft paper, it is relatively inexpensive and in some instances is an appropriate and efficient procedure to use. For the collection of hairs and fibers, shaking/scraping works well on smoother, non-adherent garments such as nylon jackets. For particles such as glass and paint, this method is efficient on articles that are more adherent and which shed easily, such as wool sweaters.

The biggest drawback to this technique is that some trace evidence can become airborne and lost. Contamination is thus more of a potential problem with this method, so proper precautions must be taken. As explained earlier, choose an area in the laboratory with minimal drafts and minimal foot traffic, and establish a large, clean workspace to contain

Figure 1.18 The scraping technique in which a spatula is used to scrape trace evidence off the article and onto clean kraft paper.

the debris for collection. Note that scraping may not be the best technique for heavily bloodstained items.

1.5.9.3 Tape Lifting

This technique was previously discussed. In the laboratory, there are several ways of using the tape-lifting method. In the authors' laboratory, a tape dispenser that holds 2-in. wide tape is utilized, and one is kept on each examination table. The strips of tape with collected trace evidence are then stuck on transparency film. The transparency sheets are 8.5 by 11 in., and they are cut down the middle lengthwise. Each half of transparency film accommodates two strips of tape, each approximately 2 by 10 in. Other substrates for sticking the tape lifts include clear plastic bags (such as zip-lock bags or sealable polyethylene bags), glass sides, clear plastic or glass Petri dishes. There are also commercially available tape lifters, such as those used for palm prints, and they can be adopted for trace evidence collection. These tend to be more expensive, but are efficient and satisfactory for collecting debris. It is important to remember to use a new piece of tape fairly regularly. This can help ensure that the tape still has enough bare adhesive to stick onto the transparency film or the substrate of your choice.

The tape-lifting method is an excellent choice for trace evidence collection, especially for hairs and fibers. In fact, tape lifting is typically a better collection method than shaking or scraping for the collection of hairs and fibers, although it does have some limitations. Special care must be taken when tape lifting very smooth surfaces, such as a nylon jacket. If the technique is performed too quickly and/or violently, hairs and fibers can actually become airborne. A slow, gentle approach works best. For collecting particulate trace evidence from articles that are more adherent and/or that are composed of fibers that shed easily (such as wool sweaters), the analyst can generally collect more particles using the shake/scrape procedure than with the tape-lifting method. Figure 1.21 depicts the tape lifting procedure.

Figure 1.21 The tape-lifting technique in which clear packing tape is pressed to the surface of an article for the purposes of collecting trace evidence. In this example, the clear tape will be preserved on the transparency sheet that is visible in the background.

1.5.9.4 Vacuum Sweeping

Vacuum sweeping is typically used in the laboratory far less than at the crime scene. It is generally more tedious to sort through vacuumed debris than debris collected from the other collection methods. It is, however, a very efficient method and there are instances where it does make the most sense to use this technique.

When trace evidence needs to be collected from large items of evidence, such as comforters, area rugs or sections of carpeting, vacuum sweeping is often the most efficient collection method to employ. For these types of items, as well as items with greater amounts of debris, tape lifting can be very time-consuming. In addition, tape lifting would generally require numerous pieces of tape to accomplish the task. Shaking/scraping is often not even a viable option simply because the item cannot be held high enough to allow for the proper collection of trace evidence. Also, as stated earlier, vacuum sweeping can collect debris that has become embedded in an item. Thus, if a lot of time has passed between the incident and when the item was collected, vacuum sweeping is typically the best technique to help ensure that this embedded material is collected.

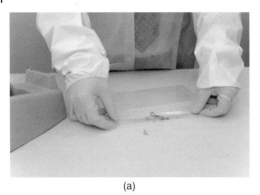
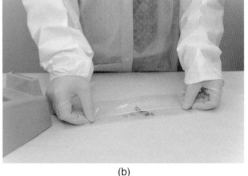

(a)   (b)

Figure 1.22 (a) Tape lifting of debris which had been previously dislodged by the shaking and scraping methods. (b) Placing the tape lift onto a sheet of clear transparency film.

1.5.9.5 Combinations of the Above Methods

It is important to remember that there are situations when multiple collection techniques can be used on the same piece of evidence. For example, it is often desirable to start by picking off any observed trace evidence. In deciding the next procedure to use on the item, many analysts prefer to search through tape lifts rather than debris collected from the shake/scrape technique. Thus, a combination of the two techniques is frequently used. A shakedown/scrape down can be conducted first, and then the dislodged debris can be tape lifted off the kraft paper (see Figure 1.22). The item itself can then be tape lifted to increase the chance that any meaningful particles of trace evidence are collected. Similarly, either of these two methods can be combined with the vacuum-sweeping procedure. As long as the desired material is collected and contamination has been avoided, the collection process will be considered a success.

1.5.10 Taking Known Exemplar Samples

After the collection of trace evidence, an examiner may consider taking known exemplar samples from an item of evidence. It is good practice to indicate the area from where the exemplar was taken. As mentioned previously, the exemplars should represent all the variation present in the item. If the item is going to be examined by another forensic discipline, it is desirable to wait for that analysis to be completed prior to taking the exemplar sample(s).

Checklist: Evidence Examination in the Laboratory

Initial Examination

☐ Document packaging: type of packaging used, the condition of the seals, and any relevant markings.
☐ Properly label packaging and/or the opening of the packaging (as per laboratory policy).
☐ Open package and remove item in a way that minimizes contamination.
☐ Retrieve all potential trace evidence from inside the packaging.
☐ Place case number and initials on the item or do this at the completion of the examination (as per laboratory policy).
☐ Examine item for other types of evidence: impression evidence, bloodspatter patterns, gunshot residue, etc.

Describe Evidence

☐ Provide an initial description of the item.

☐ Record additional details in the notes.

☐ Document the manufacturer's information observed on tags and labels, if present.

☐ Take overall photographs to document the evidence.

Macroscopic Examination

☐ Record any stains present, including the colors and locations of the stains.

☐ Record any pattern evidence.

☐ Record any damage, including holes present, and include location(s) and measurements.

☐ Record any observable debris present.

☐ Use proper lighting and/or an alternate light source if necessary.

☐ Examine pockets or concealed areas if present.

☐ Take close-up photographs of areas of interest if necessary.

Stereomicroscopic Examination

☐ Searches for targeted evidence (i.e. fibers, paint chips, gunpowder particles, and any other debris of interest).

☐ Record observations, photograph, and collect debris of interest.

☐ Examine the edges of holes and damaged areas if present; record observations and document if necessary.

Collection of Trace Evidence from Items of Evidence

☐ Choose the appropriate method of collection and document the method used.

☐ Choose the appropriate packaging material for the collected trace evidence.

Completion of Examination

☐ Take known exemplar(s) if necessary.

☐ Return item to the packaging and reseal.

☐ Change gloves and the evidence paper prior to the examination of the next item.

☐ Clean tools, equipment, and bench tops used during the examination.

☐ Remember to change PPE and locations prior to examining items from another source.

1.6 Summary

Most of the subsequent chapters in this book deal with individual types of trace evidence. One aspect of analysis that is universal to all types of trace evidence is the proper recognition, documentation, and collection of the material. If these preliminary steps are not carried out correctly, it's possible that the eventual analysis could be compromised. It is our hope that the theories and procedures presented in this chapter will lead to a better understanding of trace evidence, its proper collection and preservation, and ultimately to more meaningful analyses.

Acknowledgments

The authors would like to thank their families and especially their spouses Elayne, Nancy, and John; The Westchester County Forensic Laboratory; Keith Mancini for his assistance with the photographs; and Barbara Solomon for reading and editing the content of this chapter.

References

Baker, M., Rothenberg, D., Benjamin, B. Schwartz, T. (2005). To shake, tape or scrape. Part II: Glass and paint. Presented at the Northeastern Association of Forensic Scientists 31st Annual Meeting, Newport, RI (11 November, 2005).

Eyring, M.B. and Gaudette, B.D. (2005). An introduction to the forensic aspects of textile fiber examination. In: *Forensic Science Handbook*, 2e, vol. II (ed. R. Saferstein), 231–295. Upper Saddle River, NJ: Pearson/Prentice-Hall.

Lowrie, C.N. (1991). Transfer of fibres to head hair; their persistence and retrieval. *Forensic Science International* 50: 111–119.

Palenik, S. and Palenik, C. (2005). Microscopy and microchemistry of physical evidence. In: *Forensic Science Handbook*, 2e, vol. II (ed. R. Saferstein), 175–230. Upper Saddle River, NJ: Pearson/Prentice-Hall.

Pounds, C.A. (1975). The recovery of fibres from the surface of clothing for forensic examinations. *Journal of the Forensic Science Society* 15: 127–132.

Robertson, J. and Roux, C. (1999). Transfer, persistence and recovery of fibres. In: *Forensic Examination of Fibres*, 2e (eds. J. Robertson and M. Grieve), Philadelphia: Taylor and Francis Group.

Salter, M.T. (1996). Transfer of fibres to head hair; their persistence and retrieval. *Forensic Science International* 81: 211–221.

Schwartz, T., Applebome, B., Rothenberg, D. et al. (2004). To shake, scrape or tape: that is the question: A comparison of common trace evidence collection techniques. Presented at the Northeastern Association of Forensic Scientists 30th Annual Meeting, Mystic, CT (2 October, 2004).

Taupin, J.M. and Cwiklik, C. (2011). *Scientific Protocols for Forensic Examination of Clothing*. Boca Raton, FL: Taylor and Francis Group.

Further Reading

Ashcroft, C.M., Evans, S., and Tebbett, I.R. (1988). The persistence of fibres in head hair. *Journal of the Forensic Science Society* 28: 289–293.

ASTM Standard E1188-11 (2011). *Collection and preservation of information and physical items by a technical investigator*. West Conshohocken, PA: ASTM International. http://dx.doi.org/10.1520/E1188-11 www.astm.org.

ASTM Standard E1492-11 (2011). *Receiving, documenting, storing, and retrieving evidence in a forensic science laboratory*. West Conshohocken, PA: ASTM International. http://dx.doi.org/10.1520/D1492-11 www.astm.org.

Bergsilen, E. (2012). *An Introduction to Forensic Geoscience*. New York: Wiley.

Cwiklik, C. (1999). An evaluation of the significance of transfers of debris: criteria for association and exclusion. *Journal of Forensic Science* 44: 136–1150.

De Forest, P.R. (2001). What is trace evidence. In: *Forensic Examination of Glass and Paint* (ed. B. Caddy), 1–25. New York: Taylor and Francis.

De Forest, P.R., Gaensslen, R.E., and Lee, H.C. (1983). *Forensic Science: In Introduction to Criminalistics*. New York: McGraw-Hill.

Fisher, B.A.J. and Fisher, D.R. (2012). *Techniques of Crime Scene Investigation*, 8e. New York: CRC Press, Taylor and Francis Group.

Gaudette, B.D. and Tessarolo, A. (1987). Secondary transfer of human scalp hair. *Journal of Forensic Sciences* 32: 1241–1253.

Grieve, M.C., Dunlop, J., and Haddock, P.S. (1989). Transfer experiments with acrylic fibres. *Forensic Science International* 40: 267–277.

Houck, M.M. (ed.) (2001). *Mute Witnesses: Trace Evidence Analysis*. New York: Academic Press.

Kirk, P.L. (1974). Chapter 4 the collection of physical evidence and chapter 9 preliminary examination of microscopic evidence. In: *Crime Investigation*, 2e (ed. J.I. Thornton), 33–49, 107–111. New York: Wiley.

Lee, H.C. and Harris, H.A. (2000). *Physical Evidence in Forensic Science*. Lawyers and Judges Publishing Co.

Moore, J.E., Jackson, G., and Firth, M. (1986). Movement of fibres between working areas as a result of routine examination of garments.

Journal of the Forensic Science Society 26: 433–440.

Parybyk, A.E. and Lokan, R.J. (1986). A study of the numerical distribution of fibres transferred from blended fabrics. *Journal of the Forensic Science Society* 26 (1): 61–68.

Pearson, E.F., May, R.W., and Dabbs, M.D.G. (1971). Glass and paint fragments found in men's outer clothing – report of a survey. *Journal of Forensic Sciences* 16 (3): 283–300.

Petraco, N. and De Forest, P.R. (1993). A guide to the analysis of forensic dust specimens. In: *Forensic Science Handbook*, vol. III (ed. R. Saferstein), 24–70. Englewood Cliffs, NJ.: Regents/Prentice Hall.

Pounds, C.A. and Smalldon, K.W. (1978). The distribution of glass fragments in front of a broken window and the transfer of fragments to individuals standing nearby. *Journal of the Forensic Science Society* 18: 197–303.

Scott, H.G. (1985). The persistence of fibres transferred during contact of automobile carpets and clothing fabrics. *Canadian Society of Forensic Science Journal* 18: 185–199.

Springer, F. (1999). Collection of fibre evidence from crime scenes. In: *Forensic Examination of Fibres*, 2e (eds. J. Robertson and M. Grieve), 101–115. Philadelphia: Taylor and Francis Group.

2

Polarized Light Microscopy for the Trace Evidence Examiner

Andrew M. Bowen

United States Postal Inspection Service, National Forensic Laboratory, Dulles, VA, USA

Preface

Trace evidence encompasses a wide range of materials, each of which has different properties that are most useful for their characterization. As a result, it is difficult to put together a one-size-fits-all microscopy chapter for trace evidence examiners. Depending on the sub-discipline of the examiner, different sections of this chapter will be of value in the examiner's training. For the hair examiner, an in-depth knowledge of image-formation and the basic optical performance of the light microscope will suffice for most work. The hair examiner has relatively little need to become proficient in optical crystallography. The glass examiner will be analyzing an amorphous, and therefore isotropic, substance as their primary material of interest. While it is useful for them to understand the difference between isotropic and anisotropic substances, and to be able to distinguish between these types of substances using a polarized light microscope, no in-depth optical crystallography background is needed for routine forensic glass analysis. In addition to general microscopy knowledge, the glass examiner requires a deep understanding of the concepts of refraction of light, refractive index and its measurement, dispersion of refractive index with wavelength, the temperature-coefficient of refractive index,

and how these concepts can be applied to the examination of glass evidence. The forensic fiber examiner needs to have an understanding of the optical performance of the light microscope and must be knowledgeable about refractive index values and their measurement. Beyond this, however, the fiber examiner should also have a deep understanding of how anisotropic materials interact with light. A full grasp of concepts such as birefringence, retardation, and the use of compensators to locate the slow vibration direction in a material are necessary for competent fiber examination. However, much of the more complex optical crystallography theory goes beyond the needs of the fiber examiner. It is not common practice to study fibers conoscopically, as this type of examination rarely yields probative information. Given that most fibers behave as though they are uniaxial materials, an understanding of the optical properties of biaxial substances is not required for typical fiber casework. The trace evidence examiner who examines explosive materials, soil evidence, unknown chemicals, and to a lesser degree tape and paint, will routinely encounter a wide range of crystalline substances. As a result they could benefit tremendously from a thorough understanding of optical crystallography concepts. These examiners will likely benefit from reading this chapter in its entirety as well as several of the recommended references. This chapter attempts to introduce optical crystallography theory at a fairly basic level, emphasizing practical applications of the techniques. In that sense the chapter will cover applied light microscopy. Additional references for recommended reading are provided for the reader who is interested in pursuing some of the theory further.

2.1 Introduction

Most trace evidence examiners have a strong chemistry background and are knowledgeable about the many different types of analytical instruments that are used by chemists for identifying and characterizing chemical substances. The light microscope is sometimes considered simpler or less sophisticated than these other instruments, but this perception is largely unjustified. The light microscope is in many ways similar to the infrared spectrometer, energy dispersive X-ray spectrometer, Raman spectrometer, and other instruments considered to be state of the art. In all of these instruments, electromagnetic radiation interacts with evidence samples in a particular manner and the resulting phenomena are observed. Typically the wavelength (or range of wavelengths) of the incident radiation is controlled by the examiner, and the sample is monitored for specific phenomena that occur upon interaction with the incident radiation (absorption, scattering, fluorescence, etc.). In this respect, the light microscope is not very different from these other instruments. The primary difference is that the examiner's eyes serve as the instrument detectors, and the examiner's brain processes the information generated. It is fair to state that human performance plays a larger role in light microscopy than it does in many other areas of analytical chemistry. However, this can be an advantage if the human performance is informed by appropriate training

and experience. The human mind is extremely adept at recognizing things that are seen and instantaneously classifying them. Humans can easily pick their mother out of a crowd, identify a banana or an apple, or even tell their car apart from another with the same color, year, make, and model by small details like a scratch on the side panel. This ability can be harnessed and used to rapidly make tentative identifications of a wide range of substances that examiners have experience studying microscopically.

In light microscopy, the range of wavelengths used to study samples are those that span the visible spectrum, namely from about 400 nm (at the blue end) to 700 nm (at the red end). Electromagnetic radiation in this range is directed toward the sample (typically from below, more rarely from above), and the resulting interactions are observed. The formation of a magnified, inverted, virtual image of the specimen is what most people imagine when they think about light microscopy. While this is certainly a large part of the desired information (especially for the hair examiner), quite a range of other phenomena occur that can prove very useful for identification, characterization, and/or comparison of materials. This is particularly true when the substance to be studied is placed on a rotating stage in between two polarizing filters. This will hopefully become apparent throughout the remainder of this chapter. In order to extract the maximum amount of useful information from a sample during examination, it is necessary to understand some of the various ways in which visible light interacts with matter. In truth these interactions are extremely complex and require an understanding of quantum mechanics in order to fully grasp the theory behind them (Feynman 1985). However, simplified explanations are more generally useful for pedagogical purposes and will be used here. Before these interactions can be fully appreciated, however (even at a simplified level), a basic understanding of the nature of light is required.

2.2 The Nature of Light

As stated above, the term "light" refers to electromagnetic radiation in the visible range, from roughly 400 to 700 nm. Like all electromagnetic radiation, light has both an electric vector and a magnetic vector associated with it (hence the term electromagnetic). These vectors undergo periodic oscillations as the radiation travels through space. Electromagnetic radiation behaves in a very different manner than materials that people interact with on a macroscopic scale in day-to-day life. Despite centuries spent studying electromagnetic radiation, physicists still have a less than complete understanding of this mysterious form of energy (and the author's understanding of light is even more limited). Light is composed of photons, which exhibit both phenomena typically associated with particles (they have discrete amounts of energy and can be counted) and phenomena commonly associated with waves (interference, diffraction, etc.). As a result of this behavior, light is often discussed as though it consists of discrete particles (the particle theory of light) or as though it consists strictly of waves (the wave theory of light), although in reality it is more complicated than either of these theories would suggest. For an interesting discussion of this duality, read *QED: The Strange Theory of Light and Matter* (Feynman 1985). For the purposes of light microscopy and the explanations of phenomena provided in this chapter, it is most practical to use the wave theory of light. As most of the interactions of interest to the light microscopist can best be explained on the basis of interactions between the electric vector of light and electrons, the magnetic vector associated with light can essentially be ignored. Thus this chapter will treat light as though it is made up of waves that consist of an oscillating (vibrating) electric vector; this is a simplification of reality, but a useful one for the material presented here. In the following discussions of light waves interacting with matter there are references to a variety of wave properties, including the propagation direction or ray direction (the direction the waves are traveling), the vibration direction (the direction of displacement of the electric vector), the wavelength (the length that a wave travels during one complete vibration, represented by the Greek letter λ), and amplitude (height of the wave, represented by the letter A) (Figure 2.1).

For visible light, waves with different wavelengths are perceived by the human eye as having different colors, and waves with different amplitudes are perceived as having differences in intensity (brightness). While traveling through air (or any isotropic medium), the vibration direction of light is always perpendicular to its propagation direction. As will later become clear, in anisotropic media the vibration direction is often not perpendicular to the propagation direction of the light.

When light is coming from a typical light source such as a tungsten halogen bulb or light-emitting diode, it is generally in the state that is described as unpolarized light. This term means that the light is composed of many light rays/waves vibrating in all of the possible planes perpendicular to its propagation direction (Figure 2.2).

It is possible, however, to isolate only the portion of that light that is vibrating in one

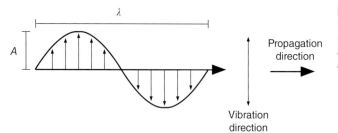

Figure 2.1 A wave of light showing its wavelength (λ), amplitude (A), propagation direction (large arrow), and vibration direction (small arrows).

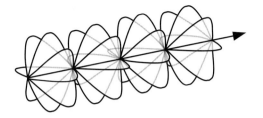

Figure 2.2 Unpolarized light composed of light waves vibrating in all possible planes perpendicular to its propagation direction.

single plane (called plane polarized light, linearly polarized light, or simply polarized light) (Figure 2.3).

Plane polarized light is required to study certain types of materials by polarized light microscopy in order to obtain the maximum amount of information from them.

2.2.1 Reflection

Generally speaking, when light encounters an interface between two different transparent substances, some of the light reflects off the surface and some of the light transmits into the second substance. Consider light traveling through air and encountering a glass window. The light that impinges on the surface of the glass is called the incident light. A portion

of the incident light will typically reflect off the surface of the window, and this portion is called the reflected light. The amount of reflection that occurs depends on the properties of the two substances as well as the angle of incidence. When discussing the angles between light rays and the surfaces with which they interact the convention is to report angles relative to a line perpendicular to the surface, termed the surface normal (Figure 2.4).

While reflection of light off a surface (like the surface of a glass window) is actually a fairly complex process that involves the entire thickness of the glass (Feynman 1985), in practice a very simple law is sufficient for predicting the path of the reflected light. Called the Law of Reflection, it provides sufficient basis for studying materials in reflected light for the purpose of identifying, characterizing, and comparing them. The Law of Reflection states that the angle of the reflected ray is equal to the angle of the incident ray (Figure 2.4). The reflected light is partially polarized, meaning that the light is no longer vibrating equally in all planes perpendicular to its propagation direction. The reflected light is vibrating preferentially in the plane parallel to the surface of the glass, and the degree to which the light

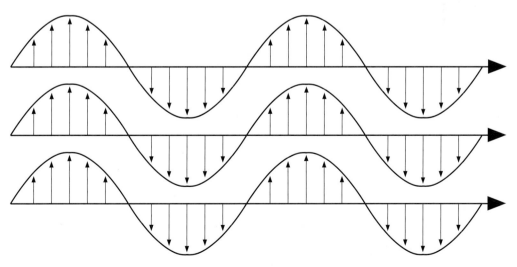

Figure 2.3 Plane polarized light. As opposed to Figure 2.2, the light waves shown here are all vibrating in a single plane (the plane of the paper).

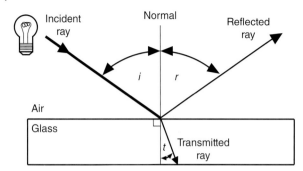

Figure 2.4 Light partially reflecting off a glass surface. The angles of incidence (i) and reflection (r) are measured relative to a line perpendicular to the surface (the normal). The Law of Reflection states that the reflected angle is always equal to the incident angle.

is polarized depends on the properties of the glass and on the angle of incidence.

Trace evidence examiners primarily study materials in transmitted light because most substances are transparent at the small sizes appropriate for microscopical examination and because a greater number of properties can typically be determined for a substance when it is examined in transmitted light than in reflected light. When reflected light is used, it is typically because the specimen is poorly suited to study in transmitted light. The most common reason for using reflected light is because the material being studied is opaque, meaning that it does not transmit visible light. Most common opaque substances are either totally absorbing materials (e.g. combustion products) or totally reflecting materials (e.g. metals). In practice, trace evidence examiners observing opaque materials in reflected light are primarily interested in the color, texture, and reflectivity of the materials. The color of a particle in reflected light can be very useful for identifying and characterizing a substance. A white spray paint sphere and black oil soot sphere will be virtually indistinguishable via transmitted light, but will have very different appearances in reflected light. The texture and reflectivity are important for distinguishing metals (highly reflective with smooth surfaces) from materials with rougher surfaces (such as soot and other combustion products). In general, materials with smooth surfaces will exhibit strong, regular (specular) reflection, while rough materials will exhibit dull, diffuse reflection (Figure 2.5).

2.2.2 Refraction

As shown in Figure 2.6 a portion of the light incident upon the glass window transmits into the glass. This portion of the light undergoes refraction.

Refraction is a phenomenon that is closely related to the velocity of light as it travels in different substances. In a vacuum light travels at a speed of roughly $3 \times 10^8 \, \text{m s}^{-1}$ (typically represented by the letter c). In other transparent substances light travels more slowly, its velocity depending on the properties of the substance. In air, a substance with very low density of molecules and composed primarily of low molecular weight compounds, light travels at very nearly its speed in a vacuum. In solid transparent substances such as glass, however, light slows down substantially. In a typical soda-lime window glass light only travels at a velocity of about $2 \times 10^8 \, \text{m s}^{-1}$. The velocity of light in a substance depends primarily on the number of atoms per unit volume and the atomic polarizability of the atoms of which it is composed (Bloss 2000). Materials having a high-density value generally have a large number of atoms per unit volume. High molecular weight substances generally have high polarizability values, as their electrons occupy more distant outer shells. Anions, with extra electrons in their electron shells, also have relatively high polarizability values. Thus light is slowed down more dramatically by substances having higher density values, higher molecular weights, and containing negatively charged species (Bloss 2000; Hartshorne and Stuart 1960).

Figure 2.5 The top image illustrates regular reflection off a smooth surface; the bottom image illustrates diffuse reflection off a rough surface. The two materials also exhibit different colors in reflected light, namely green (top image) and red (bottom image).

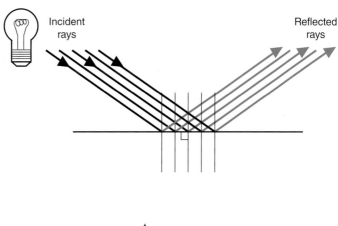

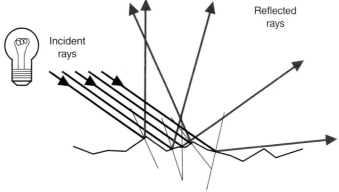

The velocity of light in a substance is typically measured in relative terms, specifically as the ratio of the velocity of light in a vacuum to the velocity of light in the substance. This ratio is known as the refractive index of the substance, typically denoted by the letter n. The relationship between refractive index (n), the velocity of light in a substance ($v_{substance}$), and the velocity of light in a vacuum (c) is shown in Eq. (2.1). Because refractive index is a ratio, the units cancel out and it is a unit-less property.

$$n_{substance} = \frac{c}{v_{substance}} \qquad (2.1)$$

Another phenomenon that is closely related to the velocity of light, and what refraction of light is commonly understood to refer to, involves a change in direction as light travels from one substance into another. As discussed above, the portion of the incident light that transmits from the air into the glass slows down. If the incident light is normal to the

surface of a block of glass, this velocity change will be the only noticeable effect. If, however, the light has an incident angle greater than 0°, the light will appear to change direction upon entering the glass. This change of direction is evident for the transmitted ray traveling in the glass in Figure 2.6. This phenomenon can be understood by considering the incident light to be composed of numerous parallel rays, each vibrating in phase with each other. The line connecting the crests (or troughs) of each individual wave (ray) define the wavefront of the incident light. A line drawn perpendicular to the wavefront is called the wave normal and is coincident with the propagation direction for light traveling in isotropic media (Figure 2.7).

The concepts of wavefront and wave normal will be useful for understanding other phenomena later in this chapter. In Figure 2.8 a part of the wavefront enters the glass first (point A) and slows down, while the rest

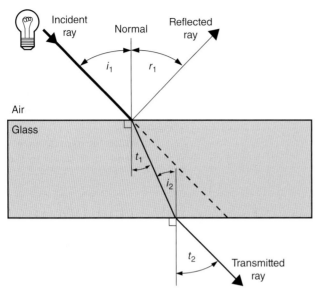

Figure 2.6 In addition to reflection, a portion of the light incident on a piece of glass may transmit through the glass and undergo refraction. The relationship of the refracted angle of the transmitted light (t) to the incident angle (i) can be determined for isotropic substances using Snell's Law (see Eq. (2.2)).

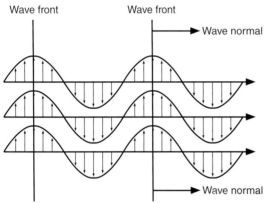

Figure 2.7 A bundle of parallel light rays with a line connecting portions of the waves that are in phase. This line defines the wave front of the bundle of light waves, and a line perpendicular to the wave front indicates the direction of the wave normal. The wave normal coincides with the propagation direction for light traveling in isotropic media.

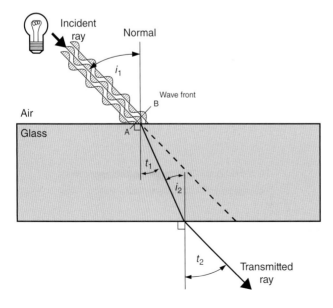

Figure 2.8 Figure 2.6 shown again with the incident light redrawn as a parallel bundle of light waves. The line AB defines the wave front of the parallel bundle of rays. Point A of the wavefront enters the glass before point B of the wavefront. The portion of the wavefront that enters the glass first slows down while the portion remaining in the air continues to travel at a higher velocity, resulting in a change in the direction of the wave normal.

of the wavefront is still in the air (point B) and traveling at a higher velocity. Once the entire wavefront is in the glass, the direction of propagation of the wave (the wave normal) has changed, and it appears to an observer as though the light ray is bent. Once again, for a more accurate discussion of this phenomenon see Feynman (1985).

This phenomenon is similar to what happens when a pair of wheels joined by an axle roll from concrete onto grass at an angle other than 90°. The wheel that first rolls onto the grass slows down while the other wheel continues to travel at a higher velocity on the concrete. Once both wheels are on the grass, they will continue to travel at the new (lower) velocity after changing direction. This example is taken from Elizabeth Wood, who uses it in her excellent book on optical crystallography (Wood 1977) (Figure 2.9).

Both the degree to which the light ray bends and the direction it bends are related to the refractive index values of the two substances. The light ray angles and refractive indices are

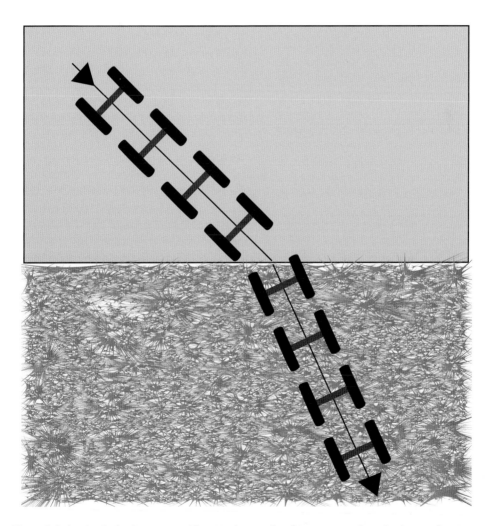

Figure 2.9 A pair of wheels connected by an axle traveling from concrete (gray background) onto grass. As with the wavefront in Figure 2.8, the direction of travel changes for the wheels because the lower wheel encounters the grass first and slows down while the top wheel continues on the concrete (at a higher velocity than the lower wheel) for a short time before also entering the grass.

related to each other by Snell's Law (Eq. (2.2)), which is commonly rearranged into Eq. (2.3), where n_1 and n_2 are the refractive indices of the first and second substances, respectively, i is the incident angle, and t is the transmitted angle:

$$n_1 \sin i = n_2 \sin t \tag{2.2}$$

$$\frac{n_1}{n_2} = \frac{\sin t}{\sin i} \tag{2.3}$$

The important takeaways from Snell's Law are that when the two refractive indices are similar, the two angles are similar, and the light does not bend very much. Conversely, when the two refractive indices are very different in magnitude, the two angles are very different and the light bends a lot. The direction the light bends depends on whether it is slowing down (it will bend toward the normal, $t < i$) or speeding up (it will bend away from the normal, $t > i$). Importantly, the incident light does not change direction at all when the two refractive indices are equal or when the incident angle is 0° (normal incidence).

2.2.3 Dispersion

The refractive index values of substances are very useful properties to determine for identification purposes. It is evident from Table 2.1 that knowing the refractive index of an unknown substance could narrow down the identity of the substance.

However, certain variables must be controlled in order to measure refractive index values and compare them to known substances or literature reference data. One important variable is the wavelength of light. It turns out that the refractive index of a substance varies with the wavelength of light used to measure it. In typical, non-absorbing (colorless) transparent substances, the refractive index value is greater for shorter wavelengths (near the blue end of the spectrum) than it is for longer wavelengths (near the red end of the spectrum) (Figure 2.10).

Table 2.1 A list of common isotropic substances and their refractive index values.

Substance	Refractive index
KCN (potassium cyanide)	1.410
CaF_2 (fluorite)	1.434
NaCN (sodium cyanide)	1.452
KCl (potassium chloride)	1.490
$NaClO_3$ (sodium chlorate)	1.515
NaCl (sodium chloride)	1.544
KBr (potassium bromide)	1.560
$Ba(NO_3)_2$ (barium nitrate)	1.571
$Sr(NO_3)_2$ (strontium nitrate)	1.588
$NaBrO_3$ (sodium bromate)	1.617
NH_4Cl (ammonium chloride)	1.643
KI (potassium iodide)	1.667
As_2O_3 (arsenic trioxide)	1.755
$Pb(NO_3)_2$ (lead nitrate)	1.782

This variation is termed dispersion (or, more precisely, dispersion of refractive index with wavelength). It can be understood by recalling that the interaction between the oscillating electric field of the light and the electron cloud in the material determines the velocity of light in a material. Shorter wavelength light has a higher frequency, which means there are more vibrations in a given time. A greater frequency of vibrations results in a greater number of interactions in that period of time, slowing the light down relative to light composed of longer (lower frequency) waves. It is convention to measure refractive index values using light with a wavelength of approximately 589 nm (the sodium D line of Fraunhofer). Historically, sodium vapor lamps were an inexpensive, readily available source of monochromatic light, and this wavelength was used out of convenience. Other wavelengths commonly used to determine refractive index and dispersion are the hydrogen C (486 nm) and hydrogen F (656 nm) lines. Dispersion of refractive index varies for different substances and can be used as an additional means of identification or characterization. This fact is

Figure 2.10 A typical dispersion curve, illustrating how refractive index changes with wavelength for a colorless transparent substance.

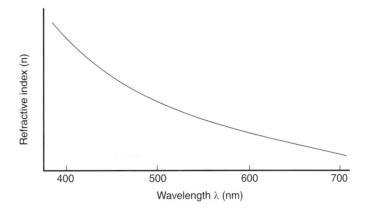

exploited by some forensic glass examiners during comparisons of glass evidence.

2.2.4 Temperature Coefficient of Refractive Index

For very accurate work, it is also necessary to control (or measure) the temperature of the sample during refractive index determinations. That is because the density of materials varies with temperature, and refractive index is dependent on density. The change in refractive index of a substance with temperature is called the material's temperature coefficient of refractive index. For the vast majority of solid substances the temperature coefficient is very small and contributes very little to the overall uncertainty of measurement. However, for many liquids the temperature coefficient of refractive index is much greater, making it a significant factor in the measurement process. The most common means of measuring refractive index involves immersing a solid sample in a liquid of known refractive index and comparing the two. In order to make accurate determinations, the temperature of the liquid must be controlled or measured so that its refractive index is accurately known. The temperature can be controlled with a hot stage or measured with a thermometer. As will be seen later in this chapter, the relatively high temperature coefficient of refractive index of liquids is exploited by forensic glass examiners

in order to make very precise refractive index measurements and comparisons.

2.2.5 Absorption of Light

When light transmits through a substance or reflects off the surface of a substance, some or all of the light may be absorbed. White light is composed of all the wavelengths (colors) of visible light mixed together. If one or more of these wavelengths is preferentially absorbed by a substance, the resulting mix of wavelengths is interpreted by the human brain as color. The substance will appear to be a color that is complementary to that of the preferentially absorbed wavelength. For example, if yellow light is absorbed, the substance will appear blue.

2.2.6 Other Interactions Between Light and Matter

There are many other types of interactions that can occur when light is directed at or through matter, including scattering, interference, and diffraction. In fact, many of these interactions are intimately related to each other, as well as to reflection and refraction. However, a rather basic understanding of reflection, absorption, and refraction of light in a practical sense will prepare the trace evidence examiner to measure refractive index values, to predict the behavior of substances during microscopical examination, and ultimately to identify and characterize a wide range of trace evidence materials. These are the most important interactions to understand for the majority of the practical applications of light microscopy. Diffraction of light will be discussed in the following section as it is critical to understanding the theory behind image formation through the light microscope, and interference is a phenomenon that underlies some of the optical crystallography theory covered later in the chapter. Additional theory related to these various interactions between light and matter can be found in Feynman (1985).

2.3 Light Microscopy

Every trace evidence examiner should have some basic knowledge of optics and image formation in the light microscope, although in-depth knowledge of the theory of optics is not a requirement. A deep understanding of this subject will be advantageous, of course, and those interested in pursuing this subject

further are referred to a number of excellent books on the topic (Ziegler 1972, 1973). At a minimum, however, the examiner should understand how to properly align and set up a polarized light microscope, and they should have knowledge of what aspects of the image they can control by adjusting various components of the microscope. Figure 2.11 shows a modern polarized light microscope with some of its important parts labeled.

2.3.1 Image Formation in a Compound Light Microscope

The polarized light microscope is a specialized type of compound light microscope. Compound microscopes are so named because they use two sets of lenses, namely the objective lens and the ocular (eye piece) lens that work together to form the final image. The magnifications of the two lens systems are multiplied to obtain the total magnification of the microscope.

Microscope objectives form magnified images of the objects on the stage in much

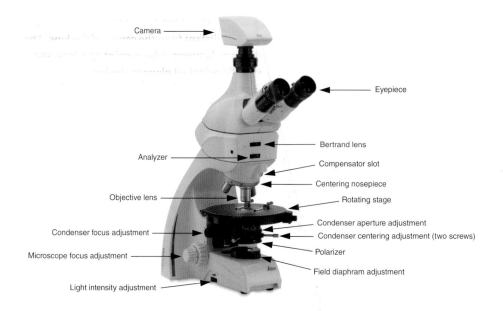

Figure 2.11 A modern polarized light microscope with most of its components labeled. Source: Courtesy of Leica Microsystems.

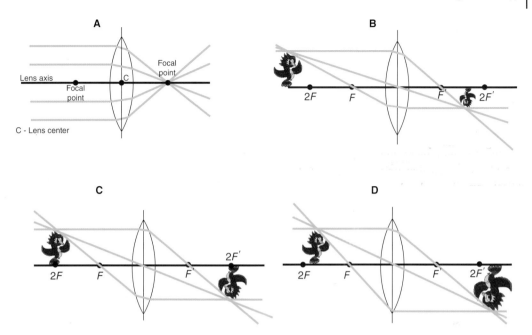

Figure 2.12 Diagram A illustrates some important terms related to image formation by glass lenses. As shown, a series of parallel light rays converge on a single point (the focal point, F) on the opposite side of the lens. Diagrams B, C, and D show image formation for an object placed further away than twice the focal length of the lens (2F), exactly 2F away, and closer than 2F, respectively. Source: Hawk drawing courtesy of Alexandra Bowen.

the same way that a camera lens forms an image in the plane of the film or sensor. To understand how an objective works, consider how an image is formed through a simple biconvex lens. A lens is a piece of glass (or other transparent material) that has at least one curved surface. Lenses come in many shapes, and their names typically indicate the type(s) of curved surfaces they have. As its name implies, a biconvex lens is bounded by two convex curved surfaces (Figure 2.12).

There are a few terms that are necessary to learn in order to understand image formation by lenses. One is the lens axis, which is the line connecting the physical center of the lens and its center of curvature. In Figure 2.12 both the center of the lens and the lens axis are indicated. Figure 2.12 also depicts a series of light rays parallel to the lens axis that are incident on the lens from one side. For an ideal biconvex lens, all such rays will converge at a single point on the opposite side of the lens; this point is designated the focal point of the lens. A biconvex lens has two focal points, one on each side of the lens. The two focal points are equidistant from the center of the lens. The distance between a focal point of a lens and a specific principal plane in the lens (close to the lens center for a thin biconvex lens) is the focal length of that lens. To understand how this type of lens forms images, an object is placed on one side of the lens and three specific types of lines are drawn from a point on the object. The first line is parallel to the lens axis, and it will therefore pass through the focal point of the lens on the opposite side. The second line is drawn such that it passes through the focal point of the lens on the same side as object. This ray will be refracted parallel lens axis on the opposite side of the le final ray is drawn such that it passe the center of the lens. This ray straight line. The intersection rays on the opposite side of where this point on the object will be focused in the newly formed image. By drawing these lines from each point on the object, the image formed by the lens on its opposite side can be constructed. If this process is repeated for objects that are placed at various distances from the lens, the images formed are magnified whenever the distance between the object and lens is between the focal length (*F*) and twice the focal length (*2F*). For objects farther away than *2F*, the image formed is smaller than the object. For an object placed at exactly *2F*, the image and object are of the same size. The image formed for an object under these circumstances is inverted (it appears to be upside down and flipped horizontally), and it is also a real image, meaning that the light rays are actually present in the location where the image appears. In a compound microscope, the instrument is constructed such that the objective forms a magnified, real, inverted image (called the intermediate image) in a plane in the microscope termed the intermediate image plane. Because the light rays actually pass through this plane, it is possible to magnify this image further. This additional magnification is accomplished by use of the oculars (eye pieces) on the microscope.

The oculars produce a magnified image in a somewhat different manner because the object is placed closer to the lens (ideally at the focal point of the lens) and the examiner's eye is located on the other side of the lens. Under these circumstances the ocular lens ~~tions much like a magnifying glass does.~~ ~~glass works by overcoming a~~ ~~of the human eye, called~~ ~~.~~ The human eye ~~ntains a lens~~ ~~rial.~~ ~~the~~ ~~ngth.~~ ~~ws the~~ ~~t is far~~ ~~to focus~~ ~~later. The~~ ~~the greater~~

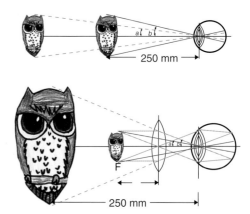

Figure 2.13 The top portion of the figure illustrates how the visual angle changes as an object is moved closer to the eye. An object far away has a smaller visual angle (a) than the same object viewed closer (b). The lower portion of the figure illustrates how a glass lens (hand magnifier) placed in between an object and the eye refracts the light rays coming from the object such that they both take up a larger visual angle and appear to originate from farther away. Source: Owl drawing courtesy of Katherine Bowen.

the visual angle of the object. As the visual angle of the object increases, the area on the retina that is involved in the image formation also increases (Figure 2.13).

The greater this area, the more rods and cones are involved. The resulting increase in detail can be thought of as analogous to having more pixels in a digital image. The greater the number of pixels in a digital image, the higher its resolution and the larger it can be blown up while still maintaining crisp detail. The eye works in a similar manner. The closer an object comes to the eye, the greater its visual angle, the more rods and cones are involved in the image formation of the object, the larger and more detailed it appears. However, there is a limit to how much the eye muscles can change the shape of the eye lens. As an object is brought closer to the eye than about 25 cm or so, the eye is no longer able to focus on the object. This distance is referred to as the limit of accommodation of the eye. However, if a lens is placed in between the eye and the object, it is possible to bring the object closer than 25 cm away while still keeping it in focus. The lens refracts the light rays in a manner that "tricks" the eye into perceiving that the object remains approximately 25 cm away. The viewer then perceives a virtual, upright, magnified image of the object. This image is considered to be a virtual image because the light rays do not actually converge in the plane in which the viewer perceives them to.

Together, the objective and ocular lenses produce the final image that is observed through the microscope. The objective produces a magnified, real, inverted image in the intermediate image plane. The oculars further magnify this image by increasing the visual angle that this intermediate image takes up on the retina. The microscopist perceives a virtual, magnified, inverted image with a total magnification equal to the magnification of the objective multiplied by the magnification of the ocular.

For the interested reader, the book on geometric image formation in a light microscope by Ziegler (1972) is an excellent resource for learning more about this subject.

2.3.2 Numerical Aperture and Resolution

Many chemists have had little instruction in the use of the light microscope. The cursory introduction that is typical may only address how to focus on a preparation on the microscope stage, and possibly how to take a picture of the field of view. There are, however, a number of microscope components located below the microscope stage that play an important role in image formation. Because they are rarely discussed, it is not surprising that these components are often poorly understood by beginning microscope users.

The most important of these underappreciated parts of the light microscope is the substage condenser. This component consists of a series of lenses, along with an adjustable iris, that are located directly below the stage. The vertical positioning of the substage condenser relative to the preparation is critical for achieving optimum performance of the microscope and maximum control over the image. Just as the objective lenses need to be focused on the preparation, so do the condenser lenses.

What is meant by achieving optimum performance of the microscope? One common measure of the performance of a light microscope is an evaluation of its resolving power. The resolving power of microscope is a measure of the smallest distance between two points that can be distinguished from each other. Any details more closely spaced than this distance will blur together. In a practical sense, the microscopist will not be able to perceive any details that are more finely spaced than the resolving power (Figure 2.14).

The resolving power of the optical system depends on both the numerical aperture of the objective lens and the numerical aperture of the substage condenser lens, among other variables. The term numerical aperture refers to the light-gathering ability of a lens. It is generally considered to be the most important property of a lens, so it is critical for the microscopist to have a firm understanding of it. This number is always printed on the side of an objective lens, ranging from approximately 0.10 to 1.25 depending on the objective. The numerical aperture of an objective (or condenser) lens system depends on two variables, namely the angular aperture of the lens and the refractive index of the medium between the specimen and the lens (Eq. (2.4)). In Eq. (2.4), NA is the numerical aperture of the lens, AA is the angular aperture of the lens, and n is the refractive index of the medium in between the lens and the preparation.

$$NA = n \times \sin\left(\frac{AA}{2}\right) \tag{2.4}$$

The angular aperture of a lens is the angle of light it is able to collect. The refractive index number in this equation is equal to approximately 1.0 for most objectives, for which air is the medium between specimen and objective. The only exception to this occurs for immersion objectives (oil being the most commc

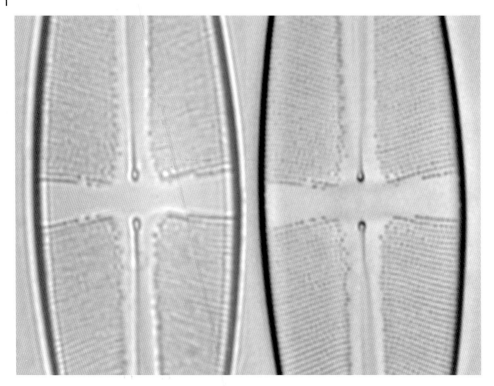

Figure 2.14 Two images of the same diatom, taken at the same magnification but with different microscope settings. In the image on the left, there are portions of the diatom in which individual punctae (dots) are blurring into one another, and other areas in which the rows of punctae are blurring into each other. The diatom appears to either have horizontal stripes or be devoid of internal structure. In the image on the right, all of the rows of punctae are clearly resolved and some of the individual punctae are also resolved, providing a much more accurate image of the internal structure in the diatom.

immersion medium), which are designed to be dipped into a drop of immersion liquid on top of the coverslip. The immersion liquid decreases the refraction of light as it travels from the sample to the objective. Figure 2.15 shows several objective lenses with different numerical apertures. Additional details may be found in Ziegler (1972).

The reason the angular aperture of the objective impacts the resolving power of the microscope has to do with the diffraction of light that occurs when it transmits through the lens. Ernst Abbe studied the relationship resolving powder and diffraction, and series of specimens with regularly signed to demonstrate these several of these speci- As these test specimens

illustrate, when light passes through a narrow slit (or several narrow slits), the slit opening acts as if it were a point source of light, with light spreading out from the slit in all directions (Figure 2.16). The phenomenon of light spreading out as it passes through one or more openings is known as diffraction.

When two or more closely spaced slits are involved, the light passing through the different slits interacts to produce a series of maxima (bright areas) and minima (dark areas). The angle between consecutive maxima (θ) depends on the wavelength of light used (λ) and the spacing between the slits (d) (Eq. (2.5)). In Eq. (2.5), n is any integer value (e.g. 0, 1, 2, 3…).

$$\sin \theta = \frac{n\lambda}{d} \qquad (2.5)$$

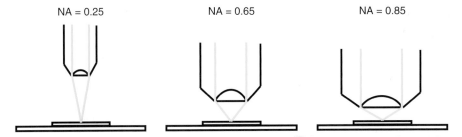

Figure 2.15 Three objectives with different numerical apertures. Lenses with higher numerical apertures capture wider angles of light from the object and typically have smaller working distances.

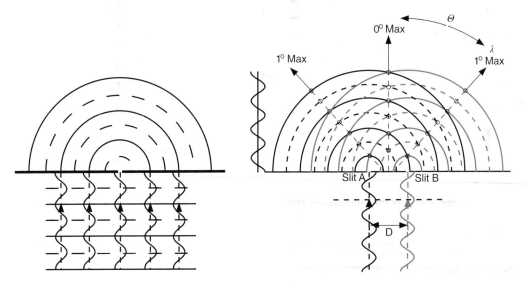

Figure 2.16 Diffraction of light waves passing through a single slit (left) and through two slits (right). Upon passing through multiple slits having a regular spacing, bright areas called diffraction maxima are formed at specific angles due to constructive interference of the light waves diffracting through the different slits. Source: Adapted from Ziegler (1972).

The significant of Eq. (2.5) is that the closer the spacing between the slits, the further apart consecutive diffraction maxima are. Abbe's experiments demonstrated that in order to resolve detail in a sample (such as a series of slits), at least two diffraction maxima must be captured by the objective lens and participate in image formation. Without at least two diffraction maxima, the slits blend together and appear as one single, slightly blurry, slit. The slits are not resolved because one single slit produces a diffraction pattern consisting of a single maximum, the same pattern as that captured by the objective lens when only one maximum from a series of closely spaced slits is captured. If the diffraction pattern collected from the objective is similar to that produced by one slit, the image formed will look like one slit, regardless of the true nature of the specimen (Figure 2.17).

A two-dimensional pattern of dots produces diffraction maxima in several directions due to the regular spacing of the dots in these directions. For any particular direction of spacing, at least two diffraction maxima are required to resolve the detail in that direction. By manipulating the diffracted maxima that participate in image formation (by use of stops

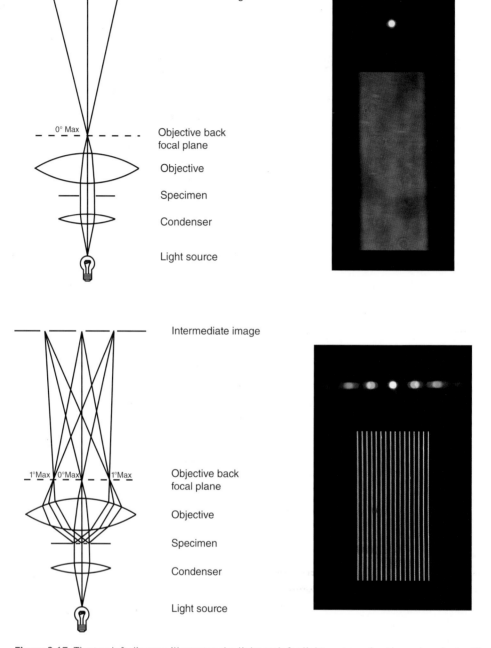

Figure 2.17 The top left diagram illustrates the light path for light rays passing through a single slit on a microscope stage. This sample produces a single diffraction maximum (the bright spot on the top right image) in the objective back focal plane, and the intermediate image formed consists of a single (in this case fairly wide) slit. The lower left diagram illustrates the light path for light rays passing through multiple slits with regular spacing on a microscope stage. They produce multiple diffraction maxima at angles determined by Eq. (2.5) in the objective back focal plane (the bright, colored spots in the lower right image) and the intermediate image formed consists of multiple slits. Source: Reproduced with permission of Microscope Publications.

Figure 2.18 The upper images illustrate a specimen consisting of a series of dots (top left) and the diffraction pattern produced by this specimen (top right). By inserting a stop consisting of a thin slit into the back focal plane of the objective, all of the diffraction maxima can be blocked except those in one direction (bottom right). This diffraction pattern is similar to the pattern that a series of slits produces, and the intermediate image formed is thus a series of parallel slits (bottom left). Note that changing the diffraction pattern alters the image produced, despite the fact that the specimen still consists of an array of dots. As this example clearly demonstrates, the diffraction maxima captured by the objective play an important role in determining the character of the image formed by the microscope system. Source: Reproduced with permission of Microscope Publications.

in the objective back focal plane), the image produced can be manipulated. The series of dots can be made to resemble slits, for example by blocking diffraction maxima in all but one direction (Figure 2.18).

The slits and dots in Abbe's specimens are analogous to details in a sample that the microscopist wishes to resolve (e.g. scales on a hair or pigment particles in a paint chip). Because finely spaced details in the specimens being studied behave as diffraction gratings, capturing widely spaced diffraction maxima

coming from the specimen is a requirement in order to resolve that detail. The ability of the objective lens to capture widely spaced diffracted maxima depends on its numerical aperture, which is why this property is critical to the ability of the objective lens to resolve fine detail.

In addition to the relationship between the numerical aperture of the objective lens and resolving power, Abbe's experiments demonstrated the importance of the illumination coming from below the sample. In experiments

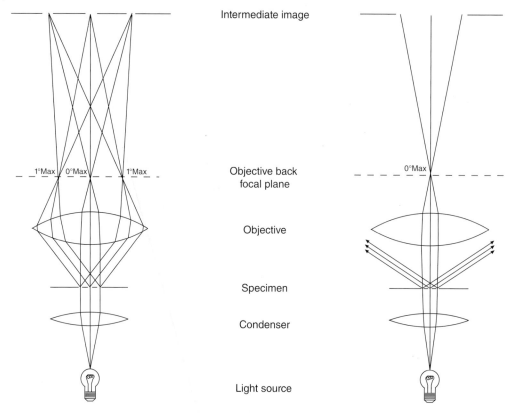

Intermediate image

1°Max   0°Max   1°Max

0°Max

Objective back
focal plane

Objective

Specimen

Condenser

Light source

Figure 2.19 A series of slits illuminated by unidirectional axial illumination. As the spacing of the slits gets smaller, the diffraction maxima are produced at higher angles of inclination to the microscope axis. If the first-order maxima are formed at an angle greater than half of the angular aperture of the objective, they will not be captured by the objective. This is the case for the diagram on the right. In this case, a single maximum is produced in the objective back focal plane, and the intermediate image consists of a single slit (see Figure 2.17). Source: Adapted from Ziegler (1972).

using unidirectional axial illumination (light coming up directly from below the sample, along the microscope axis), diffracted maxima separated by an angle up to half the objective's angular aperture can be collected (Figure 2.19). However, if the illumination was directed at the sample from an appropriate angle relative to the microscope axis (unidirectional oblique illumination), two diffraction maxima separated by an angle equal to the entire angular aperture of the objective can potentially be captured (Figure 2.20).

If multidirectional oblique illumination (essentially a cone of light coming from wide angles in all directions) is used, the finest possible details in all directions can be resolved,

getting the most out of the objective lens that is possible with respect to resolving power (Figure 2.21).

The maximum resolution can only be achieved, however, if the illumination comes in at as large an angle as the objective can capture. In other words, the numerical aperture of the condenser illumination must equal the numerical aperture of the objective to achieve the best possible resolving power.

It turns out that if the substage condenser is not properly focused, its full numerical aperture is not accessible, and the resolving power of the microscope suffers as a result. Under this condition the illumination approximates unidirectional axial illumination, and effectively

Figure 2.20 A series of slits illuminated by unidirectional oblique illumination. In this case, due to the inclination of the illuminating light, two diffraction maxima (the zero-order and one first-order maximum) can be captured by the objective provided the first-order maximum is produced at an angle smaller than the angular aperture of the objective. The inclined illumination effectively doubles the angle between diffracted maxima that can be captured as compared to unidirectional axial illumination (compare to Figure 2.19). Source: Adapted from Ziegler (1972).

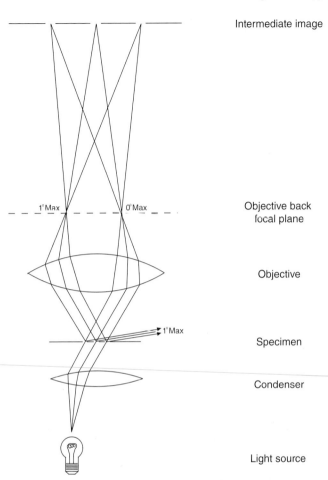

Intermediate image

1°Max 0°Max Objective back focal plane

Objective

1°Max Specimen

Condenser

Light source

only half of the objective's angular aperture is utilized for image resolution (Figure 2.22).

The importance of focusing the substage condenser on the sample becomes clear once the relationship between a focused condenser and the available angle of illumination is understood, along with the relationship between the angle of illumination and resolving power. The bottom line is that in order to illuminate a sample with multidirectional oblique illumination (which is necessary for maximum resolving power) the substage condenser must be focused on the sample. Once the condenser is properly focused, the condenser aperture (an adjustable iris inside the substage condenser) can be adjusted to control the angle of illumination. A narrow beam of unidirectional axial illumination can be achieved by closing down the aperture; a wide cone of multidirectional oblique illumination can be achieved by opening up the aperture (Figure 2.23). The two images of the diatom in Figure 2.14 were both taken using the same objective lens and a focused condenser. However, the image on the left was taken with the condenser aperture closed down, while the image on the right was taken with the condenser aperture somewhat open, increasing the resolution of the instrument.

While the prior discussion would seem to suggest that maximizing resolving power is the goal, there are two other factors that must be taken into consideration when evaluating the image produced by the microscope. The most important of these factors is image contrast. Resolving fine detail is only useful if there

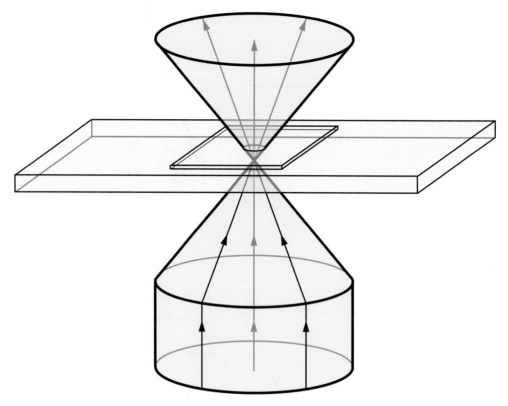

Figure 2.21 Multidirectional oblique illumination is achieved by illuminating the specimen with a cone of light rays traveling at wide angles relative to the microscope axis. This type of illumination maximizes the resolving power of the microscope system for finely spaced details in all directions within the specimen.

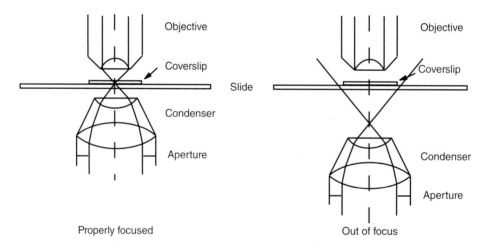

Properly focused

Out of focus

Figure 2.22 A properly focused substage condenser (left) illuminating the sample with multidirectional oblique illumination. The diagram on the right shows an improperly focused substage condenser. While the condenser is producing highly inclined illuminating rays, the rays are not being directed through the sample. The only rays actually illuminating the sample are those that are parallel to the microscope axis. This situation approximates unidirectional axial illumination.

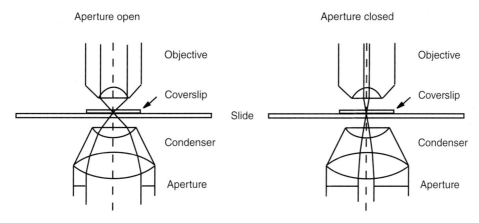

Figure 2.23 The impact of the size of the condenser aperture opening on the angle of the illuminating rays. The aperture is open in the left-hand diagram and closed down substantially in the right-hand diagram.

is sufficient contrast present in the resulting image for the fine detail to be seen. Unfortunately, for any given objective, the contrast decreases as the cone of illumination increases (i.e. as the condenser aperture is opened). In practice the microscopist must adjust the condenser aperture position for each sample depending on what they are trying to observe. Typically, the condenser aperture should be opened as wide as is possible without losing acceptable contrast in the image. Ultimately, however, the proper placement depends on what the microscopist is trying to see. Experienced microscopists typically periodically adjust the condenser aperture position, along with the fine focus, as they examine samples. When maximum resolving power is desired, and where practical, contrast can be increased by selecting a mounting medium with a refractive index far away from that of the sample. It should be noted that the depth of field of the image also depends on the position of the condenser aperture. The more open the condenser aperture, the smaller the depth of field of the resulting image. This relationship can be used to the advantage of the microscopist to present an image that is a thin slice of a specimen, or alternately to bring into focus a greater depth of the sample. In addition to the effects of the condenser aperture, depth of field typically increases as the numerical aperture

of the objective lens decreases. The bottom line is that a focused substage condenser gives the microscopist maximum control over the features of the image formed by the system by adjusting the position of the condenser aperture.

Given the importance of having a properly focused substage condenser, the next logical question is, how is that achieved? Fortunately, it is very easy to accomplish. There is a second adjustable iris in the microscope that is located below the substage condenser, typically in the base of the microscope. This iris is called the field diaphram, and its name comes from its primary role in defining the field of view that is illuminated. When the substage condenser is properly focused, an image of the field diaphram should be in focus in the plane of the preparation. The process for focusing the substage condenser involves closing the field diaphram (so that its outline is visible in the field of view) and adjusting the height of the substage condenser until the image of the field diaphram is in sharp focus (Figure 2.24).

The height of the substage condenser is adjusted by rotating the condenser focus knob. The condenser must be adjusted with a focused sample in place on the stage of the microscope. Another way of stating this is to say that the plane of the field diaphram should be in conjugate focus with the plane of the specimen.

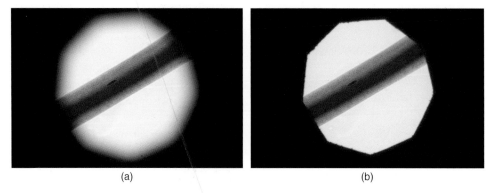

(a)   (b)

Figure 2.24 The image on the left shows a red nylon fiber with the field diaphram closed down all the way; field diaphram outline is visible, but it is out of focus as shown by the blurry nature of the outline. The image on the right shows the same field of view after the height of the substage condenser was adjusted to focus the image of the field diaphram; the edges of the diaphram outline are now sharp.

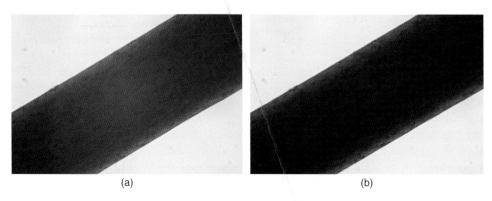

(a)   (b)

Figure 2.25 Two photomicrographs of a dark polyester wig fiber taken under similar microscope conditions. For the photograph on the left, the field diaphram was open beyond the edges of the field of view, letting in stray light. For the photograph on the right, the field diaphram was set just to the edges of the field of view, eliminating stray light. The effect of the stray light is to produce glare in the image, which is responsible for the washed-out appearance of the center of the fiber in the image on the left.

Once it is properly focused, the field diaphram should be adjusted (opened) so that it is just outside the edge of the field of view. These microscope conditions will eliminate stray light from outside the area being studied. Stray light is especially apparent when observing dark objects (Figure 2.25).

In summary, a properly set up light microscope will have a focused sample, a substage condenser whose height has been adjusted to bring a focused image of the field diaphram onto the sample image, and a field diaphram that has been opened so that it is just outside the field of view. Once the microscope is

properly set up, the position of the condenser aperture will be adjusted as needed by the microscopist in order to maximize resolving power (open), maximize contrast (closed), or, more typically, to find a compromise between these two extremes that best enables the microscopist to study the sample features of interest.

Older microscopes may require one additional adjustment, specifically to achieve even illumination across the field of view (especially noticeable at low magnifications). Older microscopes use tungsten halogen light bulbs for illumination, as opposed to the light-emitting diodes (LEDs) favored in most new instruments. These bulbs contain filaments consisting of tungsten ribbons, and as a result they are a fairly uneven source of illumination. In order to obtain even illumination across the field of view, the filament must be completely out of focus in the plane of the preparation. This condition can be achieved one of two ways. A common method employed primarily in recent decades (considered by purists to be less than ideal) is to place a ground-glass diffuser in front of the filament that defocuses it in all subsequent planes. This approach comes, however, at the expense of light intensity. Another way is to focus an image of the filament in the plane of the objective back focal plane. This plane is not normally visible in a light microscope, but can be viewed by inserting a Bertrand lens, by removing an eyepiece and looking down the empty eye tube, or by exchanging an eyepiece with a phase telescope. An adjustable lens in front of the filament (called the lamp condenser) is required for this operation. Most modern microscopes employ either LEDs or diffusers, removing the need for this last step in setting up the microscope.

The microscope setup just described is called Kohler illumination, named after the microscopist Auguste Kohler. Other methods of setting up the light microscope have been suggested, but this particular one has become the most widely used method, especially amongst trace evidence examiners.

For most microscopists working in a modern laboratory, an understanding of the concepts of resolving power, numerical aperture, and the purpose and operation of the substage condenser will suffice for routine casework. Those working with older microscopes will also want to familiarize themselves with the lamp condenser and its use in order to achieve even illumination across the field of view. Readers who are interested in understanding more about the performance of the light microscope are directed to the excellent books by Ziegler (1972, 1973).

2.4 Introduction to Crystallography

Crystallography is a very complicated subject. However, there is a beauty to its order, rules, and resulting systematic classification of materials. These concepts are extremely useful for understanding the behavior of a wide range of materials and for interpreting results from a variety of analytical techniques.

There is unfortunately not space in this chapter to do this subject justice, but this subject is extremely valuable knowledge for any trace evidence examiner who studies crystalline substances as a routine part of their work (with, for example, chemical unknowns, explosives, soil, building materials, and crystalline additives in paint, polymers, and adhesives). It would therefore be advisable for the reader to consult some additional texts on the subject, and there are some excellent options available (Bloss 2000; Dyar et al. 2008).

2.4.1 Symmetry

Crystals are solids in which there is long-range, three-dimensional order with respect to the position and orientation of their building blocks (which may be atoms, ions, or molecules). Crystals are classified based on their symmetry. Specifically, they are organized into groups based on the combination of symmetry elements present in their internal three-dimensional structure. Symmetry elements are planes, axes, or points about which operations can be performed on a crystal with the result of the operation being indistinguishable from the starting state. The operations performed are called symmetry operations. A survey of symmetry elements and operations applicable to external crystal forms follows. One example of a symmetry element that occurs in many crystal forms is a mirror plane. In a crystal containing a mirror plane, reflecting each side of the crystal across this plane would leave the crystal apparently unchanged (Figure 2.26).

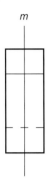

m

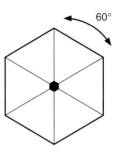

60°

Figure 2.28 The hexagon in the center of the crystal indicates the presence of a sixfold axis of symmetry. A rotation of 60° about this axis results in a crystal that resembles its starting state. Another way of stating this is to say that for any point on the crystal there is an equivalent point an equal distance from the axis, a 60° rotation away.

Figure 2.26 The line designated m indicates the presence of a mirror plane in a crystal. Every point on the right of the line has an equivalent point an equal distance from the line on the opposite side.

The symmetry operation is reflection, and the symmetry element is a mirror plane (designated by the letter m). If a crystal possesses rotational symmetry, then rotation around an axis in the crystal would leave the crystal apparently unchanged. The symmetry operation is rotation, and the symmetry element is a rotational axis of symmetry in the crystal. Rotational axes are given a designation based on the number of times during a complete 360° rotation the crystal resembles its starting state. A crystal that resembles its starting state four times on complete rotation (or every 90°) is said to have a fourfold rotational axis of symmetry (designated by a square) (Figure 2.27).

A crystal that resembles its starting state six times on complete rotation (every 60°) is said

to have sixfold rotational symmetry, designated by a hexagon (Figure 2.28).

The types of rotational axes of symmetry that occur in crystals are limited to twofold (Figure 2.29), threefold (Figure 2.30), fourfold, and sixfold axes.

An additional type of symmetry that some crystal forms exhibit is point symmetry. If a crystal possesses point symmetry then reflecting every part of a crystal across a point in the center of the crystal would leave the crystal apparently unchanged (Figure 2.31).

The symmetry operation is inversion about a point, and the symmetry element is a center of symmetry (designated by a circle enclosing a dot). In addition to the elements and operations above, there is one final type of symmetry that is less intuitive to grasp. This

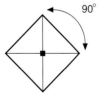

90°

Figure 2.27 The square in the center of the crystal indicates the presence of a fourfold axis of symmetry. A rotation of 90° about this axis results in a crystal that resembles its starting state. Another way of phrasing this is to state that for any point on the crystal there is an equivalent point an equal distance from the axis, a 90° rotation away.

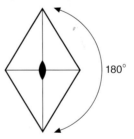

180°

Figure 2.29 The dark eye shape in the center of the crystal indicates the presence of a twofold axis of symmetry. A rotation of 180° about this axis results in a crystal that resembles its starting state.

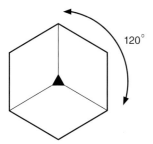

Figure 2.30 The triangle in the center of the crystal indicates the presence of a threefold axis of symmetry. A rotation of 120° about this axis results in a crystal that resembles its starting state.

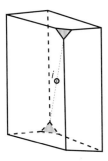

Figure 2.31 The circle enclosing a dot in the center of the crystal indicates the presence of a center of symmetry. Every point on the crystal has an equivalent point an equal distance from the center on the opposite side of the crystal.

final type of symmetry is called roto-inversion symmetry, and it involves a combination of rotation about an axis and inversion across a point. In a crystal that possesses a fourfold roto-inversion axis, the symmetry operation of a 90° rotation followed by inversion about the center of the crystal would leave the crystal apparently unchanged (Figure 2.32).

The types of roto-inversion axes that can occur in crystals are limited to onefold (which is the same as a center of symmetry), twofold (which is the same as having a mirror plane perpendicular to this axis), threefold, four-fold, and sixfold. The last three of these roto-inversion axes are brand new symmetry elements. Table 2.2 lists all of these symmetry elements, their associated symmetry operations, and the symbols that are commonly used to designate them.

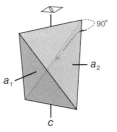

Figure 2.32 The red symbol above the crystal indicates the presence of fourfold axis of roto-inversion. A rotation of 90° about this axis, followed by inversion through the center of the crystal, results in a crystal that resembles its starting state.

2.4.2 Crystal Point Groups

Only certain combinations of symmetry elements can pass through a common point in a crystal. This statement is true because the combination of certain symmetry elements requires the presence of others and also because certain combinations do not occur in nature. Hessel (1830), Bravais (1849), and Gadolin (1867) all independently demonstrated that there are 32 unique combinations of symmetry elements that can operate about a central point in a crystal, and these are known as the 32 point groups. Crystallographers organize crystals into these point groups based on the combination of symmetry elements that they possess. Bloss (2000) provides an excellent discussion of these point groups, along with an explanation of why certain symmetry elements are compatible with each other and others are not. This book is an extremely valuable resource to the reader who is interested in learning more about crystallography than is offered here. The first several chapters, in particular, are highly recommended as additional reading.

A simpler classification system places each of these 32 point groups into one of six crystal systems based on the number, relative orientation, and spacing of atoms/ions/molecules along their crystal axes. This relatively simple means of classifying crystals is helpful for understanding the optical properties of

Table 2.2 Symmetry elements and their symbols.

Symmetry Element	Symmetry Operation	Symbol	Graphic Symbol
Twofold rotation axis	180° rotation	2	
Threefold rotation axis	120° rotation	3	
Fourfold rotation axis	90° rotation	4	
Sixfold rotation axis	60° rotation	6	
Mirror plane	Reflection across a plane	m	
Center of symmetry (same as onefold roto-inversion axis)	Inversion about a central point	i	
Twofold roto-inversion axis (same as mirror plane)	180° rotation followed by inversion about a central point	$\bar{2}$	
Threefold roto-inversion axis	120° rotation followed by inversion about a central point	$\bar{3}$	
Fourfold roto-inversion axis	90° rotation followed by inversion about a central point	$\bar{4}$	
Sixfold roto-inversion axis	180° rotation followed by inversion about a central point	$\bar{6}$	

different types of crystals that will be discussed later in this chapter, and will be used throughout the remainder of this chapter. In order of decreasing symmetry, the six crystal systems are cubic (isometric), tetragonal, hexagonal (trigonal), orthorhombic, monoclinic, and triclinic.

2.4.3 Six Crystal Systems

2.4.3.1 Cubic (Isometric) System

Crystals in the cubic, or isometric, class have three mutually perpendicular crystal axes, with their building blocks having the same spacing along each axis. The axes are commonly designated a_1, a_2, and a_3, with the use of the same letter for all axes (a) indicating that they all have the same spacing. Other books designate the three axes as a, b, and c, and define cubic crystals as those having $a = b = c$. The angles between crystal axes are designated by the Greek letters α (the angle between b and c), β (the angle between a and c), and γ (the angle between a and b). Note that the two axes and the angle collectively make up the first three letters of the alphabet, with the angle represented by a Greek character. For cubic crystals, $\alpha = \beta = \gamma = 90°$. From the standpoint of symmetry, every cubic crystal possesses four threefold axes of rotational symmetry (or four threefold roto-inversion axes). When

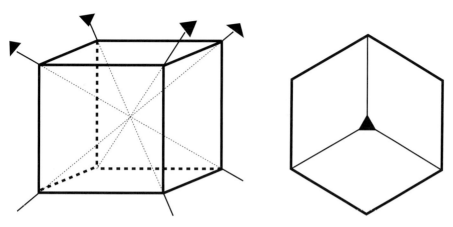

Figure 2.33 The cubic crystal system is characterized by the presence of four threefold axes (or threefold roto-inversion axes) of symmetry, located at the corners of a cube. They are shown for a cube in perspective (left) as well as looking down one of the corners of the cube (right).

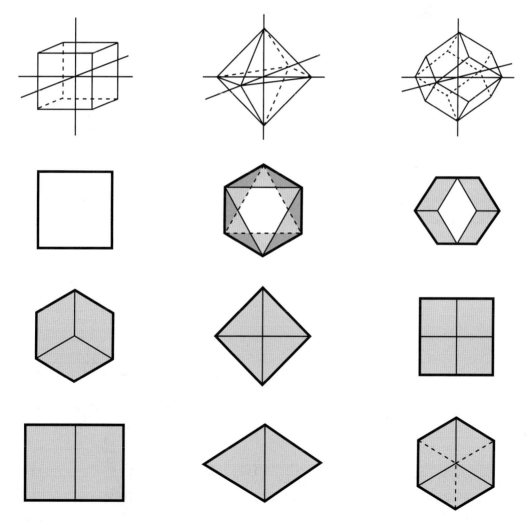

Figure 2.34 Three cubic crystal forms shown in perspective (top) and in several different orientations (bottom). The forms are a cube (left), octahedron (middle), and dodecahedron (right).

looking down at the intersection of the three crystallographic axes from a point equidistant from all three axes, one would be looking down a 3 or $\bar{3}$ axis. In crystals whose external forms are cubes, the threefold axes run between opposite corners of the cube (Figure 2.33).

Many other symmetry elements are possible in cubic crystals, including fourfold rotational axes of symmetry, twofold axes of symmetry, mirror planes, and centers of symmetry. While it is easy to see the relationship between a simple cube, or even an octahedron, and the internal cubic structure, some cubic crystals have shapes that are more challenging to visually relate to their cubic internal structure. Several cubic crystals are shown in Figure 2.34.

2.4.3.2 Tetragonal System

Crystals in the tetragonal system are those having three mutually perpendicular crystal axes with identical spacing along two of these axes, but different spacing along the third axis. The two equivalent axes are labeled a_1 and a_2, and the axis with the unique spacing is labeled c. Some texts refer to the three axes as a, b, and c, with $a = b \neq c$ for tetragonal crystals. For tetragonal crystals, the angles are $\alpha = \beta = \gamma = 90°$. One could imagine making a tetragonal crystal by starting with a cubic crystal and compressing or stretching it along just one of the axes (which would then become the c axis). All tetragonal crystals possess one unique fourfold axis of rotational symmetry (or fourfold roto-inversion axis) that coincides with the c axis. This symmetry is sometimes readily apparent (Figure 2.35), and in other forms less so, with crystals containing a roto-inversion axis being less intuitive. Several common tetragonal crystal forms are shown in Figure 2.36.

2.4.3.3 Hexagonal System

Crystals in the hexagonal class have four crystal axes. Three of these axes, labeled a_1, a_2, and a_3, are all in one plane and are 120° apart from

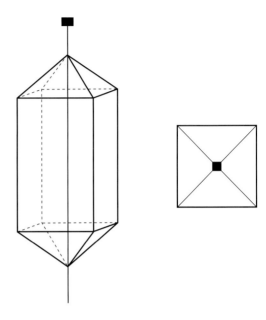

Figure 2.35 The tetragonal crystal system is characterized by the presence of a unique fourfold axis (or fourfold roto-inversion axis) of symmetry that coincides with the c axis of the crystal. This axis is shown for a tetragonal prism terminated by pyramids in perspective (left) as well as looking down the c axis of the crystal (right).

each other; the spacing along all three of the a axes is identical. The fourth crystal axis, designated the c axis, is perpendicular to the plane containing the a axes. The spacing along the c axis is different from that along the a axes. All hexagonal crystals possess one unique six- or threefold axis of rotational symmetry (or roto-inversion symmetry) that coincides with the c axis. This symmetry is sometimes readily apparent, and in other forms less so (Figures 2.37 and 2.38). In some classification systems this crystal system is further subdivided into crystals having sixfold symmetry along their c axis (termed hexagonal) and those having threefold rotational or roto-inversion symmetry along this axis (termed trigonal). Note that the axes of hexagonal crystals are also referred to as a, b, and c, with $a = b \neq c$, the third equivalent axis being implied. Using this notation the angles are $\alpha = \beta = 90°$, $\gamma = 120°$.

Figure 2.36 Three tetragonal crystal forms shown in perspective (top) and in several different orientations (bottom). The forms are a tetragonal prism terminated by basal pinacoid (left), a tetragonal bipyramid (middle), and a tetragonal prism terminated by pyramids (right).

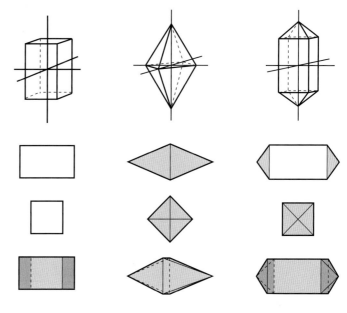

Figure 2.37 The hexagonal crystal system is characterized by the presence of a unique sixfold or threefold axis of symmetry (or roto-inversion axis of symmetry) that coincides with the c axis of the crystal. This axis is shown for a hexagonal bipyramid in perspective (left) as well as looking down the c axis of the crystal (right).

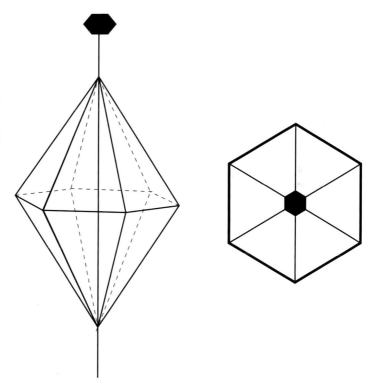

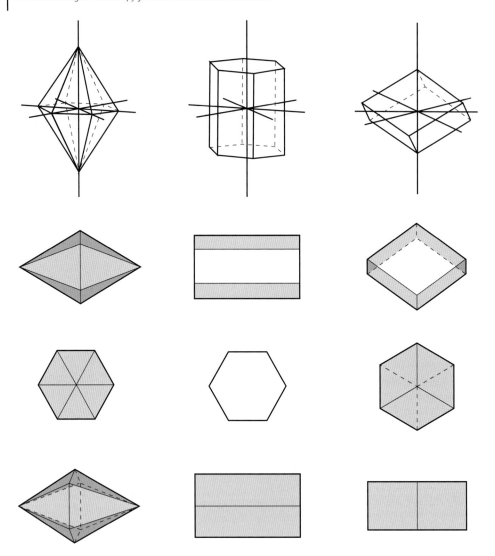

Figure 2.38 Three hexagonal crystal forms shown in perspective (top) and in several different orientations (bottom). The forms are a hexagonal bipyramid (left), a hexagonal prism terminated by basal pinacoid (middle), and a trigonal rhombohedron (right).

2.4.3.4 Orthorhombic System

Crystals in the orthorhombic class are those having three mutually perpendicular crystal axes with different spacing along all three. By convention the axis with the smallest spacing is designated the c axis, the axis with the longest spacing is designated the a axis, and the remaining axis is the designated the b axis ($a \neq b \neq c$). These crystals have either three twofold axes of symmetry, a combination of a twofold axis of symmetry and two mirror planes, or three each of twofold axes of symmetry and mirror planes (Figure 2.39). For orthorhombic crystals, $\alpha = \beta = \gamma = 90°$.

2.4.3.5 Monoclinic System

Crystals in the monoclinic class are those having three crystal axes, two of which are inclined (not perpendicular to) each other. The two axes that are not perpendicular to each

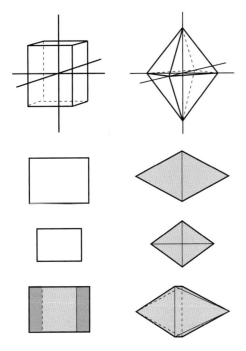

Figure 2.39 Two orthorhombic crystal forms shown in perspective (top) and in several different orientations (bottom). The crystal on the left consists of three pinacoids, while the crystal on the right is an orthorhombic dipyramid.

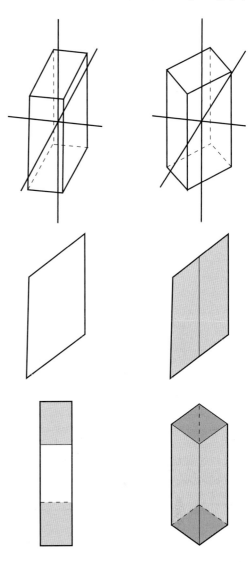

Figure 2.40 Two monoclinic crystal forms shown in perspective (top) and in two different orientations (bottom). The crystal on the left is composed of three pinacoids, while the crystal on the right is a combination of a prism and pinacoid.

other are designated the c and a axes, the c axis being the one with the smaller spacing. The third axis, designated the b axis, is perpendicular to the plane containing both the c and a axes. The spacing in monoclinic crystals is different along all three axes ($a \neq b \neq c$). The b axis is a special direction in monoclinic crystals, either coinciding with a unique twofold axis of symmetry in the crystal, being perpendicular to a unique mirror plane in the crystal, or both (Figure 2.40). For monoclinic crystals, $\alpha = \gamma = 90°$, $\beta \neq 90°$.

2.4.3.6 Triclinic System

Crystals in the triclinic class are those having three mutually inclined crystal axes, with different spacing along all three axes ($a \neq b \neq c$). They have no mirror planes, no rotational axes of symmetry, and no roto-inversion axes. At most they have a center of symmetry, although some have no symmetry elements at all (Figure 2.41). For triclinic crystals, $\alpha \neq \beta \neq \gamma \neq 90°$.

It is worth noting that wherever a crystal system is defined as having different spacing along different axes, it is possible by sheer coincidence that the spacing along two axes may be almost identical. Similarly, it is possible

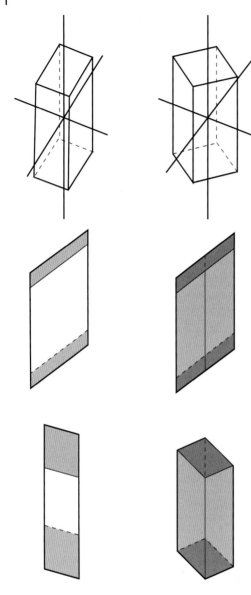

Figure 2.41 Two triclinic crystal forms shown in perspective (top) and in several different orientations (bottom). These forms both have centers of symmetry and are therefore each composed of three pinacoids.

2.4.4 Crystal Morphology

The microscopist can study crystallography from two perspectives that are inter-related, namely the external crystal morphology and the optical crystallographic properties. Not all crystalline particles have clearly developed external crystal forms, however. When crystal forms are well-developed, they are called euhedral; when crystal forms are non-existent, the crystals are described as anhedral. More typically, crystal forms fall somewhere in between these two extremes and are termed subhedral (Figure 2.42).

The value of the external crystal morphology comes from the fact that the stable external faces are determined by the internal crystal structure, so the external crystal form provides insights into the internal structure. For all crystals with well-developed crystal forms, the external form must contain all of the symmetry elements present in the internal structure. It is possible, however, for the external form to contain additional symmetry elements not present in the internal structure. The specific combination of faces that form in a crystal are characteristic of that substance, although external conditions during growth can influence the stability of growing crystal faces and thereby influence their relative development.

As a result of the relationship between internal symmetry and external symmetry, if symmetry elements can be recognized in the external shape of the crystal, the possible crystal class of the crystal can be narrowed. The presence or absence of certain symmetry elements can point definitively to a particular crystal system. It is useful when discussing the external morphology of crystals to be able to refer to specific crystal faces and directions (zones) in a crystal using clear, simple language. The need for an unambiguous means of communicating about crystal faces and zones resulted in the development of the Miller Index system by W.H. Miller in the early 1800s.

that by coincidence one of the angles α, β, or γ in a triclinic crystal (or β in a monoclinic crystal) could be very close to 90°. However, these angles are not required to be 90° by the internal symmetry of the crystal and as a result these coincidences rarely occur.

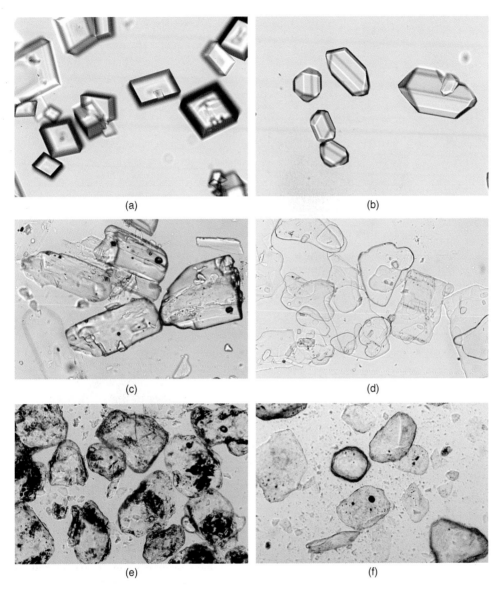

Figure 2.42 Examples of crystals with well-developed forms (euhedral, top), with partially developed forms (subhedral, middle), and with virtually no evident crystal forms (anhedral, bottom).

2.4.4.1 Miller Indices

Crystallographers use notations called Miller Indices to refer to the specific faces that form in a crystal (along with other important crystal directions). Assigning a Miller Index involves first defining a unit face for the crystal. Originally, a crystal was assigned to one of the six crystal systems described above, and the face with the largest area that intersected all three crystal axes was designated the crystal's unit face. Modern crystallographers use lattice spacings determined by X-ray diffraction to define the unit face. For example, the lattice spacings for anhydrite are $a = 6.99\,\text{Å}$, $b = 7.00\,\text{Å}$, $c = 6.24\,\text{Å}$, so the unit face would intercept the axes at ratios of $6.99 : 7.00 : 6.24$ (Nesse 2004). Once the unit face is defined, the relative number of units at which a face of

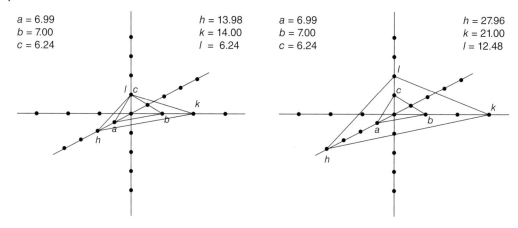

$a = 6.99$	$h = 13.98$
$b = 7.00$	$k = 14.00$
$c = 6.24$	$l = 6.24$

$a = 6.99$	$h = 27.96$
$b = 7.00$	$k = 21.00$
$c = 6.24$	$l = 12.48$

Figure 2.43 The intercepts of the anhydrite unit face (a, b, c) are shown along with the intercepts of an imaginary face hkl having $h = 2a$, $k = 2b$, and $l = 1c$. The Miller Index for this face is 112.

Figure 2.44 The intercepts of the anhydrite unit face (a, b, c) are shown along with the intercepts of another imaginary face hkl, this time having $h = 4a$, $k = 3b$, and $l = 2c$. The Miller Index for this face is 346.

interest intersects each of the crystallographic axes in the crystal is determined. For example, one of the possible faces on an anhydrite crystal intercepts the crystal axes at ratios of 13.98a, 14.00b, and 6.24c units; this face has intercepts of 2a, 2b, and 1c (Figure 2.43). It turns out that this calculation (ignoring very small errors) always results in integer numbers for the intercepts. This observation is referred to as the Law of Rational Intercepts (or Haüy's Law).

The Miller Index of this face is determined by taking the reciprocals of these intercepts, or 1/2, 1/2, 1/1, and multiplying them by the smallest number necessary to reduce all fractions, in this case 2. The resulting Miller Index is 112, read as "one, one, two." A second example is shown in Figure 2.44, with another possible face on an anhydrite crystal. This second face intercepts the crystal axes at ratios of 27.96a, 21.00b, and 12.48c units; it has intercepts of 4a, 3b, 2c. As for the first example, the Miller Index is determined by taking the reciprocals of these intercepts (1/4, 1/3, 1/2) and multiplying them by the smallest number necessary to reduce all fractions, in this case 12. The resulting Miller Index is 346, read as "three, four, six." The general equation for the Miller Index of face *hkl* is a/h, b/k, c/l.

Miller Indices are always reduced to the lowest integer numbers possible by dividing by a common denominator. There is no 224 face, for example, because all three numbers could be divided by 2 to give a Miller Index of 112 for this face. Where a face does not intersect a crystal axis, the intercept is considered to be infinity, with $1/\infty = 0$. If a face intersects the negative side of an axis, a negative sign is placed above the Miller Index for that axis, and the number read with the word "bar" preceding it: face $10\bar{1}$ would be read as "one, zero, bar one."

For orthorhombic, monoclinic, and triclinic crystals, the Miller Index is always written in the order a, b, c. For cubic crystals, the Miller Index is provided in the order a_1, a_2, a_3, for tetragonal crystals the order is a_1, a_2, c, and for hexagonal crystals it is a_1, a_2, a_3, c. It turns out that the sum of the first three Miller Indices of a hexagonal crystal (referring to the a_1, a_2, and a_3 axes) always equal zero. Thus the a_3 numeral is sometimes replaced with an asterisk in the Miller Index for hexagonal crystals, or alternatively left out entirely. The rhombohedron face in a typical calcite rhomb can therefore alternatively be written as $(10\bar{1}1)$, $(10*1)$, or (101).

When looking at a Miller Index, remember that a 0 value indicates that the face is parallel to that axis, and the value of any numeral is inversely proportional to the distance (in unit cells) from the center of the crystal to that intercept. A bar above a number indicates that the face has an intercept along the negative side of that axis. For example, the 111 face intercepts all three crystal axes at equal numbers of unit cells from the crystal center. The 012 face of a monoclinic crystal is parallel to the *a* axis and intercepts the *b* axis at twice the number of unit cells as the *c* axis. The 100 face of a triclinic crystal intercepts the *a* crystal axis, but is parallel to both the *b* and *c* axes of the crystal.

Because it is critical to understand the importance of the orientation of a crystal in determining the optical properties observed, anyone attempting to understand optical crystallography will need to be able to discuss crystal orientations. Crystal orientations are usually discussed in terms of the crystal plane (using Miller Indices) that is parallel to the microscope stage, typically referred to as the crystal section being examined. For example, this chapter will refer to the properties observed when studying the 001 section of a hexagonal crystal and distinguish those from the properties observed on the 100 section. For more detailed discussion of Miller Indices, along with conventional notations for zones (directions) in crystals, crystal forms, and more, the reader is directed to Bloss (2000) and Wood (1977).

2.4.4.2 Crystal Forms and Crystal Habit

Crystal forms are combinations of one or more crystal faces that are related to each other by symmetry elements in a crystal. For example, if one crystal face is present on a crystal that contains a center of symmetry, this symmetry element requires a second crystal face, equal in size and shape, to be present on the opposite side of the crystal (Figure 2.45).

These two faces would together constitute a crystal form termed a pinacoid. If one face

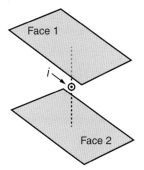

Figure 2.45 In this example, the presence of a center of symmetry (*i*) and Face 1 requires a second face (Face 2) to be present on the crystal reflected through the center of symmetry. The two faces, related to each other by the center of symmetry, are collectively called a pinacoid form.

is parallel to a fourfold axis of symmetry in a tetragonal crystal, the operation of the axis would require three additional, equivalent faces to exist in the crystal, each 90° apart. Together these four faces constitute a tetragonal prism. There exists a tremendous variety of possible crystal forms, depending on the specific symmetry of a crystal and the orientation of a face relative to the symmetry elements in that crystal. Bloss (2000) does an excellent job of expanding on this concept. The terminology used to discuss crystal forms should only be used when the symmetry relating those forms to each other is known with certainty, as these terms have very specific meanings to crystallographers. This terminology is the language of crystal morphology and it is extremely valuable for those communicating about crystals. However, for the characterization, identification, and comparisons of substances during forensic casework, this language is not necessary. It is typically sufficient (and often more practical) to use less formal descriptive language during casework, specifically by describing crystal habits.

The "habit" of a crystal is essentially a qualitative description of its general external appearance. Because the terms used are primarily descriptive in nature, there are no

Table 2.3 Several habit terms that are commonly used by mineralogists, along with their descriptions.

Habit	Description
Acicular	Crystals are shaped like needles
Bladed	Crystals are shaped like blades
Blocky	Crystals have similar dimensions in all directions (equant)
Columnar	Crystals are shaped like columns
Dendritic	Crystals are shaped like diverging tree branches
Fibrous	Crystals are shaped like thin fibers
Globular	Crystals are round, nearly spherical
Granular	Crystals are roughly equant, anhedral to subhedral grains with limited size range
Platy	Crystals are shaped like thin sheets
Prismatic	Crystals are shaped like elongated, slender prisms
Rosette	Crystals radiate outward from a central point, or intersect in a central point, resembling flower petals
Tabular	Crystals are shaped like tablets

rigorous rules applied to their use and there is some subjectivity to their application. Introductory mineralogy textbooks are good sources for possible terms that may be used to describe crystal habits (Dyar et al. 2008). A few common examples are listed in Table 2.3.

2.4.4.3 Crystal Morphology Through the Light Microscope

One of the biggest challenges facing the trace evidence examiner studying crystal morphology through a light microscope is the fact that these three-dimensional objects can only be seen in two dimensions at a time. The ideal way to study crystal morphology is to examine three-dimensional crystal models and then observe well-formed crystals through the microscope having the same morphology as those models. Crystals of many compounds may be grown on a microscope slide and can provide valuable experience

reconciling two-dimensional views of these three-dimensional objects. With practice, by adjusting the condenser aperture and focus, noting the areas of a crystal that are shaded, and looking at retardation colors (covered later in this chapter), the three-dimensional shape of a crystal can become apparent despite the imaging limitations of the light microscope.

Once an examiner has some experience studying two-dimensional crystals and extrapolating from the views presented what the three-dimensional crystal looks like, they can begin to exploit crystal morphology for the identification of unknown substances. The best way to gain insights into the crystal morphology of a compound (and therefore tentatively identify it on this basis) is to grow well-formed crystals of the substance. However, crystallization is time-consuming, requires more sample than is often available to the forensic scientist, and may be virtually impossible for insoluble materials such as silicate minerals. It is more practical to simply be aware of the potential value of crystal morphology and exploit it when the opportunity presents itself. Some substances are frequently found in commercial products or in nature as subhedral to euhedral crystals. For these compounds, the crystal morphology should be observed and characterized. This property can be a valuable clue to the identity of the substance, and together with its optical properties may enable nearly instantaneous recognition of many common substances. Several common minerals that can be recognized in part on the basis of their crystal morphology are shown in Figure 2.46.

While the morphology is an immediate clue, any hypothesis of identity should be followed up by checking as many optical properties as practical (or appropriate instrumental analysis) in order to confirm the tentative identification. A strong understanding of optical crystallography and optical orientation enables a sufficiently large number of properties to be rapidly compared to reference data that a misidentification becomes extremely unlikely.

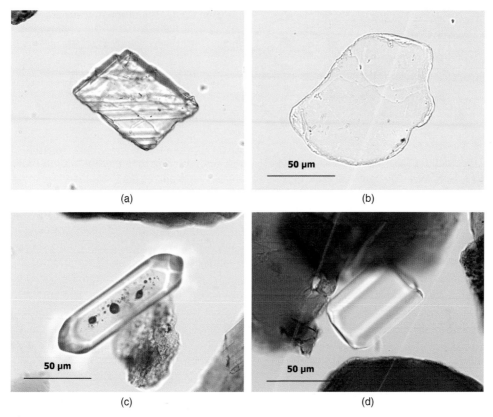

(a)

(b)

50 µm

(c)

50 µm

(d)

50 µm

Figure 2.46 One important property useful for the identification of mineral grains in soil, building materials, and other types of evidence is crystal morphology. Shown are several minerals with distinctive morphology. (a) Calcite grains commonly occur as trigonal rhombohedra; (b) muscovite mica occurs as thin flakes; (c) zircon grains commonly occur as tetragonal prisms terminated by pyramids; (d) apatite commonly occurs as hexagonal prisms.

2.5 Introduction to Optical Crystallography

Optical crystallography is the study of how light interacts with crystalline substances. As this section discusses, light behaves very differently as it interacts with different types of crystals. An understanding of optical crystallography can help the examiner interpret the interaction of light with various types of non-crystalline substances as well, such as fibers and polymer films. The simplest crystals to study with light are cubic (isometric) crystals, so those will be discussed first. Because cubic crystals behave similarly to glass with respect to how they transmit light, they will be discussed together.

2.5.1 Optics of Isotropic Substances

Isotropic substances include both amorphous substances such as glass and cubic (isometric) crystals. It is critical that the forensic glass examiner has a strong understanding of the optical properties of isotropic substances. The optical properties of isotropic substances are much more limited than those of anisotropic (non-isotropic) substances, and are essentially limited to refractive index and dispersion values.

As discussed earlier, cubic crystals have the same spacing of atoms/molecules/ions along all three of their mutually perpendicular crystal axes. Due to their symmetry, light travels at the same speed regardless of the plane in the

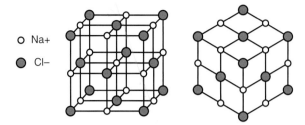

○ Na+

● Cl–

Figure 2.47 The crystal structure of sodium chloride (table salt) shown in perspective (left) and again looking down one of the threefold axes of symmetry (right).

crystal in which the light vibrates. Because the refractive index of a substance is determined by the velocity of light in that substance, the refractive index of light traveling through an isotropic substance is the same regardless of the path taken through the crystal and regardless of the plane in which the light vibrates as it travels through the crystal. In order to understand why light behaves this way, it is useful to consider the structure of a simple cubic crystal such as sodium chloride (table salt). This material is composed of sodium cations and chloride anions, in a 1 : 1 ratio, stacked in a face-centered cubic lattice (Figure 2.47).

The sodium cation can be imagined as a positively charged sphere. Each sodium cation is surrounded by six chloride anions, each of which can be considered as a negatively charged sphere. In turn, each chloride ion is surrounded by six sodium ions. The electrons in the chloride ion are attracted to all of the surrounding cations. For each sodium ion next to a given chloride ion there is another sodium ion on the opposite side of the chloride and an equal distance away. Whatever attraction is felt by the electrons toward one sodium ion, there is another cation "pulling" in the opposite direction with an equal attractive force. The result is that all attractions cancel each other out and the electron polarizability of the chloride ion is the same in all directions. A single light ray that encounters the electric field associated with this chloride ion's electrons will encounter the same electron polarizability regardless of the plane in which the light vibrates. Consider that a single light wave in the visible range of the spectrum (≥400 nm wavelength) is considerably larger

than a single chlorine or sodium atom (both between 100 and 200 pm), and therefore interacts with multiple chloride and sodium ions at once, encountering an electron density and polarizability that is averaged over a number of atoms. The net result of these conditions is that no matter what the plane of vibration of the light is, it encounters the same average electron density and polarizability, and therefore travels at the same velocity. Because refractive index is related to velocity, the refractive index is the same for light vibrating in any plane as it travels through this substance (this is the definition of optical isotropy).

The variation of refractive index (or, in this case, lack thereof) with the path of light traveling through a substance is typically depicted graphically by means of a three-dimensional figure called the optical indicatrix (or simply indicatrix) of the substance. This figure is constructed by drawing lines outward from the center of the substance, with the magnitude of the line being proportional to the refractive index value encountered by light vibrating parallel to the line as it travels through the substance. These lines are drawn for every possible direction through the crystal, and the surface defined by the ends of the lines is a three-dimensional shape called the indicatrix. By definition, the refractive index is the same for light vibrating in all directions within an isotropic substance. The magnitudes of all lines used to construct an isotropic indicatrix are therefore equal in size. The shape of the figure thus constructed (and the shape of the optical indicatrix of any isotropic substance) is a sphere. The radius of the sphere is proportional to the refractive index value for the

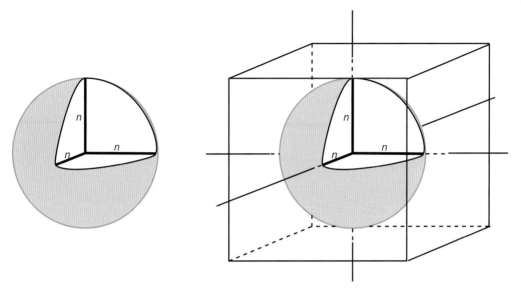

Figure 2.48 The indicatrix of an isotropic substance with refractive index = *n* (left), and the relationship between the indicatrix and the crystal morphology of sodium chloride (right).

substance. A substance with a higher refractive index would have as its indicatrix a sphere with a greater radius. The indicatrix for sodium chloride is shown in Figure 2.48.

While refractive index in an isotropic substance does not depend on the orientation of the vibrating light relative to the crystal structure, the refractive index does vary with the wavelength of light (see discussion of dispersion in Section 2.2.3). Thus a complete description of the optical properties of an isotropic substance would include the refractive index values for several different wavelengths of light (commonly n_C, n_D, and n_F). This dispersion can be depicted by drawing different indicatrix figures for different wavelengths of light (Figure 2.49). For a cubic substance, all indicatrices will be spheres. However, the spheres will have different radii due to the different refractive index values for the various wavelengths of light. For the identification of unknown isotropic compounds this additional information is rarely needed. However, for the forensic comparison of glass samples the dispersion of glass fragments may have probative value. As a result some forensic glass examiners that use refractive

index values of glass particles as a means of comparison include measurements made at several different wavelengths.

When using an indicatrix to understand the behavior of light in a substance, it is important to keep clear the distinction between the propagation direction of light (the direction the light is traveling) and the vibration direction of the light (the direction of displacement of the electric vector of the light). For light traveling through an isotropic substance, the vibration direction is always perpendicular to the propagation direction of the light. If the plane perpendicular to the light's propagation direction is located and highlighted, it is possible to visualize all of the possible vibration directions for light traveling in a particular direction. To understand how this relates to the indicatrix of a crystal, imagine a light ray traveling through the sodium chloride indicatrix. Next, take a cross-section of the indicatrix that includes the center of the sphere and is perpendicular to the propagation direction of the light. For light traveling through the crystal in the chosen direction, this section of the indicatrix defines all of the possible vibration directions for the light (Figure 2.50).

$n_C = 1.541$ $n_D = 1.544$ $n_F = 1.553$

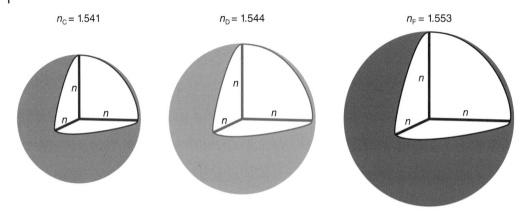

Figure 2.49 Sodium chloride indicatrices for different wavelengths of light (size differences exaggerated).

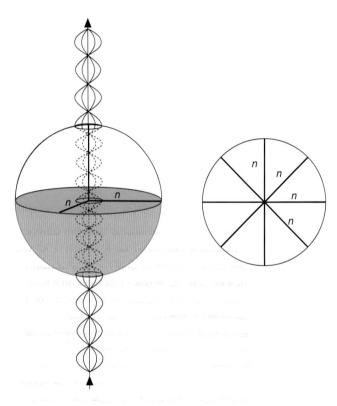

Figure 2.50 A cubic crystal's indicatrix illuminated from below with unpolarized light (left). The cross-section of the indicatrix that is perpendicular to the light's propagation direction is shaded orange on the left and shown again on the right side from above. This section contains all possible vibration directions for light passing through the crystal in this direction. The radii of the section are proportional to the magnitude of the refractive index encountered by light vibrating in any particular direction.

The refractive index encountered by light as it travels through the crystal in this particular direction is equal to the radius of this indicatrix section. The indicatrix of a substance thus becomes a tool for determining the possible refractive index values encountered by light traveling through a crystal in a particular direction. For an isotropic substance, whose indicatrix is a sphere, any section through the indicatrix that includes its center will be a circle. The radius of the circle is the refractive index value for light vibrating in that direction. Since a sphere has a single radius, the radii of all circular sections containing the center of the sphere will be equal. This statement is another way of saying that the refractive

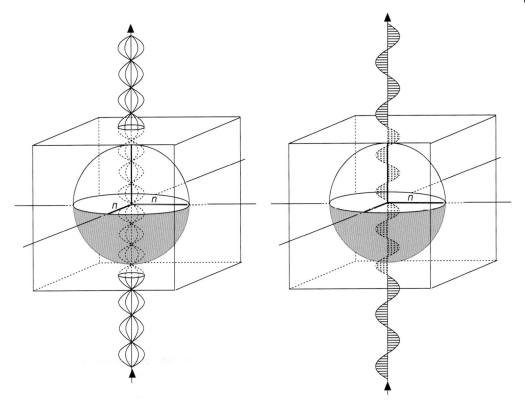

Figure 2.51 A cubic crystal's indicatrix illuminated from below with both unpolarized light (left) and polarized light (right). Unpolarized light remains unpolarized as it transmits through the crystal. Polarized light transmitting through the crystal remains polarized in the same plane as the incident light.

index of the light is the same regardless of the path it takes through the crystal (its propagation direction) and regardless of its plane of vibration (its vibration direction).

As will be seen in the following section on measuring optical properties, it is advantageous when studying crystals to illuminate them with plane polarized light (Figure 2.3). For an isotropic substance, polarized light will remain polarized and continue to vibrate in the same plane as the incident light during passage through an isotropic substance. Similarly, unpolarized light remains unchanged during its passage through an isotropic substance (Figure 2.51).

For more complex crystal systems, the direction in which light travels through the crystal does indeed impact its velocity (and potentially other properties as well). It is therefore useful

to consider the relationship between different orientations (sections) of a crystal and the respective sections of that crystal's indicatrix. For a cube lying on one of its faces on a microscope slide, the section of the crystal being examined is the 001 section (because the 001 face is parallel to the plane of the microscope). The indicatrix should be oriented such that this section of the indicatrix is parallel to the microscope slide (while the orientation makes no difference for a sphere, with other types of crystals the orientation of the indicatrix is very important). Light propagating along the axis of the microscope would be vibrating in the plane perpendicular to its propagation direction, namely the plane parallel to the stage. When light enters the crystal, it would be vibrating in the 001 section as it travels through the crystal perpendicular to this section (Figure 2.52).

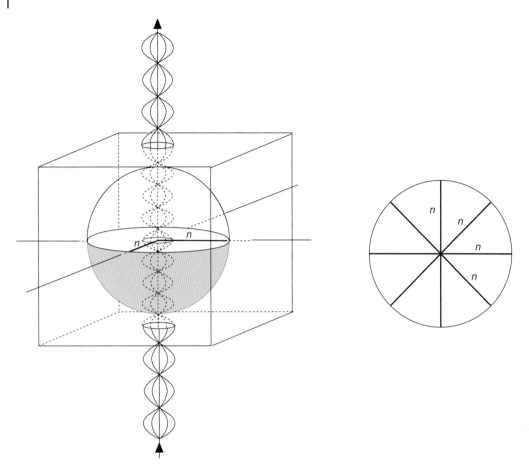

Figure 2.52 A cubic crystal illuminated from below with unpolarized light, oriented with its 001 section parallel to the plane of the microscope stage (left). The cross-section of the indicatrix that is perpendicular to the light's propagation direction (in this case the cross-section in the 001 plane) is shown on the right side.

If the same cube were tipped up so that it is lying on a corner, the section of the crystal being examined would now be the 111 section. The light traveling through the cube would now be vibrating in the 111 plane as it travels through the crystal (Figure 2.53).

To understand the refractive index values encountered by light traveling through the cube in these two different directions, simply take sections of the indicatrix parallel to these crystal sections, and the radii of the indicatrix sections are equal to the refractive index values encountered by the light. For a cubic crystal, whose indicatrix is a sphere, there is no refractive index difference for light traveling through crystals in these different orientations (as is evident from the sections shown in Figures 2.52 and 2.53). However, these concepts will be important when applied to more complex crystals.

A useful concept to grasp when studying the interaction of light with crystals is that of an "optic axis." By definition, an optic axis in a crystal is any direction in a crystal that is perpendicular to a circular section of the crystal's indicatrix. Since a sphere has an infinite number of circular sections, it also has an infinite number of optic axes. In fact any direction through a cubic crystal can be considered an optic axis of that crystal. Because

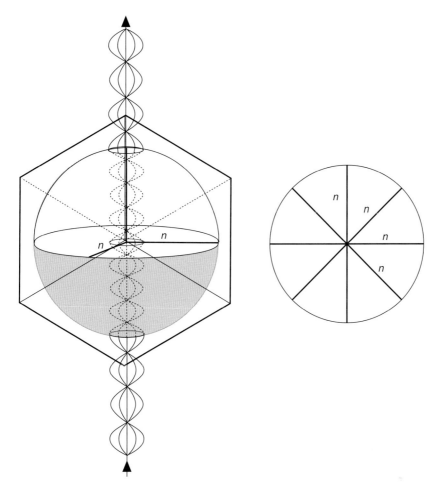

Figure 2.53 A cubic crystal illuminated from below with unpolarized light, oriented with its 111 section parallel to the plane of the microscope stage (left). The cross-section of the indicatrix that is perpendicular to the light's propagation direction (in this case the cross-section in the 111 plane) is shown on the right side. Refraction at the crystal surface is being ignored.

there is nothing special about the directions in a cubic crystal that are optic axes, it is not common to discuss the optic axes of cubic crystals. As will be seen, optic axes occur in only special directions in other crystal systems, and the concept of an optic axis becomes much more important for studying crystals in the other crystal systems.

Because of the simple nature of the isotropic indicatrix, it is not a particularly useful tool for understanding the behavior of light in isotropic materials. It is fairly straightforward to grasp the important concepts of how light interacts

with these substances without resorting to this type of discussion. For the more complex anisotropic substances, however, indicatrix theory is extremely useful for understanding their optical behavior.

2.5.2 Optics of Uniaxial Substances

For tetragonal and hexagonal crystals, the interaction between light and the crystals is much more complicated. These crystals have two principal refractive index values, and light traveling through these crystals behaves in a manner that surprised the early scientists who first observed it. Light incident on the cleavage face of a calcite rhomb will break into two separate rays as the light travels through the crystal. The waves of the two rays vibrate in planes perpendicular to each other and travel through the crystal at different velocities. The faster ray emerges from the crystal slightly ahead of the slower ray. In addition, the two rays emerge from the calcite rhomb in slightly different locations and with different apparent depths. This phenomenon is easily observed in calcite in the following manner. If a cleavage rhomb of calcite is placed over an image on a piece of paper, two images are seen (a phenomenon known as double refraction). As the rhomb is rotated, one of these images is seen to rotate about the other (Figure 2.54). If the viewer moves their head from side to side as they observe the two images, one image will appear to be deeper than the other. Because

light behaves differently when it vibrates in different planes in calcite, calcite is said to be anisotropic (not isotropic).

Given that the image is being viewed between two parallel faces of the crystal, and considering the discussion of refraction of light at the beginning of this chapter, the astute reader will notice that something is amiss. Snell's Law dictates that, given normal incidence, all light passing through the crystal should continue without deviation (its velocity changing, but not its direction). It was clear to early investigators that the light passing through a crystal of this type was separated into two components, one of which obeys Snell's Law (termed the Ordinary ray or O ray) and one of which does not (termed the Extraordinary ray or E ray). This observation in calcite makes it clear that in anisotropic crystals (those with different refractive index values in different crystal planes), there is a more

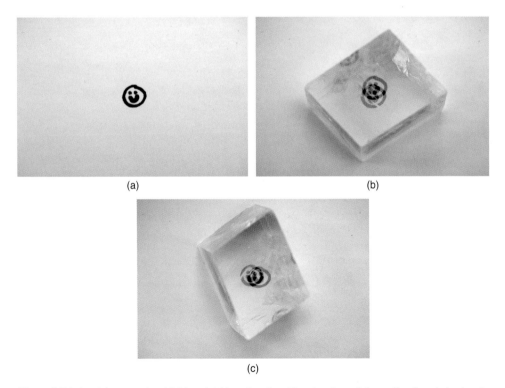

(a)

(b)

(c)

Figure 2.54 A calcite crystal exhibiting double refraction. The drawing of the smiley face is broken into two separate images, one that remains stationary as the crystal is rotated (the ordinary ray) and one that appears to rotate with the crystal (the extraordinary ray).

complicated relationship between incident angles, refracted (transmitted) angles, and refractive index values than Snell's Law suggests. The complete theory behind this unusual behavior requires an in-depth discussion of the concepts of wave normals, wave vibration directions, ray directions, and wave fronts. Many of these details are beyond the scope of this chapter, but an excellent treatment of the subject can be found in the classic book on optical crystallography by Bloss (1961). Some basic concepts will be covered here, however.

In an isotropic substance, the polarizability of the electric field with which light interacts is the same in all directions within the substance, at least on the scale of light waves.

In anisotropic substances, however, the average electron polarizability may be very different in different planes in the crystal. Imagine light traveling through a calcite crystal. The carbonate ions (with multiple C–O bonds) all lie in a single plane within the crystal. Perpendicular to this plane, the bonding is purely ionic. The carbonate ion is trigonal planar (it is shaped like a triangle and all of the atoms lie in a single plane). Calcium ions are located in between the planes containing the carbonate ions (Figure 2.55).

The polarizability of the electrons in an atom is affected (sometimes dramatically) by other atoms nearby. As a result of the influence of neighboring atoms, the electrons in

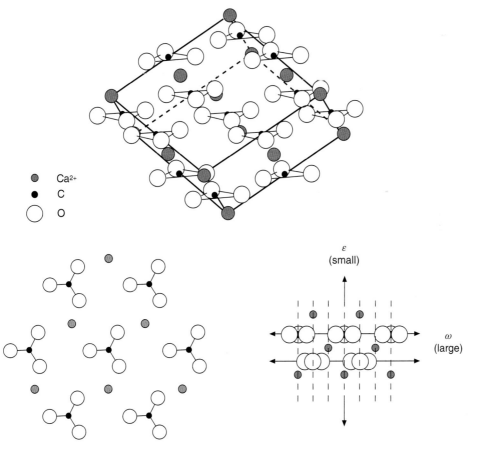

Figure 2.55 The crystal structure of calcium carbonate (calcite) shown in perspective (top) and again looking down the *c* axis (lower left) and looking down one of the *a* axes (lower right). The *c* axis coincides with the unique threefold axis of symmetry in calcite, as can be appreciated in the lower left view. Source: Figure adapted from Hartshorne and Stuart (1960).

the carbonate ion are more easily distorted within the plane of the ion than perpendicular to this plane. Thus the polarizability of the carbonate ion is not equal in all directions (as was the case for ions in the cubic example, sodium chloride). Light waves vibrating in the plane of the carbonate ion encounter significantly greater electron polarizability than those vibrating perpendicular to it. The reader is directed to Hartshorne and Stuart (1960) for additional details. Light waves vibrating in a plane intermediate between those two extremes encounters intermediate electron polarizability. Within the plane containing the carbonate ions, however, the electron polarizability is the same in all dimensions when averaged over many atoms (as is the case for relatively large waves of visible light). The result is that light vibrating anywhere within the plane of the carbonate ions (the plane containing the a axes) travels more slowly, and the crystal has a relatively high refractive index for light vibrating in this plane as it travels through the crystal (1.658). The refractive index of the crystal in the plane of the a axes is represented by the Greek letter ω. Light vibrating perpendicular to this plane (parallel to the c axis), can travel much faster, and as a result the crystal has a relatively low refractive index for light vibrating parallel to the c axis (1.486). The refractive index of the crystal parallel to the c axis is represented by the Greek letter ε. Light vibrating in a plane intermediate between these two directions experiences a refractive index somewhere in between these two values and is represented by ε'. When a substance has more than one refractive index (when it is anisotropic) a new optical property can be defined for the substance: its birefringence. Birefringence is the difference between the highest and lowest refractive index values in a substance, and is typically designated by the Greek letter δ. For calcite, the birefringence is $\delta = 1.658 - 1.486 = 0.172$.

There is one more feature of the behavior of the extraordinary ray in the calcite rhomb that still needs to be explained, namely its apparent deviation from Snell's Law. The asymmetric nature of the electric field inside a calcite crystal can distort light waves such that their vibration direction is no longer perpendicular to the propagation direction of the light wave. The wave normal is the direction perpendicular to the wave front and perpendicular to the vibration direction. In an isotropic medium, the wave normal and ray direction coincide, both being perpendicular to the vibration direction of the wave. In an anisotropic substance, however, they do not always coincide. Figure 2.56 shows the behavior of an extraordinary ray (E ray), whose wave normal does not coincide with its propagation direction.

It turns out that while the propagation direction of the E ray in calcite behaves in an "extraordinary" manner, the wave normal direction does, in fact, follow Snell's Law in calcite. The fact that the E ray propagation direction does not obey Snell's Law, while the O ray's propagation direction does, is what results in separation of the two images viewed through the calcite crystal (Figure 2.57).

When a hand specimen of a calcite rhomb is observed this separation in space of the two rays is quite significant. This notable separation is due both to the very high birefringence of calcite and to the significant thickness of the crystal. When studying crystals with a polarized light microscope, however, the separation in space is usually much smaller because the dimensions of particles being studied under a microscope are typically very small. As a

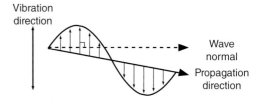

Figure 2.56 A wave of light traveling through an anisotropic substance as an E ray. The vibration direction of the wave is not perpendicular to its propagation direction. The wave normal direction, however, is, by definition, perpendicular to the vibration direction of the wave.

Figure 2.57 The light path for both the O ray (blue) and the E ray (green) through calcite when incident on a rhombohedral face. The E ray vibrates in the plane containing the *c* axis (in this case the plane of the paper). Its wave normal obeys Snell's Law, although its propagation direction does not. The O ray vibrates in the plane perpendicular to the E ray vibration (perpendicular to the plane of the paper). Both its wave normal and its propagation direction obey Snell's Law. Source: Figure adapted from Dyar et al. (2008).

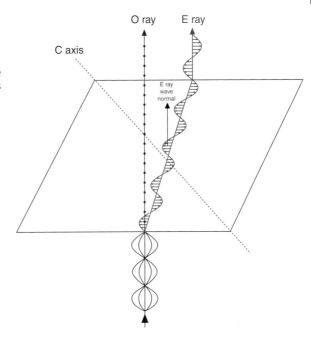

result of the very small thicknesses of typical microscopic subjects, the deviation of the extraordinary ray path from that predicted by Snell's Law is negligible. Correspondingly it has a negligible impact on the phenomena observed. In order to simplify the following discussions, this detail will be ignored for the remainder of this chapter. The interested reader is encouraged to pursue the matter further after mastering the more basic concepts covered here. An excellent place to start are the classic books on the subject by Bloss (1961) and by Hartshorne and Stuart (1960). These references present much more thorough treatments of the variables affecting ray paths, wave fronts, wave normals, and vibration directions in anisotropic materials with various angles of incidence and incident on different crystal sections. Despite the fact the following explanations are oversimplified (ignoring some of the details mentioned above), they will allow accurate predictions to be made of the phenomena discussed, and enable identification and characterization of materials during forensic examinations to be successfully completed based on observations of these phenomena.

That is ultimately the goal of the trace evidence examiner – to identify unknown substances, thoroughly characterize them, and compare them to known materials on the basis of the microscopical properties observed.

As discussed above, the velocity of light in a calcite crystal varies with the vibration direction of the light traveling through the crystal. Light behaves in this manner because the electron polarizability of calcite is different in different planes in the crystal. By definition, for all crystal systems other than the cubic system, the spacing of the crystal's building blocks is different along different crystal axes in the crystal (and often the type of bonding is different along different crystallographic axes as well). It follows that with different spacing and/or types of bonding, the electron density and electron polarizability will differ along different crystallographic directions, and therefore the velocity of light will as well. These crystals are therefore all anisotropic, meaning that light rays traveling through them will have refractive index values that vary with their vibration direction. As was the case for the calcite rhomb, with only a few exceptions for special paths through them (covered below), light is split into two components as it travels through all anisotropic crystals. The two components vibrate in planes that are perpendicular to each other, and they travel at different velocities while inside the crystal. Their wave normals always obey Snell's Law, but their ray directions may not. These crystals all have more than one principal refractive index, and the difference between the highest and lowest refractive index in any anisotropic crystal is its birefringence.

With an understanding of how light interacts with anisotropic substances, it is possible to construct an indicatrix for anisotropic substances like calcite. As discussed above, calcite has two principal refractive index values, namely ω (for light vibrating perpendicular to the c axis) and ε (for light vibrating parallel to the c axis). If lines are drawn outward from the center of the calcite crystal, with the size of each line representing the refractive index value for light vibrating in that direction, and the ends of these lines are connected to form a surface, the surface thus formed is the calcite indicatrix. For calcite, $\omega = 1.658$. Since the refractive index is the same in all directions in the plane of the a axes, this section of the indicatrix will be a circle with radius 1.658. The refractive index perpendicular to this circle (parallel to the c axis) is considerably smaller ($\varepsilon = 1.486$). The refractive index values for light vibrating in planes intermediate between

these two extremes will be equal to some value in between 1.658 and 1.486 (designated ε', its value can be calculated based on its inclination Θ to the c axis as shown in Eq. (2.6)).

$$\varepsilon' = \frac{\omega}{\sqrt{1 + \left(\frac{\omega^2}{\varepsilon^2} - 1\right)\cos^2\theta}} \tag{2.6}$$

The shape thus constructed is called an ellipsoid of revolution. It is convention to draw indicatrix figures with the c axis oriented vertically (Figure 2.58).

To fully appreciate the phenomena that occur when light transmits through a calcite crystal it is useful to consider the three different types of sections that exist in a uniaxial indicatrix (or any ellipsoid of revolution) that pass through the center of the ellipsoid. The first type of section is a circular section. There is one (and only one) circular section in a uniaxial indicatrix. The circular section coincides with the plane that contains the a axes (and ω refractive index values) in the crystal, and is perpendicular to the c axis (and ε refractive index). Given the definition of an optic axis as a direction perpendicular to a circular section of a crystal's indicatrix, the c axis is thus an optic axis in a calcite crystal. Since this plane is the only circular section in the indicatrix, there is only one optic axis and this type of crystal is considered to be uniaxial (having one optic axis). The second type of section to be considered is what is termed a principal section of the indicatrix. A principal section is any

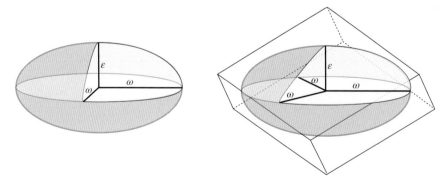

Figure 2.58 The indicatrix of a uniaxial substance with refractive indices having the magnitudes ε and ω (left), and the relationship between the indicatrix and the crystal morphology of calcite (right).

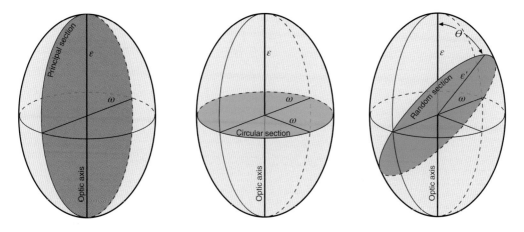

Figure 2.59 The three types of sections that occur in a uniaxial indicatrix. The left image shows one principal section, colored orange; this section includes the optic axis. The center image shows the unique circular section that is perpendicular to the optic axis, colored blue. Finally, the right image shows a random section that is neither perpendicular to the optic axis nor contains it, colored green.

section that contains the optic axis. There are an infinite number of principal sections in a uniaxial indicatrix. Any other section (neither perpendicular to the optic axis nor containing it) is considered a random section. Figure 2.59 illustrates these three types of sections for a uniaxial indicatrix.

How do these three types of sections through a uniaxial indicatrix relate to light traveling through a uniaxial crystal? To understand this relationship it is useful to discuss light rays traveling through a calcite crystal in three different directions. Consider light traveling parallel to the c axis of the crystal (Figure 2.60). The light encounters the 0001 section of the crystal (parallel to the plane containing the three a axes). Thus the plane in which light vibrates is the plane containing the a axes, and the refractive index in this plane is the same in all directions, specifically $\omega = 1.658$. This plane is the unique circular section of the uniaxial indicatrix. Light traveling in this direction, along the unique optic axis in calcite, behaves the same as light traveling through an isotropic substance. Unpolarized light would pass through this crystal and emerge as unpolarized light. Plane polarized light would emerge as a single component vibrating in its original plane.

All light rays obey Snell's Law when traveling through calcite in this direction. This section would exhibit zero birefringence, or $\delta = 0$. This example brings up an important point, namely that sections of a crystal can exhibit a birefringence lower than the true birefringence of the crystal. This concept is an important one that often causes confusion for microscopy students. If they observe a crystal whose birefringence is much lower than that of the literature value for calcite, they conclude that the crystal cannot be calcite. In practice an anisotropic crystal can exhibit birefringence values ranging from zero up to its true (maximum) birefringence, depending on its orientation.

Next, consider a light ray traveling perpendicular to the c axis of the crystal, encountering the $10\bar{1}0$ section of the crystal. The plane in which the light can vibrate contains both the c axis and a direction perpendicular to the c axis (in the plane containing the a axes). This plane is a principal section of calcite's indicatrix (Figure 2.61).

When light passes through a calcite crystal in this direction, the light is resolved (broken) into two separate components vibrating in planes perpendicular to each other. The refractive index values encountered will be $\varepsilon = 1.486$

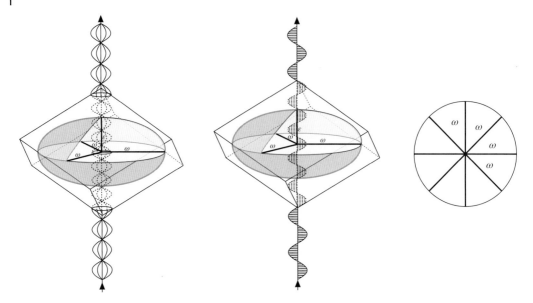

Figure 2.60 A hexagonal (uniaxial) calcite crystal illuminated from below with unpolarized light (left) and plane polarized light (middle), oriented with its 0001 section parallel to the plane of the microscope stage. The cross-section of the indicatrix that is perpendicular to the light's propagation direction (in this case the cross-section in the 0001 plane) is shown on the right side as seen from above. Refraction at the crystal surface is being ignored.

for light vibrating parallel to the c axis and $\omega = 1.658$ for light vibrating perpendicular to the c axis. These vibration directions coincide with the major and minor axes of the ellipse that is the indicatrix section in this plane. In this particular direction, the wave normals and ray directions will obey Snell's Law for both rays. They are thus both considered to be O rays.

For light incident upon any other crystal section, the indicatrix section encountered is an ellipse with one axis equal to ω, and another in between ω and ε (termed ε'). For example, light incident upon the $10\bar{1}1$ face of a calcite rhomb encounters a section of the indicatrix with one axis equal to 1.658 (ω) and one equal to 1.566 (ε'). The $10\bar{1}1$ section is an example of a random section through the uniaxial indicatrix, albeit a commonly encountered random section in calcite because crystals often lie on flat faces (Figure 2.62).

The light is resolved into two separate components, vibrating parallel to the major and minor radii of the elliptical section of the

indicatrix. The component vibrating in the plane perpendicular to the c axis will have a refractive index equal to 1.658; this component is the O ray, and both its wave normal and ray direction obey Snell's Law. The component vibrating in the plane parallel to the c axis will have a refractive index equal to $\varepsilon' = 1.566$; this component is the E ray. Its ray direction does not obey Snell's Law, although its wave normal direction does (as always). While the true birefringence of calcite is equal to 0.172, the birefringence of this section (one that calcite rhombs commonly lie on in a grain mount) is equal to $\delta = 0.092$.

Close examination of all possible directions of light passing through a calcite crystal would reveal that all sections of the indicatrix not discussed above would be elliptical sections with their major radius equal to 1.658 and their minor radius in between 1.486 and 1.658.

As mentioned above, there is only one circular section in the indicatrix of calcite and as a result there is only one optic axis in the crystal (it is uniaxial). All crystals in the tetragonal

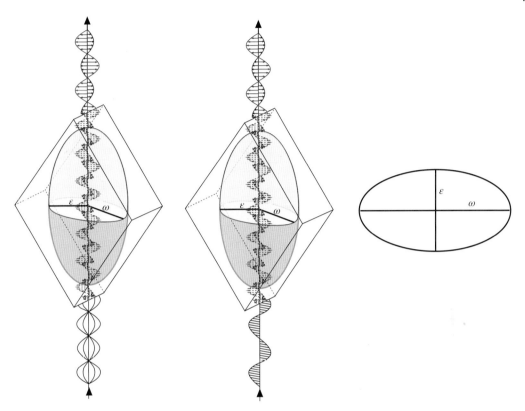

Figure 2.61 A hexagonal (uniaxial) calcite crystal illuminated from below with unpolarized light (left) and plane polarized light (middle), oriented with its $10\overline{1}0$ section parallel to the plane of the microscope stage. The cross-section of the indicatrix that is perpendicular to the light's propagation direction (in this case the cross-section in the $10\overline{1}0$ plane) is shown on the right. Refraction at the crystal surface is being ignored.

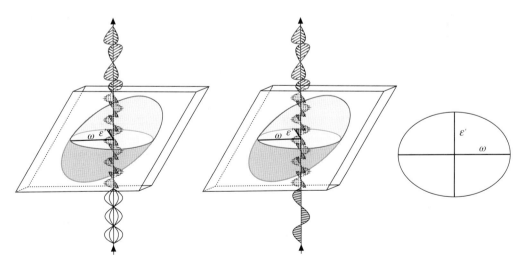

Figure 2.62 A hexagonal (uniaxial) calcite crystal illuminated from below with unpolarized light (left) and plane polarized light (middle), oriented with its $10\overline{1}1$ section parallel to the plane of the microscope stage. The cross-section of the indicatrix that is perpendicular to the light's propagation direction (in this case the cross-section in the $10\overline{1}1$ plane) is shown on the right.

and hexagonal crystal systems behave in a manner analogous to that of calcite. They all have indicatrices that are ellipsoids of revolution, and they all have one unique optic axis. They are all therefore considered to be uniaxial crystals.

Uniaxial crystals can be divided into two groups based on the shapes of their indicatrices. Some uniaxial crystals (like calcite) have a higher refractive index in the plane of their a axes than they do parallel to their c axis (more simply stated as $\omega > \varepsilon$). Their indicatrices are oblate in shape. These crystals are defined as having a negative optic sign. All other uniaxial crystals have a lower refractive index in the plane of their a axes than they do parallel to their c axis ($\omega < \varepsilon$); their indicatrices are prolate in shape. These crystals are considered to have a positive optic sign. The shapes of their respective indicatrices (oblate vs. prolate) and the definition of optic sign for uniaxial crystals are given in Figure 2.63.

As for cubic crystals, the refractive index values in uniaxial crystals vary with the wavelength of light (dispersion). For uniaxial substances, however, there are different refractive index values (ω and ε) that each have their own dispersion values. Thus the size and shape of the indicatrix may vary with wavelength of light, and uniaxial crystals have both dispersion of refractive index values and dispersion

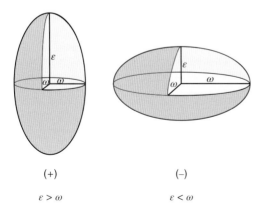

(+)   (−)

$\varepsilon > \omega$ $\varepsilon < \omega$

Figure 2.63 Examples of indicatrices for uniaxial positive (left) and negative (right) substances.

of birefringence. Some rare crystals are even optically positive for some wavelengths of light and optically negative for others (being isotropic for some intermediate wavelength).

While technically not uniaxial crystals, most synthetic fibers behave very much like uniaxial crystals. They have a single refractive index in the plane perpendicular to their length ($n_\perp$), analogous to ω, and a different refractive index parallel to their length ($n_\parallel$), analogous to ε. The preceding discussion therefore applies to most synthetic fibers as well. One major difference, however, is that synthetic fibers essentially always lie down with their $n_\parallel$ in the plane of the microscope stage. They exhibit their maximum possible birefringence in this orientation, making them easier to characterize than uniaxial crystals.

2.5.3 Optics of Biaxial Substances

The interaction of light with three of the six crystal systems has been covered (cubic, tetragonal, hexagonal). The remaining three crystal systems (orthorhombic, monoclinic, triclinic) will now be addressed. All crystals in these three crystal systems have three crystal axes (a, b, c) with different spacing along all three axes ($a \neq b \neq c$). Because the electron polarizability of any given atom is impacted by other atoms nearby, and the nearby atoms have different spacings in different planes in these crystals, the electron polarizability is likely to differ in different directions in these crystals. Consider an anhydrite ($CaSO_4$) crystal (Figure 2.64).

Being an orthorhombic crystal, the atomic spacing and electron polarizability is different along all three of the crystal axes in anhydrite. Light traveling through this crystal will travel at three different velocities when vibrating parallel to the three different crystal axes. As a result anhydrite has three principal refractive indices, designated α, β, and γ, with α being the lowest index in the substance and γ the highest. For anhydrite, the refractive index values are $\alpha = 1.572$ (for light vibrating parallel to the b axis), $\beta = 1.577$ (for light vibrating

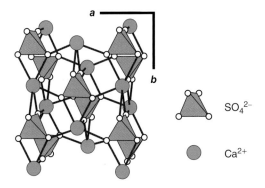

Figure 2.64 The crystal structure of anhydrite (calcium sulfate) looking down the *c* axis. Source: Adapted from Nesse (2004).

parallel to *a*), and $\gamma = 1.614$ (for light vibrating parallel to the *c* axis). The vibration directions for light vibrating parallel to α, β, and γ are sometimes represented by the letters X, Y, and Z, respectively. Light vibrating in planes intermediate between any pair of axes will encounter a refractive index value intermediate between the two principal refractive index values associated with these axes.

Given this behavior, an indicatrix for anhydrite can now be constructed. Imagine lines being drawn outward from the center of the anhydrite crystal, with the size of each line representing the refractive index value for light vibrating in that direction. If the tips of these lines are connected to form a surface, this surface will represent the indicatrix for anhydrite. Since the refractive index is different along the three (mutually perpendicular) crystal axes, the shape of the indicatrix is a triaxial ellipsoid (a three-dimensional ellipsoid having three principal axes each with a different magnitude) (Figure 2.65).

The refractive index values of the principal axes of the ellipsoid are considered to be the principal refractive index values of the crystal. The largest refractive index in the crystal (for light vibrating parallel to the largest axis of the ellipsoid) is designated γ. The smallest refractive index in the crystal (for light vibrating parallel to the smallest ellipsoid axis in the indicatrix) is designated α. The refractive index

for light vibrating perpendicular to the plane containing γ and α is designated β. The value of β is somewhere in between α and γ (it must be, since those are defined as the smallest and largest refractive index values in the crystal, respectively). It should be noted that β may fall anywhere in between α and γ, however, and is only rarely equidistant from them. Sections of the indicatrix that include two principal refractive index values are considered special and are called principal sections. Light vibrating perpendicular to these planes can provide particularly useful information during the study of these crystals. Light rays vibrating in planes that are intermediate between two principal refractive indices encounter refractive index values that are termed α' (if in between α and β) or γ' (if in between β and γ).

To appreciate the phenomena that result from light passing through an anhydrite crystal, it is necessary to consider light passing through several different sections of the crystal (five examples will be considered). Principal sections are those planes that include two primary refractive index values. There are three such planes in a biaxial indicatrix, specifically the α–β plane, the α–γ plane, and the β–γ plane (Figure 2.66). Light vibrating in a principal section as it travels through a crystal is resolved into two components, both of which behave as O rays. Two principal refractive index values can be measured on a crystal oriented with a principal section in the plane of the microscope stage.

Two special sections of this indicatrix will be discussed next. Consider taking sections of the indicatrix that include the β refractive index as one of their axes, and have as their second axis a direction somewhere in between α and γ. In taking all possible sections whose major and minor axes include β and a value between α and γ, exactly two circular sections will be encountered. Given that α is less than β and γ is greater than β, it follows that some intermediate between these two values must be equal to β. Because this intermediate can be encountered by heading from γ toward α

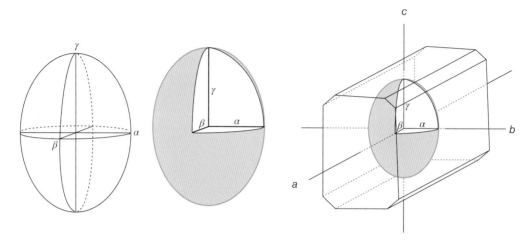

Figure 2.65 The indicatrix of a biaxial substance with refractive indices having the magnitudes α, β, and γ (left, middle), and the relationship between the indicatrix and the crystal morphology of anhydrite (right).

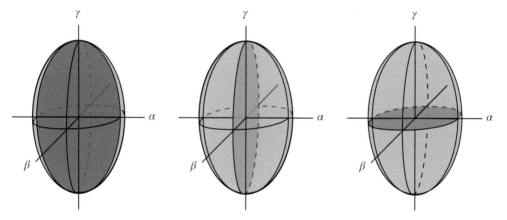

Figure 2.66 The three principal sections in a biaxial indicatrix, namely the α–γ plane (left, shaded orange), the β–γ plane (middle, shaded blue), and the α–β plane (right, shaded green).

in either of two directions, there are exactly two such circular sections in an orthorhombic anhydrite crystal (Figure 2.67).

Based on the previously provided definition of an optic axis, the direction perpendicular to each of these circular sections is an optic axis in the crystal. Anhydrite is therefore considered to be a biaxial crystal (having two optic axes). Light traveling parallel to either optic axis encounters a circular section of the indicatrix with a radius equal in magnitude to β. The velocity of light is thus the same regardless of the vibration direction within either of these two planes. Light traveling along either of these optic axes behaves the same as light traveling through an isotropic substance. Light vibrating in a circular section is not resolved into two components. Unpolarized light would pass through this crystal and emerge as unpolarized light. Plane polarized light would emerge as a single component vibrating in its original plane. All light rays obey Snell's Law when traveling through anhydrite in either of these two directions, so rays of light encountering circular sections behave as O rays. The β principal refractive index can be measured on a

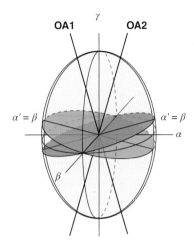

Figure 2.67 A biaxial indicatrix shown with its two circular sections indicated (shaded in blue and green). The two optic axes are the directions perpendicular to the circular sections, labeled OA1 and OA2.

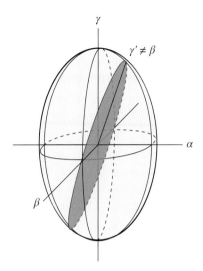

Figure 2.68 A semi-random section in a biaxial indicatrix that includes one principal refractive index value only (in this case β) along with a γ' refractive index value. The semi-random section is shaded green.

crystal oriented with a circular section in the plane of the microscope stage.

Note: Due to the difference between ray directions and wave normals in anisotropic substances, the optic axes of a biaxial crystal actually behave slightly differently from the optic axes in a uniaxial crystal, with something termed conical internal refraction occurring. This concept is expanded upon in Bloss (1961). As with other details regarding wave normal and ray directions, when dealing with very thin crystals like those fitting on a microscope slide the distinction causes little practical effect and will be ignored in this chapter.

In addition to principal sections and circular sections, biaxial indicatrices also have useful section that are known as semi-random sections. A semi-random section is one that includes one principal refractive index value (α, β, or γ), with its other vibration direction being α' or γ' (Figure 2.68). Light vibrating in a semi-random section as it travels through a crystal is resolved into two components, one of which behaves as an O ray (the one associated with the principal refractive index), the other behaving as an E ray. One of the principal refractive index values can be measured on a

crystal having a semi-random section in the plane of the microscope stage.

Finally, for any section of the anhydrite crystal that does not include a principal refractive index, the indicatrix section encountered by the light would be an ellipse with one axis having a magnitude somewhere in between β and γ (γ'), and another between β and α (α') (Figure 2.69). These sections are termed random sections. Light transmitting through an anhydrite crystal perpendicular to a random section will be resolved into two components vibrating in mutually perpendicular planes defined by the major and minor axes of the elliptical indicatrix section encountered. The magnitudes of the refractive index values encountered are defined by the magnitudes of the ellipse axes. Both rays will behave as E rays, with their wave normals obeying Snell's Law, but not their ray directions.

As with calcite (the uniaxial crystal example), it is instructive to discuss light traveling through an anhydrite crystal in several different directions in order to understand how the orientation of a crystal on the microscope

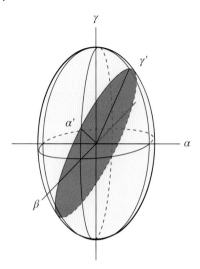

Figure 2.69 A random section in a biaxial indicatrix that does not include any of the principal refractive index values, shaded orange. All random sections have α' and γ' as their refractive indices.

stage impacts the section of the crystal and its indicatrix that are encountered by the light. First, consider a light ray traveling parallel to the *c* axis of the crystal (parallel to γ). The light encounters the 001 section of the crystal (parallel to the plane containing the *a* and *b* axes) (Figure 2.70).

Since the spacing along these two axes is different, the electron polarizability will also be different, and the refractive index will differ for light vibrating in these two different planes (α and β). The section of the indicatrix encountered by the light is an ellipse. As was the case in calcite, light incident upon this section of the crystal will be resolved into two components, vibrating along the major and minor axes of the ellipse, and the refractive index values for the two components will be equal to the magnitude of these axes (α and β for this particular section). This plane is a principal section of the indicatrix, and as a result the wave normals and ray directions of both components will obey Snell's Law (they both behave as O rays).

Similarly, a light ray traveling parallel to the *b* axis of the crystal (parallel to α), encounters the 010 section of the crystal (parallel to the plane containing the *a* and *c* axes) (Figure 2.71). Again, the light will be resolved into two components vibrating in mutually perpendicular planes, encountering refractive index values equal to the magnitude of the major and minor axes of the elliptical section of the indicatrix (β and γ for this particular section). Being a principal section of the indicatrix, both components will again behave as O rays.

A light ray traveling parallel to the *a* axis of the crystal (parallel to β), encounters the third and final principal section of the indicatrix, in this case the 100 section of the crystal (parallel to the plane containing the *b* and *c* axes) (Figure 2.72). The behavior is similar to that of the other two principal sections, with light resolved into two components, both behaving as O rays, in this case encountering refractive index values α and γ.

All crystals in the orthorhombic, monoclinic, and triclinic crystal systems behave in a manner analogous to that of anhydrite. They all have indicatrices that are triaxial ellipsoids, and they all have two optic axes. They are all considered to be biaxial crystals. The birefringence of biaxial crystals is equal to the difference between their highest and lowest refractive index values, namely $\delta = \gamma - \alpha$. For anhydrite, $\delta = 0.042$.

2.5.3.1 Optic Axial Plane and Optic Normal

There is a very important plane in biaxial crystals that is in practice fairly easy to locate and that can provide a wealth of information about the optical properties of a biaxial crystal, specifically the plane perpendicular to the β principal refractive index direction. By definition, the β direction is perpendicular to the plane that includes the largest (γ) and smallest (α) refractive index values in a biaxial indicatrix. The circular sections in biaxial crystals always include the β principal refractive index direction. Since an optic axis is (by definition) perpendicular to a circular section in an indicatrix, the two optic axes in a biaxial crystal are always perpendicular to the β principal refractive index direction.

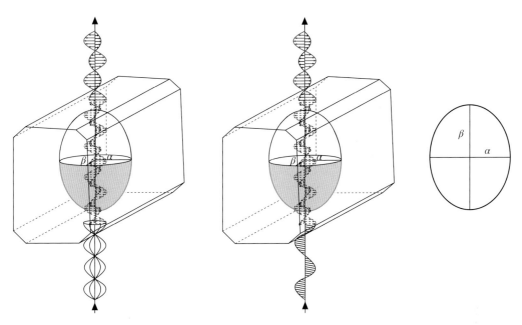

Figure 2.70 An orthorhombic (biaxial) anhydrite crystal illuminated from below with unpolarized light (left) and plane polarized light (middle), oriented with its 001 section parallel to the plane of the microscope stage. The cross-section of the indicatrix that is perpendicular to the light's propagation direction (in this case the cross-section in the 001 plane) is shown on the right.

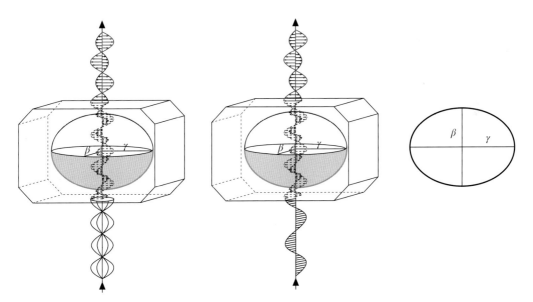

Figure 2.71 An orthorhombic (biaxial) anhydrite crystal illuminated from below with unpolarized light (left) and plane polarized light (middle), oriented with its 010 section parallel to the plane of the microscope stage. The cross-section of the indicatrix that is perpendicular to the light's propagation direction (in this case the cross-section in the 010 plane) is shown on the right.

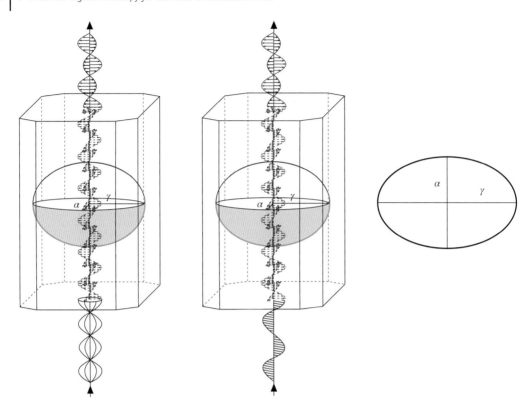

Figure 2.72 An orthorhombic (biaxial) anhydrite crystal illuminated from below with unpolarized light (left) and plane polarized light (middle), oriented with its 100 section parallel to the plane of the microscope stage. The cross-section of the indicatrix that is perpendicular to the light's propagation direction (in this case the cross-section in the 100 plane) is shown on the right.

Thus the plane in biaxial crystals that is perpendicular to β contains α, γ, and both of the optic axes in the crystal. Because it contains so many important directions, this special plane is called the optic axial plane (OAP), or simply the optic plane. The β principal refractive index direction, being perpendicular (normal) to the optic plane, is termed the optic normal (often abbreviated ON). If the optic plane can be located in a biaxial crystal then the direction perpendicular to this plane (β) can also be located, which is of great importance in identifying biaxial crystals.

2.5.3.2 Acute Bisectrix, Obtuse Bisectrix, Optic Sign, and Optic Axial Angle

While the optic axes always lie in the OAP, their position within this plane differs for different biaxial crystals. Their position depends on the values of α, β, and γ (which together define the exact shape of the indicatrix). For example, if the values of β and α are very close together, then the circular sections will be close to the $\alpha–\beta$ principal section and the optic axes will be close to γ (Figure 2.73, left). On the other hand, if the values of β and γ are close together, the circular sections will be close to the $\gamma–\beta$ principal section and the optic axes close to α (Figure 2.73, right). The principal refractive index (either γ or α) that is closest to the two optic axes is termed the acute bisectrix (AB) because it bisects the acute angle between the optic axes. For example, if the optic axes are closer to the γ refractive index direction, then γ is the acute bisectrix. In this case, α is referred to as the obtuse bisectrix (OB) because it bisects the obtuse angle between the optic axes. Biaxial crystals are given an optic sign

Figure 2.73 Indicatrices of biaxial positive (left) and negative (right) substances. For biaxial positive crystals, β is closer to α, and as a result the circular sections are closer to α. In these crystals, γ is the acute bisectrix. For biaxial negative crystals, β is closer to γ, and as a result the circular sections are closer to γ. In these crystals, α is the acute bisectrix. Circular sections are shaded blue.

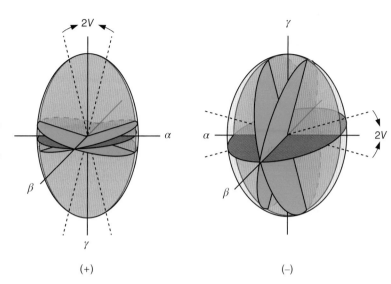

(+)   (−)

based on which principal refractive index in the crystal is the acute bisectrix. If γ is the acute bisectrix (which occurs when β is closer to α), the crystal is considered to be optically positive. If α is the acute bisectrix (which occurs when β is closer to γ), the crystal is considered to be optically negative. Note that when β is exactly halfway between α and γ, the crystal is neither optically positive nor negative (it would be considered optically neutral, although optically neutral crystals are rare). In this case neither α nor γ is the acute bisectrix as the angle between the optic axis and both of these indicatrix axes is equal to 45°.

One additional optical property of biaxial crystals that can be determined and used for identification purposes is something called their optic axial angle. As the name implies, this is the angle between the two optic axes in a biaxial crystal, and typically refers to the acute angle between the two optic axes. This angle is represented by $2V$ (V being the angle between an optic axis and α or γ) (Figure 2.74).

Sometimes the axis about which the optic axial angle was measured is specified using $2V_z$ (the angle about γ) or $2V_x$ (the angle about α). However, in practice the acute angle between the optic axes is typically measured, and it is common to drop the subscript and assume that $2V$ refers to the acute angle. The

reason the acute angle is used is because it is considerably easier to measure than the obtuse angle, as will be seen later in this chapter. Relatively speaking, the optic axial angle will be small whenever β is very close in value to either α or γ. If β and α are similar in value, the circular sections will fall very close to the β–α plane, and the optic axes will define a relatively small acute angle about γ. Similarly, if β and γ are very close in value, the circular sections will fall very close to the β–γ plane, and the optic axes will define a small acute angle about α. When the value of β is nearly equidistant between α and γ, the optic axial angle will be large (close to its maximum value of 90°).

2.5.3.3 Optical Orientation

As mentioned above, all crystals in the orthorhombic, monoclinic, and triclinic crystal systems behave in a manner analogous to that of anhydrite, in that they all have indicatrices that are triaxial ellipsoids and they all have two optic axes. However, these different crystal systems have differences with respect to the symmetry constraints on their optical orientations. The optical orientation of a crystal is the relationship between its indicatrix and its crystallographic axes. For all orthorhombic crystals (including anhydrite), the three principal refractive index directions coincide with

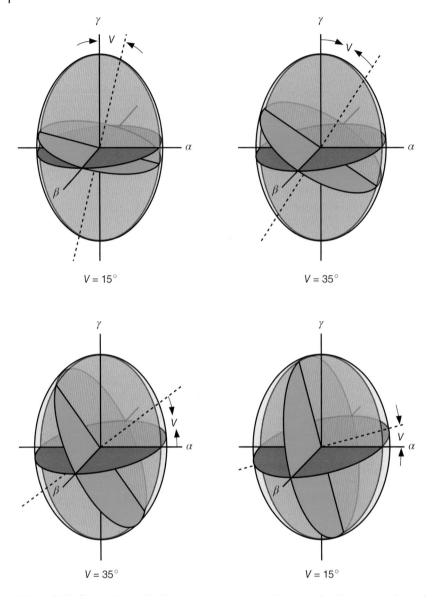

Figure 2.74 Several biaxial indicatrices are shown, each one having the same values of γ and α. The magnitude of the β refractive index increases from upper left to lower right. As β increases, the angle V measured relative to γ increases from 15° to 35° (top images), and then becomes large enough that α is the acute bisectrix (bottom images). Source: Figure adapted from Bloss (1961). Circular sections are shaded blue.

the three crystal axes. However, any particular principal refractive index direction can coincide with any crystal axis. In other words, α may coincide with the a, b, or c crystallographic axis depending on the particular orthorhombic crystal being studied; α will always coincide

with one of these axes. In anhydrite, α happens to coincide with the b axis, β with the a axis, and γ with the c axis (Figure 2.75).

In monoclinic crystals, one of the principal refractive index directions will always coincide with the b crystallographic axis. However,

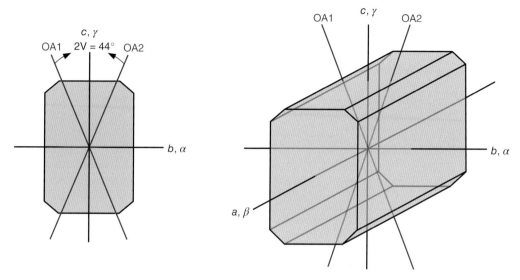

Figure 2.75 The optical orientation of anhydrite, for which β is parallel to the a axis, α is parallel to the b axis, and γ is parallel to the c axis. The crystal is biaxial positive, making γ the acute bisectrix. The optic axial angle $2V = 44°$.

any principal refractive index direction (α, β, or γ) may be the one that coincides with b. The other two principal refractive index directions may fall anywhere within the plane containing the a and c crystallographic axes. If a principal refractive index direction happens to be parallel to either the a or c axis, it is only by coincidence. Because the a and c axes are inclined (not perpendicular to each other) in monoclinic crystals, and the principal refractive index directions are always mutually perpendicular, it is impossible for all three principal refractive index directions to coincide with the three crystallographic axes in a monoclinic crystal. In gypsum, a monoclinic crystal, the β refractive index coincides with the b crystallographic axis and the γ refractive index makes an angle of 52° with the c axis (Figure 2.76).

In triclinic crystals, none of the principal refractive index directions is constrained by symmetry to coincide with any of the crystallographic axes. If one refractive index direction happens to be parallel to a crystallographic axis, it does so only by coincidence. It is impossible for more than one refractive index direction to coincide with a crystallographic axis in a triclinic crystal because principal refractive index vibration directions are always mutually perpendicular and triclinic crystallographic axes are mutually oblique.

2.5.3.4 Dispersion in Biaxial Crystals

As for all of the other crystals discussed, the refractive indices of biaxial crystals (α, β, γ) are different for different wavelengths of light. In addition to dispersion of the refractive index values, there are many more properties in biaxial crystal that can change with wavelength. Biaxial crystals can exhibit dispersion of their birefringence, dispersion of their optic axial angle, and dispersion of their optic orientation. However, the symmetry of the dispersion pattern must be equal to or greater than that of the crystal. For orthorhombic crystals, mirror planes and twofold rotation axes in their symmetry restrict the types of dispersion that can occur. Specifically, the three refractive index values (principal indicatrix axes) must coincide with the three crystallographic axes for all wavelengths of light. For monoclinic crystals, the single mirror plane and/or twofold axis

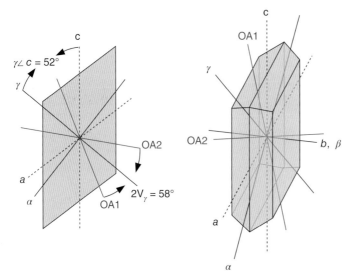

Figure 2.76 The optical orientation of gypsum, for which β is parallel to the *b* axis, and γ makes an angle of 52° with the *c* axis. The crystal is biaxial positive, with an optic axial angle $2V = 58°$.

must be present for all wavelengths of light, again restricting the types of dispersion that can occur (but being less restrictive than for orthorhombic crystals). Specifically, one refractive index direction (one principal indicatrix axis) must coincide with the b crystallographic axis for all wavelengths of light. No such symmetry elements are present in triclinic crystals, which can exhibit dispersion of their optical orientation without any of these restrictions. Dispersion of these various optical properties results in differences observable in the interference figures formed by these crystals, as well as in extinction angles. The next section of this chapter discusses the measurement of the various optical properties introduced above.

2.6 Measurement of Optical Properties

If this is the first time the reader has been introduced to crystallography, the subject may seem very complicated and perhaps a little confusing (especially for biaxial crystals). However, in practice the polarized light microscope can be applied to the solution of numerous problems with only a fairly basic understanding of the theory behind all of the

phenomena observed. With practice, experience, and additional reading, the deeper theory can be slowly learned. The benefit of learning the theory in greater detail is primarily one of efficiency, as this knowledge enables the examiner to measure optical properties much more rapidly and with smaller sample sizes. Once a student becomes comfortable with much of the theory, what initially seemed like a disadvantage of the instrument (the complexity of optical crystallography) begins instead to become an advantage. That is because mastery of the theory enables the measurement of additional optical properties. When trying to identify an unknown biaxial substance, there are numerous properties that can be determined. An examiner can observe its morphology, measure the crystal's principal refractive index values (α, β, γ), determine its birefringence, optic sign, and optic axial angle, and make additional observations related to its optic orientation and dispersion. With all of this information it is extremely unlikely that two chemically different substances would coincidentally happen to share all of these properties. Thus if a large number of these properties compare favorably to those listed in a reference, or to those of a known substance being studied, the chances of an incorrect identification are extremely low. The optical properties of a substance are highly discriminating, enabling the examiner to distinguish between different polymorphs of the same compound (due to differences in the orientation and spacing of their atoms), different members of a solid solution series that share a crystal structure (e.g. olivine grains with different compositions), and different hydration states of a compound (such as the numerous hydrated sodium phosphate phases). These examples can be problematic for some of the other instruments available to the forensic scientist. However, these properties can only be used for identification, characterization, and comparison purposes if they can be measured for a sample. The following section is focused on the measurement of optical properties. As usual, the simplest substances will be discussed first before moving on to more complex materials.

2.6.1 Measurement of Refractive Index Values: Isotropic Substances

For isotropic substances the only optical properties to be determined are refractive index and dispersion values. A very useful observation can be rapidly made to obtain information about how close (or far away) the refractive index value of a particle is to that of its mounting medium, namely a particle's contrast or relief. The contrast of a particle in a particular mounting medium is essentially a qualitative assessment of how clearly defined its edges are. The contrast depends in part on the difference in refractive index values between the particle and its mounting medium, especially when unidirectional axial illumination is used. This relationship is due to the refraction of light that occurs at the edges of the particle. As Snell's Law dictates for isotropic substances, the change in the propagation direction of the incident light is related to the change in the velocity of the light transmitted into the crystal. The change in velocity is determined by the refractive index values of the mounting

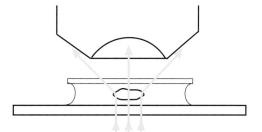

Figure 2.77 A particle having a refractive index relatively far from that of the mounting medium will cause light to change direction substantially where the illuminating rays have angles of incidence other than zero. If light rays are refracted sufficiently, they miss the objective lens and these areas of the particle become dark, resulting in high contrast.

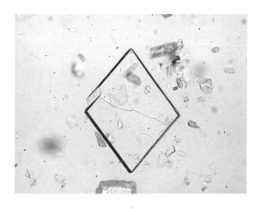

Figure 2.78 A calcite crystal exhibiting high contrast against its mounting medium.

medium and particle. Where a large difference in refractive index exists between the two, or when the incident angle is large, light incident on the particle deviates greatly from its original path and fails to enter the objective lens (Figures 2.77 and 2.78).

This deviation results in a dark appearance to areas of the particle with other than normal incidence (typically true of the edges of particles). Where a small difference in refractive index exists, the incident light deviates only slightly from its original path, resulting in a slight darkening of particle edges (Figures 2.79 and 2.80).

In the event that the two refractive indices are equal, the light passing through the particle

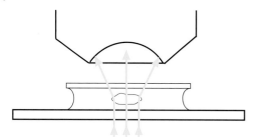

Figure 2.79 A particle having a refractive index relatively close to that of the mounting medium will cause light to change direction only slightly where the illuminating rays have angles of incidence other than zero. Fewer light rays are refracted sufficiently to miss the objective lens, so the particle is generally brighter, resulting in low contrast.

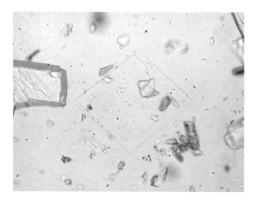

Figure 2.80 A calcite crystal exhibiting low contrast against its mounting medium.

does not deviate at all, and the particle remains invisible (Figure 2.81).

In practice the refractive indices of the particle and mounting medium typically only match at one wavelength, with other colors of light deviating slightly from their path. As a result, colored fringes are apparent at the edges of the particle (Figures 2.82 and 2.83). The exact colors visible can be used to estimate the magnitude of the refractive index difference between the particle and its mounting medium for 589 nm light (the value most references report) (Bloss 1961).

While being able to qualitatively assess the difference in refractive index between the mounting medium and a particle is certainly

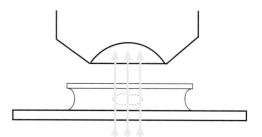

Figure 2.81 A particle having a refractive index that matches that of the mounting medium will not refract the illuminating rays at all. The light passing through the particle behaves the same as light passing through the empty mounting medium, and the particle becomes invisible.

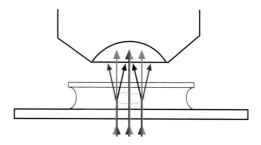

Figure 2.82 In practice, a particle will only have a refractive index that matches that of the mounting medium for one wavelength in the visible spectrum. All other wavelengths will be refracted. As a result, colored fringes become visible in areas of the particle having other than normal incidence (typically most pronounced near the edges of the particle).

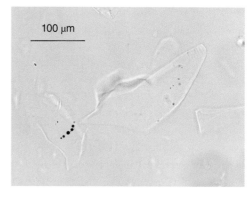

100 μm

Figure 2.83 Photomicrograph of barium nitrate particles with pale blue and yellow dispersion colors visible at their edges.

useful, it is also desirable to know whether the particle has a refractive index higher or lower than that of the mounting medium. This question can be answered by a rapid observation called the Becke line test. The Becke line test makes use of the fact that small particles behave much like lenses, refracting light in a manner that depends on the relative refractive index values of the particle and mounting medium. If a particle with a higher refractive index is mounted in a medium of lower refractive index, the particle will focus axial illuminating rays toward a point above the particle. Even a particle with vertical faces will direct light in this direction because slightly oblique rays will undergo total internal reflection at the internal faces of the particle, resulting in the same effect. Thus particles having virtually any shape will direct light toward a point above the center of the particle if they have a refractive index value that is higher than that of the mounting medium (Figures 2.84 and 2.85).

If the microscope is focused on the edges of the particle, and the focus is then raised a very small amount, a small line of bright light will appear to move into the particle. This line is called the Becke line and is most easily observed when the particle is illuminated with unidirectional axial illumination (in other words, with the condenser aperture closed down).

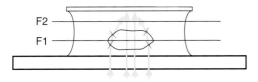

Figure 2.84 A particle having a refractive index greater than that of the mounting medium will act as a positive lens, refracting light toward a point above the particle. As the focus of the microscope is changed from plane F1 to plane F2, a halo of light will appear to move into the particle. This halo of light is called the Becke line, and it moves into the particle when the particle has a higher index than the mounting medium.

In the alternative situation, where a lower refractive index particle is mounted in a higher refractive index medium, both the refraction of light and the reflection of light combine to direct the incident light in the opposite direction. As a result, light is refracted and reflected away from the particle, and the small bright Becke line will appear to move out of the particle and into the mounting medium as the focus is raised (Figures 2.86 and 2.87).

Thus the Becke line moves into the higher refractive index substance (either the particle or the mounting medium) when the focus of the microscope is raised. One must take care to focus in the correct direction, as the Becke line appears to move in the opposite direction when the focus is lowered.

The Becke line test therefore reveals to the examiner which of the two substances (the particle or the mounting medium) has the higher refractive index. In order for the test to provide information of value, the refractive index of the mounting medium must be known. The contrast of the particle in the mounting medium, together with dispersion colors at its edges (when visible), can be used to estimate how far the particle's refractive index is from that of the mounting medium.

2.6.1.1 Becke Line Immersion Method

The most common technique used for measuring the refractive index value of a substance, known as the Becke line immersion method, takes advantage of this information. The method involves mounting an unknown substance in a liquid of known refractive index and comparing the two (determining which is higher and estimating the difference between the two). Particles of the substance are mounted in successive liquids with a goal of finding a liquid whose refractive index matches that of the particles. The liquids used are typically those available from Cargille Laboratories (Figure 2.88).

An initial liquid must be chosen (the author uses $n_D = 1.540$, although any liquid will do). The unknown substance is mounted in this

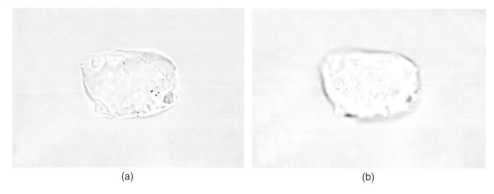

| (a) | (b) |

Figure 2.85 A particle shown at best focus (left), and again after raising the focus of the microscope (right). A bright halo of light (the Becke line) has moved into the particle because it has a higher refractive index than its mounting medium.

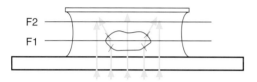

Figure 2.86 A particle having a refractive index less than that of the mounting medium will act as a negative lens, refracting light outwards from the particle. As the focus of the microscope is changed from plane F1 to plane F2, a halo of light will appear to move out of the particle and into the surrounding mounting medium. This halo of light is called the Becke line, and it moves into the mounting medium when the mounting medium has a higher index than the particle.

liquid, an assessment of the degree of contrast (low, moderate, high) is made, and then the Becke line test is conducted. If the unknown substance were potassium chloride, for example, the particles would be found to have moderate contrast and be lower in index than the liquid. A new liquid would then be chosen (perhaps $n_D = 1.440$) and the observations repeated. In the second liquid, the particles would be observed to have moderate contrast and be higher in index than the liquid, so a new liquid would be chosen. The process continues until the liquid is found in which the sample has the lowest contrast; in this case it would be the liquid with $n_D = 1.490$. The refractive index of this liquid is approximately equal to that of the particle. As discussed above, the dispersion of a solid substance such as potassium chloride typically differs from that of the liquid mounting medium. As a result, the refractive index values of the two match only for one color of light, and other colors of light will refract (bend) slightly at the edges of the particle, producing colored fringes, or colored Becke lines. The exact colors observed and their behavior during the Becke line test can be used to estimate when an exact match at the sodium D line (or other wavelength) has been achieved. For additional details see Bloss (1961). Alternatively, a monochromatic filter with a wavelength of 589 nm can be placed in the light path of the microscope to measure the n_D value of the sample more precisely. For the purposes of identifying an unknown substance, the uncertainty of measurement that results from the use of white light is small enough that it does not impede identification. Refractive index also varies with temperature, but again the uncertainty of measurement due to the temperature of the liquid is small enough that it does not prevent identification. For precise work, as is required for forensic comparison of glass, these variables must be taken into account. The commonly employed methods that control these variables are called the single variation method and the Emmons double variation method.

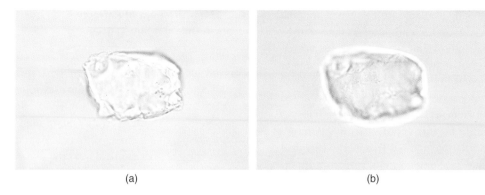

(a)   (b)

Figure 2.87 A particle shown at best focus (left), and again after raising the focus of the microscope (right). A bright halo of light (the Becke line) has moved out of the particle and into the mounting medium because the particle has a lower refractive index than its mounting medium.

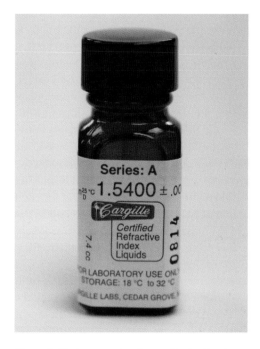

Figure 2.88 An example of a certified refractive index liquid from Cargille Laboratories.

2.6.1.2 Single Variation Method

For precise measurement of refractive index of glass samples (as is required for forensic glass comparison) the differences in the temperature coefficient of refractive index in the liquid and solid substances are taken advantage of. The glass particles are mounted in a liquid having a refractive index that is higher than

that of the glass at room temperature. The wavelength of the illuminating light is fixed by use of a monochromator or a narrow band pass filter (typically at $\lambda = 589$ nm, the sodium D line). The sample is placed on a hotstage and slowly heated. As the temperature increases, the refractive index of the liquid decreases much more rapidly than that of the glass because liquids have a significantly higher temperature coefficient of refractive index than solids do. The temperature at which the contrast is a minimum (at which the refractive index of the liquid matches that of the glass) is recorded. A common variation on this method involves automatic determination of the matching temperature by a computer application that uses imaging software and automated temperature control. The computer alternately heats and cools the sample on the hotstage, recording the temperature values at which the image contrast is at a minimum. An average of the matching temperature values recorded for several heating and cooling cycles provides a highly precise matching temperature value. Different glass particles that have matching temperature values within a narrow, pre-defined window are considered to have comparable refractive index values. This approach is sometimes called the single variation method of refractive index determination because one variable (temperature) is changed during the measurement process. The liquids commercially available for this work are typically provided with manufacturer data on their refractive index values at various temperatures, enabling the matching temperature value to be converted to a refractive index value if desired.

2.6.1.3 Emmons Double Variation Method

A variation on this approach is the Emmons double variation method. This method involves both a hotstage and a monochromator. In this method, an initial temperature is selected and the wavelength of illuminating light is varied until the contrast is a minimum. The matching wavelength for this temperature is recorded. The temperature is then changed (perhaps by 5°C) and the process repeated. Once the matching wavelength has been determined for several temperatures, the data are plotted on a special graph called a Hartmann Net (Figure 2.89). This graph enables the dispersion curve of the glass to be determined. If the dispersion curves of two different glass particles are within a pre-determined window, the glass particles are considered to have comparable optical properties. This approach is called the double variation method because two variables (temperature and wavelength) are both changed during the process.

While the single variation method and double variation method are both used by forensic scientists for comparison of the optical properties of glass particles, there is no reason these methods cannot be applied to the measurement of refractive index values on other types of evidence. These methods can be applied to both isotropic and anisotropic substances, although the latter must be oriented appropriately for the measurement of principal refractive index values (with the help of interference figures or a spindle stage, for example). The remainder of this chapter will focus on applications using the Becke line immersion method, however, as this method is the most commonly used technique by forensic scientists and generally the most efficient method for identifying unknown substances based on their optical properties.

2.6.2 Measurement of Refractive Indices in Uniaxial Substances

As discussed earlier, when light enters a uniaxial crystal such as calcite, the light is separated into two components (with the only exception occurring for light traveling parallel to the unique optic axis in the crystal). One of these rays vibrates parallel to the c axis (ε or ε') while the other vibrates perpendicular to the c axis (ω). Because the light is separated into two components, each having its own refractive index value, it is more challenging to measure refractive index values in these crystals than it is for isotropic substances. These refractive index values can only be measured if the vibration direction of the transmitted light is restricted such that the light only vibrates in a single plane in the crystal. Once restricted to a single vibration direction, the crystal can be oriented such that the vibration direction of the illuminating light is perfectly aligned with one of the principal vibration directions in the crystal (ω, for example). Thus restricted, the observations made related to contrast and the Becke line test provide information about the ω value of the crystal.

In order to restrict the vibration plane of the light to a single principal vibration direction in an anisotropic substance such as calcite, plane polarized light must be used. As discussed earlier, there are several ways of taking ordinary (unpolarized) light and isolating only the portion of that light that has its electric vector vibrating in a single direction (plane polarized light, or simply polarized light) (Figure 2.3). The most common means of obtaining plane polarized light in modern polarized light microscopes is with the use of a Polaroid filter. This filter is a material that absorbs light vibrating in all but one plane. In most microscopes the light illuminating the sample first passes through a Polaroid filter (called the polarizer) that is oriented such that the light incident on the sample is vibrating in the E–W plane of the field of view (Figure 2.90). The polarizer is typically located just below the substage condenser.

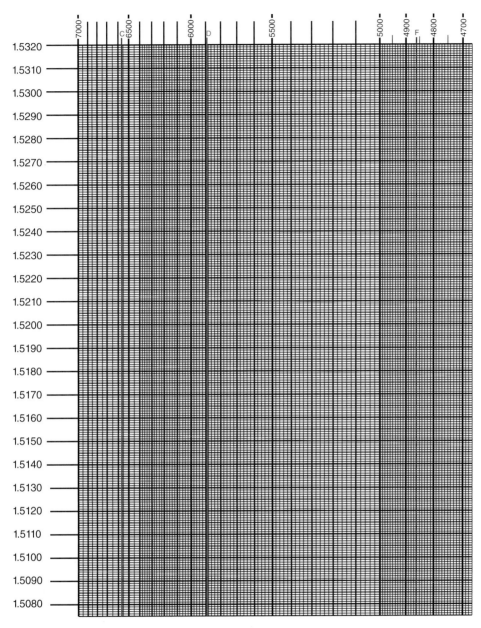

Figure 2.89 This graph is an example of a Hartmann net, which is used to plot refractive index values for different wavelengths. By determining the matching wavelength between the glass and liquid at three temperatures and plotting those data on this type of diagram, the refractive index of the glass can be extrapolated for all wavelengths of light in the visible spectrum.

For a uniaxial crystal mounted on the stage of a polarized light microscope, the orientation of vibration directions in the crystal relative to the vibration direction of the illuminating light is very important in determining what is observed. Imagine that a calcite rhomb is mounted on the stage and being studied in plane polarized light. Depending on how the stage is rotated, orientations of the crystal (relative to the polarizer vibration direction)

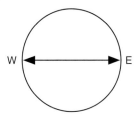

Figure 2.90 The standard orientation of the polarizer's principal vibration direction relative to the microscope's field of view. Some microscopes have their polarized oriented N–S, however, so the polarizer orientation must be checked on any microscope before it is used.

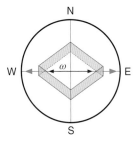

Figure 2.91 A calcite rhomb oriented such that its ω vibration direction (blue) is parallel to the polarizer vibration direction (green). In this orientation, all of the plane polarized light illuminating the crystal will vibrate in the ω plane in the crystal. Contrast and Becke line test behavior are determined by the relationship between ω and the mounting medium.

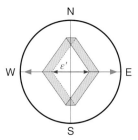

Figure 2.92 A calcite rhomb oriented such that its ε' vibration direction (red) is parallel to the polarizer vibration direction (green). In this orientation, all of the plane polarized light illuminating the crystal will vibrate in the ε' plane in the crystal. Contrast and Becke line test behavior are determined by the relationship between ε' and the mounting medium.

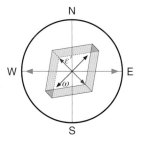

Figure 2.93 A calcite rhomb oriented such that the principal vibration directions in the crystal (ω and ε') are 45° from the polarizer vibration direction. In this orientation, the plane polarized light illuminating the crystal will be split equally into two components, one vibrating in the ω plane and the other in the ε' plane in the crystal.

will be encountered that enable the light to interact only with ω, only with ε', or to be split into two components, one vibrating in each of the two possible refractive index directions. In Figure 2.91, the rhomb is oriented such that the plane of the ω vibration is aligned with the polarizer vibration direction. In this orientation all of the light will vibrate in the ω direction. The light will not be resolved into two components. Observations related to contrast and the Becke line test will provide information about the value of ω relative to the mounting medium. If the stage is rotated by 90° from this position, the ε' vibration direction will be aligned parallel to the polarizer vibration direction (Figure 2.92). In this orientation all of the light will travel through ε'.

Observations related to contrast and the Becke line test will provide information about the value of ε' relative to the mounting medium. At 45° from either of the first two positions light will be roughly equally split into ω and ε' components upon entering the calcite crystal (Figure 2.93). In any other orientation the light from the polarizer will be split into two components, but unequally so in amounts determined by the angle of the incident light's vibration direction relative to ω and ε'.

If the crystal morphology is evident and allows the trace of the c axis to be located, then the ω vibration direction can be oriented

Figure 2.94 A recrystallized potassium dihydrogen phosphate crystal (tetragonal prism terminated by pyramids). The crystal can be oriented with either ω or ε parallel to the polarizer on the basis of its crystal morphology. In the image the c axis is aligned approximately N–S, so ω is aligned with the E–W polarizer. In this orientation, contrast and Becke line behavior are determined by ω.

by aligning the c axis perpendicular to the polarizer. In a calcite rhomb, the trace of the c axis bisects the obtuse angle, so a well-formed rhomb can be oriented based on its morphology. A re-crystallized tetragonal prism terminated by pyramids could easily be oriented on the basis of its morphology as well (Figure 2.94).

In the absence of recognizable crystal morphology, the microscopist must either use interference figures to orient grains (see Section 2.6.8), use a device such as a spindle stage to orient a grain, or use a "brute force" method to observe many randomly oriented grains and estimate ω and ε values based on the behavior of a population of grains. The latter method will be discussed first.

Generally speaking, in a population of randomly oriented grains of a uniaxial substance there are three possibilities for the orientation of grains and the resulting refractive index values that can be determined from them. A very few will be oriented with the c axis perpendicular to the plane of the microscope stage. For these crystals, light will vibrate in the plane of the a axes and encounter only ω, no matter how the stage is rotated. For grains

in this orientation, Becke lines and contrast will enable information to be determined for ω. A few grains will be oriented with the c axis in the plane of the microscope stage. For these crystals, light will vibrate in the principal indicatrix section containing the c axis (Figure 2.59, left). As the stage is rotated, that crystal will enable the ε refractive index value to be observed whenever the c axis is parallel to the polarizer. If the stage is rotated 90° the ω refractive index would be observed. On grains in this orientation, information on both ω and ε can be obtained. All of the remaining grains (typically the vast majority) have their c axis tipped at some oblique angle to the microscope stage. In this orientation the grains exhibit ω and ε' values on rotation of the stage (as is the case for the calcite rhomb example above). For these crystals information about both ω and ε' can be obtained by observing their contrast and Becke line behavior.

Of note in the above discussion is that every grain of a uniaxial substance, regardless of its orientation, will exhibit ω in at least one position as the stage is rotated. This fact makes the determination of ω fairly straightforward (even if potentially time-consuming). The primary challenge is in knowing what position of stage rotation permits ω to be determined. While it can be difficult to determine the ω value using a single grain (without additional information), this value can be readily determined if a population of grains is available for study. To understand how to measure ω using a population of grains, consider the refractive index values exhibited by grains in various orientations as listed for calcite in Figure 2.95. If samples of these grains are mounted in several different mounting media and the contrast and Becke lines studied, it is possible to obtain fairly accurate measurements of both ω and ε as discussed below.

If a liquid having a refractive index higher than ω is chosen (liquid 5 in Figure 2.95), the Becke lines will go out for all grains regardless of their orientation. Most grains will exhibit variations in the degree of contrast on

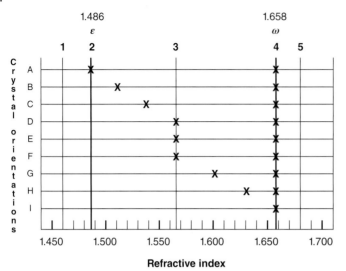

Figure 2.95 Possible refractive indices presented by calcite grains in various orientations. The different crystal orientations are represented by the horizontal lines A–I. Refractive index values are plotted on the *x* axis. Liquids selected for refractive index determination are represented by vertical lines.

rotation (all except grain I), while a few will not (grain I).

If a liquid having a refractive index lower than ε is chosen (liquid 1 in Figure 2.95), Becke lines will go into the grains in all orientations. Most grains will exhibit variations in the degree of contrast on rotation (all except grain I), while a few will not (grain I).

If a liquid having a refractive index equal to ω is selected, then every single grain will exhibit extremely low contrast (matching refractive index) at least once on rotation of the stage (liquid 4 in Figure 2.95). If the stage is rotated 90° from this position the contrast will increase for most grains, with the degree of contrast observed varying with grain orientation. For these grains the Becke line will go out in this second orientation because the liquid has a higher refractive index than any ε' value. A very small number of grains will retain their very low contrast on stage rotation (grain I).

If a liquid having a refractive index equal to ε is chosen (liquid 2 in Figure 2.95), then every single grain will exhibit high contrast with the Becke line going in when light vibrates in their ω direction (ω being considerably higher than 1.468). Rotating the stage 90° from this position the vast majority of grains (exhibiting ε' values) will have Becke lines going in and will exhibit varying degrees of contrast, from low to

high. A very few grains will exhibit one position of extremely low contrast (matching refractive index) in this orientation (grain A).

If a liquid having a refractive index anywhere in between ε and ω is chosen (liquid 3 in Figure 2.95), then every single grain will have Becke lines going in when light vibrates in their ω direction. Rotating 90° from this position, some grains will have Becke lines going in (grains G–I), some will have Becke lines going out (grains A–C), and a few will exhibit extremely low contrast (matching refractive index) (grains D–F).

Some materials have preferred orientations, and for these materials the distribution of grain orientations is not random. Calcite exhibits $10\bar{1}1$ (rhombohedral) cleavage. As a result, a significant number of calcite grains in a typical sample lie on their $10\bar{1}1$ face. These grains exhibit an ε' value of 1.566. In Figure 2.95, a disproportionate number of calcite grains are in exactly this orientation and their ε' values match liquid 3.

By choosing mounting media with a range of refractive index values and recording observations made on a number of grains, the ω and ε values of a uniaxial crystal can be determined. While it may be time consuming to determine ω and ε values in this manner, it is also effective, especially for measuring ω. As

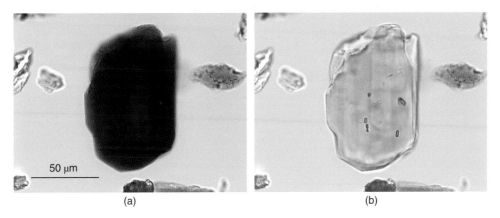

Figure 2.96 A tourmaline crystal exhibiting strong pleochroism, with a pleochroic formula of ω = dark brown, ε = pale brown. The polarizer is oriented E–W in the left-hand image, and N–S in the image on the right.

will be discussed later, ω is the more important principal refractive index to measure for identification purposes.

If a colored uniaxial substance is studied, there will typically be an observable difference in the absorption color of the crystal when light is vibrating parallel to the two principal vibration directions in the crystal. Tourmaline, for example, is a hexagonal mineral that strongly absorbs light vibrating parallel to its a axes but absorbs significantly less light vibrating parallel to its c axis (Figure 2.96). This phenomenon, namely the existence of different visible absorbance curves for different planes of vibration in a crystal, is called pleochroism. The pleochroic formula for this substance would be ω = dark brown, ε = pale brown.

2.6.3 Measurement of Refractive Index in Biaxial Substances

Light is also split into two components when it transmits through biaxial crystals, with the exception of light traveling parallel to one of the two optic axes. This phenomenon poses the same challenge for the measurement of refractive index values as it did for uniaxial crystals. As for uniaxial crystals, it is necessary to use a polarizer to restrict the vibration of light to a single plane, enabling the light to

vibrate parallel to one principal refractive index at a time. The primary difference is that there are now three principal refractive index values to determine (α, β, γ), as opposed to two for uniaxial crystals.

For biaxial crystals it is more challenging to rely on morphology to orient crystals than it is for well-formed uniaxial crystals. As a general rule the examiner must either use interference figures to orient grains, use a device such as a spindle stage to orient a grain, or use a "brute force" method to observe many randomly oriented grains and estimate α, β, and γ values based on the behavior of a population of grains. The latter method is discussed here.

In a population of randomly oriented grains of a biaxial substance there are more possible grain orientations to consider than for uniaxial materials. A very few will be oriented with one of their optic axes perpendicular to the plane of the microscope stage. For these grains, light vibrates in a circular section of the indicatrix and they exhibit only β. A small number of grains will be oriented with one of their three principal indicatrix sections in the plane of the microscope and will exhibit one of the following: α and γ, α and β, or β and γ. Some will have only one of their three principal refractive indices in the plane of the microscope (a semi-random section). The

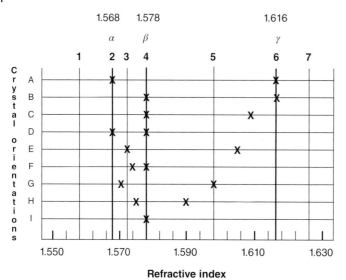

Figure 2.97 Possible refractive indices presented by anhydrite crystals in various orientations. The different crystal orientations are represented by the horizontal lines A–I. Refractive index values are plotted on the x axis. Liquids selected for refractive index determination are represented by vertical lines.

majority of the grains, however, will exhibit random sections (α' and γ').

Despite this complexity, if the behavior of a population of randomly oriented biaxial grains in several different refractive index liquids is studied, it is possible to determine the three refractive indices.

If a liquid higher than γ is chosen, Becke lines will go out in all orientations for all grains (liquid 7 in Figure 2.97). Some grains will exhibit variations in the degree of contrast upon rotation. Similarly, if a liquid lower than α is chosen, Becke lines will go into the grains in all orientations (liquid 1 in Figure 2.97), with variations in contrast in some grains.

If a liquid matching the β refractive index is selected (liquid 4 in Figure 2.97), then most grains will exhibit Becke lines going into the grain in one orientation (γ'), and 90° away Becke lines will go out of the grain (α'). For a few grains there will be extremely low contrast in one position (matching refractive index), and for even fewer there will be extremely low contrast that does not change with stage rotation (those crystals oriented with their optic axis perpendicular to the stage, grain I).

If a liquid having a refractive index equal to α is chosen (liquid 2 in Figure 2.97), then every single grain will have Becke lines going in when light vibrates in their γ' direction. Rotating the stage 90° from this position the vast majority of grains (exhibiting α' values) will have Becke lines going in and will exhibit varying degrees of contrast. A very few grains will exhibit one position of extremely low contrast (matching refractive index) in this orientation (grains A and D).

If a liquid having a refractive index equal to γ is chosen (liquid 6 in Figure 2.97), then every single grain will have Becke lines going out when light vibrates in their α' direction. Rotating the stage 90° from this position the vast majority of grains (exhibiting γ' values) will have Becke lines going out and will exhibit varying degrees of contrast. A very small number of grains will exhibit one position of extremely low contrast (matching refractive index) in this orientation (grains A and B).

If a liquid in between α and β is chosen (liquid 3 in Figure 2.97), then every single grain will have Becke lines going in when light vibrates in their γ' direction. Rotating 90° from this position some grains will have Becke lines going in, some will have Becke lines going out, and some will exhibit extremely low contrast (matching refractive index).

If a liquid in between β and γ is chosen (liquid 5 in Figure 2.97), then every single grain will have Becke lines going out when light vibrates in their α' direction. Rotating 90° from this position some grains will have Becke lines going in, some will have Becke lines going out, and some will exhibit extremely low contrast (matching refractive index).

While it is time-consuming to determine α, β, and γ values in this manner, it can be effective if sufficient sample is available, in particular for measuring β. As will be seen later, β is the most important principal refractive index value to measure for identification purposes.

In practice it is much more efficient to use additional information related to retardation values, birefringence, optic sign, extinction positions, and interference figures to more rapidly determine refractive index values for both uniaxial and biaxial crystals. These observations will be covered in the remaining sections of this chapter. However, armed only with knowledge of how to conduct the Becke line test, and how different types of crystals behave in various refractive index liquids (Figures 2.95 and 2.97), these values can all be determined for an unknown substance using the methods described above. While there is some uncertainty in the measurements, the values obtained in this manner are typically sufficiently accurate for the identification of unknown substances.

While numerous small grains are required for the brute force method, a single sugar crystal from a typical granulated sugar source is sufficiently large that it can be crushed and used to make several preparations, each consisting of numerous small crystal fragments.

Thus the sample size requirements for this method are still relatively small.

If a colored biaxial substance is studied, there will typically be an observable difference in the absorption color of the crystal when light is vibrating parallel to the three different principal vibration directions in the crystal (pleochroism). Hornblende, for example, is a monoclinic crystal that more strongly absorbs light vibrating perpendicular to its γ vibration direction than it does for light vibrating parallel to its α or β vibration directions (Figure 2.98). The pleochroic formula for a particular variety of hornblende might be expressed as follows: α = light yellow-green, β = yellow-green, γ = dark green.

2.6.4 Retardation

The following sections of the chapter will cover a number of additional observations that can be made on crystals that are studied in between two polarizing filters that have their privileged directions perpendicular to each other (a setup called crossed polars).

As the reader now knows, when light enters a uniaxial crystal such as calcite the light is separated into two components (except for light traveling parallel to the crystal's optic axis). One of these rays vibrates in the plane of the a axes (ω), while the other vibrates perpendicular to this plane (ε or ε'). These two components of light travel through the

50 μm

(a)   (b)

Figure 2.98 A hornblende grain exhibiting strong pleochroism. The polarizer is oriented E–W in the left-hand image, and N–S in the image on the right.

crystal at two different velocities (the exact velocities determined by the values of ω and ε'). Because their velocities are different, one ray travels faster than the other while inside the crystal. This ray is called the "fast ray" and the other is termed the "slow ray." Because it is traveling with a greater velocity, the fast ray will get ahead of the slow ray as they both travel through the crystal and the fast ray will emerge from the crystal ahead of the slow ray. The slow ray is said to be retarded behind the fast ray, and the exact distance that the slow ray falls behind is called the retardation, designated by the letter R (Figure 2.99).

Exactly how far ahead the fast ray gets (the magnitude of the retardation) depends on two variables, namely the relative velocities of the two rays and the thickness of the crystal. The difference between the two velocities is proportional to the difference between the two refractive indices, or the birefringence of the section. Thus retardation is directly proportional to the thickness of the sample and the birefringence of the section. A large birefringence value indicates that the fast ray travels at a much greater velocity than the slow ray while a small birefringence value means that the fast and slow rays travel at only slightly different velocities. Since refractive index is a unitless number, birefringence is also unitless. Thickness is typically measured in micrometers, while retardation is commonly measured in nanometers. The equation relating retardation to birefringence and thickness is provided in Eq. (2.7), where R is retardation, B is birefringence, and T is thickness.

$$R_{(nm)} = B \times T_{(\mu m)} \times 1000 \left(\frac{nm}{\mu m} \right) \quad (2.7)$$

If a uniaxial crystal such as calcite is examined in crossed polars (in between two polarizing filters that are perpendicular to each other), colors are seen that are produced by the light rays that have passed through the crystal. The exact color seen depends on the magnitude of the retardation produced by the crystal. The second polarizing filter, which must be located above the sample, is called the analyzer. It is made of the same material

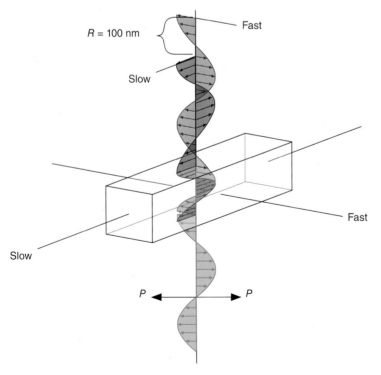

Figure 2.99 This diagram depicts a ray of plane polarized light entering an anisotropic crystal and being resolved into two components, the fast ray and the slow ray. Upon emerging from the crystal the fast ray is ahead of the slow ray by a distance called the retardation (100 nm in the example shown).

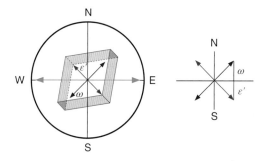

Figure 2.100 A calcite crystal shown with its vibration directions at a 45° angle to the polarizer vibration direction. Upon entering the calcite crystal, the E–W vibrating plane polarized light from the polarizer is resolved into two components, both vibrating at 45° from the polarizer. These two vectors each have some intensity in the N–S plane, and as a result a portion of the light is able to pass through the analyzer. In this orientation the crystal is in a position of brightness in between crossed polars.

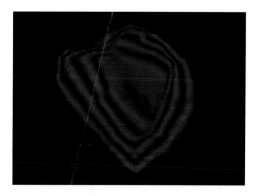

Figure 2.101 An anisotropic crystal (olivine) shown in between crossed polars, illuminated with monochromatic orange light. As the retardation increases from zero up to several thousand nanometers, there are alternating bands of orange and black observed in the crystal. The black bands correspond to areas where the retardation is equal to multiples of 590 nm (0 nm, 590 nm, 1180 nm, 1770 nm, etc.). The orange bands correspond to areas where the retardation is halfway between multiples of 590 nm (295 nm, 885 nm, 1475 nm, etc.).

as the polarizer, but given a different name to enable clear communication about the two. The analyzer is commonly oriented such that its vibration direction is perpendicular to that of the polarizer (North–South, N–S). This setup is called "crossed polars" because the two polars are crossed, or perpendicular to each other. With no sample in place, the field of view becomes black when viewed in crossed polars. That is because all of the light passing through the polarizer is vibrating in the East–West (E–W) plane, and only light with its vibration in the N–S plane can pass through the analyzer. Under these conditions, the only way that light can pass through the analyzer is if something happens to it in between the polarizer and analyzer that changes the plane of vibration of the light. As discussed above, in most orientations plane polarized light incident on a uniaxial calcite rhomb is resolved into two components, each vibrating in a new plane (determined by the orientation of the crystal's indicatrix). In Figure 2.100, these new vibration planes have some of their amplitude in the N–S plane. It is therefore possible for light to pass through the analyzer if a uniaxial crystal is placed in between the two crossed

polars in an appropriate orientation. The calcite crystal in Figure 2.100 will rotate the plane of vibration of plane polarized light, enabling it to pass through the analyzer above.

This phenomenon explains how light from the polarizer can be made to pass through the analyzer if an appropriately oriented anisotropic crystal is being studied. However, it does not explain the various colors observed or their relation to retardation. To understand these retardation colors, as they are called, consider what happens when an anisotropic crystal of olivine is illuminated with monochromatic light (light of a single wavelength, or color). If the crystal is illuminated with monochromatic orange light (590 nm), alternating bands of orange and black are observed in the crystal as the thickness increases from zero at its very edge to some maximum in its center (Figure 2.101).

The bands are due to changing thickness values in the crystal resulting in a range of retardation values. If the retardation could be measured and correlated with the colors

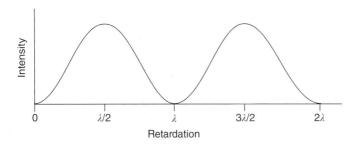

Figure 2.102 The variation in intensity of monochromatic light as a function of retardation for an anisotropic substance viewed in between crossed polars.

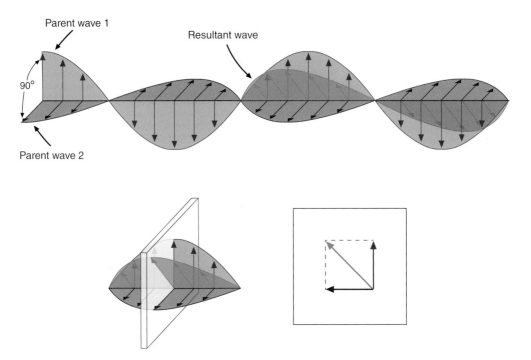

Figure 2.103 The top image shows two parent waves (blue and red) vibrating in planes perpendicular to each other. They recombine (interfere) to produce a new wave (green) that is vibrating in a new plane. The lower image shows a cross-section of one area where the parent waves are interfering both in perspective (left) and looking at the waves head-on (right).

observed, an orange band would be found to be present at retardation values of $N + \frac{1}{2}\lambda$, and a black band at retardation values of $N\lambda$, N representing any integer value. The intensity of the light of any given wavelength varies with retardation as shown in Figure 2.102.

The orange light that has passed through the crystal emerges from the crystal and the fast and slow rays "re-combine" to produce a new light wave. This phenomenon is often described as interference in perpendicular

waves. The new re-combined light wave can be thought of as a vector combination of each ray at each point in space as the wave travels away from the crystal. Figure 2.103 illustrates two parent light waves, vibrating in planes that are perpendicular to each other, recombining to produce a new wave in this manner.

If one of the waves from Figure 2.103 were shifted by $\frac{1}{2}\lambda$ relative to the other, the plane of polarization of the new recombined wave

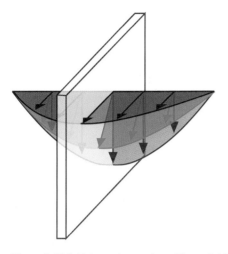 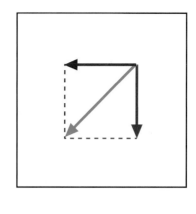

Figure 2.104 If the red wave from Figure 2.103 were shifted by ½λ, the parent waves would interfere to produce a resultant green wave with a plane of polarization that is rotated by 90° relative to the wave in Figure 2.103. This interference is shown both in perspective (left) and looking at the waves head-on (right).

would be rotated by 90° compared to its original plane of vibration (Figure 2.104).

If considered in this manner, then depending on the exact retardation, this new combined wave will be one of the following: plane polarized in its original plane (E–W), plane polarized 90° from its original plane (N–S), circularly polarized, or elliptically polarized.

Note: Technically two light waves can only re-combine, or interfere, if they are vibrating in the same plane. As a result, only the N–S components of light passing the analyzer actually re-combine. However, treating light as though it can interfere in perpendicular planes produces correct solutions to problems and is often easier to visualize.

The new, combined wave will be plane polarized in its original plane (E–W) whenever the fast and slow rays emerge from the crystal in phase with each other (Figure 2.105). They were in phase prior to entering the crystal (being a single wave), so by ending up in phase upon leaving the crystal, it is as if nothing at all happened to the wave. The new wave (while having had quite an adventure inside the anisotropic crystal) looks just like the original wave. The new, re-combined wave has its vibration entirely in the E–W plane,

and this light that passed through the crystal is indistinguishable from light that did not pass through the crystal. Because there is no vibration component in the N–S plane, this light is totally absorbed by the analyzer and a black retardation color is produced. This absorption is the origin of the black bands in the olivine crystal in Figure 2.101.

The new, combined wave will be plane polarized 90° from its original plane whenever the fast and slow rays emerge from the crystal exactly out of phase with each other (Figure 2.106). Under these conditions the new, re-combined wave is plane polarized parallel to the privileged direction of the analyzer (N–S). As a result, the entire wave (100% of its intensity) will pass through the analyzer, producing the brightest orange color observed in the crystal. This phenomenon is the origin of the orange bands in the olivine crystal in Figure 2.101.

For all other retardation values (those having values in between $N\lambda$ and $N + \frac{1}{2}\lambda$ values of the wavelength), the light will be either elliptically or circularly polarized. These are complicated concepts that will not be covered here. Suffice it to say that in these cases a portion of the original light is passed through the analyzer,

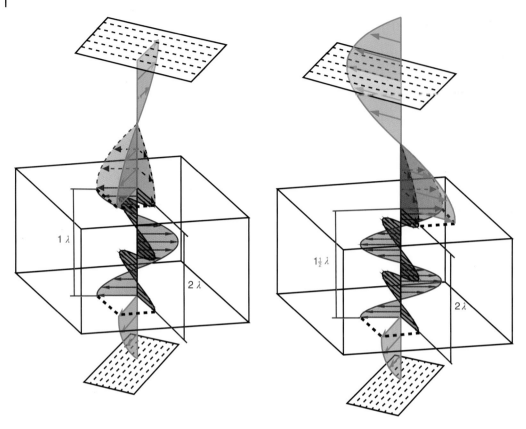

Figure 2.105 The behavior of plane polarized light passing through an anisotropic crystal that produces a retardation of λ. The incident light (green wave) is resolved into two separate components when it enters the crystal (blue and red waves). Upon exiting the crystal the waves interfere to produce a new wave with zero intensity in the privileged direction of the analyzer (the upper green wave). This wave is completely absorbed by the analyzer.

Figure 2.106 The behavior of plane polarized light passing through an anisotropic crystal that produces a retardation of $\lambda/2$. The incident light (green wave) is resolved into two separate components when it enters the crystal (blue and red waves). Upon exiting the crystal the waves interfere to produce a new wave with maximum intensity in the privileged direction of the analyzer (the upper green wave). This wave completely passes through the analyzer.

but not all of it. The result is an orange color with lower intensity. For a more thorough discussion of the concepts of elliptically and circularly polarized light and the conditions that produce them, see Bloss (1961).

If the olivine crystal is illuminated with monochromatic light of a different wavelength (blue, for example), a similar pattern will be observed in the crystal as was seen with orange light. Careful inspection, however, will reveal that the position of the blue bands is not exactly the same as the position of the orange bands.

That is because blue light, with a shorter wavelength than orange light (about 400 nm for blue compared to 590 nm for orange), will meet the conditions for total absorption by the analyzer (in phase, retardation of $N\lambda$) and maximum brightness (out of phase, retardation of $N + \frac{1}{2}\lambda$) at different retardation values than blue light did. Orange light is most intense for retardations of 295 nm, 885 nm, 1475 nm, etc. Orange light is totally absorbed for retardations of 0 nm, 590 nm, 1180 nm, and so on. Blue light, on the other hand, is most intense when retardation values are 200 nm, 600 nm, 1000 nm, and totally absorbed for retardation values of 0 nm, 400 nm, 800 nm, etc.

When illuminating the olivine crystal with white light, various colors are observed in the crystal that are the result of all the wavelengths in the visible spectrum simultaneously undergoing the phenomena described above (Figure 2.107).

To understand the colors, first consider just one retardation value, namely 550 nm. At this retardation, green light (550 nm) is in phase and therefore completely absorbed by the analyzer. The resulting color is the complementary color to green (a magenta hue) made up by the violet and red light at either end of the spectrum that is transmitted. The retardation colors resulting from white light for a range of retardation values are shown in a chart in Figure 2.108. This chart is called the Michel-Lévy chart, named after its creator, the French geologist Auguste Michel-Lévy.

While most anisotropic substances will exhibit a series of retardation colors closely resembling those shown in Figure 2.108, some substances produce a slightly different series of colors, called anomalous retardation colors. The anomalous colors are typically due to either dispersion or absorption caused by the substance. Materials that have strong dispersion of their birefringence have different birefringence values for different wavelengths of light. Therefore the retardation experienced by blue light will differ significantly from the retardation experienced by red light, the result being a somewhat different series of colors than depicted in Figure 2.108. For example, RDX (cyclotrimethylenetrinitramine) crystals exhibit anomalous retardation colors in certain orientations (Figure 2.109).

Substances that are colored in transmitted light appear colored because they selectively absorb wavelengths of light in the visible region. If these wavelengths are absorbed, they cannot participate in the production of retardation colors (Figure 2.110).

An additional valuable use of retardation colors is in gaining insights into the three-dimensional shape of a given particle. Because the retardation color observed depends on the thickness of the sample, lines of constant retardation color (called isochromes) are similar to contours on a topographical map. These isochromes define areas of constant thickness for a given sample. Where the colors observed indicate decreasing retardation, the examiner can deduce that the particle thickness is decreasing. A common application of this deductive reasoning is in determining the cross-sectional shapes of fibers. Fibers with four common cross-sectional shapes are shown in crossed polars in Figures 2.110–2.113. For a fiber with a round cross-section, moving in from the edge of the fiber toward the center the retardation colors increase rapidly at first and then more slowly as the fiber center is approached. The colors are symmetrical about the fiber center and the observed diameter remains constant (Figure 2.110). For a trilobal fiber, the retardation colors initially change slowly moving in from the edge of the fiber toward the center. The rate of change in retardation increases suddenly just before the center of the fiber. The retardation color pattern may or may not be symmetrical about the center of the fiber, depending on how the fiber is lying (Figure 2.111). For fibers with a dog bone shaped cross-section, the retardation increases slowly moving from the edge of the fiber toward the interior, and then the retardation decreases again as the center of the fiber is approached (Figure 2.112). The diameter of the fiber appears to change when the fiber is lying up on an edge, typically where the fiber is curving. Finally, for fibers with triangular cross-section, the retardation will be low at one edge of the fiber and increase toward the other edge of the fiber (Figure 2.113).

2.6.5 Birefringence

If the retardation of a section can be accurately estimated then Eq. (2.7) can be used, slightly

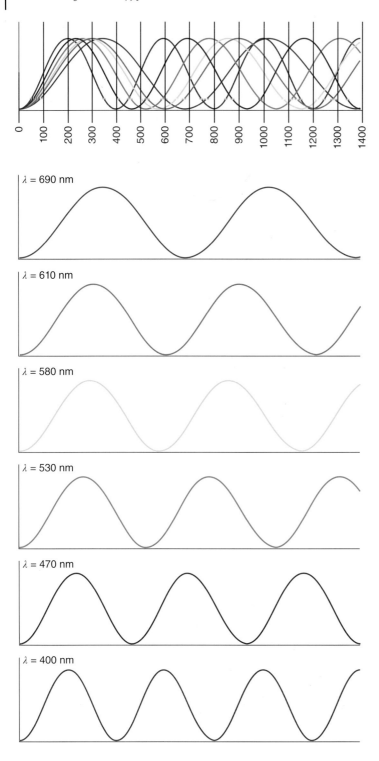

Figure 2.107 The individual wavelengths of light each exhibit intensity maxima at retardations of $N + \frac{1}{2}\lambda$, and intensity minima at retardations of $N\lambda$. The bottom plots show several selected colors of light and their relative intensities for different retardation values. The top plot superimposes the individual color plots. These colors combine to produce the interference colors observed for each particular retardation value. For example, for 550 nm of retardation, red and purple light have relatively high intensities, while green light is at minimum intensity. The resulting interference color has a magenta hue.

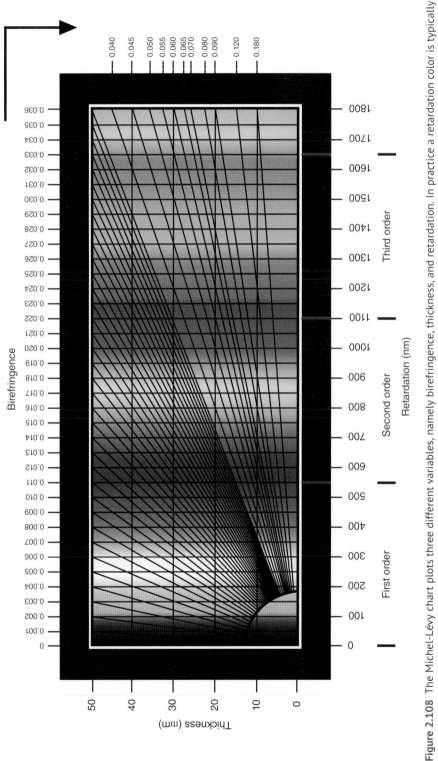

Figure 2.108 The Michel-Lévy chart plots three different variables, namely birefringence, thickness, and retardation. In practice a retardation color is typically observed in a sample (vertical lines are lines of constant retardation), the thickness of the sample is estimated (horizontal lines are lines of constant thickness), and the intersection between these two variables on the chart is located. The diagonal line that intersects this point is the birefringence exhibited by the sample (diagonal lines are lines of constant birefringence). For example, if a particle that is 20 μm thick exhibits a retardation of 800 nm, the diagonal line that crosses the intersection of these values corresponds to a birefringence of 0.040. While determination of birefringence is most common use of the chart, in practice if any two variables are known for a sample, the third may be determined.

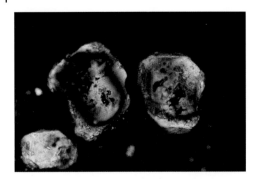

Figure 2.109 Due to its high dispersion, the retardation colors shown by RDX crystals in certain orientations are different from the series of colors on the Michel-Lévy chart. These different colors are called anomalous retardation colors.

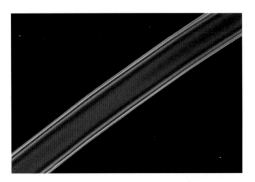

Figure 2.110 A round fiber shown in between crossed polars. The pattern of retardation colors observed in the fiber is consistent with a circular cross-section, increasing rapidly at the edges and then more slowly toward the center of the fiber, with the color pattern symmetrical about the fiber center. Note that this fiber exhibits anomalous retardation colors because it is a colored fiber (due to absorption).

rearranged to Eq. (2.8), to determine the birefringence of that section.

$$B = \frac{R_{(nm)}}{T_{(\mu m)} \times 1000 \left(\frac{nm}{\mu m} \right)} \qquad (2.8)$$

Thickness can be estimated using a calibrated fine focus scale (although there are caveats related to the refractive index of the particle), or alternately thickness can be estimated by measuring the other particle dimensions and making an educated guess as to the sample thickness. Another approach is to pass a sample through a series of sieves to isolate a limited size range; that size range can then serve as the estimated thickness. Once estimated, the retardation and thickness values are plugged into Eq. (2.8) and a reasonable estimate of the birefringence results. While not terribly precise, in practice this type of estimate is very effective for distinguishing substances having significant birefringence differences.

If the sample being studied is small enough (thickness less than 50 μm), the Michel-Lévy chart can easily be used to estimate its birefringence (Figure 2.108). This chart is such a useful tool for the microscopist that it is worth spending some additional time on. The colors shown are the retardation colors observed in between crossed polars. The retardation values (in nm) are listed along the bottom of the chart (x axis), and the colors above each number depict the color observed for that particular retardation. The vertical lines represent constant retardation values. Thickness values (usually given in either μm or mm) are listed along the left (y axis) of the chart, and the horizontal lines represent these thickness values. What makes this chart different from many the reader has likely used in the past is that there is a third variable, namely birefringence, also plotted on it. The birefringence values are listed along the top and right side of the chart. The diagonal lines represent these birefringence values. In practice, the microscopist is usually trying to estimate the birefringence of a sample on the basis of its thickness and the retardation it exhibits. The birefringence is estimated by approximating both the thickness and retardation of the sample and locating the position on the chart at which the two intersect. The diagonal line that coincides with this intersection indicates the birefringence exhibited by the particle. For example, a grain that is about 20 μm thick exhibiting a retardation of about 800 nm would coincide with the diagonal birefringence line of 0.040. A grain that is about 20 μm thick exhibiting a retardation of about 200 nm would coincide

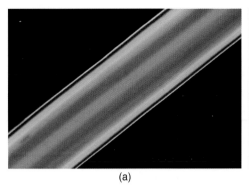 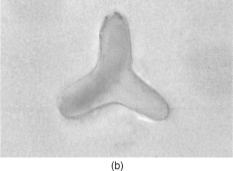

(a)   (b)

Figure 2.111 A trilobal nylon fiber shown in cross-section (left), and in between crossed polars (right). The pattern of retardation colors observed in the fiber is consistent with a trilobal cross-section.

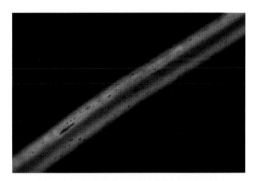

Figure 2.112 A dog bone-shaped acrylic fiber shown in between crossed polars. The pattern of retardation colors observed in the fiber is consistent with a dog bone cross-section, being lower in the center than it is on either side of center.

with the diagonal birefringence line of 0.010. Note that the second grain exhibits one quarter of the retardation exhibited by the first grain, and the birefringence of the second grain is therefore one quarter of the birefringence of the first grain (since they have the same thickness). The same birefringence values could be calculated using Eq. (2.8), and this equation is a necessity for grains that exhibit retardation values exceeding 1800 nm, or for grains thicker than 50 μm, as these grains would plot off of the Michel-Lévy chart.

While birefringence determination is the typical way the chart is used, in practice if any two variables are known the third can be determined from the chart. Thus the retardation

color that would be observed for a given substance of a particular thickness can be predicted, and the thickness of a substance having a known birefringence can be determined on the basis of its retardation color. Petrologists prepare thin sections of rock for microscopical study. They typically aim to prepare sections that are 30 μm thick. Quartz, being very common in most rocks, is often used to assess the thickness and determine when to stop polishing the section. With a birefringence of 0.009, at a thickness of 30 μm quartz will exhibit a maximum retardation of 270 nm (a very pale yellow). A great advantage of having a thin section prepared is that the thickness is no longer a variable, but rather a known constant. Variations in retardation colors observed in a thin section therefore originate only from the birefringence differences in the crystal sections being studied.

The primary difficulty that microscopy students have in using the Michel-Lévy chart is the fact that certain colors repeat themselves. In addition, there are colors observed for higher retardation values that are not included on the Michel-Lévy chart. Finally, many particles are thicker than 50 μm, making them too large to use the chart. For this last problem, the thickness and retardation values may simply be plugged into Eq. (2.8). For the first two problems, it is useful to consider this chart as being a small part of a larger picture.

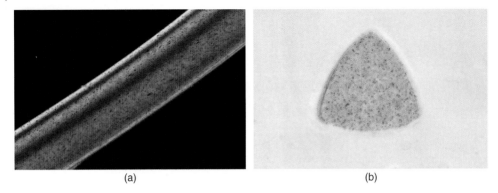

(a)   (b)

Figure 2.113 A triangular polypropylene fiber shown in cross-section (left), and in between crossed polars (right). The pattern of retardation colors observed in the fiber is consistent with a triangular cross-section, increasing from one edge to the other.

As mentioned above, the colors obtained for certain retardation values (e.g. 550 and 1100 nm) are similar in quality. In order to clearly communicate about retardation colors, the chart is divided into "orders" of retardation. A new order of retardation colors begins every 550 nm, marked by a red color for the first several orders. All of the colors for retardation values ranging from 0 to 550 nm are considered first-order colors, often designated with the order number followed by the degree sign (e.g. 1° yellow at 400 nm). All colors for retardation values ranging from 550 to 1100 nm are second-order colors, such as 2° blue at 650 nm.

It is useful to consider the entire range of possible retardation colors to be divided into three different regions. The first region is that depicted on the Michel-Lévy chart and consists of the first three orders of retardation colors. These orders are characterized by a variety of colors (gray, while, yellow, red, blue, green, etc.), and the retardation colors in the first several orders are vibrant (Figure 2.114). The second region consists of the next five orders (fourth- to eighth-order retardation colors). This region is characterized by dull (pastel) pink and green colors that repeat, becoming paler with increasing order of retardation (Figure 2.115). The third region is that containing all retardation values above the eighth order (>4400 nm). For this region a single color, namely a creamy white color called "high-order white," is observed (Figure 2.116). Table 2.4 lists the colors and retardation ranges just described.

There are several colors that serve as useful landmarks to help one determine the exact retardation value they are observing in a crystal. If a black color is observed, it corresponds to a retardation value of 0. Thus black is the color that will be seen for all isotropic substances (glass and cubic crystals), as well as for all anisotropic crystals oriented with a circular indicatrix section in the plane of the microscope stage. There is only one retardation range for which a gray color may be obtained, namely 1° gray around $R = 100$ nm (Figure 2.114). If a white color is observed, it must correspond to either 1° white (200 nm) (Figure 2.114) or high-order white ($R > 4400$ nm) (Figure 2.116). There are only two blue retardation colors on the chart, namely 2° blue ($R = 650$ nm) and 3° blue ($R = 1200$ nm) (Figure 2.114). The exact order of a particular color can usually be determined on the basis of the colors next to it, provided the thickness is not constant. As an example, the thickest area of the olivine grain in Exhibit 115 exhibits a pale green color (just north of its center), and it is not clear from examining the color alone which order of retardation it represents. At the bottom edge of the grain, however, first-order white is evident. By starting at first-order white and moving toward the center of the grain, each red color

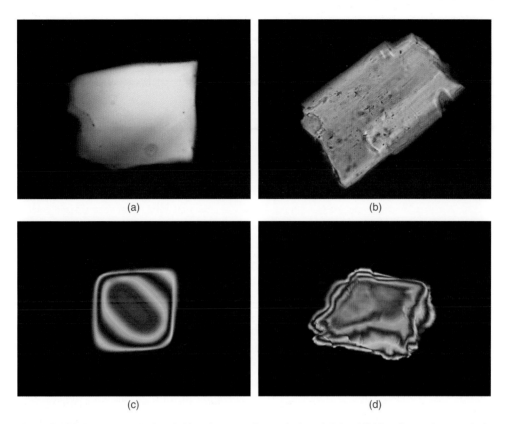

(a)

(b)

(c)

(d)

Figure 2.114 A quartz grain (top left) and a tremolite grain (top right) exhibiting first-order retardation colors, along with a quartz grain (bottom left) and a pyroxene grain (bottom right) exhibiting the vibrant, varied retardation colors characteristic of the first several orders of retardation colors.

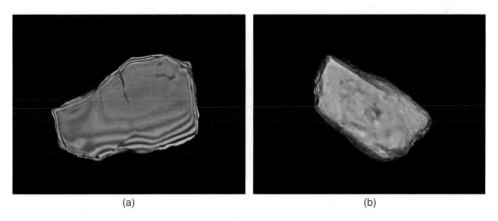

(a)

(b)

Figure 2.115 An olivine grain (left) and a carbonate grain (right) exhibiting the pale pinks and greens typical of the fourth through eighth orders of retardation. Lower order colors are visible at the edges of the olivine grain.

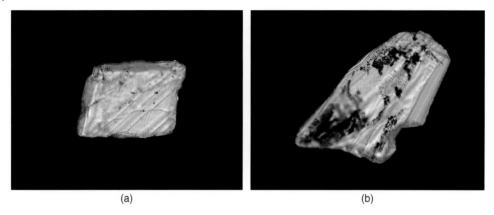

(a)   (b)

Figure 2.116 Two calcite grains exhibiting high-order white retardation colors.

Table 2.4 Retardation values and corresponding retardation colors.

Retardation value	Retardation colors
Zero	Black
First through third orders	Variety of colors, vibrant colors (see Figure 2.108)
Fourth through eighth orders	Pastel pinks and greens, paler at higher orders
Above eighth order	High-order white

encountered represents one order of retardation. If the red bands are counted, it becomes apparent that there are six red/pink bands encountered prior to reaching the pale green color in the grain center. This observation indicates that the green color in the thickest area of the grain is seventh-order green. This green retardation color is about halfway in between seventh-order red (3850 nm) and eighth-order red (4400 nm), indicating the grain has a retardation of approximately 4125 nm. In the rare situations where the retardation color remains ambiguous despite careful consideration, additional microscope accessories (compensators) may be used to clarify the retardation value.

The typical purpose of estimating retardation values is for the determination of the birefringence of a substance. If it is necessary to know the birefringence of a substance accurately, the birefringence can be determined by measuring the refractive index values of the substance and taking their difference ($|\omega - \varepsilon|$, $\gamma - \alpha$). What the Michel-Lévy chart method lacks in accuracy, however, it more than makes up for with efficiency. Measuring α and γ for a biaxial crystal can take a considerable amount of time and effort. Some substances have refractive index values so high that it is challenging to find liquids with indices high enough to use the immersion method. Estimating the birefringence of these crystals using the Michel-Lévy chart takes only seconds, requires minimal sample size, and is not dependent on the refractive index of the mounting medium.

2.6.6 Extinction Characteristics

If an anisotropic crystal such as the now familiar calcite rhomb (lying on a rhombohedral face) is rotated on the microscope stage in between crossed polars, it will disappear (go black) at positions 90° apart. The intensity of the retardation colors (but not the actual hue of the colors) varies during rotation from one position of darkness to the next, achieving maximum brightness exactly halfway between (45° away from) positions of darkness. Positions of darkness for an anisotropic crystal in between crossed polars are called extinction positions, and the phenomenon of a crystal going dark is termed extinction. An anisotropic crystal will be extinct whenever one of the privileged vibration directions in the crystal is aligned parallel to the privileged vibration direction of the polarizer. Extinction characteristics are best studied with the condenser aperture mostly closed (unidirectional axial illumination).

As was discussed above, if a calcite rhomb is mounted on the stage and is studied in plane polarized light, depending on the orientation of the crystal relative to the polarizer vibration direction the light may interact with either only ω, only ε', or the light may be split into two components (Figures 2.91 and 2.92). In one position (when ω is aligned with the polarized) the light will vibrate entirely in ω and none of the light will be rotated into the N–S plane (Figure 2.117). If rotated 90°, the light will vibrate entirely in ε' and again none of the light will be rotated into the N–S plane (Figure 2.117).

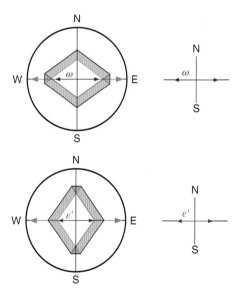

Figure 2.117 When the vibration direction of the incident plane polarized light is parallel to a principle vibration direction in an anisotropic sample, the light is not resolved into two components but rather when it passes through the anisotropic sample the light maintains its plane of vibration. The images depict two positions for a calcite rhomb for which the incident light is parallel to a principle vibration in the crystal (ω in the upper image, ε' in the lower image).

Because the crystal does not change the plane of vibration of the incident light in either of these positions, the light that transmits through the crystal will all be absorbed by the analyzer and the crystal will appear dark. At 45° from either of these first two positions, light will be roughly equally split into ω and ε' components on entering the calcite crystal (Figure 2.100). This orientation will be a position of brightness (maximum intensity for the retardation colors). In any other orientation, the light from the polarizer will be split unequally into two components. Retardation colors are still visible in these orientations, but they are not as intense as they are in the 45° position.

Extinction in single crystals is important because it can be used to locate principal vibration directions in a crystal. For grains of uniaxial calcite, extinction positions will occur when ω is parallel to the polarizer and when ε' or ε is parallel to the polarizer. Since measuring these values is useful for identifying unknown substances, it is helpful to be able to locate these planes.

Where a crystal exhibits evidence of its external form(s), the orientation of principal vibration directions can be related to the crystal morphology. For a sodium nitrate crystal lying on a rhombohedral face, for example, the planes of vibration (extinction positions) in the crystal always bisect the interfacial angles (Figure 2.118). This phenomenon is termed symmetrical extinction. For a well-formed 2,4,6-trinitrotoluene (TNT) crystal lying on a pinacoid face (Figure 2.119), however, the planes of vibration in the crystal are parallel to the crystal faces in this orthorhombic substance. A monoclinic 2,4-dinitrotoluene (DNT) crystal lying on a pinacoid face, on the other hand, would exhibit some planes of vibration that are neither parallel to crystal faces nor bisecting interfacial angles (Figure 2.120). This phenomenon is termed oblique extinction.

Generally speaking, observing parallel or symmetrical extinction in a crystal is an indication of higher symmetry (triclinic crystals

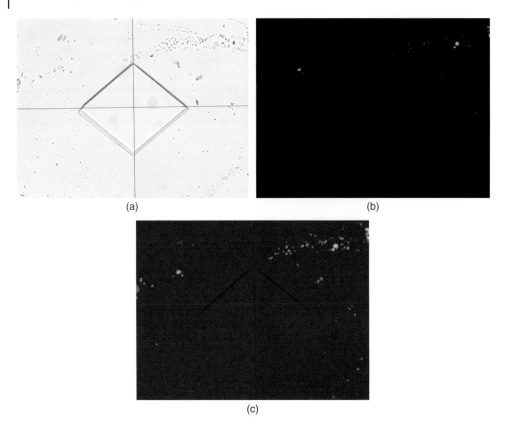

(a)

(b)

(c)

Figure 2.118 A sodium nitrate crystal exhibiting symmetrical extinction. The crosshairs perfectly bisect the inter-facial angles in the crystal, indicating that the vibration directions of light in the crystal (aligned with the crosshairs at extinction) could coincide with mirror planes in the crystal.

are unlikely to ever exhibit these types of extinction). For any particular view of a crystal, the presence of parallel or symmetrical extinction is consistent with the presence of a mirror plane existing in that plane of the crystal, whereas oblique extinction is conclusive evidence of the lack of mirror symmetry in a particular plane (Figure 2.121).

If numerous randomly oriented biaxial crystals are studied and their extinction behavior documented, it may be possible to determine the crystal system to which the substance belongs. However, care must be taken when using extinction type to make determinations about crystal symmetry. That is because extinction type is only a reliable indication of symmetry when the section being studied is a principal section of the indicatrix. Principal

sections of crystals from different systems will exhibit different types of extinction based on their symmetry elements (Table 2.5).

It must be stressed that a random section (*hkl*) of a tetragonal, hexagonal, or orthorhombic crystal can exhibit oblique extinction, and a triclinic crystal could (by chance) exhibit very nearly parallel or symmetrical extinction on a particular section. It is therefore necessary to understand optical orientation in order to use Table 2.5. The best way to determine whether a principal section of the indicatrix is being examined is by use of interference figures (see Section 2.6.8). In practice, however, many substances crystallize with simple faces (110, 101, 100, etc.), and often lie on these faces when being studied on a microscope stage. As a result it is often possible to gain

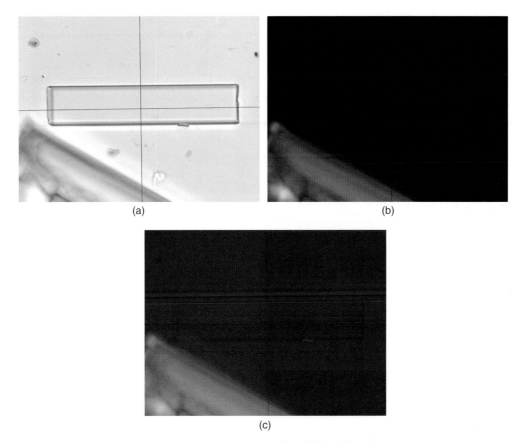

(a)

(b)

(c)

Figure 2.119 A 2,4,6-trinitrotoluene (TNT) crystal exhibiting parallel extinction. The crosshairs are parallel to the edges of prominent faces in the crystal, indicating that the vibration directions of light in the crystal (aligned with the crosshairs at extinction) could coincide with mirror planes in the crystal.

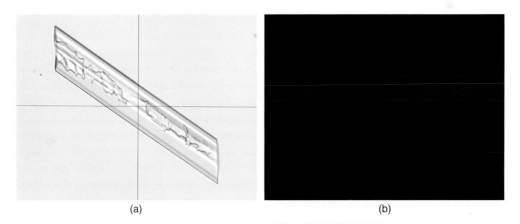

(a)

(b)

Figure 2.120 A 2,4-dinitrotoluene (DNT) crystal exhibiting oblique extinction. The crosshairs are neither parallel to crystal faces nor bisect inter-facial angles in the crystal at its extinction position. This observation indicates that the vibration directions of light in the crystal (aligned with the crosshairs at extinction) are unlikely to coincide with mirror planes in the crystal.

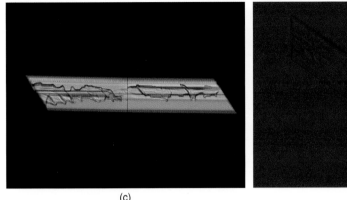

(c)   (d)

Figure 2.120 *(Continued)*

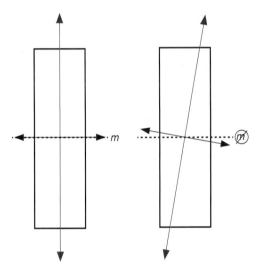

Figure 2.121 Two crystals with their vibration directions indicated by the red and blue lines. The crystal on the left could have a mirror plane in the plane indicated by the dotted line. The crystal on the right, however, cannot have a mirror plane in the indicated location because the vibration directions of light, reflected across this plane, do not exhibit this symmetry. The crystal on the left would exhibit parallel extinction, and the crystal on the right would exhibit oblique extinction. Extinction behavior can therefore provide insights into the possible presence or absence of certain symmetry elements in a particular crystal section.

insights into the likely crystal system using simple extinction observations. These insights should be considered tentative, however, unless conoscopy or some other means

Table 2.5 Extinction types on principal sections for different crystal systems.

Crystal system	Extinction types on principal sections
Cubic	Not applicable
Tetragonal	Parallel or symmetrical
Hexagonal	Parallel or symmetrical
Orthorhombic	Parallel or symmetrical
Monoclinic	Parallel or symmetrical on two principal sections, oblique on third principal section
Triclinic	Oblique

(spindle stage) is used to confirm the orientation of a crystal being studied.

For monoclinic and triclinic crystals that exhibit oblique extinction, it can be useful to determine the angle(s) between principal vibration directions in a crystal (extinction positions) and crystal faces (which often coincide with crystal axes). In practice, this angle is determined by first rotating the crystal to an extinction position (reading off the stage vernier) and then rotating the stage to the nearest crystal face (again reading off the stage vernier). The difference in degrees between the stage readings at the two positions is the extinction angle (Figure 2.122). References often indicate what these angles are (e.g. for gypsum the angle would be 52° if measured from γ to the trace of the c axis, Figure 2.76).

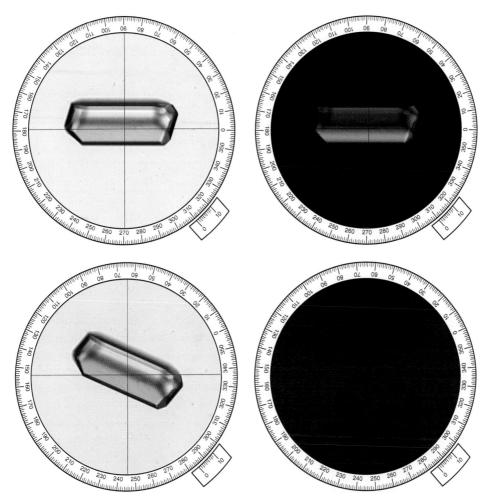

Figure 2.122 An extinction angle is measured by first aligning the crystal face of interest with a crosshair and noting the value on the microscope stage that coincides with the fixed stage vernier (top images). In the example shown above this angle is 310°. The crystal is then rotated to its nearest extinction position (bottom images) and the new value on the stage that coincides with the vernier is read. In the above example this angle is 285°. The difference between these two values is the extinction angle, which is 25° for this particular section of the copper sulfate pentahydrate crystal shown.

Some anisotropic particles do not exhibit extinction for one of several possible reasons. This lack of extinction is potentially valuable information, particularly when the reason for the incomplete extinction can be determined. Several of the possible reasons for this phenomenon are explored below.

Sometimes, a particle does not exhibit complete extinction because it is actually composed of numerous small crystals. Particles composed of numerous crystals are called polycrystalline particles. In these particles, each individual (typically very small) crystal does exhibit complete extinction every 90°. However, since the particle is made up of numerous small crystals, randomly oriented relative to each other, there is no single extinction position for the entire particle (Figures 2.123 and 2.124).

A similar reason for lack of complete extinction in a single particle is twinning. Like polycrystallinity, twinned particles are composed of multiple single crystals in different

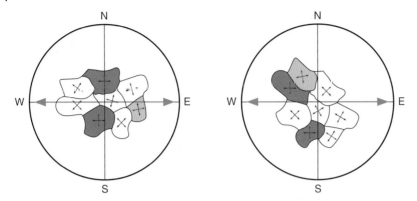

Figure 2.123 A diagram depicting a polycrystalline particle in two different orientations in between crossed polars. The vibration directions are shown for each individual crystal (the blue and red lines). Any crystal with a vibration direction parallel to the polarizer (the green line) will be at extinction. Any crystal with its vibration directions 45° from the polarizer direction will be at a position of brightness. Other crystals will have an intermediate intensity. As the stage is rotated, individual crystals will go extinct every 90°, but the particle as a whole will never be completely dark.

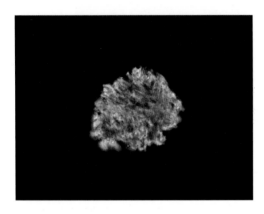

Figure 2.124 A photomicrograph of a polycrystalline grain from a fine-grained volcanic rock.

orientations. However, in twins there is a specific relationship between the relative orientations of their crystal lattices. The angles between the crystal lattices of twins are consistent and related to the symmetry and internal structures of the twins. There is no such relationship between the crystals in polycrystalline particles. The angles between planes in twins can sometimes be determined and may provide insights into the composition of the crystals. The plagioclase feldspar series is a group of minerals with compositions ranging continuously from that of albite (the

sodium-rich end member) to anorthite (the calcium-rich end member). The extinction angle to the twin plane for these minerals varies with composition. This measurement performed on a properly oriented twinned grain can provide insights into the grain's chemical composition (Figures 2.125 and 2.126).

Some materials commonly form twins, while twinning is rare to non-existent in other substances. The type of twinning varies among different substances, so recognizing a particular type of twinning can help an examiner recognize and identify an unknown substance. Further, twinning can sometimes provide insights into the "history" of the particle. The presence of tartan twinning in the mineral microcline indicates that it cooled very slowly (Figure 2.126(a)).

Some crystals appear to change color rather than go extinct every 90° in between crossed polars (Figures 2.127 and 2.128). This phenomenon is typically due to dispersion. For monoclinic and triclinic crystals, the optical orientation (angle between vibration directions of light and crystallographic axes) may vary with wavelength of light. When this dispersion of vibration directions occurs, the extinction position of the crystal will also vary with wavelength of light. If the crystal is rotated

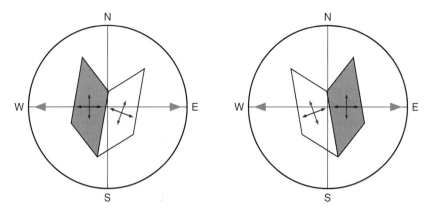

Figure 2.125 A diagram of a grain composed of two crystal twins. The behavior of the grain is similar to that of a polycrystalline particle, but in crystal twins there is a specific crystallographic relationship between the two crystal lattices, and the angle between the two extinction positions (for a particular section) has a specific value that is constant for a particular type of twins.

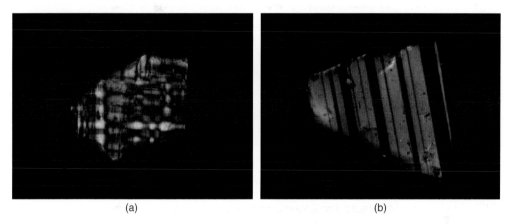

(a)   (b)

Figure 2.126 Photomicrographs of (a) microcline twins and (b) plagioclase twins. The type of twinning observed is a useful feature for the identification of certain materials, such as these two different types of feldspar minerals.

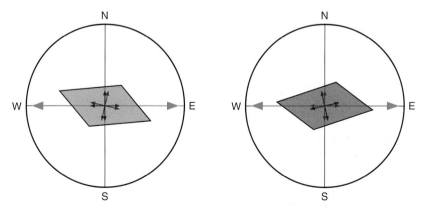

Figure 2.127 A diagram depicting a crystal exhibiting dispersed extinction. The vibration directions for red light (red lines) and blue light (blue lines) in the crystal are shown. For the crystal on the left, blue light is extinct but red/orange/yellow light is not, and the crystal exhibits an orange hue as a result. For the crystal on the right, red light is extinct (but not blue light) and the crystal exhibits a blue or violet hue.

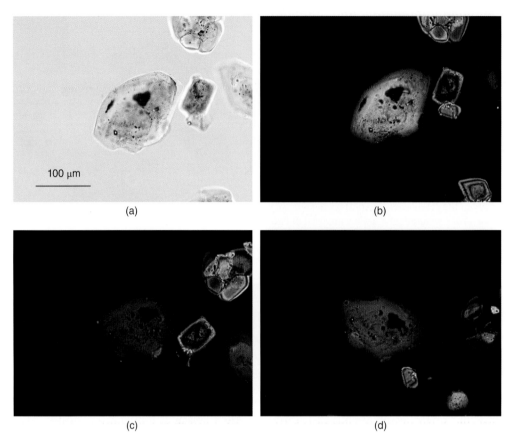

Figure 2.128 Photomicrographs of an RDX crystal shown at a position of brightness (top) and again in two orientations near its extinction position (bottom). This crystal exhibits dispersed extinction.

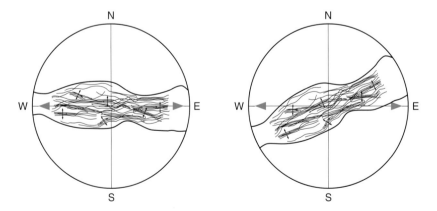

Figure 2.129 A diagram depicting the orientation of cellulose polymer chains within a cotton fiber. Some areas have a high degree of crystallinity, while others are nearly amorphous. Vibration directions are indicated in some of the highly crystalline areas, depicted by red and blue lines. There is sufficient local crystallinity for the fiber to exhibit anisotropy, but the structure is too poorly organized for the entire fiber to go extinct at any position.

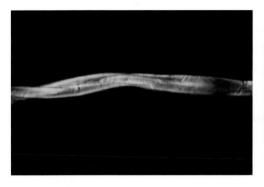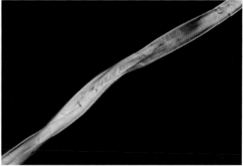

Figure 2.130 Photomicrographs of a cotton fiber shown in two positions in between crossed polars. The intensity of the retardation colors stays nearly constant as the fiber is rotated in between crossed polars.

to an extinction position for blue light, the crystal will appear to have an orange hue to it (due to all the other colors of light that are not at extinction). A slight rotation will bring the crystal into the extinction position for red light, at which point the crystal will appear to be a blue-purple color (again, because of the other wavelengths of visible light that are not at extinction).

This phenomenon (a change in color during rotation in crossed polars) may also be due to a biaxial grain oriented with its optic axis nearly perpendicular to the microscope stage, with dispersion of the optic axes. This possibility can be checked by observing the interference figure produced by the grain (see Section 2.6.8).

Some materials do not exhibit complete extinction because they are poorly crystalline. Cotton fibers, for example, are composed of cellulose polymers that are generally oriented with their lengths parallel to the length of the fiber. While the general orientation of most fibers is sufficient to slow down light vibration parallel to the fiber length (relative to light vibrating parallel to the fiber width), the internal structure is too poorly ordered to behave like a true crystal (Figures 2.129 and 2.130). Cotton fibers therefore do not go extinct. They have a roughly constant intensity to their retardation colors when rotated in between crossed polars. Some localized areas are more highly crystalline than others and may change intensity more during rotation.

Starch grains provide another interesting example of incomplete extinction in a poorly crystalline substance. Starch grains are composed of polysaccharide chains that radiate outward from a central point (the hilum). These polymer chains are generally aligned with each other and some areas are highly ordered. However, because they radiate outward in all directions, some chains are aligned parallel to the polarizer (and therefore behave as though they were a crystal at extinction) while other chains are aligned 45° to the polarizer (and behave as though they were a crystal at a brightness position). The result is a dark cross with bright areas in the four quadrants (Figures 2.131 and 2.132). The dark cross appears to pass through the grain like a wave when the grain is rotated, giving rise to the term undulose extinction.

The above discussion does not provide a comprehensive list of reasons for poor extinction in particles, but it covers some of the most common causes. The extinction behavior of particles is something that should be closely studied, and with experience the extinction characteristics of a material can provide insights into its internal structure.

2.6.7 Use of Compensators and Sign of Elongation

Polarized light microscopes typically have slots in their nosepieces or intermediate tubes for using a type of accessory called a compensator. There are a wide variety of compensators that have slightly different applications. However, they all work on a similar principle, namely

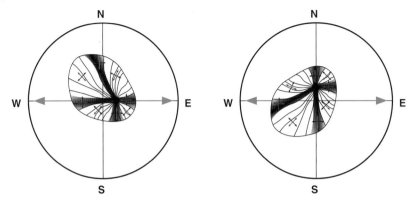

Figure 2.131 A diagram depicting the orientation of the carbohydrate polymer chains in a starch grain. The polymer chains radiate outward from the hilum of the starch grain, with sufficient local crystallinity to exhibit anisotropy. The approximate vibration directions for light in several different localized areas are shown by blue and red arrows. Any region of the grain for which a vibration direction is parallel to the polarizer (the green line) will exhibit extinction and will be dark. Other regions exhibit retardation colors, with the brightest areas being those in positions of brightness, with their vibration directions 45° from the polarizer. The result is the appearance of a dark cross inside a bright grain in between crossed polars. As the grain is rotated, the cross appears to undulate through the grain as different regions of the starch grain go extinct.

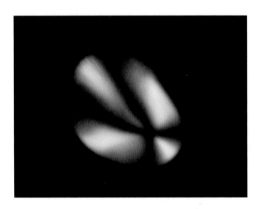

Figure 2.132 A potato starch grain shown in between crossed polars.

by introducing retardation into the light path of the microscope. The most commonly used compensator is called a full wave plate (also called a λ compensator, a red I plate, or a 530 nm compensator). This type of compensator is a crystal, typically quartz or gypsum, which produces a retardation equal to about one full order (these compensators commonly have retardation values of approximately 530 nm). When no sample is in place and the compensator is introduced into the microscope

in crossed polars, the entire field of view turns a magenta color. Compensators are usually marked with the retardation they introduce along with the direction of their high refractive index (i.e. their slow vibration direction).

Note: It is slightly misleading to refer to the slow component of light as the "slow vibration direction," as the frequency of vibration of the light does not decrease, but rather the velocity of the light slows down. This language is commonly used in references, however, so it will be used in the following sections of this chapter with the understanding that the slow vibration direction refers to the vibration direction of the component of light with the slower velocity.

When a crystal is studied in crossed polars with the compensator in place, the retardation values of the crystal and compensator are either added together or subtracted from each other depending on the relative orientation of the slow vibration directions of the two. If the slow vibration direction of the crystal is aligned with the slow vibration direction of the compensator, the two retardations are added together. If the slow vibration direction

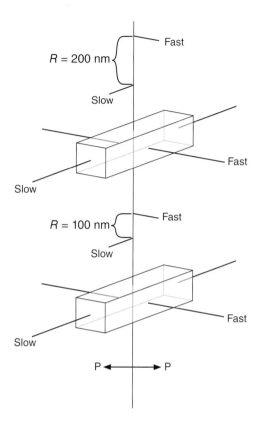

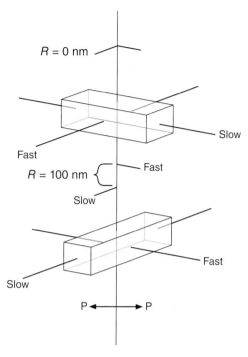

Figure 2.133 This diagram shows two identical crystals that are both in the path of the light traveling through the microscope, with their slow vibration directions parallel to each other. The light passes through the lower crystal first and this first crystal introduces 100 nm of retardation. The two components of light then enter the upper crystal and this crystal introduces an additional 100 nm of retardation. The total retardation caused by the two crystals is 200 nm. When the higher refractive index vibration directions (designated "slow" in the figure) are parallel to each other, the retardation values of the two crystals are added together.

Figure 2.134 This diagram shows the same crystals that are depicted in Figure 2.133. However, the upper crystal has now been rotated by 90° so that its fast vibration direction is parallel to the slow vibration direction in the lower crystal. As in Figure 2.133, the light passes through the lower crystal first and this crystal introduces 100 nm of retardation. When the two components of light enter the upper crystal, however, the component of light that had fallen behind by 100 nm travels more rapidly in the upper crystal and catches up to the component that had been ahead. After passing through both crystals, the total retardation is 0 nm. When the slow vibration directions are perpendicular to each other, the retardation values of the two crystals are subtracted and the retardation observed is equal to the difference between them.

of the crystal is aligned with the fast vibration direction of the compensator, the result is the difference between the two retardation values. The slow vibration direction of most compensators is oriented from lower-left to upper-right, but this is not universal and should be confirmed prior to use. Figure 2.133 illustrates the addition of retardation values for two identical crystals that are superimposed on each other in the light path with

their slow vibration directions parallel to each other. Figure 2.134 illustrates the subtraction of retardation values for two identical crystals that are superimposed on each other with their slow vibration directions perpendicular to each other.

Fibers and elongated crystals can be assigned a "sign of elongation" that can be helpful for identification purposes. Elongated samples whose refractive index parallel to their length

$(n_{\parallel})$ is greater than the refractive index perpendicular to their length $(n_{\perp})$ are defined as having a positive sign of elongation. Alternatively, elongated samples whose refractive index parallel to their length $(n_{\parallel})$ is less than the refractive index perpendicular to their length $(n_{\perp})$ are considered to have a negative sign of elongation. The terms "length slow" and "length fast" are sometimes used in place of positive elongation and negative elongation, respectively.

It is common for compensators to have two positions, one that is empty and one that holds the compensator plate (the crystal). The most commonly used compensator is the full wave plate, with a retardation of approximately 530 nm. Figure 2.135 shows an elongated crystal of celestine with a retardation of approximately 100 nm (first-order gray) in between crossed polars as viewed through the empty position of the compensator (on the left). In celestine crystals the slow vibration direction of light is parallel to the crystal length. Celestine is length slow or has a positive sign of elongation. On the right is an image of the celestine crystal after the compensator plate has been superimposed on the field of view.

The entire field of view becomes a first-order magenta color (approximately 530 nm of retardation). The retardation of the crystal has been added to that of the compensator, and as a result the crystal exhibits a second-order blue retardation color (approximately 630 nm).

Figure 2.136 shows an elongated crystal of apatite with a retardation of approximately 100 nm (first-order gray) in between crossed polars as viewed through the empty position of the compensator (on the left). In apatite crystals the slow vibration direction of light is parallel to the crystal width. Apatite is length fast or has a negative sign of elongation. On the right is an image of the apatite crystal after the compensator plate has been superimposed on the field of view. As before, the field of view becomes a first-order magenta color. The retardation of the crystal has been subtracted from that of the compensator, however, and as a result the crystal exhibits a first-order yellow retardation color (approximately 430 nm).

As Figures 2.135 and 2.136 illustrate, this observation can be a quick, easy test for distinguishing otherwise similar materials. Forensic fiber examiners can use the sign of elongation

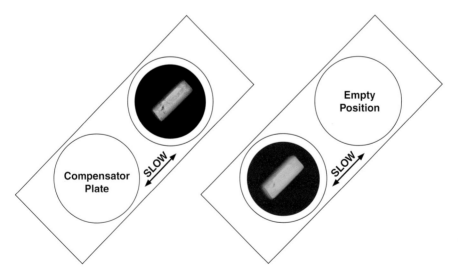

Figure 2.135 The appearance of a celestine crystal with a positive sign of elongation shown with no compensator (left) and again after insertion of a 530 nm compensator (right). The retardation values of the crystal (approximately 100 nm) and the compensator (approximately 530 nm) are added together, and the new retardation visible in the crystal is approximately 630 nm, second-order blue.

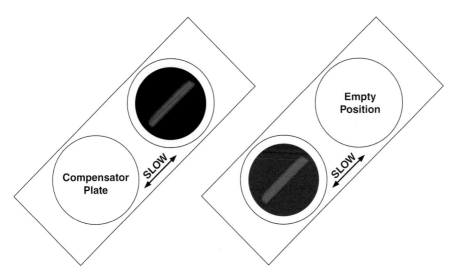

Figure 2.136 The appearance of an apatite crystal with a negative sign of elongation shown with no compensator (left) and again after insertion of a 530 nm compensator (right). The retardation values of the crystal (approximately 100 nm) and the compensator (approximately 530 nm) are subtracted from each other, and the new retardation visible in the crystal is approximately 430 nm, first-order yellow.

test to rapidly distinguish certain fiber types from each other. Figure 2.137 shows an acetate rayon fiber (a material with a positive sign of elongation), while Figure 2.138 shows an acrylic fiber with similar retardation but a negative sign of elongation.

All of the examples so far have involved small initial retardation values (near 100 nm). These retardations values are typically very easy to interpret. However, when a specimen has higher retardation values, it is sometimes more challenging to interpret what happens when the compensator is inserted. In Figure 2.139, a trilobal nylon fiber is exhibiting several orders of retardation colors in between crossed polars. When the compensator is inserted, one order of retardation is added to each color (first-order red becomes second-order red, seen close to the edge of the fiber). If the fiber is rotated 90°, one order of retardation is subtracted from each color (first-order red become zero retardation, which is black). It is valuable to spend some time studying known materials to observe the changes associated with addition and subtraction of retardation for a range of starting retardation values.

For crystals that are not elongated, a compensator can be helpful for determining the optical orientation of the crystal. Specifically, the compensator can be used to locate the higher index (slow) vibration direction in any view of the crystal. This information can be used to determine the optic sign of uniaxial crystals where morphology can be used to locate the trace of the c axis. For biaxial crystals, this information can be used to provide insights into the locations of α, β, and γ relative to the crystal faces. For example, the high and low refractive index directions could be located on the gypsum crystal in Figure 2.76 and related to the crystal shape. If the orientation of these directions is consistent with the optic orientation depicted in Figure 2.76, this information would add confidence to a tentative identification of a substance based on its optical properties.

Additionally, compensators can be used to assist in estimating retardation values in particles. Retardation estimates can be made more accurate using a full wave plate or one of several other types of compensators (e.g, quarter wave plate, quartz wedge). In addition,

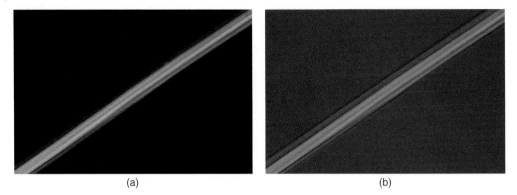

(a)   (b)

Figure 2.137 An acetate rayon fiber shown in between crossed polars (left) and again with the compensator inserted into the microscope (right). Acetate rayon has a positive sign of elongation.

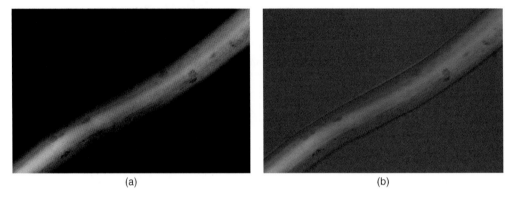

(a)   (b)

Figure 2.138 An acrylic fiber shown in between crossed polars (left) and again with the compensator inserted into the microscope (right). Acrylic fibers typically have a negative sign of elongation.

specific types of compensators have been developed for accurate measurement of very small retardation values (de Senarmont) and very high retardation values (Berek). The use of these accessories is beyond the scope of this chapter.

2.6.8 Conoscopic Observations of Uniaxial Substances

Normal observations made through the microscope as described to this point are sometimes termed "orthoscopic" observations, and in the typical microscope setup the instrument is being used as an orthoscope. However, if a few adjustments are made to the microscope, it can be converted into a conoscope, which enables the examiner to make an entirely new set of "conoscopic" observations on the sample. The

term conoscopic refers to the study of a cone of light that has passed through a substance in between crossed polars. The wider the cone of light used, the more information can be obtained regarding a sample. As was discussed earlier, the NA of an objective is a relative measure of its ability to collect a wide angle of light from the object. Thus it is desirable to use the highest NA objective available for conoscopy. In order to take full advantage of the objective's NA, it is imperative that the substage condenser is properly focused and that the condenser aperture is open as wide as the NA of the objective. With the condenser focused, aperture open, and a high NA objective in place, the sample is illuminated with a wide cone of light (Figure 2.21).

The final adjustment that is needed is to make a modification to the microscope that

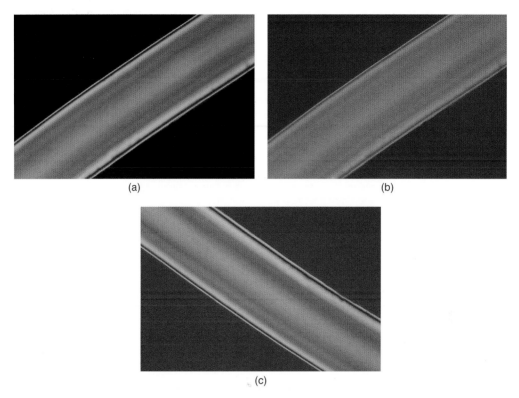

(a)   (b)

(c)

Figure 2.139 For fibers with higher retardation colors, such as the nylon fiber illustrated above (top left), it is useful to observe the fiber oriented both with its length parallel to the slow direction of the compensator (top right) and with its length perpendicular to the slow direction of the compensator (bottom). The retardation colors are adding in the upper right image, and subtracting in the lower image, indicating that the fiber has a positive sign of elongation. The appearance of black bands (zero retardation) near the edges of the fiber in the lower image is a clear indication that subtraction has occurred in this fiber.

enables the back focal plane of the objective to be observed. This plane is located above the sample, but below the intermediate image plane. By focusing on this plane it becomes possible to see the cone of light that has passed through the crystal in a variety of directions then emerged and spread out above the crystal. The typical means of observing the objective back focal plane is by inserting a Bertrand lens (Figure 2.11). Common alternatives include a phase telescope, a pinhole eyepiece, or simply by removing an eyepiece and looking down the empty eye tube. Most polarized light microscopes come equipped with a Bertrand lens, making this lens the most practical method for making conoscopic observations.

So what types of observations may be made in this back focal plane under these conditions?

Consider the now familiar calcite crystal illuminated in this manner. First imagine what will happen to a wide cone of light passing through a crystal that is oriented with its c axis (its optic axis) perpendicular to the stage. In order to understand what will be observed conoscopically, it is helpful to consider what will happen to light rays passing through the crystal from a variety of directions within the illuminating cone of light.

First, consider a ray of light traveling parallel to the optic axis (OA), right along the microscope axis. This light ray will encounter a circular section of the calcite indicatrix. There will be no retardation produced, and this ray will produce a black color in crossed polars. This light ray will emerge in the center of the back focal plane. This black spot due to light

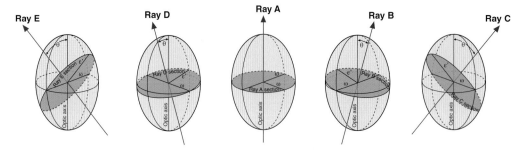

Figure 2.140 A depiction of the indicatrix sections that are encountered by light rays traveling through a uniaxial crystal in different directions. For each ray, the shaded blue section indicates the indicatrix section encountered by the ray, and ω and ε' are indicated for each section.

that traveled along the optic axis is called the melatope (ray A in Figure 2.140).

Second, consider a ray of light traveling at a small angle to the optic axis, near the center of the cone (ray B in Figure 2.140). This ray will encounter an elliptical section of the indicatrix, with its principal axes having refractive index values of ω and ε'. Since the ray is only slightly inclined to the optic axis, ε' will be close to ω, giving this section a low birefringence. As a result this ray will experience a small retardation.

Third, consider a ray of light traveling at a relatively large angle to the optic axis, near the perimeter of the cone (ray C in Figure 2.140). This ray will also encounter an elliptical section of the indicatrix, with its principal axes having values equal to ω and ε'. However, due to its greater inclination to the optic axis, the ε' value for ray C will be farther away from ω than for ray B. The ray will encounter a section with greater birefringence, and will therefore have a greater retardation value than ray B.

Ray D is inclined to the optic axis at the same angle as ray B, so they will both encounter the same retardation. However, ray D is traveling along a different path than ray B and will therefore emerge at a different position in the objective back focal plane. Rays B, D, and any other ray with the same inclination to the OA will emerge with the same retardation. As a result, there will be a circle of constant retardation this distance from the OA.

Ray E is inclined to the optic axis at the same angle as ray C, so they will both encounter the same retardation. However, ray E is traveling along a different path than ray C and will therefore emerge at a different position in the objective back focal plane. Rays C, E, and any other ray with the same inclination to the OA will emerge with the same retardation. As a result, there will be a circle of constant retardation this distance from the OA (higher retardation than that for rays B and D). For rays with inclinations in between those of B and C, there will be intermediate retardation values. These rays together produce concentric circles of constant color (retardation) around the melatope. Lines of constant color in interference figures are called isochromes. Uniaxial interference figures are characterized by circular isochromes (Figures 2.141, 2.142).

There is one additional feature that will be superimposed on the interference figure, namely extinction positions. Any light rays in the cone of illumination whose vibration directions are parallel to either of ω or ε' are not broken into two components, but rather pass through the crystal and are totally absorbed by the analyzer (extinction). In order to determine the locations of emergence for these light rays that are extinct, it is necessary to locate the vibration directions for rays traveling through the crystal at various angles within the cone of illumination. Figure 2.142 has those vibration directions indicated for several rays. The ω vibration direction is always tangent to the

Figure 2.141 The rays indicated in Figure 2.140 are shown after they have passed through a uniaxial crystal with its optic axis parallel to the axis of the microscope. The pattern of retardation colors produced in the back focal plane of the objective by the cone of rays is shown near the top of the figure.

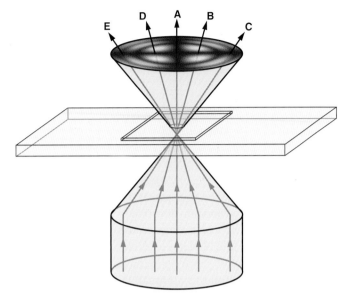

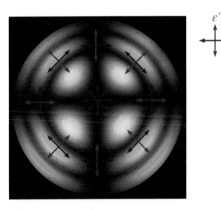

Figure 2.142 The vibration directions for several rays that have traveled through a uniaxial crystal and emerged in the objective back focal plane are shown superimposed on a uniaxial interference figure. The blue lines represent the ω vibration directions for the rays, while the red lines represent the ε' vibration directions.

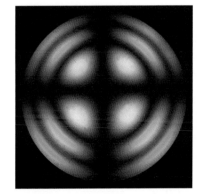

Figure 2.143 A centered uniaxial interference figure. The melatope (emergence of the optic axis) exhibits zero retardation and is located at the center of the cross. Rays that traveled through the crystal at an inclination to the optic axis exhibit non-zero retardation, with their retardation values increasing with inclination to the optic axis. This phenomenon produces a pattern of concentric circles of constant retardation (isochromes) that increase in retardation as they move away from the melatope. Superimposed on the isochromes is a dark cross produced by rays that experienced extinction as they traveled through the crystal.

circular isochromes and ε' is always perpendicular to ω. Given these vibration directions, light that emerges in two lines marking a cross centered at the melatope will exhibit extinction. There is therefore a dark cross superimposed on the circular isochromes in a uniaxial interference figure. The dark bands in the interference figure due to extinction are called isogyres (Figure 2.143).

If a perfectly centered interference figure is located, then in orthoscopic viewing this crystal will exhibit ω in all positions of stage rotation. A Becke line test on this crystal will provide information about ω relative to the mounting medium regardless of the stage position and this crystal will exhibit zero retardation.

A uniaxial interference figure like the one in Figure 2.143 offers an opportunity to determine the optic sign of the crystal. As discussed above, a uniaxial crystal is said to have a positive optic sign if $\varepsilon > \omega$ and a negative optic sign if $\varepsilon < \omega$. In other words, if ε (and therefore ε') is the slow vibration direction, the uniaxial crystal is positive. If ω is the slow vibration direction, the uniaxial crystal is negative. As discussed above, the slow vibration direction in a substance can be located with a compensator. The locations of the ω and ε' vibration directions in the uniaxial interference figure have now been determined. With this information, it is possible to insert the compensator and determine whether ε' is the slow or fast vibration direction in the crystal. This observation will indicate what the optic sign of the material is. Examining Figure 2.142, it is apparent that in the upper-right and lower-left quadrants of the interference figure ε' is oriented from lower-left to upper-right (aligned with the slow vibration direction of the compensator). In the upper-left and lower-right quadrants, however, ε' is oriented from upper-left to lower-right (parallel to the fast vibration direction of the compensator). Upon insertion of the compensator there will therefore be addition in two of these quadrants and subtraction in the other two. If addition occurs in the upper-right and lower-left quadrants, that means that ε' is the slow direction and the crystal is optically positive. In this case there will be subtraction in the upper-left and lower-right quadrants. Alternatively, if subtraction occurs in the upper-right and lower-left quadrants, that means that ε' is the fast direction and the crystal is optically negative. For negative crystals there will be addition in the upper-left and lower-right quadrants. Figure 2.144 indicates the regions of a uniaxial interference figure for which ε' is parallel to the slow direction of a compensator. Figure 2.145 shows both a uniaxial positive interference figure and a uniaxial negative

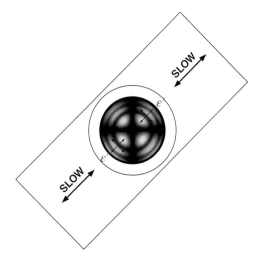

Figure 2.144 A centered uniaxial interference figure shown with the compensator orientation superimposed. The regions of the interference figure for which ε' is parallel to the slow direction in the compensator are indicated (the upper-right and lower-left quadrants of the interference figure).

interference figure as they would appear with the compensator inserted, with regions of both figures that exhibit addition and subtraction of the compensator retardation indicated.

While it is fairly straightforward to interpret a centered uniaxial interference figure like the one in Figure 2.143, it can be a bit trickier to interpret the interference figure produced by a crystal whose optic axis is tipped at some angle to the microscope axis. The interference figure shown in Figure 2.146 is due to a uniaxial crystal with its optic axis tipped a small angle relative to the microscope axis. The center of the cross can be seen near the bottom edge of the field of view. Once the center of the cross is located, it is fairly straightforward to visualize the rest of the interference figure and understand the portion of the figure that is visible in the field of view (Figure 2.147). As the stage is rotated, the center of the cross (the melatope) will be seen to precess about the center of the field of view (Figure 2.148). Other than the cross not being centered, this figure offers exactly the same information as a centered uniaxial interference figure.

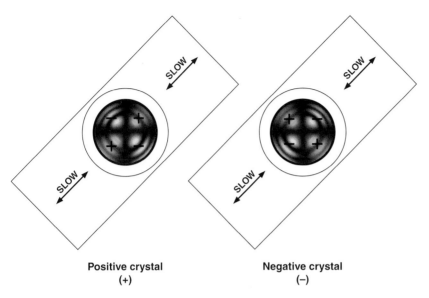

Positive crystal
(+)

Negative crystal
(−)

Figure 2.145 The appearance of centered uniaxial interference figures for a crystal with a positive optic sign (left) and a crystal with a negative optic sign (right) after the compensator has been inserted. Quadrants exhibiting addition and subtraction of the compensator retardation are indicated by plus and minus signs, respectively.

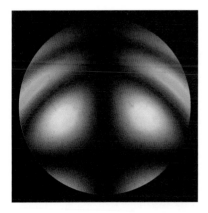

Figure 2.146 A slightly off center uniaxial interference figure with its optic axis (the center of the cross) emerging near the bottom of the field of view.

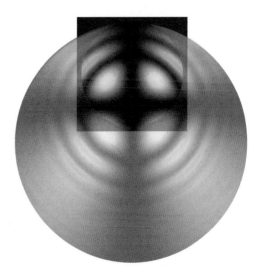

Figure 2.147 An expanded view of the uniaxial interference figure in Figure 2.146 with the portion of the figure visible in Figure 2.146 indicated to illustrate the relationship between Figure 2.146 and the rest of the uniaxial interference figure.

The optic sign can be determined by inserting the compensator and observing addition or subtraction in the appropriate quadrants of the figure (Figure 2.149).

In orthoscopic study this crystal would exhibit both ω and ε'. The interference figure can be used to orient the crystal such that ω is parallel to the polarizer. Whenever the melatope is due South or due North, with the vertical isogyre aligned with the N–S crosshair, the ω refractive index value will be aligned with the polarizer in orthoscopic viewing

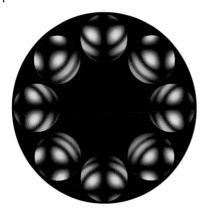

Figure 2.148 As the stage is rotated, the appearance of the interference figure in Figure 2.146 will change as the optic axis precesses around the microscope axis. The smaller circles depict the appearance of the interference figure every 45° during a complete rotation of the microscope stage.

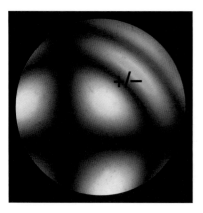

Figure 2.149 If a compensator is inserted into the microscope, the upper right and lower left quadrants of the off center uniaxial interference figure will exhibit addition for crystals with a positive optic sign and subtraction for crystals with a negative optic sign. These observations are identical to those made on a perfectly centered uniaxial interference figure.

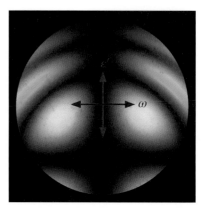

Figure 2.150 When the melatope (center of the cross) is due South (or due North), and the vertical isogyre (dark line) is aligned with the vertical cross-hair in the microscope, the crystal will be oriented in an extinction position with the ω refractive index direction parallel to the polarizer vibration direction. In this orientation, any orthoscopic observations made on the crystal (e.g. contrast, Becke line behavior) will provide data on the ω refractive index value.

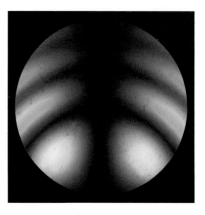

Figure 2.151 An off center uniaxial interference figure with its optic axis (the center of the cross) emerging outside the field of view.

(Figure 2.150). The crystal will also be at extinction in this orientation. In fact, whenever an isogyre passes through the center of the field of view, the crystal will be at extinction in orthoscopic viewing.

If the optic axis of a uniaxial crystal is tipped even further from the microscope axis, such that the melatope is outside the field of view of the objective back focal plane, the interference figure becomes more challenging to interpret. It may still be possible to observe concentric circles of isochromes and to see the isogyres passing through the field of view as the stage is rotated (Figure 2.151). Again, once the center of the cross is located, it is possible to visualize

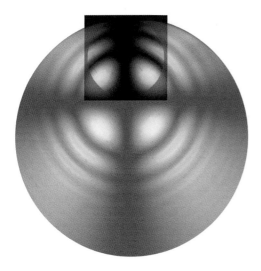

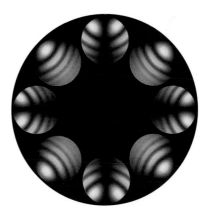

Figure 2.153 As the stage is rotated, the appearance of the interference figure in Figure 2.151 will change as the optic axis precesses around the microscope axis. The smaller circles depict the appearance of the interference figure every 45° during a complete rotation of the microscope stage.

Figure 2.152 An expanded view of the uniaxial interference figure in Figure 2.151 with the portion of the figure visible in Figure 2.151 indicated to show the relationship between this portion of the figure and the rest of the interference figure.

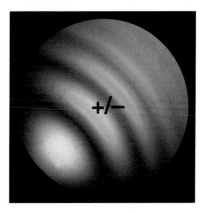

Figure 2.154 The interference figure shown in Figure 2.151, rotated into a position where the upper-right quadrant of the figure is visible in the field of view. As with all uniaxial interference figures, this quadrant will exhibit addition for crystals with a positive optic sign and subtraction for crystals with a negative optic sign when a compensator is inserted.

the rest of the uniaxial interference figure (Figure 2.152). The appearance of the figure will change as shown in Figure 2.153 as the stage is rotated. Once the relationship between the portion of the interference figure visible in the field of view and the location of the melatope is understood, it is a straightforward process to orient the crystal for optic sign determination (Figure 2.154) or for measurement of ω (Figure 2.155). As a general rule, in uniaxial interference figures isochromes are always circular and isogyres are always straight and oriented N–S and E–W. One must be cautious in interpreting significantly off-center figures, however, as some off-center biaxial interference figures may strongly resemble off-center uniaxial interference figures. Determinations made on highly off-center figures should be considered tentative.

When the optic axis is in the plane of the microscope stage (perpendicular to the microscope axis), the interference figure produced is called a flash figure. In a flash figure, two very diffuse, broad isogyres rapidly enter and then leave the field of view near each (orthoscopic) extinction position of the crystal. If the stage is

rotated slowly, the quadrants that the isogyres move into mark the trace of the optic axis. Locating the optic axis permits its orientation parallel to the polarizer. In this orientation the ε refractive index can be determined and with a 90° rotation ω can be measured. By rotating the stage, the optic axis can be aligned

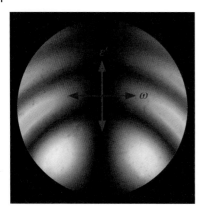

Figure 2.155 The interference figure shown in Figure 2.151 oriented such that the melatope is due South and the vertical isogyre is aligned with the vertical cross-hair in the microscope. In this orientation the ω refractive index can be measured in orthoscopic examination.

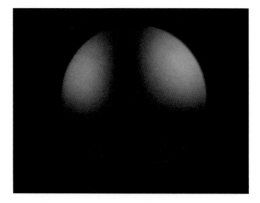

Figure 2.156 The interference figure of a low birefringent uniaxial substance (apatite).

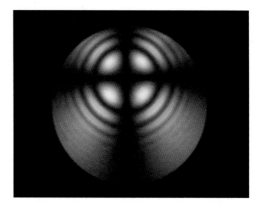

Figure 2.157 The interference figure of a highly birefringent uniaxial substance (sodium nitrate).

parallel to the slow vibration direction of a compensator, and the optic sign of the crystal may be determined by determining whether ε is the slow or fast vibration direction of the specimen.

The appearance of uniaxial interference figures varies dramatically for substances with different birefringence and/or thickness values. For low birefringent substances, or very thin crystals, the highest retardation for the isochromes may be a first-order gray or white. The figure will resemble a very diffuse dark cross and will appear to be out of focus (Figure 2.156). For highly birefringent substances, or very thick crystals, numerous narrow isochromes will be visible around a sharp, well-defined cross (Figure 2.157).

Interference figures can also be helpful for the determination of a crystal's retardation value. The retardation color observed in the center of the field of view for an interference figure is equal to that exhibited by the crystal in orthoscopic study. The advantage of an interference figure, however, is that there are often multiple isochromes visible that provide insights into the order of the retardation color in the crystal. For a crystal that is brick-shaped and exhibiting a third-order red color, for

example, the exact order of the color may be hard to determine orthoscopically. However, observation of the interference figure can make it clear exactly what order retardation color coincides with the center of the field of view. A crystal producing the interference figure in Figure 2.158, for example, would exhibit a retardation of third-order red (approximately 1650 nm) at the center of the crystal in orthoscopic examination.

2.6.9 Conoscopic Observations on Biaxial Substances

The interference figures produced by biaxial crystals differ from those produced by uniaxial crystals in a number of ways. They are easiest to

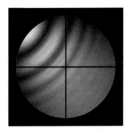

Figure 2.158 An off-center interference figure with a third-order red retardation color in the center of the field of view. This crystal will exhibit a retardation of approximately 1650 nm in orthoscopic examination.

interpret when obtained from a crystal having its acute bisectrix perpendicular to the microscope stage (looking down this direction), particularly for crystals with small optic axial angles. For such a crystal in this orientation there will be two melatopes visible in the objective back focal plane, produced by light rays that have traveled parallel to the two optic axes (rays B and C in Figure 2.159). Rays emerging from both melatopes will have zero retardation, and the melatopes will therefore be black spots in the interference figure. Light rays that travel through the crystal along paths that are inclined relative to either optic axis will exhibit some retardation (ray A in Figure 2.159). As the inclination from an optic axis (and therefore the distance from a melatope) increases, so does the retardation. This relationship was discussed for uniaxial crystals earlier. However, because a biaxial crystal has two optic axes, the retardation of rays inclined to one optic axis will start to decrease as the ray begins to approach the second optic axis. The result is a "figure eight" pattern to the isochromes that surround the melatopes, with more distant isochromes becoming elliptical in shape (Figures 2.160, 2.161).

The retardation colors increase more rapidly moving from the melatopes toward the obtuse bisectrix (away from the center of the field of view) than they do toward the acute bisectrix (toward the center of the field of view). This type of interference figure is called a centered Bxa (acute bisectrix) figure. A typical Bxa

figure is shown in Figure 2.161. If the stage is rotated, the isogyres come together at the center of the field of view to form a diffuse cross. While the cross may loosely resemble that seen for a uniaxial crystal, close examination will reveal that the isochromes are not circular, but retain their figure eight shape. In addition, one line of the cross will be broader and more diffuse than the other.

The optic sign of a biaxial crystal can be determined using a centered Bxa figure if the trace of the optic normal (β) and the obtuse bisectrix (Bxo) (either α or γ) can be located. Recall that the OAP (a special plane in biaxial crystals) contains both optic axes, the Bxa, and the Bxo. Thus if a line is drawn on the centered Bxa interference figure that goes through the two melatopes, this line represents the trace of the OAP (Figure 2.162). Perpendicular to this plane is the optic normal (β). For a centered Bxa figure, β lies in the plane of the microscope stage and can be measured. The β refractive index direction is located perpendicular to the OAP (it is the optic normal). The obtuse bisectrix also lies in the plane of the microscope stage and can be measured; it is perpendicular to the optic normal. The acute bisectrix is perpendicular to the plane of the microscope stage and it also lies in the OAP (Figure 2.162). Now consider how a compensator could be used to determine the optic sign of a biaxial crystal in this orientation.

By definition, in a positive biaxial crystal γ is the acute bisectrix and α the obtuse bisectrix. Thus if the crystal in Figure 2.162 is optically positive, the examiner is looking down γ with β and α in the plane of the microscope stage. If the stage is rotated to orient the crystal with β aligned from lower-left to upper-right and insert the compensator, there will be addition in area in between the melatopes. That is because for positive crystals β is the slow direction (it is greater than α), and therefore the slow vibration direction of the crystal is parallel to the slow vibration direction of the compensator, resulting in addition (Figure 2.163).

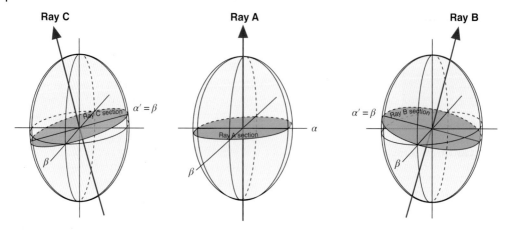

Figure 2.159 A depiction of the indicatrix sections that are encountered by several light rays traveling through a biaxial crystal in different directions. For each ray, the shaded blue section indicates the indicatrix section encountered by the ray, and the refractive index values are indicated for each section by their major and minor axes. Rays B and C both encounter circular sections of the indicatrix.

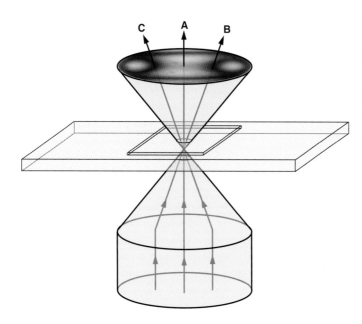

Figure 2.160 The rays indicated in Figure 2.159 are shown after they have passed through a biaxial crystal with its acute bisectrix parallel to the axis of the microscope. The pattern of retardation colors produced in the back focal plane of the objective by the cone of rays is shown near the top of the figure.

In a negative biaxial crystal α is the acute bisectrix and γ the obtuse bisectrix. If a negative biaxial crystal is being examined, therefore, the examiner will be looking down α with β and γ lying in the plane of the microscope stage. In this case when β is aligned lower-left to upper-right there will be subtraction on inserting the compensator. For these crystals β is the fast vibration direction (because it is smaller than γ), and as a result the fast vibration direction of the crystal is parallel to the slow vibration direction of the compensator (Figure 2.164).

The optic axial angle of a biaxial crystal can be estimated on a Bxa interference figure by comparing the distance between the melatopes and the diameter of the field of view for a particular objective. The angle can be approximated as being low (both melatopes easily visible within the field of view), moderate

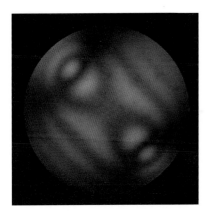

Figure 2.161 A centered acute bisectrix (Bxa) biaxial interference figure. The two melatopes (emergence of the optic axes) exhibit zero retardation. Rays that traveled through the crystal at an inclination to either optic axis exhibit non-zero retardation, with their retardation values increasing with inclination to either optic axes. These rays combine to produce the pattern of isochromes and isogyres shown.

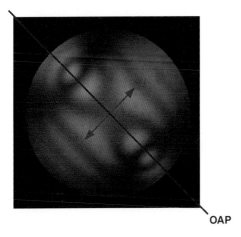

OAP

Figure 2.162 A centered Bxa interference figure with the trace of the optic axial plane (OAP) indicated. Perpendicular to this plane is the optic normal (β), and for a centered Bxa figure β will lie in the plane of the microscope stage parallel to the red line indicated in the image.

(melatopes near the edge of the field of view), or high (both melatopes outside the field of view). The ability of an objective to capture a wide cone of light depends on the NA of the objective, so this type of estimate should be

made with the NA of the objective in mind. Ideally this assessment should be "calibrated" using standard materials with known properties. The estimate of the optic axial angle is made much more accurate if the β refractive index and numerical aperture of the objective are taken into account in a formal manner. With this knowledge, the distance between the two melatopes (d) can be measured using an ocular scale along with the diameter of the field of view (D). The ratio d/D can be used, along with the NA of the objective and the β refractive index of the substance, to determine the optic axial angle. There is a detailed description of this process along with the necessary tables in McCrone et al. (1999). Figure 2.165 shows three Bxa interference figures for crystals with different values of 2V.

As with uniaxial substances, the appearance of a biaxial interference figure depends on the birefringence and thickness of the crystal being studied. For low birefringent substances, or very thin crystals, the highest retardation for the isochromes may be a first-order gray or white. A Bxa figure for such a crystal will have two diffuse parabolic brushes that appear to be out of focus (Figure 2.166). For highly birefringent substances or very thick crystals numerous narrow figure eight shaped isochromes will be visible around two sharp, well-defined black parabolas (Figure 2.167).

If biaxial crystals with very low retardation in orthoscopic examination are observed, they are likely to have one of their optic axes perpendicular to the microscope stage (or nearly so). The interference figure obtained for a biaxial crystal in this orientation is called a centered optic axis interference figure (Figure 2.168).

In this orientation, the curvature of the isogyre as the stage is rotated and the shape of the isochromes can be used to locate the trace of the OAP, the direction to the other melatope, and the proper orientation for determination of optic sign. For crystals with very high optic axial angles (near 90°) it may be impossible to determine optic sign due to the difficulty in distinguishing the acute bisectrix from

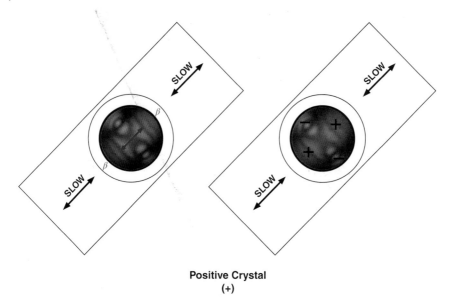

Positive Crystal
(+)

Figure 2.163 The appearance of centered Bxa interference figures for a crystal with a positive optic sign shown before the compensator has been inserted (left) and again after the compensator has been inserted (right). The crystal has a positive optic sign, so it exhibits addition in the area between the two melatopes. The orientation of β relative to the slow direction of the compensator is indicated.

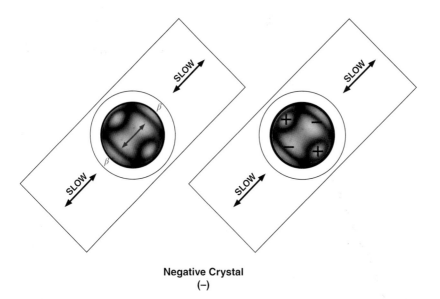

Negative Crystal
(−)

Figure 2.164 The appearance of centered Bxa interference figures for a crystal with a negative optic sign shown before the compensator has been inserted (left) and again after the compensator has been inserted (right). The crystal has a negative optic sign, so it exhibits subtraction in the area between the two melatopes. The orientation of β relative to the slow direction of the compensator is indicated.

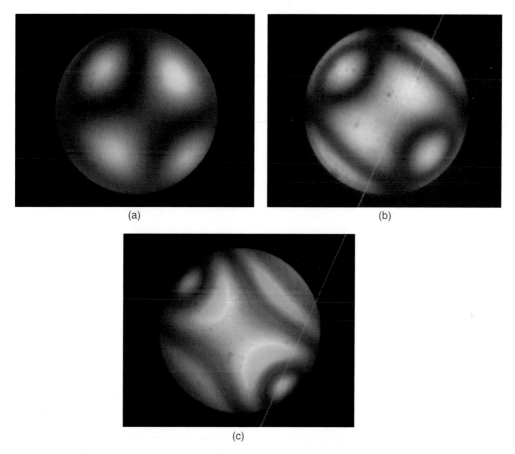

(a)

(b)

(c)

Figure 2.165 Bxa interference figures for crystals with different optic axial angles.

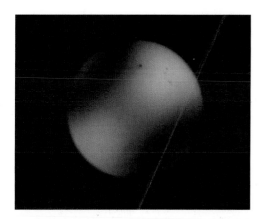

Figure 2.166 The Bxa interference figure of a biaxial substance with low birefringence (muscovite).

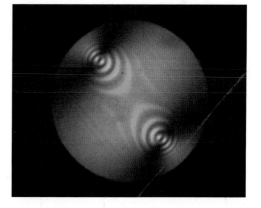

Figure 2.167 The Bxa interference figure of a biaxial substance with high birefringence (highly crystalline polyester film).

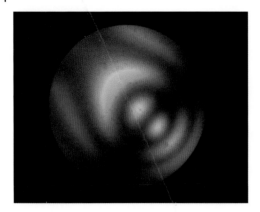

Figure 2.168 Nearly centered optic axis figure for a biaxial substance (TNT).

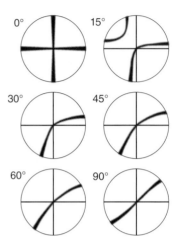

the obtuse bisectrix. If $2V$ is small enough that both melatopes are inside the field of view, the d/D method may be used to determine $2V$, as for Bxa figures. The β refractive index may be determined orthoscopically on crystals with centered optic axis figures, regardless of the stage rotation.

An approximation of the optic axial angle can also be obtained by observing the curvature of the isogyre around a melatope, and centered optic axis interference figures are well suited for making this observation. In order to make this estimate, the interference figure should be rotated until the trace of the OAP is diagonal (lower-right to upper-left). The curvature of the isogyre at the melatope in this orientation decreases with increasing optic axial angle. For a biaxial crystal with a very small $2V$ the isogyre makes a nearly 90° angle where it curves. For a biaxial crystal with a very high $2V$ (close to 90°) the isogyre becomes essentially a straight line. Simple diagrams like the one in Figure 2.169 can be used to estimate $2V$ on this basis. If the interference figure of TNT shown in Figure 2.168 is compared to the diagrams in Figure 2.169, the curvature of the TNT isogyre is similar to the curvature of the 60° isogyre in the diagrams. The optic axial angle of TNT may be estimated as approximately 60°.

Off-center Bxa and optic axis interference figures provide much of the same information

Figure 2.169 The appearance of centered optic axis interference figures for a uniaxial crystal (top left) and for biaxial crystals with different optic axial angles (all others). The curvature of the isogyre for a centered optic axis interference figure can be used to estimate the angle between the melatopes (the optic axial angle $2V$ for biaxial substances). Source: Adapted from McCrone et al. (1999).

about a biaxial crystal as centered figures do (Figure 2.170). However, if the interference figure is not centered it may not be possible to determine principal refractive index values on the crystal because the crystal may exhibit α' and γ' orthoscopically.

In addition to Bxa and optic axis interference figures, there are two other types that are worth briefly discussing. They are centered Bxo and optic normal figures. A centered Bxo figure is similar in appearance to a centered Bxa figure with a large optic axial angle (Figure 2.171). It is not possible with common objectives to see both melatopes in the field of view for a Bxo figure. The isochromes form a figure eight or oval shape as they do in a Bxa figure. On stage rotation the isogyres enter the field of view to form a diffuse cross every 90°. As

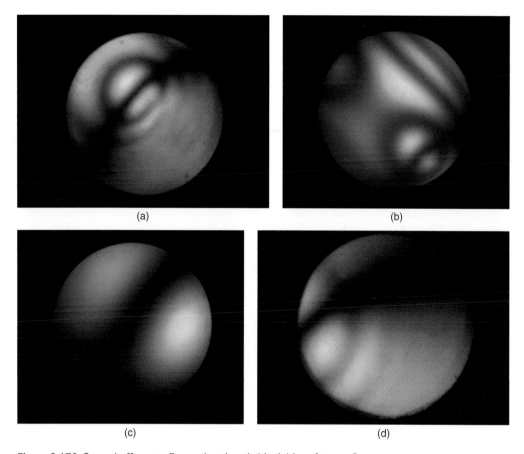

(a)

(b)

(c)

(d)

Figure 2.170 Several off-center Bxa and optic axis biaxial interference figures.

for Bxa figures, the pattern of the isochromes can be used to locate the trace of the OAP. Once this plane is located, the optic normal (β) is perpendicular to this trace and can be oriented for refractive index determination. In this orientation, however, the acute bisectrix lies in the plane of the microscope stage along the trace of the OAP. Thus the compensator produces the opposite effect from that seen on a Bxa figure of the same crystal. If a microscopist mistakes a Bxo figure for a Bxa with a high optic axial angle, the optic sign determined would be incorrect. It is important to be aware of this potential for error when dealing with possible Bxo figures. For a crystal oriented such that a centered Bxo figure is obtained, both β and the acute bisectrix can be determined orthoscopically by the Becke line

immersion method. For a crystal with a high $2V$ value (close to 90°) it can be challenging to distinguish a Bxa figure from a Bxo figure. In that case the crystal can safely be classified as biaxial and the β refractive index can be reliably located for the Becke line test. However, caution should be taken in attempting to determine the optic sign or estimate $2V$ for a crystal in such an orientation.

Finally, a centered optic normal figure for a biaxial crystal resembles a uniaxial flash figure. Two broad, diffuse isogyres rapidly enter and leave the field of view during stage rotation. If the substance being studied is known to be biaxial (based on study of other grains) then a crystal oriented to produce this type of figure can be valuable. In this orientation both α and γ can be determined orthoscopically by the

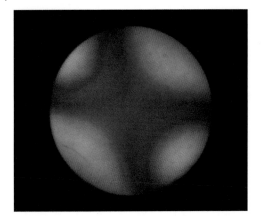

Figure 2.171 A centered Bxo biaxial interference figure.

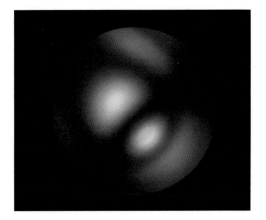

Figure 2.172 A nearly centered optic axis interference figure obtained for an RDX crystal exhibiting strong dispersion of the optic axes.

Becke line test. However, if the substance is not known to be biaxial, this type of interference figure should be interpreted with caution. A crystal exhibiting such a figure could be either uniaxial or biaxial. For either crystal type, however, two principal refractive index values can be determined in this orientation, and this section exhibits the maximum (true) birefringence of the substance.

For a crystal that exhibits very little dispersion, the pattern of colors forming the isochromes will be that seen on the Michel-Lévy chart in Figure 2.108. However, for crystals having considerable dispersion the colors visible in their interference figure may be different on opposite sides of the melatopes, or on opposite sides of one or more principal indicatrix planes (Figure 2.172). Careful examination of the dispersion pattern exhibited by the crystal can provide insights into the symmetry constraints that exist for the indicatrix (e.g. orthorhombic symmetry, monoclinic symmetry, triclinic symmetry). Further, for a monoclinic crystal exhibiting dispersion in its interference figure, the dispersion pattern will differ depending on which indicatrix axis (Bxa, Bxo, ON) is parallel to the crystal's *b* crystallographic axis. For an expanded discussion of dispersion in monoclinic crystals, see Hartshorne and Stuart (1960) and Bloss (1961).

2.6.10 Updated Measurement of Refractive Index Values: Uniaxial Substances

Given the ability to determine the retardation exhibited by a particular grain, to locate the vibration directions in a grain by rotating the grain to extinction, to distinguish the fast and slow vibration directions in the grain with a compensator, and to interpret interference figures on appropriately oriented grains, the task of measuring the optical properties of a uniaxial material becomes much more efficient. The ω refractive index value is the easiest and most important one to measure for identification purposes. In order to determine ω the largest grains that exhibit low retardation values (first-order gray) should be located. These grains are most likely to have a circular section nearly parallel to the microscope stage (and therefore are most likely to exhibit only ω orthoscopically). The interference figure of such a crystal can be used to confirm that it is uniaxial, to determine the optic sign, and (if off-center) to align ω with the polarizer. The microscope can then be converted to an orthoscope by removing the Bertrand lens and the Becke line test performed. This process is repeated in different liquids until ω is determined. If contrast and colored Becke lines are correctly interpreted the number of liquids required is fairly low and the process takes a matter of minutes. At that point, with ω measured and the optic sign determined, the birefringence can be estimated on the smallest grain exhibiting the largest retardation. This grain likely has a principle section nearly parallel to the microscope stage, something that can be confirmed by the grain's interference figure. These determinations usually produce sufficient information for identification purposes. If a measurement of ε is desired, however, the birefringence can be used to estimate which liquid to begin with. In this liquid, the smallest grains exhibiting the largest retardation are examined conoscopically to find one exhibiting a flash figure. Once one is located ε can be determined using the Becke line immersion method.

2.6.11 Updated Measurement of Refractive Index Values: Biaxial Substances

As for uniaxial substances, refractive index determination for biaxial crystals becomes much more efficient when retardation, extinction, and conoscopic observations are used. For biaxial substances β is both the easiest and the most important refractive index value to measure for identification purposes. As for uniaxial substances, the largest grains that exhibit low retardation values (first-order gray) should be located first. These grains are most likely to have a circular section nearly parallel to the microscope stage (and therefore are most likely to exhibit only β orthoscopically). The interference figure of such a crystal can be used to confirm that the crystal is biaxial, to determine its optic sign, to estimate $2V$, and (if off-center) to align β with the polarizer. The microscope can then be converted to an orthoscope and the Becke line test performed. This process is repeated in different liquids until β has been measured. At that point, with β determined and the optic sign known, the birefringence should be estimated on the smallest grain exhibiting the largest retardation. This

information is typically all that is required for the identification of an unknown substance. If measurement of additional properties is desired, however, α and γ can be determined fairly quickly. The smallest grains exhibiting the largest retardation are examined conoscopically to find one exhibiting an optic normal figure. The values of α and γ can be determined using the Becke line immersion method on grains in this orientation. Once α, β, and γ have been measured, the estimate of the optic axial angle can be refined using Eq. (2.9). The equation on the top is for negative crystals, and the one on the bottom is for positive crystals, with V being half of the optic axial angle.

$$\cos^2 V_\alpha = \frac{\gamma^2(\beta^2 - \alpha^2)}{\beta^2(\gamma^2 - \alpha^2)};$$

$$\cos^2 V_\gamma = \frac{\alpha^2(\gamma^2 - \beta^2)}{\beta^2(\gamma^2 - \alpha^2)} \qquad (2.9)$$

Equation (2.9) can be rearranged to solve for any one of these four variables (α, β, γ, V) provided the other three are known. This equation is particularly useful for biaxial substances having very high γ values (too high to be determined by the immersion method). Alternatively, these optical properties can be accurately measured using the spindle stage method.

2.6.12 The Spindle Stage

While the Becke line immersion method is the most common approach for refractive index determination, there are other means of accurately measuring the optical properties of anisotropic substances. The most relevant additional technique is the spindle stage method. This method involves gluing a single small crystal to the tip of a needle (typically using nail polish) and inserting the needle into a small accessory called a spindle stage (Figure 2.173).

The spindle stage enables the crystal to be rotated about an additional axis, the spindle axis, making it possible to orient many more

Figure 2.173 A Bloss detent spindle stage. Source: Reproduced with permission of Microscope Publications.

directions in the plane of the microscope stage for measurement. In practice the spindle axis is initially set to 0° and the mounted crystal is rotated (using the microscope stage) until it goes extinct; the angle of stage rotation is then recorded. The spindle axis is then rotated 10° and the extinction position determined again. This process is repeated for spindle axis positions from 0° to 180° in 10° increments. The data are entered into a software application (Excalibr) and the application outputs the optic axial angle (for biaxial crystals) as well as the spindle axis and stage positions required to orient the principal refractive index directions (ε, ω, or α, β, γ) in the plane of the stage and aligned with the polarizer. Once aligned, an oil cell is used to introduce different liquids to the crystal until a matching liquid is found. The process can be repeated using different wavelengths of light to determine the dispersion of anisotropic crystals. It is a fairly efficient and very accurate method for determining all of the optical properties of a substance. This process is generally more than what is required for identification purposes, but it is very useful for characterizing the optical properties of a standard substance whose optical properties are not published. An introduction to the spindle stage is provided by Gunter et al. (2004) and an in-depth

treatment is available in Bloss's book on the subject (1981).

2.7 Identification of an Unknown Using Optical Properties

This chapter has now covered quite a bit of ground, and some of the material is challenging to learn completely the first time it is encountered. However, the novelty and complexity of the information should not discourage the trace evidence examiner from continuing their education in microscopy. The final section of this chapter is meant to put all of the preceding information into the context of casework.

As discussed below, some of the optical properties of an unknown crystalline substance can be determined using even relatively basic methods. Of specific interest to the examiner identifying an unknown substance are the single refractive index of an isotropic substance, the ω refractive index of a uniaxial substance, the β refractive index of a biaxial substance, and the birefringence of both uniaxial and biaxial substances. These refractive index values can be determined using the Becke line immersion method (Figures 2.95 and 2.97). Birefringence can be roughly estimated using the Michel-Lévy chart (Figure 2.108) or Eq. (2.8). Once these properties have been determined, the examiner can turn to an appropriate reference. The most generally useful references are two books, one for organic substances (Winchell 1987) and one for inorganic substances (Winchell and Winchell 1989). These books have several different sets of determinative tables for identifying unknown substances. Inside the inorganic book there is one table for isotropic substances and one for anisotropic substances. The isotropic substances are listed in order of increasing refractive index value. It is very simple to narrow down the list of possible substances using this list. The reference then offers additional information related to each substance such as color, crystal forms and/or habits, melting points, solubility information, etc. for each candidate substance. These additional properties offer clear avenues for confirming tentative identifications or distinguishing between a small number of possible alternatives. The determinative tables for anisotropic substances are more complex. Anisotropic substances are placed on different pages based on the ω or β values. For example, all of the substances in the reference having ω or β values in between 1.5700 and 1.5799 appear on page 366 (Winchell and Winchell 1989). Within this group substances are listed in order of increasing birefringence. Thus after measuring ω or β and estimating the birefringence, the list of possible substances can be narrowed down to a handful. For each of these candidates the reference again offers additional information including additional optical properties, color, crystal system, crystal forms and/or habits, planes of cleavage, and much more. The determinative tables for the organic book are slightly different, being plotted on a large table, but work in a similar manner. For example, one of the charts has refractive index plotted along its x axis (n, ω, or β) and birefringence along its y axis. While knowing one refractive index and having an estimate of birefringence enable the use of these resources, the determinative tables also include other information that is useful for narrowing down potential substances (in particular optic sign and optic axial angle).

It is instructive to consider a couple of examples. If an unknown sample composed of calcite were being examined, the examiner would initially determine that the ω value is close to 1.658 and the birefringence is very high. There is only one other substance in the reference with optical properties consistent with these initial observations ($BaNi(CN)_4 \cdot 4H_2O$). Calcite is a much more

common substance than the other candidate, making it the most likely identity of the unknown. On looking up the properties of the alternative candidate, the reference states that it is orange-yellow in color, soluble in water, and its lowest refractive index is 1.569. Calcite on the other hand is colorless, sparingly soluble in water, and has $\varepsilon = 1.468$. Thus distinguishing between the two would be straightforward in a variety of ways.

If the unknown substance were sodium bicarbonate (baking soda), the examiner would initially determine that β is approximately 1.500 and that the birefringence is very high. There are perhaps 10 other substances in the reference that meet these initial criteria. However, looking at all of the candidates makes it clear that baking soda is the only substance in the list of candidates that has both one index much higher than 1.500 ($\gamma = 1.586$) and one index much lower than 1.500 ($\alpha = 1.380$). Thus simply by observing the strong contrast present in some grains with Becke line going in, and in other grains with Becke lines going out, the list can be narrowed to one candidate. Other optical properties could also be used to distinguish between baking soda and the other candidates on the list, but this observation is the fastest way to do so. If the unknown substance had been characterized in more detail initially, then the fact that the unknown was biaxial negative with a large optic axial angle would have narrowed the initial list of candidates down to only one.

The two books by Winchell (1987) and Winchell and Winchell (1989) are both secondary references that include information compiled from numerous different primary sources. As such the entries for all substances are not uniform, and some have more complete information than others. Nonetheless these references are the best available sources for identifying unknown chemicals based on their optical properties. There are specialized references (books and journal articles) that are useful for subsets of materials such as minerals, drugs, pigments, fibers, etc. The nature of all of these references is such that despite the large number of optical properties that could be determined for an unknown substance (especially a biaxial one), in practice it is rarely necessary to determine more than a few of them in order to use the available determinative tables for identification purposes.

Even if no measurements of optical properties are made, the polarized light microscope can make a meaningful practical impact on the examination of an unknown substance. This contribution is particularly evident for mixtures; the majority of the unknown white powder cases in the author's laboratory turn out to be commercial products containing multiple components. It is recommended that the polarized light microscope be used early in the examination process to help determine the complexity of this type of sample. Microscopy is very well suited to determining whether a sample is homogeneous or a mixture. If both isotropic and anisotropic substances are present, it will immediately be clear that the substance is a mixture. If some particles have all of their Becke lines going in, while others have all of their Becke lines going out, this observation will also provide clear evidence of a mixture. If great differences are observed with respect to crystal form and/or habit, that is additional evidence that the sample may be a mixture (although some substances may exhibit more than one habit, even within a single sample). By assessing a sample in this manner, the examiner can obtain useful information about the likely number of components as well as their approximate relative abundances. This information makes interpretation of instrumental data much clearer.

After this initial assessment, additional analysis should be performed using the available instrumentation as appropriate (Fourier transform infrared spectroscopy, Raman spectroscopy, gas chromatography/mass spectrometry,

scanning electron microscopy, energy dispersive X-ray spectroscopy, X-ray diffraction, etc.). A confocal Raman micro-spectrometer is particularly useful as a complementary instrument to the polarized light microscope for identification of solid particles (Bowen 2013a). If the data obtained from one or more of the available instruments indicate a particular compound is present, the polarized light microscope can be used to confirm the identification. The candidate compound can be looked up in an appropriate reference and the compound's optical properties noted. A mounting medium can be selected to quickly confirm one or more refractive index values. If it is believed that a uniaxial substance is present, the examiner should choose the liquid that matches ω for the target analyte. As Figure 2.95 demonstrates, all grains of the uniaxial substance will exhibit very low contrast in one orientation during every 180° of stage rotation when mounted in a liquid matching ω. Conoscopy can quickly confirm that the substance is uniaxial and confirm its optic sign. The birefringence can be estimated rapidly and compared to the literature value. For a biaxial substance it is recommended that the liquid matching the literature value for β is selected. As Figure 2.97 shows, every grain will have one orientation for which the Becke line goes in (or for which contrast is very low). On rotating the stage 90°, the Becke line will go out (or the contrast will be very low). There will be no grains for which the Becke lines go out in all orientations upon rotation of the stage. Likewise, there will be no grains for which the Becke lines go in in all orientations on rotation of the stage. Conoscopy can rapidly confirm that the substance is biaxial, confirm its optic sign, estimate its optic axial angle, and potentially determine aspects of its optical orientation. The birefringence can also be estimated and compared to the literature value. These observations may be made and compared to a reference very efficiently once a candidate substance has been identified and can add significant confidence to the identification.

Ideally a standard should be obtained and examined; this is a necessity if a candidate substance cannot be found in any reference. The optical behavior of both the unknown and the reference should be identical in any mounting medium selected.

2.7.1 Applications of Light Microscopy to Trace Evidence

The theory and techniques described in this chapter can be applied on some level to virtually any type of trace evidence. Hair evidence is by its very nature microscopic in size and requires a properly set-up microscope and an understanding of optics to examine effectively. Glass particles must be recognized as such before they can be studied. Glass can be distinguished from anisotropic substances because it will not exhibit retardation in crossed polars (unless it is strained). Cubic crystals can often be distinguished from glass by the presence of recognizable crystal faces or cleavage, while glass exhibits conchoidal fracture. Once recognized and recovered, the refractive index (and dispersion, if desired) can be determined and used for comparison to other glass samples. The shape, size, and other morphological features of fibers can be very useful for identification purposes. In addition, fibers behave in most respects like uniaxial crystals. Their refractive index values, birefringence, and sign of elongation can be determined and used to identify the fiber type. Additionally, extinction properties can provide insights into their crystallinity (distinguishing some poorly crystalline natural fibers from more highly crystalline man-made fibers). Polymer films such as those found in the backing of tapes, when highly oriented, behave in many respects like biaxial crystals. They have refractive index and birefringence values that can be determined, they often produce biaxial interference figures, and they may have

extinction angles relative to the edge of the tape or film. These properties can be useful for identifying the type of polymer present and for comparing two different tape or polymer samples. Pigments in paint and other coatings are often too small for meaningful optical characterization. However, other fillers may include larger crystalline materials such as talc, calcite, mica, etc. These materials can be characterized and identified on the basis of their optical crystallographic properties using the methods described above. Explosives are generally crystalline substances, and unconsumed explosives are excellent candidates for identification by microscopy. Sample sizes too small for many other analytical techniques are more than sufficient for microscopical examination. Many reaction products present in post-blast explosive residues are crystalline as well, although generally poorly formed and small in size due to their rapid crystallization. It is common for some unreacted materials to be present in post-blast residues, making microscopy a very useful tool for their examination. Most soil samples and many building materials are composed largely of minerals, which are by definition crystalline and are very well-suited to identification by polarized light microscopy due to the great volume of literature references specific to optical mineralogy. Unknown chemicals often end up in the trace evidence section of the forensic laboratory, and these more often than not contain at least one crystalline component. The polarized light microscope is ideally suited for their examination, including for initial sample assessment, for identification of components on the basis of their optical properties, and for confirmation of any identifications that are based on data from other instruments.

The remaining chapters in this book will expand on some of the common types of trace evidence and their collection, preservation, and examination. A skilled microscopist will be at a distinct advantage during examination of all of these varied classes of evidence.

References

Bloss, F.D. (1961). *An Introduction to the Methods of Optical Crystallography*. New York, NY: Holt, Rinehart and Winston.

Bloss, F.D. (1981). *The Spindle Stage: Principles and Practice*. New York, NY: Cambridge University Press.

Bloss, F.D. (2000). *Crystallography and Crystal Chemistry*. Washington, DC: Mineralogical Society of America.

Bowen, A.M. (2004). A closer look at resolution: Abbe's diffraction test kit. *The Microscope* 52 (3/4): 173–180.

Bowen, A.M. (2013a). Will Raman save the polarized light microscope? *The Microscope* 61 (3): 131–142.

Bowen, A.M. (2013b). Optical crystallography of silver sulfadiazine. *The Microscope* 57 (1): 11–18.

Bravais, A. (1849). Memoir sur les polyedres de forme symmetrique. *Journal de Mathématiques Pures et Appliquées* 14: 137–180.

Dyar, M.D., Gunter, M.E., and Tasa, D. (2008). *Mineralogy and Optical Mineralogy*. Chantilly, VA: Mineralogical Society of America.

Feynman, R.P. (1985). *QED: The Strange Theory of Light and Matter*. Princeton, NJ: Princeton University Press.

Gadolin, A.V. (1867). Deduction of all crystallographic systems and their subdivisions by means of a single general principle (in Russian). *Ann. Imp. St. Petersburg Mineral Soc. Ser.* 2 (4): 112–200.

Gunter, M.E., Weaver, R., Bandli, B.R. et al. (2004). Results from a McCrone spindle stage short course, a new version of EXCALIBR,

and building a spindle stage. *The Microscope* 52 (1): 23–39.

Hartshorne, N.H. and Stuart, A. (1960). *Crystals and the Polarising Microscope: A Handbook for Chemists and Others*. London: Edward Arnold (Publishers) Ltd.

Hessel, J.F.C. (1830). Krystall. In: *Gehler's Physikalische Wörterbuch Bd*, 5e (eds. H.W. Brandes, L. Gmelin, J. Horner, et al.), 1023–1340. Leipzig, Germany: E.B. Schwickert.

McCrone, W.C., McCrone, L.B., and Delly, J.G. (1999). *Polarized Light Microscopy*. Chicago, IL: McCrone Research Institute.

Nesse, W.D. (2004). *Introduction to Optical Mineralogy*. New York, NY: Oxford University Press.

Winchell, A.N. (1987). *The Optical Properties of Organic Compounds*. Chicago, IL: McCrone Research Institute.

Winchell, A.N. and Winchell, H. (1989). *The Microscopical Characters of Artificial Inorganic Solid Substances: Optical Properties of Artificial Minerals*. Chicago, IL: McCrone Research Institute.

Wood, E.A. (1977). *Crystals and Light: An Introduction to Optical Crystallography*. New York, NY: Dover Publications, Inc.

Ziegler, H.W. (1972). *The Optical Performance of the Light Microscope: Geometrical Optical Aspects of Image Formation*. Chicago, IL: Microscope Publications Ltd.

Ziegler, H.W. (1973). *The Optical Performance of the Light Microscope: Physical Optical Aspects of Image Formation*. Chicago, IL: Microscope Publications Ltd.

3

Paints and Polymers

Robyn B. Weimer[1], Diana M. Wright[2], and Tamara Hodgins[3]

[1] *Virginia Department of Forensic Science, Richmond, VA, USA*
[2] *Chemistry Unit, Federal Bureau of Investigation Laboratory, Quantico, VA, USA*
[3] *Royal Canadian Mounted Police, National Forensic Laboratory Service, Edmonton, Alberta, Canada*

3.1 Introduction to the Paint and Polymer Discipline

A vehicle fled the scene following a fatal strike to a bicyclist. Paint chips were recovered from the scene which revealed the suspect vehicle had originally been black, then later repainted two times, first green and then silver. A damaged silver vehicle was located in an automotive repair shop, though the owner denied any connection to the fatal accident. Paint collected from the suspect's vehicle was compared to the chips found at the scene and ultimately revealed no differences (Firth 1945). This is not a hypothetical tale or a retelling of a recent accident, but rather originates from a 1945 publication about forensic paint analysis. The scenario serves to demonstrate that paint and polymer analysis has a long history that includes analytical advancements, manufacturing improvements, and product diversification.

Automotive paints are not the only polymers with a long forensic history. Tape from an explosive device was compared to a roll discovered in a defendant's workshop in a 1936 bombing case (Anon. 1937). In 1937, an investigative lead in a kidnapping was developed when red paint on a wooden ladder was traced back to a particular shipment of lumber (Koehler 1937). A burglary case in 1939 involved the comparison of paint particles found on suspects' clothing to paint used on a school office safe from which money was taken (Anon. 1940). Though not all-inclusive, these cases are examples which demonstrate the importance paint and polymer analyses have had in criminal investigations.

Polymers are encountered as forensic evidence in a variety of materials. In addition to paints, polymers are also examined when forensically analyzing fibers, tapes, adhesives, and plastics such as zip ties, automotive lenses, and sandwich or trash bags. Although this chapter will focus on the forensic examination of paints and coatings, the analytical scheme presented here can be adapted for a variety of other polymeric materials. Consideration should be given to include tests which are meaningful given the material's commercial manufacturing production process. For example, noting the distance between the bottom edge and heat seal or observing extrusion die lines are important and specific to plastic bags due to their manufacturing process (Bily 2010). Refer to Chapter 5 for comprehensive information regarding polymeric fiber examinations.

Handbook of Trace Evidence Analysis, First Edition. Edited by Vincent J. Desiderio, Chris E. Taylor, and Niamh Nic Daéid.
© 2021 John Wiley & Sons Ltd. Published 2021 by John Wiley & Sons Ltd.

Paint often becomes forensic evidence when transferred in hit-and-run incidents, as in the case cited above where forcible contact occurred between an automobile and a bicyclist. Hit-and-runs may involve a variety of paint types as different substrates often require different coating formulations: automobiles, bicycles, mopeds, motorcycles, marine vessels, wood, or traffic signs. Paint transfers may occur in breaking and entering cases, for example when a person crawls through a painted window frame. Cross-transfers may occur when two painted objects come into contact, such as a tool used to pry open a safe. Paint may be used to vandalize property or to conceal other evidence, such as blood on a wall.

The variety of cases expands when considering how other polymeric materials become involved in criminal events. Tapes or zip ties may be used to bind victims or as a component in improvised explosive devices. Plastic bags may be used in the transfer of drugs or to dispose of evidence. Plastic buttons may become separated from clothing during sexual assaults. Disposable gloves may be used in an attempt to prevent the transfer of fingerprints or DNA evidence. Plastic jewelry or false nails may become broken or left at a scene following a struggle. Broken plastic lens fragments can be recovered at hit-and-run scenes. Prisoners may use available polymeric sources to make contraband, such as shank handles. Clearly, polymeric materials surround us and therefore the cases that require their analysis are diverse.

Due to their ubiquity, polymers are often encountered and easily obtainable. Most polymeric materials are available in a wide range of color options. Even within one color category, product ingredients and properties can vary widely when considering cost of materials, product purpose, and exposure to environmental conditions or other performance factors. Each item may have additional manufacturing variation present within the class (e.g. buttons – shape, size, thickness, and number of holes if any). Painted surfaces tend to be repainted over time, thereby producing

a characteristic history and layer sequence. It is the availability, variety, and ease of transfer that renders forensic paint and polymer evidence significant and meaningful.

When encountered as evidence, paint may be present in the form of particles, chips, flakes, smears, powders, or mixtures contaminated with impurities. Otherwise, an entire painted object may be received, such as a mailbox or an automotive panel. Forensic paint analysts have the ability to identify unknown material as paint and, more often, are requested to compare recovered paint from objects associated with a crime scene to a known paint source. In some cases, the request may be to compare two or more paint samples each with an unknown source, also referred to as questioned samples. If automotive paint is recovered, it may be possible based on the paint chemistry to provide color, make, model, and model year range information as an investigative lead (e.g. hit-and-run cases where a suspect vehicle has yet to be identified). Once the suspect vehicle is located, paint samples may be collected and submitted for subsequent comparisons.

A specialized application of forensic paint analysis includes the examination of art for authentication purposes. Generally, these determinations rely heavily on pigment identification and dates of pigment availability. Art authentication is not the focus of this chapter and will not be discussed further.

In examinations of other polymeric materials, comparisons are the most common request. Comparisons typically involve a questioned item and a source of others like it, or a small portion compared to a larger unit. In comparison scenarios, the evidence may support that polymeric samples could or could not share a common origin.

What began as a microscopical and microchemical forensic examination (Nissen 1934), through time has progressed to an analytical scheme including instrumentation for the comparison and identification of chemical components (SWGMAT 2011a,b; ASTM 2018a; Gross et al. 2015). Instruments have become more sensitive and reproducible, with enhanced signal-to-noise responses while being able to examine smaller sample amounts (Low 1969; Postek et al. 1980; Kawaoka 1984; Ryland 1995; Vergne et al. 2007). Each of these advances remains critical to trace evidence analysis and has made more paint and polymer formulations distinguishable. Conclusive determination of the polymeric source is still only possible, however, with a physical reconstruction (i.e. physical fit, physical match, fracture match).

This chapter is intended to provide foundational information on polymeric materials with special emphasis on paint types, chemistry, and manufacturing. The forensic analytical scheme for paint and polymer examination will be presented along with tips for sample preparation. There will be less emphasis on specific instrument education or operating parameters as that information may be found in other sources which are provided in additional readings at the end of the chapter. Strengths and weaknesses will be presented along with how to address the challenges of interpreting results.

3.2 Overview of Polymer Chemistry

3.2.1 Introduction to Polymers

Polymers are long chain-like chemical structures formed from the linking together of smaller units, called monomers. Both natural and synthetic polymers exist, though synthetic polymers are far more prevalent in the mass-produced paints and other polymeric materials that are commonly found in the marketplace today. Polymers are analogous to trains in that their overall lengths can vary, as can the class of trains/polymers, and each railcar/monomer can be different or the same as those it is linked to. Monomer construction and the polymeric arrangement determine a material's properties.

3.2.2 Polymer Synthesis

Monomers become polymers via a process called synthesis or polymerization. For the purposes of this chapter, this generally occurs by one of two methods: the reaction of monomer functional groups to form a covalent bond (step growth) or an initiated reaction whereby monomers are linked to an active site on the growing polymer chain (chain growth). "Step" or "chain" growth refers to the reaction mechanism, or how polymerization happens.

Alternatively, the terms "condensation" or "addition" polymerization are used to refer to the type of products resulting from the polymerization reaction. Following addition polymerization, with chain growth via an active growth site, only the polymer is produced. Examples of addition, chain-growth polymers include polyethylene, polypropylene, polystyrene, polyvinyl chloride, and polyacrylonitrile. In condensation polymerization, the polymer is produced as well as a small molecule with low molecular weight (e.g. water, methanol, carbon dioxide, hydrochloric acid). Where most step-growth polymers are also classified as condensation polymers, not all step-growth polymers release condensates. Polyurethane is an example of a step-growth polymer where no small molecule is released. Polyester, on the other hand, is an example of step-growth, condensation polymerization where water is released when carboxylic acid and alcohol functional groups react (Harris 1981; Prane 1986).

A polymer's properties are the result of the monomers used in its formation. If only one type of monomer is present as repeating units, it is described as a homopolymer. If two or more different monomers are used during polymerization, a copolymer is formed. Copolymers tend to use a combination of monomers to improve properties (Harris 1981; Prane 1986). For example, alternating clear and inflexible styrene with strong, hard, heat-resistant, and solvent-resistant acrylonitrile produces styrene-acrylonitrile (SAN)

(Encyclopaedia Britannica 2015), which is used for clear plastic lenses.

The simplest polymer structure is linear. Branched polymers, those with side chains extending from the long straight chain, tend to be stronger though may be less flexible than linear polymers. When used to make films, long linear or lightly branched polymer chains are often in close proximity following solvent evaporation and form weak, secondary valence attractions. These thermoplastic polymers can be dissolved by heat or with an appropriate solvent. As temperature increases, the linear or lightly branched chains are able to move and undergo no chemical change throughout the melting and solidifying process. If the appropriate solvent is added, polymer chains are pushed apart, breaking the weak, secondary attractions in favor of the stronger bonds with the solvent. Examples of thermoplastic materials include those used in injection-molded products, polyethylene plastic bags, and polyvinyl chloride plastics and coatings (Prane 1986; Hare 1989; Causin 2015).

Thermoplastic polymers are also used to make lacquers. Lacquers are clear or pigmented coatings formed via quick solvent evaporation, as opposed to production via oxidation or polymerization. Fingernail polish is the most frequently encountered lacquer today. It dries quickly after application and can be dissolved in acetone nail polish remover or other like solvents. Latex paint, the most common type of architectural paint, primarily employs thermoplastic polymers as well. In latex paints, polymerization occurs within surfactant micelles dispersed in water. Micelles are aggregated molecules which form a boundary, like a fence around a growing polymer, allowing only monomers or initiators to pass through. As water evaporates, polymer chains are left crowded together and ultimately fuse. Being water-based, latex paints can be cleaned with soap and water rather than harsh solvents (Fuller 1973; Prane 1986; Wicks Jr. et al. 2007).

Cross-linking polymer chains complicate the structure further by forming covalent bonds between neighboring chains. Cross-linking can be caused by the application of heat or pressure, or via a chemical reaction. It provides memory such that a material will return to its original shape following stretching. As crosslinking increases, so do brittleness and hardness. Following crosslinking, a three-dimensional network is formed with primary bonded linkages. These crosslinked thermoset polymers are insoluble and have excellent thermal stability and rigidity. Common crosslinkers include melamine, epoxy, and urea. Examples of thermosetting polymers include thermoplastic polymers modified by the addition of a crosslinking agent, polyurethanes used in coatings or adhesives, and phenolic resins (produced from reacting phenol and formaldehyde) used in high temperature adhesives. Thermoset polymers are generally used to form enamel coatings (hard, glossy, pigmented coatings) (Harris 1981; Prane 1986; Hare 1989).

3.3 Overview of Coatings

3.3.1 Chemistry and Terminology of Coatings

The terms paint and coating will be used interchangeably throughout this chapter. Paint is a pigmented coating. Coating, being the generic term, includes paints and other liquids that convert to a solid following application to form a protective and/or decorative film (ASTM 2018a). Colorless layers, such as those applied to automobiles, or layers where dye has been used to impart color may be referred to as paint in this chapter even though they lack pigment.

Resin is another term which may be encountered, especially in older references. Resin is a generic term for polymer (Prane 1986) that occasionally indicates a thermoset polymer, and most often can be used interchangeably with the term binder. Historically, "resin" was restricted to natural-based products, specifically originating from trees. As more synthetic polymers emerged, "resin" expanded to include both plant-based products as well as synthetic counterparts. In some texts, both binder and resin are used synonymously, but more and more, binder is being used in place of resin.

Paints are complex mixtures of the following ingredients: binder(s), pigments, additives, and volatile components.

3.3.1.1 Binders

Binders form the paint film backbone and, as their name implies, are responsible for binding the pigment particles together (ASTM 2018a) and providing adhesion to the surface being coated (Wicks Jr. et al. 2007). Binder composition often indicates specific coating end uses, so if unknown, this determination may help narrow the possibilities (Ryland 1995). Table 3.1 provides examples of binder types and their end uses (Ryland 1995; Beveridge et al. 2001; Wicks Jr. et al. 2007).

3.3.1.2 Pigments

Pigments are insoluble solid particles dispersed throughout the binder during film formation (ASTM 2018a). Through reflection, absorption, scattering, and interference, or a combination thereof, pigments alter the appearance of an object (Dössel 2008a). Pigments are used to impart color and/or provide anti-corrosion protection. When used for other purposes, such as to hide substrates, modify properties, and/or to reduce cost, they are designated as extender pigments (Wicks Jr. et al. 2007). Extender pigments are inert, make little to no contribution to color, and may be referred to as fillers as they are added to take up space within the film (Morgans 1982; Wicks Jr. et al. 2007). Extenders have a refractive index close to that

Table 3.1 Associated binder types and crosslinkers with their respective end uses

Automotive top coats	*Original finishes:* acrylic, acrylic-epoxy, acrylic-melamine, acrylic-urethane, alkyd-melamine, polyester-melamine, polyurethane
	Refinishes: acrylic, acrylic-alkyd, acrylic-urethane, alkyd, nitrocellulose, polyurethane
Automotive primers	*Original finishes:* acrylic, acrylic-melamine, acrylic-urethane, alkyd-melamine, alkyd-urea, epoxy, epoxy-polyester, epoxy-urea, polyester-melamine, polyurethane, alkyd- or epoxy-benzoguanamine
	Refinishes: acrylic, epoxy, nitrocellulose-acrylic, polyurethane
Architectural	Acrylic, polyvinyl acetate (PVA), acrylic-PVA, alkyd
	Less common: polyurethane, nitrocellulose, styrene-butadiene, PVA-polyethylene
Spray paint	Alkyd (most common) or polyester – both often modified with vinyl toluene or nitrocellulose
	Less common: acrylic, epoxy, silicone (high temperature applications), acrylic-alkyd
Tools	Alkyd, alkyd-melamine, nitrocellulose
	Less common: acrylic, acrylic-styrene, epoxy, polyester
Bicycle	Alkyd, acrylic, alkyd-melamine, alkyd-urea
Nail polish	Nitrocellulose, acrylic
Marine	Alkyd, acrylic-urethane, epoxy, polyvinyl chloride, polyurethane
Aircraft	Acrylic, alkyd, acrylic-urethane, polyurethane, epoxy

Table 3.2 Common extender pigments used in coatings

Calcium carbonate
Aluminum silicates (clays) – kaolin, mica
Magnesium silicates – talc
Silicon dioxides – diatomaceous silica, quartz
Barium sulfate

of the binder and therefore cause negligible light scattering. See Table 3.2 for common extender pigments (Morgans 1982; Wicks Jr. et al. 2007). A large variety of pigments are used in coatings, including organic, inorganic, and metallic pigments (Crown 1968; Guy 2004a; Wicks Jr. et al. 2007; Eppler 2012).

Although comprehensive coverage of colored pigments is beyond the scope of this chapter, some pigments deserve special mention. Titanium dioxide is arguably the most significant white pigment used in coatings. Titanium dioxide's relatively high refractive index causes light to scatter, resulting in excellent hiding power. Due to its high refractive index, heat and chemical stability, and non-toxic nature, titanium dioxide has largely replaced other white pigments, including lead carbonate, zinc oxide, and lead sulfate. Two crystalline forms of titanium dioxide are prevalent in coatings: anatase and rutile. Anatase is said to be a more vivid white when compared to the slightly yellowish rutile, which is attributable to rutile's absorption of wavelengths in the far blue end of the visible spectrum. Greater hiding power, roughly 20% more, is achieved with the use of rutile (refractive index ≈ 2.7) than with anatase (refractive index ≈ 2.5) and is therefore the predominant form of titanium dioxide used in coatings (Morgans 1982; Guy 2004a; Wicks Jr. et al. 2007; Braun 2012).

Dyes may be used to impart color. Unlike pigments, dyes are soluble and as such do not contribute to hiding power. Instead, dyed coatings produce a transparent or translucent film (Guy 2004a). This is important for some wood applications, such as in staining where dyed or pigmented solutions are applied to wood to impart color (Wicks Jr. et al. 2007).

Metallic pigments are widely used in automotive topcoats and industrial finishes to achieve a deeper color and shade that varies as the viewing angle is changed. Metallic pigments may also be used in many high performance primers to provide functional anticorrosive protection. Pigment grade will depend upon the substrate (metal vs. plastic) and end use.

Aluminum flakes are predominantly used in metallic finishes and can be used in combination with other colored pigments. Aluminum flakes are generally irregular corn-flake or silver-dollar shaped, and range from 0.05 to 2 μm thick. Aluminum flakes differ from other decorative flakes in that they are opaque (Morell n.d.; Guy 2004a; Dössel 2008a; Ferguson 2012).

In addition to aluminum flakes, zinc, nickel, stainless steel, and copper alloy pigments are also widely used for a variety of coating applications. Of these, zinc will be the best known to forensic analysts for its use as a corrosion inhibitor pretreatment for steel in automotive coatings. Nickel pigments, though less well known, are also used for corrosion resistance as well as electrical conductivity in coatings and plastics. Stainless-steel pigments (combinations of iron, chromium, nickel, manganese, and molybdenum) are used in specialized coatings where environmental conditions or waterborne systems challenge durability. Copper alloy pigments are flake-like and will orient parallel to the substrate and film surface. These alloys may be referred to as "gold-bronze" or "bronze" pigments, but are typically copper or a copper-zinc alloy. Altering the alloy elemental ratio will produce colors ranging from greenish-yellow to reddish-gold (Wicks Jr. et al. 2007; Ferguson 2012).

As a complement to or in place of metallic flakes, effect pigments have swelled in popularity in the last 40 years of coatings technology. Effect pigments are used to reflect, diffract, or otherwise interfere with light to create colors and color combinations that impart a pearlescent or iridescent opulence to a coating.

Their purpose is singularly esthetic-based, but the science of pigments and their manufacture has become increasingly complex. These pigments are particularly prevalent in automotive basecoats.

Effect pigments, also known as interference pigments, are translucent, generally have more uniform shapes, and provide color by means of interference. Interference is achieved by coating thin flakes with one or more layers. The thickness and composition of the layer(s) affects the subsequent color. Light will reflect off various interfaces of the multilayered pigment, resulting in interference. The dominant visual color will vary depending on the reflection angle observed. In pearlescent pigments, mica flakes are covered with layers of iron oxide or titanium dioxide to achieve a mother-of-pearl appearance. Other interference pigments work on the same principle, but vary in the choice of core flake, the number and thickness of layers applied, and the layer compositions. Pigments marketed under tradenames such as Chromaflair®, Xirallic®, Colorstream®, and Variochrome® consist of multiple layers of semi-transparent, highly reflective metal oxides over a low refracting, dielectric film (e.g. magnesium fluoride, borosilicate glass, alumina, or silica), with an optional metal or crystalline central core (Guy 2004a; Maile et al. 2005; Wicks Jr. et al. 2007; Dössel 2008a; Nowak 2012).

3.3.1.3 Additives

Additives are substances added to paint in small quantities with the purpose of improving specific properties (ASTM 2018a). The category of additives is vast and wide-ranging. Present in small quantities, additives are often proprietary constituents that are typically present in quantities below the detection limits of commonly used instrumentation. Therefore, they are not as forensically dependable as the main components of a coating. Examples include corrosion inhibitors, ultraviolet (UV) light absorbers, surfactants (e.g. wetting/dispersing agents), foam control agents, biocides, freeze-thaw stabilizers, adhesion promotors, driers, fire retardants, and thickening agents (Guy 2004a).

3.3.1.4 Volatile Components

For most paints, the primary volatile component is referred to as the solvent. The solvent is responsible for dissolving the binder and providing the proper consistency (Montemayor and Yuhas Jr. 2012). In some paints, the binder is not fully soluble in the liquid volatile components, such as in water-based latex paints and powder coatings (Guy 2004a; Wicks Jr. et al. 2007). The fluid portion of paint in which the pigments are dispersed, meaning the binder and the volatile components, comprise the paint vehicle.

Being volatile, these components evaporate as the coating is applied and eventually a formed film results. While they play a major role during manufacture and application, they are rarely involved in any forensic examination due to continuous evaporation post application. Should wet paint be submitted for comparative exams, solvent comparisons or identifications with the use of headspace gas chromatography (GC) or GC/mass spectrometry (MS) could be conducted.

3.3.2 Manufacturing Considerations

Binders, pigments, additives, and volatile components are mixed together to form the final paint product. The choice of ingredients is dependent upon a number of factors, including regulation compliance, application method, cost, and performance factors such as longevity, necessary protection and/or decoration, and film thickness (Guy 2004b). Generally no chemical reactions take place during the mixing process, but proper blending is critical. The most challenging step in the mixing process is pigment dispersion because pigments tend to aggregate and must be broken apart (Fuller 1973; Morgans 1984; Bentley 2001).

As a result of environmental pressure and legislative actions, paint manufacturers have adapted formulations accordingly. Lead-containing architectural paints were banned by the United States government in 1978 (EPA n.d.). Lead was removed from automotive coatings by the early 2000s. Additionally, there have been successive legislative measures since the 1970s limiting the emission of volatile organic compounds (VOCs) due to their harmful atmospheric affects. As a result, formulations have had to accommodate less solvent. Water-based paints, such as those used for architectural latex paints and electrocoated automotive primers, were introduced due to the VOC restrictions. Concern over solvent emissions has also lead to the introduction of high-solids paint and powder coatings. As VOC restrictions continue to tighten and there is more focus on environmental and human health, paint formulations and/or technologies will continue to be modified to meet those measures (Warnon 2004; Wicks Jr. et al. 2007; Streitberger 2008a).

Coatings manufacturing relies heavily on batch production. The components are often added via raw ingredients from silos, bags, or other storage containers rather than producing them in-house. Large batches will then be dispersed into numerous paint cans, such as for architectural paints (as many as 10 000 gal per batch), or applied to a large number of products such as vehicles (~1 quart of paint per automotive layer, originating from paint batches which can range from many hundreds to thousands of gallons) (Technical Contacts, Valspar and PPG Industries, pers. commun., 2015). Batch sizes will vary due to a number of factors, including manufacturer size, plant equipment, and color (e.g. white more popular than pink). When considering a multi-layered paint, these factors further decrease the number of objects which are coated in the same manner (i.e. same layer sequence, formulations, colors). While batch-to-batch discrimination may be achievable, the fact remains that other objects can be coated with paint originating from the same batch.

For architectural paints, manufacturers tend to produce a white base designed for in-store color adjustment. Depending upon the customer's color choice, the store will mix the appropriate colorants into the base. Manufacturers may provide several base options to deliver the widest spectrum of color choices for the various sheens. The base intended for pastel colors will differ in formulation from the base intended for deep or dark colors. Bases intended for flat sheens will differ from those used for glossy sheens. The differences are primarily in the pigment content and less frequently in the binder.

3.3.3 Application Processes

Paint formulation will vary as a function of the application method. The application process may also be prone to specific types of defects or imperfections which may indicate the type of paint present. Application imperfections can also assist in orienting or aligning particles during physical reconstructions. Not all application processes are identifiable by physical examination; however, the various methods requiring specific formulation considerations only further diversify paint chemistries.

Brushes and rollers are common methods of application as these are most popular amongst do-it-yourself applications. Imperfections or defects left by these mechanisms are based on excessive paint application or poor leveling (i.e. the inability of paint to flatten out after application to cover brush or track marks) (Morgans 1984; Wicks Jr. et al. 2007). Other methods of application include spraying, dipping, and electrodeposition.

3.3.3.1 Spraying

Spraying is a common method which is based on the atomization of paint. Droplets of paint in a fine spray are directed toward the surface to be coated. A variety of spray guns are available. The oldest method, still in use today, involves compressed air (pneumatic) spray guns, which are well suited for some architectural and automotive-refinish applications. For larger scale paint jobs (e.g. ships, bridges), airless spray guns are more suitable. Airless sprayers use a combination of compression within the gun and expansion after exiting the nozzle to atomize paint. Both pneumatic and airless spraying methods suffer from the same shortcoming: inefficiency. Only a fraction of the droplets reach the intended surface being coated. Some droplets fall out of the spray pattern due to gravity while others, called overspray, miss the target and deposit on unintended surfaces (Morgans 1984; Marrion 2004; Wicks Jr. et al. 2007). While often problematic for the painter, overspray is a valuable feature during forensic paint comparisons.

One method to diminish waste and overspray is electrostatic spraying. Paint droplets are charged and sprayed toward an electrically grounded substrate relying on the electrostatic attraction to restrict droplet deposition. Another advantage to electrostatic spraying is the wrap-around effect, where droplets deposit on surfaces not directly facing the sprayer. Atomization can be achieved with centrifugal forces where paint enters the center of either a flat disk or curved bell unit which is spinning at very high speeds. Paint is propelled away from the center, making its way outward, and is atomized upon separation from the unit's edge. Alternatively, as is used for powder coatings, an airborne powder of finely ground paint particles is electrically charged. The powder is electrostatically bonded to the grounded surface until cured (Morgans 1984; Thornton 2002; Marrion 2004; Wicks Jr. et al. 2007).

Powder coating application benefits from less overspray, no or low VOCs, and less waste in that any overspray is recoverable and reusable. Color matching is difficult with powder coats and the effect of metallic flake is lessened. In the automotive industry, powder coats have not achieved widespread use due to appearance and cost limitations. Leveling continues to be a challenge for thin automotive powder coats, as can happen with other spray coatings, commonly leaving an irregular surface resembling the surface of an orange (Wicks Jr. et al. 2007). For automotive coatings, powder coats have been relegated primarily for use in primer layers. A limited number of

automotive manufacturers have implemented powder clearcoats (Dössel 2008a). Powder coats are also used for coating tools, household appliances, patio furniture, and lawn equipment.

3.3.3.2 Dipping

Dip coating generally involves submersion of the item into a tank. The excess coating that drips off can be recovered to reduce loss. To overcome problematic draining, the object can be rotated while immersed. For intricate objects, the coating may alternatively flow over the object. Flat objects, such as metal doors, may be passed through a "curtain" of coating. Common defects seen in dip-coated objects include gradient thickness from one end to the other and formation of drips or tear drops. Dip coating is used for tools, agricultural parts, and even automotive primers via electrodeposition (Morgans 1984; Wicks Jr. et al. 2007).

3.3.3.3 Electrodeposition

Electrodeposition coating is predominantly used for the application of a corrosion-resistant, protective first primer layer. Electrocoated primers are used on over 98% of all automotive bodies manufactured globally (Krylova 2001). The metallic body is submerged in an aqueous bath where, with the help of an electric current, the coating or primer layer is deposited onto the metal. Electrocoating was introduced in the 1960s, with anodic systems (deposition occurring at the anode) dominating until the late 1970s (Krylova 2001; Wicks Jr. et al. 2007; Streitberger 2008b). Cathodic systems (deposition occurring at the cathode) have since become widely adopted due to their improved performance and versatility (Wicks Jr. et al. 2007; Streitberger 2008b). Cathodic electrodeposition is the leading method of electrocoating in use today (Wicks Jr. et al. 2007; Streitberger 2008b). Electrodeposition layers may also be referred to as electrocoats, electropaints, or e-coats.

In cathodic electrocoating, positively charged coating particles dispersed in the water bath are attracted to the submerged electrically grounded metal substrate. The metal bodies may be rotated in order to avoid air pockets. Due to the attraction of opposite charges, the coating deposits onto all charged surfaces thereby coating interior, exterior, recessed, and enclosed areas of the substrate. As the film thickens, the coating begins to repel particles remaining in the bath and the deposition process slows. Film thicknesses of 10–25 μm are typical. E-coating capitalizes on the use of waterborne technology for reduction of VOC usage, provides highly controllable film thicknesses, and reduces loss, which is more prevalent in other application methods (Morgans 1984; Thornton 2002; Wicks Jr. et al. 2007).

Epoxy and acrylic binders are considered the best binders today for electrodeposition, either anodic or cathodic. Anodic epoxy e-coats are applied to some automotive parts and agricultural tools, while anodic acrylic e-coats may be used on metal office furniture and hangers. Cathodic epoxy e-coats prevail in automobiles and automotive parts though cathodic acrylic e-coats are more common for wheels and trim (Krylova 2001).

3.3.4 Types of Coatings and End Uses

Coatings can be subcategorized based on their end use. Generally speaking, the five types of coatings are: automotive, architectural, vehicular non-automotive, tool, and specialty/other.

3.3.4.1 Automotive Coatings

The automotive painting process is a multi-step procedure, which begins with one or more substrate preparation steps (Gehmecker 2008). A sequence of layers is then applied, each of a uniform thickness, and each serving a different purpose. For proper adhesion, all layers must be compatible with the other layers in the paint system although they may not be supplied by the same paint manufacturer, even within a given assembly plant. Those paint layers applied by the manufacturer are referred to as original or original equipment manufacturer (OEM) finishes. What follows is the general OEM painting process:

(1) *Pretreatment*: In order to achieve optimal corrosion protection and/or subsequent paint layer adhesion, automotive body parts are subjected to a pretreatment. The pre-treatments for steel and aluminum are sometimes referred to as conversion coatings (Wicks Jr. et al. 2007) because the surface is converted to promote paint adhesion. After the metal surface is cleaned to remove contaminants such as grease, it is then subjected to electroplating producing a sacrificial conversion layer, usually zinc phosphate (Thornton 2002; Wicks Jr. et al. 2007; Gehmecker 2008). Many manufacturers replace zinc phosphate with zirconium oxide as it minimizes the environmental impact (i.e. less waste sludge produced) without compromising performance (Ehinger et al. 2008). A thin galvanized layer may be seen on the bottom surface of paint particles as a shiny, silver metallic finish (see Figure 3.1). The phosphate-free zirconium oxide pretreatment has a similar appearance but is an order of magnitude thinner than the 1–3 μm conventional galvanized

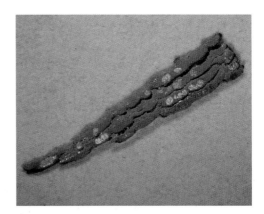

Figure 3.1 Paint chip with bottommost surface visible with areas appearing shiny, metallic. These areas are portions of the galvanized layer and indicate this chip originated from a metal substrate.

layer (Simko et al. 2009). Attempts to characterize this layer by traditional instrumental means may not be possible, but it is important to know that it exists in order to better interpret whether the presence of zinc is inherent to the e-coat or contamination from metal substrate pretreatment.

(2) *Undercoats (primers)*: Once the frame is ready for paint, there is typically an application of at least one primer layer, though two primer layers are more common. Primer layers provide protection for the underlying material (be it metal or plastic), fill imperfections, and promote adhesion between the topcoat layers and the substrate. Primer thicknesses typically range from 15 to 25 μm for liquid applied primers to as thick as or thicker than 30–40 μm for powder primers. The first applied primer on metal parts is usually an electrodeposited primer, known as the e-coat, followed by a baking process. E-coats are typically a shade of gray. Lack of color variation and the similarity of e-coat chemical formulations make this the least discriminating layer in an automotive paint system. They are commonly comprised of epoxy, polyurethane, and titanium dioxide. Barium sulfate, kaolin, zinc phosphate, silicon dioxides, and urea (instead of polyurethane) can also be present in e-coats.

Once the base primer is set, one or more additional primer layers may be applied. Generally, the primer above the electrodeposited primer is referred to as the primer surfacer. Primer surfacers used in OEM automotive paint on metal substrates are typically alkyd-based and often contain melamine, titanium dioxide, and a silicate such as talc. Primer surfacer layers are commonly, though not exclusively, gray in color but often differ in shade from the e-coat layer, allowing the two layers to be visually distinguished. Alternatively, primer surfacers can be color coordinated with the basecoat above.

Color-coordinated primers are most often seen with black, red, or white basecoats, such that the primer is also black, red, or white, respectively.

The application of an anti-chip primer layer is also possible. Anti-chip primers are applied between the e-coat and primer surfacer layers, and are more common on lower sections and leading edges of the vehicle for protection purposes. Anti-chip primers provide abrasion resistance against road debris and further protect the metal body from corrosion. Primer surfacer and anti-chip primers often share the same chemistry. These can be two separate layers or a thick primer surfacer may be present which is meant to serve as an anti-chip primer as well. Primer surfacers and anti-chip primers are typically applied via electrostatic spraying and usually go through a baking process prior to the application of any topcoats.

Plastic parts generally require a conductive, adhesion promoting primer. Primers over plastic substrates (e.g. bumpers) are typically very thin, black, and are often difficult to detect when applied over a black plastic substrate. Acrylonitrile butadiene styrene (ABS) plastic parts such as grilles, mirror housings, and headlight assemblies often do not have a primer due to the adhering qualities of the polymer itself. Plastic parts do not have the same paint system as the metal parts of the same vehicle and are often not painted at the same manufacturing plant.

(3) *Topcoats (basecoat/clearcoat)*: Following primer application, a basecoat approximately 10 μm thick is applied. The basecoat is the layer predominantly responsible for the visual color and therefore may be called the color coat, a misnomer since a tinted clearcoat can also impart color. Each manufacturer creates a palette of appearance options available for each model line: solid/non-metallic, metallic, pearlescent, or combinations of these and

other effect finishes. With approximately 1000 new colors coming to market every year (Dössel 2008b), color availability can range from a single special edition year to over a decade of use, particularly for solid basecoat colors such as white or black. Popular colors may be available at several plants for a number of years. When only a single topcoat is present above the primer(s), the paint system is said to be monocoat. This single layer incorporates the properties of color from the basecoat as well as the anti-chip and UV protection associated with the clearcoat. Monocoats were prevalent on vehicles until the introduction and subsequent proliferation of the basecoat/clearcoat system. Monocoats continue to have automotive applications, including though not limited to white trucks and sports utility vehicles.

Clearcoats were thoroughly integrated in the auto industry in the 1980s. Clearcoats provide shine or luster, durability against abrasion, and protection against environmental factors including UV light. Clearcoats are usually 30–40 µm in thickness, three to four times the thickness of its underlying basecoat. Tinted clearcoats are also available in a wide variety of hues including red, black, green, yellow, and blue. Although OEM automotive clearcoats typically have a small number of chemical components, it is often the most discriminating layer. The presence, absence, and variations in the amount of melamine, styrene, and polyurethane along with the variety of different acrylics available are valuable features when making comparisons and make/model/year inquiries.

When two clearcoats are present over a basecoat and one of the clearcoat layers includes effect pigments as in Figure 3.2, the system is described as a tri-coat. Tri-coats are most common in white paint systems. Four topcoat layers are used in quad-coat systems. Quad-coat topcoats

Figure 3.2 Cross-section of tri-coat paint sequence: clearcoat, clearcoat with effect pigment, white color coat, gray primer. Magnification ∼400×. In both reflected and transmitted light.

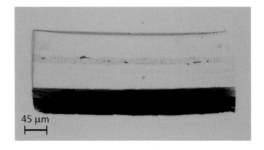

Figure 3.3 Cross-section in transmitted light of quad-coat paint sequence: clearcoat, blue transparent color coat with effect pigment, clearcoat, blue color coat with effect pigment, gray primer.

include two clearcoat layers, separated by a tinted transparent basecoat, above a layer with metallic or pearlescent flakes (ASTEE 2018) as in Figure 3.3. This type of layering system is an ever expanding area in topcoat technology.

Baking may not occur between topcoat layers, with full drying and curing achieved only following clearcoat application. If the clearcoat is applied to a wet or partially dried basecoat, the process is described as a wet-on-wet application. Some plants such as Mercedes Rastatt, BMW Mini Oxford, Mazda Japan, and Ford Mexico are further eliminating baking following the primer surfacer application, described as a wet-on-wet-on-wet process. Eliminating baking decreases energy consumption and manufacturing line length. Without full baking, an optional short (i.e. 1 to 8 minutes) "flash off" drying between topcoats may be used to diminish defects such as solvent or water popping (Dössel 2008a). Wet-on-wet applications retain layer separation but the polymers within, such as melamine and polyurethane, can migrate. This migration can be problematic during instrumental analysis if sampling from different layer depths, as component concentrations may appear to vary.

Further capitalizing on reduced energy costs and line length, other plants are eliminating the primer surfacer layer from their coating process. BMW, Ford, General Motors, Nissan, Toyota, and Volkswagen are all known to use this coating process at select plants in North America and Europe (Dössel 2008a; Technical Contacts Valspar and PPG Industries, pers. commun., 2015). Referred to as primerless, EcoConcept, or the B1 : B2 compact process, these manufacturers also benefit from reduced material consumption contributing to further cost savings. Primerless processes modify the basecoat with polyurethane so it can mimic the chip resistance and UV protection traditionally provided by the primer surfacer (Dössel 2008a).

During the OEM paint process, defects requiring in-plant repairs may result. It has been estimated that more than 80% of cars produced require at least some touchup to one or more layers of the paint system, usually a topcoat (Dössel 2008b). Sanding is typically used to repair damage to primer layers. A combination of sanding and polishing is used on the majority of minor defects in the clearcoat. More extensive spot or panel repairs may be necessary to correct severe topcoat defects. Spot repairs are small areas which are sanded and, with surrounding areas masked, additional basecoat/clearcoat layers are applied. These factory repair layers typically use the same paint as that originally used and are applied via spray guns. Panel repairs of non-removable parts such as the roof or fender result in repainting of the entire panel. Following panel sanding and optional masking, the

Figure 3.4 Cross-section of OEM repair with three basecoat/clearcoat topcoat repairs. Note the consistency in color and thickness for the clearcoat and basecoat layers, respectively, as well as the uniformity of layer thicknesses which physically indicate factory repair rather than aftermarket refinish. Chemically, layers of like appearance would not differ.

entire car traverses the topcoat manufacturing paint line again (Dössel 2008b). In a study of automotive paint layers, over 1000 layer systems were examined for the presence of OEM repair layers (Wright and Mehltretter 2015). The sample set revealed that a single OEM basecoat/clearcoat repair system was applied to 67 of the 1057 samples, two basecoat/clearcoat repairs were used on 12 of the samples, and three basecoat/clearcoat repairs were used on three samples (see Figure 3.4 for an example). Research has demonstrated factory repair paint layers are needed about 8% of the time, while manufacturers estimate as many as 10–20% of cars require spot or panel repairs (Dössel 2008b; Wright and Mehltretter 2015).

Aftermarket refinishes or repaints are those applied, as their name suggests, after OEM paint application to a completely assembled vehicle. Aftermarket refinishes can be applied for a number of reasons, including for esthetic purposes or following damage. Aftermarket refinish layers vary in colors, chemistries, and layer thicknesses (see Figure 3.5). They are generally more crudely applied and have less stringent quality assessments. Furthermore, baking temperatures on the order of those

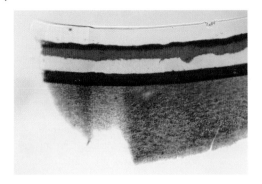

Figure 3.5 Example of aftermarket automotive refinish paint layers above OEM layers in cross-section. Magnification ~280×. Layer sequence is as follows (top to bottom): clear colorless, dark red with decorative flake, gray primer, tinted clear, dark red with decorative flake, black primer, black plastic substrate. Note the uneven paint layer thicknesses in the upper three aftermarket layers, the presence of primer above topcoats, and basecoat layer thickness inconsistencies.

used for OEM-applied layers are not feasible due to the variety of temperature-sensitive materials present in a fully assembled vehicle. As a result, physical characteristics and some specific chemical components can distinguish repaint layers, for example:

- defects, delamination (the separation at layer interfaces), or sanding marks
- layer thicknesses tend to be uneven, irregular, and thicker than OEM layers
- debris or overspray paint droplets (from other commissioned paint jobs in close proximity) at layer interfaces
- incomplete, feathered layers resulting from partial layer elimination during sanding
- clearcoats covered by additional non-transparent paint layers (other physical and/or chemical characterization may be necessary to distinguish factory repair layers from aftermarket refinish layers)
- primer applied over a topcoat
- body fillers or spot putties
- chemical indications: nitrocellulose; alkyd without melamine; high amounts of talc, clay, and/or calcium carbonate in undercoats; high amounts of polyurethane (There

are exceptions, such as the use of OEM nitrocellulose lacquers on vehicles until the 1950s or 1960s depending upon the manufacturer. Additionally, there are terephthalic alkyd-epoxy OEM powder coat primers without melamine and isophthalic alkyd primers that use benzoguanamine as a crosslinker instead of melamine (Wright 2010).)

- aftermarket replacement parts are often received with a black e-coat. These will be chemically similar to OEM e-coats and will have epoxy, kaolin, and polyurethane (no titanium dioxide). Any paint layers above this would be aftermarket refinish paint.

Chemical components have historically played a major role in distinguishing OEM from aftermarket refinish layers. As the automotive coating industry has continued to evolve over time, the well-defined borders between the two have blurred. For example, polyurethane in topcoats used to indicate a refinish until its incorporation into OEM topcoats began in the late 1990s. For a long time, melamine (which requires high temperature curing) was a clear indication of OEM, so much so that the lack of melamine was considered by the forensic community to be indicative of a refinish. Examples of non-melamine OEM finishes (e.g. acrylic polyurethane styrene) and the incorporation of low-temperature ovens in some refinish paint shops suggests melamine can no longer be used as the gold standard for distinction between an OEM application and an aftermarket refinish. With the number of paint chemistries indicative of OEM application diminishing, physical characteristics are generally a better way to evaluate whether a layer system is OEM or aftermarket.

At times, physical characteristics have also been important indicators of manufacturer. For example, there was a time when a red-brown primer was thought to indicate that a paint chip originated from a Ford vehicle. However, as other manufacturers followed this practice in some plants, Ford began to use other primer

Figure 3.6 Image of a paint chip viewing the bottom side of the chip such that the uppermost visible layer is the gray e-coat which has been scraped away to reveal the recycled powder coat primer layer. This layer appears like a mosaic, a mottled multicolored assemblage that is chemically consistent throughout, despite its visual heterogeneous appearance. Magnification ~50×.

colors and with the onset of color-coordinated primers this is not a reliable means of identifying the manufacturer or assembly plant. Another example of a recognizable physical characteristic would be General Motors' use of a recycled powder coat primer (e.g. in the Lordstown, OH plant from 2006 to 2011). As can be seen in Figure 3.6, this recycled powder primer appears multi-colored, mottled, and chemically consists of terephthalic alkyd-epoxy, titanium dioxide, and barium sulfate.

Not all trends are as physically distinctive as those described above, but many can be traced to the industry's efforts to cut costs, improve performance, eliminate solvents and heavy metals, and improve consumer fuel efficiency as well as production energy efficiency. Table 3.3 is a list of automotive coating trends that have been introduced in response to these initiatives.

3.3.4.2 Architectural Coatings

Architectural coatings may be referred to as structural paints or house paints. A number of factors influence consumer choice of architectural paints, such as color, sheen, cost, binder, odor, and ease of application. Architectural paints differ from automotive paints in some

physical and chemical attributes which help distinguish them.

Examination of the paint layer sequence and structure may indicate an architectural origin because layers tend to be applied over time in no predictable sequence. Colorless layers, with the exception of specialized applications such as furniture, are uncommon in architectural paints as are decorative metallic or interference flakes. Primers in architectural applications, when used, are usually white or tinted to the topcoat color. Layer thicknesses are not as uniform as that observed in OEM automotive finishes. All layers can appear grainy in texture due to their high pigment and extender loads. Adhering substrate is an indication of an architectural coating as well if wood, drywall, or masonry remnants are present.

Architectural coatings may be submitted as smears, particularly if transfer occurred prior to cure. When wet, paint will tend to flow onto the substrate, thus wrapping around fibers or yarns in textile substrates such as clothing. It is generally possible to distinguish if transfers occurred with wet or dry paint based on this interaction with the substrate.

Conventional house paints were once solvent-borne alkyds, but today waterborne latex systems dominate the market (Wicks Jr. et al. 2007). Alkyd and polyurethane coatings are very popular for wood (Wicks Jr. et al. 2007). Polyurethane, epoxy, or acrylic binders are commonly used on concrete floors and walls (Wicks Jr. et al. 2007; Kemmann 2010). Multipurpose paints (e.g. all-in-one paint, primer, and stain blocking) and self-priming paints have gained popularity (J.D. Power and Associates n.d.). As of yet, research efforts have not identified a reliable chemical indicator for forensic analysts to recognize a multipurpose or self-priming paint, as manufacturers seem to be achieving the multiple functions using a variety of formulation modifications (Dolak and Weimer 2015). Sometimes, pigments can provide clues as to the paint's end use. Zinc oxide, for example, naturally protects against fungal growth and may indicate an anti-mold

Table 3.3 Automotive coating trends

Trend	Approximate Date
E-coats	Introduced in the 1960s
Monotone primers: primers that have the chemical properties of a topcoat	Introduced in the early 1970s and used until 2000 at some General Motors plants in North America
Monocoats	Predominant on vehicles until basecoat/clearcoat combination introduced in the 1980s; continues to have automotive applications, e.g. still common for white trucks and sports utility vehicles
Lacquers	Predominantly on pre-1990s OEM coatings or refinish automotive coatings
Tri-coats	Introduced in 1995
Removal of lead from paint layers	Mandated for post-2000; still detectable due to wash-out through 2002
Primerless systems	Introduced in 2005
Primer surfacer composed of recycled (multi-colored) paint	2006–2011 at some General Motors plants
Matte clearcoats	Introduced in 2012
Self-cleaning clearcoats	Introduced in 2014
Zirconium oxide pretreatment for steel or aluminum	Introduced in 2014
Quad-coats	Introduced in 2015

or mildew product (Morgans 1982; Wicks Jr. et al. 2007; Dolak and Weimer 2015). The lack of zinc does not exclude this type of paint, however, as some mildew resistant products do not contain it or the concentration may be below detection limits (Dolak and Weimer 2015).

Unused architectural paints, representing roughly 10% of the hundreds of billions of cans sold annually, pose challenges to municipal waste management (American Coatings Association 2016; Look 2009). Architectural paint recycling programs have been introduced and implemented in an attempt to divert non-hazardous, reusable waste from landfills. These programs are predominantly available for latex water-based architectural paints. There are two types of recycled paint, which differ in the amount of recycled material used. Re-blended paints, or consolidated paints, contain a higher percentage than reprocessed, or remanufactured paints (Green Seal

2013; Look 2009; Schuster 2004). The recycling process begins with collection, assessment, and sorting. Paint cans are sorted based upon product type, color, and sheen before being emptied into a vat with similar cans. These vats get emptied into larger mixing vessels that disperse the components, break up solids, and allow for sample testing. Small adjustments may be made such as to alter color or viscosity, but as few additional components are added as possible. There is post-processing filtration to remove debris or larger solids, quality testing to ensure it meets specific performance criteria, and packaging for distribution or sale (BMR 2018; CanadaPaintExport 2009; Green Planet Films 2014). Recycled paints are appealing to the consumer due to their lower cost, similar performance to mid-range non-recycled paints, and/or smaller environmental footprint. To the forensic examiner, recycled paints have greater batch-to-batch variation than off-the-shelf paint products and may result in unexpected analytical data (e.g. an unusual element present in a particular colored paint).

3.3.4.3 Vehicular Non-automotive Coatings

Coatings from bicycles, motorcycles, mopeds, boats, other marine vessels, and airplanes are included in this category. These coatings often share physical characteristics and similar chemistries to those used in automotive coatings. Sometimes a tinted transparent layer may be seen in bicycle paint sequences over a metallic layer. This metallic layer is typically thinner than automotive metallic layers and either foil-like or contains more densely packed flakes than what is seen in automotive applications (Ryland 1995). It is not uncommon for bicycles, mopeds, and motorcycles to have layer sequences and structures like those on automobiles.

Marine coatings can vary depending on their location on the boat. Above the water line, boats may be painted with topside marine paint, generally undifferentiated from high-quality automotive paint. To prevent growth below the water line, boats that are not removed from water use "bottom paint." Bottom paints prevent growth of plants and animals, tend to have a high metal content (e.g. copper, zinc, or historically tin), and are typically thick. As they are optional on smaller boats, owners can customize bottom paint with their preferred color choice prior to dealer application. An epoxy barrier coat may be applied between the boat hull and bottom paint (Wicks Jr. et al. 2007; Hardin 2011).

Gel coats are pigmented polyester coatings applied within molded forms (Wicks Jr. et al. 2007). They are generally observed as a relatively thick outer layer (as compared to automotive paint layers) with a shiny surface and may or may not be painted. Sometimes when cutting into a gel coat it may appear that there is a colorless layer on top. Usually, however, it is binder alone with no clear delineation between a colorless and pigmented layer. During manufacturing, gel coats are sprayed into molds and then fiber reinforcement is applied (Wicks Jr. et al. 2007). Fiberglass is used as reinforcement for the vast majority of boat composites (>90%). Variation in the orientation of fiberglass filaments is possible and therefore a potential point of comparison, if present. Fiberglass filaments may be found in mat form, woven or knit, or as a random arrangement of short staple-length fragments (Hardin 2011).

Function may determine the presence of other physical or chemical properties. Due to heavy traffic on ship decks, anti-skid additives in the form of sand particles, polymer beads, or bauxite (aluminum mineral) are added to the binder, generally epoxy or polyurethane (Guy 2004a; Wicks Jr. et al. 2007). Chlorinated alkyd binders or antimony trioxide extender pigments may be used to enhance fire retardant properties for ship interiors (Wicks Jr. et al. 2007). Anticorrosion in a salt-filled environment is important and may be achieved by using zinc-rich primers or fluorinated urethane coatings (Wicks Jr. et al. 2007).

Airplane exterior surfaces may be painted or polished. Financial considerations, substrate type, environmental impact, and strategic marketing are factors which influence that decision (Hansen n.d.). Eliminating paint layers greatly diminishes weight, which affects fuel consumption, an increasingly important issue. When painted, exterior aircraft coatings are applied in a layer structure similar to automobiles, with an anticorrosive primer and topcoats. Self-priming topcoats which combine the necessary properties of both layers can also be found (Hegedus et al. 2012). Unlike automotive coatings, aircraft tend to be stripped prior to repainting for inspection of the underlying airframe, therefore any characteristic repaint layer history is lost. Interior surfaces may be coated as well, but are generally neither stripped nor re-coated during the aircraft's lifetime. With the exception of a few special applications, most interior surfaces (e.g. hold or cargo areas) are primed but do not receive topcoats (Marrion 2004; Wicks Jr. et al. 2007).

3.3.4.4 Tool Coatings

Tool coatings rely predominantly on alkyd, alkyd-melamine, or nitrocellulose binders. Care must be taken when obtaining known paint from a tool for examination purposes. Instead of being applied to the entire tool length, some coating layers have more limited application, such as a colorless layer. Known samples should be cut from an area adjacent to the possible transfer, close to but outside of the damaged area.

Tools are also a valuable source of questioned paint which may be found, for example, on a hammer face, the jaws of a bolt cutter, or screwdriver head. Due to the nature of tool usage, paint may be smeared when transferred either to or from a tool. Subsequent color comparisons and layer isolations may be difficult due to layer mixing caused by smearing (see Figure 3.7). Further complicating forensic paint examinations, tools may have numerous

Figure 3.7 Note the smearing of the architectural paint layers within the deposits on the screwdriver (top, magnification ~20×). Those served as the questioned sample for comparison to the known multilayered architectural paint (cross-section seen in bottom, magnification ~200×). Note the uneven layer thicknesses and variety of colors present in the known architectural paint cross-section.

paint deposits or smears due to a lifetime of previous use. Observations of texture, weathering, and relative age may assist in determining which smears or deposits to pursue further.

3.3.4.5 Other/Specialty Coatings

Spray Paints In most paint applications, proper mixing is critical and highly desired. Spray paint coatings, in contrast, may not be thoroughly mixed, resulting in pigment and binder concentration variations. Attempting to duplicate the extent of shaking and pigment dispersion can be challenging when cans are submitted for comparison to dried samples from the scene. It is generally accepted practice for the analyst to collect control samples of spray paint from an unshaken can as well as after time intervals of shaking until well mixed to create a gradient of dispersed pigment (Zeichner et al. 1992; Muehlethaler et al. 2014; Gates 2015). If a known paint sample cannot be obtained from within a suspect can, a sample could be taken from the can's nozzle. Greater heterogeneity should be anticipated from nozzle samples if the paint accumulated from a number of uses which varied in mixing.

Research has found that when spraying from an aerosol spray paint can, paint droplets from the produced mist are highly likely to fall on surfaces in close vicinity (Krausher 1994; Marsh 2007). These droplets may be found on clothing or shoes using a stereomicroscope with at least 40× magnification. Droplets are not readily visible with the unaided eye as the majority range in size from 10 to 30 μm (Marsh 2007), though some roughly 40 μm or as large as 60 μm have been reported (Olderiks et al. 2015). The droplets dry quickly but due to close proximity during spraying, it is not uncommon to find droplets wrapped around fibers (see Figure 3.8) (Marsh 2007; Olderiks et al. 2015). Spray droplets can establish a link between a suspect and a scene even when no spray paint can is recovered.

Wrinkle Finishes With humble beginnings, wrinkled finishes were originally viewed as

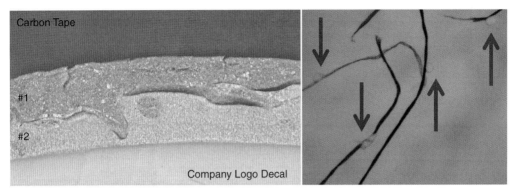

Figure 3.8 Following a homicide, one suspect stated that they, along with a partner, used spray paint, simultaneously, to cover a company logo on the victim's truck. Two spray paint cans were submitted for comparison to the paint on the truck door. These two paints could be distinguished chemically, but not physically. Above, left is a SEM-EDS backscatter image (magnification ∼250×) of paint from the truck door where two "layers" of paint can be seen mixing at the interface, corroborating the suspect's statement. During examination of the partner's jacket, which was submitted for other testing purposes, numerous white paint droplets were recovered. In the image on the right (magnification ∼75×), note the white droplets adhering to and occasionally wrapped around the black jacket fibers (indicating they were wet when contact made with jacket fibers). There were three distinguishable populations within the paint droplets from the jacket: some like spray paint 1, some like spray paint 2, and some which were mixtures of spray paints 1 and 2. The spray paint droplets on the jacket further corroborate the suspect's statement and support the jacket's close proximity during spraying, which established a link between the partner and the scene. At trial, paint was the only evidence that tied the partner to the acts other than the co-defendant's testimony. Source: Brenda Christy, Virginia Department of Forensic Science.

a defect. These are coatings where the surface looks shriveled, with hills and valleys. Wrinkling is caused by more rapid solvent loss or crosslinking at the surface versus the film bottom. Some producers exploited this "mistake" and wrinkle finishes became deliberately applied to a variety of products including office equipment, safes (see Figure 3.9), and metal castings such as tools. They can range from prominent wrinkles easily observed to a slightly low gloss surface where the wrinkles are only visible under magnification (Wicks Jr. et al. 2007).

Figure 3.9 Paint from a safe. Visually very distinctive due to hills and valleys of wrinkles. This paint was very brittle and multi-layered, making layer isolation difficult (scale = mm).

Matte Automotive Clearcoats Increasingly popular, matte automotive finishes have become available as an OEM option by several automotive manufacturers such as BMW (Bruzek 2012), Hyundai for the Veloster Turbo (Wood 2012), Dodge for the Viper (Siu 2015), and as an aftermarket product for any vehicle type. These clearcoats rely on matting or flattening agents to reduce gloss and scatter, rather than reflect incident light like traditional high gloss clearcoats (Guy 2004a). The most common approach is the addition of small (less than 10 μm) silica particles (e.g. silicon dioxide, diatomaceous earth) to create a rough, textured surface (Guy 2004a; Wicks Jr. et al. 2007).

Other matting agents include polymethylurea binders and polyethylene waxes (Guy 2004a).

Body Fillers and Spot Putties Body fillers and spot putties are used during repair to provide bulk within damaged areas and a suitable flat surface for subsequent paint layer application. Due to poor adhesion (McNorton et al. 2008), the interface between the repair material and the car body is a convenient location for cleavage. Body fillers and spot putties may be present as a thick layer on or within paint particles left at a crime scene. Body fillers tend to be muted colors such as light pink, tan, yellow, or green. Spot putties tend to be more bright or vivid colors including reds, blues, and greens. Body fillers are commonly composed of a polyester binder with styrene crosslinker, talc, titanium dioxide, and glass/silica balls (McNorton et al. 2008). As can be seen in Figure 3.10, an air bubble-like appearance is the distinguishing factor of body fillers. Spot putties are more diverse in their composition and typically include talc, calcium carbonate, barium sulfate, and/or nitrocellulose (McNorton et al. 2008).

Films Though not OEM paint, these materials are paint imposters. During the late 2000s, 3M introduced an aftermarket paint protective film, also called a "clear (car) bra." Typically a clear urethane film, this product is applied to the leading edges and rocker panels for protection against rock chips, road debris, or bird/bug acids. Colored films are also available for whole vehicle wrapping, such as customizable vinyl wrapping films (Tokic 2010; 3M Europe 2015). These films are offered in a wide range of colors, patterns, and effects. Where vinyl wrapping is intended to be removable, other films are permanent. Soliant's Fluorex® paint film, for example, can be applied to plastic substrates in a variety of methods including during plastic injection molding, laminated with heat, or applied with an adhesive (Soliant n.d.).

Road Paint Also known as traffic paint, road paints are special purpose paints where rapid drying is important (Morgans 1984; Wicks Jr. et al. 2007). Conventional alkyd binders have for the most part been replaced with epoxies, polyureas, and acrylic latexes, and this coating type may be one of the few that still contain lead and chrome pigments (Beveridge et al. 2001; Wicks Jr. et al. 2007). Road paints can be distinguished quickly from other types of paints based on color (white or yellow) in conjunction with the presence of glass beads used for reflective purposes (see Figure 3.11) (Beveridge et al. 2001). Craters may be observed when those glass beads separate from the paint. These glass beads, with or without adhering

Figure 3.10 Side view of a paint chip, magnification ~55×. Note the thick tan body filler on the bottom with the air bubble appearance. This side view also illustrates the danger in assessing layer structure using this method alone as the topcoat layers (clear colorless, red metallic) are difficult to distinguish accurately above the gray primer.

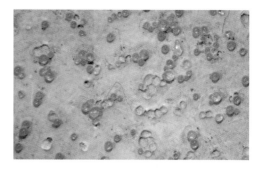

Figure 3.11 Road paint (magnification ~12×), notice the distinctive glass balls and craters.

road paint, are often recovered in the debris from a hit-and-run victim's clothing.

Self-Cleaning Coatings For obvious reasons, economical self-cleaning coatings are highly sought. News-making examples include (i) an aftermarket clearcoat option to Nissan Notes in Europe (Nissan News Release 2014), (ii) Mercedes-Benz testing a PPG self-cleaning OEM clearcoat for which PPG received an Innovation Award in 2015 (Olson and Schuenemann 2015), (iii) to curb public urination on buildings in large cities such as Hamburg, Germany, and San Francisco, California (Imam 2015; Noack 2015), and (iv) to protect memorials or historical sites from debasement with the use of anti-graffiti coatings (Ouroussoff 2005). Self-cleaning coatings are generally super-hydrophobic (repel water) or super-hydrophilic (water spreads allowing "contaminants" to be removed by water). Titanium dioxide nanoparticles, or other semiconductor materials, are commonly used in super-hydrophilic coatings because these materials, due to their photocatalytic properties, break down organic pollutants when stimulated by sunlight. Titanium dioxide also repels oily substances. The hydrophilic surface allows water to spread, thus cleaning is achieved from water rinsing, even from rainfall (Olveira et al. 2015). Super-hydrophobic coatings commonly rely on fluorinated or silicon-modified resins (Guy 2004b; Deschamps et al. 2013). One approach is the use of a highly textured surface. Hydrophobic nanoparticles, such as silica, create peaks that protect the lower lying surface from contact with dirt or water (Guy 2004b; Su 2012). The textured surface results in light diffusion and therefore high gloss finishes are impossible (Guy 2004b). Additional limitations with self-cleaning paints are the high cost and less-than-stellar durability (Sakr 2014; Imam 2015).

Self-Healing Clearcoats Theoretically, self-healing coatings will repair themselves when damaged. Nissan created a self-healing automotive clearcoat in 2005 that repaired small scratches with the help of UV light. Scratches would disappear in anywhere from a few hours to up to a week. The self-healing clearcoat was described as more elastic than the traditional more rigid, plastic-like clearcoats (MacGregor 2011). Offered on at least some Infiniti models, the self-healing clearcoat was available on various Nissan cars until 2011 (PhysOrg.com 2005; MacGregor 2011; Popa 2011). This clearcoat was claimed to last 3 years yet caused greater difficulties when attempting to fix deeper scratches. Though the exact binder chemistry of Nissan's Scratch Guard is unknown, active research seeks to improve on this concept (Esteves and Garcia 2015).

3.3.5 Other Polymeric Materials

While coatings bind to substrates and have a much greater surface area to volume ratio (Krylova 2001), the examination of other polymeric materials may require the use of different analytical approaches. Some examples are provided here.

3.3.5.1 Buttons, Hair Beads, Jewelry, and Synthetic Fingernails

These polymers all tend to be fairly generic in chemical composition and can be best distinguished by physical features. Examination should include documenting sizes, shapes, thicknesses, colors, insignias, and other notable visual characteristics. These materials are also good sources of other evidence types thus increasing the value and strength of a reported association.

3.3.5.2 Gasoline Cans

Red extruded polyethylene plastic gasoline cans lack distinguishing features to allow for differentiation. They are available generally anywhere gasoline is sold. If red plastic is recovered from an arson scene, the ability to distinguish this plastic from a known red plastic gasoline can is unlikely. Red gasoline cans

Figure 3.12 Two trash-sized plastic bags side-by-side over a light box. Bag tops can be seen to the right of the image and bottoms seen to the left. Each bag is ~44 in. long. Notice the corresponding extrusion markings.

have significantly less evidential value than the association of plastics used in other applications or those that contain more discriminating features.

3.3.5.3 Plastic Bags

Extruded polyethylene plastic bags have little variation in chemical composition. Physical features such as manufacturer notations, closure mechanisms, and extrusion markings are the best comparative features (von Bremen and Blunt 1982; Pierce 1990; Castle et al. 1994; Vanderkolk 1995; Sim et al. 2015). Extrusion markings can be observed by viewing over a light box (see Figure 3.12). The use of polarizing films, one below and another rotated above the bag, may assist in visualization of some markings. It has been demonstrated with plastic trash-size bags that these extrusion markings extend across the serrated tear edge and can allow physical reconstruction of successive bags in a box (Ryland and Houck 2001).

3.3.5.4 Gloves

Disposable gloves are generally blown films with limited discriminating physical characteristics. With the instrumentation commonly available in a forensic laboratory, it is typically not possible to distinguish between brands or lots/boxes of the same brand (Causin 2015). For this reason, many laboratories will not accept gloves for comparative examinations of the manufactured material.

3.3.5.5 Automotive Parts and Panels

Several different polymers are common in automotive parts, including acrylic lens covers, ABS in fascia and unpainted side mirrors, and thermoplastic polyolefin (TPO) in bumpers. Chemical analysis of these parts (generally infrared spectroscopy is sufficient) may be helpful in identifying them as a possible vehicle-related polymer. Further, classifying the polymer may aid in research as to which types of polymers are used in certain automotive applications. Documenting any codes on these parts is the best way to utilize these polymers in casework, particularly in make/model/year investigations. Often these codes will indicate certain features that can be used to readily identify a make (e.g. manufacturer's insignia), placement on a vehicle (e.g. RH for right hand/passenger side), polymer composition (e.g. ABS), or a series of letters and/or numbers of varying size and relative position which in conjunction with these other symbols can be sent to a manufacturer or part supplier to develop a shortlist of possible models and perhaps a model year range.

3.3.5.6 Decals

Decal materials can be both physically and chemically similar to coatings. They are paper or plastic sheets, with an image or text imprinted, and an adhesive coating used for fixing to the substrate (U.S. Customs and Border Protection 2007). Decals may be found on the side of an automobile, bicycle, or boat, but a common application also includes license plates. Due to their placement on a vehicle, front license plates are likely to make contact during hit-and-run incidents and can be a source and repository of cross-transferred material.

License plates can be manufactured by first affixing the pre-assembled decal sheet to the metal plate. Next, the plates are stamped or pressed to produce the raised letters and characters, which ultimately are coated with ink or paint (Made How n.d.; Anon. 2007). The pre-assembled decal sheet has the main plate color and will usually contain a series of layers including a colorless layer and glass beads. The uppermost colorless layer is usually more like plastic and not like the colorless layer in automotive paints. Glass beads can be clear, frosted, or a combination of the two. Additional reflection may be achieved with the incorporation of a very thin, almost foil-like aluminum layer beneath the glass beads. The series of layers may differ according to plate type and geographic location. The analytical scheme for license plate decal transfer is the same as for paint, though some consideration should be made during interpretation due to its commonness.

3.3.5.7 Paintballs

Paintballs are exploding capsules ejected from compressed gas-fitted guns, used to mark or "tag" a player in a combat-simulating sport. The capsules are intended to splatter when contact is made at high velocity. Due to their intended purpose, paintballs must be non-toxic and water soluble. Paintballs generally have a thin gelatin shell surrounding a dyed polyethylene glycol-based mixture (Harris n.d.; Woodward n.d.; Listman 2004; Sterling Paintballs 2011; How It's Made 2013). Therefore, when analyzing, expect unconventional ingredients and not those typically found in paints.

3.3.5.8 Glitter

Glitter particles are forensically significant due to their ease of transfer, widespread use in commercial products, tendency to persist following transfer, and wide variation in properties (Aardahl et al. 2005; Blackledge and Jones Jr. 2007; Gross et al. 2010; Vernoud et al. 2011). Glitter particles, although minute in size, can consist of a single polymer film or can contain a sequence of polymer film, coating, and metal layers (Gross et al. 2010). Vernoud et al. reported observing 11 distinct layers in a single glitter particle (2011). Polyester, polyvinyl chloride, polypropylene, and/or poly(methyl methacrylate) polymers are common (Blackledge and Jones Jr. 2007; Gross et al. 2010), though different polymeric layers can be present within the same particle as can polymer blends (Blackledge and Jones Jr. 2007; Vernoud et al. 2011). Highly reflective, thin metal layers are usually aluminum foil or vacuum-deposited aluminum (Blackledge and Jones Jr. 2007; Gross et al. 2010). Care should be taken to physically characterize glitter particles for comparison, to include size, shape, layer structure, and color (Blackledge and Jones Jr. 2007; Gross et al. 2010). If glitter particles require further analysis for comparative purposes, they may be treated much like multilayered paint particles. Discrimination may be achieved via instrumental color or chemical composition comparisons such as with IR analysis, microchemical tests, and/or elemental analysis (Blackledge and Jones Jr. 2007; Gross et al. 2010; Vernoud et al. 2011).

3.3.5.9 Foam

Polyurethane foam is the most common forensically encountered foam due to its use in clothing, automotive seat cushions, and a variety of household items such as furniture, carpeting, bedding, and pipe insulation (Wiggins et al. 2002; Parsons and Mountain 2007; Reed et al. 2010). Gas bubble incorporation during foam manufacture (Causin 2015) results in an easily recognizable physical appearance. Microscopically, polyurethane foam appears like a three-dimensional network of connected polygons (most often tetra-, penta-, or hexagons). In technical terms, the sides of the polymeric polygon are called "struts" while the voids enclosed by the polygon are called "cells" or "pores" (Parsons and Mountain 2007). In smaller fragment form, when the polygons have broken, the particles have a tetrahedral geometry, like the molecular arrangement of methane (CH_4), or if several of these remain connected they can appear like a dog-shaped balloon animal.

Color, strut structure, and cell size are comparable physical characteristics worth examining using stereomicroscopy as well as compound microscopy. Comparison using fluorescence microscopy may further discriminate samples (Parsons and Mountain 2007; Reed et al. 2010). Differences in production methods and additives such as flame retardants and antioxidants cause chemical differences, though minor components are undetectable by IR analysis (Parsons and Mountain 2007). IR analysis will distinguish polyurethane foams from other types (e.g. cellulose or polyethylene) and can differentiate two polyurethane types: poly(ether urethane) and poly(ester urethane) (Causin 2015). Seeking additional discrimination, researchers have sought methods to elucidate minor chemical components though most techniques have employed instrumentation less common to forensic laboratories: VOC analysis via solid-phase microextraction (SPME) coupled to GC/MS (Parsons et al. 2013), trace tin analysis by inductively coupled plasma-optical emission spectrometry (ICP-OES) (Parsons et al. 2010), and time domain nuclear magnetic resonance (TD-NMR) (Mauri et al. 2013). Parsons et al. found comparing trace organic profiles by gas chromatography-flame ionization detection (GC–FID) provides additional discrimination but requires solvent leaching and is a lengthy process (Parsons et al. 2010).

3.4 Forensic Examination

3.4.1 Recognition, Collection, and Preservation

Depending upon circumstances, collection of paint and polymer trace evidence may occur in a forensic laboratory or under non-ideal conditions at the scene, a hospital, or the morgue. As collection is preferred in the laboratory, entire items such as clothing, automotive parts or panels, or bicycle frames may be submitted. Alternatively, a section of the substrate can be physically removed from the larger object leaving any transfers in situ. Once in the laboratory, these items will need to be assessed appropriately in order to best elucidate the evidential value.

3.4.1.1 Gross Examination

Overall observation of submitted items is necessary. During this initial assessment, the evidence should be marked according to the analyst's laboratory protocols to include labeling the item with its unique identifier, laboratory number, and analyst initials. Examination of evidential materials will include noting the basic information about the item(s) such as any manufacturer's labels or markings, item type (e.g. fender, garment, drywall section), size, color, any logos or insignias, damage, and the condition as received. Any observed streaks or smears and the general location of suspected transfers (e.g. blue smear on left arm of shirt) should be documented. Transfer of paint is frequently, though not necessarily (see Figure 3.13), accompanied by smearing at or around the site of the suspected transfer. As circumstances dictate, observations of general location and appearance should also be noted for non-paint/polymer materials (e.g. apparent grass stains, biological fluids, stray ink marks).

Initial observations may be made with the unaided eye, but a magnifier and adjustable lighting can assist in overall assessments. When handling items of evidence, care must be taken to ensure any debris dislodged from the object is preserved. This is most easily accomplished by opening evidence on top of paper and handling carefully when rotating evidence.

If damage to a coated substrate is observed, then known exemplars adjacent to the damage will be necessary. Ideally, a portion of the substrate, leaving the transferred material unaltered, will be physically removed and submitted to the laboratory for examination. If the substrate is a large or immovable object such as a wall, or vehicle, samples should be

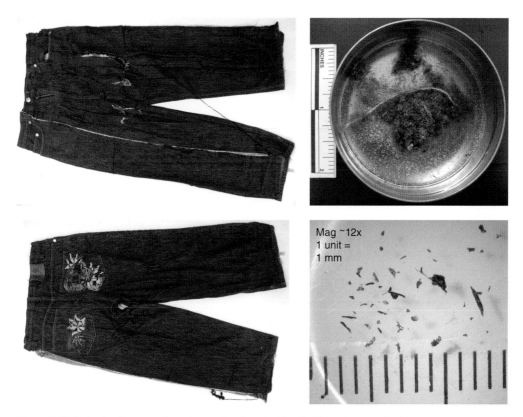

Figure 3.13 Paint is often transferred to pedestrian clothing in hit-and-runs, whether or not a smear can be visualized. The above jeans were submitted requesting a fiber comparison only as no visible paint smears were present and yarns were found within the suspect vehicle's broken bumper. In addition to the medical cuts, damage can be seen on the jeans front. The jeans were scraped and debris collected in a round metal tin, above right. The debris was searched using a stereomicroscope and paint particles were isolated, bottom right. More than 30 dark green paint particles with decorative flake were recovered, representing two layer sequences: one from a plastic substrate and one from a metal substrate. Known paint samples were requested from the suspect vehicle, from both damaged metal and plastic panels. The particles recovered from the jeans were then compared to the submitted respective knowns and no differences were observed. Additionally, no differences were observed between the yarns and fibers recovered from the vehicle and those comprising the jeans. Thus the resulting report drew attention to the cross-transfer of material that appeared to have occurred and its increased significance.

collected such that the damaged areas and substrate are adequately represented.

Straight edged razors or scalpel blades are acceptable tools to sample transferred paint from a surface. Avoid scraping and shaving the questioned paint and instead use deep, angled cuts down to the substrate to maintain an intact layer sequence. It may be helpful to imagine scooping ice cream: angle the blade or razor edge in, press down, and then angle out. This technique can be more challenging depending upon the substrate and sampling angle, but it is critical to attempt to collect all paint layers down to the substrate in one cutting. Any loose paint adhering to the blade can be gently tapped into the collection vessel (e.g. paper fold). Paint samples should not be placed directly into an envelope or plastic bag due to the potential for loss and static electricity, respectively. Only after due diligence is exercised to ensure that all paint is encapsulated in the primary collection vessel can a labeled plastic resealable, zipper-lock storage bag, or envelope be employed to store the collected paint chips.

3.4.1.2 Visual Recovery and Collection

Once any areas of damage, discoloration, or other visible disturbances have been located, further inspection is appropriate. Use of low magnification, such as that from a stereomicroscope, can aid in the recovery. Any observed paint chips or smears that can be pried from the surface with forceps should be isolated in an appropriately sized and labeled storage container, such as a metal box, glassine envelope, paper evidence fold, or glass well slide. When searching for questioned paint, oblique or alternate lighting may be helpful as paint particles may reflect the light differently and draw attention.

3.4.1.3 Recovery by Scraping

If no foreign paint is recovered after visual examination (unaided eye and low magnification), textile items such as clothing may be scraped for microscopical searching of associated debris. Often, clothing is collected from a victim at the scene, hospital, or morgue and may have already encountered numerous sources of trace debris from each or any of these locations. This clothing is usually recovered from the road or hospital floor and packaged together in a single container. If each garment submitted has been packaged separately, it should be examined and processed individually. The preferable container for packaging clothing is a brown paper bag, but it could also be a plastic hospital patient garment storage bag or even a plastic trash bag. Plastic is non-ideal for textile storage due to its inability to release the moisture and odor associated with biological contaminants, which can foster insect and mold growth. Additionally, dislodged paint evidence within plastic packaging can preferentially adhere to the plastic surface due to static electricity, making detection and recovery of foreign paint difficult. Regardless of the outer packaging,

clothing associated with a hit-and-run victim should be assumed to be biohazardous and treated and labeled as such.

The examination of clothing for foreign paint or polymer fragments begins with preparation of the work area. The ideal work surface is a flat, wide counter or tabletop that can be wiped down with a cleaning solution to remove dust and debris. Once dry, the surface should be covered with a large piece of kraft or butcher paper to catch any material dislodged from the clothing during handling and examination. Personal protective equipment such as a laboratory coat, gloves, mask, and eyewear should be worn during processing to protect the analyst from biological material.

If multiple items are packaged together, it is preferable to process them together in order to accumulate the debris as a single collection from the commingled garments. It may seem counterintuitive to process undergarments that are not likely to contain paint chips or smears from a hit-and-run, but if garments were collectively packaged, there is the potential that loose paint chips could have shifted and become lodged in any of the items. Often, the analyst may not know if items were packaged separately at the time of retrieval or if they were sorted by an evidence technician after clothing had been commingled. If processed together, any recovered paint should be reported as part of the general clothing population rather than attempting to speculate where it was originally deposited.

Once a garment has been inspected for smears or loose paint chips (inside and out, front and back with care to keep the garment on the paper at all times), it should be hung from a position above the paper such that it is suspended a few inches above the work surface. The garment may be suspended using a clothesline with wooden pegs or a frame containing metal hangers that can be raised or lowered according to the garment's length (see Figure 3.14). After the garment is suspended, a tool such as a large flat spatula should be swept down the garment in a

Figure 3.14 The shirt is suspended above a paper covered surface. The spatula to the left is used to sweep down the shirt surface toward the paper, resulting in debris accumulation on the paper.

systematic fashion to allow debris to fall onto the paper. The sweeping motion should be continuous and the spatula swept in a downward motion beginning at one edge of the garment and proceeding in a steady, slightly overlapping motion to ensure that entire side of the garment is agitated to release possible paint particles. Once one side has been swept, the analyst should repeat the process on the other side. Pockets and hoods should be inverted, and the interior of long sleeve shirts or pant legs should be agitated with the spatula to dislodge any particles that may have collected there during handling or transport. The innermost container that housed the item should also be inverted over the debris pile and the spatula should be lightly tapped into all the corners and crevices in order to dislodge any paint or polymeric materials. Once all relevant debris has been thoroughly gathered, the garment should be returned to the container.

Once the debris has been collected on the underlying paper it must be concentrated into a more manageable pile. The edges of the paper can be raised, the spatula can be used to gently tap on the outer sides or above the debris on the same side, or the flat spatula edges can be used to guide debris in a manner such as that used to gather crumbs by hand sweeping them into a pile. As the debris is concentrated into successively smaller areas of the paper, the outer edges can be cut away for ease of paper handling. Eventually the paper may be shaped into a cone for transfer of the debris into a container. The container should be labeled with the item identifier, laboratory number, and analyst's initials so that any paint or polymeric evidence recovered from the debris can be traced back to the item of origin.

Each debris-filled container should be examined stereomicroscopically using appropriate lighting (e.g. a ring light positioned at 90° to the plane of the microscope stage, or bifurcated fiber optic arms positioned at a ~45° angle from the stage) and a systematic approach to searching for paint particles. Some analysts will deposit the container's contents onto a piece of paper in order to increase the surface area and redistribute debris confined within or around fiber bundles. White or black paper may be used for optimal contrast purposes. Other analysts prefer to keep the debris contained and will use a metal probe and/or forceps to separate the debris. Regardless of the analyst's approach, the system used should be methodical to ensure that all of the debris is inspected. In the event that no evidentiary materials are recovered from the debris, some laboratories have a second search policy in which a second analyst will independently search the debris or the same analyst may repeat the debris search to ensure no paint or polymeric materials were overlooked during the first search. If any paint or polymers are observed within the debris, these items should be isolated into a separate, appropriately labeled container.

3.4.2 Analytical Scheme

Whether the questioned paint or polymeric evidence is submitted by the contributor or recovered from debris by the analyst, the analytical scheme is the same. Each item's physical features must be documented such that observable differences between samples are noted. A preliminary evaluation of physical features includes assessing the suitability for physical fit and further testing. If a physical fit is found, no further testing is necessary because this result is conclusive. In the absence of physical differences or physical fits, further testing is performed for comparison of chemical composition. See Figure 3.15 for a general analytical flow.

3.4.2.1 Physical Fit

After the physical features of the submitted items have been at least preliminarily assessed and documented, and any loose adhering evidence has been collected and preserved, it may be possible to identify fractured edges which appear similar between like items. If the realignment of these pieces allows aspects of the aligned edges, any underlying layers, microscopic markings, surface features, etc. to be in agreement, then the pieces have formed a physical reconstruction (e.g. fracture match, physical fit) (VanHoven and Fraysier 1983; Cortner and Hamman 1996; Katterwe 2005). It could be concluded that these pieces were once a part of the same larger item and were forcibly separated at this re-established juncture

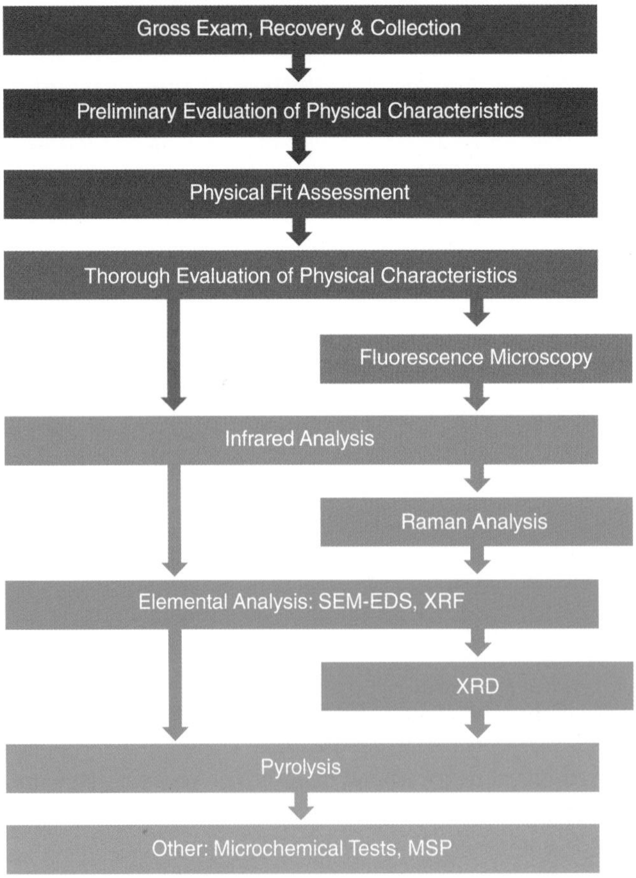

Gross Exam, Recovery & Collection

Preliminary Evaluation of Physical Characteristics

Physical Fit Assessment

Thorough Evaluation of Physical Characteristics

Fluorescence Microscopy

Infrared Analysis

Raman Analysis

Elemental Analysis: SEM-EDS, XRF

XRD

Pyrolysis

Other: Microchemical Tests, MSP

Figure 3.15 Analytical scheme for forensic paint analysis. Optional, less common instrumental techniques are included in the smaller boxes to the right where best appropriate in the analytical scheme.

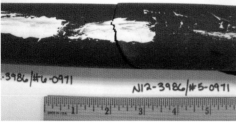

Figure 3.16 Examples of physical reconstructions. Fits were confirmed with stereomicroscopic examination using interior edge topography, and exterior features. Top: three plastic fragments, with manufacturer's text crossing the fractured edges. Bottom: two pieces of foam pipe insulation with white paint smears across fractured edge. One piece recovered in suspect's possession, the other piece found at the scene where copper pipe was stolen.

(see examples in Figure 3.16). This conclusion is the most definitive opinion an analyst can render and should be well documented to allow a technical reviewer, other subject matter expert, or the trier of fact to understand the parameters that were assessed and how the individual features support the conclusion.

3.4.2.2 Comparison

Examinations of like items in the absence of a physical fit cannot provide as strong an associative conclusion but can nonetheless yield significant results. A paint comparison involves a thorough comparison of physical properties and chemical composition to determine if the paints could have shared a common

origin. Still, the strongest conclusion that can result from any side-by-side comparison would be discrimination of the compared items. Discrimination can result from exclusionary differences noted between any of the observable or measurable properties documented for a paint or plastic. For example, automotive paint systems that contain the same number of layers, relative layer thicknesses, basecoat color, and layer sequences might be discriminated by chemical differences in the primer surfacer, the layer between the basecoat and the electrocoat.

By contrast, a color difference in a layer sequence of an aftermarket automotive paint or an architectural paint may not be indicative of different paint formulations, but rather different areas of the same larger source. For this reason, it cannot be overemphasized that known samples submitted for comparison to questioned items *must* be collected from a site immediately adjacent to the area where the questioned paint is thought to have originated. Differences between polymeric materials are generally more obvious on a macroscopic scale (e.g. color, construction, manufactured thickness, markings) and should be noted accordingly when observed in comparative casework.

Unaided visual and stereomicroscopic examinations can reveal a wealth of information regarding a suspected transfer of paint. Documentation of these examinations should include information about the material's layer system, color(s), thickness or relative layer thicknesses, textures, and imperfections such as air voids in a latex-like system. These details might serve to classify an unknown material as visually consistent with a particular type of paint or polymeric material (e.g. rubber-like based on aforementioned physical properties described). Images are sometimes the best descriptor available, but even materials that are difficult to photograph due to size or surface topography can be adequately visualized by a technical reviewer (or jury) if enough written detail is provided to support the stated conclusions.

A relative scale should be included in descriptive notes about paint and polymer evidence and a physical scale should be included in images to provide context to what is being depicted. Relative thicknesses should be noted in sketches of paint layers within a paint chip. The latter is of particular importance to support an architectural paint assessment because layer thickness can vary greatly within a sample. The same is true when documenting an automotive layer system that consists of both OEM and aftermarket layers, which can vary significantly in relative layer thicknesses.

3.4.2.3 Exposing of Layers

Physical features tend to be the most discriminating characteristics pertaining to paint and polymeric evidence. Viewing all coating layers simultaneously provides a large number of comparable features. Layer sequences of paint systems can be indicative of a particular end use (e.g. automotive, architectural, maintenance/tool) and can often distinguish an OEM versus an aftermarket automotive refinish. More than one mechanism for exposing paint layers may be necessary for different instrumental techniques. See Figure 3.17 for illustrations of different layer exposure mechanisms. The method used may depend on the sample amount, condition, or testing to be done and, therefore, achieving sampling proficiency in more than one technique is recommended.

Cross-Sections and Thin Peels Cross-sections can be obtained either manually or using a microtome. When executed manually, the paint chip is held by forceps with one hand so the chip is on-edge and all layers are visible while the opposite hand uses a clean, sharp scalpel blade to cut across the surface.

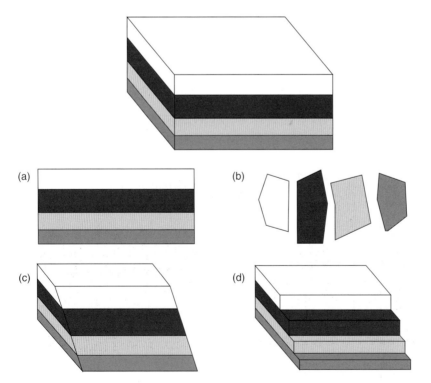

Figure 3.17 Paint chip (top) and the manual methods of exposing layers: (a) cross-section, (b) thin peels, (c) wedge cut, and (d) stair-step exposure.

Alternatively, a microtome equipped with a glass or diamond knife can be used to section a paint chip which has been secured within a hardening medium, such as a two-part epoxy. The excised portion of the chip is referred to as a "cross-section" and encompasses each layer present in the paint chip's layer system. All of the physical features of the layer system (e.g. number, sequence, relative thicknesses, colors) can be documented and verified using cross-sections.

Cutting thin cross-sections is a skill that requires practice and patience. Novice analysts may be tempted to solely view a paint chip on its side to observe the layer sequence without cutting a cross-section. This is a mistake as layers may be missed and colors may not be accurately represented (e.g. dark blue may appear black or colorless layers may not appear colorless due to light reflecting from adjacent layers). It may also be tempting to chop down through all the layers of the paint chip, from one surface to the other. This practice is also discouraged because it produces sections that are not thin enough for light transmission and may cause smearing of layers which will affect instrumental testing. In rare instances where sample size precludes other methods, chopping may be necessary, but it should be used as a last resort.

"Thin peels" refer to a thin cutting of a single layer, generally horizontally across the layer surface. Single layer thin peels may be cut by hand or with a microtome. If several cross-sections and/or thin peels are taken from the sample, these may be used for further testing.

Wedge Cut (Bevel Cut, Oblique Cut) A wedge cut is created by cutting the intact layer system at an oblique angle using a clean, sharp scalpel blade. The result is an angled surface on the chip. This technique exposes a larger surface area of each layer (the lower the angle, the greater the surface area exposed). Wedge cuts are most useful when an interior layer is very thin and difficult to observe with cross-sectioning or to isolate with thin peels. With more area exposed, wedge cuts may ease the process of sampling from a thin layer.

Stair-Step This method requires skill in manipulation of the paint chip and manual layer separation. Stair-step exposure of the layers can be achieved with the sample held stationary on a glass microscope slide (e.g. on double-sided tape, mounting media, or manually with forceps placed on a corner) with the larger surface face down on the slide. Depending upon the size, shape, and mode of separation from the substrate, the larger surface may be the topmost side or the side closest to the substrate. With step-by-step layer exposure, a section of the surface layer is gently removed using successive manual thin peels with a clean, sharp scalpel blade to expose the layer underneath. This process is then repeated on the exposed layer to reveal the layer below it and so on until all of the layers can be microscopically viewed simultaneously. This method can serve as the preparation step for instrumental analysis of each exposed layer when transmission of light is not the objective, such as scanning electron microscopy-energy dispersive X-ray spectroscopy (SEM-EDS).

Other Helpful Hints It is critical that known and questioned samples are viewed side-by-side using the same background color. Some analysts preferentially use one background color routinely to view paint samples, but alternating between black, gray, and/or white backgrounds may facilitate color determinations.

When using any of the aforementioned hand-sectioning methods, it is best practice to use a smooth, shallow, skimming motion with a fresh scalpel blade while holding the sample gently with forceps. If the cut is too deep, the resulting section will be too thick. Cutting under increased magnification may assist in preventing thick sections because the perception of thick versus thin is improved. The placement of the sample within the forceps and its relationship to scalpel placement is critical. The scalpel should be placed so that when pressure is applied, the scalpel does not cause chip movement, rotation, fracture, or loss. Generally, cutting should proceed from an inner location on the paint edge rather than from a corner.

Pre-cleaning of the work area, prior to evidence examination, is a practice that cannot be overemphasized, especially for instances where a particle may have been dropped or lost during examination. In these instances, recovery may be difficult or impossible. The surrounding table top can be searched using oblique lighting in an attempt to relocate the errant chip. As a last resort, the surrounding area may be "taped" (i.e. a piece of office tape can be applied and removed from the tabletop surface) in the area proximal to the stage and then viewed microscopically.

Optimal lighting conditions may include the use of reflected light and/or transmitted light. Transmitted light is particularly helpful at higher magnifications for observing pigment distribution or decorative flake arrangement in thinly sectioned samples. Reflected light is helpful for evaluating dark layers, white layers, or textures. Often, the successive use of reflected and transmitted light is beneficial because these lighting conditions will highlight different characteristics. The simultaneous use of both reflected and transmitted light may be helpful, such as to distinguish layers that are very similar in color and texture.

Mounting thin peels or cross-sections of paint in a medium of refractive index closer to 1.5 (similar to the refractive index of paint) may further elucidate some physical characteristics because it minimizes light reflection and refraction. Likewise, it is helpful when attempting to photograph features or for fluorescence observations. Addition of a mounting medium and a coverslip will visually smooth rough edges and can flatten manual cross-sections. Commercially available optical adhesives or certified refractive index liquids have refractive index ranges that better approach 1.5, but water can alternatively be used with a refractive index ~1.3 (McCrone et al. 1984). Water is not ideal, however, because although it permits recovery and reuse of the paint sample, it is also prone to problematic air bubbles.

Layer assessments, particularly of automotive OEM systems, should be conducted with caution. The analyst should be cognizant of the use of color-coordinated primers, which can be particularly challenging to distinguish from the basecoat in some systems. For example, what appears to be a thick, white, non-metallic paint layer could be a basecoat over a color-coordinated primer (where both layers are generally consistent in relative thicknesses) or a basecoat over a powder primer (where the primer can be 2–3× thicker than the basecoat). Infrared analysis of the top and bottom of the layer(s) will readily demonstrate if two layers are present in the sequence based on differences in chemical formulation. Alternatively, fluorescence microscopy or a backscatter electron image of the layer system using SEM may better elucidate layer thicknesses than a stereo- or compound microscopic examination of a cross-section.

3.4.2.4 Physical Characteristics to Note

– *Color*: Color is highly discriminating and arguably the most important characteristic to compare in paint samples. Color, or more importantly how it is perceived, can be influenced by a number of factors such as formulation differences, environmental conditions, age of the sample, the visual acuity of the analyst, the substrate, sample size, and the color of the surrounding area. Color comparisons should be made with samples side-by-side on a color neutral background or using more than one background color (e.g. black and white).

  Color is best noted using descriptors that convey hue, value, and chroma (e.g. bright/intense medium-toned red layer). Instrumental methods or a paper color reference, such as the Munsell system, may be of assistance. The Munsell color system uses three coordinates to describe a color as it is located within a three-dimensional color space. The first coordinate is the hue. The Munsell color space consists of five principle hues and five combination hues, each divided into ten uniform steps similar to a color wheel. The second coordinate is the value and is measured along the vertical axis of the space. The axis represents the neutral scale from black to white and measures the darkness or lightness of a coordinate within the space. The third coordinate is the chroma and is measured outwards or perpendicular to the vertical axis and measures the intensity of a color. Due to the difficulty in communicating color clearly, the relative comparison of colors (i.e. whether two colors appear the same or not) is more useful and more reproducible for analysts than the way in which colors are described.

Complicating factors further, the same visual paint color can be achieved by more than one pigment formulation. This capability is important when a vehicle is partially refinished following damage, for example, or a customer wants to buy a gallon of paint to duplicate a wall color where the original paint manufacturer is unknown. In refinish situations, color matching is occurring rather than a duplication of chemical formulations. Two objects that are visually indistinguishable may be quite different chemically. Metamerism occurs when two colors, achieved using different pigment formulations, are visually indistinguishable under at least one light source but can be differentiated under other lighting conditions. Spectrophotometric means of assessing color, such as microspectrophotometry (MSP), are used by some laboratories to impart a more objective evaluation to color comparisons and to possibly distinguish metameric pairs. Keep in mind that two objects that look visually different may have come from different sources or different areas of the same source material exposed to different conditions.

– *Approximate amount/size*: Sample size should be noted to document condition but also is important in assessing sample preparation options, suitability for further instrumental examinations, and the order in which tests are performed. Enough sample must be used to ensure examination of homogeneous, contaminant-free aliquots yet retain sufficient material for possible future testing by another analyst. In limited sample size scenarios, destructive tests such as pyrolysis or microchemical tests may be excluded or at least saved until all other tests have been performed and no differences found. With small samples, wedge cuts and stair-step layer exposures are not practical and thin peels, for example, may not be possible without the high risk of losing the particle. Sample preparation methods should be selected based on the amount of sample present.

– *Texture(s)*: Textures can provide points of discrimination, as well as an indication of end use. Surface topography can vary, but if appropriate knowns are collected, samples from adjacent areas will exhibit the same features. Noteworthy indicators would be a smooth glass-like surface, a highly uneven rough surface, or a pitted surface with air voids due to solvent loss. The term orange peel, for example, is used to describe uneven surface topography which looks like the surface of an orange. In interior architectural and other decorative coatings, an orange peel appearance may be desirable in that it gives surface texturing, as in a faux finish. In automotive applications, the presence of orange peel is indicative of poor quality control measures such as paint thinner evaporating too quickly, applying too much or too little paint, low air pressure (poor atomization) in spray applicators, or spraying the paint at an incorrect angle (i.e. other than perpendicular) (Glasurit n.d.). Individual layer textures (e.g. grainy, smooth, rough) may help distinguish primer layers from basecoat layers if color coordinated, for example where the primer may appear grainier than the basecoat. Noticing the texture while cutting can also be helpful, as more flexible paints are typical of architectural latexes and automotive plastic parts. Older paints or those with a low binder/pigment ratio will tend to be brittle and break apart.

- *Layer sequence*: As painted surfaces tend to be repainted over time, noting the layer sequence is essential in assessing evidential significance. The more layers that transfer, the lower the number of paint systems that could share this common source. That is not to say that the layer sequences must be exactly the same between questioned and known samples for an association. The comparison could be limited if layers are added post-incident to conceal the previous known source paint color; these layers would obviously not be present on any transferred paint. It is possible that only a portion of a layer sequence will transfer due to poor adhesion between layers, such as at a body filler/lower layer interface. Incomplete removal of a layer by sanding may result in a feathering layer beneath any refinish layer(s). These are only a few scenarios where differences in layer sequences would not prohibit an association if no other differences were found throughout the analytical scheme. As addressed previously, layer sequence can also help determine the paint type (architectural, automotive, etc.).

- *Relative thickness of layers*: Uniformity in layer thicknesses is an indication of manufactured products such as OEM automotive or tool paints. On the other hand, uneven thickness with greater variation is more common in refinish automotive paint layers or architectural paints. Layer differences should be assessed keeping those factors in mind. Feathered layers are by nature varying in thickness within a sample and therefore variation in thickness between comparative samples may be explained. The cutting angle used by the analyst to expose a layer system

may also impact the perceived relative layer thicknesses.

- *Decorative flake*: If decorative flake is present in either comparison sample, then it must be present in the other for an association to be reported. Other factors such as color, orientation, distribution (including how flakes are arranged and general density), and flake shape can be compared as well. Flakes may be aligned parallel to the layer structure or at varying angles. A paint film may contain relatively few flakes or be heavily filled, with flakes present in clumps or more evenly dispersed. Flakes may be translucent as with an effect pigment or opaque if the flakes are metallic. Most of these properties will be better examined with the use of cross-sections or thin peels on a compound or polarized light microscope (PLM).

- *Size and distribution of pigments*: The size and distribution of all extender and colored pigments are comparative features. These are strictly controlled in some paints (e.g. OEM automotive and bicycle basecoats) so a difference in pigment characteristics would indicate different sources. Physical attributes of pigments are known to vary in other paints, such as spray paints, and this must be considered during sample preparation. The relative amount of pigments of like size, the number of different sized pigments present, and the spatial distribution will affect the color visually perceived. Higher magnification and viewing in transmitted light are generally necessary for these observations and can potentially allow for pigment identification with the use of PLM.

- *Defects/imperfections*: Defects or imperfections may give insight as to the type of paint or the method of application. These features will be present in both questioned and known samples if appropriate known samples are collected. As these are unintended characteristics, the significance of observing like features of this type is slightly elevated since the chances of randomly finding a different paint source with all the same properties is reduced.

o *Weathering characteristics*: Exposure to environmental influences over time can result in flaws, defects, and failure. Exposure to UV light can cause loss of gloss or color fading, and may be more apparent on horizontal automotive panels such as the hood rather than vertical panels such as doors. Texture is also affected by UV exposure where over time the paint becomes more brittle and harder to cut during sampling. Surface roughness may be due to weathering, such as in the case of chalking exterior architectural coatings with intentional inclusion of anatase titanium dioxide so white paint looks brighter as the film erodes. Oxidation of the surface can cause microcracking to occur, which will ultimately lead to polymer breakdown (Nichols et al. 1997). Delamination, the separation of coating layers, can be caused by weathering in an older vehicle or more commonly is a sign of a refinish with poor adhesion between layers.

o *Dirt/debris*: Debris can be used to determine whether two items were exposed to the same environment. Debris between layers is an indication of refinish layers in automotive paint. Dirt or debris within and between layers is more common in exterior architectural coatings due to poor substrate preparation. If the chip is too small to remove any observed contaminants, analysis of it along with the paint should allow for subtraction techniques to determine the contribution that is made by the unwanted surface materials.

o *Sag*: Observed as curtain-like or as tear drops of paint, sag is a defect which results in thickness variability. Formulators attempt to combat sag with viscosity and thickness controllers as well as anti-sag pigments (Wicks Jr. et al. 2007). Regardless of the formulation management, sag can be caused by excessive paint load during application. Most often seen with the use of brushes or rollers, sag via spraying is possible. Due to the downward flow, there may be chemical differences observed when comparing paint from within the sag "curtain" to the adjacent non-sagging paint, therefore control samples should be taken from visually similar surfaces.

o *Overspray*: Overspray is caused by spray applications where areas surrounding the substrate can be subjected to paint droplets that go beyond the intended surface (Wicks Jr. et al. 2007). In automotive applications, overspray between layers indicates refinish layers. With regards to OEM applications, overspray may be observed inside doors, on undercarriages, or within hoods or trunk lids. These areas can be of great benefit to the analyst if the original exterior OEM coating has been refinished. For architectural or spray paint applications, overspray can connect a suspect's clothing to a scene if spraying occurred in close proximity to the clothing.

o *Solvent popping/trapping*: The appearance of solvent pops is common in architectural coatings where craters or voids occur during film curing. This is particularly apparent in matte finishes where the absence of gloss tends to magnify surface imperfections. In a semi-cured film, some solvent may still exist within the layer which can be characterized by analytical means, thereby deriving another characteristic of the formulation that is normally absent from a cured film.

o *Sanding marks*: Sanding marks are due to repairs and indicate a refinish. These are most easily seen with oblique lighting on the bottommost surface. Sanding is an intentional act, but the resulting marks will be random. Alignment of sanding marks may support physical reconstructions.

3.4.2.5 Further Testing

Based on the physical characterization of a paint chip, the best analytical approach for chemical analysis can be determined. Sample size, physical characteristics, and available instrumentation must be factored into the order of instrumental analysis. Faster techniques (considering sample preparation, instrument quality assurance checks, and data acquisition) that are highly discriminating are generally performed first. Nondestructive tests are generally prioritized before destructive tests. As an example, a sample suspected of containing several white architectural paint layers may initially be examined with the use of fluorescence microscopy, microchemical tests, Fourier transform infrared spectroscopy (FTIR), or SEM-EDS backscatter imaging in order to help determine the number of white paint layers present. Each of these paths may lead to sample/layer discrimination, but sample size should be considered before selecting a destructive test.

Time considerations can also be a significant concern in forensic analysis. For identification of an unknown particle as paint, a shorter scheme may suffice. An experienced paint analyst may use physical characteristics alone (e.g. layer sequence, texture, sheen) to identify a particle as paint. Infrared analysis can identify the binder when confirmation is necessary.

For comparison purposes, an analytical approach which examines all main constituents in paint (binder, pigments, volatile components, additives) is sought. The volatile components are not available for comparison once the paint has cured. Additives may be difficult to identify given their proprietary nature and their low concentrations. Each technique will be briefly reviewed, highlighting advantages and limitations, with less emphasis on specific instrument use or operating parameters.

Fluorescence Microscopy Fluorescence microscopy involves the exposure of typically thin peels or cross-sections to specific wavelengths of light where some of that light may be absorbed and re-emitted as fluorescence at a longer wavelength. When conducting a comparison, samples should be mounted side-by-side such that the resulting color and intensity of each layer can be documented and any differences easily observed. A variety of filter sets are commercially available (pairing excitation and barrier filters), but those used for forensic fiber comparisons are also applicable to other polymer types. Short excitation filter wavelengths are used, such as the 300–400 nm wavelengths of the UV region and the 400–500 nm wavelengths of violet and blue regions (Allen 1994). Observed fluorescence may originate from organic pigments, additives, and/or the binder (ASTM 2018a) though specific chemical information is not obtainable. Fluorescence is quick, nondestructive, and requires relatively little sample preparation. It has proven particularly helpful in distinguishing multilayered white architectural layers or automotive primer layers (Ryland et al. 2006). Caution should be employed when discriminating between samples with the use of fluorescence. Fluorescence is a subjective test and slight differences may be explainable due to environmental factors (e.g. sun exposure differences) or a contaminant (e.g. wax).

Infrared Analysis Infrared (IR) spectroscopy is arguably the second most essential tool in forensic paint analysis after stereomicroscopy. Samples are exposed to infrared radiation; as a result of the chemical composition, some of that radiation is absorbed. Ultimately, a graphical representation, or spectrum, is produced plotting the wavelengths or frequency of IR radiation on the x axis versus the intensity of radiation absorbed or transmitted on the y axis. Specific chemical component information on binders, pigments, and additives may be obtained from spectral interpretation (Beveridge et al. 2001; ASTM 2018a).

FTIR is preferable over dispersive IR, and offers a variety of analytical approaches. For example, use of attenuated total reflectance (ATR) accessories results in surface analysis requiring very little if any sample preparation and providing an opportunity to analyze smears in situ. A microscope accessory couples aperture adjustment with the ability to analyze microscopic amounts of sample. This is particularly useful for layer isolations when analyzing cross-sections. If a layer is too thin, the resulting aperture is too small and produces noisy spectra of limited value. Smaller apertures are also negatively impacted by heterogeneity. Here again, proficiency in more than one technique for paint layer exposure is of value. Overall, IR analysis is relatively quick, minimally destructive, and requires fairly little sample preparation (Ryland 1995; Ryland et al. 2006; ASTM 2018b).

As IR radiation must pass through the sample for transmission or absorption measurements, it is important that the sample be thin. Sufficiently thin samples are often accomplished by flattening sections or peels. Hand-tightened compression cells with diamond windows allow for easy sample preparation for the microscope accessory, though a variety of other sample preparation techniques are available. Compression cells flatten the sample between two window faces and provide a convenient sample holder as the window material is non-IR absorbing. Alternatively, sections or peels may be flattened using a roller or other similar technique and placed on a potassium bromide pellet. Over-absorption results from samples which are too thick and is indicated by spectral peaks which fall below 10% transmission or above 1.0 absorbance (ASTM 2018b).

Component identification can confirm a particle is paint, help classify a particular end use (e.g. polyvinyl acetate [PVA] binder in architectural paint), and support chemical discrimination (e.g. sample 1 differs from sample 2 in polyurethane concentration). Component identification is also a critical step when attempting to provide make/model/year information of an automotive paint (see Section 3.5.1) (Ryland 1995; Beveridge et al. 2001; ASTM 2018a).

The application of IR analysis to paints produces significant discrimination power (DP). With the application of IR analysis alone, a DP of 77.3% was found for red spray paints (Govaert and Bernard 2004), 95% for green spray paints (Buzzinni and Massonnet 2004), and 99.1% for black spray paints (Ryland 2010). A discrimination power of as high as 94.45% for single layer white architectural paints was found with IR analysis alone (Wright et al. 2013), and 99.99% for architectural paints when both IR and microscopical examinations were considered together (Wright et al. 2011). Likewise, when applying microscopical and IR examination to automotive paint analysis, a DP of more than 99.99% was calculated from Edmondstone et al.'s work (100 [32 669 discriminated pairs/32 670 possible pairs]) (Edmonstone et al. 2004). Although a high discrimination power is possible with the application of microscopical and IR analysis, typical forensic examinations include additional techniques to gather more information, further increase the discrimination power, and overcome the limitations of IR.

Paints can be complex mixtures rendering spectral interpretation challenging as components may be masked or undetected. Components must be present in quantities of at least 5% by weight for IR detection (Ryland et al. 2006). Many additives do not reach this limit and therefore do not produce absorption bands. Pigments and/or fillers may dominate the spectra in some highly filled architectural paints and primers which can mask peaks attributable to the binder (Ryland et al. 2006). Some pigments, though sensitive to IR, are unable to be identified because their dominant absorbance peaks appear below detector cut-off limits. A compromise between detector sensitivity and cut-off has resulted in detector lower limits generally around 650 cm^{-1}. With many pigment absorption bands below 700 cm^{-1}, these remain undetectable by IR. Identification of pigments such as iron oxide, zinc oxide, and titanium dioxide would require extended-range capability for confident identification based solely on IR spectroscopy (Beveridge et al. 2001; Ryland et al. 2006).

Elemental Analysis Critical for the analysis and comparison of pigments and additives, elemental analysis is employed to characterize the elemental composition of paint. Primarily accomplished with the use of SEM-EDS or X-ray fluorescence (XRF), elemental analysis can support or expand component identification and can provide information about components in lower concentration, though neither alone can identify chemical components.

SEM-EDS is a type of microscopy in which electrons rather than light interact with the sample, and simultaneously provide elemental composition information. The electron beam will displace electrons within the sample, and when a higher energy electron fills the vacancy in an inner shell an X-ray is emitted to release the excess energy. The X-rays emitted are specific to the elements present within the sample. The resultant spectrum depicts the X-ray energy in electron volts on the x axis versus the X-ray counts on the y axis. Relative peak ratios can be compared in addition to peak, or element, presence/absence as X-ray counts are proportional to the concentration of the element present (Ryland and Suzuki 2012).

SEMs are high powered microscopes reaching magnifications of up to 100 000×. Imaging is typically achieved with the use of backscattered electrons, those electrons from the beam which are reflected or scattered back from the sample. A backscattered electron image can provide layer differentiation that may not be visible with other microscopy techniques because higher atomic number elements appear brighter than lower atomic number elements. Component distribution and heterogeneity can be qualitatively evaluated in the resulting image (Ryland and Suzuki 2012; ASTM 2018a).

Sample preparation is critical for data evaluation. Generally, thicker cross-sections or a stair-step layer exposure are employed, though at the risk of electron beam penetration beyond the specific layer of interest. Using thin peels would ensure that data originates from a particular layer, but may result in the loss of elemental data of some minor components. Paint, a non-conducting material, must be pretreated with a coating (i.e. carbon) to dissipate surface charging in high-vacuum instruments. Variable pressure SEMs have the advantage of using air to dissipate the charge, thereby mitigating the need for coating. A tradeoff with variable pressure SEMs is that the partial vacuum causes beam scattering which may result in the detection of elements in adjacent paint layers (Ryland et al. 2006; Ryland and Suzuki 2012; ASTM 2013a).

Sample orientation and surface texture are important factors to consider as well. The orientation relative to the detector is important to prevent the analysis of other layers, and similar orientation between compared samples is desirable. Smooth sample surfaces are necessary for the most consistent peak ratios. The smoothest surface can be achieved by microtoming and polishing after embedding the paint sample in a resinous curing medium (Ryland et al. 2006; Ryland and Suzuki 2012; ASTM 2013a).

SEM-EDS is fast, generally non-destructive, and sensitive to low concentrations (minimum detection limit theoretically ~0.1% by weight for median atomic weight elements with the best optimal conditions, realistically closer to ~1%) (Ryland and Suzuki 2012; Dolak and Weimer 2015). When sample size is limited, SEM-EDS analysis is usually still possible if IR analysis was performed. Samples examined by IR could be transferred to an SEM stub for analysis as needed.

In XRF, X-rays are used to interact with the sample, rather than an electron beam, though the emission process mirrors that of SEM-EDS. As a result, sample charging is not a concern and therefore sample coating is not necessary. The limit of detection is approximately tens of parts per million, lower than SEM-EDS. XRF is preferentially more sensitive to higher atomic weight elements and may miss some of the lower atomic weight elements detectable by SEM-EDS. Larger sample sizes are necessary for XRF than for SEM-EDS and due to greater beam penetration thin peels are the preferred sample preparation technique. Samples for comparison should have similar thicknesses to ensure peak ratio differences are not due to thickness variation. Cross-sections would only be analyzed as a bulk sample since layers cannot be isolated during analysis. Micro-XRF systems allow the analysis of smaller samples but result in a higher minimum detection limit (~0.005% by weight) (Ryland et al. 2006; Ryland and Suzuki 2012).

Pyrolysis Pyrolysis (py) is the breaking apart of chemical bonds using thermal energy in order to detect the resulting fragments. Pyrolysis is a powerful means of discriminating between binders of the same class as well as identifying minor components left unresolved by other techniques (e.g. IR response to high pigment loads).

The decision to use pyrolysis on polymeric samples is based largely on size, condition, and chemical characteristics of the material. Pyrolysis is a destructive technique where replicate analyses are necessary to better evaluate possible variation. Polymers can pyrolyze by different degradation mechanisms depending upon how they were formed. The traditional degradation paths are random scission where fragmentation can occur at any of the carbon-carbon junctures in a long-chain molecule (i.e. polyethylene), side group scission where loss of a side group causes the unsaturated backbone to reform as an aromatic (i.e. poly[vinyl chloride] when HCl is cleaved during heating), and monomer reversion where the starting monomer is cleaved (i.e. methyl methacrylate pyrolyzates from poly[methyl methacrylate]). Wampler's handbook includes chapters that provide sufficient detail on the mechanisms and applications of forensic pyrolysis (2006). Similarly, Tsuge et al.

have provided detailed examples of the pyrograms produced by many types of synthetic polymers (2011).

Pyrolysis is the mechanism for breaking the sample apart. A small amount of sample is rapidly heated in order to minimize degradation and maximize adequate fragmentation. Approximately 10 μg of sample may be sufficient for clear and/or colorless binders; up to 150 μg is preferable for samples with high filler content. Once pyrolysis is completed, the carrier gas (helium or neon) transfers the pyrolyzates to an inert capillary column where the separation and detection process of GC begins. The best practice for pyGC or pyGC/MS of paint systems is to analyze individual paint layers. This process is quite simple for clearcoat automotive paints and spray paints where the available sample size is generally sufficient, able to be sampled cleanly, and ironically, requires very little sample due to the abundance of binder relative to additives. Sampling becomes progressively more important in architectural paint and automotive undercoats (i.e. primers or body fillers in refinish systems) where inorganic pigment loads can be large relative to the amount of binder available. Separation of architectural paint and automotive undercoats can be complicated by multiple layers of like-colored materials that contain different chemical properties. If necessary, complementary layers such as automotive primers can be combined to increase sample size. Relatively proportional amounts of each layer in comparative samples should be carefully attempted.

The majority of forensically significant polymers can be pyrolyzed at temperatures between ~400–800 °C depending upon the degree of desired fragmentation and the properties of the polymer being pyrolyzed (e.g. paint, tape, or a molded polymer). Most laboratories employ a medium polarity GC column if the samples will be further transferred to a mass spectral detection system. Alternatively, two GC columns of differing polarities can be used to obtain two separate chromatographs for comparison (Wampler 2006; Tsuge et al. 2011).

Applications of pyrolysis and its discrimination power specifically with respect to paint systems have been covered extensively by the art conservation community. As for forensic laboratories, there appears to be a lesser tendency to implement pyrolysis, possibly due to its destructive nature, potentially challenging sample preparation, or the perception that the data is not as reproducible as other techniques. A number of published discrimination studies, however, suggest that irreproducibility does not afflict all pyGC methodologies.

Plage et al. found major variations in the type of acrylate or methacrylate used in 25 automotive clearcoats, originating from eight IR classification groupings (2008). As a result, 19 of the samples were able to be further discriminated while three pairs remained undifferentiated. These results indicate that when possible, pyrolysis should be considered in clearcoat layer comparisons.

Further discrimination has also been achieved for architectural paints and spray paints. Wright et al. used pyGC/MS to analyze architectural paint samples left undiscriminated by visual/microscopical examinations, FTIR, and SEM-EDS. One additional sample pairing was discriminated using this technique, again due to differences in acrylate composition. The ten remaining indistinguishable pairs were determined to be comprised of sample sets that shared a common source within each pairing (Wright et al. 2011). In a follow-up study, Wright et al. analyzed single-layered white architectural coatings. Following pyGC/MS analyses on 32 specimens, eight additional paints were discriminated based on formulation differences such as acrylate composition or the presence of phthalic anhydride (Wright et al. 2013). Similarly, Ryland achieved discrimination for two pairs of black spray paints through the use of pyGC equipped with high and low polarity columns and dual detection systems (Ryland 2010).

Russell et al. used pyGC/MS to identify synthetic organic pigments used in a variety of coatings applications. The final pyrolysis temperature for all of the studied pigments was 600 °C with replicate analysis conducted at a final temperature of 800 °C for those samples that failed to fully pyrolyze at the lower temperature. The authors also reported that solvent extraction facilitated analysis of pigment mixtures (Russell et al. 2011). Additionally, Challinor reported on the use of derivative pyrolyzates for elucidating structural features and thereby simplifying the resultant chromatographic profiles. This technique is particularly well suited to alkyd enamels and polyesters (Challinor 2006).

Other Instrumental Techniques

- *Raman*: Though more routine in art conservation work (Deneckere et al. 2012), Raman spectroscopy has been well studied in Europe for forensic polymer examinations and is growing in popularity in North America. The technique is non-destructive and provides complementary, and at times supplementary, binder and pigment information to that obtained by IR. Carbon black, a pigment used in paints and plastics, is identifiable with Raman but not with IR. Raman has the added ability to discriminate between crystalline polymorphs such as anatase and rutile forms of titanium dioxide. Both IR and Raman spectroscopy result from the interaction of molecules with incident light. Whereas the response in IR results from a change in dipole moment (i.e. unequal sharing of electrons in a molecule causing charge separation such that one area is partially positive and another is partially negative), the Raman signal is the inelastic scattering response to a change in polarizability (i.e. the electron cloud of a molecule changing as a function of interaction with an external electric field). Since each technique exploits a different aspect of the interaction of light with matter, they are a natural complement to one another for analysis of polymeric materials. Weak signals in the IR are usually stronger in Raman and strong IR responses (e.g. water) are weak in Raman.

Following the interaction of a monochromatic laser with the sample's electron cloud, excited molecules emit photons to return to the ground state. Most of the emitted photons produced by this interaction are elastically scattered (Rayleigh scattered, of the same energy as the incoming radiation), making the inelastic scattered photons (Raman scattered) a highly inefficient process. Fluorescence can also result, a highly efficient process which can easily overwhelm weak Raman peaks in a spectrum. A number of laser wavelengths are available, though common laser options are green (532 nm), which is a higher energy but can more easily damage a sample, and red (785 nm), which is more gentle on samples, producing less fluorescence and weaker Raman signal. Although costly, having more than one laser can maximize Raman's utility. A variety of methods may be necessary to reduce fluorescence, including decreasing laser power, use of short laser exposures, use of long laser exposures in an attempt to quench the fluorophore, adjusting focus, or switching to a longer wavelength laser (Ryland and Suzuki 2012).

Raman spectroscopy, like IR, is non-destructive for the most part and requires minimal sample preparation if the surface is contaminant free. Thin peels, cross-sections, and stair step exposures can be placed on a potassium bromide or metal substrate (e.g. aluminum foil-covered slide). Flat surfaces are preferable. The coupling of a Raman instrument with a microscope permits focusing on extremely small sample diameters (even 1–3 µm in size) (Buzzini et al. 2006) and allows individual layer analysis of cross-sectioned paint samples.

Raman is not a new technique, but its widespread application to forensic samples has yet to be realized in North America. In 1994, Kuptsov touted Raman's ability to distinguish polymers and minor components in plastic lenses, provide IR-complementary binder information for paints, and more successfully identify paint pigments (Kuptsov 1994). A collection of Raman spectra for organic and inorganic pigments commonly found in paints and other polymers can be found in Palenik et al.'s report along with a classification scheme for pigment identification (2013).

Bell et al. compared architectural paint binders using both IR and Raman to demonstrate the added discrimination power that Raman can provide to binder classification (2005a,b I and II). Additional work by this group reported on the analysis of pigmented paint samples as a means of demonstrating how Raman spectroscopy could provide both complementary organic and inorganic information to IR (Bell et al. 2005c). It should be noted that these studies were all conducted on paint samples prepared in the laboratory on aluminum slides, so environmental effects could not be evaluated. Similar conclusions have been drawn for the analysis of spray paints and automotive coatings and continue to demonstrate the utility of adding Raman to an analytical paint scheme, particularly for small samples (Massonnet and Stoecklein 1999; Suzuki and Carrabba 2001; Buzzinni and Massonnet 2004; Lv et al. 2012; Lambert et al. 2014; Muehlethaler et al. 2014).

- *X-ray diffraction*: Not nearly as common as other analytical techniques for forensic paint analysis, X-ray diffraction (XRD) is best used for the identification of crystalline pigments and extenders. Unlike elemental analysis where inferences are made based on specific element peaks, XRD benefits from the non-destructive identification of crystalline compounds and can often distinguish polymorphs. For example, one may deduce the presence of titanium dioxide through detection of a titanium peak in elemental analysis, but anatase and rutile may be identified and distinguished by XRD. Calcium carbonate is another compound that can be definitively identified by XRD, along with the calcite or aragonite polymorphs which could not be positively identified by SEM-EDS due to the presence of carbon either in an anti-charging coating or in the tape on the sample holder.

When a sample is exposed to a beam of X-rays, crystalline materials within the sample will diffract the beam. The difference in the incident X-ray beam angle and the angle of diffraction is precisely measured as is the intensity of the diffracted beam. Each crystalline phase produces a unique XRD pattern based on the three-dimensional atomic arrangement, allowing component identification (Snider Jr. 2012).

Historical complaints regarding the long analysis times for XRD have been largely alleviated with detector advances (Snider Jr. 2012). Sample preparation remains somewhat of a concern. While many samples do not require much preparation, the size requirement is generally larger than that required for other techniques (i.e. ~20 μm rather than a cross-section or thin peel) (Ryland and Suzuki 2012). The analysis of individual layers is preferred (ASTM 2018a), allowing components to be identified and compared per layer. Concentrations of 1–2% are generally required for detection, though the limit of detection is affected by a number of factors, including the instrumentation, operating conditions, and analyte(s) of interest (Snider Jr. 2012).

- *Microchemical tests*: In the hit-and-run case from 1945 described in the chapter introduction, microchemical testing was critical to the reported association. Even after the introduction of more sophisticated instrumentation, there remains some information that is arguably best achieved via microchemical tests. The low cost associated with microchemical tests along with lack of equipment maintenance, fast testing times, and little sample preparation keep microchemical tests still in use today. Though destructive, very small sample sizes are necessary because chemical tests are best performed under a stereomicroscope, allowing observation of any reaction which may occur.

During microchemical tests, thin peels or cross-sections are typically placed within a spot plate, welled slide, or on a slide. Reagents, acids, and/or solvents are added dropwise or via capillary action and any resulting reactions noted. Reactions include solubility observations as well as any other effect, such as color changes, effervescence (release of air bubbles), or swelling. While generally no specific chemical information is obtained, paints with different pigments or binders will tend to behave differently. Thus, differences in microchemical reactions provide visual discrimination of binder and pigment composition. Background color is again important and it is best to use a color-neutral background or more than one colored background (e.g. black and white).

Microchemical tests also allow some paint classification. Minimal chemicals are necessary to differentiate between enamels, lacquers, and the type of lacquer (see Table 3.4). Dispersion and solution acrylic lacquers differ in cure mechanism. Once in a cured film, only the solution lacquer has cellulose acetate butyrate, a flow controller, though its peaks are masked by acrylic bands in IR analysis (Ryland 1995).

Acids and reagents are best used for side-by-side comparisons and can help distinguish similarly colored layers (e.g. whites). Differing chemical reactions can help establish the number of layers and their relative layer thicknesses. A number of microchemical testing schemes exist and their use often varies from laboratory to laboratory (Thornton 2002; Ryland and Suzuki 2012; Ryland et al. 2006).

- *Microspectrophotometry*: Known by a number of terms (microspec, microspectrometer,

Table 3.4 Microchemical reactions helpful for paint classification

	Chloroform	Acetone	Toluene or Xylene	Diphenylamine Reagent
Enamel	Insoluble	Insoluble	Insoluble	No reaction
Acrylic dispersion lacquer	Soluble	Soluble	Soluble	No reaction
Acrylic solution lacquer	Soluble	Soluble	Insoluble	No reaction
Nitrocellulose lacquer	Insoluble	Soluble	Insoluble	Dark blue

microscope spectrophotometer, etc.), micro-spectrophotometry (MSP) is an instrumental technique generally employed to compare colors. While our eyes are very sensitive to color differences, environmental factors can affect color perception. Color differences are easier to detect when comparing large samples and much harder to distinguish when dealing with very small sample sizes. Metameric pairs may appear the same visually, but can be differentiated with the use of MSP. The MSP can be used to graphically compare the response from microscopic paint samples to the simultaneous exposure of a range of wavelengths. Wavelengths, in the visible range (~380–800 nm) and often extending into the UV range (~190–380 nm), will be absorbed, transmitted, or reflected based on the pigments and additives present in the sample (ASTM 2019e1). If extending into the UV region, it is critical that the microscope be equipped with mirrored or quartz objectives, the sample is mounted using quartz slides and coverslips, and the mounting medium is non-UV absorbing. The resulting graphical representation, or spectrum, plots wavelength on the x axis versus the intensity of light absorbed, transmitted, or reflected on the y axis. Transmission or reflectance techniques are possible, but transmission is favored (Ryland et al. 2006; ASTM 2019e1). Reflectance techniques, while requiring less sample preparation, are limited to wavelengths in the visible range and are problematic due to the influence of surface texture, sample curvature, specular reflection, and diminished spectral reproducibility (ASTM 2019e1;

Ryland and Suzuki 2012). For batch-to-batch discrimination or differences based on concentrations, transmission measurements prevail; however, careful sample preparation is necessary to ensure equivalent section thicknesses in compared samples (Stoecklein 2001; Ryland et al. 2006; ASTM 2019e1; Ryland and Suzuki 2012). Controlled thicknesses of approximately 3 µm for pigmented layers and 20 µm for clearcoats are best achieved with the use of a microtome for cutting embedded samples (ASTM 2019e1).

3.5 Paint Databases

It is difficult to imagine a paint database comprehensive enough to encompass every type of coating that one may encounter in casework. Even within a particular type of paint, no database is complete. Products are forever changing and it is quickly understood that what was once up to date can become outdated rather quickly because manufacturers continuously seek to make their products cheaper, better, and more desirable to the consumer. Through the years, various researchers have embarked on searchable databases, such as Govaert and Bernard's red spray paint library in 2003 or Skenderovska et al.'s FTIR and Raman spectral database of automotive paints (Madariaga 2012). These internal databases are not well maintained or updated, have limited access, and consequently tend to be useful for only very short periods of time. Often manufacturers will create internal libraries of their products as well as their competitors. For this reason, developing manufacturer contacts can be critical to the process of determining a coating's possible end use.

There are some published databases which, due to the publishing process, are more useful for historical information as opposed to the most recent additions to the market. A widely used collection is The Federation of Societies for Coatings Technology's collection of over 2500 pigment, binder, filler, and additive IR spectra (1991). A possible resource for general formulations by category is a 2005 publication by Flick (2005a), which describes over 2500 trade and industrial paint and ink formulations. Similarly, Flick released a cosmetics and toiletries formulations database in the same year which includes more than 10 000 formulations for a number of household products (2005b).

Web-based databases have the ability to be more current, but are mostly devoted to pigments. The open web e-VISART database contains FTIR and Raman spectra of pigments and artist's materials (Castro et al. 2003; Castro and Pérez-Alonso n.d.). The Color of Art Pigment database includes color index names, numbers, and some chemical composition (Myers n.d.). The Infrared and Raman Users Group has a searchable spectral database which includes over 2000 contributed spectra of "artists' and cultural heritage materials" (Infrared & Raman Users Group 1993–2015). Additionally, a mineral database including Raman, FTIR, and XRD spectra is available online from the RRUFF project (Lafuente et al. 2015). Generally, if analysis can yield some pigment information, internet searches or these web-based databases can often serve to exclude or provide direction to a class of pigments, if not to a specific pigment.

The most comprehensive and readily available automotive OEM paint databases to law-enforcement affiliated forensic practitioners are European Union Collection of Automotive Paints (EUCAP) and Paint Data Query (PDQ). EUCAP is maintained by the Bundeskriminalamt (BKA) in Wiesbaden, Germany. In order to access EUCAP, one must be a member of the European Paint and Glass (EPG) Group. PDQ is owned by the Royal Canadian Mounted Police (RCMP) and maintained in Edmonton, Alberta, Canada. In order to access PDQ, a laboratory must be affiliated with a law enforcement organization which is an active partner in the submission of PDQ samples. Fortunately, EUCAP and PDQ have an agreement whereby they share samples obtained from plants in North America, Europe, and Asia. In this way, the most comprehensive set of automotive paint formulations is annually updated. The PDQ database is described more fully in this chapter as the context for the utility of databases particularly in make, model, and model year range investigative lead examinations.

3.5.1 The Royal Canadian Mounted Police Paint Data Query Database

Scientists at the RCMP forensic laboratories demonstrated in studies conducted before 1980 that vehicles could be differentiated by comparing the color, layer sequence, and chemical composition of each individual layer in an OEM paint system (Cartwright and Rodgers 1976; Rodgers et al. 1976a–c I–III). To make those comparisons possible, a database was developed as a means of searching and retrieving the information (Buckle et al. 1997). Today this database, known as PDQ, contains data for over 81 000 individual paint layers collected from over 20 000 paint systems. With approximately 100 PDQ partner laboratories from 22 countries submitting paint samples, PDQ contains samples that represent the paint systems used on most domestic and foreign vehicles marketed in North America, as well as many vehicles marketed abroad. Currently, international partners from Europe, the United Kingdom, Australia, New Zealand, Singapore, South Africa, and the United Arab Emirates submit paint samples for inclusion in the database.

In order to be a PDQ Partner, a forensic laboratory must be affiliated with a recognized, publicly funded police agency, sign a non-disclosure agreement, and submit a minimum of 60 OEM automotive street samples per year. All samples received are assigned a unique PDQ number and catalogued. It is from these sample submissions that a minimum of 500 new samples are selected, analyzed, and added to the database each year.

As described earlier, automotive OEM systems consist of a minimum of one topcoat over one or more primer layers. A typical modern OEM automotive paint system has four layers: a clearcoat over a colored basecoat, over a primer surfacer over an electrodeposited primer or e-coat. Although manufacturing plants in the same geographical region may share a paint formulation for a particular layer from a common supplier (e.g. e-coat, clearcoat), it remains a rare occurrence to have multiple plants that are using chemically indistinguishable layer systems. A single automotive manufacturing plant may use different paint suppliers for each paint layer on a vehicle, where each layer may have its own unique formulation of pigments and binders. This results in a layer system that helps forensic analysts determine the possible make, model, and year range for a vehicle from which a paint chip may have originated.

Figure 3.18 illustrates how the layer sequence for a typical four-layer OEM automotive paint system is designated in the PDQ database. A line is drawn at the interface where the topcoats meet the undercoats, and the layers are numbered sequentially above and below this line. Original topcoats are given

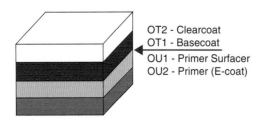

Figure 3.18 Example of layer designators on a typical four-layer OEM automotive paint system.

the prefix OT and original undercoats are given the prefix OU.

Spectra for the database are collected using Thermo Scientific™ Nicolet™ 6700 FTIR spectrometers each equipped with a cesium iodide (CsI) beam splitter and a deuterated triglycine sulfate (DTGS) detector. Thin peels are collected from the middle of each layer and placed in a high pressure diamond anvil cell. The diamond cell is placed in a 6× Harrick beam condenser. Each layer is analyzed over the wavelength range 4000–250 cm^{-1} at a resolution of 4 cm^{-1} and a gain of 8; 100 scans are normally collected for each layer, except for highly reflective metallic basecoats, for which 256 scans are collected. The raw data is used to create a spectral library using Bio-Rad's KnowItAll® software, which must be purchased by each PDQ Partner. This searchable library is distributed along with the PDQ update annually.

Forensic analysts examine an unknown paint chip microscopically and analyze all possible layers by FTIR. If an OEM system is present, spectral interpretation is done on all OEM layers using PDQ guidelines for component identification (see Figure 3.19).

The PDQ Program comprises three components: the PDQi software, the PDQ Spectral Library, and the PDQ Help Line. The PDQ Help Line provides support to all PDQ Partners. The PDQ Maintenance Team is available to assist and consult with spectral interpretation, PDQ searches, spectral searches, and provide opinion reports when requested.

PDQi is a text-based database that contains the complete color, chemical composition, layer sequence, and sourcing information for each of the paint systems in the database along with images of the spectra (see Figure 3.20).

The chemical composition and layer sequence information derived from the examination and analysis of an unknown paint chip by FTIR is entered into PDQ as a search parameter using the *Layer System Query* (see Figure 3.21). Given that basecoat

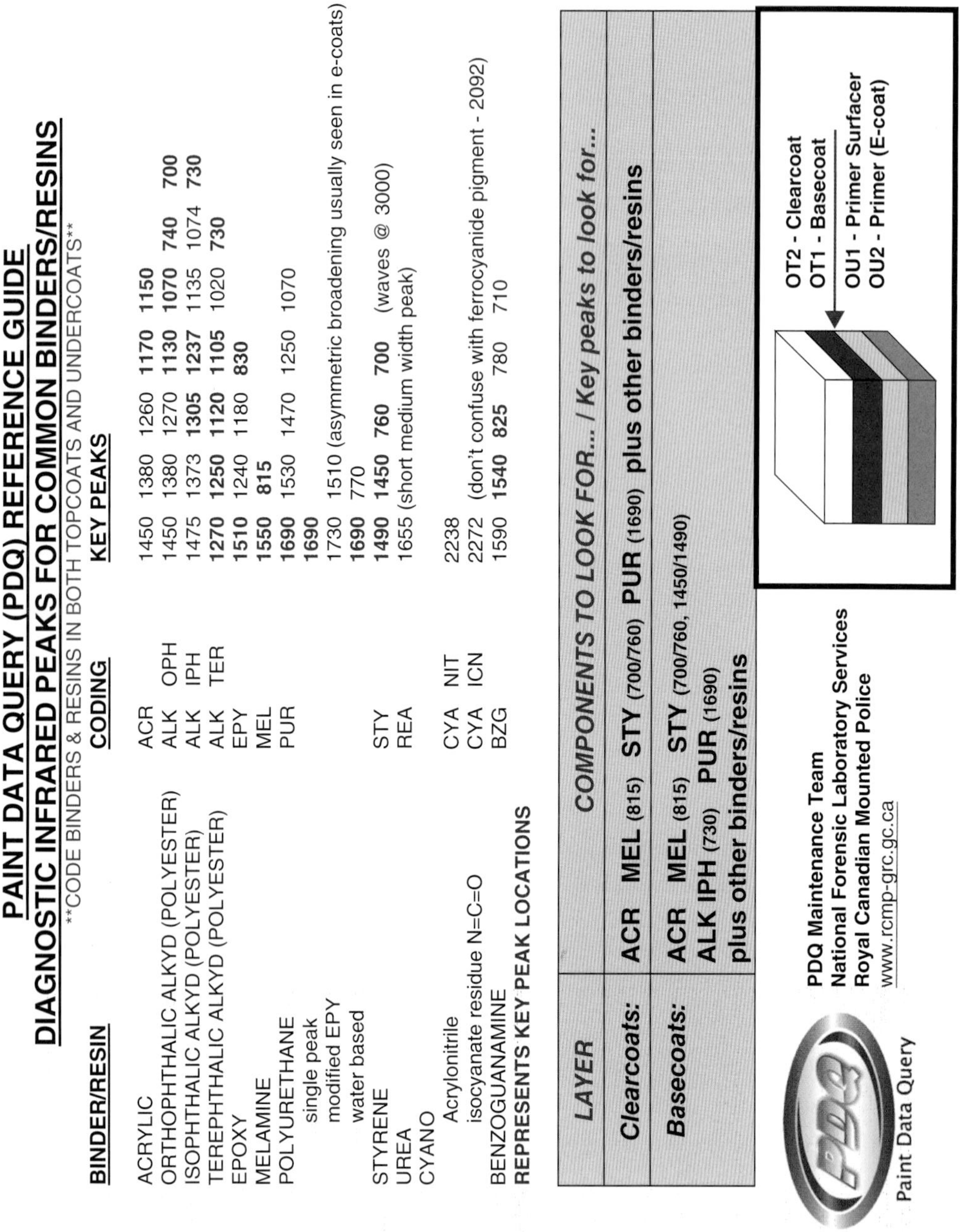

PAINT DATA QUERY (PDQ) REFERENCE GUIDE
DIAGNOSTIC INFRARED PEAKS FOR COMMON BINDERS/RESINS

CODE BINDERS & RESINS IN BOTH TOPCOATS AND UNDERCOATS

BINDER/RESIN	CODING	KEY PEAKS
ACRYLIC	ACR	1450 1380 1260 **1170** **1150**
ORTHOPHTHALIC ALKYD (POLYESTER)	ALK OPH	1450 1380 1270 **1130** **1070** **740** **700**
ISOPHTHALIC ALKYD (POLYESTER)	ALK IPH	1475 1373 **1305** **1237** 1135 1074 **730**
TEREPHTHALIC ALKYD (POLYESTER)	ALK TER	1270 **1250** **1120** **1105** 1020 **730**
EPOXY	EPY	**1510** 1240 1180 **830**
MELAMINE	MEL	**1550** **815**
POLYURETHANE	PUR	**1690** 1530 1470 1250 1070
single peak		**1690**
modified EPY		1730 1510 (asymmetric broadening usually seen in e-coats)
water based		**1690** 770
STYRENE	STY	**1490** **1450** **760** **700** (waves @ 3000)
UREA	REA	1655 (short medium width peak)
CYANO		
Acrylonitrile	CYA NIT	2238
isocyanate residue N=C=O	CYA ICN	2272 (don't confuse with ferrocyanide pigment - 2092)
BENZOGUANAMINE	BZG	1590 **1540** 825 780 710

REPRESENTS KEY PEAK LOCATIONS

LAYER	COMPONENTS TO LOOK FOR... / Key peaks to look for...
Clearcoats:	ACR MEL (815) STY (700/760) PUR (1690) plus other binders/resins
Basecoats:	ACR MEL (815) STY (700/760, 1450/1490) ALK IPH (730) PUR (1690) plus other binders/resins

OT2 - Clearcoat
OT1 - Basecoat
OU1 - Primer Surfacer
OU2 - Primer (E-coat)

PDQ Maintenance Team
National Forensic Laboratory Services
Royal Canadian Mounted Police
www.rcmp-grc.gc.ca

Paint Data Query

Figure 3.19 PDQ reference guide, an aid to coding binders and pigments in automotive paint for PDQi purposes.

layer chemistry can vary within a single plant depending on the hue and pigments, it is advised that the basecoat not be included in the layer system query search. Once layers have been entered, the software searches the database comparing all records for samples having a similar paint system to the unknown to generate a "hit list" (see Figure 3.22). The "hit list" is a text-based pre-screen of the database.

PAINT DATA QUERY (PDQ) REFERENCE GUIDE
DIAGNOSTIC INFRARED PEAKS FOR COMMON PIGMENTS/EXTENDERS
CODE PIGMENTS & EXTENDERS IN UNDERCOAT LAYERS ONLY

OT2 - Clearcoat
OT1 - Basecoat
OU1 - Primer Surfacer
OU2 - Primer (E-coat)

PIGMENT AND EXTENDER	CODING			KEY PEAKS									
CALCIUM CARBONATE	CAR	CAC											
Aragonite	CAR	CAC	ARA	1445	870	857	712	317					
Calcite	CAR	CAC	CAL	1445	870		712	317					
CHROMATE	CHR												
Potassium Zinc	CHR	KZC		950	880	805							
Strontium	CHR	SCH		911	887	875	844						
OXIDE	OXI												
Iron Oxide (Red)	OXI	FEO	RED	560–530	480–440	350–310							
Iron Oxide (Yellow)	OXI	FEO	YEL	899	797	606	405	278					
SILICON DIOXIDE	OXI	SIO											
Opal, diatomaceous silica	OXI	SIO	OPA	1099	795	475							
Quartz	OXI	SIO	QUA	1081	798	779	512	460	397	373			
TITANIUM DIOXIDE	OXI	TIO											
Rutile	OXI	TIO	RUT										
ZINC PHOSPHATE	PHO	ZNP		600 (Broad suppression)		410	340						
SILICATE	SIL			1120	1080	1020	950	630					
Magnesium (Talc)	SIL	MGS	TAL	3676	1015	670	465	450	420	390	345		
Aluminum (Kaolinite)	SIL	ALS	KAO	3695	3620	1035	1005	940	915	540	470	430	350 280
BARIUM SULPHATE	SUL	BAS		1174	1115	1080	984	630	610				

REPRESENTS KEY PEAK LOCATIONS

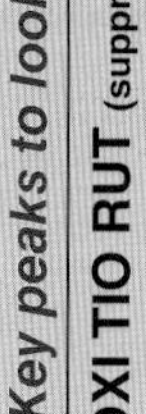

LAYER	COMPONENTS TO LOOK FOR… / Key peaks to look for…
Primer surfacer:	ALK's (730 or 740) MEL (815) EPY (830 and 1510 trace) OXI TIO RUT (suppression 600) SIL's (3600 region) SUL BAS (980 and 630/610 doublet), PUR plus other binders, resins, pigments & extenders
E-coat:	EPY (830) OXI TIO RUT (huge 600) SIL ALS KAO (3600 region) PUR (1730 and 1510 asymmetry) PHO ZNP (950), SUL BAS (newer) plus other binders, resins, pigments and extenders

SPECTRAL STANDARDS CAN BE FOUND IN PDQi UNDER LOOKUP TABLES, LAYER CHEMISTRY

Figure 3.19 (*Continued*)

Any information that is captured in a PDQi record is searchable. A *Fill In The Blank* (FITB) query can be performed to mine the data available in the PDQ database, such as determining the number of vehicles in PDQ from a given plant, year, manufacturer, or from a specific topcoat color of interest. A FITB search can aid in locating reference samples as well as providing a list of vehicle models that were produced at a particular plant during a specific

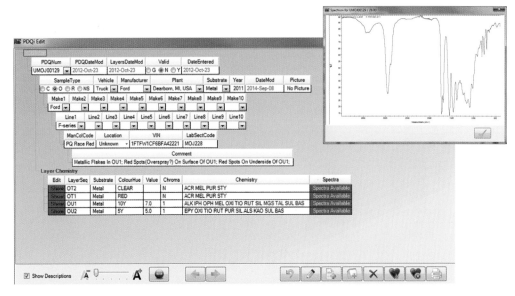

Figure 3.20 A PDQ record capturing source information, layer sequence, chemistry, and images of the spectra for each layer.

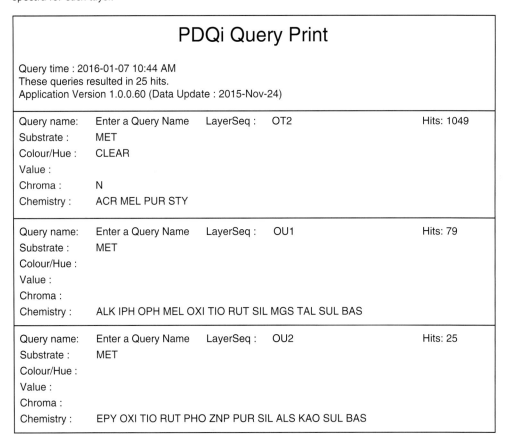

Figure 3.21 Parameters of a layer system query search.

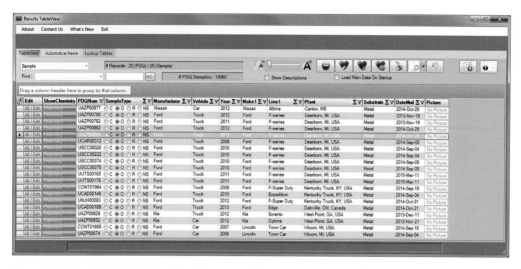

Figure 3.22 The PDQ Hit List is a list of known vehicles that are similar in layer sequence and in chemistry to the unknown paint sample.

year range. This function can also be used to search through PDQ's inventory of nearly 50 000 physical paint samples in the event a specific make/model/year and color is needed for comparison to an unknown. Physical samples are available to agency partners on an "as needed" basis and may be requested via the PDQ help line for direct comparisons.

The PDQ Spectral Library contains the FTIR spectra for each paint layer present in the PDQ database. By conducting a combination search of the FTIR spectrum of an unknown paint layer along with the plant and year information obtained from a PDQ search "hit list," analysts perform spectral comparisons to exclude manufacturing plants that have differences in chemistry or relative amounts of chemical components in one or more layers. Those hits that cannot be eliminated must be considered a possible source of the unknown paint system.

Single layer spectral searches can also be done by searching an unknown layer against the PDQ Spectral Library or subgroups of specific layer types. For example, an unknown clearcoat can be searched against a subgroup of clearcoats in the library. Likewise, the same could be performed with primers and e-coats.

Alternatively, multi-layer spectral searching, a feature added in the KnowItAll 2013 software release, allows an analyst to search more than one layer simultaneously against the appropriate subgroups in the PDQ Spectral Library. For instance, an analyst may load and search the spectrum of a clearcoat, a primer and an e-coat of an unknown paint system, and the software will then return full systems that are most similar to the unknown. Multilayer searches can be used to confirm or test a working PDQ hit list.

Once a possible assembly plant and year range has been developed, manufacturing information can be used to determine makes and models produced. For plants located in North America, manufacturing information can be found under the "Automotive News" tab where production information is reprinted by permission of Crain Communications, Inc. For plants outside of North America, PDQi can be used to perform FITB searches to view the samples in the database from a specified plant and year range. Internet searches or contacts with manufacturing representatives may also be helpful.

A paint chip may be compared to refinish pages such as those produced by DuPont, PPG, and BASF. These books are published annually and contain color chips representing the colors available by manufacturer (and sometimes models) produced each year. By identifying a likely color code, it may be possible to further narrow a year range or model list based on color availability and usage information.

PDQ is not a comprehensive population database. It does not contain data on all vehicles produced, all paint systems used on different substrates or vehicle areas, nor does it contain all topcoat colors, trial run paints, or information on all batch differences. PDQ is a representative database, therefore the potential hits are limited by what is in the database.

With the possibility of multiple types of substrates on a single vehicle including metal, plastic, and fiberglass, there may be multiple paint systems on a single vehicle. Paint systems applied to each type must be specifically formulated for the substrate. This allows the application of flexible paints on flexible parts and more rigid paints where there is less likely to be flex in the substrate. Many plastic and fiberglass parts are received pre-primed at the manufacturing plant or pre-painted if the plant is not equipped with facilities to paint plastic substrates. This makes narrowing down a manufacturing plant or identifying a manufacturer more difficult when performing searches on paint systems on vehicle substrates other than metal.

3.6 Interpretation and Report Considerations

Limited research exists to indicate how long transferred paints or polymers persist once they have deposited onto a surface. Willis et al. hypothesize paint and glass fragments persist for a similar duration (Willis et al. 2001). They report the majority of glass particles, including the larger ones, are lost within the first 30 minutes, with continual loses for 8 hours following transfer. Based on Buzzini et al.'s research on crowbars, cross-transfers of paint can be expected between prying tools and wooden surfaces (Buzzini et al. 2005). Prying simulations with crowbars were performed in repetition resulting in transferred paint retention following three subsequent uses. Therefore, retention on tool surfaces allows the opportunity for secondary transfers, or in this scenario, for foreign paint on the tool to transfer in a later use.

Frequency of occurrence surveys have demonstrated that the vast majority of paint particles retained on garments are single-layered and less than $1\,mm \times 1\,mm$ in size (Lau et al. 1997; Moore et al. 2012). Two-layered particles are more than three times less likely to be present, with successively less representation of three-, four- or more layered particles. Further, paint particles larger in size and number are more likely found in garment pockets when compared to those from exterior surfaces (Moore et al. 2012). Though more research could be helpful with regards to transfer and persistence, the analyst still must be able to evaluate the significance of any associations in a report format.

In the late 2000s, there was a shift in thinking with regards to report writing. Some argue it was precipitated by the National Academy of Science's (NAS) Report "Strengthening Forensic Science in the United States: A Path Forward" (National Research Council 2009). Significant points that were made during this time included the inconsistent reporting of the methodologies used in laboratory reports, inconsistent use and/or misinterpretation of report terminology, misuse of forensic reports in court, and the misunderstanding of report significance due to the absence of conclusion(s) strength. Comparative associations can vary in strength based on a variety of factors, including the quantity and quality of evidence and the commonness of the evidence type in the environment. The shift in thinking caused by the NAS report and/or its aftermath has emphasized the responsibility of relaying the strength of conclusion in the report wording such that a police officer, investigator, attorney, judge, or juror can understand its significance.

The North American trace evidence community began seeking an interpretation approach that lends consistency to report language. At the 2009 Trace Evidence Symposium, Christopher Bommarito presented an interpretation approach he had been developing and implementing for several years (Bommarito 2009). In this "Tiers of Association" model, all possible tiers, along with the one selected, are provided to the reader for context in describing the relative strength of the reported association. In 2011, significance in reports was further addressed by the American Society of Crime Laboratory Directors/Laboratory Accreditation Board's (ASCLD/LAB) Supplemental Requirements adding "When associations are made, the significance of the association shall be communicated clearly and qualified properly in the test report" (ASCLD/LAB 2011). It was roughly at this point that the original Bommarito Scale, colloquially named after the presenter, propagated. Many state, local, and federal laboratory systems have since adopted the Bommarito Scale tiers or levels of association, making some accommodations to best fit their system. A similar approach was also adopted by Germany's BKA.

A benefit to using levels of association is that minimal case knowledge is needed for interpretation as conclusions are drawn from the evidence itself. Having a range of possible conclusions provides the analyst context to explain limitations or added significance based on the evidence at hand. Once the conclusion has been rendered and the interpretation has been presented within the context of the possible conclusions that could be reached, further statements to justify why the analyst believes that the interpretation is appropriate can be provided. The justification is the link between the findings and the knowledge (of the manufacturing process, transfer, and persistence, etc.) that the analyst has developed for a particular trace material. Providing the rationale for the conclusion as well as the entire range of possible conclusions is intended to facilitate significance assessments.

Furthermore, when two or more different paints, polymers, or materials are undifferentiated within a given case, additional statements can be added to the report to explain that the significance of the association(s) may be increased by the presence of multiple materials transferring in one direction or by the cross-transfer of materials (e.g. a two-way transfer). An example of a cross-transfer, in addition to that described in Figure 3.13, would be the exchange of automotive paint between different colored vehicles. Statements which draw attention to and describe the increased significance of the presence of multiple associations or a cross-transfer are important. These statements serve to inform the reader that given multiple associations, a coincidental transfer of materials between two unrelated objects is less likely than contact having occurred between the two considered sources.

In a scaled approach to interpretation, there are at least four categories: (i) physical match, (ii) associations of evidence with class characteristics, (iii) inconclusive, and (iv) elimination/exclusion. A physical match is the strongest association possible with paint or other polymeric evidence. Inconclusive means no conclusion could be reached regarding an association or elimination between the items because there is not enough information. For elimination or exclusion, an exclusionary difference was found in physical properties and/or chemical composition between the items confirming they did not originate from the same source. In the absence of a physical match, but with no exclusionary differences detected, the paint analyst describes the strength of association between items based on the specific class characteristics present.

Associations of evidence with class characteristics require sub-categories in order to account for the breadth of scenarios that can be common to trace evidence, particularly paint. Generally the following association sub-categories are included: one with atypical characteristics, one with typical characteristics, and one with limited characteristics or examinations. With each of these levels of association, no individual source, to the exclusion of all others, can be determined. The questioned paint or polymer could have come from the submitted known source or any other source with the same properties. These associations with examples can be seen in Table 3.5.

There can be instances where characteristics are neither typical nor atypical. For example, the presence of OEM repair layers within an automotive paint system is not commonplace but is not unexpected either. Research supports the rate of OEM repair to be roughly 8% of vehicles (Wright and Mehltretter 2015). Given that a typical production year yields over 16 million vehicles in North America alone, the presence of an OEM repair is certainly random and not the preferred OEM coating process; however, it can be expected to occur on occasion and in that sense is not as atypical as the use of non-automotive coatings for refinishing. In a comparison of two paint systems containing the same number, color, sequence, and chemical composition of OEM repair layers, the use of additional language in the report to convey the unusual aspects of the associated items would be appropriate to convey an association beyond that which is typically encountered.

Within the scale approach to interpretation, there is scope for two analysts to choose different levels of association regarding the same evidence. This result could seem

Table 3.5 Associations of evidence and examples

Conclusion	Examples
Physical match	– Corresponding individual characteristics indicating that items were once part of the same larger entity/polymeric system
Association with atypical characteristics: shared unusual features that are unlikely to be encountered in the "typical" population of like materials	– Architectural paint layers on automotive paint chips – Aftermarket automotive refinish layers above OEM layers – Defect that is consistent between two compared polymers but cannot be physically realigned – Unusual features that are not a deliberate part of the manufacturing process and would not be expected or controlled in the mass production of these materials
Association with typical characteristics: other items have been manufactured which share the properties and may likely be encountered in the population of like materials	– Portions from mass-produced items that exhibit no differences (OEM automotive paints, tool paint, bike paint, plastic fragments with morphology, buttons, etc.) – Can range from single layers of architectural paint to multiple layers of OEM repair on top of a standard OEM system – Added significance of unusual features (e.g. color, extra OEM layers, cross-transfer) could be conveyed with additional statements of interpretation
Association with limited characteristics/examinations: there are a limited number of characteristics or a limited analysis is performed due to condition and therefore the strength of the reported association must convey those limitations	– Polymers that have few attributes available for comparison (e.g. fragments that lack physical features attributable or applicable to end use, are clear/colorless, and when analyzed are of a common polymeric class such as polystyrene or polyethylene) – An OEM automotive paint where only some of the layers are available for comparison – Sample too small or too contaminated to conduct the full typical analytical suite of examinations
Inconclusive	– Insufficient known sample provided and unable to evaluate heterogeneity – Smearing of layers prevents layer isolation and the ability to assess the significance of chemical differences
Elimination	– Exclusionary differences including, but not limited to, those found in color, texture, pigments (size, distribution, type, etc.), or layer chemistry

counterintuitive and undermine the process of "standardizing" report language and interpretation. However, with the appropriate caveats and justifications for the significance chosen for the opinions rendered, it is reasonable to allow for this apparent difference in report writing. For example, consider a scenario where two analysts independently conduct comparisons on OEM paint chips that contain multiple factory repair topcoats. After the application of all available analytical techniques, one analyst reports an association with typical characteristics and uses additional statements to convey increased significance based on the additional factory repair topcoat layers. The other analyst reports an association with atypical characteristics based on the presence of the factory repair layers and an uncommon topcoat color. The uncommon color further limits the available population of OEM vehicles which contain this particular layer system. Both conclusions are deemed appropriate and reasonable by the technical reviewer(s). The important factor is whether each analyst appropriately articulated justification for the respective association reported. This same logic would be flawed, however, if wildly disparate conclusions were reported for the same set of samples (e.g. an association versus elimination or the difference between a physical match versus a class association). However, within the context of class associations, suitably stated justifications for a conclusion versus its nearest neighbor should be permissible.

Regardless of how common or unusual a paint system or polymer appears to an analyst, the most critical aspect of the examination is how it is reported and interpreted by that analyst. It cannot be assumed that even a technical reviewer will derive the same interpretation from the stated results if the writer does not clearly indicate what is intended by the significance that is conveyed. Worse, if no significance is conveyed, any reader, technical or not can easily misinterpret what is meant by the conclusion. As an example, there is not much that can be stated about a clear, colorless polymeric fragment with no discernible physical features, regardless of whether the

report is comparing unknown polymers or discussing the classification/identification of a polymer. For example, a reported classification/identification conclusion might read as follows:

> Item X was identified as polystyrene based on the following analytical techniques: visual and microscopical examinations, Fourier transform infrared spectroscopy (FTIR), and pyrolysis gas chromatography with mass spectral detection (PyGC/MS). No physical features were observed to determine the manufacturer or end use of Item X. However, polystyrene is commonly used in the manufacture of CD jewel cases, disposable food containers and cutlery, as well as other mass produced commercially available materials.

While this information may seem too vague or already available to the general public, it does give some context to what item X may not be attributable to and may serve to inform a reader not familiar with technical reports. Regardless as to how context and interpretative significance is conveyed to the reader, it is important to provide the reader with context as well as the results and methodology used to derive those results.

As in North America, there has been considerable discussion in Europe and Australia regarding ways to interpret trace evidence results in an objective manner. In contrast to a scale approach, the European Network of Forensic Science Institutes (ENFSI) has adopted an approach that uses statistics-based likelihood ratios. Likelihood ratios attempt to provide the probability or degree of support, given the forensic findings, for one theory of events versus at least one other. These theories of events often originate from the prosecution and defense propositions regarding the accused's involvement in the crime. ENFSI has published a guide to the use of likelihood ratios in forensic sciences and it is this model that ENFSI working groups will advance in their approach to report writing interpretation (2015). Likelihood ratios and by extension Bayesian statistics have not gained as much popularity worldwide for trace evidence because they require approximations to be made and/or comprehensive relevant databases and greater knowledge of the details of the case than what the trace analyst is usually privy to. See Chapter 7 for a more thorough discussion of this approach to interpretation.

In developing ways to provide report context, some laboratories have a slightly different perspective regarding the scale approach. One derivative approach, for example, is the use of a verbal support scale, such as weak support, moderate support, moderately strong support, strong support, very strong support, and extremely strong support. The verbal support scale has also been used to convey a particular likelihood ratio range (e.g. >1–10 = weak support) when it is not possible to calculate a numerical likelihood ratio (Mullen et al. 2014; ENFSI 2015; Martire and Watkins 2015). Users of this significance assessment system may or may not provide the entire scale and/or the numerical context in the written report or testimony. Studies have reported that this version of interpretation has been misunderstood by laypersons (Mullen et al. 2014; Martire and Watkins 2015), though this version of interpretation is one of the few interpretation models that has been studied in this manner. Therefore, the unflattering aspects of the reported perceptions are not necessarily exclusive to this version of significance assessments.

It is still difficult to determine the best approach to interpreting trace evidence results for a lay audience. It seems logical that working toward consistency is a key aspect of whatever system is chosen. That consistency must begin with a single analyst in terms of a written report today versus one that will be written at a later date where all other factors are equivalent. Likewise, how the results will be interpreted by the technical reviewer must align with how the writer intended the significance to be interpreted, such that either could testify to the results in court without changing the intended meaning. Once a level of consistency can be incorporated into a discipline in one laboratory system, it will be easier to develop foundational arguments that allow other disciplines and/or laboratory systems to work together to better align laboratory reports and the language used in them.

Disclaimer

This is publication number 16-07 of the FBI Laboratory Division. Names of commercial manufacturers are provided for identification purposes only, and inclusion does not imply endorsement of the manufacturer, or its products or services by the FBI. The views expressed are those of the authors and do not necessarily reflect the official policy or position of the FBI or the U.S. Government.

Additional Reading

See the accumulated bibliography provided by SWGMAT in Paint Daubert Final – Appendix A (available on www.asteetrace.org, in SWGMAT option on the Resources Tab, under Paint Subgroup).

References

3M Europe (2015). 3M™ Wrap film series 1080 product bulletin. http://multimedia.3m.com/mws/media/731671O/product-bulletin-1080.pdf (accessed 9 August 2015).

Aardahl, K., Kirkowski, S., and Blackledge, R. (2005). A target glitter study. *Science and Justice* 45 (1): 7–12.

Allen, T. (1994). *Effects of Environmental Factors on the Fluorescence of White Alkyd Paint*. Aldermaston, UK: Home Office Central Research Establishment.

American Coatings Association. (2016, April). ACA and PaintCare®: steering a post-consumer paint solution. Issue Backgrounder 24(1).

American Society of Trace Evidence Examiners (2018). New terminology to be aware of – 'quadcoat'. *ASTEE Newsletter* (February), p. 10.

Anon (1937). Scientific evidence in a bombing case: identification of wire, tape, etc.; determination of type of explosive used. *Journal of Criminal Law and Criminology* 27 (5): 739–740.

Anon (1940). Microscopic evidence: the analysis of fibers, soil and paint in a burglary case. *Journal of Criminal Law and Criminology* 30 (5): 768.

Anon. (2007). Making license plates (Florida State Prison). https://www.youtube.com/watch?v=oklKAMEOT7I (accessed 5 July 2015).

ASCLD/LAB (2011). *Supplemental Requirements*. ASCLD/LAB.

ASTM (2019e1). *E2808-19e1: Standard Guide for Microspectrophotometry and Color Measurement in Forensic Paint Analysis*. West Conshohocken: ASTM International.

ASTM (2013a). *E2809-13 Standard Guide for Using Scanning Electron Microscopy/X-Ray Spectrometry in Forensic Paint Examinations*. West Conshohocken: ASTM International.

ASTM (2018b). *E2937-18 Standard Guide for Using Infrared Spectroscopy in Forensic Paint Examinations*. West Conshohocken: ASTM International.

ASTM (2018a). *E1610-18 Standard Guide for Forensic Paint Analysis and Comparison*. West Conshohocken: ASTM International.

Bell, S., Fido, L., Speers, S. et al. (2005a). Forensic analysis of architectural finishes using Fourier transform infrared and Raman spectroscopy: I, the resin bases. *Applied Spectroscopy* 59 (11): 1333–1339.

Bell, S., Fido, L., Speers, S. et al. (2005b). Forensic analysis of architectural finishes using Fourier transform infrared and Raman spectroscopy: II. White paint. *Applied Spectroscopy* 59 (11): 1340–1346.

Bell, S., Fido, L., Speers, S., and Armstrong, W. (2005c). Rapid forensic analysis and identification of "lilac" architectural finishes using Raman spectroscopy. *Applied Spectroscopy* 59 (1): 100–108.

Bentley, J. (2001). Composition, manufacture and use of paint. In: *Forensic Examination of Glass and Paint: Analysis and Interpretation* (ed. B. Caddy), 123–141. New York: Taylor & Francis.

Beveridge, A., Fung, T., and MacDougall, D. (2001). Use of infrared spectroscopy for the characterisation of paint fragments. In: *Forensic Examination of Glass and Paint: Analysis and Interpretation* (ed. B. Caddy), 183–242. New York: Taylor & Francis.

Bily, C. (2010). The evidence is in the bag. *Evidence Technology Magazine* (July–August), pp. 22–27.

Blackledge, R. and Jones, E. Jr., (2007). All that glitters is gold! In: *Forensic Analysis on the Cutting Edge: New Methods for Trace Evidence Analysis* (ed. R. Blackledge), 1–32. Hoboken: Wiley.

BMR. (2018, June 5). Boomerang recycled paint – How is it made? [YouTube video]. BMR. Retrieved from https://www.youtube.com/watch?v=SX0Z7X6qby0 (accessed 10 March 2020).

Bommarito, C. (2009). Significance of report writing presentation. http://projects.nfstc.org/trace/2009/day2.htm (accessed 13 September 2015).

Braun, J. (2012). White pigments. In: *Paint and Coating Testing Manual*, 15e (ed. J. Koleske), 185–203. West Conshohocken: ASTM International.

von Bremen, U. and Blunt, L. (1982). Physical comparison of plastic garbage bags and sandwich bags. *Journal of Forensic Sciences* 28 (3): 644–654.

Bruzek, J. (2012). BMW's matte paint requires sharp attention. https://www.cars.com/articles/2012/11/bmws-matte-paint-requires-sharp-attention (accessed 9 August 2015).

Buckle, J., MacDougall, D., and Grant, R. (1997). PDQ – paint data queries: the history and technology behind the development of the Royal Canadian Mounted Police Forensic Science Laboratory Services automotive paint database. *Canadian Society of Forensic Science Journal* 30 (4): 199–212.

Buzzini, P., Massonnet, G., Birrer, S. et al. (2005). Survey of crowbar and household paints in burglary cases – population studies, transfer, and interpretation. *Forensic Science International* 152 (2–3): 221–234.

Buzzini, P., Massonnet, G., and Sermier, F. (2006). The micro Raman analysis of paint evidence in criminalistics: case studies. *Journal of Raman Spectroscopy* 37 (9): 922–931.

Buzzinni, P. and Massonnet, G. (2004). A market study of green spray paints by Fourier transform infrared (FTIR) and Raman spectroscopy. *Science and Justice* 44 (3): 123–131.

CanadaPaintExport (2009). CanadaPaintExport recycled paint. [YouTube video]. CanadaPaintExport. Retrieved from https://www.youtube.com/watch?v=w9U5dH4D7XA ().

Cartwright, N. and Rodgers, P. (1976). A proposed data base for the identification of automotive paint. *Canadian Society of Forensic Science Journal* 9 (4): 145–154.

Castle, D., Gibbins, B., and Hamer, P. (1994). Physical methods for examining and comparing transparent plastic bags and cling films. *Journal of the Forensic Science Society* 34 (1): 61–68.

Castro, K. and Pérez-Alonso, M. (n.d.). Welcome to e-vibrational spectroscopic databases. http://www.ehu.eus/udps/database/database1.html; login: spectra, password: database (accessed 12 September 2015).

Castro, K., Pérez, M., Dolores Rodríguez-Laso, M., and Madariaga, J. (2003). FTIR spectra database of inorganic art materials. *Analytical Chemistry* 75 (9): 214A–221A.

Causin, V. (2015). *Polymers on the Crime Scene: Forensic Analysis of Polymeric Trace Evidence*. Basel: Springer International Publishing.

Challinor, J. (2006). Examination of forensic evidence. In: *Applied Pyrolysis Handbook* (ed. T. Wampler), 175–199. Boca Raton: CRC Press.

Cortner, G. and Hamman, J. (1996). Physical match: a focus on its forensic use and interpretation in criminal cases. *TIELINE* 20 (1): 32–49.

Crown, D. (1968). *The Forensic Examination of Paints and Pigments*. Springfield: Charles C Thomas.

Deneckere, A., Vandenabeele, P., and Moens, L. (2012). Vibrational spectroscopy as a tool for tracing art forgeries. In: *Infrared and Raman Spectroscopy in Forensic Science* (eds. J.M. Chalmers, H.G.M. Edwards and M.D. Hargreaves), 369–381. Chichester: Wiley.

Deschamps, C., Bemert, L., Gibbs, H., and Groteklaes, M. (2013). Permanent hydrophobic and easy-to-clean effects. *European Coatings Journal* 7 (8): 34–39.

Dolak, E. and Weimer, R. (2015). The physical and chemical characterization of multipurpose architectural paint. *Journal of the American Society of Trace Evidence Examiners* 6 (3): 21–45.

Dössel, K. (2008a). Top coats. In: *Automotive Paints and Coatings*, 2e (eds. H. Streitberger and K. Dössel), 175–210. Weinheim: Wiley-VCH Verlag GmbH & Co. KGaA.

Dössel, K. (2008b). In-plant repairs. In: *Automotive Paints and Coatings*, 2e (eds. H. Streitberger and K. Dössel), 377–380. Weinheim: Wiley-VCH Verlag GmbH & Co. KGaA.

Edmonstone, G., Hellman, J., Legate, K. et al. (2004). An assessment of the evidential value of automotive paint comparisons. *Canadian Society of Forensic Science Journal* 37 (3): 147–153.

Ehinger, E., Moyle, R. and Simpson, M. (2008). High-performance 'green' pretreatment. *PCI Magazine*. http://www.pcimag.com/articles/95435-high-performance-green-pretreatment (accessed 10 August 2015).

Encyclopaedia Britannica (2015). Styrene-acrylonitrile copolymer (SAN). http://academic.eb.com.proxy.library.vcu.edu/EBchecked/topic/570375/styrene-acrylonitrile-copolymer (accessed 14 June 2015).

EPA (n.d.). Protect your family. http://www2.epa
.gov/lead/protect-your-family (accessed 20
June 2015).

Eppler, R. (2012). Extender pigments. In: *Paint
and Coating Testing Manual*, 15e (ed. J.
Koleske), 242–249. West Conshohocken:
ASTM International.

Esteves, A. and Garcia, S. (2015). Self-healing
polymeric coatings. In: *Functional Polymer
Coatings: Principles, Methods, and
Applications* (eds. L. Wu and J. Baghdachi),
133–162. Hoboken: Wiley.

European Network of Forensic Science Institutes
(ENFSI) (2015). *ENFSI Guideline for
Evaluative Reporting in Forensic Science*.
ENFSI.

Federation of Societies for Coatings Technology
(1991). *An Infrared Spectroscopy Atlas for the
Coatings Industry*, 4e. Blue Bell: Federation of
Societies for Coatings Technology.

Ferguson, R. (2012). Metallic pigments. In: *Paint
and Coating Testing Manual*, 15e (ed. J.
Koleske), 250–255. West Conshohocken:
ASTM International.

Firth, J. (1945). Forensic science. *Journal of the
Royal Society of Arts* 93 (4689): 228–244.

Flick, E. (2005a). *Cosmetics & Toiletries
Formulations Database*. Norwich: William
Andrew Publishing.

Flick, E. (2005b). *Paint and Ink Formulations
Database*. Norwich: William Andrew
Publishing.

Fuller, W. (1973). *Federation Series on Coatings
Technology, Unit One: Introduction to Coatings
Technology*. Philadelphia, PA: Federation of
Societies for Paint Technology.

Gates, K. (2015). The effect of pigment type on
pigment variation due to differential mixing in
spray paints. *Journal of the American Society of
Trace Evidence Examiners* 6 (2):
3–16.

Gehmecker, H. (2008). Pretreatment of
multimetal car bodies. In: *Automotive Paints
and Coatings*, 2e (eds. H. Streitberger and K.
Dössel), 61–87. Weinheim: Wiley-VCH Verlag
GmbH & Co. KGaA.

Glasurit (n.d.). Orange-peel effect. http://www
.glasurit.com/uk/orange-peel-effect (accessed
14 September 2015).

Govaert, F. and Bernard, M. (2004).
Discriminating red spray paints by optical
microscopy, Fourier transform infrared
spectroscopy, and X-ray fluorescence. *Forensic
Science International* 140 (1): 61–70.

Green Planet Films (2014). Recycling paint. In:
Curiosity Quest Goes Green [Television Series].
San Francisco, CA: Kanopy Streaming.

Green Seal (2013). *GS-43 Green Seal Standard for
Recycled Latext Paint*. Washington, DC: Green
Seal, Inc.

Gross, S., Igowsky, K., and Pangerl, E. (2010).
Glitter as a source of trace evidence. *Journal of
the American Society of Trace Evidence
Examiners* 1 (1): 62–72.

Gross, S., Duevet, R., Wilson, J., and Almirall, J.
(2015). Evaluation of automotive lenses for
forensic applications by FTIR, PGC, and
Raman spectroscopy. *Journal of the American
Association of Trace Evidence Examiners* 6 (2):
27–54.

Guy, A. (2004a). Coatings components beyond
binders. In: *The Chemistry and Physics of
Coatings*, 2e (ed. A. Marrion), 267–316.
Cambridge: The Royal Society of Chemistry.

Guy, A. (2004b). The science and art of paint
formulation. In: *The Chemistry and Physics of
Coatings*, 2e (ed. A. Marrion), 317–359.
Cambridge: The Royal Society of Chemistry.

Hansen, D. (n.d.). Painting versus polishing of
airplane exterior surfaces. http://www.boeing
.com/commercial/aeromagazine/aero_05/
textonly/fo01txt.html (accessed 19 November
2015).

Hardin, J. (2011). Study module 3 composite
materials for boat building. Presented at
Grady White Boats, Greenville, NC,
November 8, 2011.

Hare, C. (1989). Materials technology: anatomy
of paint. *Journal of Protective Coatings &
Linings* 6 (11): 89–102.

Harris, F. (1981). Introduction to polymer
chemistry. *Journal of Chemical Education*
58 (11): 837–843.

Harris, T. (n.d.). How paintball works. http://
entertainment.howstuffworks.com/paintball
.htm (accessed 5 July 2015).

Hegedus, C., Spadafora, S., Eng, A. et al. (2012).
Aerospace and aircraft coatings. In: *Paint and
Coating Testing Manual*, 15e (ed. J. Koleske),
739–749. West Conshohocken: ASTM
International.

Holmes, G.S. (n.d.). How products are made:
license plate. Made how. http://www
.madehow.com/Volume-5/License-Plate.html
(accessed 5 July 2015).

How It's Made (2013). Paintballs. https://www
.youtube.com/watch?v=3AKrzgUSsoA
(accessed 5 July 2015).

Imam, J. (2015). San francisco starts using
'pee-proof' paint to stop public urination.
http://www.cnn.com/2015/07/25/us/san-
francisco-pee-proof-paint (accessed 8 August
2015).

Infrared & Raman Users Group (1993–2015).
About the IRUG spectral database initiative.
http://www.irug.org/about-us/the-database
(accessed 12 September 2015).

J.D. Power and Associates (n.d.). J.D. power and
associates reports: manufacturers and retailers
are making it easier for do-it-yourself painters
to succeed. http://www.jdpower.com/
content/press-release/3OBtPvN/2012-u-s-
interior-paint-satisfaction-study.htm
(accessed 4 July 2015).

Katterwe, H. (2005). Fracture matching and
repetitive experiments: a contribution of
validation. *AFTE Journal* 37 (3):
229–241.

Kawaoka, K. (1984). *Characterization of Polymers
by Pyrolysis-Gas Chromatography-Mass
Spectrometry*, 39–49. Quantico: U.S.
Department of Justice, Federal Bureau of
Investigation.

Kemmann, K. (2010). *Forensic Analysis of
Architectural, Industrial, and Marine Coatings*.
Quantico: Federal Bureau of Investigation.

Koehler, A. (1937). Technique used in tracing the
Lindbergh kidnaping ladder. *Journal of
Criminal Law and Criminology* 27 (5):
712–724.

Krausher, C. (1994). Characteristics of aerosol
paint transfer and dispersal. *Canadian Society
of Forensic Science Journal* 27 (3): 125–142.

Krylova, I. (2001). Painting by electrodeposition
on the eve of the 21st century. *Progress in
Organic Coatings* 42 (3-4): 119–131.

Kuptsov, A. (1994). Applications of Fourier
transform Raman spectroscopy in forensic
science. *Journal of Forensic Sciences* 39 (2):
305–318.

Lafuente, B., Downs, R.T., Yang, H., and Stone,
N. (2015). The power of databases: the RRUFF
project. In: *Highlights in Mineralogical
Crystallography* (eds. T. Armbruster and R.M.
Danisi), 1–30. Berlin: W. De Gruyter http://
rruff.info/about/downloads/HMC1-30.pdf.

Lambert, D., Cyril, M., Gueissaz, L., and
Genevieve, M. (2014). Raman analysis of
multilayer automotive paints in forensic
science: measurement variability and depth
profile. *Journal of Raman Spectroscopy*
45 (11–12): 1285–1292.

Lau, L., Beveridge, A., Callowhill, B. et al. (1997).
The frequency of occurrence of paint and glass
on the clothing of high school students.
Canadian Society of Forensic Science Journal
30 (4): 233–240.

Listman, D. (2004). Paintball injuries in children:
more than meets the eye. *Pediatrics* 113 (1):
e15–e18.

Look, M. (2009). Recycling mysteries: paint.
Earth911. Retrieved from https://earth911
.com/home-garden/recycling-mysteries-paint
(accessed 16 July 2019).

Low, M. (1969). Infrared Fourier transform
spectroscopy. *Analytical Chemistry* 41 (6):
97A–108a.

Lv, J., Feng, J., Liu, Y. et al. (2012).
Discriminating paints with different clay
additives in forensic analysis of automotive
coatings by FT-IR and Raman spectroscopy.
Spectroscopy 27 (4): 36–43.

MacGregor, R. (2011). Does self-healing car paint
really exist? http://www.theglobeandmail
.com/globe-drive/culture/commuting/does-
self-healing-car-paint-really-exist/
article622334 (accessed 19 September 2015).

Madariaga, J. (2012). Identification of dyes and pigments by vibrational spectroscopy. In: *Infrared and Raman Spectroscopy in Forensic Science*, 1e (eds. J. Chalmers, H. Edwards and M. Hargreaves), 383–399. Chichester: Wiley.

Maile, F., Pfaff, G., and Reynders, P. (2005). Effect pigments – past, present and future. *Progress in Organic Coatings* 54 (3): 150–163.

Marrion, A. (2004). Application and applications. In: *The Chemistry and Physics of Coatings*, 2e (ed. A. Marrion), 347–359. Cambridge: The Royal Society of Chemistry.

Marsh, L. (2007). Some call it art: case studies investigating the spraying of illegal graffiti in the uk. http://projects.nfstc.org/trace/docs/final/marsh.pdf (accessed 9 August 2015).

Martire, K. and Watkins, I. (2015). Perception problems of the verbal scale: a reanalysis and application of a membership function approach. *Science and Justice* 55 (4): 264–273.

Massonnet, G. and Stoecklein, W. (1999). Identification of organic pigments in coatings: applications to red automotive topcoats: Part III: Raman spectroscopy (NIR FT-Raman). *Science and Justice* 39 (3): 181–187.

Mauri, M., Dibbanti, M., Calzavara, M. et al. (2013). Time domain nuclear magnetic resonance: a key complementary technique for the forensic differentiation of foam traces. *Analytical Methods* 5 (17): 4336–4344.

McCrone, W., McCrone, L., and Delly, J. (1984). *Polarized Light Microscopy*. Chicago: McCrone Research Institute.

McNorton, S., Nutter, G., and Siegel, J. (2008). The characterization of automobile body fillers. *Journal of Forensic Sciences* 53 (1): 116–124.

Montemayor, R. and Yuhas, S. Jr., (2012). Solvents. In: *Paint and Coating Testing Manual*, 15e (ed. Koleske), 149–182. West Conshohocken: ASTM International.

Moore, R., Kingsbury, D., Bunford, J., and Tucker, V. (2012). A survey of paint flakes on the clothing of persons suspected of involvement in crime. *Science and Justice* 52 (2): 96–101.

Morell, S. (n.d.). Metallic pigments – the science of optics. http://www.spmorell.com/newsletters/metallic_pigments/metallic_pigments.html (accessed 20 August 2015).

Morgans, W. (1982). *Outlines of Paint Technology: Materials*. New York: Wiley.

Morgans, W. (1984). *Outlines of Paint Technology: Finished Products*. New York: Wiley.

Muehlethaler, C., Massonnet, G., and Buzzini, P. (2014). Influence of the shaking time on the forensic analysis of FTIR and Raman spectra of spray paints. *Forensic Science International* 237 (4): 78–85.

Mullen, C., Spence, D., Moxey, L., and Jamieson, A. (2014). Perception problems of the verbal scale. *Science and Justice* 54 (2): 154–158.

Myers, D. (n.d.). The art is creation: color of art pigment database. http://www.artiscreation.com/Color_index_names.html (accessed 12 September 2015).

National Research Council (2009). *Strengthening Forensic Science in the United States: A Path Forward*. Washington: National Academy of Sciences.

Nichols, M., Gerlock, J., and Smith, C. (1997). Rates of photooxidation induced crosslinking and chain scission in thermoset polymer coatings – I. *Polymer Degradation and Stability* 56 (1): 81–91.

Nissan News Release (2014). Nissan develops first "self-cleaning" car prototype. http://nissannews.com/en-US/nissan/usa/releases/nissan-develops-first-self-cleaning-car-prototype (accessed 8 August 2015).

Nissen, C. (1934). Recent criminal cases. *Journal of Criminal Law and Criminology* 24 (5): 960–962.

Noack, R. (2015). When peeing in public in this german city, beware walls that pee back. https://www.washingtonpost.com/news/worldviews/wp/2015/03/12/when-peeing-in-public-in-this-german-city-beware-walls-that-pee-back (accessed 8 August 2015).

Nowak, P. (2012). Effect pigments. In: *Paint and Coating Testing Manual*, 15e (ed. J. Koleske), 256–271. West Conshohocken: ASTM International.

Olderiks, M., Baiker, M., van Velzen, J., and van der Weerd, J. (2015). Recovery of spray paint traces from clothing by beating. *Journal of Forensic Sciences* 60 (2): 428–434.

Olson, K. and Schuenemann, M. (2015) Shaping the future with easy-to-clean coated car surfaces: global trends, vision and dream. http://cannes.surcarcongress.com/discover-the-winners-of-surcar-cannes-2015 (accessed 17 August 2015).

Olveira, S., Stojanovic, A., and Seeger, S. (2015). Superhydrophilic and superamphiphilic coatings. In: *Functional Polymer Coatings: Principles, Methods, and Applications* (eds. L. Wu and J. Baghdachi), 96–132. Hoboken: Wiley.

Ouroussoff, N. (2005). A forest of pillars, recalling the unimaginable. http://www.nytimes.com/2005/05/09/arts/design/a-forest-of-pillars-recalling-the-unimaginable.html (accessed 8 August 2015).

Palenik, C., Palenik, S., Groves, E., and Herb, J. (2013). *Raman Spectroscopy of Automotive and Architectural Paints: In Situ Pigment Identification and Evidentiary Significance.* Washington, DC: National Institutes of Justice.

Parsons, N. and Mountain, C. (2007). Investigating polyurethane foam as a form of trace evidence. *Science and Justice* 47 (1): 24–33.

Parsons, N., Lam, M., Hamilton, S., and Hui, F. (2010). A preliminary investigation into the comparison of dissolution/digestion techniques for the chemical characterization of polyurethane foam. *Science and Justice* 50 (4): 177–181.

Parsons, N., Lam, M., and Hamilton, S. (2013). Chemical characterization of automotive polyurethane foam using solid-phase microextraction and gas chromatography-mass spectrometry. *Journal of Forensic Sciences* 58 (S1): S186–S191.

PhysOrg.com (2005). Scratches no match for nissan's new car paint. http://www.physorg.com/printnews.php?newsid=8675 (accessed 19 December 2005).

Pierce, D. (1990). Identifiable markings on plastics. *Journal of Forensic Identification* 40 (2): 51–59.

Plage, B., Berg, A., and Luhn, S. (2008). The discrimination of automotive clear coats by pyrolysis-gas chromatography/mass spectrometry and comparison of samples by a chromatogram library software. *Forensic Science International* 177 (2–3): 146–152.

Popa, B. (2011). Automotive magic: self-healing car paint. http://www.autoevolution.com/news/automotive-magic-self-healing-car-paint-41252.html (accessed 19 September 2015).

Postek, M., Howard, K., Johnson, A., and McMichael, K. (1980). *Scanning Electron Microscopy: A Student's Handbook* (ed. M.T. Postek Jr.,). Ladd Research Industries, Inc.

Prane, J. (1986). *Federation Series on Coatings Technology: Introduction to Polymers and Resins.* Philadelphia: Federation of Societies for Coatings Technology.

Reed, G., Lofts, C., and Coyle, T. (2010). A population study of polyurethane foam fragments recovered from the surface of 100 outer-garments. *Science and Justice* 50 (3): 127–137.

Rodgers, P., Cameron, R., Cartwright, N. et al. (1976a). The classification of automotive paint by diamond window infrared spectrophotometry. Part I: binders and pigments. *Canadian Society of Forensic Science Journal* 9 (1): 1–14.

Rodgers, P., Cameron, R., Cartwright, N. et al. (1976b). The classification of automotive paint by diamond window infrared spectrophotometry. Part II. Automotive topcoats and undercoats. *Canadian Society of Forensic Science Journal* 9 (2): 49–68.

Rodgers, P., Cameron, R., Cartwright, N. et al. (1976c). The classification of automotive paint by diamond window infrared spectrophotometry. Part III. Case histories. *Canadian Society of Forensic Science Journal* 9 (3): 103–111.

Russell, J., Singer, B., and Perry, J. (2011). The identification of synthetic organic pigments in modern paints and modern paintings using pyrolysis-gas chromatography-mass spectrometry. *Analytical and Bioanalytical Chemistry* 400 (5): 1473–1491.

Ryland, S. (1995). Infrared microspectroscopy of forensic paint evidence. In: *Practical Guide to Infrared Microspectroscopy* (ed. H. Humecki), 163–243. New York: Marcel Dekker, Inc.

Ryland, S. (2010). Discrimination of retail black spray paints. *Journal of the American Society of Trace Evidence Examiners* 1 (2): 109–126.

Ryland, S. and Houck, M. (2001). Only circumstantial evidence. In: *Mute Witnesses: Trace Evidence Analysis* (ed. M. Houck), 117–138. San Diego: Academic Press.

Ryland, S. and Suzuki, E. (2012). Analysis of paint evidence. In: *Forensic Chemistry Handbook* (ed. L. Kobilinsky), 131–224. Hoboken: Wiley.

Ryland, S., Jergovich, T., and Kirkbride, K. (2006). Current trends in forensic paint examination. *Forensic Science Review* 18 (2): 97–117.

Sakr, S. (2014). Nissan's dirt-phobic paint keeps a car spotless for the duration of a PR video. http://www.engadget.com/tag/paint/http:// www.engadget.com/2014/04/25/nissan-ultra-ever-dry-self-cleaning-paint (accessed 8 August 2015).

Schuster, J. (2004). Free paint! Like new! *Painting & Wallcovering Contractor I* 66 (5): 14.

Scientific Working Group for Materials Analysis (SWGMAT) (2011a). Forensic fiber examination guidelines: introduction to forensic fiber examination. http://swgmat .org/Introduction%20to%20Fibers%20Chapter %202011%20update.pdf (accessed 16 June 2015). Now available here: https://drive .google.com/file/d/0B1RLIs_ mYm7eaGRJUHEyRnhOSTA/view.

Scientific Working Group for Materials Analysis (SWGMAT) (2011b). Guideline for forensic examination of pressure sensitive tapes. *Journal of the American Society of Trace Evidence Examiners* 2 (1): 88–97.

Sim, Y., Koh, A., Lim, S., and Yew, S. (2015). Snap-lock bags with red band: a study of manufacturing characteristics, thermal and chemical properties. *Forensic Science International* 255 (10): 50–55.

Simko, S., Schneider, B., Tardiff, J. et al. (2009). Characterization of zirconium oxide-based pretreatment coatings Part 1 – variability in coating deposition on different metal substrates. *SAE International Journal of Materials and Manufacturing* 2 (1): 416–424.

Siu, J. (2015). 2016 dodge viper now available with matte paint finishes. http://www .autoguide.com/auto-news/2015/06/2016-dodge-viper-now-available-with-matte-paint-finishes.html (accessed 9 August 2015).

Snider, A. Jr., (2012). X-ray analysis. In: *Paint and Coating Testing Manual*, 15e (ed. J. Koleske), 920–940. West Conshohocken: ASTM International.

Soliant (n.d.). Fluorex® paintfilms: it's all about the finish. http://www.paintfilm.com/pdf/ brochure-soliant.pdf (accessed 9 August 2015).

Sterling Paintballs (2011). Making paintballs. https://www.youtube.com/watch? v=PAmy2W1eaaw (accessed 5 July 2015).

Stoecklein, W. (2001). The role of colour and microscopic techniques for the characterisation of paint fragments. In: *Forensic Examination of Glass and Paint: Analysis and Interpretation* (ed. B. Caddy), 143–164. New York: Taylor & Francis.

Streitberger, H. (2008a). Introduction. In: *Automotive Paints and Coatings*, 2e (eds. H. Streitberger and K. Dössel), 1–11. Weinheim: Wiley-VCH Verlag GmbH & Co. KGaA.

Streitberger, H. (2008b). Electrodeposition coatings. In: *Automotive Paints and Coatings*, 2e (eds. H. Streitberger and K. Dössel), 89–127. Weinheim: Wiley-VCH Verlag GmbH & Co. KGaA.

Su, C. (2012). A simple and cost-effective method for fabricating lotus-effect composite coatings. *Journal of Coatings Technology and Research* 9 (2): 135–141.

Suzuki, E. and Carrabba, M. (2001). In situ identification and analysis of automotive paint pigments using line segment excitation Raman spectroscopy: I. inorganic topcoat pigments. *Journal of Forensic Sciences* 46 (5): 1053–1069.

Thornton, J. (2002). Forensic paint examination. In: *Forensic Science Handbook*, 2e (ed. R. Saferstein), 429–478. Upper Saddle River: Prentice Hall.

Tokic, A. (2010). Smart wraps up the fortwo with customized vehicle wraps. http://www .autoguide.com/auto-news/2010/07/smart-wraps-up-the-fortwo-with-customized-vehicle-wraps.html (accessed 9 August 2015).

Tsuge, S., Ohtani, H., and Watanabe, C. (2011). *Pyrolysis-GC/MS Data Book of Synthetic Polymers*. Oxford: Elsevier.

U.S. Customs and Border Protection (2007). What every member of the trade community should know about: decals, decorative stickers and "window clings". http://permanent .access.gpo.gov/LPS112057/LPS112057_icp87 .pdf (accessed 5 July 2015).

Vanderkolk, J. (1995). Identifying consecutively made garbage bags through manufactured characteristics. *Journal of Forensic Identification* 45 (1): 38–50.

VanHoven, H. and Fraysier, H. (1983). The matching of automotive paint chips by surface striation alignment. *Journal of Forensic Sciences* 27 (2): 463–467.

Vergne, M., Hercules, D., and Lattimer, R. (2007). A developmental history of polymer mass spectrometry. *Journal of Chemical Education* 84 (1): 81–90.

Vernoud, L., Bechtel, H., Martin, M. et al. (2011). Characterization of multilayered glitter particles using synchrotron FT-IR microscopy. *Forensic Science International* 210 (1): 47–51.

Wampler, T. (2006). *Applied Pyrolysis Handbook*. Boca Raton: CRC Press/Taylor and Francis Group.

Warnon, J. (2004). Present and future coatings legislation and the drive to compliance. In: *The Chemistry and Physics of Coatings*, 2e (ed. A. Marrion), 8–25. Cambridge: The Royal Society of Chemistry.

Wicks, Z. Jr.,, Jones, F., Pappas, S., and Wicks, D. (2007). *Organic Coatings: Science and Technology*, 3e. Hoboken: Wiley.

Wiggins, K., Emes, A., and Brackley, L. (2002). The transfer and persistence of small fragments polyurethane foam onto clothing. *Science and Justice* 42 (2): 105–110.

Willis, S., McCullough, J., and McDermott, S. (2001). The interpretation of paint evidence. In: *Forensic Examination of Glass and Paint: Analysis and Interpretation* (ed. B. Caddy), 273–287. New York: Taylor & Francis.

Wood, C. (2012). Hyundai veloster turbo gets 201-HP, matte-gray paint: 2012 detroit auto show. http://www.autoguide.com/auto-news/ 2012/01/hyundai-veloster-turbo-gets-201-hp-matte-gray-paint-2012-detroit-auto-show .html (accessed 9 August 2015).

Woodward, A. (n.d.). How products are made: paintball. http://www.madehow.com/ Volume-6/Paintball.html (accessed 5 July 2015).

Wright, D. (2010). A make-model-year case involving unusual primer chemistry and good resources. *Journal of the American Society of Trace Evidence Examiners* 1 (2): 137–148.

Wright, D. and Mehltretter, A. (2015). The prevalence of original equipment manufacturer (OEM) factory repairs in automotive paint samples. *Journal of the American Society of Trace Evidence Examiners* 6 (3): 4–20.

Wright, D., Bradley, M., and Mehltretter, A. (2011). Analysis and discrimination of architectural paint samples via a population study. *Forensic Science International* 209 (1): 86–95.

Wright, D., Bradley, M., and Mehltretter, A. (2013). Analysis and discrimination of single-layer white architectural paint samples. *Journal of Forensic Sciences* 58 (2): 358–364.

Zeichner, A., Levin, N., and Landau, E. (1992). A study of paint coat characteristics produced by spray paints from shaken and nonshaken spray cans. *Journal of Forensic Sciences* 37 (2): 542–555.

4

Forensic Hair Microscopy

Jason C. Beckert

Microtrace, LLC

4.1 Introduction

This chapter will focus on the microscopical examination of hair in the forensic domain. The relevant biological aspects of hair will be discussed to provide the necessary background information upon which forensic hair examinations are based. With this foundation in place, the chapter will focus on the methodologies and techniques used by forensic hair examiners. Finally, the interpretation and significance of the results obtained through a microscopical hair examination will be considered along with the limitations of the technique.

4.1.1 History

The scientific study of hair has a long history. Its microscopical examination can be traced back to the dawn of the field and the seminal text *Micrographia* by Robert Hooke (Hooke 1665). From these auspicious beginnings, our knowledge of hair has grown through the efforts of scientists encompassing a wide variety of disciplines over the centuries. The earliest advances in our understanding of the form and structure of hair were primarily brought about by medical doctors, anatomists, anthropologists, and zoologists. While their

understanding was incomplete, as ours is now, it is rather amazing to realize how much was known by the second half of the nineteenth century (Browne 1853; Leonard 1879).

Significant numbers of research papers were published in peer-reviewed journals beginning in the 1920s. Two of the most prolific authors of this early period were Dr. Leon Augustus Hausman, a zoologist, and Dr. Mildred Trotter, an anatomist and anthropologist. Dr. Hausman was interested in the microscopic structure of both animal and human hair, publishing at least 23 papers between 1920 and 1944.[1] Unsurprisingly, Dr. Trotter and many other anthropologists were interested primarily in human hair. Much of their work dealt with describing basic hair morphology and characterizing the hair of various populations or ethnic groups.

As with all other scientific endeavors, our knowledge of hair has steadily increased with the passage of time. The scientific disciplines that laid the initial foundation of knowledge were augmented by chemists, histologists, molecular biologists, mycologists, cosmetic scientists, textile scientists, environmental scientists, toxicologists, and criminalists, among

---

1 Dr. Hausman was not limited to academic endeavors as he applied his knowledge to several forensic cases during his career (Anon 1950).

Handbook of Trace Evidence Analysis, First Edition. Edited by Vincent J. Desiderio, Chris E. Taylor, and Niamh Nic Daéid.
© 2021 John Wiley & Sons Ltd. Published 2021 by John Wiley & Sons Ltd.

others, in the pursuit of elucidating all that there is to know about hair. With all these interested parties, the number of publications regarding the scientific examination of hair has increased dramatically over time. The modern forensic scientist would be wise to study the work of those who came before them, for there is much to learn.[2]

While the potential utility of hair regarding criminal investigations dates to at least the seventeenth century, its value wasn't demonstrated until the middle of the nineteenth century (i.e. essentially contemporaneous with the birth of forensic science) (Thorwald 1967). In one of the first recorded applications of hair microscopy to a criminal case, hairs on the suspected murder weapon were determined to be of animal origin, eventually leading to the acquittal of the accused (Ollivier 1838).[3]

A rudimentary description of a microscopical hair comparison involving two suspected eyebrow hairs recovered from a hammer and the known eyebrow hairs of the victim was reported in England in 1851 (Anon 1851). An interesting aspect of this case was the opinion put forth at trial that the hairs on the hammer were "bruised or partly divided, as if squeezed between two blunt substances." This was an early demonstration of the ability of microscopy to provide contextual information regarding the history of the hairs in question.

More thoroughly described case studies of microscopical hair comparisons appeared in the French literature a few years later (Lassaigne 1857; Robin 1858). In the latter case, bloody hairs recovered from the doorway of the decedent's house were determined to be consistent with known head hairs of the victim. This indicated that the victim was initially

attacked at his house, and not in the field in which he was found.

The limitations of microscopical hair comparisons were described as early as 1861 in Germany, when Rudolf Virchow determined that while questioned hairs recovered from a defendant's handkerchief were indistinguishable from the known hairs of the victim, including the presence of lice eggs, it could not be claimed that the unknown hairs definitively originated from the victim (Marx 1906). This opinion was reaffirmed a few years later in a review of forensic hair microscopy (Oesterlen 1873). In short, it has been understood for over 150 years that microscopical hair examinations do not result in individualization (i.e. it cannot be said that any given questioned hair originates from a specific person based upon microscopy alone).

In another milestone case, Dr. Paul Jeserich of Westphalia (in modern-day Germany) examined a hair recovered from a murdered woman originally believed to have originated from the beard of a male suspect (Anon 1895). Dr. Jeserich determined that the unknown hair was most likely a dog hair, clearing the original suspect. His further characterization of the suspected dog hair provided investigative leads to the police which resulted in the naming of another suspect. Hairs from this suspect's dog were determined to be indistinguishable from the hair recovered from the body, and this second suspect subsequently confessed to the crime.

The forensic examination of hair has continued uninterrupted since the pioneering scientists initially demonstrated its ability to answer a variety of questions relating to legal matters. Books recognizing the utility of hair identification regarding forensic matters became widely available in the first half of the twentieth century, e.g. Lambert and Balthazard (1910)[4] and Glaister (1931). Near the end of the century, reviews of forensic

---

2 There are literally thousands of books, academic papers, reports, etc. that focus on the scientific study of hair.

3 It is worth noting that this examination was conducted in court using a hand lens by a physician who merely happened to be present at the time.

4 Dr. Victor Balthazard's analysis of hair played a critical role in the highly publicized investigation into the murder of Germaine Bichon (Thorwald 1967).

hair examination were published in several now canonical sources (e.g. Seta et al. (1988), Robertson (1999), and Bisbing (2002)[5]).

The interest in the forensic examination of hair has historically been a world-wide endeavor with significant contributions emanating from across the globe (e.g. the US, Canada, the UK, France, Germany, Russia, Japan, and Australia). In the United States, forensic hair examinations have been a fixture of crime laboratories for more than half a century.

At least a portion of this adoption can be traced to Dr. Paul Leland Kirk, a professor of biochemistry and criminalistics at the University of California, Berkeley, widely considered to be the "father of criminalistics" in the United States.[6] A proponent of the forensic examination of hair, he authored or co-authored numerous scientific papers on the forensic aspects of hair analysis and he devoted a chapter of his classic book to the subject (Kirk 1940, 1953; Gamble and Kirk 1941; Greenwell et al. 1941; Kirk and Gamble 1942; Goin et al. 1952). His journal articles focus on attempts to identify several physical characteristics that could be used to distinguish hair samples, with the ultimate goal being hair individualization. These properties (including refractive index, density, and scale count[7]) are quantifiable features which can be measured on individual hairs and then compared to ranges obtained from known samples. While the use of these features to compare hairs has generally fallen out of favor for a variety of reasons, they are worth noting because they attempted to develop objective measures to discriminate hairs from different individuals. However,

Kirk also recognized that the forensic analysis of hair was not limited to establishing identify, and that vital facts could be determined through the careful examination of the hairs themselves (Kirk 1953). This important point is often lost on those who only evaluate the strengths and limitations of forensic hair comparisons.

Throughout the twentieth century, the forensic examination of hair was established as one of the core disciplines in trace evidence sections across the country, and warranted its own SWGMAT[8] subgroup which produced guidelines regarding examination and training (SWGMAT 2005).

The early twenty-first century is shaping up to be a pivotal time in the history of forensic hair microscopy. The value of microscopical hair comparisons has been repeatedly questioned, and its continued widespread application to criminal matters may be in jeopardy. However, the fact remains that the examination of hair continues to provide valuable, often critical, information to a wide variety of forensic investigations.

4.2 Chemistry and Histology

4.2.1 Basic Chemistry

Hairs are composed primarily of protein, specifically keratins.[9] Keratins are a group of fibrous, sulfur-containing polyamides found in many vertebrate groups. Mammalian tissues are composed of alpha-keratins while other groups (e.g. birds and reptiles) utilize both alpha- and beta-keratins (Alibardi et al. 2009). In addition to hair, numerous mammalian

---

5 This chapter was originally published in the first edition of the *Forensic Science Handbook* in 1982.
6 The Paul L. Kirk award is the highest recognition bestowed to trace evidence scientists by the criminalistics section of the American Academy of Forensic Sciences.
7 The value of scale counts to distinguish hairs from different individuals was both supported and disputed by other contemporary scientists (Beeman 1942; Beeman 1943; Trotter and Duggins 1950).

8 Scientific Working Group for Materials Analysis. The Scientific Working Groups were reorganized under the National Institute of Standards and Technology's (NIST) Organization of Scientific Area Committees (OSAC).
9 Human hair is composed of approximately 65–95% protein with water (up to 32% by weight) being the primary cause for the wide variation. Lipids ($\sim$1–9%), melanin (i.e. pigments), and trace elements (<1%) are also found in hair (Robbins 2002).

structures including skin, horns, nails/claws, hooves, quills, and baleen are composed of keratinized tissue (Marshall et al. 1991).

Hairs are remarkably stable tissues, both chemically and physically. In the appropriate conditions, they can persist for thousands of years, nearly unchanged, even at the ultra-structural level (Wu and Wang 1980). This stability is one of the characteristics that make hairs well-suited as forensic trace evidence.

Twenty-one amino acids have been identified in human hair (Robbins 2002).[10] One of the defining chemical characteristics of hair is the relatively high concentration of the sulfur-containing compound cystine. Cystine is a dimer composed of two cysteine amino acids joined together by a disulfide bond. These disulfide bonds have a large influence on the three-dimensional morphology, mechanical strength, and elasticity of hair (Marshall et al. 1991). Additionally, their ability to be broken and reformed is the basis for intentional cosmetic changes altering hair conformation (e.g. curling and straightening).

The conversion of cystine to cysteic acid is one of the key means of measuring the degradation of hair. It has been demonstrated to occur in a wide variety of conditions, including sunlight weathering, bleaching, and permanent waving (Robbins 2002).

However, because all true hairs have the same basic chemistry, it is generally not practical to differentiate them using chemical techniques, although this is an area of active research (Goodpastor et al. 2003; Manheim et al. 2016).[11]

4.2.2 Basic Histology

Hairs may appear relatively simple when viewed macroscopically but they are actually

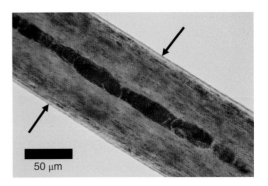

Figure 4.1 Human head hair exhibiting a distinct cuticle (arrows), cortex, and medulla (mounted in xylene and viewed using transmitted light).

complex composite structures. The first hint of this complexity can be observed when hairs are viewed using transmitted light with a compound microscope. Three main histological layers are typically found in hair: the cuticle, the cortex, and the medulla (Figure 4.1).[12] These layers can be recognized on the basis of their microscopic morphology and they impart different properties to the hair shaft as they are both chemically and structurally distinct. While not visible as a distinct layer, the cell membrane complex (CMC) represents a fourth major histological component of hair. Its primary function is to hold other cellular structures together.

A common analogy relates the hair shaft to a pencil (Bisbing 2002). The cuticle of the hair is analogous to the thin layer of paint on the surface of the pencil, which offers protection to the underlying cortex, represented by the wood of the pencil. The cortex provides structural integrity to the hair and surrounds the medulla, analogous to the graphite core of the modern pencil. The rounded eraser can be likened to the root of the hair and the sharpened tip of the pencil resembles the naturally tapered tip of an uncut hair. While perhaps overly simplistic, this analogy is typically a good starting point when describing the microscopic morphology of hairs to students or lay members of a jury.

---

10 Cosmetically treated or naturally weathered hair will contain numerous derivatives of these amino acids. Many of these derivatives are formed through oxidation.

11 However, there are certain instances where detailed chemical analysis can be useful in differentiating hairs (Espinoza et al. 2008).

12 The medulla is not found in every hair and it is commonly absent from thinner hairs.

Figure 4.2 Human head hair with the free ends of the cuticular scales pointing toward the upper right, indicting the distal end of the hair (mounted in xylene and viewed using transmitted light).

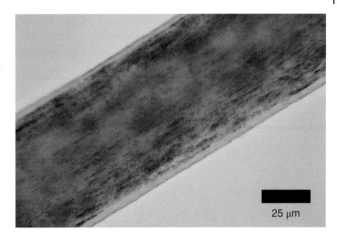

25 μm

4.2.3 Cuticle

The outermost layer of a hair is known as the cuticle. It is composed of overlapping scales which are somewhat analogous to the shingles on a roof. The free ends of the scales always point toward the distal portion of the hair (just as the free ends of roofing shingles always point down and toward the ground) (Figure 4.2). The fact that the scales point away from the skin helps hairs trap dirt and debris, thus keeping these particles from reaching the skin surface (Swift 1999a).

The cuticle is largely responsible for the chemical resistance of hair. This is likely due to the high cystine concentration in these cells relative to other tissues within the hair (Robbins 2002). The cuticle also helps maintain the integrity of the cortex, which easily becomes damaged in its absence.

Individual cuticular scales are approximately 0.5 μm thick (Swift 1999a). Transmission electron microscopy (TEM) demonstrates that human head[13] hairs typically have approximately 5–10 overlapping scales (Wolfram and Lindemann 1971; Takahashi et al. 2006) although lower numbers have been reported (Kim et al. 2006). In contrast, the cuticle layer of wool fibers is typically only one or two scales thick (Rudall 1941).

Detailed histochemical analysis has elucidated the ultrastructure of the cuticle and provided numerous insights into its mechanical and chemical properties. Each individual cuticle scale is composed of at least five layers (Swift and Smith 2001; Robbins 2002):

- the outermost epicuticle[14]
- the A layer (which has a relatively high cystine concentration)
- the B layer (also known as the exocuticle)
- the endocuticle (with a relatively low cystine concentration)
- the undermembrane (also known as the inner layer; its protein chemistry is thought to be similar to the epicuticle).

Individual cuticular scales are separated from each other by a CMC, itself believed to be composed of three layers (Swift and Smith 2001).

The epicuticle is composed of an inner layer of protein with an outer layer of covalently bound lipids, specifically the fatty acid 18-methyleicosanoic acid (18-MEA) (Jones and Rivett 1997). The epicuticle, especially its covalently bound lipid layer, plays an important role in the surface characteristics of hair, including chemical resistance, friction, hydrophobicity, and chemical diffusion (Jones

---

13 The terms "scalp hairs" and "head hairs" are used interchangeably throughout this chapter.

14 This layer is responsible for the Allwörden sacs observed when hairs are placed in chlorine water (Swift and Smith 2001).

and Rivett 1997; Swift 1999a; Robbins 2002). As such, it is an important area of research in cosmetic science.

It has been demonstrated that each cuticular scale has its own independent epicuticle layer (i.e. there is not a continuous layer covering the surface of the hair) (Leeder and Bradbury 1971).

4.2.4 Cortex

The cortex is composed of tightly packed spindle-shaped cells which are oriented parallel to the long axis of the hair. It is largely responsible for the mechanical properties of a hair. In humans, cortical cells are approximately 50–100 μm long and 1–6 μm wide (Swift 1977; Robbins 2002). A thin layer of CMC separates these cells from each other.

As with cuticular cells, cortical cells have a complex ultrastructure. Each cortical cell is made up of macrofibrils surrounded by an intermacrofibrillar matrix (IMM) (Swift 1977). Each macrofibril is in turn composed of intermediate filaments (also known as microfibrils) surrounded by amorphous matrix proteins (Robbins 2002).

The intermediate filaments can be arranged in different patterns within the macrofibrils. Based on these patterns, wool cortical cells (the most extensively studied) are classified as orthocortex, paracortex, or mesocortex. There is evidence for a general bilateral distribution along the long axis of high-crimp wool fibers, with orthocortical and paracortical cells comprising approximately half of the total area of the hair (the paracortical cells are located on the inner, concave, portion of the crimp) (Mercer 1954; Rogers 1959).[15] Low crimp wool fibers do not show this pattern, and have a proportionately higher number of mesocortical

cells (Kaplin and Whitely 1978). This suggests a relationship between the type of cortical cell and the macroscopic contour of the fiber, at least in wool.

The ultrastructure of human cortical cells is not as well understood, although it is an area of ongoing research. In general terms, it appears that the distinct differentiations between cortical cell types found in wool fibers are not present in human hair (Harland et al. 2014). However, because wool research has served as a model, there is disagreement in the literature describing the ultrastructure of human cortical cells (i.e. some scientists have attempted to adopt the terminology used to describe wool fibers (Thibaut et al. 2007) while others have suggested using new terms (Bryson et al. 2009)). The current understanding is that human cortical cells are significantly more complex than wool cortical cells, and exhibit variations in the three-dimensional ultrastructure within a single cell (Harland et al. 2014).

Pigment granules are the other main histological structure found within the cortex, although they may also be found within the medulla and, less commonly, the cuticle. It has been recognized for over 100 years that there are two types of pigment in hair (Davenport and Davenport 1909). Brownish-black pigment is known as eumelanin[16] and reddish-yellow pigment is termed pheomelanin (also spelled phaeomelanin). Combinations of these two pigments are primarily responsible for the color of hair, although many other physical features affect a hair's macroscopic appearance (e.g. the condition of the cuticle, and the presence or absence of a medulla). While their exact chemistries are not fully understood, even after extensive study, both eumelanin and pheomelanin are composed of complex heterogeneous macromolecules biochemically synthesized from the amino acid tyrosine (Meredith and Sarna 2006). Both pigments appear to be present in all human hairs and estimates of their relative proportions in

---

15 While direct observations of the ultrastructural differences require examination using TEM, the bilateral distribution of these cortical cells was first detected using dyed wool fibers with light microscopy (Horio and Kondo 1953). Bilateral differential dye uptake can also be observed in modern wool textile fibers, presumably as a result of these ultrastructural variations.

---

16 Eumelanin may also be referred to as "tyrosine-melanin" (Fitzpatrick et al. 1958).

different hair colors have recently been made (Borges et al. 2001; Ito and Wakamatsu 2011).

4.2.5 Medulla

From a histological perspective, the medulla is by far the least studied structure within hair. It is not present in all hairs, and is not believed to significantly contribute to the chemical or physical properties of the hair (Robbins 2002; Wagner and Joekes 2007). It is composed primarily of vacuoles, which are often air-filled, resulting from the dehydration of cells during hair growth. It lacks the histological organization of other hair layers and the loose aggregations of cells present appear to have essentially random orientations. For example, structures resembling deformed cortical cells (i.e. macrofibrils composed of intermediate filaments) have been identified within the medulla although they are not aligned parallel to the long axis of the hair (Wagner and Joekes 2007).

The chemistry of the medulla is different from that of the cortex and cuticle, a fact which can be demonstrated using picro-carmine staining (Stoves 1958).[17] One notable chemical difference is the presence of the amino acid citrulline in the medulla (Harding and Rogers 1999).

4.2.6 Cell Membrane Complex

The CMC is a general term used to describe the material between cortical and cuticle cells. It contains relatively low amounts of sulfur-containing amino acids and it acts as natural adhesive, binding adjacent cells to each other (Robbins 2002). In this capacity, the CMC is important for understanding how hairs respond to mechanical stresses (e.g. stretching and torsion).

The CMC and the endocuticle are sometimes collectively known as the nonkeratinous regions. These nonkeratinous regions are important from a chemical perspective as they

are believed to be the major avenues through which chemical compounds penetrate and diffuse into the hair (Robbins 2002).

4.2.7 Follicle

Each hair grows from a follicle, which is the invagination of the epidermis into a small sac, or pouch. The follicle is deepest (~4–5 mm) when the hair is actively growing, and it shrinks in size while migrating toward the surface of the skin as the hair cycle progresses (Harding and Rogers 1999). Because the lower portion of the follicle regenerates with each hair cycle, only the upper portions of the follicle, known as the isthmus and the infundibulum, are permanent (Randall 2008).

Histologically, the follicle is composed of multiple tubes wrapped around each other. The outer root sheath envelopes the inner root sheath (IRS), which is composed of three separate layers: Henle's layer, Huxley's layer, and the IRS cuticle (Harding and Rogers 1999).

The leading edges of the IRS cuticle point downwards and interlock with the upwardly pointing cuticular scales of the hair shaft (Stenn and Paus 2001). The resulting friction helps physically hold the hair in the follicle. The interlocking of the cuticles necessitates the IRS to move upward with the hair shaft as it grows before being degraded by enzymes (Alibardi 2004).

It is known that multiple hairs can originate from the same pore, or follicular ostium (Loewenthal 1947; Cottington et al. 1977; Messenger 2011). It has been demonstrated that at least some of these "compound hairs" result from individual follicles merging into one canal beneath the skin's surface (Montagna and Van Scott 1958).

4.3 Physiology

4.3.1 Hair Cycle

Each individual hair progresses through a regular and predictable cycle. This cycle is classically described as having three major

---

17 The medulla will stain red while the cortex stains yellow.

phases: anagen, catagen, and telogen.[18] Anagen is the active growing phase of the hair in which there are high rates of mitotic activity in the basal portion of the root (Stenn and Paus 2001). As the cells continually divide, the hair extends progressively outward from the skin. The follicle extends to its deepest position relative to the surface of the skin in the anagen phase. Cell division occurs at the base of the follicle as pluripotent cells become differentiated into the histological layers which make up the hair. These tissues keratinize and dehydrate as they rise in the follicle. Melanocytes actively produce pigment granules throughout this phase of continual growth (except in colorless hairs).

The anagen phase continues until a complex, and not fully understood, biochemical pathway causes hair growth to slow and eventually stop.[19] This transitional phase is known as catagen. Melanin production ceases as the melanocytes revert to seemingly multipotent epithelial cells (Kligman 1959). The hair root begins to move up with the follicle as it distances itself from the underlying dermal papilla. The root itself begins to form a partially keratinized bulbous club with a column of undifferentiated epithelial cells connecting it to the dermal papilla. These cells will eventually separate from the papilla and the column will shorten into a small germinal nipple just below the completely keratinized bulb (Kligman 1959).

With the transition complete, the hair root enters the latent telogen, or resting phase (i.e. it is no longer actively growing). In human scalp hairs, telogen roots consist of enlarged, keratinized bulbs which help to mechanically anchor the hairs within the follicles. Once the

remnants of the follicular sac are eliminated, there are no soft tissues connecting the root to the follicle.

At this point hair can be removed with minimal force (at least compared to the force required to remove hairs at other stages of the growth cycle), and they will eventually fall out naturally of their own accord. This natural shedding of hairs is known as exogen, while the time between shedding and the start of anagen is known as kenogen (Rebora and Guarrera 2002). These phases are sometimes considered to be subdivisions of telogen (Messenger 2011) but relatively recent research indicates that exogen is a distinct phase in which the tissues anchoring the telogen root to the follicle are lost through apoptosis, allowing the hair to be shed (Milner et al. 2002; Stenn 2005; Van Neste et al. 2007). Staining methods have been proposed to distinguish telogen and exogen roots in humans (Van Neste et al. 2007).[20]

4.3.1.1 Timing

In humans, the growth of each hair is largely independent of other hairs (i.e. there is no visual synchronization of the hair cycles). This mosaic pattern of hair growth is in contrast to some animals in which there are either seasonal molts or synchronized hair cycles which result in waves of hair replacement (Allen 1894; Collins 1918; Dry 1926; Chase and Eaton 1959).

Because of this lack of synchronization, approximately 85–90% of human head hairs will be in the anagen phase, 10–15% will be in the telogen phase, and relatively few (1–2%) will be in the catagen phase at any given time on the typical human scalp (Van Scott et al. 1957; Lynfield 1960; Kligman 1961; Maguire and Kligman 1964; Barman et al. 1965).[21] For typical adult human head hair, studies

---

18 Histologists further subdivide some of these phases based on the appearance of histologically prepared thin sections of skin (Schneider et al. 2009). This specificity is not applicable for forensic purposes because the growth phase determination is made on hair roots which have been removed from their follicles.

19 It is known, however, that the dermal papilla, located just below the anagen root bulb, is involved in the chemical signaling which regulates the hair cycle (Schneider et al. 2009).

---

20 From a forensic perspective, the ability to determine the presence or absence of follicular material on the root is more important than the term used to classify the root (i.e. telogen versus exogen).

21 It is important to recognize that these numbers are averages and only apply to human head hairs. In other words, they cannot be extrapolated to other somatic regions or to animal hairs. In fact, the vast majority of

indicate that anagen lasts several years (2–6), catagen lasts several weeks, and telogen lasts a few weeks to a few months (Kligman 1959; Robbins 2002).

The above summary is somewhat of an oversimplification as there are significant amounts of individual variation. Additionally, at least in temperate regions, there is evidence of seasonal changes in the relative ratios of hairs in the different phases of the hair cycle (e.g. elevated numbers of telogen hairs in the late summer and early fall) (Randall and Ebling 1991; Courtois et al. 1996).

Age also effects the hair cycle. For example, children younger than 10 tend to have a slightly higher percentage of anagen hairs (>90%), with a corresponding lack of telogen hairs, compared to adults (Pecoraro et al. 1964). There are also indications that the percentage of hairs in the telogen phase increases post-puberty through at least the fifth decade of life (Barman et al. 1965). Similarly, it has been demonstrated that the length of the anagen phase decreases as adults age, and that there is a corresponding increase in the duration of the kenogen phase (Courtois et al. 1995).

There are a few deviations from the typical mosaic hair growth in humans. The first exception, experienced by all humans, is the synchronized growth of head hair which progresses in waves in utero and immediately after birth (Barman et al. 1967).[22] The transition to the typical mosaic pattern is generally believed to occur within one year (Messenger 2011).

The effect of pregnancy represents another deviation on the hair cycle of head hairs. It has been demonstrated that beginning in the second trimester, the progression from anagen to telogen slows in the head hairs of pregnant women (Lynfield 1960; Pecoraro et al. 1969). There is then a corresponding increase in the

conversion of hairs to the telogen phase after parturition (e.g. higher than baseline percentages of telogen hairs were demonstrated both 6 weeks and 3 months after giving birth). This provides an explanation for the large amounts of head hair that typically fall out in the weeks and months after delivery. In other words, increased hair loss postpartum is not the symptom of a disease but rather a restoration of the scalp hairs to the normal (i.e. not pregnant) state. This is a second non-pathological cause of telogen effluvium (Eckert et al. 1967; Sperling 2003). It has also been demonstrated that the growth rate of axillary hairs decreases during pregnancy while pubic hairs are unaffected with regards to growth rate and hair cycle (Pecoraro et al. 1971; Astore et al. 1979).

4.3.1.2 Shedding

It is estimated that there are between 100 000 and 110 000 hairs on the average human scalp (Orentreich 1969; Robbins 2002) although higher estimates (e.g. up to at least 200 000) can be found in the literature (Cottington et al. 1977).

It is commonly stated in the forensic literature that the average human naturally sheds approximately 100 head hairs per day. This is a difficult area of study with numerous variables (e.g. age, sex, and health) making it hard to reduce the answer to a single number. For example, in temperate zones there is evidence of short-term cycles superimposed on longer seasonal cycles with the most hair loss occurring in the fall (Orentreich 1969; Randall and Ebling 1991). While different researchers using different methodologies have produced varied results, the consensus is that lower rates of daily head hair loss, between ~30 and 75, are more typical (Kligman 1961; Stroud 1987; Ihm and Lee 1991). It may be more accurate to state that shedding 100 head hairs daily is an upper limit of normal hair loss (Kligman 1961; Robbins 2002). These studies also demonstrate the large variability between individuals, and caution must be exercised when applying this information to forensic casework. While it is a fact that the daily shedding of hair is normal in

---

animal hairs are in the telogen phase (Favarato and Conceição 2008).

22 Infants often shed significant amounts of scalp hair in the months after birth as large numbers of anagen hairs transition to telogen hairs. This is one of the physiological causes of telogen effluvium (diffuse hair loss) (Sperling 2003).

Table 4.1 Human head hair growth rates (in µm/day) for three different ancestral groups

Study	Asian				African				European			
2001	NA				$n = 38$				$n = 45$			
	Average	SD	Min	Max	Average	SD	Min	Max	Average	SD	Min	Max
	NA	NA	NA	NA	256	44	150	356	396	55	281	537
2005	$n = 188$				$n = 216$				$n = 107$			
	Average	SD	Min	Max	Average	SD	Min	Max	Average	SD	Min	Max
	411	53	244	611	280	50	129	436	367	56	165	506

Source: Reproduced with permission of John Wiley & Sons.

humans, it is impossible to state with any kind of certainty the number of head hairs a given individual will be expected to lose daily without subjecting that person to a clinical study. It should also be noted that the rate of hair loss is not expected to be constant throughout the day (i.e. most hair loss is believed to occur during washing, grooming, or other activities which disturb the hairs).

4.3.2 Growth Rates

There have been many studies focused on determining the growth rates of human hair. These studies have demonstrated that there are numerous variables affecting growth rates including, but not limited to, somatic origin, age, sex, pigmentation, and time of year (Hamilton 1958; Pecoraro et al. 1964, 1971; Barman et al. 1964; Saitoh et al. 1969; Miyazawa and Uematsu 1992; Randall and Ebling 1991; Hayashi et al. 1991; Nagl 1995; Potsch 1996; Courtois et al. 1996; Loussouarn 2001; Lee et al. 2005; Loussouarn et al. 2005; LeBeau et al. 2011).

Forensic literature commonly states that human head hair grows approximately 1 cm per month. Many of the above studies support this approximate average but delving into the details shows how much variation is present between individuals. Individual rates have been reported as low as 0.36 cm per month[23]

and as high as 2.2 cm per month (Loussouarn et al. 2005; Potsch 1996).

One particularly interesting result is the evidence suggesting relative differences in head hair growth rates between different ancestral groups (Loussouarn 2001; Loussouarn et al. 2005). While there is overlap between the groups, this research demonstrates that, on average, Asian head hair grows faster than European head hair, which in turn grows faster than African head hair. Table 4.1 displays some of the relevant data from these two studies.

Another general trend exhibited in a number of the hair growth studies is that hair growth slows with increasing age across multiple somatic regions (Myers and Hamilton 1951; Astore et al. 1979; Tajima et al. 2007). It should also be noted that several studies have demonstrated that shaving does not have an effect on the rate of hair growth, at least with respect to beard and leg hair (Danforth 1925; Trotter 1928; Saitoh et al. 1969; Lynfield and Macwilliams 1970).

While beyond the scope of this chapter, hair growth rates are often important in interpreting the results of drug tests that have used hair as the sample matrix (Wennig 2000; LeBeau et al. 2011).

4.3.3 Changes with Age

There is no way to determine the absolute age of an individual based on a microscopical examination of their hair. There are, however, several generalized changes in the morphology of hair that occur as individuals age. Not

---

23 This monthly growth rate was calculated from the daily growth rate data in the reference with 1 month equaling 28 days after LeBeau et al. (2011).

surprisingly, these changes are typically associated with early childhood and later adulthood.

Trotter and Duggins authored a series of articles in which they examined a number of morphological traits as their child subjects aged.[24] They reported a distinct increase in the cross-sectional area (and hence diameter) of head hairs during the three years after birth which continued at a lower, and sometimes negligible, rate until adolescence (Trotter and Duggins 1948). This was confirmed in later studies (Atkinson et al. 1959) and corresponds with the commonplace observation that the hair of young children is typically fine and then becomes thicker as they get older. They also noted a distinct decrease in the circularity of these head hairs in the first two years after birth.[25] There are also some indications that head hair diameter eventually begins to decrease slightly with increasing age in adults (i.e. in individuals in their 40s and beyond) (Trotter 1930; Atkinson et al. 1959; Birch et al. 2001). Their other studies did not show significant correlations between the degree of medullation, scale count, or refractive index and age (Duggins and Trotter 1950; Trotter and Duggins 1950; Duggins 1954).[26] However, there are indications that the medullary index (i.e. the thickness of the medulla relative to the overall thickness of the hair) tends to increase with advancing age (Luell and Archer 1964; Longia 1966).

------

24 While these studies were conducted primarily from an anthropological perspective, some of these articles were clearly inspired by the series of articles published by Kirk et al. in the early 1940s, and the authors are cognizant of the potential forensic implications of their work.

25 Only white (i.e. of European ancestry) children were included in this study and this decrease in circularity may not apply to children of different ancestries.

26 However, they did observe a direct correlation between hair diameter and degree of medullation after the age of two (i.e. thicker hairs are more likely to have medullae) (Duggins and Trotter 1950). This corresponds to earlier observations made by Hausman and his student, Wynkoop, relating degree of medullation to diameter in human head hairs (Hausman 1925a; Wynkoop 1929).

4.3.3.1 Hair Color, Graying, and Baldness

Many studies have shown that the head hair of children of European ancestry tends to darken with increasing age (Hrdlička 1922; Trotter 1930; Trotter and Dawson 1934; Bean 1935; Steggerda 1941; Prokopec et al. 2000).

Hair color is more stable during adulthood, although inevitable change occurs as colorless hairs, commonly called white or gray hairs, begin to be produced. The onset of graying varies from individual to individual but also it appears to correlate with ancestry (i.e. ethnic group). The typical onset of graying begins sometime during a person's 30s or 40s, affecting almost all people once they are in their 60s (Keogh and Walsh 1965; Tobin and Paus 2001; Panhard et al. 2012). There is limited evidence to suggest that colorless hairs have relatively wider medullae compared to pigmented hairs from the same individual (Longia 1966).

Contrary to colloquial expressions, hair doesn't turn gray (i.e. a fixed pigmented portion of hair shaft doesn't become gray suddenly, or over time, since the pigment deposited in the hair is both chemically stable and spatially removed from any of the active biological processes occurring in the follicle) (Hausman 1925b). Gray hairs arise when melanocytes cease pigment production, and hence the emerging hair appears white or gray macroscopically (Commo et al. 2004). The absence of pigment causes the cortices of these hairs to appear colorless when viewed microscopically using transmitted light.[27] The exact biochemical mechanisms of melanocyte failure are not fully understood, but it is thought to be caused by the oxidative damage resulting from hydrogen peroxide accumulation (Tobin 2009; Wood et al. 2009).

This transition can be captured in a single strand of hair which gradually changes from its pigmented form to a complete lack of pigmentation, sometimes over the span of several

------

27 Diffuse reflectance is the primary cause for colorless hairs to appear white or gray macroscopically in the same way that colorless sugar or salt grains appear white when viewed with the unaided eye.

Figure 4.3 Human head hair exhibiting a natural progression from a proximal colorless area (left) to a distal pigmented area (right) (mounted in xylene and viewed using transmitted light). The photomicrograph in the middle depicts a transitional region approximately 2 cm from each of the other areas (i.e. these three photomicrographs span a total of ~4 cm).

centimeters (i.e. several months of growth) (Figure 4.3).[28]

The typical graying process cannot account for popularized reports of hair suddenly becoming gray, typically in the aftermath of a shocking event or great stress, a condition known as *canities subita*. The most scientifically supported explanation for these cases is that the pigmented hairs of these people preferentially fall out leaving predominantly white hairs on the head, although a recent review of the literature suggests that this explanation does not sufficiently explain all well-documented examples (Tobin and Paus 2001; Nahm et al. 2013).

Typical male pattern baldness, androgenetic alopecia, results from the miniaturization of terminal hairs to the vellus state (i.e. fine, colorless, and essentially macroscopically invisible hairs) (Hoffman 2002; Mirmirani 2015). The onset varies by individual and ancestry (i.e. ethnic group), but it is driven by male sex hormones and appears to have a strong genetic basis (Nyholt et al. 2003). Interestingly, the effect of androgens on hairs has been termed an "endocrine paradox" in that the same hormones may both cause vellus hairs to become coarse terminal hairs (e.g. pubic and axillary) and cause some terminal scalp hairs to transform to vellus hairs (Randall 2008). Female pattern hair loss also results from a miniaturization of hairs to the vellus state, although it

is not clear if this is driven primarily by androgens as in males (Birch et al. 2002; Messenger and Sinclair 2006).

4.4 Collection and Isolation

4.4.1 Questioned Samples

Dr. Kirk believed that hair was critical physical evidence which should always be collected and studied thoroughly when it occurs (Kirk 1953). Hairs of unknown origin (i.e. questioned or Q hairs) can be recovered from nearly any physical object (e.g. clothing, footwear, upholstery, vehicles, bodies [living and deceased], weapons, and tools).

4.4.1.1 Techniques

While a variety of methods can be used, forceps and tape lifts are the two most commonly employed techniques for collecting questioned hairs.

Individual hairs observed during the examination of an item can be isolated using forceps. Oblique lighting is often advantageous when manually searching for hairs. It is important to handle the hairs gently because too much pressure will cause localized areas of damage if the hair is crushed (Figure 4.4).[29] Isolated hairs can be transferred to appropriately sized

---

28 While it has not been demonstrated, it may be presumed that the next hair to arise from this follicle will be colorless over its entire length.

29 Examiners should become familiar with the appearance of hairs that have been crushed using forceps as they will likely see them if they analyze hairs collected by others. When encountered in casework, examiners may not be able to definitively determine

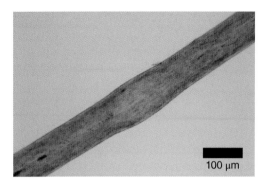

Figure 4.4 Example of a bulge on a human hair caused by excessive force applied with forceps (mounted in xylene and viewed using transmitted light).

storage containers (e.g. plastic bags and Petri dishes[30]). A stereomicroscope can be used to locate hairs that are too small to be seen by the unaided eye. These hairs should generally be transferred directly to microscope slides and protected with coverslips. Tungsten needles can be used to transfer exceptionally small hairs (those less than about 1 mm). Aside from potentially damaging hairs, the main disadvantages of manual isolation are the tediousness of collecting significant numbers of hairs and the potential for missing hairs (especially dark hairs on dark substrates and light hairs on light substrates).

Tape lifts solve these problems as they are the most efficient means of collecting hairs from large surfaces. Most objects are suitable for taping, although certain items make tape lifts impractical due to their inaccessible regions (e.g. recessed areas, deep cracks/cervices, and tight corners). Standard colorless packing tape can be pressed onto the surface of the object in question and then secured to a fresh transparency sheet for later examination. A piece of tape can be pressed multiple times onto an object until it begins to lose its adhesiveness.

Separate pieces of tape can be used for different regions to increase spatial resolution or one-to-one tape lifts[31] can be used to pinpoint a more precise location.

Once secured to the tape, potential hairs of interest can be noted, photographed, and then carefully isolated. In practice, a clean razor may be used to circumscribe an incomplete loop around the hair (e.g. cutting on three sides).[32] This area of the tape can be separated from the transparency, and a small aliquot of solvent (e.g. xylene) can be applied using a drawn micro-capillary to dissolve the adhesive surrounding the hair. This releases the hair from the tape and ensures that a minimum amount of force is required to remove it.[33] One drawback of tape lifts is that the inherent adhesive properties of the tape, combined with the use of a solvent, can remove particles/residues adhering to the hair.

Combings are commonly employed in efforts to isolate foreign hairs (and other materials) from the pubic and head hair of individuals (both living and deceased). Generally, most of the hairs recovered from these combings originate from the individual being sampled, but it remains the only practical method for isolating any foreign hairs that may be present.

Additional techniques (e.g. sonication, density separation, and sieving) may be useful when unusual samples are encountered. For example, various combinations of these methods have proven valuable when searching for human hair in desiccated carnivore feces and slurries of various compositions. While not typically utilized by the author, it should be noted that some hair examiners are proponents

---

the significance of an area with this appearance, but they should recognize that it may be an artifact of careless handling.

30 Glass Petri dishes are preferred over plastic ones since they are relatively free from electrostatic charge.

31 The object being sampled is covered in strips of tape, the locations of which are mapped, allowing each tape lift to be associated with a specific portion of the item. This time-consuming method is generally only applicable to field sampling.

32 The cutting should be conducted with the aid of a stereomicroscope to ensure that other potentially important materials (e.g. fibers and other hairs) are not bisected.

33 Obviously, careless handling can also damage hairs during their removal from tape lifts.

of other sampling methods (e.g. vacuuming and scraping).

4.4.1.2 Other Considerations

Collecting hairs from objects can be conducted in the field or at the laboratory and there are benefits and disadvantages for each. The laboratory offers a controlled, clean, well-lit, and comfortable environment. These advantageous conditions speak for themselves and are virtually impossible to practically replicate in the field. However, it is unrealistic, and sometimes truly impossible, to package and transport evidence from the field to the laboratory (e.g. large pieces of furniture, walls, trees, and oversized trucks/trailers). In these cases, field sampling may be justified or required.

One advantage of field sampling is that it eliminates the chance of losing trace evidence during packaging or transportation to the laboratory. For example, loosely adhering hairs can fall off an item while it is being placed into a bag or swept off a vehicle as it is being towed to a laboratory's garage. In contrast, if a hair is observed on an item at the scene, its location can be photographed, and it can be placed into an appropriate container. This ensures that the hair is secured as evidence before the item is moved and that its original location is documented. Utmost caution must be utilized when collecting hairs in the field as these environments are typically less forgiving than the laboratory, especially in adverse conditions (e.g. wind or rain). For example, in the laboratory when a short hair gently held using forceps is dropped while transferring it from an object to a container, it generally falls a few inches onto the underlying paper placed below the item being examined. The fallen hair can be easily relocated and placed into the desired location. In the field, a dropped hair may never be recovered and, depending on the circumstances, its uncertain provenance may render it meaningless for future examination

even if it is located.[34] Conducting tapings in the field, before evidence is packaged, is a good way to minimize sample loss. These tape lifts can be especially valuable if they are spatially resolved (i.e. one-to-one tapings where each strip of tape is only used to sample one specific area of the item being sampled).

Another consideration is the fact that hairs can change positions once they are placed into a package (Chewning et al. 2008). For this reason, a loose hair recovered on an item removed from a package cannot be assumed to be in the original location it was deposited. For example, a hair observed lying on the left sleeve of a sweatshirt removed from an evidence bag could have originally been located on another portion of the sweatshirt. This intrasample movement can be minimized through careful packaging (e.g. placing clean paper between the folded surfaces of the item being placed in the bag) (Lee and De Forest 1984). Also, while discouraged, it is not uncommon to find multiple items in the same package (e.g. shirt, pants, socks, and shoes from the same individual). Loose hairs found on one of the items could have originated from any of them. Hairs can also be transferred to the inner surfaces of the packaging and thus these surfaces should be examined as well.

It should be noted that certain details not visible to the unaided eye may be overlooked when hairs are collected in the field. One of the advantages of bringing items back to the laboratory is the ability to make additional observations using a stereomicroscope before the hair is disturbed (assuming the item has been properly packaged). Stereomicroscopes offer an unparalleled ability to note, and document if equipped with a camera, features that cannot be discerned with the unaided eye. For example, a stereomicroscope can differentiate a hair lying on top of a dried blood residue from

---

34 For this reason, it is often advisable to hold or secure a fresh sheet of paper underneath the hair during sampling in the field.

one partially or completely embedded within the blood. The facts regarding the depositional order of the hair and the blood can have a significant impact on the interpretation of the evidence as it relates to the larger questions being asked during the investigation. Similarly, when dealing with a collection of hairs, a stereomicroscope can be used to determine if all the hairs are oriented in the same direction (e.g. a clump of hairs pulled out together will have all of their roots facing in the same direction, at least initially).[35]

Hopefully, the above discussion has demonstrated that the decision to collect hairs in the field or to package items for examination at a laboratory is not always a simple one. In summary, there is no prescribed answer that applies to all scenarios and the decision should be based upon the nature of the evidence, the personnel available, the environmental conditions, the circumstances of the investigation, and any other relevant considerations that present themselves.

4.4.2 Known Samples

Known hair samples are commonly collected from individuals to determine if they could be a potential source of one or more questioned hairs recovered during an investigation. Typically, only head hairs and possibly pubic hairs are collected, depending on the circumstances of the case. Hairs should be collected from different sub-areas of these somatic regions (e.g. the front, top, back, and sides of the head) (Bisbing 2002). This is important because hairs from different portions of the same generic somatic area (e.g. head) can have different macroscopic and microscopic morphologies. Obviously, the individual doing the sampling should try to collect hairs that represent any variation that can be observed at the macroscopic level (e.g. different lengths, colors, or textures).

Because the hairs within a given somatic area exhibit inherent microscopical morphology variations, the goal is to collect a representative hair sample which captures most, if not all, of this variability.[36] There is no absolute minimum number of hairs that constitutes a representative standard because hairs from some individuals exhibit a wider range of variation compared to others. However, a larger sample has a better chance of capturing any variation present. Multiple examiners have offered their opinions as to what constitutes a recommended sample size. These estimates typically range from 25 to 100 for head hairs and from 25 to 50 for pubic hairs (or other somatic regions) (Lee and De Forest 1984; Bisbing 2002; Deedrick and Koch 2004a; SWGMAT 2005; Houck and Bisbing 2005).[37] A recent European guideline recommends collecting 20 hairs from each of the five head regions (for a total of 100) and packaging them separately (ENFSI 2015). This source also recommends collecting a minimum of 20 pubic hairs.

While not ideal, a comparison can still be attempted when the known standard is composed of less than the recommended number of hairs. After all, it *theoretically* only takes a single known hair to make an association with a questioned hair. The context of the case, as well as the quantity and condition of the samples, should be carefully considered before performing these examinations. If the examination is attempted and an association is not made, the conclusion may need to be caveated

35 These types of observations have played important roles in cases the author has worked on, and were anticipated by R. Austin Freeman's scientific detective, Dr. John Evelyn Thorndyke, in the short story "A Message from the Deep Sea" (Freeman 1909).

36 At least one experienced hair examiner has discussed atypical hairs which represent distinct outliers within the sampled region (Gaudette 1985).
37 It should be noted that not every hair constituting the known sample will necessarily be mounted for detailed microscopical analysis.

that the lack of a sufficient standard has limited the ability of the examiner to conduct a complete comparison (i.e. there is an increased risk of false exclusions). Alternatively, and depending on the circumstances of the case, additional known hairs can be requested with the aim of augmenting the original known standard.

Known hairs can be collected either by plucking or combing, or, preferentially, a combination of the two. Combed hairs are generally shorter and thinner compared to pulled head hairs.[38] Some examiners prefer combed hairs because they are thought to more closely resemble the shed hairs typically encountered in casework, but combing often results in the known sample being composed of relatively few hairs (Peabody et al. 1985). Another point of consideration is that any foreign hairs in the area being sampled will likely be collected along with known hairs from the individual being sampled. Because of this, combings may be conducted in two stages with the first round used to isolate foreign hairs (with the understanding that hairs from the individual being sampled will also be collected), and the second combing reserved for the collection of known hairs. In these instances, the first round should be relatively gentle, and the second should be more vigorous.

Regardless of the sampling method utilized, it is important to collect complete hairs (i.e. hairs with intact roots) because incomplete hairs inherently limit the value of a microscopical comparison (e.g. the original length of a hair cannot be determined if it is a fragment). For this reason, using scissors to cut hairs is not a recommended collection technique. Similarly, the collection method should not induce significant damage to the hair. It should be obvious that a known standard composed of damaged hair fragments without roots is of limited value for a microscopical examination.

The known hair standard should ideally be collected as close to the incident in question as possible. This is because the macroscopic and microscopic appearance of hair can change over time. Easily recognizable macroscopic changes including haircuts and cosmetic treatments (e.g. bleaching, dyeing, permanent waving, and straightening) require little time (i.e. they are effectively instantaneous). Changes in microscopic morphology are generally relatively slow and gradual, tending to occur and accumulate over much larger timeframes.[39] The time required for noticeable natural changes in hair length due to growth fall somewhere between these two extremes.

For the reasons mentioned above, caution must be heeded when a microscopical hair comparison is conducted using a hair standard collected a significant amount of time after the incident occurred (e.g. a time difference of more than one year for head hairs (Deedrick and Koch 2004a; Oien 2009)).[40] The ensuing report may include a statement indicating that the comparison was limited due to the extended period of time between the incident and the collection of the known standard.

For example, in one of the author's cases, a known hair standard was collected more than a year after the questioned hairs were recovered. The questioned hairs could not be distinguished from the known hairs based on their microscopic morphology but they were significantly shorter than the known hairs. In fact, assuming a hair growth rate of ~1 cm

---

38 Experimental data demonstrating that the amount of force required to pluck a hair correlates with hair diameter can at least partially explain the tendency for combed hairs to be thinner (Van Neste et al. 2007).

39 Although not rigorously studied, many forensic hair examiners have anecdotally recognized changes in the hair morphology of people who have been incarcerated for significant amounts of time. It is hypothesized that the conditions of prison life itself (e.g. restricted exposure to natural sunlight) augment any changes that may have accumulated due to the normal passage of time.

40 It has been suggested that compared to head hairs, the microscopic characteristics of pubic hairs are more constant over time and may be suitable for comparison after relatively longer elapsed temporal periods (Deedrick 2000).

per month, the known hairs would have had to have grown continuously without undergoing a haircut for the entire time interval (~16 months) to obtain their current length if they were as short as the questioned hairs at the time of the incident. A report was written explaining this and later it was learned that the source of the known hairs stated that he had not had a haircut in the time between the incident and the collection of his known hairs. As anticipated, a legitimate explanation existed for the large difference in hair lengths between the questioned and the known hairs.

While known standards should be collected as soon as possible, there is no empirically derived upper limit on the amount of time that can pass before the value of a comparison becomes limited. However, the value of collecting known hairs after significant time intervals have passed should be evaluated on the specifics of the case at hand. For example, in the investigation of a cold case, if the suspect was known to have long black hair at the time of the incident, and he has short, naturally white hair now, there is little to be gained from a microscopical hair comparison, and consequently it may be decided that there is no point in collecting a known standard.

Because of these temporal limitations, hair standards should be collected from suspects as soon as realistically possible, even if there are currently no questioned hairs to compare them to. Questioned hairs may be recovered years, even decades after the event, and the most reliable comparison will be ensured if contemporaneous hair standards were collected and stored properly. As discussed above, failure to obtain the known standard in a timely manner may negatively impact the ability of an examiner to conduct a meaningful comparison.

In summary, the proper collection of a high-quality known standard at least partially determines the significance of a subsequent hair comparison. The quality of a known standard is determined primarily by the care and thoroughness of the individual collecting it.

4.5 General Hair

True hairs are only found in mammals (class Mammalia) and their presence is one of the defining characteristics of the class, separating them from all other forms of life (Noback 1951).[41]

The field of hair microscopy has typically been divided into two sub-disciplines: human and animal.[42] This split is somewhat artificial as both sub-disciplines use the same instruments to examine the same histological tissue. The specialization arises principally because the focus of the examination is typically different. For example, animal hair examinations are concerned primarily with taxonomic identifications (i.e. determining the type of animal from which the hair originated). In contrast, human hair examinations have historically been focused on comparisons and other contextual questions (e.g. whether the hair was forcibly removed from the skin).

4.5.1 Types of Hair

4.5.1.1 Human

In humans, hairs are most commonly divided into one of three types[43]:

- *Lanugo*: These hairs are formed in utero and are typically described as being fine, unmedullated, and unpigmented (Montagna 1976; Harding and Rogers 1999) although it has also been reported that

---

41 The conceptual understanding of hair is so universal that the word "hair" has been appropriated by other disciplines. Trichomes and setae may be colloquially referred to as "plant hairs" and "insect hairs," respectively. Unlike true keratinous hairs, trichomes are composed primarily of cellulose while setae are formed mainly from chitin.

42 It is acknowledged by the author that humans are in fact animals and that the term "non-human animal hair" has been used to more correctly describe animal hair. However, for ease of reading, the simplified terms "human" and "animal" will be used throughout this chapter.

43 It should also be recognized that some hairs exhibit intermediate morphologies between these major types (Danforth 1926; Bogaty 1969).

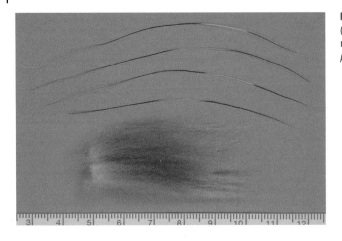

Figure 4.5 Examples of guard hairs (top) and fur hairs (bottom) from a raccoon dog (*Nyctereutes procyonoides*).

they may be pigmented (Bogaty 1969). Lanugo hairs can grow to significant lengths (~15 cm) (Robbins 2002) and are typically shed before or shortly after birth.

- *Vellus*: These are fine, short (~1 mm), unmedullated, typically unpigmented or lightly colored hairs present on almost all skin surfaces including seemingly hairless areas such as the forehead, nose, ears, and the bald scalp (Harding and Rogers 1999; Robbins 2002). They are not found on the palms of the hands or the soles of the feet.
- *Terminal*: These are the typical hairs macroscopically visible on children and adults. They may be further subdivided into primary hairs (e.g. head, eyelash, and eyebrow) and secondary hairs. Secondary hairs, also called secondary sex hairs, arise at puberty in specific somatic regions (e.g. pubic, axilla, and beard) and are the result of vellus hairs being replaced by terminal hairs.

Aside from potential infanticide investigations involving lanugo hair (Gallard 1879; Bisbing 2002), the forensic analysis of hair is generally restricted to the examination of terminal hairs, most commonly head and pubic hair.

4.5.1.2 Animal

Animal hairs may also be divided into three types:[44]

- *Guard hairs*: Also called overhairs, these are the longer, stiffer hairs in the main pelage of the animal (Figure 4.5). Taxonomic identifications are possible due to the microscopical morphological variations present within guard hairs.[45]
- *Fur hairs*: Also called underhairs, these are the fine, often undulating hairs in the main pelage of the animal. Typically, these hairs are relatively uniform in diameter and devoid of microscopical characteristics useful for identification purposes.
- *Vibrissa*: Also called whiskers, these hairs are long, stiff, and primarily provide a tactile sensory function to the animal. They are rarely encountered in forensic casework.

Guard hairs often have a distinctly thicker region in their distal portions. This is known as the "shield", with the thinner proximal region referred to as the "shaft" (Figure 4.6). The shield is particularly important for hair microscopy as morphological characteristics useful for identifications are often most pronounced in this region.

It should also be noted that the division of the main pelage of animal hair into two types is an oversimplification. There generally exists a continuum between the finest fur hairs and the

---

44 A wide variety of terms and classification systems are used to describe animal hairs in the literature. In some instances, the same term (e.g. overhair) can have different meanings (Brunner and Coman 1974; Teerink 1991).

45 Guard hairs may be subdivided based on their macroscopic morphology (e.g. GH 0, GH 1, or GH 2) (Teerink 1991). Regardless of the terminology used, similarly sized hairs should be compared to each other when identifications are being attempted.

Figure 4.6 Guard hairs from an American mink (*Neovison vison*) exhibiting distinct shaft (left) and shield (right) regions.

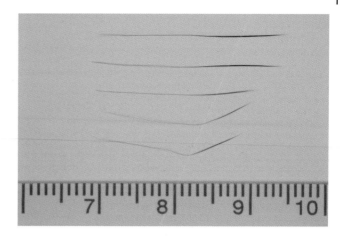

coarsest guard hairs (Hardy and Hardy 1942; Noback 1951).

4.5.2 Basic Microscopy

Microscopy is essential to hair examinations. While the fundamentals of microscopy are beyond the scope of this chapter, it must be recognized that microscopes are scientific instruments, not machines that are turned "on" and "off." Failure to take full advantage of the microscope's capabilities will lead to substandard images which obscure fine details of the specimens being examined. Simply put, one cannot become a good hair examiner without first becoming a competent microscopist.

Detailed hair examinations are conducted primarily with a compound light microscope using transmitted light. This has traditionally been, and remains so today, the preferred instrument for the forensic examination of human and animal hairs. One major advantage of light microscopy is that it is the only technique that can be used to study all three of the major histological layers of hair (i.e. the cuticle, cortex, and medulla) without advanced preparation techniques.[46] In short, a great deal of information can be obtained from a hair mounted on a slide within an appropriate mounting medium.

There are numerous parameters that should be evaluated when selecting a mounting medium. Concerning optical characteristics, it should be colorless, have a refractive index relatively close to that of hair,[47] and it should not fluoresce. Additionally, it should not degrade the hair or any dyes that may be present within the hair, and it should not inhibit any subsequent DNA analyses (De Forest et al. 1987; Roe et al. 1991).

Hairs can be mounted for microscopy as either temporary or permanent mounts. Temporary mounts use media that do not harden and most will evaporate to dryness after relatively short periods of time (e.g. xylene). Permanent mounts use media that cure to a hardened, resinous solid. The term "permanent" is a misnomer in that the media can be removed if necessary, typically through dissolution. Additional factors must be considered when selecting a permanent mounting medium. Principally, it should be easy to work with and it should be stable over time (i.e. it should not discolor or crystallize).

There are benefits and disadvantages to each general type of mounting medium. It takes longer to mount a hair in a permanent medium compared to a temporary medium, but it only needs to be done once. In contrast, hairs in temporary mounts may need to be "refreshed" with media as it evaporates. Additionally, permanent mounts secure the hair in

---

46 It should be noted that more advanced sample preparation techniques, discussed later in this chapter, can be used to obtain additional information which cannot be determined or documented using hairs in longitudinal mounts.

47 Hairs typically have refractive indices in the range of 1.54–1.56 (Greenwell et al. 1941; Duggins 1954).

solid resin, allowing them to be readily transported. Consequently, they require additional efforts to isolate hairs for other preparation techniques or DNA analyses. Hairs in temporary mounts can be easily removed but they need to be transferred to other storage containers for transport. In summary, there is no perfect mounting medium and each laboratory should select appropriate media based upon their scientific and practical requirements.

Scanning electron microscopy (SEM) can also be used to examine hairs. This technique is more common in the examination of animal hairs, especially in Europe and Russia. A more detailed discussion of the potential benefits and disadvantages regarding electron microscopy can be found in Section 4.10. Finally, TEM can be used to study the ultra-structural features of hair. While providing important fundamental information that is relevant to hair microscopy in general, there are currently no practical applications of TEM to forensic casework involving hair.

4.5.2.1 Cuticle

In longitudinal mounts, the cuticle is most easily observed at the margins of a hair, where the optical axis of the microscope is tangential to the surface of the hair. The thickness of the overall cuticular layer depends on the number of overlapping cuticular scales (each scale in human hair is ~0.5 μm thick) (Tolgyesi et al. 1983; Swift 1999a). The cuticle will appear as a distinct layer if it is relatively thick, but the individual cuticular scales comprising the layer will not be resolvable using a compound light microscope, and it will not be possible to accurately count the number of scales using this technique. When thin, the cuticle may only be recognized by the edges of the cuticular cells which protrude from the margins of the hair.

The leading edges of the cuticular scales always point toward the distal portion of the hair. Therefore, the proximal and distal ends of a hair fragment can be determined if recognizable cuticular scales can be identified.

The natural cuticle is typically colorless, although it may appear slightly yellowish in some cases. It is generally free from pigment,

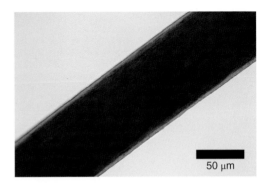

Figure 4.7 Example of a human head hair exhibiting a distinctly colored cuticle indicative of dyeing (mounted in xylene and viewed using transmitted light).

but individual granules can occasionally be found in some hairs. A colored cuticle, aside from a slight yellowing, is generally a sign of artificial dyeing (Figure 4.7). The cuticle may appear isotropic when viewed using crossed polars but this layer exhibits measurable birefringence (~0.005) (Duggins 1954; McCrone 1977).

All hairs have a cuticular layer when they are formed. However, hairs without a cuticle may be encountered in forensic examinations. Two common causes for the absence of a cuticle are:

- *Natural weathering*: The cuticle layer can be gradually removed through repeated physical abrasion. This is more common at the distal ends of long hairs (i.e. hairs that have been exposed to the environment for relatively long periods of time).
- *It originated from a hairpiece (e.g. wigs, toupees, or extensions)*: The cuticular scales are often chemically removed from hairs destined for use in hairpieces, especially those of lower quality.[48] The surfaces of these hairs are typically quite smooth in appearance, almost resembling man-made fibers (Figure 4.8).

---

48 Removing the cuticle simplifies the manufacturing process because directionality does not need to be maintained for hairs without cuticular scales. However, remnants of the cuticle, arranged in thin strips oriented parallel to the long axis of the fiber, may remain on the hair after some wig pretreatment processes (Takaki et al. 2012).

5kV   X600   20µm   13 50 SEI

Figure 4.8 SEM photomicrograph of a human hair from a wig, lacking a cuticle.

4.5.2.2 Cortex

All hairs have a cortex, although it may be reduced to a thin margin in the hairs of some animals (e.g. deer). While difficult to observe in pristine hair, the boundaries of individual cortical cells may be observed in mechanically or chemically damaged hair. Cortical cells are easily discerned in frayed tips, appearing as splayed, brush-like fibrils (Figure 4.9). Cortical cells are anisotropic, exhibiting parallel extinction with a positive sign of elongation and relatively low birefringence (typically <0.01) (McCrone and Delly 1973; McCrone 1977). When viewed between crossed polars in a non-extinction position, straight hairs will have uninterrupted bands of interference colors aligned parallel to the long axis of the fiber (Figure 4.10). Subtle disruptions to the form of

50 µm

Figure 4.9 Frayed end of a human head hair with individual cortical cells visible (mounted in xylene and viewed using transmitted light).

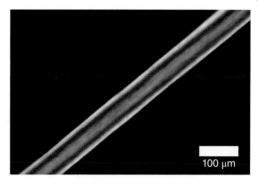

100 µm

Figure 4.10 Parallel interference colors in a straight human head hair (mounted in xylene and viewed between crossed polars).

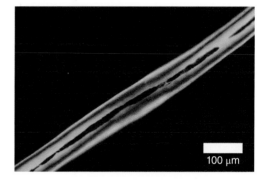

100 µm

Figure 4.11 Distorted interference colors in a slightly twisted human head hair (mounted in xylene and viewed between crossed polars).

the hair shaft (e.g. twisting or shouldering) that may be difficult to observe using transmitted light will manifest themselves as more easily visible irregularities of these interference color bands (Figure 4.11).

Minute air spaces between cortical cells, known as cortical fusi, appear as slightly elongated (oriented parallel to the long axis of the hair), high contrast, dark voids (Hausman 1932) (Figure 4.12).[49] Cortical fusi are most commonly observed in the proximal regions of a hair shaft above catagen or telogen roots but they may be found throughout the shaft. In general, cortical fusi are more likely to be found in colorless or lightly colored hair (Hausman 1932; Seta et al. 1988).

---

49 It can be demonstrated that cortical fusi are composed of air by viewing them using reflected light, as they appear white under this illumination condition.

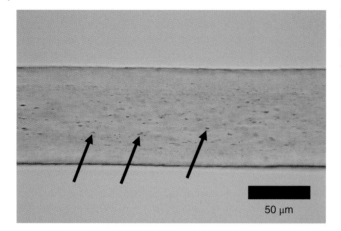

Figure 4.12 Cortical fusi, a few of which are marked with arrows, in the shaft of a human head hair (mounted in xylene and viewed using transmitted light).

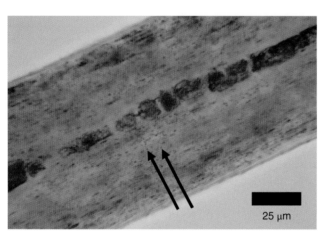

Figure 4.13 Distinct pigment granules, a few of which are marked with arrows, in the shaft of a human head hair (mounted in xylene and viewed using transmitted light).

In humans, the pigment responsible for giving hair its color is commonly located within the cortex, although it can also be found within the medulla and traces of it may occur in the cuticle. Individual pigment units are known as granules (Figure 4.13). These discrete granules vary in color, size, and shape. Regarding color, pigment typically appears black, brown, reddish-orange, or yellowish when viewed using transmitted light. The largest discrete pigment granules are a few micrometers in size while the smallest cannot be resolved using a light microscope. Pigment granules are typically round or slightly elongated, in which case they will be aligned roughly parallel to the long axis of the hair.

Larger, seemingly solid, agglomerations of undispersed pigment found within the cortex are known as ovoid bodies, as they are typically elliptical in shape (aligned parallel to the long axis of the hair) (Figure 4.14).

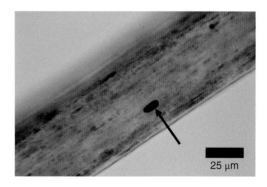

Figure 4.14 Example of an ovoid body, marked with an arrow, in the shaft of a human head hair (mounted in xylene and viewed using transmitted light).

Figure 4.15 Continuous medulla in the shaft of a human head hair, mounted in xylene and viewed using transmitted (left) and reflected (right) light.

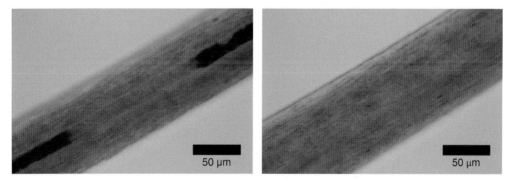

Figure 4.16 Examples of partially (left) and completely (right) fluid-filled medullae in human head hairs (mounted in xylene and viewed using transmitted light).

4.5.2.3 Medulla

The medulla typically appears as an opaque band in the central region of the hair when viewed using transmitted light. It appears opaque because it is filled with air.[50] A seemingly opaque medulla will appear white when the hair is viewed using reflected light, thus confirming the presence of the entrapped air (Figure 4.15). A fluid-filled medulla will appear translucent and while identifiable, it will not be as distinct compared to an air-filled medulla (Figure 4.16).

The internal cellular structure of the medulla cannot be critically examined when it is filled with air. However, there are multiple techniques for "clearing" the hair (i.e. replacing the air with a suitable medium), some of which are discussed in Section 4.10. In contrast, certain characteristics such as the medullary index[51] and the contours of the medullary margin are best viewed with an opaque (i.e. air-filled) medulla.

Unlike the cuticle and the cortex, medullae are not present in all hairs and they are frequently absent from relatively thin hairs.

4.5.3 Basic Hair Identification

The first step to a hair examination is confirming that the material being studied is in

---

50 More specifically, the medulla appears opaque because of the large difference between the refractive indices of the entrapped air within the medulla and the surrounding cortical cells.

51 The medullary index is the ratio of the thickness of the medulla relative to the thickness of the hair.

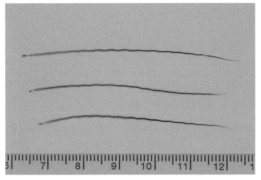 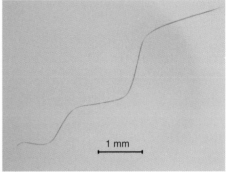

Figure 4.17 Moose (*Alces alces*) hair exhibiting undulations (left) and a short-tailed shrew (*Blarina brevicauda*) hair exhibiting a distinct zig-zag (right).

fact hair. This is typically a trivial matter, but the importance of this identification should not be overlooked.[52] In some cases, industrially processed or severely degraded hair fragments require careful observation before a firm identification can be made.

In general, hairs can be distinguished from other fibrous objects (e.g. natural cellulosic fibers, man-made fibers, and feather fragments) by the identification of the different histological tissues of which they are composed (i.e. the cuticle, the cortex, and possibly the medulla). The identification of recognizable cuticular scales or a true medulla (i.e. not another centrally located morphological feature such as a lumen) is of significant value. It should be reiterated that not all hairs possess a medulla and that only air-filled medullae will appear opaque when viewed using transmitted light.

The evaluation of optical and chemical properties can also be useful with regards to hair identification. For example, hairs should display appropriate retardation colors for their approximate thicknesses when viewed between crossed polars in a non-extinction position. Similarly, when they are immersed in a solution of iodine-azide, all hairs should give a positive microchemical reaction in the

form of the evolution of nitrogen gas bubbles, as they contain significant amounts of sulfide groups (Feigl and Anger 1972) (Figure 4.18).

Finally, a hair examiner should be familiar with the microscopical morphology, optical properties, and chemistry of other fibrous materials. This will help the examiner appreciate the differences that exist between hair and the materials that could potentially be confused with hair.

4.5.4 Human Versus Animal Hair

Once a specimen has been identified as a hair, the next step is generally determining if it originated from a human or an animal. This determination is often straightforward but there are instances when it requires considerable attention.

Some hairs may be recognized as originating from an animal based on macroscopic observations. For example, only animal hairs have distinct shield regions. Similarly, only animal hairs exhibit multiple abrupt coloration changes, known as banding.[53] Finally, some animal hairs have contour patterns (e.g. undulations or zig-zags) not observed in human hairs (Figure 4.17).

---

52 Our laboratory has been asked to examine "hairs" after their "roots" did not produce a nuclear DNA profile. The subsequent microscopical examination revealed that they were in fact synthetic fibers.

53 Human hairs may be dyed different colors, but the true banding patterns observed in animal hairs are a result of pigmentation differences. Microscopical examination can determine whether a hair's color changes are the result of dyes or pigments if there are any doubts after the initial examination.

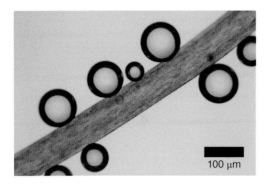

100 μm

Figure 4.18 Nitrogen gas bubbles forming on a human head hair upon exposure to an iodine-azide solution (viewed using transmitted light).

There are many microscopic characteristics that can be used to differentiate human and animal hairs. The size and form of the medulla are often the most diagnostic features. In general, the medulla in a human hair occupies no more than approximately one-third of the total width of the hair (i.e. it has a medullary index $\leq \sim 0.33$). The medullae of many, but not all, animal hairs are considerably wider. In other words, wide medullae are indicative of animal hairs, but narrow medullae are not necessarily indicative of human hairs.

The medullary morphology of human hair is typically described as amorphous. In contrast, the medullae of most, but not all, animal hairs have definite patterns. These medullary patterns are best observed after the hair has been "cleared," but features useful for distinguishing human and animal hairs can be observed without advanced sample preparation techniques. Again, in simplified terms, distinct medullary patterns are indicative of animal hairs, but amorphous medullary patterns do not necessarily indicate human hair.

It has been stated that the medullary ultrastructure of human hair, as observed using electron microscopy of sectioned hair, is unique and distinguishable from all other animals, although it most closely resembles other apes (e.g. chimpanzees or gorillas) (Clement et al. 1981, 1982). While intriguing,

the ultimate conclusions of this work have not been replicated[54] and this level of examination is not practically possible in a forensic laboratory routinely examining large numbers of hairs.

Microscopic features of the cuticle and cortex may also offer clues relevant for distinguishing human and animal hairs. The cuticular scales of some animal hairs significantly protrude from the margins of the hair. Humans and other animals have cuticular scales that lie close to the surface of the hair.[55]

In human hair, most of the pigment is found within the cortex, and is evenly distributed or somewhat concentrated near the periphery (i.e. closer to the cuticle than to the medulla), although red-headed individuals have been cited as exceptions to this general trend (Figure 4.19) (Harvey 1938; Vernall 1963; Deedrick and Koch 2004a; Koch et al. 2019).[56] Animals often have significant amounts of pigment within both the cortex and the medulla.

Individual pigment granules are typically $\leq 1\,\mu m$ in human hair (Robbins 2002) but larger granules can be found in animal hairs (e.g. many rodent species have large granules which are principally located within the medulla) (Figure 4.20).

Lastly, human hairs have relatively small, bulbous, club-shaped telogen roots. Many animal hairs have larger or more elaborate root morphologies which are easily distinguished from those of humans (Figure 4.21).

---

54 It should be noted that other researchers have described the same medullary ultrastructure in human hairs (Wagner and Joekes 2007), but have not confirmed the claim that it is specific to humans.
55 Human cuticular scales can become frayed or ragged after physical damage (e.g. back-combing) or cosmetic treatment. Consequently, these scales may protrude significantly from the main body of the hair. However, the irregularity of these scales should be easily differentiated from animal hairs with naturally prominent cuticular scales.
56 The radial distribution of pigment is best observed directly in a transverse cross-section, but it may be inferred by optically sectioning the hair (both techniques are discussed in Section 4.10).

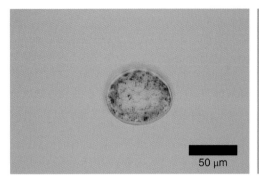 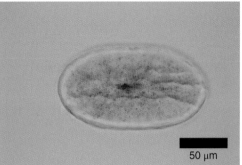

Figure 4.19 Transverse cross-sections of a brown human head hair exhibiting peripherally concentrated pigment (left) and a red human head hair exhibiting centrally concentrated pigment (right) (mounted in xylene and viewed using transmitted light).

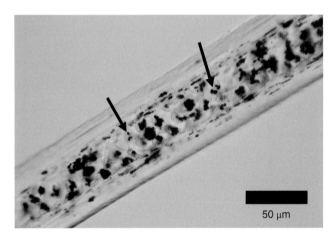

Figure 4.20 Cleared longitudinal cross-section of a hair from a pet rat (*Rattus norvegicus*) exhibiting large, globular pigment granules in the medulla, a few of which are marked with arrows (mounted in glycerin and viewed using transmitted light).

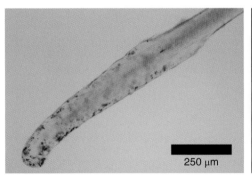 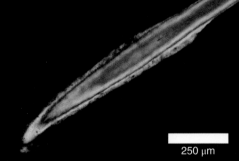

Figure 4.21 Large, elongated root of a brown bear (*Ursus arctos*) mounted in xylene and viewed using transmitted light (left) and between crossed polars (right).

4.6 Human Hair Examinations

Most forensic hair cases involve the examination of human hair. Historically, the emphasis has been placed on human hair comparisons (i.e. determining if a questioned hair *could* have originated from a given person). However, it must be stressed that the microscopical examination of hair can provide information relating to many other discrete questions, including, but not limited to:

- What somatic (i.e. body) region did the hair originate from?
- What is the ancestry of the person from whom the hair originated?
- Has the hair been cosmetically treated?
- Does the hair exhibit shaft abnormalities indicative of disease?
- Was the hair forcibly removed from the skin?
- Does the hair exhibit morphological characteristics indicative of discrete events or the environmental conditions to which it may have been subjected prior to its recovery?

In most cases, microscopy is the only practical means by which these questions can be answered, and it is almost always the most efficient and cost-effective.

4.6.1 Somatic Origin

It is obvious that terminal hairs from different areas of the human body exhibit gross macroscopical differences (e.g. length, contour, and thickness). The hairs from these locations can also exhibit distinct microscopical differences. As such, human hairs are generally classified as originating from a specific somatic origin (e.g. scalp, eyebrow, eyelash, beard, axillary, body, or pubic). While appearing relatively straightforward, there are significant complexities regarding the determination of the somatic origin of an unknown hair.

First, there is no universal agreement as to the number or location of different hair regions. For example, four different references define six,[57] nine,[58] ten,[59] and twelve[60] different somatic regions. Second, it is not true that all examples of hairs from these different body areas are truly distinctive. For example, pubic and axillary hairs often exhibit many morphological similarities, as mentioned in all four of the references listed above. Third, there are inherent biological limitations on the entire concept of assigning distinct body locations to individual hairs. In men, for example, there are transitional regions between head hairs and beard hairs, nape of the neck and back hairs, and between pubic hairs and leg or abdominal body hairs. Even from a macroscopic standpoint, there is no definitive line that can be drawn separating these areas. In summary, there are significant amounts of biological variation that cannot always be satisfactorily quantized into distinct types.

The above is not written to dismiss the ability of a trained examiner to express an opinion regarding the assignment of a hair to a specific body region. It is intended to address the fact that this is not always a straightforward task.

Given this complexity, it is the author's opinion that there is more justification for the classification of relatively fewer somatic categories. The best way to learn about the differences and similarities between the hairs of various somatic regions is to examine many examples of each type from different people. The following generalized summary, adapted primarily from the sources listed above, is not a substitute for the experience gained by directly observing hairs themselves:

---

57 Head, eyebrow/eyelash, beard/mustache, body, pubic, and axillary (Garn 1951b).
58 Head, pubic, limb, beard/mustache, chest, axillary, eyebrow, eyelash, and trunk (Hicks 1977).
59 Head, eyebrows, eyelashes, beard, ear, nose, axillary, pubic, body, limb (Danforth 1925).
60 Head, pubic, vulvar, chest, beard, axillary, eyebrow, eyelash, limb, ear, buttock, and nose (Bisbing 2002).

- Head
  - Diameter varies greatly between hairs (typical range ~25–125 μm) but it is relatively uniform for a given hair.
  - Length varies greatly from a few millimeters to over a meter.
  - The medulla, if present, is relatively narrow.
  - Typically possess cut or frayed tips, except in young children which have naturally tapered tips until their hair is cut.
- Pubic
  - Generally coarse and wiry.
  - Irregular cross-sectional shapes and contours with twists and constrictions.
  - Distinct "buckles" often visible using microscopy (Figure 4.22).
  - Moderate in length (less than ~90 mm).
  - Medullae often relatively thick.
  - Telogen roots often possess follicular material (Figure 4.23).
- Axillary
  - Resembling pubic hairs but generally shorter (less than ~70 mm) and thinner, with less pronounced contour irregularities (i.e. straighter without distinct buckles).
  - Distal tips may be abraded or frayed and appear lighter or yellowish in color.
- Beard/mustache
  - Coarse with varying lengths (less than 1 mm to lengths more typical of head hairs).

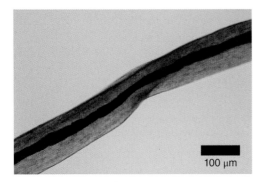

Figure 4.22 Buckle in the shaft of a human pubic hair (mounted in xylene and viewed using transmitted light).

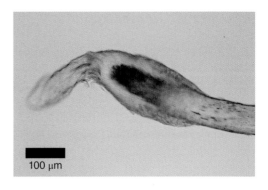

Figure 4.23 Telogen root from a naturally shed human pubic hair (mounted in xylene and viewed using transmitted light). Note the follicular material adhering to the root of the hair.

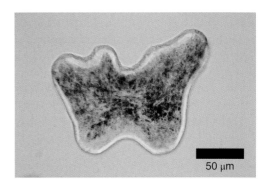

Figure 4.24 Elaborate cross-sectional shape in a human beard hair (mounted in xylene and viewed using transmitted light).

  - Many are somewhat triangular in cross-sectional shape, although there can be significant variability (Figure 4.24).
  - Medullae are often relatively thick with complex structure (a double medulla may be present (Danforth 1925; Chowdhuri and Bhattacharyya 1964)).
  - Often exhibit razor or clipper cuts.
  - Typically have a thick cuticle compared to head hairs (Tolgyesi et al. 1983).
- Eyelash/eyebrow
  - Short (less than ~1 cm) and curved but some eyebrow hairs may be longer and curled/twisted.
  - Relatively thick for length.
  - Generally tapered tip but eyebrows may be cut.

- Body/limb[61]
  - ○ Typically relatively thin and short but thickness and length are highly variable depending on body area.
  - ○ Generally possess tapered tips that may be abraded.
  - ○ Chest hairs may resemble some less distinct pubic and axillary hairs.

Due to the inherent complexities and limitations described above, it is not always possible to determine the somatic origin of an unknown hair. For example, a hair exhibiting indistinct characteristics shared by both pubic and axillary hairs may be described and identified as such.

4.6.2 Ancestry

General trends in macroscopic characteristics of hair such as color and contour are apparent amongst people who originate from different places around the world. This variation, along with variations in the microscopic morphology of hairs, has been studied for over 150 years.[62] Much of the fundamental work was conducted in the realm of anthropology (Trotter 1938; Steggerda 1940; Steggerda and Seibert 1941; Vernall 1961; Hrdy 1973; Guilbeau-Frugier et al. 2006; Lasisi et al. 2016). In more recent decades, the anthropologists have been joined by scientists in other fields, most notably cosmetic science (Takahashi et al. 2006; Loussouarn et al. 2007; Westgate et al. 2013).

In general, this research has identified three major groups with respect to hair morphology. This variation was frequently cited as one of the anthropological components used for racial classifications. The terms Caucasoid, Negroid, and Mongoloid were commonly used to describe these three races in the literature of the twentieth century. Because forensic science adopted this anthropological construct, these terms are also found in the forensic literature (Hicks 1977; Bisbing 2002).

More recently, many anthropologists have argued against the entire concept of "race" regarding the human species and most now prefer to think of an individual's genetic ancestry (Brace 1995; Kennedy 1995; Wagner et al. 2017).[63] Specifically, the terms European, African or sub-Saharan African, and Asian or East Asian may be used to describe the three broad groups. Functionally, little has changed in forensic science except that it has once again adopted, or is at least in the process of adopting, the classification terms preferred by most anthropologists.

However, it is understood that this threefold division is an oversimplification that only begins to capture the diversity exhibited in the hair from people around the world. In other words, many ethnic groups do not necessarily fit neatly within the confines of these three broad groups.

At the same time, it must also be recognized that there is overlap between the morphological variations exhibited by members of the three major groups. This means that while there are recognizable differences between the groups as a whole, not every member of each group will be distinguishable on the basis of their hair morphology. Additionally, individuals of mixed ancestry represent another layer of complexity that effectively reduces the distinctness of even these three broad groups.

For these reasons, the hair examiner must approach the subject of ancestral identification with appropriate caution. Simply put, definitive classifications are not always warranted, and the strongest opinions are only justified when hairs exhibit the "end-member" morphologies of a given group (i.e. they exhibit the classic morphologies of a group that are almost

---

61 The body/limb hair category may be used as a general term for hairs that do not appear to originate from a more specific somatic location.

62 For example, the cross-sectional shape of human head hair was first used to divide populations into three major groups in the middle of the nineteenth century (Browne 1853).

63 Specifically, different phenotypes (hair color, hair curliness, skin color, etc.) vary independently with geography and do not correlate with definable "races."

never observed in either of the two other groups). Despite their limitations, ancestral identifications can provide useful investigative leads under appropriate circumstances.

It is also important to recognize that essentially all of the research in this area has been conducted on head hair. As such, the following generalized summary applies only to head hairs and is not a substitute for the experience gained by directly observing hairs themselves (Lee and De Forest 1984; Robertson 1999; Bisbing 2002)[64]:

- Asian (Figure 4.25)
  - Generally straight contour.
  - Macroscopically dark in color.
  - Moderate to thick shaft diameter.
  - Typically circular cross-sectional shape.
  - Relatively thick cuticle.[65]
  - Relatively high pigment density, often with a reddish cast.
- European (Figure 4.26)
  - Contour varies from relatively straight to moderately curly.
  - Wide variety of natural macroscopic color (light blonde to dark brown/black).

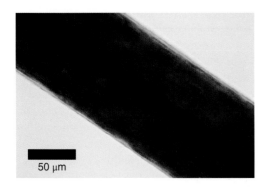

Figure 4.25 Example of a head hair from a person of East Asian ancestry (mounted in xylene and viewed using transmitted light).

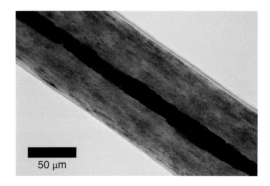

Figure 4.26 Example of a head hair from a person of European ancestry (mounted in xylene and viewed using transmitted light).

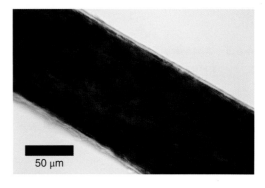

Figure 4.27 Example of a head hair from a person of sub-Saharan African ancestry (mounted in xylene and viewed using transmitted light).

  - Moderate to fine shaft diameter.
  - Typically oval cross-sectional shape.
  - Moderate cuticle thickness.
  - Relatively low to moderate pigment density.
- African (Figure 4.27)
  - Generally curly or kinked contour (sometimes tightly curled).
  - Macroscopically dark in color.
  - Relatively fine to coarse shaft diameter.
  - Typically flattened cross-sectional shape.[66]

64 Progress has been made recently in elucidating the underlying genetic factors determining some of these phenotypes (Fujimoto et al. 2009; Medland et al. 2009; Tan et al. 2013; Adhikari et al. 2016).

65 It has been demonstrated that the principal reason the cuticles of Asian hairs are generally thicker than European hairs is because they have more layers of cuticular scales (Takahashi et al. 2006; Kim et al. 2006).

66 The flattened cross-sectional shape causes the hair to have large apparent shaft diameter variations depending on whether the examiner is viewing the minor or major elliptical axis. Although there are conflicting reports in the literature, careful examinations using light microscopy and SEM demonstrate that this is primarily an artifact of the

o Relatively high pigment density often with clumps of pigment.

A number of these observations, which were originally made by light microscopy (e.g. cross-sectional shape, cuticle thickness, pigment size, and pigment density), have been augmented by quantitative research on the ultrastructure of hairs from members of these three general populations (Koch et al. 2019).

4.6.3 Cosmetic Treatment

In forensic hair examinations, "cosmetic treatment" generally refers to the alteration of the macroscopic appearance of hair and does not include "normal" cosmetic practices such as shampooing and conditioning.[67] Typically, this involves changing the hair color (i.e. bleaching or dyeing) or its contour (i.e. permanent waving or straightening). It is most commonly encountered with human hair although dyed animal hair is frequently observed in fur garments.[68] Fundamentally, these processes are degradative to the shaft of the hair.

The underlying chemistries of the processes have been studied extensively, mostly in the cosmetic sciences. A complete discussion of these topics is beyond the scope of this chapter but many relatively modern references review them in detail (Bolduc and Shapiro 2001; Robbins 2002; Harrison and Sinclair 2003; Zviak and Sabbagh 2005; Zviak and Milléquant 2005a,b,c; Morel and Chrisite 2011; Guerra-Tapia and Gonzalez-Guerra 2014).

In very general terms, both permanent waving and straightening typically involve the breaking of the disulfide bonds with reducing agents, shaping the hair to the desired form, and reforming the disulfide bonds via oxidation. Bleaching refers to the lightening of the hair through the oxidation of the melanin pigments (often using hydrogen peroxide either alone or with additional chemicals). Bleaching may be performed to achieve the desired hair color directly, or it may be used to lighten the hair in preparation for subsequent dyeing. Dyeing refers to changing the hairs' color, and the dyes utilized are often classified based on the longevity of the altered color (e.g. permanent dyes, semi-permanent dyes, and temporary dyes).

Permanent or "oxidation" dyes are the most complex dye systems and represent the vast majority of the commercial dye market (Bolduc and Shapiro 2001). They generally have three main components: primary intermediates, couplers, and an oxidizer (almost always hydrogen peroxide), referred to as an oxidant in the cosmetic literature. The primary intermediates diffuse into the hair and are oxidized by the hydrogen peroxide to form colored active intermediates. These active intermediates then react with the couplers inside the hair to form large colored complexes (i.e. dyes) (Bolduc and Shapiro 2001). This process is permanent because the resulting dyes are too large to diffuse back out of the hair (although the process needs to be repeated every 4–6 weeks to maintain a uniform appearance at the roots as new, undyed, hair is continually growing) (Robbins 2002). Permanent dyes have the ability to lighten the original color of the hair due to the presence of hydrogen peroxide but a separate bleaching step is required before the dyeing process if a significantly lighter shade of blonde is desired (Bolduc and Shapiro 2001).

Semi-permanent or "direct" dyes have low molecular weights and diffuse into the hair but do not bind strongly. They therefore slowly diffuse out of the hair and are typically expected to remain for four to eight shampoos (Bolduc and Shapiro 2001; Robbins 2002). Unlike permanent dyes, they are intrinsically colored and

---

cross-sectional shape and that hairs from individuals of African ancestry do not appear to constrict or collapse as they coil (Lee and De Forest 1984: Lindelöf et al. 1988; Harding and Rogers 1999; Khumalo et al. 2000).
67 However, haircare products that leave visible residues on the hair (e.g. hair spray and gel) can be isolated and chemically analyzed if they are recognized. Gas chromatography-mass spectrometry (GC-MS) has also been used to identify cosmetic hair care products in the residues extracted from human hairs (Fujita et al. 1987, 1989a, 1990).
68 While rare, it is also possible to encounter cosmetically treated pet hair.

therefore do not require oxidation (Harrison and Sinclair 2003). Because they do not have an oxidizing component, they cannot be used to lighten the original color of the hair.

Temporary dyes can be described as "makeup products for hair" (Zviak and Milléquant 2005b). They are composed of high-molecular weight acid dyes which are deposited on the surface of the hair (i.e. they do not penetrate the cuticle) and are expected to be removed after a single shampooing.[69]

Detecting these various cosmetic treatments is typically the principal interest of the forensic hair examiner. Abrupt changes in color (either through bleaching or dyeing) may be observed in the form of a "dye line" on the shaft of the hair (Figures 4.28 and 4.29). These well-defined changes in color may be observed macro- or microscopically and are a result of the cosmetic treatment affecting only the portion of the hair shaft above the skin's surface. Observing unnatural hair colors in the cortex or diffuse color in the cuticle, besides a slight yellowish cast, are also indications that the hair has been dyed. Additionally, when viewed in whole mounts, the color of dyed hairs is

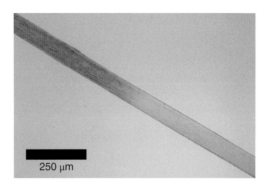

Figure 4.29 Bleach-line in a human head hair in which the proximal, brown pigmented shaft quickly transitions to a lighter, bleached color (mounted in xylene and viewed using transmitted light).

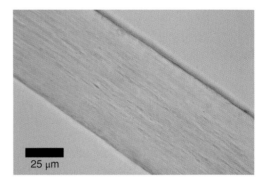

Figure 4.30 Close-up view of the cortical texture in the shaft of a heavily bleached human head hair (mounted in xylene and viewed using transmitted light).

generally homogeneously distributed throughout the cortex, in contrast to undyed hairs, in which the color arises from discrete pigment granules. Hairs that have been bleached also often exhibit a distinct wavy cortical texture resulting from the cortical cells beginning to separate from each other (Figure 4.30).

Mild bleaching or dyeing may not result in distinct "dye lines" and additional techniques have been proposed for visualizing these treatments. Historically, staining with methylene blue has been cited in the forensic literature but fluorescence microscopy has also been suggested (Turner 1949; Roe et al. 1985; Witt et al. 2016). Caution must be used with these two techniques as they both detect general

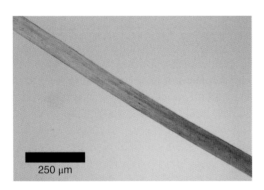

Figure 4.28 Dye-line in a human head hair in which the proximal, light brown pigmented shaft quickly transitions to a deeper, dyed, reddish-brown (mounted in xylene and viewed using transmitted light).

69 Temporary dyes may persist for longer than a single washing if they were applied to previously cosmetically treated (i.e. damaged and somewhat porous) hair (Bolduc and Shapiro 2001).

oxidative damage which can be caused by a discrete cosmetic treatment, but such damage also gradually occurs naturally through weathering (Nelson and De Forest 1999).

Permanent waving and straightening also result in oxidative damage, but these treatments do not alter the color of the hair and are thus significantly more difficult to detect using microscopy alone. It has been demonstrated using SEM that these treatments damage the cuticular scales but the damage is not necessarily diagnostic or differentiable from other forms of cumulative degradation, except perhaps in cases of severe treatment (Swift 1971; Swift and Brown 1972).[70]

Chemical techniques using infrared (IR) and Raman spectroscopy, as well as liquid chromatography-mass spectrometry (LC–MS), have been suggested for detecting changes in hair chemistry due to oxidation but they generally suffer the same drawbacks as the microscopical techniques (i.e. the ultimate cause of the oxidative damage cannot be determined) (Brenner et al. 1985; Strassburger and Breuer 1985; Panayiotou and Kokot 1999; Pudney et al. 2013; Petzel-Witt et al. 2018).

Hairs that have been dyed offer entire new avenues for color and chemical analyses analogous to the techniques used in forensic fiber examinations. For example, the color of dyed hairs can be analyzed using microspectrophotometry (MSP) (Barrett et al. 2010, 2011).

The dyes may also be extracted from the hair and analyzed using a variety of techniques (e.g. thin layer chromatography [TLC], GC-MS, and high-performance liquid chromatography [HPLC]) (Bailey 1982; Roe et al. 1985; Singh and Garg 2009; Fujita et al. 1989b; Tanada et al. 1991, 1994, 1999; Scarpi et al. 1998; Zhu et al. 2008).

Extraction systems originally developed for wool fibers can be used to extract dyes from

hair (Macrae and Smalldon 1979; Macrae et al. 1979; Roe et al. 1985; Wiggins 1999). It should be noted that dye extractions are generally considered destructive testing since the evidence is permanently altered.[71] As such, they should only be utilized after a complete microscopical examination has been conducted and appropriate precautions should be followed:

- Experiment with different extraction solvents, and eluents if performing TLC, to optimize the analysis.
- Determine the minimum amount of sample required to obtain a robust result.[72]
- Document the questioned hair in its original state before the extraction procedure.
- Preserve enough of the original questioned hair that a complete re-examination, including dye analysis, can be conducted by another scientist.
- Preserve the extracted hair fragments (and the chromatography plate if TLC is performed).

Alternatively, in situ analysis of the dyes within the hair using surface-enhanced Raman spectroscopy (SERS) and attenuated total reflection (ATR) Fourier transform infrared spectroscopy (FTIR) have been suggested (Kurouski and Van Duyne 2015; Boll et al. 2017). One major benefit of these techniques is that the dyes do not need to be extracted from the hair, and thus they are non-destructive.[73]

The identification of cosmetic treatment can provide both investigative leads and increase the significance of a hair comparison, especially if additional analytical information

---

70 Methylene blue has also been suggested for detecting permanent waving in hairs (Roe et al. 1985). This confirms that care must be used when evaluating the results of this test as the ultimate cause of the oxidative damage cannot always be discerned.

71 Although in the case of TLC analysis, nothing is actually destroyed.

72 This task is more challenging with typical hairs compared to synthetic fibers because there are generally more variations with hair morphology and dye uptake (i.e. the extraction of dye may vary considerably within the known hairs and it is difficult to ensure that the known hair, or hairs, being used in the length determination experiments will adequately represent the extraction behavior of the questioned hair).

73 It should be noted that the hairs are compressed in small areas using the ATR technique.

regarding the altered color, or the chemistry of the dyes responsible for the color, can be elucidated. Additionally, the relative timing of the cosmetic treatment can be estimated if it is found in a hair with an anagen root (i.e. a hair that was actively growing when it was removed).[74]

4.6.4 Shaft Abnormalities

Hair shafts can exhibit numerous structural abnormalities which can be distinguished using microscopy. These abnormalities are sometimes associated with specific diseases and they are often genetically inherited, but some may be acquired via certain activities.

Population statistics are difficult to find in the literature, but these morphological aberrations are not encountered frequently in casework (Robertson 1999). This relative rarity makes their identification an important point of comparison when they are present in both known and questioned hair, but they can also provide valuable investigative leads.

The literature is devoted primarily to abnormalities of scalp hair. Briefly, some of the abnormalities described in the literature are as follows (Price 1975; Whiting 1987; Rogers 1995, 1996; Messenger et al. 2010; Adya et al. 2011):

- *Monilethrix (beaded hair)*: Hair shafts appear beaded with thicker nodes separated from each other by tapering internodes (the nodes have diameters that are typical of scalp hair). The lengths of the nodes and the distances between them can vary significantly but they are classically described as being ∼ 0.7–1 mm apart. Affected hairs

---

74 It should also be understood that hairs from the same source can exhibit differences in the lengths between the dye lines and the roots (i.e. the untreated portion of the hair) as hairs can be in different stages of the growth cycle (Nelson and De Forest 1999). For example, consider two hairs: one in the middle of anagen and one just entering telogen when they are dyed. If these hairs are removed at the same time after 2 months have elapsed, there will be different lengths of untreated hair shafts between the roots and the dye lines.

break easily at the thin internodes which are non-medullated and often have longitudinal ridges/grooves on the cuticle. Other somatic regions, including eyebrows, eyelashes, axillary, pubic, limb, and body hair, may also be affected.

- *Pili torti (twisted hair)*: Hair shafts have flattened cross-sectional shapes which rotate 180° on their longitudinal axes (rotations of 90° and 360° are less commonly observed). Several of these twists (approximately three to five) are normally found on the same hair shaft, which is brittle as a result (seemingly normal hairs with an occasional twist are not classified as exhibiting pili torti). Eyebrows and eyelashes can also be affected. It is often associated with various syndromes (e.g. Menkes' syndrome and Beare syndrome, the latter of which appears for the first time in adults).

- *Trichorrhexis invaginata (bamboo hair)*: Hair shafts have "bamboo-like" nodes resembling ball-and-socket joints (the cup-like socket is always proximal) resulting from incomplete keratinization. These nodes are weak points in the brittle hair and once broken the proximal portion exhibits a "golf tee" morphology. It can affect hairs on all somatic regions and it is associated with Netherton's disease.

- *Trichorrhexis nodosa*: Hair shafts with swollen nodes resulting from physical trauma, sometimes caused by defects in the keratinization of the hair. However, this same morphology can be found in normal hairs. The nodes resemble two brushes facing each other with fibrillated cortical cells resulting from a loss of the overlying cuticle. The shaft will eventually fracture at these nodes. It can affect other somatic regions, including eyelashes, eyebrows, pubic, and body hair. It is associated with the metabolic disorder argininosuccinic aciduria but it can also be the result of excessive cosmetic treatment, brushing, or back-combing (i.e. acquired trichorrhexis nodosa).

- *Trichothiodystrophy (sulfur-deficient brittle hair)*: Hair shafts are flattened and may fold over on themselves, resembling twisted ribbons. The cuticle is irregular, incomplete, or absent and the hair exhibits alternating bands of birefringence when viewed between crossed polars.[75] The pigment may be distributed in a wavy pattern and sharp, transverse fractures associated with missing cuticle cells in the immediate vicinity of the break (trichoschisis) may be observed.[76] It can affect eyelashes and eyebrows as well.

- *Pili annulati (ringed hair)*: Hair shafts macroscopically appear to have light and dark bands. The bright bands are due to light scattering caused by air spaces in the cortex (i.e. they appear dark when viewed using transmitted light). Axillary hair may also be affected.
- *Pseudo-pili annulati*: Hair shafts appear macroscopically similar to pili annulati with light and dark bands but there are no air voids in the cortex. The bright bands are caused by twisted hairs with flattened cross-sectional shapes (i.e. specular reflection).
- *Uncombable hair syndrome (spun glass hair or pili trianguli et canaliculi)*: Hairs have triangular cross-sectional shapes with longitudinal grooves resulting in rigid shafts. Examination using crossed polars can aid in the identification of the triangular cross-sectional shape.
- *Pili bifurcati*: Recognized as a hair split into two halves, each with its own fully intact cuticle. These two shafts may reunite upon additional growth.
- *Trichonodosis (knotted hair)*: Most common in curly hair and may also affect pubic hair. Essentially, hairs become entangled with themselves, forming knots, upon physical rubbing.

There are also several examples where abnormalities are caused by foreign material adhering to the hair. Some of these cause

---

75 The entire hair is birefringent, as can be demonstrated through rotation, but the hair does not exhibit parallel extinction along its entire length.
76 Fractures with this morphology can also be observed in normal hairs.

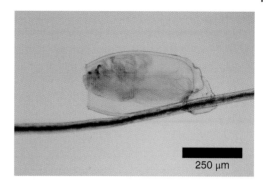

Figure 4.31 Louse egg, with a louse inside, adhering to the hair shaft from a striped skunk (*Mephitis mephitis*) (mounted in glycerin and viewed using transmitted light).

damage to the hair shaft while others are essentially benign from a structural perspective. Examples include the following (Whiting 1987; Sentamilselvi et al. 2009; Charles 2009; Adya et al. 2011):

- Nits: Oval lice eggs (~0.5–0.8 mm long) can be observed adhering to the shafts of hairs (Figure 4.31). The nits may appear white to brown, depending on the development of the louse within, if it has not already hatched. *Pediculosis capitis* affects primarily the scalp and beard while *Phthirus pubis* affects mainly pubic hair although it can be found in other somatic locations (e.g. axillary, eyelashes, and eyebrows).
- *Peripilar casts*: These are keratinous cylinders enveloping the hair shaft, composed primarily of root sheath tissue. Unlike nits, which are secured to the shaft, these cylinders can slide along the hair shaft. They are sometimes referred to as "pseudonits."
- *Trichomycosis axillaris*: A condition in which hair shafts of axillary and pubic hair exhibit nodules caused by bacteria of the genus *Corynebacterium*. These nodules can be yellow, orange, red, or black in color and adhere strongly to, and may envelope, the shaft. The bacteria penetrate and damage the cuticle and can be visualized using SEM or various staining techniques, including fluorescent probes.

- *Black piedra*: Recognized by gritty brown to black nodules that are well adhered to the hair shaft. It is caused by the fungus *Piedraia hortae* and both brown spores and hyphae may be identified through microscopical examination. It is a tropical disease primarily affecting the cortex of scalp, beard, and sometimes body hairs. The damage caused by the fungi can lead to broken hairs.
- *White piedra*: Recognized by soft, spongy, nodes that can be easily removed from hair shafts. These nodes are primarily white but may appear other colors as well. It is caused by yeast-like fungi of the genus *Trichosporon* which has spores that are essentially colorless. Pubic and beard hairs are primarily affected but it can also occur in head, eyelash, and axillary hairs. Penetration of the hair cuticle can cause structural damage leading to fractures.
- *Tinea capitis*: Caused by a variety of fungi that invade hair follicles, primarily of children. These dermatophytes can be divided into three main groups:
  - *Ectothrix*: Hairs have a characteristic gray, lusterless appearance due to fungal material on the surface of the cuticle which is damaged. Caused primarily by members of the genera *Microsporum* and *Trichophyton*, these hairs will typically fluoresce using ultraviolet (UV) light, and break a few millimeters from the skin surface.
  - *Endothrix*: Caused by fungi of the genus *Trichophyton* within the cortex. The cuticular layer remains intact but the hairs appear swollen and black, typically breaking off at scalp level. This condition is also known as black dot and the hairs do not fluoresce using UV light.
  - *Favus*: A specific endothrix infection typically caused by *Trichophyton schoenleinii*. Affected hairs have characteristic voids in the cortex with many hyphae and few spores.

Many of these conditions may be treated with topical agents. These medications may be recognized on the surfaces of hairs during a microscopical examination, even if the hairs themselves show no evidence of abnormality. Once isolated, they can be identified using various chemical techniques (e.g. FTIR and GC-MS). This information can either augment a microscopical comparison or provide investigative leads.

4.6.5 Hair End Morphology

As linear objects, hairs have both a proximal end and a distal tip. All hairs arise from a proximal root and originally possess a tapered distal tip. While this idealized state is commonly observed in animal hairs, many hairs encountered in casework will exhibit modifications at one or both ends.[77] Examining the ends of a hair in question can provide information regarding its history (i.e. by what means did it come to exist in its current condition). The following discussion will be concerned mainly with human hairs, although analogies can be drawn to animal hairs.

4.6.5.1 Typical Root Morphology

Hairs with roots are commonly encountered in forensic examinations (hairs without roots are typically described as fragments). The different growth phases of a hair (i.e. anagen, catagen, and telogen) can be identified using a compound microscope.

The roots of anagen hairs are not fully keratinized and consequently they are soft and pliable when freshly plucked (Figure 4.32). The soft tissue will dry, harden, and may become brittle upon continued exposure to air. The pigmentation of the shaft will continue unabated to the proximal end of the root, assuming it is not a white (i.e. unpigmented, hair). In general, some, or all, of the follicular sheath will adhere to, and be removed with, anagen hairs

---

77 As discussed previously, even in the absence of the natural ends (i.e. roots and tapered tips), the proximal and distal ends can be easily distinguished from each other as long as the leading edge of one, or preferably more, cuticular scales can be identified.

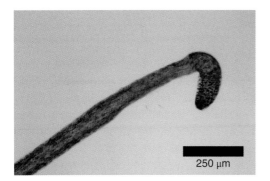

Figure 4.32 Human head hair with an anagen root (mounted in xylene and viewed using transmitted light).

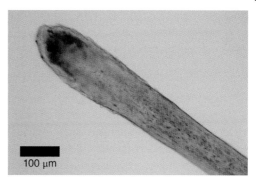

Figure 4.33 Human head hair with a telogen root (mounted in xylene and viewed using transmitted light).

that are pulled quickly (Schmid 1967; King et al. 1982; Chapman 1992).[78] Microscopically, root sheaths appear translucent, colorless, and anisotropic. In contrast, an anagen hair will generally separate from the follicle when it is pulled slowly. The friction of this separation causes the most proximal portion of the cuticle to have a "ruffled" appearance as these cuticular cells, which are not fully keratinized, are rolled backwards against the more fully keratinized IRS (Chapman 1997).

The roots of telogen hairs are highly keratinized. The shafts just above the roots of these hairs lack the pigmentation found in the more distal portions of the shaft and cortical fusi are commonly encountered. Human head hairs in this phase have a distinct, club-shaped root bulb and do not have significant amounts of follicular material adhering to them (Figure 4.33).[79] In contrast, human pubic and facial hairs may have follicular material adhering to telogen roots (sometimes described as "follicular tags" or "fleshy roots" (Petraco et al. 1988)). The medulla, even if it was present in other portions of the hair shaft, will not extend into the root of a telogen hair.

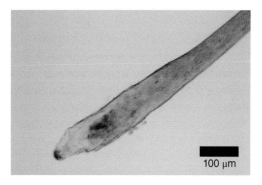

Figure 4.34 Human head hair with a catagen root (mounted in xylene and viewed using transmitted light).

Catagen roots exhibit intermediate morphologies representative of the transition between anagen and telogen (Figure 4.34). The catagen root has begun its transformation to a keratinized bulb, but it is incomplete and remnants of a root sheath are typically present. Cortical fusi may be present and there will be a reduction in the density of pigment granules.

It should be understood that the division of a hair's growth cycle into three phases is another artificial attempt to quantize a gradually occurring biological process. In other words, anagen roots do not become catagen roots from one moment to the next, nor do catagen roots instantly morph into telogen roots. A hair pulled out of its follicle at a given time can exist at any point along the continuum between anagen and telogen, and therefore it may express

---

78 Less frequently, the entire dermal papilla may also be removed when an anagen hair is plucked from the skin (Ludwig 1967).

79 Shed animal hairs with telogen roots often have more elaborate root morphologies that are quite distinct from human telogen roots.

a range of intermediary morphologies. While it is easy to distinguish anagen and telogen roots, catagen roots can be more challenging to classify. This is not surprising considering that the catagen phase is defined as the transition between the two ends of the hair cycle (anagen and telogen). Therefore, it is appropriate to classify a root as "late anagen/early catagen" or "late catagen/early telogen" if the scientist believes that is the most accurate description of the hair in question.

4.6.5.2 General Significance

When pulled, the roots of scalp hairs will typically release from their follicles before they break. It has been estimated that it takes about three times the force to break a hair as it does to pull it out (Harding and Rogers 1999). It has been demonstrated that thin hairs, as well as hairs in poor condition (e.g. exhibiting cosmetic treatment) are more likely to break compared to more "normal" hairs (Schmid 1967; Quarmby and Whitehead 1975). There is also evidence that hairs are more likely to break when they are pulled slowly compared to those pulled quickly (Maguire and Kligman 1964).

The identification of a root's growth stage may be useful in determining the manner in which it was removed from the follicle. Generally, the question at hand is determining whether the hair was "forcefully" removed or naturally shed. Anagen head hairs are secured within the follicle and require greater force, certainly compared to telogen hairs, to be removed from the skin. Therefore, the identification of anagen roots is an indication of a "forceful" action.[80] In contrast, telogen roots require minimal force to become dislodged from the skin and no significance can be attributed to their occurrence because they could have been forcibly removed or naturally shed (Ewing 1909).

However, caution must accompany these interpretations. Other actions besides those of a struggle can result in the removal of hairs with anagen roots. For example, anagen roots are commonly found on hairbrushes. Additionally, one study examining the roots of over 1000 hairs collected on outer garments during a three-month period found sheath material on ~10% of the hairs (King et al. 1982). Furthermore, all of the roots with sheath material were classified as either anagen and catagen.[81]

Also, anagen hairs from people with the pathological condition known as "loose anagen hair syndrome" can be easily removed without pain. However, in almost all cases, these hairs lack root sheaths, even when removed quickly (Price and Gummer 1989; O'Donnell et al. 1992). This condition primarily affects young children, although it also occurs in adults (Price and Gummer 1989; Dhurat and Deshpande 2010). Importantly, it has been cited in the literature as a significant factor in the investigation of a potential child abuse case (Kilbourn 1993).

4.6.5.3 Suitability for DNA Testing

The suitability of hairs for nuclear DNA testing is determined through a microscopical examination of the root, if it is present. Hairs without roots are not suitable for nuclear DNA testing. Hairs in the anagen or catagen growth stages, or any hair with attached follicular tissue (i.e. follicular tags), are good candidates for nuclear DNA testing. Telogen roots without any attached tissue are unfit for nuclear DNA testing because they lack nucleated cellular material.[82] Hairs unsuitable for nuclear DNA testing can be submitted for mitochondrial DNA (mtDNA) testing.

---

80 It has also been demonstrated that the force required to remove a hair from its follicle is dependent on the diameter of the hair. On average, it requires more force to remove a thicker hair (Chapman and Miller 1996; Van Neste et al. 2007).

81 Anagen and catagen hairs represented 4.5% and 11.2% of the total number of hairs examined in this study.

82 At least some reports in the literature of obtaining full nuclear DNA profiles from telogen hairs utilize a very liberal classification of telogen (i.e. at least some of the hairs depicted in these references should be classified as catagen) (Bourguignon et al. 2008; Brooks et al. 2010; Edson et al. 2013).

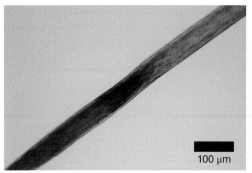 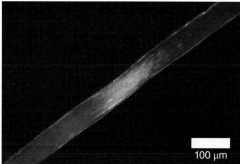

Figure 4.35 Post-mortem root band in the shaft of a human head hair, mounted in xylene and viewed using transmitted (left) and reflected (right) light.

These microscopical examinations have traditionally been conducted using transmitted light. However, there is no guarantee that hairs determined to be eligible for nuclear DNA testing will produce a full profile. For example, anagen hairs or hairs with significant amounts of follicular tissue may produce an incomplete DNA profile or none at all. In contrast, hairs with traces of follicular tissue may produce a full profile. It is possible that numerous factors including time since deposition, environmental conditions, and intrinsic variations in the hairs themselves may affect these results.

There have been numerous attempts to increase the predictive power of the microscopical examination with regards to the likelihood of obtaining DNA, especially in telogen hairs that typically would not be sent for nuclear DNA testing. These techniques have focused on methods to visualize the nuclei or, more specifically, the DNA within the nuclei. Techniques using Harris' Hematoxylin, DAPI,[83] and other fluorescent dyes have been described in the literature (Linch et al. 1998; Bourguignon et al. 2008; Brooks et al. 2010; Edson et al. 2013; Lepez et al. 2014; Haines and Linacre 2016). One logistical advantage of using Harris' Hematoxylin is that this method does not require a fluorescence microscope to visualize the stained nuclei. While not widespread, some laboratories in the United States have begun to apply these techniques to casework samples.

4.6.5.4 Postmortem Changes

It has been recognized since at least the 1970s that the incompletely keratinized portions of an anagen hair root can undergo morphological changes in postmortem samples (i.e. hairs remaining in the skin after death) (Prasad 1975).

These changes appear to be progressive and first manifest themselves as a darkening of the hair shaft above the root that may be accompanied by elongated voids oriented parallel to the long axis of the hair in this area (Koch et al. 2013; Roberts et al. 2017). Eventually, it appears that these voids coalesce into an opaque, ellipsoidal band (Petraco et al. 1988) (Figure 4.35). This is the classic morphology most commonly called "postmortem root banding" (PMRB) although it has also been called "putrid root" or "dead man's ring" (Koch et al. 2013). The band appears opaque when viewed using transmitted light because it is composed of trapped air. This can be confirmed using reflected light, which is a good technique to view PMRBs in heavily pigmented hairs.

This decomposition weakens the hair in this area and the shaft may break, forming a brush-like or pointed end (Figure 4.36) (Seta et al. 1984; Linch and Prahlow 2001).[84]

---

83 4′,6-diamidino-2-phenylindole.

84 These two morphologies are sometimes classified specifically as "putrid" roots (SWGMAT 2005).

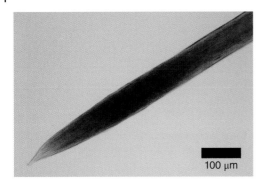

Figure 4.36 Human head hair with a pointed proximal end indicative of post-mortem conditions (mounted in xylene and viewed using transmitted light).

The brush-like morphology is a manifestation of the cortical cells becoming separated from each other. It has been reported that the brush-like morphology is more likely to occur in dry scalp areas whereas the pointed morphology is more likely to occur in wet scalp areas (Linch and Prahlow 2001).

It was initially reported that PMRBs are located ~0.5 mm above the root bulb (Petraco et al. 1988). More recent research confirms this and has indicated that the proximal margin of the band is typically located at the region where the cuticle becomes visibly distinct (i.e. the band is located just distal to the beginning of the cuticle) (Hietpas et al. 2016). Also, the proximal margin of the band is typically more abrupt and defined compared to the distal end. These same researchers determined that the average length of the root bands in their study was ~250 ± ~50 μm (1σ) and that the cuticle itself was visibly unaffected by the decomposition process.

These decompositional changes have not been observed in telogen hairs. It is hypothesized that this is due to the fact that telogen hairs are more fully keratinized and are therefore more resistant to the degradative process. Recent work suggests that PMRB may be caused by the selective degradation of the IMM in the pre-keratin/keratogenous region of the cortex (i.e. the portion of cortex that has undergone some keratinization but has not become fully keratinized) (Hietpas et al. 2016). The ultimate cause of this degradation is not known at this time (Donfack and Castillo 2018).

The timing of the degradation process is not fully understood, although it has been demonstrated that various environmental factors (e.g. temperature and submersion in water) are important (Collins 1996; Koch et al. 2013). In the largest cadaver study conducted to date, bodies were placed in a variety of different environments, and fully developed PMRBs were observed in as little as four days (these particular bodies were in cars) (Koch et al. 2013).

It should also be noted that there are significant amounts of variation both between and within individuals. For unknown reasons, the hairs from some people do not seem to develop PMRBs under conditions conducive to degradation (Linch and Prahlow 2001; Koch et al. 2013). Similarly, these studies also demonstrate that hairs in varying states of decomposition (i.e. no degradation, incomplete bands, fully developed bands, and brush-like/pointed ends) can be observed at the same time within a given individual. This is thought to result from the fact that at any given time, human hairs will be present at all growth stages along the continuum from anagen to telogen (i.e. the proximal ends will be keratinized to varying degrees).

Identifying a hair with PMRB is significant because it indicates, but does not prove, that it originated from a deceased individual. This can be an important factor in the reconstruction of events that preceded the deposition of the hair. It has also played a critical role in investigating the possibility that evidence may have been planted (e.g. hairs removed from a victim at autopsy are subsequently placed in the suspect's vehicle) (Hietpas et al. 2016).

Two studies examining antemortem hairs (i.e. hairs removed from living subjects) have demonstrated that anagen hairs can develop root morphologies mimicking this postmortem degradation (i.e. incomplete banding, fully developed bands, and brush-like/pointed ends) when they are exposed to a limited number of environmental conditions (Domzalski 2004; Roberts et al. 2017). All of the environmental conditions responsible for producing these morphologies involved soil burial or water immersion.

The bands produced in one of these studies were found ~0.05–0.3 mm from the root bulb end (Domzalski 2004). This is more proximal than typical PMRBs, which are ~0.5 mm from the root. However, the second study observed bands ~0.2–0.9 mm away from the root, with an average distance of 0.46 mm. Additionally, these bands ranged in length from ~110 to ~900 µm, with an average length of 440 µm. Furthermore, the data demonstrates that some of the individual hairs could be incorrectly identified as exhibiting PMRB (i.e. they have appropriately sized bands in the approximate locations typical of PMRB).

While tempering the significance of locating roots with classic PMRB, it must be recognized that the antemortem hairs in these studies only exhibited morphologies similar to PMRBs in a limited number of environments (i.e. buried in soil or immersed in water). Hairs in other environments have not developed morphologies that could be confused with PMRB. As always, the context of the case and the circumstances of the evidence must be evaluated during the interpretation of the results.

Finally, it should be noted that the scientific literature on this subject is devoted almost exclusively to the study of human head hairs, although recent research has demonstrated the formation of PMRBs in animal hairs (Richard et al. 2019).[85]

4.6.5.5 Other Atypical Root Morphologies
The use of methadone has been correlated with two different morphologies by researchers in Israel. Approximately 55% of the roots and follicular material of patients ($n = 21$) who had taken methadone within 24 hours were found to have a slight blue coloration (Brauner et al. 1990).[86] The authors did not independently determine the chemical identity of this colorant in the hairs but they did propose that it likely originated from the methadone itself, as a blue dye was added to methadone in Israel (trade name Adolan). This study is a good visual illustration of the fact that the hair follicle is served by the circulatory system and that compounds in the bloodstream can be incorporated into hairs. Originating from casework, it is also a reminder to be cognizant of unusual morphologies. Research that elucidates their causes not only increases the field's knowledge, but the additional information can strengthen an association or provide investigative leads in future cases.

These researchers also noted that ~62% of these patients exhibited completely opaque anagen roots in which the opacity extended into the proximal portion of the shaft (Gorski and Brauner 1992). This opacity was determined to be caused by dense clusters of dark granules, similar in appearance to pigment, and the authors hypothesize an interruption of the distribution of said pigment granules as a possible cause.

4.6.5.6 Non-root Morphologies
The distal and proximal ends of hairs can exhibit various morphologies resulting from different mechanisms of weathering and damage. These morphologies can be recognized using microscopy and provide contextual information regarding the history of the hair. Examples include, but are not necessarily limited to, the following:

- *Tapered*: A newly formed hair will exhibit a natural taper to a fine tip (Figure 4.37). These tapered tips are unmedullated and typically possess few pigment granules in human hair.
- *Cut*: Cut hairs have well-defined ends which may be classified as "square," "angled," or on

---

85 Degradation in gorilla hair roots, but not classic PMRB, has also been described in the literature (Jeffrey et al. 2007).

86 The blue coloration was observed in 62 out of the 112 hairs examined.

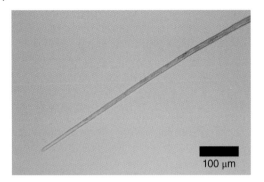

Figure 4.37 Human head hair with a naturally tapering tip (mounted in xylene and viewed using transmitted light).

Figure 4.39 Human beard hair with two razor cut ends (mounted in xylene and viewed using transmitted light).

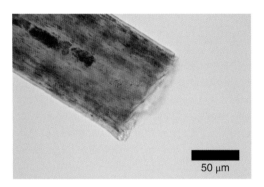

Figure 4.38 Human head hair with a scissor cut tip (mounted in xylene and viewed using transmitted light).

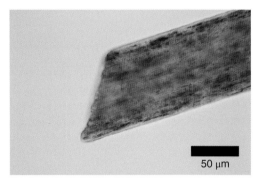

Figure 4.40 Human head hair with a clipper cut tip (mounted in xylene and viewed using transmitted light).

the basis of the implement that likely caused the cut.

- ○ *Scissor cut*: Hair has an abrupt end which may exhibit partial compression resulting from the action of the scissor blades (Figure 4.38).[87]
- ○ *Razor cut*: Hair end has an asymmetric, tapered, smooth, well-defined angle (Figure 4.39).
- ○ *Clipper cut*: Hair end possibly exhibits evidence of being both cut and broken, and the shaft *may* exhibit partial cuts (Bisbing 2002) (Figure 4.40).

---

87 It has been suggested that buried hairs can exhibit fractures similar in appearance to scissor cuts (Kundrat and Rowe 1989).

- *Rounded/abraded*: These hairs exhibit relatively smooth, convex tips resulting from the gradual abrasion of their cortical cells (Figure 4.41). This is an indication of repeated, low-intensity contact. Tapered and cut hairs will typically exhibit progressive rounding as time elapses. The degree of rounding may be used to provide some relative constraints on when the cut occurred (e.g. freshly cut or cut some time ago) (Ewing 1909; Sudo and Seta 1976; Bisbing 2002).
- *Broken*: Broken hairs can exhibit a wide range of morphologies which are discussed in more detail below. This is the most general category and is often used when hairs do not exhibit the characteristics associated with more specific end-shape morphologies (Figure 4.42).

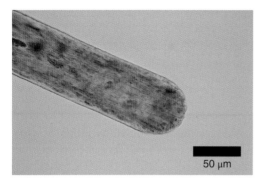

Figure 4.41 Human head hair with a rounded tip (mounted in xylene and viewed using transmitted light).

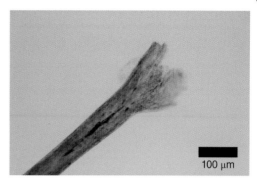

Figure 4.43 Human head hair with a crushed proximal end (mounted in xylene and viewed using transmitted light).

- *Crushed*: Crushed hair ends are flattened and widened, often forming shapes approximating a delta as a result of physical compression (Figure 4.43).
- *Frayed*: A frayed hair end has the appearance of a brush with cortical cells appearing as splayed fibrils (Figure 4.9). They are associated with normal weathering and breakage as well as certain diseases (e.g. trichorrhexis nodosa). In the medical literature, they are referred to as trichoclasis or "greenstick" fractures (Messenger et al. 2010).
- *Split ends*: Longitudinal splitting of the hair is referred to as trichoptilosis in the medical literature (Messenger et al. 2010; Figure 4.44). Split ends are associated with normal weathering, especially in longer hairs.

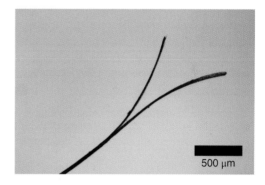

Figure 4.44 Human head hair with a split tip (mounted in xylene and viewed using transmitted light).

- *Burned*: Hair ends exhibit swelling, irregular gaseous voids, and may appear "mushroom" shaped (Figure 4.45). Burned hairs are discussed further in the degradation section of this chapter.

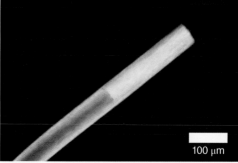

Figure 4.42 Human head hair with a broken proximal end (mounted in xylene and viewed using transmitted light (left) and between crossed polars (right)).

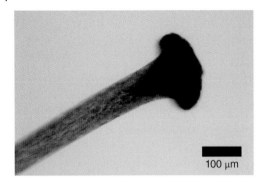

100 μm

Figure 4.45 Human head hair with a burned proximal end (mounted in xylene and viewed using transmitted light).

These morphologies are typically observed using transmitted light, but SEM can also be used to examine the ends of hairs. Residues (e.g. blood) and debris adhering to the hair may obscure the end morphologies. However, if the residue is isotropic, viewing the anisotropic hair between crossed polars in a non-extinction position may permit the microscopist to evaluate the hair end morphology without requiring the removal of this material.

The morphology of broken hairs can be complex, especially given the combination of forces (e.g. tension, torsion, and radial compression) that may be simultaneously exerted on the hair. Also, given the composite nature of hairs, it is not unexpected that they would undergo complex fracturing, as all hairs are composed of at least two, and sometimes three, major histological layers, each exhibiting their own physical and mechanical properties.

A hair broken under pure tension may exhibit a transverse fracture, resulting in a smooth, planar edge at a right angle to the longitudinal axis of the hair (i.e. the cuticle exhibits a circumferential split in the same plane as the fractured cortex) (Brown and Swift 1975; Henderson et al. 1978; Swift 1999b). Alternatively, the cortex may exhibit "stair-step" or partially fibrillated fractures with more extensive and complex cuticular splitting. It has been suggested that factors such

as the distance from the root (i.e. a proxy for progressive weathering) and relative humidity affect the preferential fracturing mechanics and subsequent morphologies observed.

Finally, it should be recognized that many different processes may be occurring nearly simultaneously in real-world situations (e.g. cutting, breaking, and crushing). This complexity should be considered when describing hair ends and interpreting the significance of the morphologies observed.

4.6.6 Degradation

Although physically and chemically resistant, hairs will degrade in the environment under certain conditions. Some of these degradation processes occur while the hair is still attached to the organism, while others occur primarily once the hair has been shed.

Many of these processes are interrelated and can produce similar morphologies on hair (e.g. cosmetic treatment and natural weathering). Because of this, it is sometimes difficult, if not impossible, to identify the exact processes that have caused the damage exhibited by individual hair shafts in practical casework.

4.6.6.1 Weathering

Weathering may be defined as the accumulated degradation of hair produced by typical cosmetic activities and normal environmental exposure while attached to the living organism (i.e. with the root in the follicle). This includes daily hair care activities (e.g. brushing, combing, and washing) and more pronounced cosmetic treatments (e.g. bleaching and permanent waving), previously discussed in this chapter. Most of the literature on the subject originates from the cosmetic sciences and consequently it involves the study of human head hair.

Cuticular Erosion Most of the investigations studying cuticular scale damage have been conducted using electron microscopy. However, this damage may also be observed on whole mounted hairs using transmitted light or with scale casts (discussed in Section 4.10).

It has been well documented that the leading edges of the cuticular scales are relatively smooth and regular when they emerge from the follicle (Bottoms et al. 1972; Swift and Brown 1972; Robinson 1976; Garcia et al. 1978). However, upon normal weathering, progressive damage can be observed along the length of the hair (i.e. the more distal portions of the hair shaft are more damaged as they have been subjected to environmental exposure for longer periods of time).

Initially the cuticular scales begin to chip, forming jagged, irregular leading edges (Figure 4.46).[88] This morphology begins to develop shortly after the hair emerges from the follicle and may be observed within the first few centimeters of the hair shaft. Upon continued exposure, this process continues until individual cuticular scales detach, revealing an underlying cuticular scale. Eventually the hair may lose its entire cuticular layer, exposing the cortex. These cortical cells will fray without the protection of the cuticular

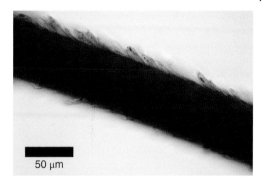

Figure 4.47 Human head hair with lifted cuticular scales (mounted in xylene and viewed using transmitted light).

scales. This causes the formation of split ends, which can ultimately lead to the fracture of the hair shaft. Cosmetic treatment exacerbates this weathering process.

It has been demonstrated that different patterns of cuticular wear can occur in hairs collected from different areas of the scalp, possibly the result of differential grooming (i.e. brushing or combing some areas more than others) (Swift and Brown 1972). This reinforces the need to collect representative known hair samples from all areas of the scalp.

Additionally, certain grooming practices such as back-combing or "teasing" will exacerbate cuticular damage. Specifically, it causes scales to lift from the surface of the hair and bend backwards. Lifted cuticular scales caused by this, and other mechanisms, can be observed in whole mounted hairs using light microscopy or SEM (Figures 4.47 and 4.48).

Light Degradation Prolonged irradiation with both visible and UV light causes observable and measurable changes to hair shafts. Physically the hairs will lighten in color, become mechanically weaker, less lustrous, drier, and rougher (Beyak et al. 1971; Dawber 1996; Signori 2004; Lee 2009). The manifestations of this degradation may be significant factors to consider during the interpretation of the morphologies exhibited by hairs in a forensic examination or comparison (e.g. color fading

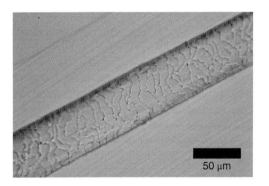

Figure 4.46 Scale cast of the shaft of a human head hair with jagged cuticular scale edges (mounted in air and viewed using transmitted light).

---

88 Ultrastructural research has demonstrated that cuticular scales fracture within the CMC or the endocuticle. Several factors have been reported to influence the fracture location, including ancestry, age, and whether the hair is wet or dry (Takahashi et al. 2006, 2015; Swift 1991).

5 kV   X500   50 µm   13 50 SEI

Figure 4.48 SEM micrograph of a human head hair with lifted cuticular scales.

in hairs exposed to significant amounts of sunlight).

Chemically, damage due to radiation has been identified within cuticular and cortical proteins, lipids, and the melanin pigments. The oxidation of cystine to cysteic acid and cystine *S*-sulfonate[89] appears to be a significant effect of photodegradation, although other amino acids are degraded as well (e.g. tryptophan, proline, valine, and histidine) (Robbins and Kelly 1970; Robbins 2002). Lipids within the hair shaft (e.g. within the CMC) are also oxidized due to photodegradation. This results in structural deficiencies as the CMC is involved in the adhesion of adjacent cellular structures.

The literature offers conflicting results concerning the relative stabilities of eumelanin and pheomelanin with regards to degradation caused by light (i.e. eumelanin is reported to be more stable and less stable than pheomelanin in different studies) (Wolfram and Albrecht 1987; Hotin et al. 1995). However, it has been demonstrated that blonde hair exhibits more color fading compared to darker hairs (Nogueira and Joekes 2007). Also, as discussed in the section on biodeterioration, the degradation of keratin itself may be partially responsible for color changes observed in hair shafts.

___
89 Photochemical oxidation of hair appears to be more complex than chemical oxidation; the latter primarily forms cysteic acid as a result of cystine oxidation (Robbins 2002).

Eumelanin pigments also protect cortical proteins and lipids from oxidation (Hoting et al. 1995; Hoting and Zimmermann 1996). This protection correlates with color (i.e. darker hairs with more eumelanin are more protected from the effects of light radiation compared to light-colored or colorless hair).

The proteins comprising the cuticle are typically more severely degraded than those of the cortex. This can be at least partially explained by the fact that the cuticle is the outermost layer of the hair, and consequently receives the most intense radiation. This is supported by the gradient of oxidative damage observed within hairs (i.e. progressively lower levels of damage are detected in the deeper portions of the hair further from the surface) (Robbins 2002). Additionally, the cortex, but not the cuticle, is partially protected from the effects of photodegradation due to the presence of pigment granules (which are not found in the cuticle, at least not in significant quantities). Consequently, sunlight radiation often physically degrades the cuticle, which may completely disintegrate, exposing the underlying cortex, in cases of severe exposure (Signori 2004).

It has been demonstrated that the processes of cortical protein, lipid, and melanin oxidation are exacerbated in cosmetically treated hair (i.e. permanently waved, bleached, or dyed hair) (Hoting and Zimmermann 1997). Additionally, the rate of these degradation processes correlates with humidity (i.e. the presence of moisture intensifies the degradation caused by radiation).

4.6.6.2 Heat

Unlike many man-made fibers, hairs do not melt when they are exposed to elevated temperatures. Being proteinaceous, they thermally degrade through a complex pyrolysis process.

The microscopical study of hairs that have been heated dates to at least the late nineteenth century (Ewing 1909). More recently, a limited number of studies have systematically examined the microscopic effects of hairs exposed to elevated temperatures (Henson and Rowe

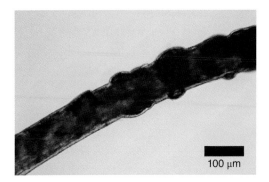

100 μm

Figure 4.49 Human hair shaft with bulges resulting from thermal degradation (mounted in xylene and viewed using transmitted light).

2002; Igowsky and Pangerl 2015). These studies have demonstrated that hairs will initially discolor at relatively low temperatures before eventually pyrolyzing at higher temperatures. The evolution of gases during pyrolysis permanently alters the structure of the hair. The overall diameter of the hair may increase as gaseous voids are formed in the cortex and the medulla. When limited pyrolysis has occurred, these voids are relatively subtle and may be mistaken for other microscopical features (e.g. medullary cells). At greater levels of thermal degradation, the voids become quite distinct and unmistakable (i.e. the pressure of the expanding gases often grossly distorts the form of the hair) (Figure 4.49). Once damaged, these hairs are quite brittle and will fracture easily. Shafts exposed to extreme temperatures may become nearly unrecognizable as hairs.

The precise temperatures at which these processes occur are not well understood at this time, as experimental design greatly affects the results. Besides variations intrinsic to different hair samples, it is likely that numerous factors, including heating rate, maximum temperature reached, and heating duration, are relevant to understanding the degradation process.

In the medical literature, these gaseous voids have been observed in patients suffering from brittle hair. The condition is known as "bubble hair" and both hair dryers and irons have been implicated as root causes in separate case

studies (Brown et al. 1986; Detwiler et al. 1994; Savitha et al. 2011). It is not a true pathological condition and normal hair will eventually replace the damaged hair upon cessation of the offending heat treatment.

It has been demonstrated that the surfaces of wet and dry hair respond differently to repeated treatment with a curling iron (Reutsch and Kamath 2004).[90] In dry hair, the cuticular cells crack both radially and axially, and there is fusion of the scales. Small pores may also be observed near these fused areas, possibly as a result of escaping hot, moist gas. In addition to the radial and axial fractures, the cuticular scales of the wet hair exhibited characteristic bulges and ripples. It is hypothesized that this distortion and lifting of the cuticular cells is caused by the pressure of trapped water being converted into steam.

Recognizing hair that has undergone thermal degradation provides information regarding its history, which may aid in the reconstruction of events (e.g. fire/arson investigations, reconstructions involving close range gunshots, and animal cruelty investigations involving burning) (Appel and Kollo 2010).

4.6.6.3 Biodeterioration
Nearly all organic matter provides nourishment for some forms of life and hair is no exception. Insects, fungi, and bacteria are some of the organisms that make use of hair for sustenance.

Insect Damage Insect damage on hair is quite distinctive and easy to recognize using a microscope. The resulting cuspate lesions on the hair shaft are perhaps the most perfect example of the miniaturizations of our normal macroscopic world to the microscopic (i.e. they look exactly as one would expect microscopic insect bites to look) (Figure 4.50).

---

90 It is important to note that this study did not attempt to recreate standard grooming practice and that the severity of the damage discussed is not expected for typical use of a curling iron.

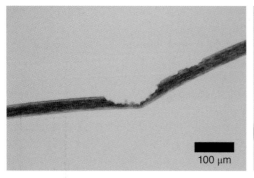 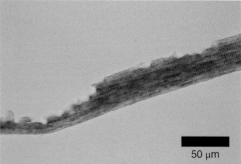

Figure 4.50 Cow (*Bos taurus*) hair shaft exhibiting insect damage, mounted in xylene and viewed using transmitted light (left). Individual cuspate lesions can be discerned in the close-up view (right).

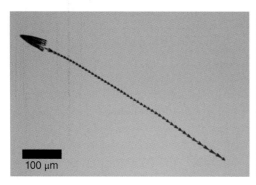 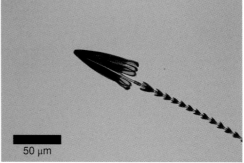

Figure 4.51 Hastiseta "hair" from the larva of a dermestid beetle (left) with a close-up view of the distal tip (right) (mounted in xylene and viewed using transmitted light). These bristles are commonly found in areas where dermestid beetle larvae have been active.

Insect damage is caused primarily by the larvae of clothes moths and dermestid beetles (Wilson 2008; Tridico et al. 2014a) (Figure 4.51). Specific examples of some commonly offending insects include the following (Rowe 1997; Chille 1989):

- Moths
  - *Hofmannophila pseudospretella* – brown house moth
  - *Tinea pellionella* – case-bearing clothes moth
  - *Tineola bisselliella* – common clothes moth
  - *Trichophaga tapetzella* – tapestry moth
- Beetles
  - *Anthrenus spp.* – museum beetles
  - *Attagenus megatoma* – black carpet beetle
  - *Attagenus pellio* – fur beetle
  - *Dermestes maculatus* – hide beetle

It has also been demonstrated that other insect species (e.g. *Gibbium* psylloides)[91] will eat hair when their preferred food is not available (Chille 1989).

Insect damage is only found on undisturbed hairs that have been in an environment conducive to insect activity, usually for an extended period of time. Because of this, insect damage can be a useful characteristic for elucidating the relative timing of hair deposition. For example, hairs exhibiting insect damage were most likely not deposited recently, although there is currently no known minimum amount of time required for this activity to occur.

---

91 This species, commonly known as the humpback beetle, is not a dermestid, but belongs to the Ptininae subfamily (spider beetles) of Anobiidae. They do not leave well-defined cuspate lesions, but rather discrete disruptions with a splintered appearance (Chille 1989).

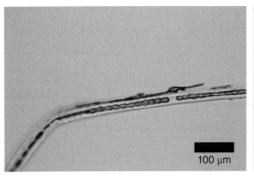 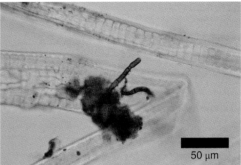

Figure 4.52 Examples of fungal hyphae on the shafts of rabbit hairs (mounted in xylene and viewed using transmitted light).

Fungal Damage Hairs deposited in the environment represent a biological source of nutrients for fungi as well as insects. Fungal activity is recognized by the presence of hyphae and spores either on the surface of, or within, hair shafts (Figure 4.52). Unlike fungal diseases affecting living patients, environmental fungal activity always occurs from the outside in.

Fungi relevant to hair degradation can be divided into two main groups (Blyskal 2009)[92]:

- keratinolytic species that are capable of digesting keratin, mainly via keratinase enzymes[93]
- keratinophilic species that can only digest more readily degradable substances (e.g. partially decomposed keratin and related materials).

Both types of fungi initially form frond-like mycelia (masses of hyphae) on the surface of the hairs. Keratinolytic fungal attacks on hairs can be divided into four general stages (Page 1950; Vanbreuseghem 1952; Daniels 1953; English 1963, 1965):

1) cuticular scale lifting – hyphae growing on the surface of the hair force their way beneath cuticular scales

2) cortical erosion – hyphae (eroding mycelia) grow longitudinally below the cuticle and within the cortex, extending from the penetrating organs, if formed

3) penetrating organs (also known as perforating organs) – modified eroding mycelia that form conical tunnels toward the core of the hair (i.e. perpendicular to the length of the hair)

4) colonization of the medulla – characterized by rapid hyphal growth within the medulla, presumably due to its relatively "soft" keratinization. The hyphae may eventually reenter the cortex from the medulla, appearing to digest the hair from the inside out (Tridico et al. 2014a).[94]

The keratinophilic fungi have similar stages of development. However, their "boring hyphae," thought to be analogous to the penetrating organs of keratinolytic fungi, remain extremely narrow, likely as a result of their inability to digest the surrounding cortical cells (English 1965).

All of these fungal structures and the resulting damage caused to the hairs have been described in the taphonomic and forensic literature, primarily in hairs in contact with soil (e.g. buried) (Serowik and Rowe 1987; Kundrat and Rowe 1989; DeGaetano et al.

---

92 While now understood to be different, these terms have been used somewhat interchangeably in the literature.
93 The enzymatic digestion of keratin only occurs after the disulfide bonds of the keratin substrate have been broken, a process known as sulfitolysis (Blyskal 2009).

---

94 The entire medulla may be consumed resulting in a "soda straw" morphology (Rowe 2010) although a similar appearance has also been reportedly caused by keratinolytic bacteria (Tridico et al. 2014b).

1992; Rowe 2010; Tridico et al. 2014a). Many of these references used SEM in addition to light microscopy to document this degradation. Histological stains (e.g. cotton blue, Trypan blue, and toluidine blue) can also be used to increase the contrast of fungal material associated with hairs (Rowe 1997; Marko and Rowe 2001).

The identification of fungal hyphae on hair may provide information regarding the environmental conditions to which the hair was subjected prior to its recovery. However, the degree of fungal activity should not be used to determine the absolute amount of time a hair may have been in a specific environment (Marko and Rowe 2001).

Bacterial Damage Keratinolytic bacteria have also been documented degrading hair but they have not been studied as extensively as the analogous keratinolytic fungi (Noval and Nickerson 1959; McBride et al. 1970; Brady et al. 1990; Tridico et al. 2014a). At least in some instances, the enzymes produced by these bacteria do not appear capable of digesting the heavily keratinized histological structures (e.g. the cortical cells themselves) (Dobson and Bosley 1963; Brady et al. 1990).

The bacteria are best observed after staining with colored stains or fluorescent probes and may also be observed on the surfaces of hair using SEM.

4.6.6.4 Other General Changes

One general effect of weathering is that the cortex may develop a coarse texture as cortical cells begin to separate from each other. This texture is more commonly encountered toward the distal portions of longer hairs (i.e. portions that have been exposed to the environment for relatively longer periods of time) and it is more easily observed in lightly colored hairs (i.e. hairs with relatively low pigment densities) (Robertson 1999). As stated previously, bleaching often results in significant expressions of cortical texturing.

Another general trend that has been documented in both the forensic and archeological literature is that hairs removed from soil/buried

environments often have a reddish cast (Wilson 2008; Tridico et al. 2014b). Multiple theories have been proposed for this phenomenon. One supposition is based on the principle that eumelanin appears to be less stable than pheomelanin with regards to chemical oxidation (Wolfram and Albrecht 1987). Therefore, the preferential degradation of eumelanin pigment granules results in the enhancement of the reddish-yellow color due to the pheomelanin pigments already present in the hair. Alternatively, it has been hypothesized that the degradation of keratin may cause the coloration, especially the nitrification and alkalinization of the amino acid tyrosine (Krefft 1969).

It has also been documented that fungal hyphae and spores can cause white hairs (i.e. hairs without pigment) to appear yellowish-orange (Rowe 1997). Additionally, brown staining resulting from the Maillard reaction has been suggested as a possible mechanism for hairs recovered from bog environments (Wilson 2008). In summary, depending on the circumstances, it is likely that multiple processes are involved in the taphonomic changes observed regarding hair color (Tridico et al. 2014a).

While most of the research has focused on hair shaft degradation in terrestrial environments, a few researchers have studied hairs in aquatic environments. For example, it has been demonstrated that continued immersion in water (both distilled and river water) results in the progressive loss of cuticular scales and the appearance of irregularly shaped "lumps" on the surfaces of hair shafts (Kupferschmid et al. 1994).

4.7 Human Hair Comparisons

The macroscopical and microscopical examination of hairs reveals that they exhibit a wide variety of different morphological characteristics. It is the comparison of these characteristics between a hair of unknown origin, typically referred to as the questioned (Q) hair, and a sample of hair from a known

(K) individual, that constitutes a forensic hair comparison.

A large portion of the forensic literature regarding human hairs has focused on their use as associative evidence. As such, many references discuss both the relevant characteristics of, and approaches for, forensic hair comparisons (Gaudette and Keeping 1974; Gaudette 1976; Hicks 1977; Robertson 1982, 1999; Shaffer 1982; Strauss 1983a; Lee and De Forest 1984; Robertson and Aitken 1986; Seta et al. 1988; Ogle and Fox 1999; Bisbing 2002; Deedrick and Koch 2004a; SWGMAT 2005; Houck and Bisbing 2005; Petraco and Kubic 2003; ENFSI 2015). Most of these references are quite similar to each other in spirit, even if they do not all use the same terminology to describe the characteristics or the potential morphologies within each characteristic.

4.7.1 Comparison Guidelines

The general guidelines for the comparison of hairs discussed below should be considered in conjunction with the general examination guidelines discussed in Section 4.11.3.

4.7.1.1 Macroscopic Observations and Stereomicroscopy

Forensic hair comparisons begin at the macroscopic level. Characteristics that may be evaluated include:[95]

- macroscopic color (e.g. colorless, blonde, red, brown, or black)
- length (measured in absolute units such as millimeters)
- general contour and degree of curliness[96] (e.g. straight, arced, wavy, curly, kinked, or peppercorn[97])
- approximate diameter (e.g. thin, medium, or thick).

These macroscopic observations may be augmented with a stereomicroscope. Additionally, the hair color may be evaluated using variously colored backgrounds to provide appropriate contrast and emphasize subtle highlights that may be present (Bisbing 2002).

4.7.1.2 Compound Light Microscopy

Upon completion of the macroscopic examination, the hairs should be mounted in an appropriate medium for examination using a compound light microscope, preferably one equipped with polarizing filters. A compound light microscope is necessary to observe the microscopic features present within hairs.

The questioned and the known hairs should be mounted in the same media. This ensures that the background color of the media and the contrast of the hair within the media are the same for both the questioned and the known hairs.[98] Once mounted, numerous microscopic features can be evaluated. These include, but are not necessarily limited to[99]:

- general color (e.g. colorless, blonde, red, brown, or black)
- cosmetic treatment (e.g. bleached or dyed)
- thickness range (measured in micrometers)
- inferred cross-sectional shape (e.g. round, oval, flattened, triangular, or other)
- shaft irregularities (e.g. buckling, shouldering, or twisting)
- cuticle
  - presence or absence
  - color (e.g. colorless, yellowed, or an unnatural color indicative of dyeing)
  - pigment granules (e.g. presence or absence)
  - thickness (e.g. thin, medium, or thick)
  - scale protrusion (e.g. indistinct, minimal, medium, or prominent)

---

95 The list of potential traits for each characteristic are provided as examples and are not meant to represent a full listing of every possible attribute within the characteristic.
96 More quantitative approaches to describing hair curliness have been described in the literature (Bailey and Schliebe 1985; Ogle and Fox 1999).
97 A tightly curled or spiraled hair.

98 The contrast is determined primarily by the refractive index of the medium. It should be noted that the refractive indices of some mounting media continually change over time as various components of the medium evaporate or degrade (De Forest et al. 1987).
99 This listing is adapted primarily from SWGMAT (2005).

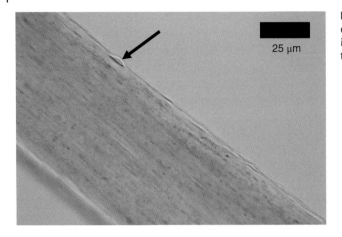

25 µm

Figure 4.53 Human hair shaft exhibiting a looped cuticle (mounted in xylene and viewed using transmitted light).

- o inner margin (e.g. distinct or indistinct)
- o damage (e.g. lifted, cracked, or looped) (Figure 4.53)
- cortex
  - o pigment granules
    - ☐ density (e.g. absent, light, medium, heavy, or opaque)
    - ☐ size (e.g. indistinct, fine, medium, or coarse)
    - ☐ shape (e.g. round or oval)
    - ☐ aggregates (e.g. absent, streaked, or clumped)
    - ☐ aggregate size (e.g. small, medium, or large)
    - ☐ distribution (e.g. uniform, peripheral, central, one-sided, or irregular)
  - o texture (e.g. fine, medium, or coarse)
  - o cortical fusi
    - ☐ distribution (e.g. only proximal or throughout length)
    - ☐ size (e.g. small, medium, or large)
    - ☐ abundance (e.g. absent, rare, or common)
  - o ovoid bodies
    - ☐ size (e.g. small, medium, or large)
    - ☐ abundance (e.g. absent, rare, or common)
- medulla
  - o distribution (e.g. absent, fragmented, discontinuous, continuous, or other[100])

- o thickness relative to shaft diameter (e.g. thin, medium, or thick)
- o appearance (e.g. opaque or translucent)
- root (if present)
  - o growth stage (e.g. anagen, catagen, or telogen)
  - o follicular material (e.g. root sheath, tag, or germinal nipple)
  - o other (e.g. discoloration, PMRB, or other abnormalities)
- non-root end morphologies (e.g. natural taper, rounded, cut, broken, crushed, frayed, split, burned, or decomposed)
- shaft abnormalities (e.g. monilethrix, pili torti, trichorrhexis invaginata, trichorrhexis nodosa, or pili annulati)
- general damage (e.g. split, frayed, partially broken, crushed, burned, or knotted)
- biological damage (e.g. insect bites, fungal activity, or bacterial activity)
- adhering materials (e.g. blood, nits, particles, or residues).

4.7.1.3 Comparison Microscopy

Hairs determined to be similar to each other should then be examined using a comparison microscope with transmitted light. A comparison microscope consists of two independent microscope bases joined by an optical bridge that allows the examiner to simultaneously view the specimens on each stage in a single field of view. A rigorous microscopical hair

---

100 For example, a double medulla (Figure 4.54).

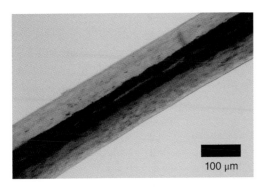

Figure 4.54 Human eyebrow hair exhibiting a double medulla (mounted in xylene and viewed using transmitted light).

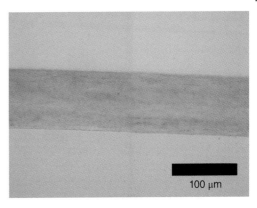

Figure 4.55 Photomicrograph taken using a comparison microscope of two head hairs from the same individual (mounted in xylene and viewed using transmitted light).

comparison cannot be completed without this instrument.[101]

It should be noted that a comparison microscope's illumination must be properly balanced before it can be used to conduct a hair comparison (i.e. the light being transmitted must be of the same intensity and color temperature on each side of the microscope). This can be checked by cutting several differently colored hairs or fibers in half and viewing each pair with the microscope (Figure 4.55). No visible differences should be observable if the illumination is properly balanced. Obviously, all the optics (e.g. condensers and objectives) should be matched on each half of the microscope.

The following are some general notes regarding the process of microscopical hair comparisons. First, it must be stated that only hairs of the same somatic origin can be compared to each other. Typically, only human head and pubic hairs are compared microscopically. Head hairs typically exhibit more variation between people than pubic hairs. Consequently, head hairs have more potential value for discrimination compared to pubic hairs. Hairs from other somatic regions are

believed to exhibit less variation between individuals and therefore there is a corresponding reduction in the value of their comparisons using microscopy.

It should also be noted that many of the microscopical characteristics listed above may change over the length of the hairs being examined. These variations should be noted when they are observed and should also be considered when conducting a comparison.

Questioned hairs with roots should ideally be compared to known hairs with roots in the same growth stage (e.g. Q hairs with anagen roots should be compared to K hairs with anagen roots).

The results of a microscopical hair comparison cannot be fully peer reviewed without a second examiner observing the hairs directly using a microscope. The second scientist should conduct their examination without knowing the conclusion obtained by the initial examiner (i.e. it should be conducted "blind") (ENFSI 2015).

Comparison microscopy is typically the final stage of a microscopical hair comparison. However, additional analytical techniques (e.g. fluorescence microscopy, MSP, TLC, and chemical analyses) may be utilized if there is reason to believe that they have the potential to provide additional discrimination.

---

101 Comparison microscopes were first designed in the late nineteenth century but became more widely commercially available in the early twentieth century (Chamot 1915). It is interesting to question how the earliest microscopical hair comparisons described in the literature were conducted without this essential piece of equipment.

Questioned hairs of significance to the investigation that cannot be distinguished from a known source using the techniques described above should be submitted for additional analysis utilizing molecular methods (i.e. DNA). The evaluation of the root, if present, will determine if a hair is suitable for nuclear DNA testing. Hairs unsuitable for nuclear DNA testing should be submitted for mtDNA testing.[102] When possible, nuclear DNA testing is preferred over mtDNA testing because of its greater discriminating potential. However, the shafts of hairs whose roots do not produce a nuclear DNA profile may be subsequently analyzed using mtDNA.

4.7.2 Conclusions and Interpretation

Trace evidence as a discipline has value because of the variations that exist, and can be detected, in the materials comprising our environment. Hair is different than many other forms of typical trace evidence in that it is of biological origin. One consequence of this is that hair exhibits significant amounts of morphological variation both within a given individual and between individuals.

It is the variation between individuals that provides the discriminating potential for forensic hair comparisons. Simply stated, hair from different individuals may appear different, and therefore it is possible to distinguish hairs from different individuals on the basis of their macroscopic and microscopic morphology (Kirk 1940; Gaudette and Keeping 1974; Gaudette 1976, 1978; Strauss 1983a; Bisbing and Wolner 1984; Wickenheiser and Hepworth 1990; Lamb and Tucker 1994; Houck and Budowle 2002; Kolowski et al. 2004). However, hair cannot be individualized on the basis of these physical characteristics alone. This means that microscopical hair comparisons are not a positive means of identification, and it cannot be determined that a given unknown hair originated from a specific individual

using only microscopy.[103] Additionally, the variation within individuals' hair limits the discriminating potential of microscopical hair comparisons as it expands the range of characteristics from which questioned hairs could be found to be indistinguishable.

In general, forensic hair comparisons can be reduced to a seemingly straightforward question: can a hair of unknown origin, often referred to as the questioned (Q) hair, be distinguished from the known (K) hairs sampled from an individual? It is important to stress that hair comparisons are fundamentally looking for differences, not similarities, between the questioned and the known hairs.[104] In this regard, the comparison of hairs is analogous to many other forms of trace evidence (e.g. fibers, paint, and glass).

A microscopical hair comparison is conducted by determining whether the characteristics of the questioned hair fall within the range of characteristics exhibited by a known source. In general, there are three main types of conclusions that can be reached after a microscopical hair comparison has been conducted: association, exclusion, and inconclusive.

It should also be noted that some hairs may be determined to be unsuitable for microscopical hair comparisons, and designated as "not suitable for comparison" or NSFC. For example, they may be exceptionally short, thin and featureless, damaged, or originate from a somatic region considered to be fundamentally ill-suited for comparisons, such as general body or limb hairs.

4.7.2.1 Association

An association is made when the questioned hair cannot be distinguished from the known sample (i.e. there are no meaningful differences between the questioned hair and the

---

102 Mitochondrial DNA profiles can be obtained with high success rates from relatively short hairs (e.g. less than 1 cm in length) (Melton et al. 2012).

103 Imaginative examples, such as a hair 26 ft long or a hair that has 50 distinctly different dye bands, challenge the certitude of this statement, and certainly approach, if not obtain, individualization (Gaudette 1985).

104 For this reason, there is no minimum number of characteristics required for a comparison to be "valid."

known sample). Practically, this means that all of the characteristics within the questioned hair are present within the known hairs. These characteristics often change along the length of a hair and, ideally, corresponding changes can be observed along the lengths of questioned and known hairs. However, no two hairs are identical and ultimately the questioned hair is compared to the range of features exhibited by the known sample. Theoretically, this signifies that if the questioned hair was mixed in a bag with the hairs comprising the known sample, it would not be possible to determine which hair was the questioned hair through a microscopical analysis.[105]

Various factors can strengthen or weaken an individual association. An association may be strengthened when the hairs being compared exhibit unusual characteristics. Some examples include, but are not limited to:

- distinctive cosmetic treatment (e.g. a hair dyed three different colors)
- shaft abnormalities (e.g. monilethrix, pili torti, or trichorrhexis invaginata)
- exceptional physical characteristics (e.g. a six-foot-long hair).

The presence of these unusual characteristics does not prove that a questioned hair originated from a specific person. They indicate that the characteristics are not commonly encountered, and therefore they provide additional support for the association.

Associations are weakened when hairs possess limited characteristics. Some examples include, but are not limited to:

- short hairs
- incomplete (i.e. fragmented) hairs
- lightly colored, colorless, or bleached hairs
- heavily pigmented hairs approaching or obtaining opacity.

A special note is warranted regarding the color and pigmentation (i.e. granule size, density, aggregations, or distribution) of hairs.

These characteristics are rightfully considered to be the most discriminating features in macro- and microscopical comparisons due to the large amounts of variation exhibited between different people (Seta et al. 1988; Robertson 1999; Bisbing 2002; Houck and Bisbing 2005). Therefore, both lightly colored (including colorless and bleached) and darkly colored hairs have limited discrimination potential for different, but fundamentally related, reasons. Lightly colored hairs have limited amounts of fine pigment granules which may be difficult to resolve using microscopy. Colorless and bleached hairs are the extreme cases of lightly colored hairs in that pigment granules may be completely absent. In contrast, opaque hairs may have so much pigment that individual granules and other microscopical characteristics of the hair cannot be observed. In summary, the hairs on opposite ends of the pigmentation spectrum have diminished value for hair comparisons because limited information can be ascertained from their pigment granules.

The range of characteristics exhibited by the known hair standard can also influence the strength of an association. For example, if the known hairs exhibit a wide range of variation, the association is weakened because more unknown hairs, relatively speaking, would be expected to fall within the expanded range. Conversely, if the known hairs exhibit a narrow range of variation, the association is strengthened because relatively fewer unknown hairs would be expected to fall within the reduced range.

Associations can also be strengthened or weakened by contextual information. For example, consider a case where a car with two people is in an accident. It is reasonable to assume that a clump of head hairs pinched within a crack in the windshield originated from one of these two people, and therefore there are only two possible sources for the unknown hair. A relatively strong association can be supported if the questioned hair can only be associated with one of the known samples collected from the two occupants.

---

105 Obviously, this thought experiment is never actually conducted in a real case.

Another way to assess the value of an association is to compare the known standards to each other. An association is strengthened if the known hairs from all of the relevant people can be easily distinguished from each other. However, the value of an association is significantly limited if an unknown hair cannot be distinguished from the known standards of multiple people.

Because the relative strength of associations can vary, some examiners specify different levels of their associative conclusions. For example, a typical association may be termed an "association with discriminating characteristics," a relatively strong association as an "association with highly discriminating characteristics," and a relatively weak association as an "association with limitations."[106]

It is important to reiterate that any association made through microscopy alone is not a positive means of identification. There is also no practical way to determine how many people have hair that would be indistinguishable from the questioned hair.

Finally, while each individual association must stand on its own merit, combinations of associations can also strengthen their overall significance (Gaudette 1985). Some examples include, but are not limited to the following:

- Two or more questioned hairs collected from the same item which appear different from each other are determined to be indistinguishable from the same known sample.
- Two or more questioned hairs of different somatic regions collected from the same item are determined to be indistinguishable from the corresponding known samples of an individual.
- A two-way transfer (e.g. a questioned hair recovered from person A is determined to be indistinguishable from the known

sample of person B, and a questioned hair recovered from person B is determined to be indistinguishable from the known sample of person A).

4.7.2.2 Inconclusive

An inconclusive conclusion is typically reached when a questioned hair exhibits some similarities and some differences with a known source, but some limiting factors are complicating the comparison. For example, a significant amount of time may have elapsed between the incident and the collection of the known sample. Alternatively, one sample of hair being compared may have been exposed to different environmental conditions (e.g. buried or exposed to direct sunlight for extended periods of time). Another possibility is that the known sample is composed of an insufficient number of hairs, and it is not possible, or worthwhile, to obtain additional hairs via resampling (e.g. the person has been cremated or 30 years have elapsed since the time of the incident).

4.7.2.3 Exclusion

An exclusion, or elimination, conclusion is reached when a questioned hair exhibits a meaningful difference compared to a known source (i.e. a characteristic of the questioned hair falls outside the range found within the known sample). This meaningful difference between the questioned and the known hairs can be encountered at any stage of the comparison process, including during macroscopic observations.

An exclusion can also be strengthened or weakened by a variety of factors (Gaudette 1985). Some circumstances that strengthen an exclusion include, but are not limited to:

- the questioned hair exhibits different ancestral characteristics compared to the known hairs
- the questioned hair is grossly different in appearance from the known hairs[107]

---

106 These terms were being discussed within the OSAC Materials (Trace) subcommittee at the time this chapter was written.

107 Examiners must always be cognizant of the possibility of contemporaneous hair alterations when

- the known standard is composed of many hairs (i.e. more than the recommended number)
- the known hairs exhibit a narrow range of variation.

Factors that weaken an exclusion include, but are not limited to:

- the questioned hair is an incomplete fragment
- the questioned hair exhibits evidence of degradation (physical or biodeterioration)
- the known sample is composed of few hairs
- the known sample is composed of incomplete hair fragments
- the known sample was collected a significant amount of time after the questioned hair would have been deposited
- the known sample is not representative of the variation exhibited by the known source.

It is important to recognize that it is impossible to determine if the known sample captures the variation that exists within a source. Collecting many hairs from multiple subareas within a somatic region is the best way to address this issue but there is no guarantee of success. For this reason, an exclusion is technically limited to the known sample that was collected, not the person from whom it was collected. Additionally, atypical hairs (i.e. those which do not resemble the vast majority of the

---

considering exclusions based on gross differences. Drastic changes in the appearance of hair (e.g. haircuts, bleaching, and dyeing) can be achieved essentially instantaneously. For example, a criminal can cut their long hair close to the scalp or bleach their black hair immediately after committing a crime (i.e. prior to having a known sample collected). These alterations will ensure that their known hairs do not resemble any hairs that they may have deposited during the commission of the crime. An astute hair examiner who did not cease the examination after observing the macroscopic differences may determine that the known hairs all appear to have been recently cut or bleached. A strong association via microscopy will not be possible, but the examination of the remaining microscopical characteristics could determine if additional DNA testing of the questioned hair is warranted.

hairs from a given somatic region of a person) may be present at trace levels (Gaudette 1985). These atypical hairs may not be present within a large known sample, even with representative sampling. Consequently, if the questioned hair being compared happens to be one of these atypical hairs, it will likely fall outside of the range of characteristics exhibited by the known standard.

For these reasons, some examiners will only report an exclusion if the questioned and known hairs originate from people exhibiting different ancestral characteristics. Other conclusion terms such as "dissimilar" or "non-association" are used for other comparisons where a questioned hair falls outside of the range of variation exhibited by a known sample. This conclusion is also used by some examiners when the questioned hair is similar, yet different from the known source.

Other examiners believe that this limited exclusion conclusion is unnecessary. They argue that an exclusion is based on the known sample provided for the comparison, and that this does not necessarily exclude the person from whom the sample was collected. Proponents of the "dissimilar" or "non-association" conclusion argue that this subtlety is often lost on those reading and interpreting the report.

4.8 Transfer and Persistence

Numerous experiments focusing on the transfer and persistence of hair have been conducted. These experiments have identified many of the variables that affect hair transfer and persistence. Some of the relevant factors include time since deposition, recipient object texture and construction, physical orientation, fiber composition (if applicable), hair length, and the activities of the individual (Robertson 1987; Gaudette and Tessarolo 1987; Dachs et al. 2003; Boehme et al. 2009). In the most general terms, experiments have demonstrated that when a known garment is spiked with a certain number of hairs, there is a continual progression of hair loss over time. As with fibers, the rate of loss is generally highest initially and it decreases with time (i.e. it approximates an exponential decay) (Robertson 1987; Gaudette and Tessarolo 1987; Dachs et al. 2003). However, on relatively short time scales (approximately eight hours), it has been demonstrated that a roughly linear rate of hair loss from woolen garments is possible (Dachs et al. 2003). It is unlikely that this linear trend would continue given previous results where persistence was tracked for extended time periods (Robertson 1987).

When considering clothing, the type of fabric has a significant effect on the persistence of hairs. In general terms, rough garments (e.g. typical woven wool)[108] are better at accepting and retaining hairs compared to smoother fabrics (e.g. tightly knitted cotton or polyester) (Robertson 1987; Gaudette and Tessarolo 1987; Dachs et al. 2003; Boehme et al. 2009). Depending on the garment, some hairs may work themselves into the fabric itself and these entrapped hairs may persist for extended periods of time (at least several days) (Robertson 1987). Other garments display almost no ability to retain hairs even for short periods of time. The presence or absence of roots and artificial dyeing does not appear to affect the retention of hairs on typical clothing items (Dachs et al. 2003).

One study examined the persistence of human head hair and animal guard hairs, from cats and dogs, on two types of fabrics (Boehme et al. 2009). The results of this study suggest that there are no statistically significant differences in the persistence of these three types of hair. While not a comprehensive survey (e.g. there were limited replicates with only a few species and fabrics studied), the results are relevant because the three species selected represent the most commonly encountered hairs in typical forensic casework.

Hairs deposited on one area of a garment will also commonly migrate to other portions of the garment before they are lost entirely (Robertson 1987; Gaudette and Tessarolo 1987). This is an important fact to remember when attempting to assess the significance of hairs found on specific areas of an object. Thus, the location on an object where a hair was recovered is not necessarily the location at which it was initially deposited.[109]

Along the same line of reasoning, a series of experiments demonstrated the possibility of secondary transfer of hairs in a variety of scenarios (e.g. from assailant's clothing to victim's clothing or from a volunteer's clothing to an upholstered chair) (Gaudette and Tessarolo 1987). Interestingly, the authors concluded that secondary transfer is more common than primary transfer.[110]

Transferred hairs may also not be truly representative of the known source, as demonstrated by a study which looked at the hairs recovered from individuals wearing hats, balaclavas, or tights on their heads (Peabody et al. 1985). Regarding the numbers of recovered hairs, the researchers demonstrated that there is both individual variation and variation between the types of headgear, with the balaclavas retaining the most, and the tights retaining the least, amount of shed hair.[111] Most interesting, however, was the fact that the hairs recovered from all three types of headgear tended to be both shorter and thinner than the control

---

108 Wool fibers also have relatively pronounced cuticular scales which likely aid in the retention of hairs, as the free ends of the scales from the wool fibers may interact with the cuticular scales of the hairs (Dachs et al. 2003).

109 This effect is obviously minimized in the absence of movement (e.g. hairs recovered from the clothing of an undisturbed decedent would be expected to have migrated less than hairs on the clothing of the suspect who was apprehended 12 hours after the homicide occurred).

110 Regarding hair, primary transfer would be directly from one person's body to another object while secondary transfer would require an intermediary object (i.e. a direct transfer of a hair from a person's head to their shirt followed by a secondary transfer to another person's clothing).

111 The authors do note that at least some of these differences may be due to the experimental design of the study which had the volunteers wear the hats in the same sequential order (hats, followed by balaclavas, and finally the tights) with a minimum interval of 2 hours between each garment.

(i.e. known) hairs collected from the volunteers.[112] The correlation between hair diameter and the amount of force required to remove it from the scalp at least partially explains the higher proportion of thinner hairs located on the headgear (Van Neste et al. 2007).

It is not surprising that foreign hairs on clothing often originate from people in close contact with the owner of the garments. One study analyzed the hairs recovered from the tape lifts collected (twice daily) from an individual's clothing over the course of a month (Quill 1985). A total of 81 hairs were recovered although only 14 were considered suitable for comparison. All 14 of these hairs were determined by the researcher to have been shed naturally and to have originated from members of his nuclear family (i.e. wife and children). It should be recognized that this is a very limited study and that variations in lifestyle would be expected to have a large effect on potential hair transfer. For example, one can hypothesize that a fastidious individual who drives their personal car to work and has a private office would be expected to have fewer hairs from unrelated individuals on their clothes compared to a slovenly person who rides public transportation and works in close physical contact with numerous individuals.

Pubic hair combings are commonly collected from the victims, and sometimes the suspects, of sexual assaults with the goal of locating foreign hairs (or other probative trace evidence). One experiment focused on the transfer of pubic hairs during consensual heterosexual intercourse (six Caucasian couples) (Exline et al. 1998). Pubic combings from each participant were collected immediately after intercourse ($n = 55$) and compared to known standards to determine origin. A total of 28 foreign pubic hairs suitable for comparison were recovered in 19 of the 110 combings (17.3%). For reasons unknown, perhaps a

Table 4.2 Summary of pubic hairs recovered from combings after sexual intercourse

Number of foreign pubic hairs in combing	Number of combings	Approximate percentage
0	91	83
1	14	13
2	2	2
3	2	2
4	1	1

Source: Adapted from Exline et al. (1998).

statistical anomaly, the transfer rate from females to males (13 of 55 combings or 23.6%) was approximately double the male to female transfer rate (6 of 55 combings or 10.9%).[113] All of the foreign pubic hairs were classified as having a catagen or telogen root. Only one two-way transfer where foreign pubic hairs were recovered from both individuals after a single event was recorded. Table 4.2 displays the number of pubic hairs found in the individual combings.

This study demonstrates that even under ideal circumstances (i.e. combings collected immediately after intercourse), pubic hair transfer occurs at a relatively low rate, and even when it does occur, only a single foreign hair is typically recovered from the combings.[114]

Unsurprisingly, it has been demonstrated that hairs can transfer from one item of clothing to another when they are laundered together (i.e. secondary, or higher order, transfer). In one of these studies, distinctly dyed head and pubic hairs were purposefully placed on a variety of questioned garments which were then washed and dried with several

---

112 The lengths and widths of the hairs from the headgear were more similar to the known hairs collected by combing as opposed to pulling, as this same study demonstrated that combed hairs are generally shorter and thinner than pulled hairs.

113 In fact, these asymmetrical results directly contradict the results of a smaller study involving 20 acts of intercourse with a single heterosexual couple (Keating 1988). In this study, hairs from the man were recovered in the combings of the women after 45% of the sexual encounters while hairs from the woman were never recovered in the combings from the man.
114 It should be noted that these sexual encounters were consensual acts and consequently they may not be representative of pubic hair transfer that occurs during unwanted sexual contact.

Table 4.3 Summary of laundered hair study

Somatic origin	Number of hairs deposited	Percentage of hairs recovered from:				Percentage of unrecovered hairs[a]
		Questioned garments	Control garments	Washing machine lint trap	Dryer lint trap	
Head	43	5	5	11	56	23
Pubic	39	8	10	10	41	31

a) The authors suggest that these hairs may have been lost down a drain or possibly retained in another area of the appliances.

Source: Adapted from Simons (1986).

control garments (i.e. without hairs) (Simons 1986). Dyed hairs were recovered from both the questioned and the control garments although most of the recovered hairs were found in the lint traps of the two appliances (Table 4.3)

Another experiment examined control garments (i.e. men's, women's, and children's underwear without hair) for the presence of hair after they had been laundered with several different families' ($n = 11$) typical laundry (Atwell et al. 2011). Three control garments (i.e. one of each) were washed in a total of 107 washing cycles (8–10 replicates per family). Human hairs were located on ~26% of these garments (82 out of 321). Only one of these hairs was determined to be a pubic hair. There was a significant amount of variation between families regarding the number of hairs recovered from the control garments (i.e. human hairs were found on 21 of 30 control garments from one family [70%] compared to zero human hairs recovered from 30 control garments from another family).

The results of these laundry studies are in accordance with what would be expected from Locard's exchange principle, and they demonstrate the provenance limitations when dealing with hairs recovered from various items which have been laundered together (i.e. it is impossible to know from which garment any given hair originated once it has been laundered with other items of clothing). The first study also shows the value of collecting and searching the debris from lint traps for hair if a relevant item of clothing is suspected of having been laundered.

Animal hairs abound in homes with cats and dogs and on the clothes of those who come into close contact with these animals. A study focused on animal hairs which were transferred to "criminals" during simulated burglaries of homes with pets ($n = 7$) and assaults of individuals recently in contact with animals ($n = 2$) (D'Andrea et al. 1998). Significant numbers of animal hairs were recovered from the clothing of the "criminals" in all scenarios. An average of ~237 animal hairs were recovered from the "burglars" (low = 24, high = 610, median = 179) while 12 and 255 hairs were recovered from the two "assailants." While exact numbers were not given, the authors state that most of the recovered hairs were secondary (i.e. fur) hairs. They offer several explanations for this observation, including (i) fur hairs outnumber guard hairs and (ii) fur hairs are finer and lighter than guard hairs, making them better candidates for transfer events. As discussed in Section 4.9.1, fur hairs possess severely limited morphological characteristics suitable for identification/comparison purposes using microscopical techniques. Because of this, they are typically not utilized in forensic investigations relying on microscopy, although they may be submitted for DNA analysis if sufficient quantities are present.[115]

There have also been several reports looking at hair transfer frequencies using casework

---

115 Combining several hairs into a single extraction process runs the risk of analyzing hairs from multiple animals, which obviously further complicates the interpretation of the resulting data.

Table 4.4 Summary of hair transfer to clothing in sexual assaults

Clothing	Subject	Number of cases	No hairs (%)	No significant transfer[a] (%)	Significant head hair transfer (%)	Significant pubic hair transfer (%)
Underwear	Victim	68	15	78	4	3
	Suspect	17	0	100	0	0
Outerwear	Victim	62	1.5	84	13	1.5
	Suspect	29	0	83	14	3

a) In this study, a significant transfer was defined as the recovery of one or more hairs which indicated an association between the subjects (i.e. the victim and the suspect).
Source: Adapted from Mann (1990).

Table 4.5 Summary of hairs recovered from victim's hands/fingernail scrapings

Type of hair recovered	Total number of cases	Number of cases with Q hairs consistent with victim's hair	Number of cases with Q hairs inconsistent with victim's hairs	Number of cases in which the somatic origin of the hairs correlate with the victim's injury
Head	53	44	9	23 (severe head trauma)
Pubic	2	2	0	2 (sexual assault)
Body	31	NA[a]	NA	18 (stabbings/strangulations)

a) Comparisons were not conducted on the body hairs.
Source: Adapted from Fallon et al. (1985).

data. Two of these studies focused on hair transfers occurring during sexual assaults. Regarding the victim's pubic hair combings, they both indicated that recovering pubic hairs differing from the victim's own hair does not occur often (~2% in ~2500 cases (Stone 1982) and ~4% in 96 cases (Mann 1990)[116]). Both reports stated that the examination of clothing led to the recovery of additional hairs indicative of a transfer event. Stone reported finding hairs (head or pubic) dissimilar to the victim in the clothing or from the crime scene in ~10–15% of the cases reviewed (Stone 1982). This transfer rate is in accordance with the other study, the findings of which are summarized in Table 4.4.

Another study looked at the presence of hairs on the hands/in the fingernail scrapings of 400 victims (Fallon et al. 1985). Hairs were

recovered in 86 (~22%) of the reviewed cases although the vast majority of the recovered head and pubic hairs were determined to have originated from the victim. The authors also noted a general correlation between the injury and the type of hairs (i.e. somatic origin) recovered from the victims' hands (Table 4.5).

In summary, experimental research has established many of the fundamental principles governing the transfer and persistence of hair. However, in almost all cases, these studies and analogous studies involving textile fibers have shown that transfer and persistence are complex issues with far too many variables to be able to predict the absolute number of hairs expected to be transferred or remain on an object in a real-world scenario.

4.9 Animal Hair

The microscopical examination of animal hairs for forensic purposes has a long history, essentially contemporaneous with that

---

116 Mann also reported the complete absence of finding pubic hairs determined to be consistent with the victim from the pubic hair combings collected from the suspect ($n = 18$) (Mann 1990).

of human hair, and classic books were published on the subject in the first half of the twentieth century (Lambert and Balthazard 1910; Friedenthal 1911; Glaister 1931; Lochte 1938).[117] In addition to these sources, there are literally hundreds of books[118] and scientific papers on animal hair microscopy, including a relatively recent review of the applications of animal hair to forensic science (Tridico 2005).

Most of these references describe a subset of animals either from a specific geographic region or taxonomic group (or a combination of the two). The literature concerning animal hair microscopy varies wildly in quality, and while it is invaluable, the scientist should conduct their own examinations of authentic reference hairs whenever possible. Additionally, many references make use of dichotomous keys. Extreme care should be taken when following these identification schemes. Even assuming the key was prepared carefully and followed correctly by the examiner, arrival at the correct identification is only possible when the target animal is present. In other words, if the true animal is omitted from the key, incorrect, yet plausible, identifications are possible when animals with similar characteristics are included. It should also be noted that almost all of these references describe the examination of guard hairs, typically from the back/body. This fact should be kept in mind since questioned hairs can obviously originate from any part of the animal's body. Finally, these references offer both written descriptions and illustrations/photomicrographs of what the authors consider to be typical of the animals they are discussing. Not every hair from the same region of the same animal will look identical and these references cannot capture the full range of variation exhibited by

the hairs of the animal being discussed. This is another reason why the examiner should make every effort to examine reference hairs themselves, preferably from multiple examples of the same species.

It should also be noted that much of the information discussed in the human section of this chapter can be directly applied to animal hairs (e.g. cosmetic treatment, hair end morphologies, and degradation).

4.9.1 Identification

The forensic analysis of animal hairs generally involves the identification of the hair to a taxonomic group.[119] However, it is not always possible to identify an animal hair to the species level using microscopy alone. It is often more realistic to identify animal hairs to the family, or perhaps genus, level. Fortunately, it is often relatively easy to identify the broader taxonomic group (e.g. order or family) to which the animal belongs, and this level of identification is often sufficient to answer the question at hand. For example, rabbits and hares (family Leporidae) are easily identifiable on the basis of their multiserial medullary morphology[120] and the presence of cytoplasmic spherules on the distal walls of the individual medullary cells (which are best observed once a longitudinal cross-section has been made) (Clement et al. 1981) (Figure 4.56). The specificity to which animal hair can be identified is dependent on numerous factors outside of the examiner's control, including, but not necessarily limited to the following:

---

117 Human hair microscopy is also addressed in all of these books.

118 A few examples of the major books on the subject include Appleyard (1960), Brunner and Coman (1974), Moore et al. (1974), Debrot et al. (1982), Teerink (1991), Meyer et al. (2002), Chernova and Tselikova (2004), and Tóth (2017).

119 Less typically, comparisons are conducted between animals of the same species or breed (as will be discussed in the following section). Also, while seldom encountered currently, additional questions may be asked of the hair examiner, especially as greater resources and attention are devoted to animal abuse cases. For example, the author has examined animal hairs to determine if they were burned or exposed to caustic compounds in multiple cases.

120 Often colloquially described as a "corn cob" morphology.

Figure 4.56 Cleared longitudinal cross-section of a dyed rabbit hair (mounted in glycerin and viewed using transmitted light). Note the cytoplasmic spherules, a few of which are marked with arrows, located on the distal walls of the medullary cells.

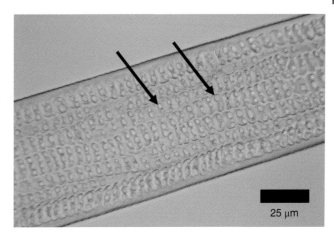

25 μm

- *The physical condition of the hair*: All things being equal, physical and morphological information is more difficult to extract from fragments or damaged hairs compared to pristine, complete hairs.
- *The type of hair (i.e. guard versus fur)*: Compared to guard hairs, very little information can be obtained from fur hairs.
- *The number of hairs that can reasonably be assumed to originate from the same source*[121]: A sample size greater than one has the benefit of potentially demonstrating the reproducibility of morphological features as well as increasing the chance that one or more hairs exhibit the "textbook" morphology.
- *The somatic location from which it originated*: While unknown to the examiner, a questioned hair from the dorsal area of an animal is more likely to resemble the description in the literature compared to a hair from another somatic region. Similarly, dorsal hairs are more likely to be in the examiner's reference collection, allowing for a more appropriate comparison.

- *The relevant animal population from which it can reasonably be expected to originate*: It is easier to identify an animal from a geographically defined group of potential animals familiar to the examiner compared to considering mammals from around the world. For example, identifying an unknown animal hair in a shipment of goods from Asia in an animal trafficking case, which could have ultimately originated from virtually anywhere on the planet, obviously presents different challenges than a wildlife poaching case in rural Wisconsin.
- *The number of closely related animals (e.g. the number of congeners within a genus)*: It is generally easier to identify specific animals when they do not have many close relatives. For example, raccoon dogs (*Nyctereutes procyonoides*) are the only extant members of their genus, and they can often be identified to the species level using hair microscopy.[122] In contrast, it is quite difficult, if not impossible, to distinguish a questioned hair of unknown somatic origin from the gray wolf (*Canis lupus*) and the coyote (*Canis latrans*) by microscopy alone.

As with human hair examinations, observations begin with the unaided eye.

---

121 Typically, each questioned hair needs to be treated independently but fortune occasionally favors the forensic scientist and sometimes it is justifiable to group multiple hairs (e.g. it is reasonable to assume that a clump of hairs with similar macroscopic appearances wedged between two car parts originated from the same animal that was hit by the car).

---

122 This identification can then be confirmed using other techniques, including DNA and MALDI-ToF mass spectrometry (Hollemeyer et al. 2007).

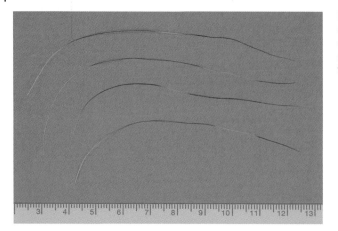

Figure 4.57 Guard hairs from a coyote (*Canis latrans*) exhibiting four distinct color bands: white, brown, off-white/yellow, and black (proximal to distal).

Characteristics to consider include, but are not necessarily limited to the following:

- *Length*: Unlike human head hairs, most animal hairs grow to a prescribed length, depending on the somatic region.
- *Color*: Macroscopic color is an especially useful characteristic when examining animal hairs. Some animal hairs are essentially uniform in color along their length but many exhibit abrupt color changes, known as banding (Figure 4.57). The number, relative lengths, and arrangement of color bands are quite discriminating and can drastically limit the number of potential species from which the question hair originated.
- *Presence or absence of a shield region*: The guard hairs of many, but not all, animals have a distinct shield region.
- *Contour*: Most animal hairs have relatively unremarkable contours (e.g. straight, gently arced, or slightly angled). However, the hair of certain groups of animals have macroscopically recognizable patterns. For example, some hairs have relatively uniform, almost sinusoidal, undulations (e.g. deer [family Cervidae]). Alternatively, some hair shafts have distinct zig-zags with sharp angles (e.g. shrews [family Soricidae]) (Figure 4.17).[123]

---

123 The thicker portions of these hairs are called the "nodes," which are separated from each other by the thin, angled "internodes" (Smith 1933). The internodes have also been termed "strictures" (Moore et al. 1974).

Additional observations are possible once the hairs are mounted for microscopical examination. Many of the relevant characteristics are analogous to human hair examinations, including, but not limited to the following:

- *Thickness*: Unlike human head hairs, the thickness of an animal guard hair may change dramatically along its length.
- *Cuticular scale protrusion*: The cuticular scales of animals protrude to varying degrees from the underlying cortex.
- *Cortical features*: For example, the presence of ovoid bodies, and the color, size, and distribution of pigment granules.
- *Distal tip condition*: Most animals have a fine, tapered tip but other morphologies may be present (e.g. the characteristically split or frayed tips of domestic pigs [*Sus scrofa*]) (Figure 4.58).
- *Root morphology*: The roots of certain animals are quite distinctive (e.g. the "wine-glass" shaped roots found in deer (Hicks 1977)) (Figure 4.59), but in general root morphology should not be emphasized for species identification purposes (see Section 4.9.2).

However, as a group, animal hairs exhibit a much wider diversity of microscopic features compared to human hairs. As such, there are many additional characteristics that are more fruitful when performing animal hair examinations:

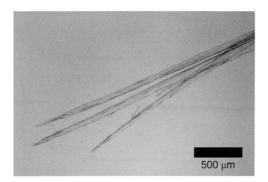

500 µm

Figure 4.58 Pig (*Sus scrofa*) hair exhibiting a split tip (mounted in xylene and viewed using transmitted light).

- *Cuticular scale morphology*: In addition to having a great diversity of possible scale shapes and sizes, the scale pattern often changes along the length of the hair and may even differ from one side of the hair to the other (i.e. scales on opposing surfaces of the hair at the same point along the length) (Figure 4.60). Detailed observations of scale morphology require additional preparations/techniques (e.g. relief casts), which are discussed later in the chapter. Other features, including the relative spacing of the scales and the form of the scale margins (e.g. smooth, rippled, or frilled), can be observed in addition to the general scale pattern (Teerink 1991).
- *Contour of the medullary margin (i.e. the boundary between the cortex and the medulla)*: Visible in whole mounts, the medullary margin can be useful in characterizing broad groups of animals (e.g. Mustelidae, Canidae, and Felidae) (Teerink 1991) (Figure 4.61).
- *Medullary index*: Also visible in whole mounts, the relative thickness of the medulla varies greatly between animals.
- *Transverse cross-sectional shape*: The cross-sectional shapes found in animal hairs varies from the commonplace (e.g. round or slightly oval) to the extreme (e.g. greatly flattened) and elaborate (e.g. dumbbell or H-shaped) (Figure 4.62). Critical

observations require making a transverse cross-section. Several techniques explaining how to do this are discussed later in the chapter.
- *Medullary morphology*: The shapes of the medullary cells are arguably the most critical microscopic features in animal hair identifications. Some indications of the shape, size, and distribution of these cells can often be made with a whole mounted hair. However, detailed observations require replacing the air in the medulla with a suitable mounting medium. Techniques to achieve this are discussed later in this chapter.

In should be noted that there is no universally accepted terminology for the wide diversity of cuticular scale patterns, cross-sectional shapes, and medullary morphologies found in animal hairs as many authors have selected their own suite of terms for their publications. Despite this verbal confusion, the illustrations and photomicrographs in the publications generally allow for easy correlations between references.

Except in rare cases, animal hair identification should not rely on a single feature. A comprehensive examination should include the consideration of multiple characteristics to provide the most accurate identification. Given the wide diversity of animal hair morphology, the value of being familiar with the literature and spending time examining reference hairs cannot be overstated.

4.9.2 Cats and Dogs

Cats and dogs are by far the most common mammalian pets in the United States, in terms of both absolute numbers and percentages of homes with them (AVMA 2012).[124] Not surprisingly, these are the most frequently encountered animal hairs in typical forensic casework. As such, numerous authors have

---

124 There are ~75 million cats and ~43 million dogs living as pets in the United States. They are found in ~30% and ~37% of American households, respectively.

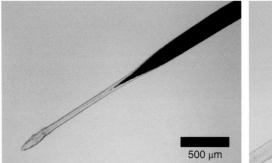 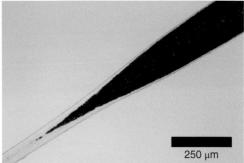

Figure 4.59 "Wine-glass" shaped root from a white-tailed deer (*Odocoileus virginianus*) (left) with a close-up view of the proximal portion of the medulla (right) (mounted in xylene and viewed using transmitted light).

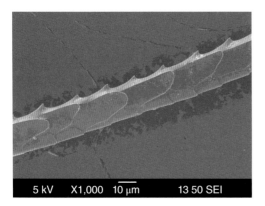

Figure 4.60 SEM photomicrograph of the shaft of a guard hair from a short-tailed shrew (*Blarina brevicauda*).

described methods for discriminating the two from each other.

Three papers have described the utility of plotting the medullary index against the hair diameter using simple Cartesian coordinates (Kind 1965; Peabody et al. 1983; Palenik 1990). These papers demonstrate that for a given diameter, cat hairs generally have a greater medullary index. This is graphically represented by a gently sloping line separating most of the data points for cats and dogs on the plot. The benefits of this technique are the objective nature of the examination and the relative ease with which the measurements are made (i.e. the hairs are simply mounted longitudinally).

However, this method is not infallible and there is some overlap between the two populations (i.e. there are examples of cat and dog data points on the "wrong" side of the lines). One paper suggests that examining the cuticular scale pattern progression is useful as a secondary technique when analyzing hairs near the line (Peabody et al. 1983). Similarly, each paper selects a slightly different line to best separate the two populations of cats and dogs selected for their respective studies.[125] Finally, each paper lacks the details necessary to precisely replicate their analytical methodologies, causing uncertainty for examiners trying to apply this technique to casework.

It has also been suggested that root morphology can be useful when attempting to distinguish cat and dog hairs (Hicks 1977; Deedrick and Koch 2004b),[126] however, root morphology in cats and dogs is often highly variable. Consequently, the author finds this characteristic to be relatively unreliable, an opinion that is shared by others within the community (Tridico et al. 2014c).

While not specific to domestic cats and dogs, Teerink discusses two characteristics useful for discriminating members of Canidae and Felidae (Teerink 1991):

---

125 While not explicitly stated in the Palenik paper, the best fit line can be estimated as
$y = 0.0048x + 0.3433$.
126 These publications describe cats as having fibrillated roots with indistinct shapes and dogs as having spade-shaped roots.

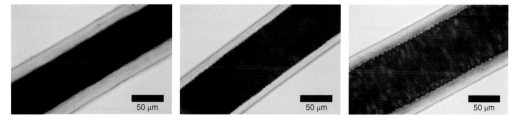

Figure 4.61 Straight (left), fringed (middle), and scalloped (right) medullary margins in the shield regions of guard hairs from a domestic dog, a domestic cat, and an American mink (*Neovison vison*), respectively (mounted in xylene and viewed using transmitted light).

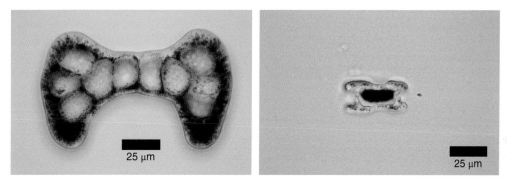

Figure 4.62 Transverse cross-sections of guard hairs from an Eastern cottontail rabbit (*Sylvilagus floridanus*) (left) and a short-tailed shrew (*Blarina brevicauda*) (right) (mounted in xylene and viewed using transmitted light).

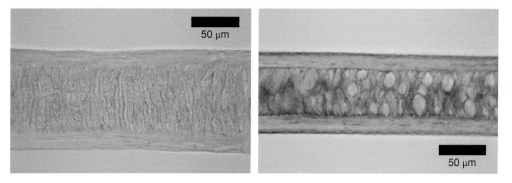

Figure 4.63 Cleared longitudinal cross-sections of a domestic cat (left) and a domestic dog (right) (mounted in glycerin and viewed using transmitted light).

- The medullary margins in the thickest portions of the shield of canids are typically straight while those of felids are typically fringed.
- The medullary morphology in the thickest portions of the shield of canids is typically cloisonné while those of felids are typically fine-grained reverse cloisonné (Figure 4.63). Additionally, the voids in dog hairs are typically rounded while those in cat hairs are generally elongated perpendicular to the long axis of the hair.

The medullary margin can be easily observed in whole mounts if the hair does not have an excess of pigment rendering it nearly opaque, while the medullary morphology is best observed once it has been "cleared" (see Section 4.10.3).

Aside from the metrical technique relating the medullary index to the diameter of the hair,[127] these characteristics are all subjective. Individually, they are all subject to error and therefore the identification of cat and dog hairs should utilize the evaluation of multiple microscopical characteristics considered in tandem with each other to minimize error. Furthermore, these techniques presuppose a closed universe of only cat and dog hairs, an unrealistic situation for forensic hair examiners performing casework.

It should also be noted that research into dog, but not cat, microscopical hair comparisons has been described in the literature (Suzanski 1988, 1989). These studies have demonstrated that there is the potential to discriminate dogs of the same breed although there are numerous limitations analogous to those found in human hair comparisons (Suzanski 1988). Obviously, dog hair microscopical comparisons are not a basis for positive means of identification (i.e. they do not result in individualization). Despite these limitations, case studies can also be found in the literature where dog hair comparisons added value to forensic investigations (Deadman 1984; Tridico 2004).

Although well beyond the scope of this chapter, DNA analyses of both cat and dog hair have been applied to forensic casework (Lyons et al. 2014; Verscheure et al. 2014; Iyengar and Hadi 2014). As with human hair associations, it is recommended that any animal hair association based on microscopy should be followed up with appropriate DNA analysis.

4.9.3 Textile Fur Fibers

Animal fur fibers (i.e. underhairs) have been used in textiles for thousands of years. The wool from sheep is certainly the most commonly encountered example in typical forensic cases. However, textile fibers have been produced from many different animals besides sheep. Some of these, classified as specialty fur fibers, are considered more luxurious and are correspondingly more expensive. Some of the more common examples include cashmere from the cashmere goat,[128] mohair from the Angora goat, angora from the Angora rabbit, as well as camel, alpaca, and vicuña hair (Langley and Kennedy 1981; McGregor 2012).

Other less common textile fibers including shahtoosh from the Tibetan antelope (*Pantholops hodgsonii*) (Rollins and Hall 1999), qiviut from muskoxen (*Ovibos moschatus*) (Rowell et al. 2001), chiengora from domestic dogs (Greer et al. 2007), and yak hair (*Bos grunniens*) (Wortmann et al. 2007) have also been produced.

The correct identification of these textile fibers is of great economic importance and has traditionally been the interest of groups involved in their production or trade (e.g. the German Wool Research Institute (DWI) and the Cashmere and Camel Hair Manufacturer's Institute (CCMI)).

Both light microscopy and electron microscopy have been used to examine these fine hairs (Wildman 1954; Wortmann and Wortmann 1991). They each have their advantages and limitations. For example, textiles with even trace amounts of rabbit hair can be easily and quickly identified using light microscopy. In contrast, cuticular scale height, an important distinguishing characteristic, is best observed using SEM (Phan and Wortmann 1996). In general, surface analysis using SEM has become the microscopical technique of choice for the examination of specialty fur fibers (Wortmann and Wortmann 1992).[129]

---

127 It should be noted that other attempts to discriminate cat and dog hairs using objective, metrical methods have been published (Sato et al. 2006).

128 The term "cashmere" has multiple definitions and it is generally regulated as a commodity in slightly different ways by various governments. Strictly speaking, it is the fine fibers (maximum average diameter ≤19 μm) produced from a specific breed of goat (*Capra hircus laniger*) living in the highlands of Central Asia (Wildman 1954; Phan and Wortmann 1996).

129 Many other techniques, including DNA analysis, have also been used to differentiate specialty fur fibers (Ji et al. 2011).

The above information is only intended to be a brief introduction to this topic as it is a highly specialized area of study with a vast amount of technical literature. Additionally, in forensic cases, these fibers are almost always the subject of a comparison. Therefore, it could be argued that the ability to accurately describe and characterize the fibers is more crucial than the absolute identification. More importantly, being textile fibers, they are almost always dyed when they are encountered in forensic cases. Analyzing the color of the fibers, and possibly the dyes themselves, provides a significant advancement of the discriminating potential of the comparison. In these situations, the examination is more akin to a typical fiber analysis.

4.10 Specialized Techniques

4.10.1 Examination of the Cuticular Surface

There are numerous techniques for viewing the morphology of the scales which comprise the cuticle (Hardy and Plitt 1940; Kirk et al. 1949; Carter and Dilworth 1971; Ogle et al. 1973; Weingart 1973; Petraco 1986; Crocker 1998). Perhaps the most common technique involves making a replicate scale cast using one of several suitable media. Colorless nail polish diluted with acetone (~1:1) works well for this technique. In this method, a thin film of nail polish is applied to a microscope slide and then the hair in question is placed onto the thin liquid film. Once the medium has set, the hair is removed, and the impression of the scales can be examined using a compound microscope (Figure 4.64). It is generally desirable to increase the contrast by swinging out the top lens of the condenser or by stopping down the condenser aperture diaphragm to view this morphology. There are several advantages to this technique, including its relative ease and the fact that it only requires small amounts of inexpensive materials that are easily obtainable.

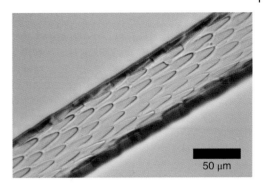

50 µm

Figure 4.64 Scale cast of the shaft of a guard hair from an American mink (*Neovison vison*) (mounted in air and viewed using transmitted light).

Before a high-quality scale cast is made, the hair needs to be cleaned to remove any oily residues and adhering debris. This can typically be accomplished by washing the hair in a watch glass containing a small aliquot of an appropriate solvent such as hexane or ethanol-ether. Polar solvents are obviously more effective for removing blood or water-soluble residues. In rare circumstances, the hair can be cleaned in a sonicating bath to remove well-adhered particles/residues. Depending on the circumstances of the case, it may be desirable to collect and retain the residue/debris removed from the hair for future analysis.

SEM can also be used to directly examine the surface of a hair (Figure 4.60). As with scale casts, the hair should be cleaned before examination. This technique allows for greater resolution and increased depth of field but has several drawbacks which typically outweigh these benefits in typical casework scenarios. The inability to quickly scan the surface of a hair from end to end is the biggest hindrance to using electron microscopy for the routine examination of cuticular scales. The time required to move the SEM stage and adjust the focus simply does not compare to the speed and efficiency of an experienced microscopist as he or she moves a slide with one hand while adjusting the fine focus knob of the microscope with the other. Also, because hairs are not good conductors, they generally need to be coated with a thin layer of conductive material (usually carbon or gold) before they are examined using SEM.[130] In addition to requiring preparation equipment and adding another step to the process, the coating itself has some drawbacks. While not destructive (the hair remains intact throughout the coating and SEM examination) the coating process certainly alters the hair in the sense that it now has a thin film deposited on it which is not easily removed. Depending on its composition and thickness, this coating will potentially interfere with any future examination of the hair using light microscopy. Therefore, hairs should generally only be coated and examined using SEM as a final step after a complete "traditional" light microscopy examination. Alternatively, a subset of a group of hairs may be coated if there is compelling reason to believe that they all originated from the same source.

It should be noted that many trace evidence laboratories use SEM in conjunction with energy-dispersive X-ray spectrometers (EDS) to obtain compositional elemental data from a wide variety of materials (e.g. paints and gunshot residue [GSR] particles). As such, they typically operate at relatively high accelerating voltages of 20 keV and greater. While useful for generating the characteristic X-rays across a broad energy range which enables elemental compositions to be determined, this voltage is detrimental to observing fine surface features because the penetration depth is relatively large. As such, the accelerating voltage should be reduced, along with the spot size as long as sufficient signal is generated to form a high-quality image. A secondary electron (SE) detector is preferable to a backscattered electron (BSE) detector for the observation of fine surficial features due to the comparatively smaller interaction volume.

Perhaps the most obvious obstacle to the routine electron imaging of hair is the instrument itself. Scanning electron microscopes are expensive pieces of equipment (especially compared to compound light microscopes) and while common, they are not present in every forensic laboratory. In the laboratories which do have scanning electron microscopes, the instruments are often dedicated to other types of analyses (e.g. searching for inorganic primer GSR particles) and may not be available to hair examiners. Additionally, while not particularly challenging, acquiring a high-quality SEM image of hair is arguably more involved than the analogous task using a compound microscope and may require supplemental training for the hair examiner. It should be noted that these are not disadvantages of the technique itself, but instead are potential practical limitations of the modern forensic laboratory.

One advantage of SEM is that it can be used to examine the surface of a physically damaged hair. In contrast, the act of making a scale cast, specifically removing the hair from the hardened resin, can inflict additional damage to the hair.

The scales on a hair can be also viewed directly in situ using transmitted light microscopy. This is generally only possible with lightly colored hairs and it helps to have the hair mounted in a medium having a refractive index quite different from the hair such as water or even air. Increasing the contrast of the microscope by swinging out the top lens of the condenser, or by stopping down the condenser aperture diaphragm, is beneficial. Unfortunately, light microscopy allows for only a small portion of the hair's surface to be in focus at a given point.[131] As a consequence, a composite image of the surface must be constructed in the microscopist's mind as the hair is optically sectioned (i.e. careful observation as the fine focus is slowly adjusted). This is not the best way to view cuticular scales for the first time, and

---

130 Electron microscopes designed to work at low vacuum (i.e. a relatively higher pressure compared to a "standard" SEM) may achieve usable images of hairs without coating, although superior images will be obtained if the sample is coated and examined at high vacuum.

---

131 Compound light microscopes have limited depths of field, especially when using higher numerical aperture (NA) objectives (McCrone et al. 1984).

thus it should be reserved for more experienced microscopists who are familiar with the suite of possible scale morphologies. This technique is not suited for detailed in-depth analyses or for documenting cuticular morphology using photomicrographs, and should really be reserved as a quick tool for obtaining additional information from whole mounted hairs. A phase contrast microscope can also be used to examine the cuticular morphology of a hair.

4.10.2 Transverse Cross-sections

The cross-sectional shapes of both human and animal hairs can provide important information during a microscopical examination. The most definitive way to determine the cross-sectional shape of a hair is to cut a transverse cross-section. This is also the best way to document the cross-sectional shape via a photomicrograph. Transverse sections are also valuable for observing (Figure 4.65):

1) the radial distribution[132] and aggregations of pigment
2) the depth of dye penetration in artificially colored hairs
3) the relative thicknesses of the three main layers (i.e. cuticle, cortex, and medulla)
4) the morphologies of the boundaries between these layers
5) the medullary morphology (although this is best studied using longitudinal sections, which are described in the next section).

There are numerous methods of cutting transverse sections but they can be divided into two major classes: bulk and single fiber techniques. While there are many methods for cutting transverse cross-sections of single hairs, one of the easiest and most versatile uses polyethylene (PE) film to embed the hair (Palenik and Fitzsimons 1990).[133] Briefly

summarized, the portion of the hair to be sectioned is sandwiched between two pieces of PE film[134] on a clean microscope slide. A smaller piece of microscope slide (sized to just cover the PE film)[135] is placed over the PE film and the assemblage is heated using a hot plate or an alcohol lamp (author's preference) until the translucent PE film becomes clear (i.e. it has melted). Gentle pressure using the blunt end of any number of tools (e.g. a tungsten needle holder, forceps, or a dissecting needle) may be applied during the heating process and should continue once the slide has been removed from the heat to ensure good adhesion between the hair and the solidifying polymer. Once cool, the top slide can be removed and the PE trimmed to present a reduced cutting surface for microtomy. Freehand sections can be made using a clean, fresh razor (preferably Teflon™ coated) while viewing the sample with a stereomicroscope. It is important to hold the razor orthogonal to the plane of the PE film to prepare cross-sections without angular distortions. While initially challenging, high-quality thin sections can be produced with a moderate amount of practice. Typically, serial sections are made one after the other, and the best are selected for additional examination. These sections are transferred to another clean microscope slide, mounted in a suitable medium such as xylene,[136] and examined using a compound light microscope.

---

132 General pigment distributions (e.g. peripheral or central) which may be inferred with whole mounted hairs are readily visible and documented in transverse sections.

133 This method was developed for making cross-sections of fibers but it is equally applicable to hairs.

134 Palenik and Fitzsimmons recommend a film thickness of 4 mil although thicker films may be used for especially thick hairs. It is also preferable for the film to lack inorganic fillers. This can be ascertained easily by viewing a portion of the film between crossed polars.

135 Wiping a small amount of forehead or nose grease onto the underside of this top slide will act as a release agent and ensure that the PE film sticks to the bottom (i.e. whole) slide instead of being removed with the top slide fragment.

136 Xylene is typically used because it has a refractive index close to PE and therefore the PE surrounding the section essentially "disappears." Alternatively, the hair cross-section can be "popped-out" of the PE and mounted without the surrounding film.

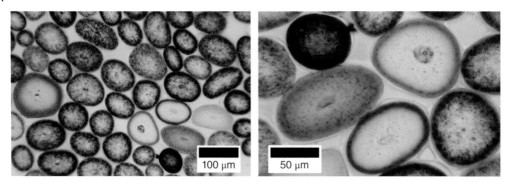

Figure 4.65 Cross-section of wig hairs made using a Schwarz microtome (left) with a close-up view on the right (mounted in xylene and viewed using transmitted light). Note the peripheral pigment distribution and the varying degrees of dye penetration.

There are also many ways to cut bulk transverse sections (i.e. cutting multiple hairs at once). These methods typically employ a microtome but they can also be cut using a Joliff plate (Palenik and Fitzsimons 1990). With Joliff plates, the thickness of the sections is entirely determined by the thickness of the plates themselves, and they are typically quite thick (~400 μm). Because of this they are typically only suited for determining the cross-sectional shape of the hairs as opposed to some of the finer observations discussed above (i.e. pigmentation distribution patterns). Superior sections are produced using microtomes specifically designed for sectioning fibers (e.g. Hardy microtomes (Hardy 1935) and the more advanced Schwarz microtomes (Schwarz 1936)). These fiber microtomes can easily produce high-quality sections between 10 and 20 μm thick and thinner sections can be produced if desired (Heyn 1954). Standard rotary microtomes can also be used to section hairs, although there is no significant advantage compared to a well-functioning fiber microtome.

There are advantages and disadvantages to both single hair and bulk cross-sectioning techniques. The most obvious advantage of bulk techniques is the ability to section multiple hairs at the same time. This advantage is at least partially offset by the loss of spatial resolution for any particular hair (i.e. it is impossible to know exactly where the section is being made along the length of any given hair). This is of primary importance when examining animal hairs, some of which exhibit dramatic changes along their lengths. Compared to the single-fiber techniques, the more mechanized bulk techniques using microtomes require additional set up time but they allow for more reproducible section thicknesses. Freehand sections (such as the PE film method) suffer from a lack of thickness reproducibility as the thickness is determined through hand-eye coordination. However, it should be noted that section thickness is not something that generally needs to be strictly controlled.

Single hair techniques such as the PE film method allow the microscopist to determine exactly where the sections are being made, although these sections must be made one hair at a time (and are thus time-consuming if several hairs are to be sectioned). Single hair techniques are required when the hairs to be sectioned are short, as the bulk techniques require longer hairs.[137] The PE film method is rather quick and it requires easily obtainable supplies.

---

137 The exact length limitations for either technique are truly determined by the manual dexterity of the microscopist. That being said, it should be relatively easy for an experienced microscopist to section a hair measuring a millimeter in length using the PE film method. It is essentially impossible to achieve this feat using a Joliff plate or a Schwarz microtome.

In summary, bulk techniques are more useful for gaining an overview of the range of cross-sectional shapes that are present within a sample. They are well-suited for the examination of human head hairs, as these hairs do not typically exhibit significant changes in their cross-sectional shapes along their lengths. Single hair techniques are better suited for higher level animal hair investigations where it is important to know exactly where the sections are being made. Single hair techniques are often used when a limited number of hairs are to be sectioned or when the hairs are too short for the bulk techniques.

In many cases, the cross-sectional shape can be inferred when the hair in question is observed as a whole mount. This can be accomplished using the optical sectioning technique described in the previous section. However, in this case the microscopist is not simply focusing on the top surface of the hair, but rather focusing through the hair from top to bottom (and vice versa). This allows the microscopist to construct a mental picture of the hair's three-dimensional cross-sectional shape as thin horizontal planes are continually brought into, and out of, focus. It is obvious that this technique is completely unsuitable for documenting the cross-sectional shape via photomicrographs.

Viewing the hair between crossed polars in a non-extinction position can also aid the microscopist in determining the cross-sectional shape of a hair. When viewed in this manner (so-called "optical staining"), the interference colors observed on the hair are analogous to contour lines on a topographical map (Garn 1951a). Both whole mount methods (i.e. optical sectioning and optical staining) are best suited for experienced microscopists who have had practice interpreting these subtle optical features.

4.10.3 Longitudinal Cross-sections

In the realm of forensic science, the need for making longitudinal cross-sections on individual fibrous elements is unique to hair microscopy (i.e. there are no analogous techniques employed with fiber microscopy). Longitudinal cross-sections, primarily on animal hairs, can be highly valuable because they allow for the visualization of the internal microscopic morphology of the medullary cells (Figures 4.56 and 4.63). This morphology can be a very important characteristic aiding the taxonomic classification of animal hairs (Clement et al. 1981).

The need for longitudinal cross-sections lies in the fact that the diagnostic medullary microstructure is typically obscured by air trapped within the medulla. More specifically, it is the large difference between the refractive indices of this air and the surrounding tissue, and the resulting refraction which commonly causes the medulla to appear opaque when hairs are viewed using transmitted light. Although seemingly counterintuitive, animal hairs containing a high proportion of air relative to medullary tissue (e.g. cervids)[138] do not appear opaque when viewed in this manner (Figure 4.66). The medulla, which takes up the vast majority of the hair in these animals, as they contain almost no cortex, is composed of extremely thin membranous films spaced relatively far apart from each other. This results in little contrast between this tissue and

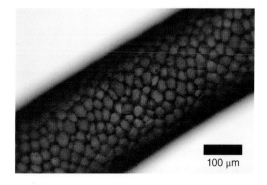

Figure 4.66 Whole mount of a guard hair from a white-tailed deer (*Odocoileus virginianus*) (mounted in xylene and viewed using transmitted light).

100 μm

---

138 Deer and their allies.

the entrapped air which allows for the direct examination of the medullary morphology using transmitted light microscopy.

A straightforward technique for making longitudinal cross-sections of single hairs has been described by Skip Palenik (1983). Briefly summarized, the area bordering the portion of the hair to be sectioned is pulled taut and secured to a microscope slide using tape. A clean, fresh razor held at an extremely low angle is then used to slice into the hair while observing it using a stereomicroscope. Palenik describes how a pair of fine forceps can then be used to peel back the flap of the hair created by this initial incision, thereby increasing the length of the exposed medulla. A slight modification of this technique has the razor remain held in a fixed[139] position while the slide (with the hair attached) is slowly slid across the base of the stereomicroscope. This modification results in a cleaner cross-section (as the medullary tissue is continually cut as opposed to being pulled apart) but it comes with the increased risk of cutting all the way through the hair (which is disadvantageous although not necessarily disastrous).

Regardless of the preferred technique, it is important to section the hair at an appropriate depth. Sectioning too shallow may not expose the medulla, and sectioning too deep might excise the medulla entirely. Needless to say, this technique requires a certain amount of practice before one becomes proficient. After all, we are literally talking about splitting hairs, but adequate sections can generally be produced by practitioners within a few hours of first learning the technique.

Once the medulla is exposed through sectioning, Palenik describes a procedure for "clearing" the hair and replacing the air in the medulla with a more suitable medium for examination of the medullary microstructure.

Glycerin provides a good "index of visibility" for viewing this morphology but it is too viscous to penetrate the fine cavities typically found within the medullae of animal hairs. The viscosity of the glycerin can be reduced by cutting it with ethanol.[140] The alcohol can then be boiled off (due to its lower boiling point compared to glycerin) leaving the glycerin filling the fine medullary cavities originally filled with air. In practice, a drop of the glycerin-ethanol solution is placed on the sectioned portion of the hair, a coverslip is placed over it, and the slide is held over an alcohol lamp or placed onto a hot plate (author's preference). The solution will begin to boil, as evidenced by the bubbles formed under the coverslip, and the slide should continue to be heated until this bubbling ceases, or at least slows considerably (heat for no more than a few minutes). The hair should now be "cleared" and its medullary microstructure can be viewed using transmitted light.[141] The clearing process will continue after heating and it may be advantageous to let the hair sit overnight in order to examine a more completely cleared hair.

Alternatively, once the medulla has been exposed through sectioning, its structure can be directly viewed using an SEM.[142] Along with the examination of the surfaces of specialty fur fibers, the visualization of the medullary micro-structure of longitudinally sectioned hairs is the main application where SEM *may* hold an advantage over transmitted light

---

139 While the razor remains ostensibly in the same position, extremely fine changes in the angle at which the razor is held are typically necessary in order to continue sectioning the hair at an appropriate plane (i.e. not too shallow nor too deep).

140 The exact ratio is relatively unimportant but a nominal solution of 65% glycerin with 35% ethanol produces good results.

141 It is important to let the slide sufficiently cool before it is placed on the stage of the microscope. Failure to do this will likely result in the breaking of the slide due to the differential cooling rates of the portions of the slide in contact with the stage of the microscope and the central portion suspended in air. Generally, placing the slide on the surface of the laboratory bench for a few moments is all that is required to avoid catastrophic slide breakage.

142 As discussed above, hair needs to be coated with a thin layer of a conductive material (e.g. gold or carbon) to obtain high-resolution images using electron microscopy.

microscopy using a conventional compound microscope. Finer features can be observed using electron microscopy, but it has not been sufficiently demonstrated that features useful for identification cannot be observed using high-powered compound light microscopy (e.g. 100X oil immersion objective used in conjunction with 12.5X oculars) (Palenik 1983).

In some cases, the hair being analyzed may simply be too thin or too short for the sectioning method described above to be of practical use. Fortunately, there are other options for "clearing" these hairs and viewing their medullary morphologies.

If the microscopist is lucky, the hair may clear itself when it is examined in a whole mount if a mounting medium with relatively low viscosity (e.g. xylene) is used (Figure 4.67). This serendipitous clearing is the result of the existence of continuous passages through the cuticle and cortex which allows the medium to reach the medulla. Damaged hairs often result in partial clearing in the areas surrounding the damage, although this may not be useful to the microscopist as the medullary structure may be damaged as well. In the case of obviously damaged hairs, it is typically best to look for areas adjacent to the damage in which the medium has managed to penetrate. Alternatively, seemingly intact hairs may also exhibit regions of serendipitous clearing, indicating that their structure must be compromised even if the damage cannot be observed. This is more common in hairs with relatively thin combined cuticular-cortical layers because there is less cellular material for the medium to penetrate to reach the medulla. Clearing hairs in this manner is advantageous because it is expedient, requiring no additional sample preparation, and it is completely non-destructive.[143]

In the absence of serendipitous clearing, making a simple transverse cut adjacent to the region of interest will often allow the mounting medium to penetrate some distance into the hair. This method is typically best suited for hairs with large, open medullary cells (Palenik 1983). This clearing may also be facilitated by adding a small droplet of detergent to the glycerin-ethanol solution. In cases where the medullary cells are truly isolated from each other (as is the case with many insectivores, for example), a single cut made nearly parallel to one edge of hair will allow several cells to be cleared and examined (Figure 4.68).

Although the above methods demonstrate that it is possible to clear hairs without making longitudinal sections, it should be noted that these methods can result in slightly lower quality images of the medullary structure compared to longitudinally sectioned hairs. This is because the medulla needs to be imaged between underlying *and* overlying layers of cortex and cuticle (compared to only underlying cortex and cuticle in longitudinally sectioned hairs). Luckily, this disadvantage is minimized in thin hairs with thin combined cuticle-cortex layers, which are precisely the types of hairs suited for or requiring alterative clearing techniques.

Figure 4.67 Example of serendipitous clearing in the shaft of a guard hair of a domestic cat (mounted in xylene and viewed using transmitted light).

---

143 It can be argued that sectioning hairs is not destructive because all portions of the original hair can be retained and are available for future re-analysis but it must be conceded that once the hair is cut, it is not in its original state. For this reason, appropriate photodocumentation should be completed before sectioning commences.

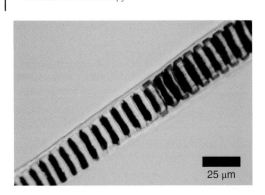

25 μm

Figure 4.68 Partial clearing of a guard hair from a short-tailed shrew (*Blarina brevicauda*) prepared with a nearly parallel cut along the lower margin of the hair (mounted in xylene and viewed using transmitted light).

4.11 Practical Considerations

4.11.1 Training

A significant amount of time is required to train a competent forensic hair examiner. This training will likely begin with a literature review, and while this first step is essential, given the astounding amount there is to learn about hair, it is clearly insufficient by itself. Simply put, hair microscopy cannot be learned from reading alone. It requires many hours of careful observation while examining hairs from a wide variety of sources with a microscope. One must learn to recognize, and interpret the significance of, the multitude of microscopic characteristics that may be found in hairs. There are no shortcuts when it comes to this training of the eye and the mind in the creation of what has been termed a "visual dictionary" (Houck 1999).

Hair microscopy is best learned by being the apprentice of an experienced examiner. He or she can help guide the novice examiner while providing challenging questions, teaching examples, and practical exercises. As in all facets of forensic science, it is critical to transmit the collective knowledge of experienced examiners to those who will be performing the work in the future. A single generation

of poorly trained hair examiners could be a death-blow to the entire discipline.

Practically speaking, the scope of the training will likely depend on the needs of the laboratory as not all modern laboratories conduct full microscopical hair examinations and comparisons (Murphy et al. 2018). When a laboratory limits the scope of their hair examinations (e.g. they only evaluate hair roots for their suitability concerning nuclear DNA testing), there is often a tendency to drastically reduce the scope of the training. Putting the obvious logistical and financial limitations aside, it is the author's opinion that a hair examiner's training should be as broad as possible. It cannot be predicted when additional knowledge (likely attained only under the auspices of a supportive agency) will provide added value during a hair examination.

Similarly, it is advantageous for the trainee to receive at least some education in other trace sub-disciplines. Many hair examiners are also trained as fiber examiners because there are some obvious overlaps in subject material (e.g. animal fibers such as wool, cashmere, and angora used in textiles are clearly animal hairs as well) and techniques (e.g. proficiency in light microscopy and the ability to cut transverse cross-sections). Despite the burden to the trainee and their laboratory, there is no reason that their training cannot be expanded, as other trace evidence (e.g. blood, paint, and glitter) may be observed adhering to hairs. The ability of the hair examiner to identify these materials and assess their significance may provide pertinent information to the investigation that would be lost if these extraneous particles were simply overlooked because they did not fit into the narrow definition of a "hair" examination.

The specifics of training a hair examiner are beyond the scope of this chapter, but guidelines have been drafted by SWGMAT and are currently being updated by OSAC's Materials (Trace) subcommittee.

Finally, it should be recognized that training never truly ends. There is always more to be learned and it is important to stay abreast of developments in the field. Everyone, and especially experienced examiners, must remember this fact or fall victim to the traps of hubris and self-satisfaction.

4.11.2 Reference Collections

The importance of reference collections in trace evidence cannot be overstated, and hair is no exception. As discussed above, the only true way to learn about microscopical hair examinations is to practice examining a wide variety of hairs using a microscope.

As such, each laboratory should maintain (and expand when possible) a reference collection of both human and animal hairs. When building a reference collection, provenance is critical. One must be certain of the origin of every sample included or else it is not a reference collection.

Regarding humans, reference collections should include hair samples:

- of people from different ancestral groups (e.g. European, African, and Asian)
- from various somatic locations (e.g. head, pubic, axilla, limb, eyelashes, and eyebrows)
- exhibiting cosmetic treatment (e.g. bleached, dyed, permed, and straightened)
- exhibiting damage (e.g. scissor cut, razor cut, broken, crushed, and burned)
- exhibiting disease (e.g. monilethrix, pili annulati, pili torti, and trichorrhexis nodosa)[144]
- exhibiting taphonomic degradation (e.g. PMRB, fungal growth, and insect damage).

Animal hairs should be collected from as many different species and breeds as can be obtained, with multiple examples when possible. These would ideally include examples of:

- domestic animals (e.g. cats, dogs, horses, cows, sheep, goats, and Guinea pigs)[145]

- commensal rodents (e.g. the house mouse, brown rat, and black rat in North America)[146]
- local fauna (e.g. deer, foxes, rabbits, rodents, raccoons, bears, and bats)
- animals commonly used in the fur trade (e.g. fox, rabbit, raccoons dog, coyote, and mink).

It is important to collect samples from various somatic areas of animals since, like humans, their hair can vary significantly over different portions of their bodies. General areas to be sampled include back, belly, tail, limbs, and face. The sampler should also emphasize the collection of guard hairs since these are the hairs that will be used in microscopical examinations. A photograph of the animal being sampled is helpful for the examiner to correlate the appearance of loose hairs and the macroscopic appearance of the animal. Photographs are also advantageous when dealing with various breeds of domestic animals. For example, a hair examiner may not know the name of every dog breed with long, white hair by name, but she can easily focus her efforts if she can scan through photographs of every dog in her reference collection.

Maintaining an animal hair database presents certain problems not encountered with other more chemistry-based reference collections. Simply put, the entire concepts of taxonomy and individual species are human constructs.[147] As such, the generally accepted classification of species can change over time. For example, as new evidence is accumulated, formerly distinct species may be reorganized into a single species[148] and, conversely, a single species may be split into two or more

---

144 Examples of diseased hair are generally difficult to obtain, and examiners must often rely on literature references and their accompanying photomicrographs.
145 Examples of multiple breeds should be collected whenever possible.

146 *Mus musculus, Rattus norvegicus,* and *Rattus rattus,* respectively.
147 Albeit ones based on scientific principles.
148 For example, the grizzly bear, once regarded as its own species (*Ursus horribilis*), is now considered a subspecies of the brown bear (*Ursus arctos*).

species.[149] In contrast, chemical names and their meanings are much more stable.[150]

Also, there is not always universal agreement with regards to a species', or a subspecies', correct classification.[151] Ostensibly simple tasks, such as the correct classification of domestic dogs and their close relatives the red wolf and the dingo are not without controversy (vonHoldt et al. 2016; Crowther et al. 2014).[152]

Because of this complexity, the curator of the reference collection should be cognizant of both the date each sample was named or entered into the collection, and the geographic location from which it originated. Recording facts such as these will help establish the provenance of the sample and allow for the most correct classification.

The physical hair reference collection should be stored in a dark, dry environment protected from insects. Dermestid beetles are the bane of reference collections and can cause irreparable damage. Once dry, loose hairs can be placed in plastic zip bags for long term storage. Samples with a higher risk of insect infestation, such as whole animal pelts, should be periodically inspected to ensure that their packaging has not been compromised. Examiners may also elect to make permanent slide preparations of specimens for quick reference. Finally, it is useful to catalogue the collection in a searchable, electronic database with all of the accompanying data entered into appropriate fields (e.g. scientific name, common name, date collected, source of sample, somatic location, and photographs).

---

149 Recently, a new species of orangutan was described (Nater et al. 2017).

150 For example, chloroform may also be called trichloromethane, but there is no reason to suspect that chemists will one day decide that it is composed of something other than three chlorine atoms and one hydrogen atom bonded to a carbon atom.

151 The International Commission on Zoological Nomenclature (ICZN) is the organization which governs the accepted scientific names of animals.

152 Seemingly academic distinctions such as these can have serious consequences for both hunting and transporting species that are regulated by state, federal, or international laws.

4.11.3 Examination Guidelines

The examination of hair, like other forms of trace evidence, does not lend itself to blind obedience of rigid protocols or flow charts. It is the responsibility of hair examiners to carefully *think* about the samples submitted to them and the questions they are attempting to answer. Every case is different and its details should be considered when deciding on the most appropriate course of action. In short, forethought is required before beginning any examination. However, there are some general guidelines that apply to a wide variety of situations and are generally relevant for "typical" casework. The following is a generalized guideline for the examination of hairs. This guideline is not necessarily applicable to hair comparisons, as these were discussed earlier.

Hairs should be photographed in the condition they were received, and then examined using the unaided eye and a stereomicroscope before they are washed or mounted on microscope slides for a more detailed microscopical examination. This allows the examiner to both evaluate the length[153] and natural contour of the hair, as well as examine it for the presence of adhering trace evidence, including potential blood, fibers, paint, or unknown residues.

Any adhering material may be photodocumented and then physically isolated at this point for further analysis. Alternatively, the hairs may be washed (and possibly sonicated) in an appropriate solvent. In addition to isolating potential trace evidence from the surface of the hair, this washing makes the hair more suitable for a microscopical examination by removing particles/residues that may have obscured details of the hair's microscopic morphology. Particles freed from the hair can be recovered using a variety of techniques (e.g. filtration). The solvent may be evaporated to

---

153 The length of the hair may be measured directly using a ruler, or it can be determined from a calibrated photograph. Hairs with significant amounts of three-dimensionality will need to be held flat with a microscope slide, or other suitable material, if their lengths are to be determined from a photograph.

Figure 4.69 Human hair shaft with a particle of glitter (circled) adhering to its surface (mounted in xylene and viewed using transmitted light).

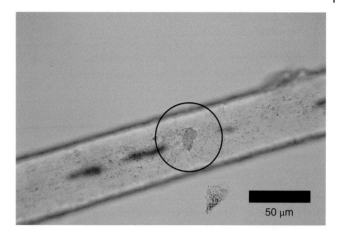

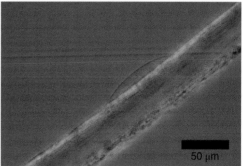

Figure 4.70 Isotropic residue on the surface of a human head hair (mounted in xylene and viewed using transmitted light [left] and between crossed polars with a first-order red compensator inserted [right]).

dryness and any remaining residue can also be analyzed.

After this initial examination, the hairs should be mounted on a microscope slide in an appropriate mounting medium. This can be either a temporary or a permanent preparation. Once mounted, the microscopic morphology of the hairs can be examined in detail using a compound light microscope, preferably one equipped with polarizing filters. If the microscope is equipped with a camera, some of these microscopic characteristics may be photographed. Microscopic traces of adhering material may also be located, photographed, and possibly identified during this examination. Any component of dust may be found on the surface of hairs, including potential blood, paint, mineral grains, starch, pollen, fungal spores, hyphae, cosmetic glitter, other crystalline particles, or amorphous residues

(Figures 4.69 and 4.70). Attempts to isolate these particles for further analyses may be conducted once they have been recognized.

The results of these microscopical examinations and the goals of the analysis will determine if additional techniques are necessary. These may include, but are not limited to:

- comparison microscopy
- fluorescence microscopy
- specialized preparation techniques (e.g. scale casts, transverse or longitudinal cross-sections)
- SEM
- microchemical staining
- MSP
- dye extraction and subsequent analyses
- solvent extraction and subsequent chemical analyses.

4.11.4 Documentation, Report Writing, and Testimony

As with any science, observations should be recorded contemporaneously with the examination of hairs. These can take the form of hand-written or typed notes and they may be augmented with drawings or photographs/photomicrographs. These notes serve to document the examination, refresh the mind of the examiner after periods of time have elapsed (i.e. before testimony), and enable another scientist to review the work that was completed. However, it is recognized that no practical amount of notes or photographs can truly record all of the observations made while looking at hairs through a microscope (Lee and De Forest 1984). Also, photomicrographs are inherently limited in that they only capture one focal plane of the hair. For these reasons, a truly independent review cannot be conducted solely from the notes and photographs of another examiner. Simply put, all examiners must conduct their own microscopical examinations before they reach their conclusions for all but the most obvious inquiries.

For comparisons, the notes themselves can be taken freehand or using a form/checklist with various categories and the possible characteristics within each category. In general, proponents of the checklist system believe that they help ensure a systematic, documented examination. Proponents of general note taking believe that it provides the examiner with the ability to more fully describe the continuum of the characteristics being observed without being restricted by the quantized nature of the checklist (Robertson and Aitken 1986). As such, even staunch proponents of using checklists recommend augmenting their use with written notes (Robertson 1999).

Laboratory policy largely determines the general form and wording of reports. While working within the confines prescribed upon them, examiners should make every effort to lucidly present their observations and results in a well-organized manner. It is the examiner's interpretation of these results that allows her to reach a conclusion. The conclusion and its significance should be written in clear, precise language along with any associated limitations, caveats, and assumptions. For example, it must be written that any association made through microscopy alone is not a positive means of identification. For hair comparisons, a "conclusion scale" listing all the possible conclusions may be included in the report as an illustration of the relative significance of the conclusion reached in the current case.[154]

The goal of clarity should continue through testimony. It is the examiner's duty to accurately explain her findings to the trier of fact. This may include educating the court on the basics of hair anatomy, hair examinations, hair comparisons, transfer principles, etc. As in the report, the conclusion and its significance should be thoroughly described and any limitations, caveats, and assumptions must be explained. This includes the statement that any association made through microscopy alone is not a positive means of identification. Additionally, the significance of an association should not be assessed using statistics. A final and perhaps more eloquently stated word of caution is provided below:

> Much has been written about the deductions which have been gleaned from the study of a strand of hair found at the scene of a crime. True, many apparently remarkable facts can be observed about a hair with the aid of a microscope, but it is equally important to be aware of the limitations imposed by this type of evidence. Moreover, the expert witness can easily be led astray by being overzealous about his findings (Turner 1949).

---

154 However, there is no current consensus within the discipline on the specifics of the possible conclusions and therefore there is no universally accepted "conclusion scale."

4.12   Criticisms

Microscopical hair examinations have witnessed a substantial amount of criticism in recent years. These criticisms have varying levels of validity, as will be discussed below.

The most significant commentary on the state of forensic science in the United States in the twenty-first century was published in 2009 by the National Academy of Sciences, the so-called NAS Report (National Research Council of the National Academies 2009). Forensic hair examinations received mostly mild criticisms which focused on the inappropriate use of statistics, the limitations of the science in general (i.e. the impossibility of individualization), and the need to incorporate DNA testing, whether nuclear or mitochondrial, to increase the significance of associations. The consensus among modern forensic hair examiners is that these are valid points to which they already adhere. Importantly, while perhaps exaggerating the limitations of microscopical hair examinations, the report did not fundamentally challenge the scientific validity of the discipline.

In 2016, the Department of Justice (DOJ 2016) released a hair examination testimony guideline, which in turn precipitated the publication of a more stinging rebuke in what is now known as the PCAST report (President's Council of Advisors on Science and Technology 2016). Despite PCAST's assertion that this was not a "comprehensive review," the report makes the far-reaching claim that "the papers described in the DOJ supporting document do not provide a scientific basis for concluding that microscopic [sic] hair examination is a valid and reliable process." The author respectfully disagrees with their conclusion. As this chapter has demonstrated, forensic microscopical hair examinations are rooted in science and despite their limitations they can result in discriminating comparisons and provide additional information that cannot be obtained by any other means.

4.12.1   Probability

One of the most criticized aspects of forensic hair comparisons concerns the use of statistics. Beginning in the mid-1970s, a series of papers, authored primarily by Barry Gaudette, appeared in the literature attempting to determine probabilities relating to microscopical hair comparisons (Gaudette and Keeping 1974; Gaudette 1976, 1978). In the ensuing decades, these papers were met with considerable criticism from within the field and elicited responses from those continuing this avenue of research (Barnett and Ogle 1982; Gaudette 1982, 1984; Strauss 1983b; Aitken and Robertson 1987; Wickenheiser and Hepworth 1990; Ogle 1991; Lamb and Tucker 1994). Criticisms regarding statistics also featured prominently in both the NAS and PCAST reports (National Research Council of the National Academies 2009; President's Council of Advisors on Science and Technology 2016).

The current consensus among hair examiners is that statistics should not be used in either reports or testimony to convey the significance of a microscopical hair examination. To date, there is no scientifically valid means of applying statistics to microscopical hair comparisons, and there might never be. This does not imply that there is no value in microscopical hair comparisons, just that there is no way to satisfactorily quantify it. Indeed, some of the largest challenges faced by all trace evidence examiners are the difficulties conveying the significance of their results to lay members of a jury.

While the papers attempting to introduce statistics may have failed in that regard, the other research presented in those publications, along with that of other scientists,[155] conclusively demonstrates that there is value in forensic hair comparisons. Although this statement may not be met with universal agreement, statistics are not a prerequisite for

---

155 For examples, see Bisbing and Wolner (1984) and Houck and Budowle (2002).

the implementation of the scientific method (Houck 1999).

4.12.2 FBI Review

Recent press releases providing preliminary results of a joint DOJ, FBI, Innocence Project, and the National Association of Criminal Defense Lawyers (NACDL) review of the FBI's hair comparison cases has arguably resulted in the most negative publicity for forensic hair examinations, and has potentially undermined the public's confidence in the science (FBI 2015). This review of cases submitted to the FBI prior to 2000 focuses on whether examiner reports and testimony given at trial exceeded the limits of science in any of three ways:

1. The examiner stated or implied that a questioned hair originated from an individual to the exclusion of all others (i.e. individualization).
2. The examiner stated or implied a statistical weight or probability regarding an association between a questioned hair and a known source.
3. The examiner referenced his ability to distinguish hairs from the large number of individuals in the cases that he has worked over the course of his career to increase the significance of an association between a questioned hair and a known source.

Initial results have indicated that inappropriate statements were given during testimony at 96% (257 of 268) of the trials reviewed (FBI 2015).

The first error is self-explanatory and particularly egregious not only because it is the most extreme overstatement, but because it has always been known that microscopical hair comparisons do not result in individualization.

The second error is both the most difficult to define[156] and comes with the most complicated backstory given the sincere efforts of past research to apply statistics to forensic hair comparisons. In some instances, it is akin to judging the past with the understanding of the present, but it is still a valid criticism, and one principle of science is the advancement of knowledge through time.

The third error walks a fine line between the use of experience to help inform an examiner's opinion (i.e. one of the privileges bestowed upon expert witnesses) and a flawed approach to convey the framework of said experience. This point is best illustrated in an example of testimony from an FBI hair examiner in one of the cases comprising this review:

> But normally, a hair examiner will have no problem separating out hairs from different people. In the last eighteen years, I've looked at hairs of thousands and thousands of people, and in that time, in that eighteen years, I've only had two, I'm sorry, three occasions where I had hairs from two different people that I could not distinguish from each other.

This statement gives the impression that the examiner has examined thousands of hairs and compared them *all to each other*, with only a few samples being indistinguishable.

First, this is not possible because the hair standards from completed cases were returned to their submitting agencies and were not available for comparison to newer submissions. Second, regardless of the physical impossibility of this scenario, the significance of this misleading statement is as follows. Assume the examiner has worked 2000 cases with two hair standards each (i.e. 4000 total hair samples). Comparing them all to each other would require approximately eight million pairwise comparisons.[157] However, instead of this one massive experiment, the examiner in this hypothetical scenario has actually conducted 2000 smaller experiments, each with

---

156 For example, the phrase "imply a statistical weight" can be interpreted in a variety of ways.

157 7 998 000 pairwise comparisons are required with 4000 samples (# of comparisons = $(n*(n-1))/2$).

a single pairwise comparison (i.e. a total of 2000 pairwise comparisons). There is a large difference between the inability to distinguish people in three out of 2000 comparisons and three out of eight million comparisons.

There are two other points to bring up regarding these pairwise comparisons. First, there is the matter of inherent bias, as the examiner knew that the standards came from different people when he was trying to determine if he could distinguish them. Second, there is no proof that the examiner could actually distinguish the hair standards examined using microscopy alone in these pairwise comparisons. In any event, there is no way to independently verify the veracity of these claims.

Looking at this large-scale review of the FBI hair examiners from a broad perspective, it is important to note that it concerns the overstatement of the significance of the results, not the results themselves. This is a critical distinction, as a flaw in the application of science is quite different than a flaw in the science itself. Nevertheless, this review has highlighted a valid point that the significance of hair evidence has repeatedly been overstated in courtrooms around the country.

However, all is not what it seems when the details of this review are scrutinized. The author has had the opportunity to work with numerous attorneys representing clients whose cases were part of the FBI review. In this capacity, it was noted that some trial transcripts demonstrate all three of the errors, and it is clear that the testimony overstated the significance of the hair comparison. However, there are also examples of cases where testimony was flagged for error, but no error was apparent given the guidelines set forth in the review. Others who have also studied examples of FBI-reviewed cases have come to similar conclusions (Kaye 2015). Examples such as these are cause to question the results of the FBI review and indeed a critical audit of the review may be warranted.

Alas, much damage has already been done to erode the public's confidence, and the "pendulum may be swinging in favor of the uncritical rejection of once unquestioned forensic science" (Kaye 2015). It is hoped that a sustained, well-reasoned counterargument will lead to a true accounting of the value and limitations of forensic hair examinations that will determine their role in the future of forensic science.

4.13 Summary: The Value of Forensic Hair Microscopy

Hair is, in many ways, the ideal form of forensic trace evidence:

- It is found on all humans and other mammals.
- It is constantly being produced and subsequently shed in their immediate environments.
- It is readily transferred from one person/object to another person/object.
- It is highly stable, resisting both physical and chemical degradation.
- It is easily overlooked by criminals involved in nefarious activities.
- Hairs from different individuals can be distinguished from each other, and with nuclear DNA testing this discrimination can approach individualization.
- Information obtained from the examination of hairs can provide investigative leads or help with the reconstruction of events in contention.

Despite these attributes, the future of microscopical hair examinations is uncertain. While exact statistics may not be available, there is anecdotal evidence that many forensic laboratories are moving away from full microscopical examinations and comparisons of hairs.[158] In their place, many examiners are tasked

---

158 Although at least one major federal laboratory is currently exploring the expansion of its hair microscopy capabilities.

solely with identifying human hairs and determining which ones are suitable for nuclear DNA testing based on their root morphologies. Quite simply, this is a myopic mistake on many levels.

It is unquestioned that molecular techniques have revolutionized forensic science, greatly enhancing the amount of information that can be obtained from biological materials, including hair. The question of identity (i.e. from whom did an unknown hair originate) is often of great importance in a forensic investigation. When a full profile is obtained, nuclear DNA testing is unrivaled at answering this question and essentially approaches true individualization. Mitochondrial DNA is maternally inherited and thus it is not nearly as discriminating as nuclear DNA. However, it is a powerful technique that can exclude large portions of the population when a profile is developed. Both nuclear and mitochondrial DNA methods find favor with the judicial system as their results are amenable to statistical interpretation. Nevertheless, despite their proven utility, each of these techniques has limitations.

Perhaps the biggest limitation is that while forensic DNA testing can provide information regarding identity, that is the only subject that it can address. It cannot answer any of the contextual questions that are often just as important to an investigation as ascertaining from whom an unknown hair originated. For example, DNA testing cannot be used to determine if a hair was forcibly removed from the skin, burnt, originated from a decomposing body, or if it is a pubic hair. Microscopy is uniquely suited to answering these and many other potential questions that may be relevant to the investigation. This contextual information is especially important when the victims and suspects share one or more environments (e.g. a house or car), and the mere presence of their hair is not particularly significant. Simply put, hair microscopy can provide critical information that cannot be obtained using any other analytical

techniques. This information can help direct an investigation, as well as support or refute claims made by victims, suspects, and witnesses.

Secondly, all DNA techniques are inherently destructive. Some or all of the hair needs to be consumed during the extraction process. Once consumed, there is no possibility of obtaining additional information through non-molecular techniques. This is especially significant because the relevant contextual questions may not immediately present themselves at the onset of an investigation, and these questions will remain forever unanswered if the hair has already been consumed for DNA testing before they are asked. Additionally, there is no guarantee that genetic information will be successfully obtained. Without a prior microscopical hair examination, no knowledge of the hair will be elucidated in these cases.

In contrast, hair microscopy is non-destructive and the appearance of the hair can be documented using both written notes and photographs. Once the hair has been photographically preserved, its images can be studied by anyone at a later time, even after it has been consumed via DNA testing. Additionally, some amount of information is always obtained at the conclusion of a microscopical hair examination. In some cases, this examination may conclusively answer a relevant question. For example, a known sample may be eliminated as a potential source, or a dye line or insect bites may be observed. This information will be permanently lost if a microscopical examination is not conducted before the hair is consumed, or if the molecular testing does not result in a profile. For these reasons alone, DNA testing should only be conducted after the completion of a microscopical hair examination.

Nuclear DNA testing is also limited in that it requires nucleated cells, which are typically absent from hairs with telogen roots. Unfortunately, the vast majority of unknown hairs encountered in forensic casework have telogen roots and are therefore unsuitable for the most discriminating form of DNA testing.[159]

Mitochondrial DNA can be used to exclude substantial portions of the population as a potential source of an unknown hair. However, its significance is often severely limited in that it cannot distinguish family members of maternal descent.[160] For example, it cannot differentiate the hair of a mother, her children, and her daughter's children. There are no analogous a priori limitations on hair microscopy, and additional discrimination potential is easily demonstrated (e.g. unlike mtDNA, even a novice hair examiner would be able to differentiate the author's head hair from that of his mother's). However, it has been demonstrated that mtDNA testing can differentiate hairs that have been determined to be indistinguishable from each other using microscopy (Houck and Budowle 2002). In short, neither technique can approach individualization but the combined discriminating potential of mtDNA testing and hair microscopy is greater than the discriminating potential of either technique alone. This is because each technique is evaluating different characteristics of the hair (i.e. molecular sequences versus physical morphology). Furthermore, it has been demonstrated that the hairs of identical twins may be discriminated using microscopy (Das-Chaudhuri 1976; Bisbing and Wolner 1984). In these rare cases, hair microscopy even has the ability to augment the discriminating potential of nuclear DNA testing.

It is also common for large numbers of hairs to be located during the investigation of a single case. Even disregarding all of the other benefits that it has to offer, microscopy is by far the most efficient and cost-effective technique for examining all of these hairs and selecting those that will be the best candidates for DNA testing given the circumstances of the case. Furthermore, regardless of the underlying inefficiency, it is not realistic to perform DNA testing on every hair with the technology, personnel, and financial resources currently available.

In summary, microscopical hair comparisons complement DNA testing, increasing the efficiency and the discriminating potential of these already powerful techniques. Equally important, hair microscopy also provides additional contextual information that cannot be obtained using any other analytical method. This is a critical point to comprehend, as so often the perceived value of forensic hair microscopy has been limited to its role in the comparison process. It is indisputable that the totality of the potential information that may be elucidated from a hair cannot be obtained without a complete microscopical examination. Any failure to recognize and appreciate this fact constitutes a regression of forensic science.

Dedication

This chapter is dedicated to all of the people who have had a positive impact on my life and career, beginning with my mother and father. In addition to loving me unconditionally, they encouraged a love of learning from an early age, especially about the physical world. I would like to thank Dr. Peter De Forest, who introduced me to criminalistics and microscopy, and whose wisdom and philosophy shaped the very foundation of how I think. Similarly, words cannot express my sincere gratitude to Skip Palenik, who has served as my main scientific mentor for the past 13 years, and who has taught me most of what I know about the scientific analysis of trace evidence, including hair microscopy. I'd also like to thank Dr. Christopher Palenik and all of the staff at Microtrace for creating a terrific work environment, and for showing

---

159 It has been estimated that as many as 95% of the questioned hairs encountered in forensic casework have telogen roots (Robertson 1999).

160 It may also face considerable limitations in geographically or socially isolated populations that do not typically marry within the general population.

me interesting hairs, among other things, to examine. Finally, this chapter could not have been written without the love and support of

my wife, Kelly Brinsko Beckert, whose suggestions and comments have greatly improved its content.

References

Adhikari, K., Fontanil, T., Cal, S. et al. (2016). A genome-wide association scan in admixed Latin Americans identifies loci influencing facial and scalp hair features. *Nature Communications* 7: 1–12.

Adya, K.A., Inamadar, A.C., Palit, A. et al. (2011). Light microscopy of the hair: a simple tool to "Untangle" hair disorders. *International Journal of Trichology* 3 (1): 46–56.

Aitken, C.G.G. and Robertson, J. (1987). A contribution to the discussion of probabilities and human hair comparisons. *Journal of Forensic Sciences* 32 (3): 684–689.

Alibardi, L. (2004). Comparative aspects of the inner root sheath in adult and developing hairs of mammals in relation to the evolution of hairs. *Journal of Anatomy* 205 (3): 179–200.

Alibardi, L., Valle, L.D., Nardi, A., and Toni, M. (2009). Evolution of hard proteins in the Sauropsid integument in relation to the cornification of skin derivatives in amniotes. *Journal of Anatomy* 214 (4): 560–586.

Allen, J.A. (1894). On the seasonal change in color in the varying hare (*Lepus americanus*). *Bulletin of the American Museum of Natural History* 6: 107–128.

Anon (1851). Trial for murder by contused wounds and fracture of the cranium. *The London Medical Gazette* 48: 729–734.

Anon (1895). Photography and the detection of crime. *The Photographic Times* 26 (3): 129–136.

Anon (1950). Zoology professor often doubles in character of Sherlock Holmes. *The Hackettstown Gazette*: 9.

Appel, O. and Kollo, I. (2010). The evidential value of singed hairs in arson cases. *Science and Justice* 50: 138–140.

Appleyard, H.M. (1960). *Guide to the Identification of Animal Fibres*. Torridon: Wool Industries Research Association.

Astore, I.P.L., Pecoraro, V., and Pecoraro, E.G. (1979). The normal trichogram of pubic hair. *British Journal of Dermatology* 101 (4): 441–444.

Atkinson, S.C., Cormia, F.E., and Unrau, S.A. (1959). The diameter and growth phase of hair in relation to age. *British Journal of Dermatology* 71 (8–9): 309–311.

Atwell, T., McCurdy, R. Shaw, D., (2011). *Is the hair probative or from the laundry? Probative value of hair in households in which the suspect and victim have co-mingled laundry*. Presented at the Trace Evidence Symposium, Kansas City, August 08–11, 2011.

AVMA (2012). *U.S. Pet Ownership & Demographics Sourcebook*. Schaumburg: American Veterinary Medical Association.

Bailey, J.G. (1982). *The Characterization of Semi-Permanent Dyes on a Single Hair*. Sacramento: Presented at the First Interamerican Congress of Forensic Sciences.

Bailey, J.G. and Schliebe, S.A. (1985). *Precision of the Average Curvature Measurement in Human Head Hairs*. Washington, D.C.: Federal Bureau of Investigation.

Barman, J.M., Pecoraro, V., and Astore, I. (1964). Method, technic and computations in the study of the trophic state of the human scalp hair. *The Journal of Investigative Dermatology* 42 (6): 421–425.

Barman, J.M., Astore, I., and Pecoraro, V. (1965). The normal trichogram of the adult. *The Journal of Investigative Dermatology* 44 (4): 233–236.

Barman, J.M., Pecoraro, V., Astore, I., and Ferrer, J. (1967). The first stage in the natural history of the human scalp hair cycle. *The Journal of Investigative Dermatology* 48 (2): 138–142.

Barnett, P.D. and Ogle, R.R. (1982). Probabilities and human hair comparison. *Journal of Forensic Sciences* 27 (2): 272–278.

Barrett, J.A., Siegel, J.A., and Goodpastor, J.V. (2010). Forensic discrimination of dyed hair color: I. UV-visible microspectrophotometry. *Journal of Forensic Sciences* 55 (2): 323–333.

Barrett, J., Siegel, J., and Goodpastor, J. (2011). Forensic discrimination of dyed hair color: II. Multivariate statistical analysis. *Journal of Forensic Sciences* 56 (1): 95–101.

Bean, R.B. (1935). Hair and eye color in old Virginians. *The American Journal of Physical Anthropology* 20 (2): 171–204.

Beeman, J. (1942). The scale count of human hair. *Journal of Criminal Law and Criminology* 32 (5): 572–574.

Beeman, J. (1943). Further evaluation of the scale count of human hair. *Journal of Criminal Law and Criminology* 33 (5): 422–424.

Beyak, R., Kass, G.S., and Meyer, C.F. (1971). Elasticity and tensile properties of human hair. II. Light radiation effects. *Journal of the Society of Cosmetic Chemists* 22: 667–678.

Birch, M.P., Messenger, J.F., and Messenger, A.G. (2001). Hair density, hair diameter and the prevalence of female pattern hair loss. *British Journal of Dermatology* 144 (2): 297–304.

Birch, M.P., Lall, S.C., and Messenger, A.G. (2002). Female pattern hair loss. *Clinical Dermatology* 27: 383–388.

Bisbing, R.E. (2002). The forensic identification and association of human hair. In: *Forensic Science Handbook: Volume I*, 2e (ed. R. Safenstein), 389–428. Upper Saddle River, NJ: Prentice Hall.

Bisbing, R.E. and Wolner, M.F. (1984). Microscopical discrimination of twins' head hair. *Journal of Forensic Sciences* 29 (3): 780–786.

Blyskal, B. (2009). Fungi utilizing keratinous substrates. *International Biodeterioration & Biodegradation* 63: 631–653.

Boehme, A., Brooks, E., McNaught, I., and Robertson, J. (2009). The persistence of animal hairs in a forensic context. *Australian Journal of Forensic Science* 41 (2): 99–112.

Bogaty, H. (1969). Differences between adult and children's hair. *Journal of the Society of Cosmetic Chemists* 20 (3): 159–171.

Bolduc, C. and Shapiro, J. (2001). Hair care products: waving, straightening, conditioning, and Coloring. *Clinics in Dermatology* 19: 431–436.

Boll, M.S., Doty, K.C., Wickenheiser, R., and Lednev, I.K. (2017). Differentiation of hair using ATR FT-IR spectroscopy: a statistical classification of dyed and non-dyed hairs. *Forensic Chemistry* 6: 1–9.

Borges, C.R., Roberts, J.C., Wilkins, D.G., and Rollins, D.E. (2001). Relationship of melanin degradation products to actual melanin content: application to human hair. *Analytical Biochemistry* 290: 116–125.

Bottoms, E., Wyatt, E., and Comaish (1972). Progressive changes in cuticular pattern along the shafts of human hair as seen by scanning electron microscopy. *British Journal of Dermatology* 86: 379–384.

Bourguignon, L., Hoste, B., Vits, K. et al. (2008). A fluorescent microscopy-screening test for efficient STR-typing of telogen hair roots. *Forensic Science International: Genetics* 3: 27–31.

Brace, C.L. (1995). Region does nor mean "Race" – reality versus convention in forensic anthropology. *Journal of Forensic Sciences* 40 (2): 171–175.

Brady, D., Duncan, J.R., Cross, R.H.M., and Russell, A.E. (1990). Scanning electron microscopy of wool fibre degradation by Streptomyces bacteria. *South African Society for Animal Science* 20 (3): 136–140.

Brauner, P., Gorski, A., and Levy, S. (1990). A case of the blues. *The Microscope* 38 (3): 241–246.

Brenner, L., Squires, P.L., Garry, M., and Tumosa, C.S. (1985). A measurement of human hair oxidation by fourier transform infrared spectroscopy. *Journal of Forensic Sciences* 13 (2): 420–426.

Brooks, E.M., Cullen, M., Sztydna, T., and Walsh, S.J. (2010). Nuclear staining of Telogen roots contributes to succesfull forensic nDNA analysis. *Australian Journal of Forensic Sciences* 42 (2): 115–122.

Brown, A.C. and Swift, J.A. (1975). Hair breakage: the scanning electron microscope as a diagnostic tool. *Journal of the Society of Cosmetic Chemists* 26: 289–297.

Brown, V.M., Crounse, R.G., and Abele, D.C. (1986). An unusual new hair shaft abnormailty: "Bubble Hair". *Journal of the American Academy of Dermatology* 15 (5): 1113–1117.

Browne, P.A. (1853). *Trichologia Mammalium; or, a Treatise on the Organization, Properties and Uses of Hair and Wool*. Philadelphia: J. H. Jones.

Brunner, H. and Coman, B. (1974). *The Identification of Mammalian Hair*. Melbourne: Inkata Press.

Bryson, W.G., Harland, D.P., Caldwell, J.P. et al. (2009). Cortical cell types and intermediate filament arrangements correlate with fiber curvature in Japanese human hair. *Journal of Structural Biology* 166: 46–58.

Carter, B.C. and Dilworth, T.G. (1971). A simple technique for revealing the surface pattern of hair. *American Midland Naturalist* 85 (1): 260–262.

Chamot, É.M. (1915). *Elementary Chemical Microscopy*. New York: Wiley.

Chapman, D.M. (1992). The bare: ensheathed anagen root ratio as a function of the speed of epilation. *Clinical and Experimental Dermatology* 17: 99–101.

Chapman, D.M. (1997). The nature of cuticular "Ruffles" on slowly plucked anagane hair roots. *Journal of Cutaneous Pathology* 24: 434–439.

Chapman, D.M. and Miller, R.A. (1996). An objective measurement of the anchoring strength of anagen hair in an adult with the loose anagen hair syndrome. *Journal of Cutaneous Pathology* 23 (3): 288–292.

Charles, A.J. (2009). Superficial cutaneous fungal infections in tropical countries. *Dermatologic Therapy* 22: 550–559.

Chase, H.B. and Eaton, G.J. (1959). The growth of hair follicles in waves. *Annals of the New York Academy of Sciences* 83: 365–368.

Chernova, O.F. and Tselikova, T.N. (2004). *The Atlas of Mammalian Hair: The Fine Structure of Guard Hair and Spines under a Scanning Electron Microscope*. Moscow: KMK.

Chewning, D.D., Deaver, K.L., and Christensen, A.M. (2008). Persistence of fibers on ski masks during transit and processing. *Forensic Science Communications* 10 (3).

Chille, E.A. (1989). *The Forensic Significance of Hair Degradation in Interior Environments (Thesis)*. New York, NY: John Jay College of Criminal Justice.

Chowdhuri, S. and Bhattacharyya, B. (1964). Paired medulla in human hair. *Current Science* 33 (24): 748–749.

Clement, J.-L., Hagege, R., Le Pareux, A. et al. (1981). New concepts about hair identification revealed by electron microscope studies. *Journal of Forensic Sciences* 26 (3): 447–458.

Clement, J.L., Le Pareux, A., and Ceccaldi, P.F. (1982). The specificity of the ultrastructure of human hair medulla. *Journal of the Forensic Science Society* 22: 396–398.

Collins, H.H. (1918). Studies of Normal moult and of artificially induced regeneration of pelage in Peromyscus. *Journal of Experimental Zoology* 27 (1): 73–99.

Collins, B.W. (1996). *The Effect of Temperature and Environment on Post Mortem Morphology of Human Hair Roots (Thesis)*. New York, NY: John Jay College of Criminal Justice.

Commo, S., Gaillard, O., and Bernard, B.A. (2004). Human hair greying is linked to a specific depletion of hair follicle melanocytes affecting both the bulb and the outer root sheath. *British Journal of Dermatology* 150: 435–443.

Cottington, E.M., Kissinger, R.H., and Tolgyesi, W.S. (1977). Observations on female scalp hair population, distribution, and diameter. *Journal of Cosmetic Science* 28 (5): 219–229.

Courtois, M., Loussouarn, G., Hourseau, C., and Grollier, J.F. (1995). Ageing and hair cycles. *British Journal of Dermatology* 132: 86–93.

Courtois, M., Loussouarn, G., Hourseau, S., and Grollier, J.F. (1996). Periodicity in the growth and shedding of hair. *British Journal of Dermatology* 134: 47–54.

Crocker, E.J. (1998). A new technique for the rapid simultaneous examination of medullae and cuticular patterns of hairs. *The Microscope* 46 (3): 169–173.

Crowther, M.S., Fillios, M., Colman, N., and Letnic, M. (2014). An updated description of the Australian dingo (Canis dingo Meyer, 1793). *Journal of Zoology* 293 (3): 192–203.

Dachs, J., McNaught, I.J., and Robertson, J. (2003). The persistence of human scalp hair on clothing fabrics. *Forensic Science International* 138 (1–3): 27–36.

D'Andrea, F., Fridez, F., and Coquoz, R. (1998). Preliminary experiments on the transfer of animal hair during simulated criminal behavior. *Journal of Forensic Sciences* 43 (6): 1257–1258.

Danforth, C.H. (1925). *Hair with Special Reference to Hypertrichosis*. Chicago: American Medical Association.

Danforth, C.H. (1926). The hair. *Natural History* 26: 75–79.

Daniels, G. (1953). The digestion of human hair keratin by Microsporum canis Bodin. *Journal of General Microbiology* 8 (2): 289–294.

Das-Chaudhuri, A.B. (1976). A twin study of the structure of human hair medulla. *Human Heredity* 26: 167–170.

Davenport, G.C. and Davenport, C.B. (1909). Heredity of hair color in man. *The American Naturalist* 43 (4): 193–211.

Dawber, R. (1996). Hair: its structure and response to cosmetic preparations. *Clinic in Dermatology* 14: 105–112.

De Forest, P.R., Shankles, B., Sacher, R.L., and Petraco, N. (1987). Meltmount 1.539 as a mounting medium for hair. *The Microscope* 35: 249–259.

Deadman, H.A. (1984). Fiber evidence and the Wayne Williams trial (conclusion). *FBI Law Enforcement Bulletin* 53 (5): 10–19.

Debrot, S., Fivaz, G., Mermod, C., and Weber, J.-M. (1982). *Atlas des Poils de Mammifères d'Europe*. Peseux: l'Quest S. A.

Deedrick, D.W. (2000). Hairs, fibers, crime, and evidence. Part 1: Hair evidence. *Forensic Science Communications* 2 (3).

Deedrick, D.W. and Koch, S.L. (2004a). Microscopy of hair. Part 1: A practical guide and manual for human hairs. *Forensic Science Communications* 6 (1).

Deedrick, D.W. and Koch, S.L. (2004b). Microscopy of hair. Part 2: A practical guide and manual for animal hairs. *Forensic Science Communications* 6 (3).

DeGaetano, D.H., Lempton, J.B., and Rowe, W.F. (1992). Fungal tunneling of hair from a buried body. *Journal of Forensic Sciences* 37 (4): 1048–1054.

Detwiler, S.P., Carson, J.L., Woosley, J.T. et al. (1994). Bubble hair. *Journal of the American Academy of Dermatology* 30: 54–60.

Dhurat, R. and Deshpande, D.J. (2010). Loose anagen hair syndrome. *International Journal of Trichology* 2 (2): 96–100.

Dobson, R.L. and Bosley, L. (1963). The effect of keratinase on human epidermis. *Journal of Investigative Dermatology* 41 (3): 131–133.

DOJ (2016). *Poprosed Language for Testimony and Reports for the Forensic Hair Examination Discipline*. Washington, D.C.: DOJ.

Domzalski, A.C. (2004). *The Effects of Environmental Exposure on Human Scalp Hair Root Morphology (Thesis)*. New York, NY: John Jay College of Criminal Justice.

Donfack, J. and Castillo, H.S. (2018). A review and conceptual model of factors correlated with postmortem root band formation. *Journal of Forensic Sciences* 63 (6): 1628–1633.

Dry, F.W. (1926). The coat of the mouse (*Mus musculus*). *Journal of Genetics* 16 (3): 287–340.

Duggins, O.H. (1954). Age changes in head hair from birth to maturity IV. Refractive indices and birefringence of the cuitlce hair of children. *American Journal of Physical Anthropology* 12 (1): 89–114.

Duggins, O.H. and Trotter, M. (1950). Age changes in head hair from birth to maturity II. Medullation in hair of children. *American Journal of Physical Anthropology* 8 (3): 399–415.

Eckert, J., Church, R.E., Ebling, F.J., and Munro, D.S. (1967). Hair loss in women. *British Journal of Dermatology* 79 (10): 543–548.

Edson, J., Brooks, E.M., McLaren, C. et al. (2013). A quantitative assessment of a reliable screening technique for the STR analysis of telogen hair roots. *Forensic Science International: Genetics* 7: 180–188.

ENFSI (2015). *Best Practice Manual for the Microscopic Examination and Comparison of Human and Animal Hair*. s.l.: European Network of Forensic Science Institutes.

English, M.P. (1963). The saprophytic growth of keratinophilic fungi on keratin. *Sabouraudia* 2 (3): 115–130.

English, M.P. (1965). The saprophytic growth of non-keratinophilic fungi on keratinized substrata, and a comparison with keratinophilic fungi. *Transactions of the British Mycological Society* 48 (2): 219–235.

Espinoza, E.O., Baker, B.W., Moores, T.D., and Voin, D. (2008). Forensic identification of elephant and giraffe hair artifacts using HATR FTIR spectroscopy and discriminant analysis. *Endangered Species Research* 9: 239–246.

Ewing, J. (1909). The examination of hair. In: *Medical Jurisprudence Forensic Medicine and Toxicology*, 2e (eds. R.A. Witthaus and T.C. Becker), 894–909. New York, NY: William Wood and Company.

Exline, D.L., Smith, F.P., and Drexler, S.G. (1998). Frequency of pubic hair transfer during sexual intercourse. *Journal of Forensic Sciences* 43 (3): 505–508.

Fallon, T.C., Stone, I.C., and Petty, C.S. (1985). *Hair on Victim's Hands: Value of Examination*. Washington, D.C.: Federal Bureau of Investigation.

Favarato, E.S. and Conceição, L.G. (2008). Hair cycle in dogs with different hair types in a tropical region of Brazil. *Veterinary Dermatology* 19 (1): 15–20.

FBI (2015). *FBI Testimony on Microscopic Hair Analysis Contained Errors in at Least 90 Percent of Cases in Ongoing Review*. Washington, D.C.: FBI.

Feigl, F. and Anger, V. (1972). *Spot Tests in Inorganic Analysis*, 6e. Amsterdam: Elsevier.

Fitzpatrick, T.B., Brunet, P., and Kukita, A. (1958). The nature of hair pigment. In: *The Biology of Hair Growth* (eds. W. Montagna and R.A. Ellis), 255–303. New York, NY: Academic Press Inc.

Freeman, R.A. (1909). A message from the deep sea. In: *John Thorndyke's Cases*, 205–235. Cornwall: House of Stratus.

Friedenthal, H. (1911). *Tierhaaratlas*. Jena: Gustav Fischer.

Fujimoto, A., Fujimoto, A., Nishida, N. et al. (2009). FGFR2 is associated with hair thickness in Asian populations. *Journal of Human Genetics* 54: 461–465.

Fujita, Y., Nakayama, M., Kanbara, K. et al. (1987). Forensic chemical study on human hair I. identification of brand of hair care products by components Remaining on human hairs. *Japanese Journal of Toxicology and Environmental Health* 33 (5): 321–327.

Fujita, Y., Nakayama, M., Kanbara, K. et al. (1989a). Forensic chemical study on human hair. II. Identification of brand of women's hair care products by remaining components on human hair. *Japanese Journal of Toxicology and Environmental Health* 35 (1): 37–48.

Fujita, Y., Yamamoto, N., Nakayama, M. et al. (1989b). Forensic chemical study on human hair. III. Identification of oxidative dyes and presumption of the brands from remaining components on human hair. *Japanese Journal of Toxicology and Environmental Health* 35 (6): 444–453.

Fujita, Y., Mitsuo, N., and Satoh, T. (1990). Forensic chemical study on human hair. IV. Identification of brand of hair sprays and hair growth promoters by components remaining on human hair, and example of forensic hair examination. *Japanese Journal of Toxicology and Environmental Health* 36 (3): 211–218.

Gallard, T. (1879). Suppression de Part Indices Fournis par l'examen des organes Génitaux de la Mère et par l'examen des Cheveux de l'enfant. *Annales D'Hygiène Publique et de Médecine Légale* 2: 371–382.

Gamble, L.H. and Kirk, P.L. (1941). Human hair studies II. Scale counts. *Journal of Criminal Law and Criminology* 31 (5): 627–636.

Garcia, M.L., Epps, J.A., Yare, R.S., and Hunter, L.D. (1978). Normal cuticle-wear patterns in human hair. *Journal of the Society of Cosmetic Chemists* 29 (3): 155–175.

Garn, S.M. (1951a). The examination of hair under the polarizing microscope. *Annals of the New York Academy of Sciences* 53: 649–652.

Garn, S.M. (1951b). Types and distribution of the hair in man. *Annals of the New York Academy of Sciences* 53: 498–507.

Gaudette, B.D. (1976). Probabilities and human pubic hair comparisons. *Journal of Forensic Sciences* 21 (3): 514–517.

Gaudette, B.D. (1978). Some further thoughts on probabilities and human hair comparisons. *Journal of Forensic Sciences* 23 (4): 758–763.

Gaudette, B.D. (1982). A supplementary discussion of probabilities and human hair comparisons. *Journal of Forensic Sciences* 27 (2): 279–289.

Gaudette, B.D. (1984). Discussion of "The Law of Probability". *The Microscope* 32: 64–68.

Gaudette, B.D. (1985). Strong negative conclusions in hair comparison – a rare event. *Candian Society of Forensic Science Journal* 18 (1): 32–37.

Gaudette, B.D. and Keeping, E.S. (1974). An attempt at determining probabilities in human scalp hair comparison. *Journal of Forensic Sciences* 19 (3): 599–606.

Gaudette, B.D. and Tessarolo, A.A. (1987). Secondary transfer of human scalp hair. *Journal of Forensic Sciences* 32 (5): 1241–1253.

Glaister, J. (1931). *A Study of Hairs and Wools Belonging to the Mammalian Group of Animals, Including a Special Study of the Human Hair, Considered from the Medico-Legal Aspect*. Cairo: Misr Press.

Goin, L.J., McKee, W.H., and Kirk, P.L. (1952). Human hair studies: applications of the microdetermination of Comparitive density. *Journal of Criminal Law, Criminology, and Police Science* 43 (2): 263–273.

Goodpastor, J.V., Drumheller, B.C., and Brenner, B.A.J. (2003). Evaluation of extraction techniques for the forensic analysis of human scalp hair using gas chromatography/mass spectrometry (GC/MS). *Journal of Forensic Sciences* 48 (2): 299–306.

Gorski, A. and Brauner, P. (1992). A morphologic abnormality noted in hair roots of patients of a methadone clinic in Israel (or the burned match phenomenon). *The Microscope* 40 (2): 103–106.

Greenwell, M.D., Willner, A., and Kirk, P.L. (1941). Human hair studies III. Refractive index of crown hair. *Journal of Criminal Law and Criminology* 31 (6): 746–752.

Greer, S., Banks-Lee, P., and Jones, M. (2007). Physical and mechanical properties of chiengora fibers. *AATCC Review* 7 (5): 42–46.

Guerra-Tapia, A. and Gonzalez-Guerra, E. (2014). Hair cosmetics: dyes. *Actas Dermo-Sifiliográficas* 105 (9): 833–839.

Guilbeau-Frugier, C., Blanc, A., Crubezy, E. et al. (2006). Hair morphology and anthropologial applications. *American Journal of Human Biology* 18: 861–864.

Haines, A.M. and Linacre, A. (2016). A rapid screening method using DNA binding dyes to determine whether hair follicles have sufficient DNA for successful profiling. *Forensic Science International* 262: 190–195.

Hamilton, J.B. (1958). Age, sex, and genetic factors in the regulation of hair growth in man: a comparison of Caucasian and Japanese populations. In: *The Biology of Hair Growth* (eds. W. Montagna and R.A. Ellis), 399–433. New York, NY: Academic Press.

Harding, H. and Rogers, G. (1999). Physiology and growth of human hair. In: *Forensic Examination of Hair* (ed. J. Robertson), 1–77. London: Taylor & Francis.

Hardy, J.I. (1935). *A Practical Laboratory Method of Making Thin Cross Sections of Fibers*. Washington, D. C.: United States Department of Agriculture.

Hardy, T.M.P. and Hardy, J.I. (1942). Types of fur Fibers. *Journal of Heredity* 33 (5): 191–199.

Hardy, J.I. and Plitt, T.M. (1940). *An Improved Method for Revealing the Surface Structure of Fur Fibers*. s.l.: United States Department of the Interior.

Harland, D.P., Walls, R.J., Vernon, J.A. et al. (2014). Three-dimensional architecture of macrofibrils in the human scalp hair. *Journal of Structural Biology* 185: 397–404.

Harrison, S. and Sinclair, R. (2003). Hair coloring, permanent styling and hair structure. *Journal of Cosmetic Dermatology* 2: 180–185.

Harvey, L.A. (1938). The examination of hairs. *The Police Journal* 1: 61–72.

Hausman, L.A. (1925a). The relationships of the microscopic structural characters of human head-hair. *The American Journal of Physical Anthropology* 8 (2): 173–177.

Hausman, L.A. (1925b). Why hair turns gray. *Scientific American* 133 (5): 306–307.

Hausman, L.A. (1932). The cortical fusi of mammalian hair shafts. *The American Naturalist* 66 (706): 461–470.

Hayashi, S., Miyamoto, I., and Takeda, K. (1991). Measurement of human hair growth by optical microscopy and image analysis. *British Journal of Dermatology* 125: 123–129.

Henderson, G.H., Karg, G.M., and O'Neill, J.J. (1978). Fractography of human hair. *Journal of the Society of Cosmetic Chemists* 29: 449–467.

Henson, C.R. and Rowe, W.F. (2002). The effect of elevated temperature on the microscopic morphology of human head hair. *The Microscope* 50 (1): 21–24.

Heyn, A.N.J. (1954). *Fiber Microscopy*. New York, NY: Interscience Publishers, Inc.

Hicks, J.W. (1977). *Microscopy of Hair: A Practical Guide and Manual*. Washington, D.C.: U.S. Government Printing Office.

Hietpas, J., Buscaglia, J., Richard, A.H. et al. (2016). Microscopical characterization of known postmortem root bands using light and scanning electron microscopy. *Forensic Science International* 267: 7–15.

Hoffman, R. (2002). Male androgenetic alopecia. *Clinical Dermatology* 27: 373–382.

Hollemeyer, K., Altmeyer, W., and Heinzle, E. (2007). Identification of furs of domestic dog, raccoon dog, rabbit and domestic cat by hair analysis using MALDI-ToF mass spectrometry. *Spectroscopy Europe* 19 (2): 8–15.

Hooke, R. (1665). *Micrographia: Or some Physiological Descriptions of Minute Bodies Made by Magnifying Glasses with Observations and Inquiries Thereupon*. London: Martyn and Allestry.

Horio, M. and Kondo, T. (1953). Crimping of wool Fibers. *Textile Research Journal* 23 (6): 373–386.

Hotin, E., Zimmermann, M., and Höcker, H. (1995). Photochemical alterations in human hair. Part II: analysis of melanin. *Journal of the Society of Cosmetic Chemists* 46: 181–190.

Hoting, E. and Zimmermann, M. (1996). Photochemical alterations in human hair. Part III: investigations of internal lipids. *Journal of the Society of Cosmetic Chemists* 47: 201–211.

Hoting, E. and Zimmermann, M. (1997). Sunlight-induced modifications in bleached, permed, or dyed human hair. *Journal of the Scoiety of Cosmetic Chemists* 48: 79–91.

Hoting, E., Zimmermann, M., and Hilterhaus-Bong, S. (1995). Photochemical alterations in human hair. I. Artificial irradiation and investigations of hair proteins. *Journal of the Society of Cosmetic Chemists* 46: 85–99.

Houck, M.M. (1999). Statistics and trace evidence: the tyranny of numbers. *Forensic Science Cmmunications* 1 (3).

Houck, M.M. and Bisbing, R.E. (2005). Forensic human hair examination and comparison in the 21st century. *Forensic Science Review* 17 (1): 52–66.

Houck, M.M. and Budowle, B. (2002). Correlation of microscopic and mitochondrial DNA hair comparisons. *Journal of Forensic Sciences* 47 (5): 964–967.

Hrdlička, A. (1922). Physical anthropology of the old Americans. *American Journal of Physical Anthropology* 5 (2): 97–142.

Hrdy, D. (1973). Quantitative hair form variation in seven populations. *American Journal of Physical Anthropology* 39 (1): 7–17.

Igowsky, K. and Pangerl, E. (2015). Changes observed in human head hairs exposed to heat. *Journal of the American Society of Trace Evidence Examiners* 6 (2): 17–26.

Ihm, C.-W. and Lee, J.-Y. (1991). Evaluation of daily hair counts. *Dermatologica* 182 (1): 67.

Ito, S. and Wakamatsu, K. (2011). Diversity of human hair pigmentation as studied by chemical analysis of eumelanin and pheomelanin. *Journal of the European Academy of Dermatology and Venereology* 25: 1369–1380.

Iyengar, A. and Hadi, S. (2014). Use of non-human DNA analysis in forensic science: a mini review. *Medicine, Science and the Law* 54 (1): 41–50.

Jeffrey, K.J., Abernethy, K.A., Tutin, C.E., and Bruford, M.W. (2007). Biological and environmental degradation of gorilla hair and microsatellite amplification success. *Biological Journal of the Linnean Society* 91: 281–294.

Ji, W., Bai, L., Ji, M., and Yang, X. (2011). A method for quantifying mixed goat cashmere and sheep wool. *Forensic Science International* 208: 139–142.

Jones, L.N. and Rivett, D.E. (1997). The role of 18-methylleicosanoic acid in the structure and formation of mammalian hair fibres. *Micron* 28 (6): 469–485.

Kaplin, I.J. and Whitely, K.J. (1978). An electron microscope study of fibril: matrix arrangements in high- and low-crimp wool fibres. *Australian Journal of Biological Science* 31 (3): 231–240.

Kaye, D.H. (2015). Ultracrepidarianism in forensic science: the hair evidence debacle. *Washington & Lee Law Review* 72: 227–254.

Keating, S.M. (1988). The laboratory's approach to sexual assault cases. Part 2: Demonstration of the possible offender. *Journal of the Forensic Science Society* 28: 99–110.

Kennedy, K.A.R. (1995). But professor, why teach race identification if races don't exist? *Journal of Forensic Sciences* 40 (5): 797–800.

Keogh, E.V. and Walsh, R.J. (1965). Rate of greying of human hair. *Nature* 207: 877–878.

Khumalo, N.P., Doe, P.T., Dawber, R.P.R. et al. (2000). What is normal black African hair? A light and scanning electron-microscope study. *Journal fo the American Academy of Dermatology* 43 (5): 814–820.

Kilbourn, H.H. (1993). Loose anagen syndrome – forensic implications (abstract). *The Microscope* 41 (2/3): 81.

Kim, B.J., Na, J.I., Park, W.S. et al. (2006). Hair cuticle differences between Asian and Caucasian females. *International Journal of Dermatology* 45: 1435–1437.

Kind, S.S. (1965). Metrical characters in the identification of animal hairs. *Journal of the Forensic Science Society* 5 (2): 110–111.

King, L.A., Wigmore, R., and Twibell, J.M. (1982). The morphology and occurrence of human hair sheath cells. *Journal of the Forensic Science Society* 22 (3): 267–269.

Kirk, P.L. (1940). Human hair studies: general considerations of hair individualization and its forensic importance. *Journal of Criminal Law and Criminology* 31 (4): 486–496.

Kirk, P.L. (1953). *Crime Investigation: Physical Evidence and the Police Laboratory*. New York, NY: Interscience Publishers, Inc.

Kirk, P.L. and Gamble, L.H. (1942). Further investigation of the scale count of human hair. *Journal of Criminal Law and Criminology* 33 (3): 276–280.

Kirk, P.L., Magagnose, S., and Salisbury, D. (1949). Casting of hairs – its technique and application to species and personal identification. *Journal of Criminal Law and Criminology* 40 (2): 236–241.

Kligman, A.M. (1959). The human hair cycle. *The Journal of Investigative Dermatology* 33 (6): 307–316.

Kligman, A.M. (1961). Pathologic dynamics of human hair loss I. Telogen effluvium. *Archives of Dermatology* 83 (2): 175–198.

Koch, S.L., Michaud, A.L., and Mikell, C.E. (2013). Taphonomy of hair – a study of postmortem root banding. *Journal of Forensic Sciences* 58 (S1): S52–S59.

Koch, S.L., Shriver, M.D., and Jablonski, N.G. (2019). Variation in human hair ultrastructure among three biogeographic populations. *Journal of Structural Biology* 205 (1): 60–66.

Kolowski, J.C., Petraco, N., Wallace, M.M. et al. (2004). A comparison study of hair examination methods. *Journal of Foensic Sciences* 49 (6): 1253–1255.

Krefft, S. (1969). Über postmortale Struktur- und Farbveränderungen der Haare und weiterer keratinhaltiger Hautanhangsgebilde. *Archiv für Kriminologie* 143: 76–81.

Kundrat, J.A. and Rowe, W.F. (1989). A study of hair degradation in agricultural soil. In: *Biodeterioration Research 2* (eds. G.C. Llewellyn and C.E. O'Rear), 91–98. Boston: Springer.

Kupferschmid, T.D., Van Dyke, R., and Rowe, W.F. (1994). Scanning electron microscope studies of the biodeterioration of human hair buried in soil and immersed in water. In: *Biodeterioration Research 4* (eds. W.V. Dashek, C.E. O'Rear and G.C. Llewellyn), 479–491. Boston: Springer.

Kurouski, D. and Van Duyne, R.P. (2015). In situ detection and identification of hair dyes using surface-enhanced raman spectroscopy (SERS). *Analytical Chemistry* 87 (5): 2901–2906.

Lamb, P. and Tucker, L.G. (1994). A study of the probative value of afro-caribbean hair comparisons. *Journal of the Forensic Science Society* 34 (3): 177–179.

Lambert, M. and Balthazard, V. (1910). *Le Poil de l'Homme et des Animaux: Applications aux Expertises Médico-Légales et aux Expertises des Fourrures*. Paris: G. Steinheil.

Langley, K.D. and Kennedy, T.A. (1981). The identification of specialty fibers. *Textile Research Journal* 51: 703–709.

Lasisi, T., Ito, S., Wakamatsu, K. et al. (2016). Quantifying variation in human scalp hair fiber shape and pigmentation. *American Journal of Physical Anthropology* 160: 341–352.

Lassaigne, J.L. (1857). De l'examen Physique des Poils et des Cheveux Considéré Sous le Rapport Médico-Légal. *Annales D'Hygiène Publique et de Médecine Légale* 8: 226–231.

LeBeau, M.A., Montgomery, M.A., and Brewer, J.D. (2011). The role of variations in growth rate and sample collection on interpreting results of segmental analyses of hair. *Forensic Science International* 210: 110–116.

Lee, W.-S. (2009). Photoaggravation of hair aging. *International Journal of Trichology* 1 (2): 94–99.

Lee, H.C. and De Forest, P.R. (1984). Forensic hair examination. In: *Forensic Science* (ed. C. Wecht), 37A-5–37A-46. New York, NY: Matthew Blender.

Lee, S.H., Kwon, O.S., Oh, J.K. et al. (2005). Bleaching phototrichogram: an improved method for hair growth assessment. *The Journal of Dermatology* 32: 782–787.

Leeder, J.D. and Bradbury, J.H. (1971). The discontinuous nature of epicuticle on the surface of keratin fibers. *Textile Research Journal* 41 (7): 563–568.

Leonard, C.H. (1879). *A Popular Treatise on the Hair: Its Growth, Care, Diseases and Their Treatment*. Detroit: Post & Tribune Job Co.

Lepez, T., Vandewoestyne, M., Hoofstat, D.V. et al. (2014). Fast nuclear staining of head hair roots as a screening method for successful STR analysis in forensics. *Forensic Science International: Genetics* 13: 191–194.

Linch, C.A. and Prahlow, J.A. (2001). Postmortem microscopic changes observed at the human head hair proximal end. *Journal of Forensic Sciences* 46 (1): 15–20.

Linch, C.A., Smith, S.L., and Prahlow, J.A. (1998). Evaluation of the human hair root for DNA typing subsequent to microscopic comparison. *Journal of Forensic Sciences* 43 (2): 305–314.

Lindelöf, B., Forslind, B., Hedblas, M.-A., and Kaveus, U. (1988). Human hair form: morphology revealed by light and scanning electron microscopy and computer aided three-dimensional reconstruction. *Archives of Dermatology* 124 (9): 1359–1363.

Lochte, T. (1938). *Atlas der Menschlichen und Tierischen Haare*. Leipzig: Paul Schops.

Loewenthal, L.J.A. (1947). "Compound" and grouped hairs of the human scalp: their possible connections with follicular infections. *The Journal of Investigative Dermatology* 8 (5): 263–273.

Longia, H.S. (1966). Increase in medullary index of human hair with the passage of time. *The Journal of Criminal Law, Criminology and Police Science* 57 (2): 221–222.

Loussouarn, G. (2001). African hair growth parameters. *British Journal of Dermatology* 145: 294–297.

Loussouarn, G., El Rawadi, C., and Genain, G. (2005). Diversity of hair growth profiles. *International Journal of Dermatology* 44 (Suppl. 1): 6–9.

Loussouarn, G. et al. (2007). Worldwide diversity of hair curliness: a new method of assessment. *International Journal of Dermatology* 24 (Suppl. 1): 2–6.

Ludwig, E. (1967). Removal of intact hair papilla and connective tissue sheath by plucking anagen hairs. *The Journal of Investigative Dermatology* 48 (2): 595–597.

Luell, E. and Archer, V.E. (1964). Hair medulla variation with age in human males. *American Journal of Physical Anthropology* 22 (1): 107–109.

Lynfield, Y.L. (1960). Effect of pregnancy on the human hair cycle. *The Journal of Investigative Dermatology* 35 (6): 323–327.

Lynfield, Y.L. and Macwilliams, P. (1970). Shaving and hair growth. *The Journal of Investigative Dermatology* 55 (3): 170–172.

Lyons, L.A., Grahn, R.A., Kun, T.J. et al. (2014). Acceptance of domestic cat mitochondrial DNA in criminal proceeding. *Forensic Science International* 13: 61–67.

Macrae, R. and Smalldon, K.W. (1979). The extraction of dyestuffs from single wool fibers. *Journal of Forensic Sciences* 24 (1): 109–116.

Macrae, R., Dudley, R.J., and Smalldon, K.W. (1979). The characterization of dyestuffs on wool fibers with special reference to microspectrophotometry. *Journal of Forensic Sciences* 24 (1): 117–129.

Maguire, H.C. and Kligman, A.M. (1964). Hair plucking as a diagnostic tool. *The Journal of Investigative Dermatology* 42 (1): 77–79.

Manheim, J., Doty, K.C., McLaughlin, G., and Lednev, I.K. (2016). Forensic hair differentiation using attenuated Total reflection fourier transform infrared (ATR FT-IR) spectroscopy. *Applie Spectroscopy* 70 (7): 1109–1117.

Mann, M.-J. (1990). Hair transferred in sexual assualt: a six-year case study. *Journal of Forensic Sciences* 35 (4): 951–955.

Marko, N.F. and Rowe, W.F. (2001). The effect of humidity on the degradation of isolated human hair by keratinolytic and nonkeratinolytic fungi. *The Microscope* 49 (4): 223–230.

Marshall, R.C., Orwin, D.F.G., and Gillespie, J.M. (1991). Structure and biochemistry of mammalian hard keratin. *Electron Microscopy Review* 4: 47–83.

Marx, H. (1906). Ein Beitrag zur Identitätsfrage bei der Forensischen Haarunteruchung. *Archiv für Kriminal-Anthropologie und Kriminalistik* 23: 75–79.

McBride, M.E., Freemna, R.G., and Knox, J.M. (1970). Keratinolytic activity in species of Corynebacterium. *Canadian Journal of Microbiology* 16: 1024–1025.

McCrone, W.C. (1977). Characterization of human hair by light microscopy. *The Microscope* 25: 15–30.

McCrone, W.C. and Delly, J.G. (1973). *The Particle Atlas: Volume II the Light Microscopy Atlas*, 2e. Ann Arbor: Ann Arbor Science Publsihers, Inc.

McCrone, W.C., McCrone, L.B., and Delly, J.G. (1984). *Polarized Light Microscopy*. Chicago: McCrone Research Institute.

McGregor, B.A. (2012). *Properties, Processing and Performance of Rare Natural Animal Fibres: A Review and Interpretation of Existing Resaerch Data*. Barton: RIRDC.

Medland, S.E., Nyholt, D.R., Painter, J.N. et al. (2009). Common variants in the Trichohyalin gene are associated with straight hair in

Europeans. *The American Journal of Human Genetics* 85: 750–755.

Melton, T., Dimick, G., Higgins, B. et al. (2012). Mitochondrial DNA analysis of 114 hairs measuring less than 1 cm from a 19-year-old homicide. *Investigative Genetics* 3 (12).

Mercer, E.H. (1954). The relation between external shape and internal structure in wool Fibers. *Textile Research Journal* 24 (1): 39–43.

Meredith, P. and Sarna, T. (2006). The physical and chemical properties of eumelanin. *Pigment Cell Research* 19: 572–594.

Messenger, A.G. (2011). Hair through the female life cycle. *British Journal of Dermatology* 165 (S3): 2–6.

Messenger, A.G. and Sinclair, R. (2006). Follicular miniaturization in female pattern hair loss: clinicopathological correlations. *British Journal of Dermatology* 155: 926–930.

Messenger, A.G., de Berker, D.A.R., and Sinclair, R.D. (2010). Disorders of hair. In: *Rook's Textbook of Dermatology*, 8e (eds. T. Burns, S. Breathnach, N. Cox and C. Griffiths), 66.1–66.100. Oxford, UK: Blackwell Publishing Ltd.

Meyer, W., Hülmann, G., and Seger, H. (2002). *SEM-Atlas on the Hair Cuticle Structure of Central European Mammals*. Hannover: Verlag M. & H. Schaper Alfeld.

Milner, Y., Sudnik, J., Filippi, M. et al. (2002). Exogen, shedding phase of the hair growth cycle: characterization of a mouse model. *The Journal of Investigative Dermatology* 119 (3): 639–644.

Mirmirani, P. (2015). Age-related hair changes in men: mechanisms and management of alopecia and graying. *Maturitas* 80: 58–62.

Miyazawa, N. and Uematsu, T. (1992). Analysis of Ofloxacin in hair as a measure of hair growth and as a time marker for hair analysis. *Therapeutic Drug Monitoring* 14: 525–528.

Montagna, W. (1976). General review of the anatomy, growth, and development of hair in man. In: *Biology and Disease of the Hair* (eds. T. Kobori and W. Montagna), xxi–xxxi. Baltimore: University Park Press.

Montagna, W. and Van Scott, E.J. (1958). The anatomy of the hair follicle. In: *The Biology of Hair Growth* (eds. W. Montagna and R.A. Ellis), 39–64. New York, NY: Academic Press Inc.

Moore, T.D., Spence, L.E., and Dugnolle, C.E. (1974). *Identification of the Dorsal Guard Hairs of some Mammals of Wyoming*. Cheyenne: Wyoming Game and Fish Department.

Morel, O.J.X. and Chrisite, R.M. (2011). Current trends in the chemistry of permanent hair dyeing. *Chemical Reviews* 111 (4): 2537–2561.

Murphy, N.E., Reynolds, A., and Hall, A.B. (2018). Little variation exists between laboratory procedures for the microscopical examination of human hair. *Journal of the American Society of Trace Evidence Examiners* 8 (1): 46–61.

Myers, R.J. and Hamilton, J.B. (1951). Regeneration and rate of growth of hairs in man. *Annals of the New York Academy of Sciences* 53: 562–568.

Nagl, W. (1995). Different growth rates of pigmented and white hair in the beard: differentiation vs. proliferation? *British Journal of Dermatology* 132: 94–97.

Nahm, M., Navarini, A.A., and Kelly, E.W. (2013). Canities subita: a reappraisal of evidence based on 196 case reports published in the medical literature. *International Journal of Trichology* 5 (2): 63–68.

Nater, A., Matte-Greminger, M.P., Nurcahyo, A., and Nowak, M.G. (2017). Morphometric, behavioral, and genomic evidence for a new orangutan species. *Current Biology* 27 (22): 3487–3498.

National Research Council of the National Academies (2009). *Strengthening Forensic Science in the United States: A Path Forward*. Washington, D.C.: The National Academies Press.

Nelson, D. and De Forest, P. (1999). Forensic examination of hairs for cosmetic treatment. In: *Forenisc Examination of Hair* (ed. J. Robertson), 229–242. London: Taylor & Francis.

Noback, C.R. (1951). Morphology and phylogeny of hair. *Annals of the New York Academy of Sciences* 53: 476–492.

Nogueira, A.C.S. and Joekes, I. (2007). Hair melanin content and photodamage. *Journal of Cosmetic Science* 58: 385–391.

Noval, J.J. and Nickerson, W.J. (1959). Decomposition of native keratin by streptomyces fradiae. *Journal of Bacteriology* 77 (3): 251–263.

Nyholt, D.R., Gillespie, N.A., and Heath, A.C. (2003). Genetic basis of male pattern baldness. *The Journal of Investigative Dermatology* 121 (6): 1561–1564.

O'Donnell, B.P., Sperling, L.C., and James, W.D. (1992). Loose anagen hair syndrome. *International Journal of Dermatology* 31 (2): 107.

Oesterlen, O. (1873). Ueber die Forensische Bedeutung des Menschlichen Haars. *Jahrbücher der in- und Ausländischen Gesammten Medicin* 157 (3): 281–304.

Ogle, R.R. (1991). Discussion of "Further Evaluation of Probabilities in Human Scalp Hair Comparison". *Journal of Forensic Sciences* 36 (4): 971–976.

Ogle, R.R.J. and Fox, M.J. (1999). *Atlas of Human Hair Microscopic Characteristics*. Boca Raton: CRC Press.

Ogle, R.R., Mitosinka, B.A., and Mitosinka, G.T. (1973). A rapid technique for preparing hair Cuticular scale casts. *Journal of Forensic Sciences* 18 (1): 82–83.

Oien, C.T. (2009). Forensic hair comparison: background information for interpretation. *Forensic Science Communications* 11 (2).

Ollivier (1838). Nouvelle Application de l'emploi du Microscope dans les Expertises Médico-Légales. *Archives Générales de Médecine* III: 455–460.

Orentreich, N. (1969). Scalp hair replacement in man. In: *Advances in Biology of Skin*, vol. 9 (eds. W. Montagna and R.L. Dobson), 99–108. Oxford: Pergamon Press.

Page, R.M. (1950). Observations on keratin digestion by Microsporum gypseum. *Mycologia* 42 (5): 591–602.

Palenik, S. (1983). Light microscopy of medullary micro-structure in hair identification. *The Microscope* 31: 129–137.

Palenik, C. (1990). The microscopical differentiation of dog and cat hairs. *The Microscope* 38: 415–420.

Palenik, S. and Fitzsimons, C. (1990). Fiber cross-sections: part II a simple method for sectioning single fibers. *The Microscope* 38: 313–320.

Panayiotou, H. and Kokot, S. (1999). Matching and discrimination of single human-scalp hairs by FT-IR micro-spectroscopy and chemometrics. *Analytica Chimica Acta* 392: 223–235.

Panhard, S., Lozano, I., and Loussouarn, G. (2012). Greying of the human hair: a worldwide survey, revisiting the '50' rule of thumb. *British Journal of Dermatology* 167: 865–873.

Peabody, A.J., Oxborough, R.J., Cage, P.E., and Evett, I.W. (1983). The discrimination of cat and dog hairs. *Journal of the Forensic Science Society* 23 (2): 121–129.

Peabody, A.J., Thomas, K.E., and Stockdale, R.E. (1985). *On the Nature of Human Head Hairs Shed into Various Types of Headgear*. Aldermaston: Home Office Forensic Science Service.

Pecoraro, V., Astore, I., Barman, J., and Araujo, C.I. (1964). The normal trichogram in the child before the age of puberty. *The Journal of Investigative Dermatology* 42 (6): 427–430.

Pecoraro, V., Barman, J.M., and Astore, I. (1969). The normal trichogram of pregnant women. In: *Advances in Biology of Skin*, vol. 9 (eds. W. Montagna and R.L. Dobson), 203–210. Oxford: Pergamon Press.

Pecoraro, V., Astore, I., and Barman, J.M. (1971). Growth rate and hair density of the human axilla. *The Journal of Investigative Dermatology* 56 (5): 362–365.

Petraco, N. (1986). The replication of hair cuticle scale patterns in meltmounts. *The Microscope* 34: 341–345.

Petraco, N. and Kubic, T. (2003). *Color Atlas and Manual of Microscopy for Criminalists,*

Chemists, and Conservators. Boca Raton: CRC Press.

Petraco, N., Fraas, C., Callery, F.X., and De Forest, P.R. (1988). The morphology and evidential significance of human hair roots. *Journal of Forensic Sciences* 33 (1): 68–76.

Petzel-Witt, S., Meier, S., Schubert-Zsilavecz, M., and Toennes, S.W. (2018). PTCA (1H-pyrrole-2,3,5-tricarboxylic acid) as a marker for oxidative hair treatment. *Drug Testing and Analysis* 10 (4): 768–773.

Phan, K.H. and Wortmann, F.J. (1996). Identification and classification of cashmere. In: *Metrology and Identification of Speciality Animal Fibres* (eds. J.P. Laker and F.J. Wortmann), 45–58. Aberdeen: European Fine Fibre Network.

Potsch, L. (1996). A discourse on human hair fibers and reflections on the conservation of drug molecules. *International Journal of Legal Medicine* 108: 285–293.

Prasad, A.N. (1975). Susceptibility of hair to the influence of bacteria. *International Criminal Police Review, Issue* 286: 86–89.

President's Council of Advisors on Science and Technology (2016). *Forensic Science in Criminal Courts: Ensuring Scientific Validity of Feature-Comparison Methods.* Washington, D.C: Executive Office of the President.

Price, V.H. (1975). Office diagnosis of structural hair anomalies. *Cutis* 15: 231–240.

Price, V.H. and Gummer, C.L. (1989). Loose Anagen Syndrome. *Journal of the American Academy of Dermatology* 20 (2–1): 249–256.

Prokopec, M., Glosová, L., and Ubelaker, D.H. (2000). Change in hair pigmentation in children from birth to 5 years in a central European population (longitudinal study). *Forensic Science Communications* 2 (3).

Pudney, P.D.A., Bonnist, E.Y.M., Mutch, K.J. et al. (2013). Confocal raman spectroscopy of whole hairs. *Applied Spectroscopy* 67 (12): 1408–1416.

Quarmby, V.E. and Whitehead, P.H. (1975). *The Significance of Sheath Cells on Plucked Hair Roots.* Aldermaston: Home Office Central Research Establishment.

Quill, J.L. (1985). *The Transfer Theory of Hairs Applied to the Normal Work Day.* Washington, D.C.: Federal Bureau of Investigation.

Randall, V.A. (2008). Androgens and hair growth. *Dermatologic Therapy* 21: 314–328.

Randall, V.A. and Ebling, F.J.G. (1991). Seasonal changes in human hair growth. *British Journal of Dermatology* 124: 146–151.

Rebora, A. and Guarrera, M. (2002). Kenogen: a new phase of the hair cycle? *Dermatology* 205: 108–110.

Reutsch, S.B. and Kamath, Y.K. (2004). Effects of thermal treatments with a curling iron on hair fiber. *Journal of Cosmetic Science* 55: 13–27.

Richard, A.H., Hietpas, J., Buscaglia, J., and Monson, K.L. (2019). Timing and appearance of postmortem root banding in nonhuman animals. *Journal of Forensic Sciences* 64 (1): 98–107.

Robbins, C.R. (2002). *Chemical and Physical Behavior of Human Hair*, 4e. New York, NY: Springer.

Robbins, C.R. and Kelly, C.H. (1970). Amino acid composition of human hair. *Textile Research Journal* 40 (10): 891–896.

Roberts, K.A., Garcia, L.R., and De Forest, P.R. (2017). Proximal end root morphology characteristics in antemortem anagen head hairs. *Journal of Forensic Sciences* 62 (2): 317–329.

Robertson, J. (1982). An appraisal of the use of microscopic data in the examination of human head hair. *Journal of the Forensic Science Society* 22: 390–395.

Robertson, J. (1987). *The persistence of hairs on clothing.* Presented at the 11th Meeting of the International Association of Forensic Sciences, Vancouver, August 02–07, 1987.

Robertson, J. (1999). Forensic and microscopic examination of human hair. In: *Forenisc Examination of Hair* (ed. J. Robertson), 79–154. London: Taylor & Francis.

Robertson, J. and Aitken, C.G.G. (1986). The value of microscopic features in the examination of human head hairs: analysis of comments contained in questionaire returns. *Journal of Forensic Sciences* 31 (2): 563–573.

Robin, C. (1858). La Comparaison de Cheveux Pourvus de Leur Racine ét Trouvés sur le Lieu Présumé d'un Assassinat, Avec Ceux de la Victime. *Annales D'Hygiène Publique et de Médecine Légale*: 434–441.

Robinson, V.N.E. (1976). A study of damaged hair. *Journal of the Society of Cosmetic Chemists* 27: 155–161.

Roe, G.M., McArdle, W., and Pole, K. (1985). *The Detection of Cosmetic Treatments on Human Scalp Hair. Screening of Forensic Casework Samples*. Washington, D. C: Federal Bureau of Investigation.

Roe, G.M., Cook, R., and North, C. (1991). An evaluation of mountants for use in forensic hair examination. *Journal of the Forensic Science Society* 31 (1): 59–65.

Rogers, G.E. (1959). Electron microscopy of wool. *Journal of Ultrastructural Rsearch* 2: 309–330.

Rogers, M. (1995). Hair shaft abnormalities: part I. *Australasian Journal of Dermatology* 36: 179–185.

Rogers, M. (1996). Hair Shaft abnormalities: part II. *Australasian Journal of Dermatology* 37: 1–11.

Rollins, C.K. and Hall, D.M. (1999). Using light and scanning electron microscopic methods to differentiate ibex goat and Tibetan antelope fibers. *Textile Research Journal* 69 (11): 856–860.

Rowe, W.F. (1997). Biodegradation of hairs and fibers. In: *Forensic Taphonomy: The Postmortem Fate of Human Remains* (eds. W.D. Haglund and M.H. Sorg), 337–351. Boca Raton: CRC Press.

Rowe, W.F. (2010). Extreme degradation of human hair by keratinophilic and keratinolytic fungi. *The Microscope* 58 (3): 115–119.

Rowell, J.E., Lupton, C.J., Robertson, M.A. et al. (2001). Fiber characteristics of quivit and guard hair from wild muskoxen (*Ovibos moschatus*). *Journal of Animal Science* 79 (7): 1670–1674.

Rudall, K.M. (1941). The structure of the cuticle. *Proceedings of the Leeds Philosophical Society* 4: 13–18.

Saitoh, M., Uzuka, M., and Sakamoto, M. (1969). Rate of hair growth. In: *Advances in Biology of Skin*, vol. 9 (eds. W. Montagna and R.L. Dobson), 183–201. Oxford: Pergamon Press.

Sato, H., Matsuda, H., Kubota, S., and Kawano, K. (2006). Statistical comparison of dog and cat guard hairs using numerical morphology. *Forensic Science International* 158 (2–3): 94–103.

Savitha, A.S., Sacchidamamd, S., and Revathy, T.N. (2011). Bubble hair and other acquired hair shaft abnormalities due to hot ironing on wet hair. *International Journal of Trichology* 3 (2): 118–120.

Scarpi, C., Ninci, F., Centini, M., and Anselmi, C. (1998). High-performance liquid chromatography determination of direct and temporary dyes in natural hair Colorings. *Journal of Chromatography A* 796 (2): 319–325.

Schmid, W. (1967). Sex chromatin in hair roots. *Cytogenetics* 6 (5): 342–349.

Schneider, M.R., Schmidt-Ullrich, R., and Paus, R. (2009). The hair follicle as a dynamic miniorgan. *Current Biology* 19 (3): R132–R142.

Schwarz, E.R. (1936). Improved rapid sectioning of fibres. *Textile Research Journal* 6 (6): 270–272.

Sentamilselvi, G., Janaki, C., and Murugusundram, S. (2009). Trichomycoses. *International Journal of Trichology* 1 (2): 100–107.

Serowik, J.M. and Rowe, W.F. (1987). Biodeterioration of hair in a soil environment. In: *Biodeterioration Research 1* (eds. C.E. O'Rear and G.C. Llewellyn), 87–93. Boston: Springer.

Seta, S., Sato, H., Yoshino, M. Miyasaka, S. (1984). *Morphological changes of hair root with the time lapsed after death*. 10th Triennial Meeting of the Internationl Association of Forensic Sciences, Oxford, September 18–25, 1984.

Seta, S., Sato, H., and Miyake, B. (1988). Forensic hair investigation. In: *Forensic Science Progress*, vol. 2 (eds. A. Maehly and R.L. Williams), 47–166. Berlin: Springer-Verlag.

Shaffer, S. (1982). A protocol for the examination of hair evidence. *The Microscope* 30: 151–161.

Signori, V. (2004). Review of the understanding of the effect of ultraviolet and visible radiation on hair structure and options for photoprotection. *Journal of Cosmetic Science* 55: 95–113.

Simons, A.A. (1986). Hair evidence on laundered items. *Crime Laboratory Digest* 13 (3): 78–81.

Singh, D. and Garg, R.K. (2009). Forensic analysis of oxidative hair dyes from commerical dyes and dyed hair samples by thin-layer chromatography. *Journal of Forensic Identification* 59 (2): 172–189.

Smith, H.H. (1933). The relationship of the medullae and cuticular scales of the hair shafts of the Soricidae. *Journal of Morphology* 55 (1): 137–149.

Sperling, L.C. (2003). *An Atlas of Hair Pathology with Clinical Correlations*. New York, NY: Parthenon.

Steggerda, M. (1940). Cross sections of human hair from four racial groups. *Journal of Heredity* 31 (11): 474–476.

Steggerda, M. (1941). Change in hair color with age. *The Journal of Heredity* 32 (11): 402–404.

Steggerda, M. and Seibert, H.C. (1941). Size and shape of head hair from six racial groups. *Journal of Heredity* 32 (9): 315–318.

Stenn, K. (2005). Exogen is an active, separately controlled phase of the hair growth cycle. *Journal of the American Academy of Dermatology* 52 (2): 374–375.

Stenn, K.S. and Paus, R. (2001). Controls of hair follicle cycling. *Physiological Reviews* 81 (1): 449–494.

Stone, I.C. (1982). Hair and its probative value as evidence. *Texas Bar Journal* 45 (3): 275–279.

Stoves, J.L. (1958). *Fibre Microscopy: Its Technique and Application*. Princeton: D. Van Nostrand Company.

Strassburger, J. and Breuer, M.M. (1985). Quantitative fourier transform infrared spectroscopy of oxidized hair. *Journal of the Society of Cosmetic Chemists* 36 (1): 61–74.

Strauss, M.A.T. (1983a). Forensic characterization of human hair I. *The Microscope* 31: 15–29.

Strauss, M.A.T. (1983b). The law of probability. *The Microscope* 31 (2): 115–128.

Stroud, J.D. (1987). Diagnosis and management of the hair loss patient. *Cutis* 40 (3): 272–276.

Sudo, T. and Seta, S. (1976). Individual identification of hair samples in criminalistics. In: *Biology and Disease of the Hair* (eds. T. Kobori and W. Montagna), 543–553. Baltimore: University Park Press.

Suzanski, T.W. (1988). Dog hair comparison: a preliminary study. *Canadian Journal of Forensic Science* 21 (1 & 2): 19–28.

Suzanski, T.W. (1989). Dog hair comparison: purebreds, mixed breeds, multiple questioned hairs. *Canadian Journal of Forensic Science* 22 (4): 299–309.

SWGMAT (2005). Forensic human hair examination guidelines. *Forensic Science Communications* 7 (2).

Swift, J.A. (1971). New developments in electron microscopy. *Journal of the Society of Cosmetic Chemists* 22: 477–486.

Swift, J.A. (1977). The histology of keratin fibers. In: *Chemistry of Natural Protein Fibers* (ed. R.S. Asquith), 81–146. s.l.: Springer.

Swift, J.A. (1991). Fine details on the surface of human hair. *International Journal of Cosmetic Science* 13: 143–159.

Swift, J.A. (1999a). Human hair cuticle: biologically conspired to the owner's advantage. *Journal of Cosmetic Sciecne* 50: 23–47.

Swift, J.A. (1999b). The mechanics of fracture of human hair. *International Journal of Cosmetic Science* 21: 227–239.

Swift, J.A. and Brown, A.C. (1972). The critical determination of fine changes in the surface architecture of human hair due to cosmetic treatment. *Journal of the Society of Cosmetic Chemists* 23: 695–702.

Swift, J.A. and Smith, J.R. (2001). Microscopical investigations on the epicuticle of mammalian keratin fibres. *Journal of Microscopy* 204 (3): 203–211.

Tajima, M., Hamada, C., Arai, T. et al. (2007). Characteristic features of Japanese Women's hair with aging and with progressing hair loss. *Journal of Dermatological Science* 45: 93–103.

Takahashi, T., Hayashi, R., Okamoto, M., and Inouw, S. (2006). Morphology and properties of Asian and Caucasian hair. *Journal of Cosmetic Science* 57: 327–338.

Takahashi, T., Mamada, A., Breakspear, S. et al. (2015). Age-dependent changes in damage processes of hair cuticle. *Journal of Cosmetic Dermatology* 14 (1): 2–8.

Takaki, T., Tachiiri, N., Ouchi, T. et al. (2012). Morphology of human scalp hair used for wigs. *Japanese Journal of Forensic Science and Technology* 17 (1): 45–51.

Tan, J., Yang, Y., Tang, K. et al. (2013). The adaptive variant EDARV370A is associated with straight hair in east Asians. *Human Genetics* 132: 1187–1191.

Tanada, N., Kageura, M., Hara, K. et al. (1991). Identification of human hair stained with oxidation hair dyes by gas chromatographic-mass spectrometric analysis. *Forensic Science International* 52: 5–11.

Tanada, N., Kageura, M., Hara, K. et al. (1994). Demonstration of oxidation dyes on human hair. *Forensic Science International* 64: 1–8.

Tanada, N., Kashimura, S., Kageura, M., and Hara, K. (1999). Practical GC/MS analysis of oxidation dye components in hair fiber as a forensic investigative procedure. *Journal of Forensic Sciences* 44 (2): 292–296.

Teerink, B.J. (1991). *Hair of West-European Mammals*. Cambridge: Cambridge University Press.

Thibaut, S., Barbarat, P., Leroy, F., and Bernard, B.A. (2007). Human hair keratin network and curvature. *International Journal of Dermatology* 46 (Suppl. 1): 7–10.

Thorwald, J. (1967). *Crime and Science: The New Frontier in Criminology*. New York, NY: Harcourt, Brace & World.

Tobin, D.J. (2009). Aging of the hair follicle pigmentation system. *International Journal of Trichology* 1 (2): 83–93.

Tobin, D.J. and Paus, R. (2001). Graying: gerontobiology of the hair follicle pigmentary unit. *Experimental Gerontology* 36: 29–54.

Tolgyesi, E., Coble, D.W., Fang, F.S., and Kairinen, E.O. (1983). A comparative study of beard and scalp hair. *Journal of the Society of Cosmetic Chemists* 34 (7): 361–382.

Tóth, M. (2017). *Hair and Fur Atlas of Central European Mammals*. Nagykovácsi: Pars Ltd.

Tridico, S.R. (2004). Hair of the dog: a case study. In: *Trace Evidence Analysis: More Cases in Forensic Microscopy and Mute Witnesses* (ed. M.M. Houck), 27–52. Amsterdam: Elsevier.

Tridico, S. (2005). Examination, analysis, and application of hair in forensic science – animal hair. *Forensic Science Review* 17 (1): 18–28.

Tridico, S.R., Koch, S., Michaud, A. et al. (2014a). Interpreting biological degradative processes acting on mammalian hair in the living and the dead: which ones are taphonomic? *Proceedings of the Royal Society B* 281.

Tridico, S.R., Rigby, P., Kirkbride, K.P. et al. (2014b). Megafaunal Split ends: microscopical characterisation of hair structure and function in extinct woolly mammoth and woolly rhino. *Quaternary Science Reviews* 83: 68–75.

Tridico, S.R., Houck, M.M., Kirkbride, K.P. et al. (2014c). Morphological identification of animal hairs: myths and misconceptions, possibilities and pitfalls. *Forensic Science International* 238: 101–107.

Trotter, M. (1928). Hair growth and shaving. *The Anatomical Record* 37 (4): 373–379.

Trotter, M. (1930). The form, size, and color of head hair in American whites. *American Journal of Physical Anthropology* 14 (3): 433–445.

Trotter, M. (1938). A review of the classification of hair. *American Journal of Physical Anthropology* 24 (1): 105–126.

Trotter, M. and Dawson, H.L. (1934). The hair of French Canadians. *American Journal of Physical Anthropology* 18 (3): 443–456.

Trotter, M. and Duggins, O.H. (1948). Age changes in head hair from birth to maturity I. Index and size of hair of children. *American Journal of Physical Anthropology* 6 (4): 489–506.

Trotter, M. and Duggins, O.H. (1950). Age changes in head hair from birth to maturity III. Cuticular scale counts of hair of children. *American Journal of Physical Anthropology* 8 (4): 467–484.

Turner, R.F. (1949). *Forensic Science and Laboratory Technics*. Springfield: Charles C. Thomas.

Van Neste, D., Leroy, T., and Conil, S. (2007). Exogen hair characterization in human scalp. *Skin Research and Technology* 13 (4): 436–443.

Van Scott, E.J., Reinerston, R.P., and Steinmuller, R. (1957). The growing hair roots of the human scalp and morphologic changes therein following amethopterin therapy. *The Journal of Investigative Dermatology* 29 (3): 197–204.

Vanbreuseghem, R. (1952). Keratin digestion by dermatophytes: a specific diagnostic method. *Mycologia* 44 (2): 176–182.

Vernall, D.G. (1961). A study of the size and shape of cross sections of hair from four races of men. *American Journal of Physical Anthropology* 19 (4): 345–350.

Vernall, D.G. (1963). A study of the density of pigment granules in hair from four races of men. *American Journal of Physical Anthropology* 21 (4): 489–496.

Verscheure, S., Backeljau, T., and Desmyter, S. (2014). Dog mitochondrial genome sequencing to enhance dog mtDNA discrimination power in forensic casework. *Forensic Science International: Genetics* 12: 60–68.

vonHoldt, B.M., Cahill, J.A., Fan, Z. et al. (2016). Whole-genome sequence analysis shows that two endemic species of North American wolf are admixtures of the coyote and Gray wolf. *Science Advances* 2 (7).

Wagner, R. and Joekes, I. (2007). Hair medulla morphology and mechanical properties. *Journal of Cosmetic Science* 58: 359–368.

Wagner, J.K., Yu, J.H., Ifekwunigwe, J.O. et al. (2017). Anthropologists' views on race, ancestry, and genetics. *The American Journal of Physical Anthropology* 162: 318–327.

Weingart, E.L. (1973). A simple technique for revealing hair scale patterns. *American Midland Naturalist* 90 (2): 508–509.

Wennig, R. (2000). Potential problems with the interpretation of hair analysis results. *Forensic Science International* 107 (1–3): 5–12.

Westgate, G.E., Botchkareva, N.V., and Tobin, D.J. (2013). The biology of hair diversity. *International Journal of Cosmetic Science* 35: 329–336.

Whiting, D.A. (1987). Structural abnormalities of the hair shaft. *Journal of the American Academy of Dermatology* 16 (1): 1–25.

Wickenheiser, R.A. and Hepworth, D.G. (1990). Further evaluation of probabilities in human scalp hair comparisons. *Journal of Forensic Sciences* 35 (6): 1323–1329.

Wiggins, K.G. (1999). Thin layer chromatographic analysis for fibre dyes. In: *Forensic Examination of Fibres*, 2e (eds. J.R. Robertson and M. Grieve), 291–310. Philadelphia: Taylor & Francis.

Wildman, A.B. (1954). *The Microscopy of Animal Textile Fibers*. Torridon: Wool Industries Research Association.

Wilson, A.S. (2008). The decomposition of hair in the buried body environment. In: *Soil Analysis in Forensic Taphonomy* (eds. M. Tibbett and D.O. Carter), 123–151. Boca Raton: CRC Press.

Witt, S., Wunder, C., Paulke, A. et al. (2016). Detection of oxidative hair treatment using fluorescence microscopy. *Drug Testing and Analysis* 8: 826–831.

Wolfram, L.J. and Albrecht, L. (1987). Chemical- and photo-bleaching of brown and red hair. *Journal of the Society of Cosmetic Chemists* 82: 179–191.

Wolfram, L. and Lindemann, M.K. (1971). Some observations on the hair cuticle. *Journal of the Society of Cosmetic Chemists* 22: 839–850.

Wood, J.M., Decker, H., Hartmann, H. et al. (2009). Senile hair graying: H_2O_2-mediated oxidative stress affects human hair color by blunting methionine Sulfoxide repair. *The FASEB Journal* 23 (7): 2065–2075.

Wortmann, F.J. and Wortmann, G. (1991). *Scanning Electron Microscopy as a Tool for the Analysis of Wool/Specialty Fiber Blends*. Guimares: EEC Comett Eurotex.

Wortmann, F.J. and Wortmann, G. (1992). Quantitative Fiber mixture analysis by scanning electron microscopy part IV: assessment of light microscopy as an alternative tool for analyzing wool/specialty fiber blends. *Textile Research Journal* 62 (7): 423–431.

Wortmann, F.J., Wortmann, G., and McCarthy, B. (2007). Cashmere/yak blends: a vexing analytical problem. *Wool Record* 166: 33.

Wu, B.M. and Wang, J.H. (1980). Female cadaver in the han tomb no. 1 X-ray diffraction studies on two kinds of fibrous protein. *Scientia Sinica* 23 (7): 915–922.

Wynkoop, E.M. (1929). A study of the age correlations of the cuticular scales, medullas, and shaft diameters of human head hair. *American Journal of Physical Anthropology* 13 (2): 177–188.

Zhu, H., Yang, Y., Zhang, W., and Zhu, Y. (2008). Determination of 22 components in hair dyes by high performance liquid chromatography. *Chinese Journal of Chromatography* 26 (5): 554–558.

Zviak, C. and Milléquant, J. (2005a). Hair bleaching. In: *The Science of Hair Care* (eds. C. Bouillon and J. Wilkinson), 246–268. Boca Raton: Taylor & Francis.

Zviak, C. and Milléquant, J. (2005b). Hair coloring: non-oxidation coloring. In: *The Science of Hair Care* (eds. C. Bouillon and J. Wilkinson), 269–294. Boca Raton: Taylor & Francis.

Zviak, C. and Milléquant, J. (2005c). Oxidation coloring. In: *The Science of Hair Care* (eds. C. Bouillon and J. Wilkinson), 296–327. Boca Raton: Taylor & Francis.

Zviak, C. and Sabbagh, A. (2005). Permanent waving and hair straightening. In: *The Science of Hair Care* (eds. C. Bouillon and J. Wilkinson), 217–244. Boca Raton: Taylor & Francis.

5

Fibers

Sandra Koch[1] and Kornelia Nehse[2]

[1] *McCrone Associates, Westmont, IL, USA*
[2] *Forensic Science Institute (LKA KTI), Berlin, Germany*

5.1 Introduction to Forensic Fiber Analysis

Fibers are encountered as forensic evidence in a variety of forms: shed or transferred as single fibers; threads lost, cut, or torn from a garment; or in the form of a textile product such as clothing, upholstery, carpeting, or cordage. A forensic fiber examination covers identifying the fiber type by analyzing the physical, optical, and chemical properties of a fiber, the comparison of unknown fiber(s) to a known reference sample in order to determine whether or not the fibers could have originated from the same source (or another of similar manufacture), and potentially examining the construction of a textile product to determine damage or whether two items could have once been joined. It is not realistically possible to determine if a fiber came from a specific clothing garment versus another textile material of similar manufacture. However, the physical, optical, and chemical properties of a fiber can provide information as to how a textile material was manufactured, the mechanical processes used to finish a fabric, the type of dye it was colored with, the processes used

to apply the colorant, and additives that may have been applied to impart properties of interest to a finished product. The features of evidential fibers can provide supporting evidence for an association between two samples or reveal differences that would indicate an alternate source other than the reference material supplied.

This chapter is intended to provide an overview of the analyses that are included in a forensic fiber examination, including how fibers transfer and are collected as evidence, the instrumentation typically used in a forensic analysis of fibers, the physical characteristics and optical properties of the fibers most commonly found in forensic casework, and the conclusions that can be drawn from such analyses. An analytical scheme for a forensic fiber examination is presented along with a discussion regarding the attendant strengths and weaknesses to the conclusions and interpretations that can be drawn from fiber evidence within the constraints of case circumstances. For additional guidance, the ASTM standards on forensic fiber examinations (ASTM D276 and ASTM E2228; ASTM International 2012, 2019a) and the relevant instrumental techniques to be used (E2224, E2225, E2227, and E2228; ASTM International 2013, 2019a–c), along with the European Textile and Hair Group: Manual of Best Practice for the Forensic Examination of Fibres should be consulted. The Scientific Working Group for Materials Analysis (SWGMAT) fiber training guidelines (SWGMAT 2004) set out an extensive training program for new fiber examiners and contain laboratory exercises that may aid in preparing a new examiner to understand the strengths and limitations of a forensic fiber examination.

5.2 Fiber Overview

Fibers comprise the basic unit of textiles and are typically defined as a unit of material whose length significantly exceeds its width. Fiber length further differentiates filament fibers from staple fibers. Filament fibers are fibers whose length is continuous during manufacture while staple fibers are cut to designated lengths during manufacture. The typical fiber recovered in a forensic examination is fragmentary in nature, either due to its inherent or manufactured length or because it broke or was cut from wear or damage. Because of the small size and the range of microscopic characteristics differentiable among fiber types, a microscope is needed to observe and characterize the evidence.

Prior to the twentieth century, fibers were primarily produced from plant or animal materials; however, the manufacture of man-made fibers and the industrialization of textile products has led to manufactured polymer compositions gaining predominance in textile productions. Nevertheless, a fiber examiner should learn to identify the varied types of fibers that could reasonably be expected to be found in casework and the range of textile materials that fibers are used to make. Natural fibers can be differentiated by the plant, animal species, or mineral from which the fiber is extracted. For plant fibers, further differentiation can indicate what part of the plant the fiber is processed from: seed, stem, leaf, or fruit. Man-made fibers can be differentiated by their natural or synthetic polymer composition and by characteristic features imparted to the fibers from production and use. Production features include diameter, cross-sectional shape, color from dyes or pigment added to the polymer solution, the addition of delustrants or other particles, and surface alterations from mechanical or chemical treatments. Post-production aspects of manufacturing include the addition of color from dyeing or the application of pigments to the surface of a fiber or textile material, spinning the fibers into yarns, the creation of a textile by weaving, knitting, or otherwise binding fibers together into a non-woven material, and the potential alterations that can affect textiles through production, wear, or exposure to various environmental conditions. Identifying the fiber type and comparing a sample to a known reference material or library is often the main objective in a forensic fiber analysis, and is accomplished through a series of analytical examinations.

5.2.1 Textile Production: Fiber – Yarn/Cordage – Fabric

Having an understanding of how fibers and textiles are produced will aid the fiber examiner in assessing the significance of a fiber association; whether it is a common type of fiber or the result of a more unusual production method. Natural fiber processing begins with cleaning the vegetable fibers of seeds and debris, and animal fibers of grease and other debris. Natural fibers are carded in order to separate fibers from each other and orient the fibers into the same direction to achieve a degree of order. Carding not only aligns the fibers, but untangles clumps and prepares the fibers to be spun. Combing further aligns fibers in preparation for spinning into yarns. Man-made fibers are produced by extruding a polymer solution or a melted pure polymer through spinnerets into liquid or gas chambers. These fibers must then be drawn to align the internal crystalline matrix and give greater strength to the fiber. Textile production starts with processing materials into fibers, which are then spun into threads or yarns and used to construct twisted yarns, cordage, or fabrics by a variety of production methods (e.g. twisting, bonding, plaiting, weaving, knitting). Yarn construction begins with untangled and oriented fibers that are then spun or twisted into a continuous yarn. Through this mechanical process the surface structure of fibers can interlock (e.g. the scales of wool, the convolutions of cotton, the irregular surface of viscose) to provide additional strength to a spun yarn. Washing and drying promotes wool yarns to further tighten and interlock their respective scales together through a type of felting process. Once a yarn has been spun, it can be twisted together with another yarn for additional strength and evenness or for design purposes to form a larger portion of a textile.

Figure 5.1 Yarn direction of twist: S and Z twists.

Cordage refers to a general category of multiple threads or yarns twisted together into twine or rope. Once fibers are spun into twisted yarns, they can be combined into plied strands of multiple yarns. A cordage examination incorporates the construction and composition of the cordage starting with a measurement of the overall diameter followed by a count of the plies making up the whole. The direction of twist for the cordage and the plies that make up the rope are assessed in terms of the direction of the downward slant (Figure 5.1). If it descends from upper left to lower right it is termed an "S" twist as you can imagine writing an S over the cordage and the middle part of the S aligns with the twist of the rope. Alternatively, if the twist goes from upper right to lower left it is a "Z" twist with the diagonal bar of the Z aligning with the twist. Alternatively, S and Z twists may be referred to as left and right twists, respectively. For cordage that is not twisted together but may be braided with or without a core, counts of the number of plies making up the braid will be the first step after measuring the diameter. If there is a distinctly colored ply within the braid, that can also be used to count from (see Figure 5.2a). For complex twisted or braided cordage or cordage of similar colors, it helps to have several small pieces of tape that can be used to label each ply as you count the ends in each direction (see Figure 5.2b).

Each ply may be made up of several strands twisted together and these will need to be characterized. If the cordage is composed of man-made filament fibers, counting the fibers within each ply or strand may be an important point of discrimination between samples. The center of a cordage material may contain a core, which can be composed of non-woven material and/or be composed of several yarns bunched or twisted together, adding strength to the cordage. These should be measured, counted, and described for comparison to a known source.

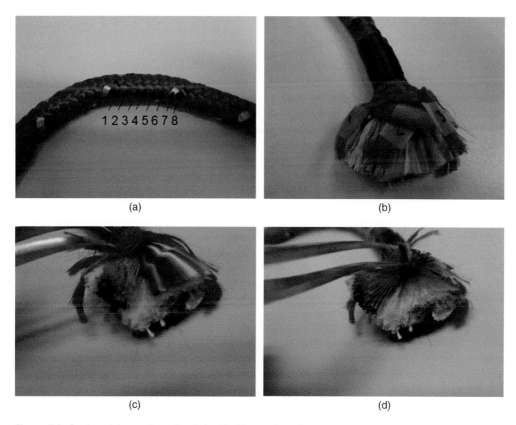

Figure 5.2 Cordage (a) counting plies in braid, (b) counting plies by labeling taped ends, (c) core filled with yarns and filament fibers, and (d) non-woven core material exposed.

Fabric is produced by weaving, knitting, or otherwise adhering fibers or yarns together into a textile material. Non-wovens are a form of textile material created by bonding, needle punching, or felting fibers together. Understanding the method by which a material is put together is important for a variety of forensic textile examinations (e.g. physical fit determinations, textile damage, fabric construction comparisons).

How fine or coarse a yarn is can be an indicator of end use. Coarse yarns, with expanded nodes or irregularities along the length of a yarn, create textiles with an uneven feel, more suitable for utilitarian use. Yarns twisted with the same amount of pull are usually more even and have more strength. Therefore, if there is a difference in the warp and weft yarns, the more uniform yarn with a tighter spin is most often used as the warp material. With mechanization and development of microfibers, finer yarns and higher thread count products have been produced.

Woven fabric is a very old form of textile production that involves a loom to create a textile material. Warp yarns run lengthwise and by interlacing weft or fill yarns in a crosswise direction a fabric is produced. In general, woven fabrics are less elastic in the longer warp direction than in weft direction. This is because warp yarns are already stretched in the loom to stop them from getting entangled and the weft yarns are not under strain when interwoven among the warp yarns. The pattern of a weave can be termed a *plain* weave (Figure 5.3a), which is in a one over, one under form (meaning the weft goes over one warp yarn and under the next warp, repeated

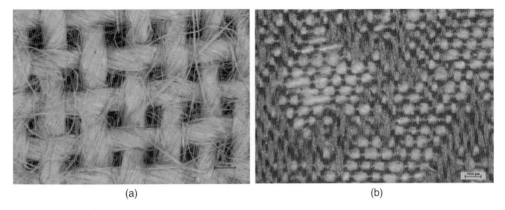

(a)   (b)

Figure 5.3 (a) Plain weave and (b) patterned weave.

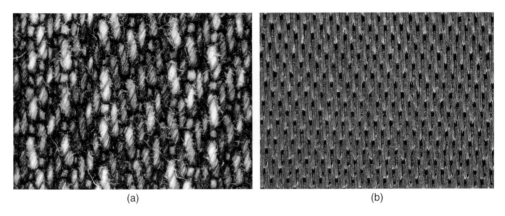

(a)   (b)

Figure 5.4 (a) Twill weave and (b) satin weave.

throughout the fabric), or more elaborate designs (Figure 5.3b) in any repeat of x warp over and n warp under.

The typical pattern found in denim has the weft going over one or more warp yarns and then under two or more warp yarns with an offset to create a diagonal line or a *twill* pattern (Figure 5.4a). *Satin* patterns (Figure 5.4b) create a very smooth closed surface that typically shows a glossy and a dull side. This is due to the fact that one side shows predominantly the warp and the other nearly only the weft material. Warp and weft satin patterns can be created by either having the warp yarns or the weft yarns floating on the show side.

Knit fabric (Figure 5.5) is produced either by hand or by machines using needles to create

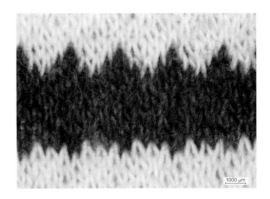

Figure 5.5 Knit fabric.

interlocking loops from a yarn to form a cohesive material. The interlocking loops allow far more elasticity to a knit fabric than the warp and weft allow in a woven fabric.

Rows of loops, or wales, run lengthwise in the same direction as warp yarns in woven material. Crosswise rows are called courses and run in the same direction as weft or fill yarns in woven textiles. Complex patterns and multiple colors can be programmed into knitting machines.

There are two main techniques involved in creating a knit fabric: warp knitting and weft knitting.

In weft knitting loops are formed one after the other by the use of at least one yarn running horizontally, creating course after course. Pulling a thread results in unraveling of the course.

In warp knitting, loops are formed perpendicular to each other forming one loop above the next, also called wales. To interlace the individual wales, loops secure loops from neighboring yarns in a defined way. This results in more or less zig-zag pattern that can be observed more easily on the back side of the fabric. The course of a warp knit cannot be unraveled.

Non-woven (Figure 5.6) materials are manufactured through a variety of methods. A sheet or web of fibers is formed by stapling, melt blowing, spun, or air laying fibers. The layers need to be interlocked for stability and different techniques can be used for bonding the fibers such as heat, water, chemicals, or mechanical methods of interlocking the fibers so they remain adhered to one another. Wool is a good material for wet felting where the physical properties of the wool fibers (i.e. having scales) in combination with hot water and friction open the scales mechanically and then entangle or interlock the fibers into a cohesive form. Non-woolen fibers (e.g. polyester fibers) can also be mechanically felted by using a needle punching technique. Other techniques use adhesive binders and/or temperature as well as chemicals for bonding. Binding fibers together with powders that have lower melting points can also be used.

Carpet production ranges from commercial tufted carpeting to woven rugs and is differentiated by the manufacturing process. Carpet manufacturers create tufts of fibers by punching looped yarns through a woven or non-woven backing material. The tufts are either cut to create a smooth pile or left as loops (Figure 5.7). While fibers may be spun and dyed prior to being incorporated into a carpet by tufting, carpet is typically dyed after the tufting process. This can be determined by examining the fiber tufts or loops to see if the dye uptake is uniform along the length of a single fiber. If the depth of color is not uniform throughout the fiber, then the dye or printing was most likely applied to the yarn, fabric, or assembled product and may appear lighter in color where the dye uptake was reduced. This is either done as a continuous piece that is fed through a heated dye bath or through a

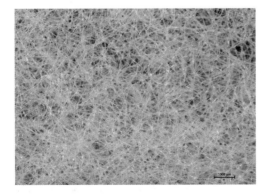

Figure 5.6 Non-woven material: fibers melt bonded together to create textile product.

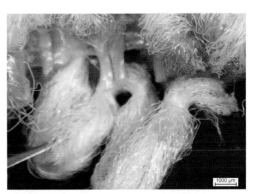

Figure 5.7 Carpet loops.

printing process where the dye is pressed into the carpet in a specific pattern (see http://www .madehow.com/Volume-2/Carpet.html).

5.2.2 Fiber Types

Fibers are formed from a variety of materials, both natural and manufactured. A new examiner should become familiar with the properties of the different materials that can be used to differentiate fiber types. Being able to identify fiber types found in or on items of evidence may be useful for providing investigative leads to law enforcement prior to searches. If investigators know to look for items of a specific color and composition (e.g. black cotton) then a search can be narrowed and the laboratory won't receive a whole closetful of clothing from a suspect, which will help streamline examinations.

5.2.2.1 Natural Fibers

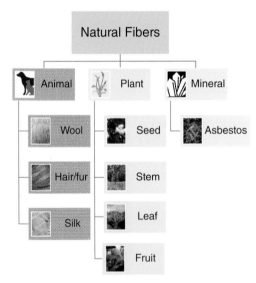

Plant fibers have a basic structure based on the type of plant and the location on the plant that the fiber is extracted from (Figure 5.8). This structure varies and is able to be differentiated among the diverse sources of plant material. A fiber's structure is based on how each cell grows and interacts within the plant and how

Figure 5.8 Cotton seed boll.

the fiber is extracted from the source. Each fiber ultimate contains a lumen, which is the central hollow core. The cell walls surrounding the lumen vary in thickness and the presence of nodes and silica cells present within the plant material as it is processed down to its fibrous components are useful features to differentiate among fiber types (Perry et al. 1975). Whether the fiber is a single cell, called an ultimate, or is clustered together into a bundle of cells (Figure 5.9) depends on the type of plant and the portion of the plant that the fiber originates from (seed, stem, leaf, or fruit).

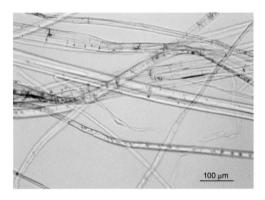

100 µm

Figure 5.9 Hemp fiber ultimates and technical fibers.

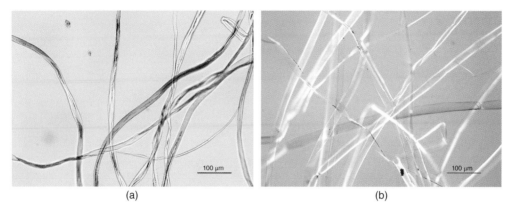

(a)   (b)

Figure 5.10 Seed fibers: (a) cotton and (b) Kapok.

Seed fibers (Figure 5.10) are from material that surrounds or is attached to the seed of a plant for protection and/or distribution. Cotton is the most common seed fiber and belongs to the *Gossypium* genus. Kapok and akund are also considered seed fibers, though these fibers are not often woven into textiles. Kapok was historically used as stuffing in lifejackets and other flotation devices but has been largely replaced with manufactured polymer materials.

Bast fibers are fibers that are processed from the stems of dicotyledonous plants (Perry et al. 1975). They are obtained by separating the elongated cells glued together in bundles from the plant's natural xylem and phloem connectivity (Perry et al. 1975). The processes that go into separating the fibrous portion of a plant stem into its useable textile material are termed retting, scutching, and heckling. *Retting* is a controlled rotting process where the plant stems are reduced to bundles of cellular material termed technical fibers or potentially down to fiber ultimates through bacterial action. This is followed by *scutching*, which is the process of scraping or beating the stems to separate out any adhering debris. The final step in breaking down plant stems to a useable fiber form is *hackling*, in which hackling combs further separate the fibers through a combing process. Pulling the fibrous material through the heckling combs further detaches the fibers from each other and any remaining impurities, and straightens them in preparation for spinning (Catling and Grayson 2004).

Examples of stem fibers are shown in Figure 5.11: flax (*Linum usitatissimum*), jute (*Corchorus capsularis* and *Corchorus olitorius*), hemp (*Cannabis sativa*), and ramie (*Boehmeria nivea*) (Perry et al. 1975; Catling and Grayson 2004).

Leaf fibers are fibrous material that is processed from the leaves or stalks of mono-cotyledonous plants (Perry et al. 1975). Agave plants (*Agave sisalana* and *Agave Americana*) are sources for sisal and maguey fibers and the abaca plant (*Musa textilis*) is the source for abaca or manila (Perry et al. 1975). The leaves of these plants are processed to separate the fibrous bundles from the leaf structure. While some plant fibers are processed down to the individual ultimates (e.g. flax used for linen), the majority of leaf fibers remain in bundles or technical fibers and are twisted into rough sack cloth or cordage.

Fruit fibers are processed from the outer husk and sometimes the inner shell of fruits like the coconut *Cocos nucifera* (Perry et al. 1975). The fiber is obtained by soaking the husks in water to remove the fibers (Perry et al. 1975). These fibers are typically used for ropes and mats as well as stuffing material

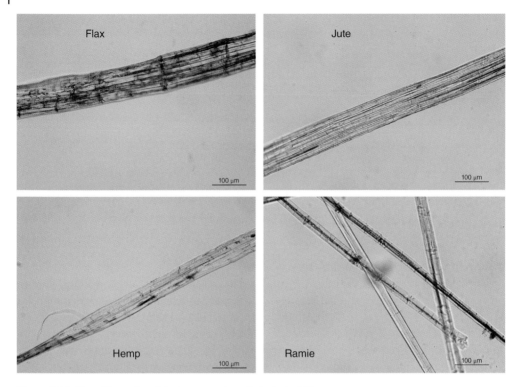

Figure 5.11 Stem fibers: flax, jute, hemp, and ramie technical fibers.

and brushes as they are not soft and flexible enough for use in clothing textiles.

Animal fibers include protein-based fibers naturally occurring as the wool, guard hairs, and underfur hairs from a variety of mammals as well as silk fibers produced from insect larvae when forming cocoons. The structure of hair is typically organized in three layers, with an outer cuticle surrounding the cortex or main body of the hair and a medulla occupying the central core. However, many wool fibers lack a medulla or it is much reduced in size relative to other non-human mammalian hairs. Wool hairs are most often shorn from the coats of sheep and goats; however, wool hair is also obtained from members of the camel family (alpaca, vicuna, llama) as well as hair from yaks, the cashmere goat, rabbits, etc. Wool is able to be is used in textiles because the cuticle scales and fiber crimp help keep

the fibers together in a twisted yarn or the scales can interlock to the extent that a mass of fibers forms a felted material. Wool fibers are typically more elastic, have a reduced medulla, higher water retention, and greater heat

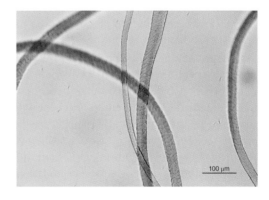

Figure 5.12 Wool fiber with variable diameter and dye uptake.

retention ability than other mammalian hairs. Dye uptake in wool can vary among the various fibers as well as at different points along a fiber (see Figure 5.12), and the diameter and cross-sectional shape will not be as uniform as in manufactured fibers.

An animal fiber distinct from mammalian hairs is the filaments produced by silk worms. Silk is extruded during cocoon production as two filaments of the protein fibroin, coated by the protein sericin (Perry et al. 1975). Silk fibers must first be unwound from a cocoon (see Figure 5.13a) and degummed or processed to remove the sericin to be useable as a fiber. Cultivated silks or mulberry silks (see Figure 5.13b) are produced from the domesticated silkworm, *Bombyx mori* (Perry et al. 1975). To avoid damage to the fiber, cocoons are processed before the larvae hatch. This results in extremely long, relatively even fibers that can easily be mistaken for a man-made filament. Cross marks originating from the spinning process of the cocoon can be observed. Wild silk, also known as tussah silk, differs from cultivated silk in color and longitudinal view as it appears more fibrillated, has a striated appearance, and the natural color appears to have shading along the fiber that is often brownish (see Figure 5.13c). Since the cocoon is most often not processed before the larvae hatch, the fibers tend to be shorter than those originating from cultivated silk.

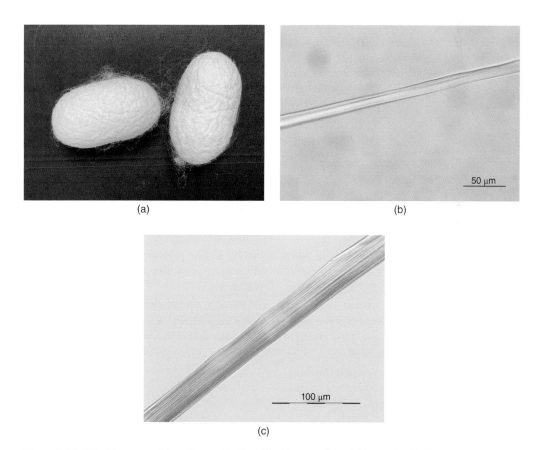

(a)

(b)

(c)

Figure 5.13 Silk: (a) cocoon, (b) mulberry silk fiber (double strand), and (c) tussah silk fiber.

5.2.2.2 Manufactured Fibers

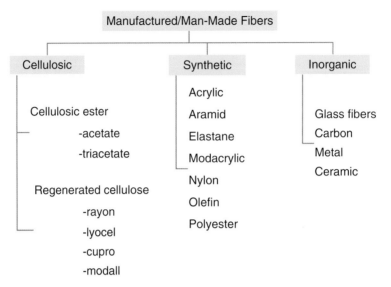

Man-made fibers made their appearance in the late 1800s with attempts to create an artificial silk. The first attempts to create manufactured fibers took place in Europe and used plant cellulose as a natural polymer. This led to the production of rayon (a cellulosic fiber) and then acetate (a modified cellulosic). Rayon was patented in the United States in 1910 and because of the high cost of silk at that time, it quickly took over the market. In 1937 DuPont patented nylon, a synthetic polymer, and began commercial production in 1939. This fiber had first been synthesized by one of their research chemists, Wallace H. Carothers, who also invented neoprene and conducted research on polyamides and polyesters (Viswanathan 2010; Smith and Hounshell 1985; Mueller 1962).

Synthetic fibers are produced from a polymer solution or melt that is extruded through spinnerets, which then coagulate into a fiber form in a heated air chamber or chemical bath. The different spinning production methods are melt spinning, dry (or solvent) spinning, wet spinning, and a combination wet-dry spinning termed gel spinning (Figure 5.14). In *melt spinning* polymer chips are melted down to create a liquefied polymer that can be forced through the holes in the spinneret and then solidifies into a fiber as it cools in air. In *dry spinning* the polymer is dissolved in a solvent prior to extrusion through the spinneret and then as it passes through a hot gas chamber the solvent evaporates and the filaments harden. In *wet spinning* the polymer is also dissolved in a solvent but is extruded through the spinneret into a liquid bath, which promotes coagulation of the filament and the removal of the solvent. *Gel spinning* combines the wet and dry spinning methods after extrusion. The filaments coming from the spinneret first form a rubbery solid, which cools initially in air and then as a further step in a liquid bath. This production method is primarily used for high-strength polyethylene fibers.

Drawing fibers aligns the polymer chains within the fiber and provides strength to the final form. Spinnerets are like shower heads and direct the liquid polymer into separate fibrous streams that are then dried and stretched into their final form (Figure 5.15). The shape of the openings in a spinneret imparts a shape to the fiber. After extrusion, a fiber is drawn and dried, which can alter its diameter and cross-sectional shape. A list of fiber types and their definitions typically comes with a commercial forensic fiber

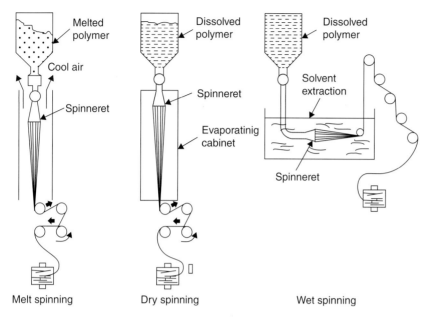

Figure 5.14 Spinning production methods.

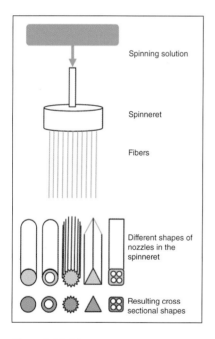

Figure 5.15 Diagram of fiber production from solution through spinneret to final fiberv form.

proficiency test, but a check of the Federal Trade Commission (FTC) and/or Bureau International pour la Standardization des Fibres Artificielles/International Bureau of Standardization of Man-made Fiber Producers (BISFA) websites will reveal any updates to what can be expected to be found among commercially available textile materials.

Some features to note in the major fiber types are noted below:

Cellulosics (Figure 5.16) are produced by dry spinning (acetate) or wet spinning (rayon) and include cupramonium rayon, viscose rayon, acetate, and lyocell. As a group, they typically have a low refractive index, with bluish or bright blue, brown and white, yellow/orange interference colors under crossed polars depending on the fiber diameter with the fiber positioned at a 45° angle to the cross hairs. Using a lambda plate the interference colors show bright blue, yellow, and orange if the fiber is placed at an angle of 45° and bluish to gray colors with orange striation near the edges when placed at 315°. Fibers often appear

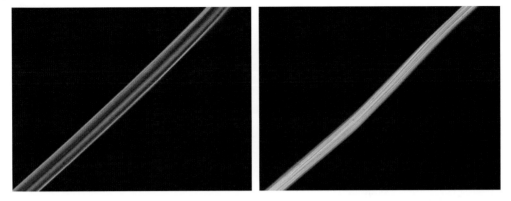

Figure 5.16 Viscose rayon fibers with bluish white and yellow-orange interference colors under crossed polars: different diameters and different cross-sectional shape. Source: Courtesy of ETHG Fibre Type Information System – FTIS.

to have a striated surface from shrinkage of the outer surface relative to the core of the fiber during formation. These fibers have a soft texture when used in textiles, are strong, and have good absorbance and dyeability. The textiles often show a laundry stiffness when still wet but soften after drying.

FTC definition of acetate: A manufactured fiber in which the fiber-forming substance is cellulose acetate. Where not less than 92% of the hydroxyl groups are acetylated, the term triacetate may be used as a generic description of the fiber.

FTC definition of rayon: A manufactured fiber composed of regenerated cellulose, as well as manufactured fibers composed of regenerated cellulose in which substituents have replaced not more than 15% of the hydrogens of the hydroxyl groups. Where the fiber is composed of cellulose precipitated from an organic solution in which no substitution of the hydroxyl groups takes place and no chemical intermediates are formed, the term lyocell may be used as a generic description of the fiber.

Acrylic fibers (Figure 5.17) are produced by wet and dry spinning and are dyed with cationic dyes. These fibers have some antimicrobial characteristics and acrylic fibers are resistant to degradation by sunlight and the environment, hold their shape, and dry quickly

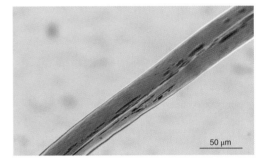

Figure 5.17 Acrylic fiber.

(Mueller 1962). The polymer allows transport of moisture along the fiber but does not absorb much moisture itself so it is often used in athletic wear (Masson 1995). Research on Orlon acrylic fibers, also invented in the DuPont laboratories, started in 1941 and acrylic fibers were patented in 1948. Under cross-polarized light acrylic fibers appear gray but with a full wave plate; fibers oriented parallel to the analyzer appear orange.

FTC definition of acrylic: A manufactured fiber in which the fiber-forming substance is any long-chain synthetic polymer composed of at least 85% by weight of acrylonitrile units.

Modacrylic fibers were patented in the 1940s, have flame-resistant as well as abrasion-resistant properties, are produced by wet spinning, and have a low birefringence so they appear gray under cross-polarized light. Modacrylic fibers can be easily dyed and are resistant to acids and alkalis. They often contain chlorinated or brominated co-monomers with acrylonitrile.

FTC definition of modacrylic: A manufactured fiber in which the fiber-forming substance is any long-chain synthetic polymer composed of less than 85% but at least 35% by weight of acrylonitrile units.

Olefin fibers are made from polyolefin such as polypropylene or polyethylene and are produced by melt spinning. Olefin fibers (Figure 5.18) typically have a large diameter, a smooth surface, and, while not able to be dyed, are colorfast because in order to color the fiber, pigment is added to the polymer matrix before spinning. These fibers are resistant to staining, mildew, abrasion, and sunlight so they are often used in carpeting. Some olefin fibers can be difficult to determine the retardation of because of the typical large diameter and the amount of pigment used to color the fibers; however, these fibers have a moderate birefringence.

FTC definition of olefin: A manufactured fiber in which the fiber-forming substance is any long-chain synthetic polymer composed of at least 85% by weight of ethylene, propylene, or other olefin units.

High-density polyethylene (HDPE) (e.g. Spectra®) fibers are specialized fibers found predominantly in technical climbing ropes

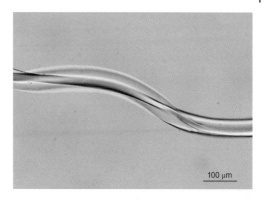

Figure 5.19 Nylon trilobal carpet-type fiber.

and in bulletproof fabric. These fibers have a very high refractive index, are produced by gel spinning, and are infrequently found in forensic casework.

Nylon (polyamide) fibers are produced by melt spinning. Nylon is a thermoplastic material so it can melt under high heat or friction (e.g. hit and run cases). The fibers are typically lustrous, strong, waterproof, and resistant to sunlight and weathering. Nylon is used in both carpeting (Figure 5.19) and clothing, so fiber shape and size can be important features for potential end use determinations. Nylon can dissolve in acids so acid dyes are not often used for this fiber but direct and vat dyes are. While many different types of nylon (polyamide) are manufactured, nylon 6 (polycaproamide) and nylon 6.6 (polyhexamethyleneadipamide) are two of the most common sub-types of nylon and relate to the chemical composition of the raw materials used, and how they combine into a polymer structure. The differences in chemical composition can be identified by Fourier transform infrared spectroscopy (FTIR) (Figure 5.20).

Nylon 6

- Weak peak at 1274 cm^{-1}

Nylon 6.6

- Dominant peak at 1274 cm^{-1}
- Small peak at 720 cm^{-1}
- Weak peaks at 935 and 1145 cm^{-1}

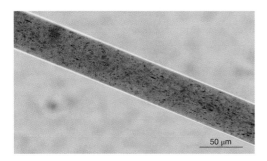

Figure 5.18 Olefin fiber.

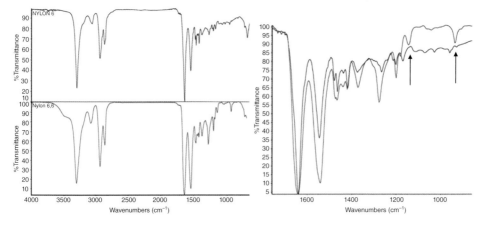

Figure 5.20 IR spectra of nylon 6 and 6.6 with the fingerprint region highlighting slight differences around 720 and 935 cm^{-1}.

Nylon 6 and 6.6 can also be identified via melting point determination with nylon 6 melting around 215–220 °C and nylon 6.6 between 255 and 260 °C.

Nylon is used in both carpeting and clothing so fiber shape and size can be important features for potential end use determinations.

FTC definition of nylon: A manufactured fiber in which the fiber-forming substance is a long-chain synthetic polyamide in which less than 85% of the amide linkages are attached directly to two aromatic rings.

Polyester (Figure 5.21) is most commonly found in fiber form as polyethylene terephthalate (PET), a copolymer of ethylene glycol and terephthalic acid; however, there are several other types of polyester fibers.

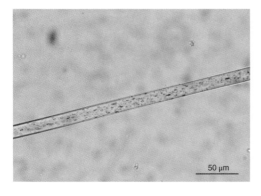

Figure 5.21 Polyester fiber.

PET, polytrimethylene terephthalate (PTT), and polybutylene terephthalate (PBT) are condensation polymer fibers.

The different polyester types can be identified by melting point determination or the presence or absence of discriminating FTIR peaks (Figure 5.22):

PET: an additional peak at ~1340 cm^{-1}
PBT: weak shoulders around 1220 and 920 cm^{-1}
PTT: shifted peak positions around 1466, 1358, and 1036 cm^{-1}.

These fibers are produced by melt spinning, have a high refractive index, and are dyed with disperse, cationic, and acidic dyes. Polyester was first patented in 1941 in the UK, and DuPont filed a US patent in 1945 after research transferred between companies under cooperative research agreements (McIntyre 2005). Polyester is also used in a variety of applications so cross-sectional shape and fiber size can be important for differentiating carpet-type fibers from upholstery or clothing textiles.

FTC definition of polyester: A manufactured fiber in which the fiber-forming substance is any long-chain synthetic polymer composed of at least 85% by weight of an ester of a substituted aromatic carboxylic acid, including but not restricted to substituted

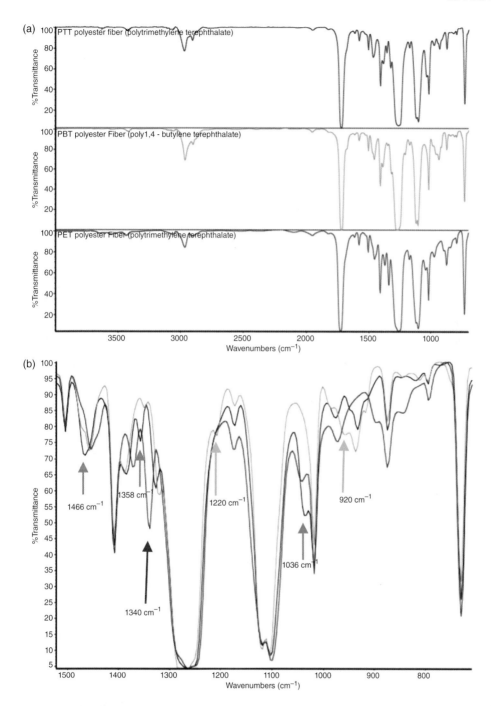

Figure 5.22 (a) IR spectra of polyesters PET (red), PBT (yellow) and PTT (blue). (b) Overlaid fingerprint regions to show differences in spectra.

terephthalate units and para substituted hydroxy-benzoate units.

Elastomeric fibers (e.g. Spandex) are elastic polymers that allow for a high degree of elongation and recovery, and are resistant to heat, sunlight, environmental degradation, and chemicals. These fibers are not lustrous but can be improved with optical brighteners. Disperse and acid dyes can be used to dye them. Under a microscope, elastomeric fibers are often opaque and have a large diameter. To examine these fibers, a small lobe or section of the fiber may need to be sampled to study the optical properties and chemical composition.

FTC definition of spandex: A manufactured fiber in which the fiber-forming substance is a long-chain synthetic polymer composed of at least 85% of a segmented polyurethane.

Aramids (Kevlar and Nomex) are produced by wet spinning, have a very high refractive index, and are infrequently found in background fiber assemblages in forensic casework. These fibers are very strong, highly flame-resistant, have a high resistance to stretching, and maintain their shape at high temperatures. A photomicrograph of a Kevlar fiber is shown in Figure 5.23.

FTC definition of aramid: A manufactured fiber in which the fiber-forming substance is a long-chain synthetic polyamide in which at least 85% of the amide linkages are attached directly to two aromatic rings.

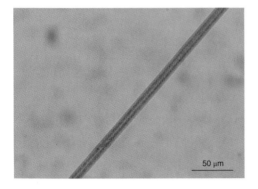

Figure 5.23 Kevlar fiber.

5.2.3 Fiber/Textile Coloration

Once fibers are spun into yarns or made into fabrics, the material can be dyed with a variety of techniques. The processes whereby color is applied to fibers varies, but there is a general difference between dyeing from dye solutions and applying color by printing with dye pastes. The method of applying color will depend on the fiber type and the composition of the dye source. Methods of dye application vary according to the solubility of the colorant in water and how well it binds to different fibers. Pretreatment of textile fibers by mordants can improve the affinity of a fiber to a particular dye, the intensity of the color, and its long-term stability or colorfastness. Pigments are insoluble to water and are attached via a binder to the outer surface of the fibers or are added into the spinning solution to color the fiber as it is made.

Printing techniques can be applied to fibers, yarns, fabrics, or garments. With fabrics, a pattern is printed to one side of the material and the color is predominant on this side of the fabric. The backside is usually paler since the dye does not always penetrate the whole fabric.

With man-made fibers color can be achieved by adding pigments to the polymer solution prior to spinning and stretching. Soluble dyes can be used to color fibers post-production as well as yarns, fabrics, or whole garments. The depth of dye penetration depends on the material, the dye method, and the stage of production. Fiber dyes achieve the most even results either as pigment dyes with man-made fibers or with soluble dyes on all sorts of fiber material. Since yarn and threads are twisted and fibers overlap, not every part of the fiber can be reached by a dye solution when fabrics and garments are dyed post production. Where the warp and weft cross in a woven textile, the dye solution is limited in its ability to penetrate the fabric completely at those locations. The fibers from the inner sides of those crossing points are often lighter colored than the outer portions of the fabric.

Direct dyes are water soluble and easily bind to fibers through direct application of the dye to the textile material in solution. These dyes are usually less stable than vat dyes or fibers that have been treated by a mordant prior to being exposed to a direct dye (Ferreira et al. 2004). Repeated exposure to light or washing thus reduces the amount of dye that remains bound to the fibers. Red dyes from insects such as cochineal, kerms, and lac are examples of natural direct dyes.

Vats dyes are used for colorants that are not soluble in water. This class of dye needs to be converted into an alkaline solution to allow for uptake of the colorant into the fiber (Ferreira et al. 2004). Once the dye has penetrated the fiber, the material is exposed to air to allow oxidation to change the dye back to its insoluble form (Cardon 2007). Through this process, the dye is trapped inside the fiber, which creates a more colorfast dye. Of the natural dyes, indigo, woad, and shellfish purple fall into this category of dyeing.

Sulfur dyes are also insoluble in water so they need a reducing agent, such as a water-soluble salt that alkalizes the dye bath, and heat to allow for absorption of the dye into fibers. Once the dye has been absorbed, it maintains good wash-fastness and colorfastness because of the insolubility of the dye in water.

Mordants are substances that are applied to fibers to assist in the uptake and retention of the dye and improve color fastness. Some natural dyes do not bind well to plant or animal fibers; however, when they interact with mordanted fibers, the color is able to bind more easily and becomes much more vibrant and colorfast. Mineral mordants from salts, mud, or metal oxides and organic materials such as urine and animal fats (Cardon 2007) have been used to alter the uptake and retention of natural dyes.

Applying color to fibers or yarns is not only done in a dye bath but can be done by printing on the surface of a textile. When printing, colorants are applied by spraying or painting the dye or a pigment onto the material. Typically, the pigment or dye does not penetrate the

yarns. *Pigments* are insoluble colorants that are not soluble in a dye bath. Olefin fibers are not able to be dyed after production, so these fibers are colored by pigments added to the polymer solution prior to extrusion and color the fibers from within. Other uses for pigments are on the surface of fibers or textiles where an extra layer is added on top of the material to color a particular area or in a specific pattern, especially with less expensive prints.

Piece dyeing involves immersing the whole fabric in the dye bath instead of the fiber or yarn components so there may be portions of the yarns that do not uptake the dye in as uniform a way because of the tightness of the twist or weave inhibiting contact with the dye bath.

5.3 Forensic Fiber Examination Background

Having a comprehensive understanding of the production of fibers, the techniques that can be used to characterize them, and potential conclusions that can be reached in a comparative analysis, along with any limitations, is essential knowledge for a forensic fiber examiner to have.

This background knowledge should include an understanding of the morphology of natural and man-made fibers and the different production processes. This will enable a more complete analysis of textile evidence to provide better and more information for the investigators. In addition, a fiber examiner will need to have a thorough comprehension of Locard's exchange principle, relevant transfer and persistence studies, and how they relate to fiber evidence in casework.

5.3.1 Transfer and Persistence

Edmund Locard has been famously attributed with stating "Every contact leaves a trace." Fibers are one type of trace material that are exchanged through contact. The clothing that we wear sheds fibers and these fibers are often transferred when two people come in contact. Transfers also occur between a person and an object and sometimes between two objects (e.g. a textile bag placed on a chair). How fibers transfer and persist depends on a wide range of influencing factors. The surface quality of the donor and recipient garments plays an important role regarding the potential sheddability of fibers and the retention of any transferred fibers. How likely an item of clothing is to shed fibers depends on the fiber's length, individual properties of the fiber type, the extent that fibers will break off due to textile finishing, and wear and tear. Fabric construction also has an impact on the number of fibers that will potentially transfer and the potential to remain attached to a material. A garment's shedding potential varies from zero or close to zero fibers up to potentially many hundreds in a contact. Thus, it is important to assess the potential of a garment to shed prior to a fiber examination and, more significantly, before interpreting results.

A number of studies have been conducted over the years on the transfer and persistence of fibers (Pounds and Smalldon 1975a–c; Lowrie and Jackson 1994; Salter and Cook 1996; Grieve and Biermann 1997a,b; Palmer 1998; Roux et al. 1999; Akulova et al. 2002; Bologna and Parent 2002; Deadman and Scully 2004; Palmer and Banks 2005; Palmer and Burch 2009; Bennett et al. 2010; Szewcow et al. 2011; Hong et al. 2014; Palmer et al. 2017; Slot et al. 2017). While some studies are decades old, they remain useful for understanding the principles of fiber transfer and persistence. Researchers have focused on the transfer of different fiber types (Grieve and Biermann 1997a,b; De Wael et al. 2011), the activities and types of recipient garments that could affect fiber retention (Pounds and Smalldon 1975a; Grieve and Biermann 1997a,b; Roux et al. 1999; De Wael et al. 2010; Slot et al. 2017), diverse environments and exposure conditions (Akulova et al. 2002; Lepot et al. 2015), and secondary transfer (Lowrie and Jackson 1994; Palmer and Banks 2005; Palmer et al. 2017) that could influence fiber transfer, persistence, and a comparison. A comprehensive review of

the fiber transfer and persistence literature was carried out by Palmer in 2016 and provides a more current basis for relating the significance of fiber evidence in forensic casework (Palmer 2016). Palmer's research distilled much of the substantive information from the forensic fiber literature, with a focus on combining data from fiber population studies, specific fiber types and colors, and data from transfer and persistence studies. While fiber populations may differ based on location, season, and changing styles, continued research on fiber populations can be useful for understanding the relative abundance of different fiber types and colors in different regions and over time (Fong and Inami 1986; Lepot et al. 2017; Palmer and Oliver 2004; Roux and Margot 1997; Watt et al. 2005 Bologna and Parent 2002; Deadman and Scully 2004). These studies can be helpful in combination with studies focused on specific colors of fibers (Biermann 2007; Buzzini and Massonnet 2015; Grieve et al. 1988, 2001, 2003, 2005; Palmer et al. 2009) and target fibers (Brüschweiler and Grieve 1997; Cook and Wilson 1986; Jones and Coyle 2011; Kelly and Griffin 1998; Palmer et al. 2017; Palmer and Chinherende 1996; Wiggins et al. 2004) to interpret the significance of fiber findings and their evidential value in a case. If fibers do transfer, they can be lost and/or redistributed on a garment through passive and active forces (e.g. gravity, running, washing clothes) (Palmer 1998; Roux et al. 1999; Palmer and Burch 2009; Szewcow et al. 2011) or through evidence transport (Chewning et al. 2008). Features of the recipient garment (tightness of weave, fiber type) greatly influence the rate of fiber persistence (Pounds and Smalldon 1975a–c). The majority of transferred fibers are typically lost within 2 hours (Pounds and Smalldon 1975b) under normal activity patterns. Some fibers can persist for far longer, especially if transferred to areas of a garment that protect fibers from loss (e.g. pockets) or if stuck to rough surfaces (e.g. a wool pullover or a hook-and-pile fastener). Washing, exposure to outdoor elements, etc. can impact the persistence of transferred fibers (Grieve and

Biermann 1997a,b; Palmer 1998; Akulova et al. 2002; Palmer and Polwarth 2011; Szewcow et al. 2011; Hong et al. 2014; Lepot and Vanden Driessche 2015). Case studies and research have shown that transferred fibers exposed to outdoor elements have a high initial loss (between 67% and 74% loss) over the first two days (Palmer and Polwarth 2011) and the majority of transferred fibers are lost within days even with no movement of the object that the fibers were transferred to or when the evidence was found in more sheltered areas (Krauß and Hildebrand 1995). Data from such studies suggest that wind and rain generally contribute to fiber loss in outdoor environments, but further outdoor studies show that even flowing water does not eliminate all fiber and fiber particles present. After washing a garment, loss of transferred fiber material can be expected, but again, a total loss is not anticipated (De Wael et al. 2010).

Fiber transfers may occur as the result of a direct contact (primary transfer) or an indirect contact (secondary and tertiary transfer). Besides the general tendency of a textile product to shed fibers, the nature, intensity, and duration of a contact play a very important role in the transfer and the resulting numbers of fibers potentially being transferred. The recipient itself may have good or poor retention qualities, which also influences the number of fibers that will persist once transferred.

An undisturbed scene and unmoved items or bodies in general provide the best conditions for persistence so that the most trace evidence can be recovered and preserved. If a crime scene is preserved soon after a crime occurs and fibers are recovered directly at the scene, the information gained from the evidence can be extremely valuable for further conclusions. If evidence is collected and later delivered or shipped to a laboratory for fiber analysis, it should be noted that fibers may change position on a garment and move from the front to back, inside to outside, etc. depending on how it was handled (Chewning et al. 2008). Accordingly, in cases where the fibers have not been directly collected or tape lifted in the

field it may not be accurate to state where a fiber was found except in the most general sense relating to the garment as a whole. The proper limitation of conclusions in such cases is necessary.

The intensity of an interaction, the number of originally transferred fibers, movement, and time influence the results and the interpretation of the evidence. Loss of fiber material can occur after movement of items, victims, and offenders. Outdoor conditions, e.g. wind and rain, have an impact and fibers may be lost or moved on the surface.

Despite time and outdoor conditions or manipulations, like washing, being crucial factors, transferred fibers might move into pockets, turned up cuffs, velcro fasteners or other places with good retention qualities.

Collecting textiles and clothing garments at an early stage in an investigation should help preserve much of the trace evidence. To prevent loss or contamination it is important that items are packaged and sealed immediately after seizing them. Care needs to be taken to ensure that the victim and offender are not transported in the same vehicle and that interrogations of the victim and offender do not take place in the same room before garments worn during the offense have been seized, packaged, and sealed.

To avoid contamination in the laboratory, fiber recovery from garments of victims and offenders need to be carried out independently. This can be done by different laboratory personnel, in different rooms, and/or at different times or days with clean laboratory coats and tools.

Donor qualities (sheddability) and recipient qualities (retention) should be checked prior to a fiber examination if inferences are to be made concerning the possible rate of transfer and persistence. While a tape lift will remove more fibers than would be typically transferred under contact, a general assessment of sheddability can be made from taping a garment. If the garment does not transfer many fibers (e.g. nylon windbreaker) it can be viewed as a low shedder. Alternatively, a garment that transfers many fibers to a tape lift (e.g. wool sweater, flock fiber fabric) can be viewed as a high shedder. The sheddability of a garment can be tested by the Martindale rub test (ASTM D4966; ASTM International 2016) or a simplified weighted rub test. These tests are designed to assess the durability of fabrics when subjected to abrasion conditions, such as would be encountered by a fabric during normal handling and wear. The test is useful for forensic purposes to count the number of shed fibers from a donor garment under pre-defined pressures, using specific weights, and a set number of intervals where the fabric is rubbed against a neutral white cotton surface. To estimate the sheddability of a garment or other textile, three different pressures (light, medium, heavy) are typically used in three replicate experiments. Under the defined pressures, a donor garment is moved on top of the recipient garment three to five times. The recipient garment must be free of potential surface fibers, and this can be ensured by tape lifting the surface before testing. For both the Martindale rub test and the weighted rub test, a defined area of fabric (e.g. a square of fabric approximately 10×10 cm or a circle of 10 cm in diameter) is designated to search and count transferred fibers.

Since garments can be made of multiple fiber types and people often wear more than one garment at a time, fiber transfers may not be restricted to the transfer of a single fiber type originating from only one item. If material and color blends are present in a garment it can be expected that different fiber types and colors originating from such an item will be transferred. Thus, it can be expected that different fiber types originating from multiple items are transferred during intense interaction when contact is made between donor and recipient garments (Decke 2000; Neubert-Kirfel 2000). Whether those fibers persist until they can be collected in the laboratory is a separate consideration. In addition, small numbers of secondary transferred fibers present on the surface of a garment have to be taken into account. Finding multiple fibers and/or different fiber types can increase the significance of findings (Palmer et al. 2017; Yesil and Sabir 2011). In the case of a cross transfer (both directions transfer and retain fibers) with multiple fibers and different fiber types involved, the value of fiber associations can also increase dramatically. The interpretation of findings should be put into context with the donor and recipient qualities of potential garments involved as well as the circumstances of the case. For instance, finding numerous transferred fibers on an acrylic windbreaker that does not retain fibers for long would have different implications than finding multiple fibers on a wool sweater that has longer retention capabilities (Decke 2000; Neubert-Kirfel 2000).

5.3.2 Collection

A fiber examination starts with the collection of evidence at a crime scene. If nothing is collected or the materials with fibers potentially adhering to their surface are not preserved for laboratory analysis, then no conclusions can be drawn. Examinations conducted in the laboratory include a fiber's physical, optical, and chemical properties to identify fibers for comparison with other evidence or against known samples, and an evaluation of whether unknown fibers are similar or dissimilar to known fiber sources or libraries to answer questions relevant to a forensic case, such as potential contact between people or objects. Similar collection and recovery methods are used for fibers as previously discussed for paint (see Chapter 4) and hairs (see Chapter 5) so are not discussed at length here.

5.3.2.1 Recognition, Collection, and Preservation

Depending upon the circumstances of the case, collection of fibers and other trace evidence may occur at a crime scene, jail, hospital, morgue, or the crime laboratory. When possible, the whole item (e.g. clothing, car seats, vehicle parts, weapons) should be submitted for evidential fibers to be collected in a controlled laboratory setting. Possible source material (e.g. carpeting, upholstery, clothing items) should be collected as reference samples at the crime scene and cuttings taken from submitted textile materials in the laboratory for comparisons to be made.

5.3.2.2 Collection

A fiber examination starts with the collection and processing of evidence. During an initial assessment, evidence should be visually inspected, described, processed to remove trace materials adhering to the evidence, and, if it won't be damaging to the evidence, labeled according to laboratory protocols to uniquely identify the item and document those who have examined it. Documentation should include a general description of the item along with information from a manufacturer's label (e.g. fiber content, size, location of manufacture), the color, type of material (knit, woven, or non-woven fabric), any damage, and the packaging conditions under which the item was received.

When assessing submitted evidence, magnification and adjustable lighting can aid in identifying and collecting fibrous evidence from submitted items. Visible fibers can be picked from the surface of items (e.g. with forceps) or taped to collect and the location they were recovered from noted. Any loose fibers adhering to objects can also be gently tapped into a sealable container or paper fold. Collecting fibers from evidence typically involves picking, scraping, taping, and/or vacuuming the evidence. It is also important to collect a known exemplar of the material for elimination and comparison purposes. These samples should represent fiber material from the visible area of potential contacts. If samples are taken from the inner hidden portions of a textile (e.g. seams) there might be differences in color that may disturb the comparison process and the result of findings.

5.3.2.3 Visual Recovery: Picking

Using low magnification, such as a stereomicroscope, fibers can be searched for and picked from the surface of items (e.g. with forceps) for further analysis. When searching for fibers, oblique or alternate lighting may also be helpful to locate loosely adhering particles as different fibers may reflect light differently or fluoresce, thus facilitating their detection and recovery. For picking, a pair of fine tweezers is used to grasp the fibers in question to place them in a small container, on tape, or on a glass microscope slide.

5.3.2.4 Other Recovery Methods: Taping, Scraping, and Vacuuming

If no foreign fibers are recovered after a visual examination (by unaided eye and low magnification), textile items such as clothing may be taped or scraped for microscopical analyses of associated debris in the laboratory.

Tapings can be carried out by lint roller tape, sticky notes, or with clear sticky tape. Such tapes typically have low to moderate adhesive properties and can be used to collect fibers from a particular area of an object while not breaking the fibers during removal. This procedure is also known as tape lifting.

Scraping is a collection process in which a garment is hung over a clean sheet of paper and lightly scraped with an elongated spatula (e.g. pastry spatula) to encourage loosely adhering fibers to fall from the garment. This evidence is then collected from the paper by tapping it into a small container for examination under a stereomicroscope. If each garment submitted has been recovered and packaged separately, they should be examined and processed individually. If items are packaged together then by already having come into contact with each other, transfer between items could have occurred and it no longer makes sense to process each item separately.

Larger items or locations that cannot be easily transported to a laboratory for processing can be vacuumed with single-use sealed collection filters specially designed to collect trace evidence. The one-time use evidence collection filters are factory sealed and can be directly submitted to the laboratory for analysis of the debris collected from a specific location. Some laboratories prefer tapings over vacuum collections, while others prefer the opposite, so it is best to check with your laboratory system prior to collecting evidence for their preferred method of trace evidence collection in the field.

The durability of a textile material in its original form is not ensured because of the potential for fibers and colorants to degrade over time. Textile materials that do survive can offer information as to how the textile was manufactured and/or used, the dyes and pigments that were applied, and potentially how the manufacturing process changed over time. As crime scenes are not pristine environments, exposure to a variety of conditions can degrade textile materials and their dyes or colorants over time. Accordingly, new fiber examiners should be aware of the analytical processes used in textile conservation and archeological laboratories in case such methods can be applied in forensic fiber examinations. A fiber examiner's training should not rely solely on forensic resources but include an overview of techniques from other scientific disciplines and the textile industry that examine fibers and textiles to best prepare a new fiber examiner to be able to accurately address the varied questions that may come up from different case situations over the course of a career.

5.3.3 Identification

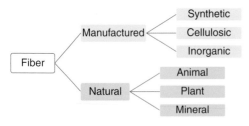

An examination of a textile material begins with characterizing its physical properties and proceeds to determining the composition of an item, its preservation, and its similarity to other evidentiary fibers or textile materials. Crime scene evidence is often exposed to environmental conditions that may adversely

impact a textile's preservation and/or the fibers that are able to be recovered as evidence. Certain environments are more conducive to recovering organic material. Wet areas with acidic, anoxic conditions, or low oxygen levels in the soil, such as bog areas, reduce the organic decomposition of many materials, including textiles (Vanden Berghe et al. 2009). Sites with dry, arid conditions such as deserts or high-altitude locations may increase the preservation of textile materials. Plant and other cellulosic fibers often preserve better in alkaline conditions, while protein-based animal fibers such as wool preserve better in slightly acidic environments (Good 2001). Even when environmental conditions lead to degradation and modifications of fiber structures, some structural information may still be detectable that can lead to an identification of a fiber as having been manufactured or have plant or animal origin. Characteristics present within a fiber can serve as indications of decomposition (e.g. dye changes, fiber degradation, fungal tunneling in animal hair). These features may also inform an examiner about the environment the textile was found in, and with additional research regarding the soil and weather conditions of the area can offer potential information concerning the general time period a garment was buried or exposed to those environmental conditions.

Beyond identifying the composition of the fibers comprising spun yarns and remnants of woven materials, knowing when raw materials were patented and in general use around the world may allow fiber examiners to indicate whether a particular type of fiber was produced or typically in use at the time of an incident. Such information may be important to a case. Such analyses can lead to a better understanding of the role textile materials play over time and how changing styles and the chemical compositions of dyes may add to an analysis. Clothing labels can provide useful information about the fiber type(s) that a garment is made of; however, care should be taken when relying on these labels for identification of a fiber type, as the fiber content listed may not accurately reflect the fiber(s) present in the garment or it may not be original to the garment. Researching when fiber types were patented, generally available in the market, and their relative abundance in current production should be a part of a forensic fiber examiner's training and background knowledge.

5.3.3.1 Natural Fiber Identification

Natural Fibers As previously described in Section 5.2.2.1, plant fibers have a basic structure that is based on the type and part of the plant that fibers are extracted from. This structure varies and is able to be differentiated among the diverse sources of plant material. A fiber's structure is based upon how each cell grows and interacts within the plant and how the fiber is extracted from the source. Each cell contains a lumen, which is the central hollow core. The cell walls surrounding the lumen vary in thickness and the presence of nodes, silica cells, etc. present within the plant material as it is processed down to its fibrous components helps to differentiate fiber types (Perry et al. 1975). Whether the fiber is a single cell, called an ultimate, or is clustered together into a bundle, called a technical fiber, depends on the type of plant and the portion of the plant that the fiber originates from (seed, stem, leaf, or fruit).

Seed fibers are staple length fibers collected from the seeds of various plants e.g., cotton and kapok.

Cotton fibers are elongated single spindle-shaped cells (Figure 5.24), meaning they are wide in the middle and taper at both ends (Catling and Grayson 2004). The cell walls are of varying thickness and surround a hollow lumen. Cotton fibers are identifiable by this cellular structure and the variable twists and convolutions that occur along their length. Typically, cotton fibers range in length from 12 to 64 mm with a diameter of approximately 11–22 µm. (Perry et al. 1975). Some of the various types found in cultivation around

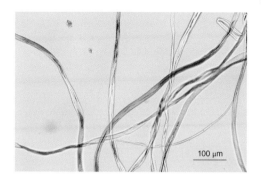

Figure 5.24 Cotton fibers.

the world are upland cotton or *Gossypium hirsutum*, Indian cotton, American cotton, Eyptian cotton, and Sea Island cotton (Perry et al. 1975). Identification of fiber provenance is not typically part of a forensic fiber examination, and examiners are more likely to exclude a fiber sample based on differences in length or morphology. Typically, yarns are not spun from just one source and there is a mixture of long and short fibers spun into the final product, so the variation in fiber morphology should be evaluated in a known sample.

Kapok fibers are smooth, hollow, cylindrical forms with thin cell walls that often bend sharply. The trapped air inside the cell walls and the lower density of these fibers relative to water made them ideal stuffing material for life jacket because of their buoyancy. Kapok fibers are readily identifiable with light microscopy (Figure 5.25). Specialized synthetic fibers, such as hollow polyester fibers, have generally replaced kapok as stuffing material; however, kapok fibers may still be encountered in casework.

Bast fibers (e.g. flax, hemp, jute, ramie) can be differentiated by the shape of their ultimates, the transverse joints where the ultimates join one another in a bundle, the cross-sectional shape, and the variable form of their lumens (Catling and Grayson 2004) (Figures 5.26–5.29). The morphological characteristics useful for differentiate these fibers are described in Table 5.1.

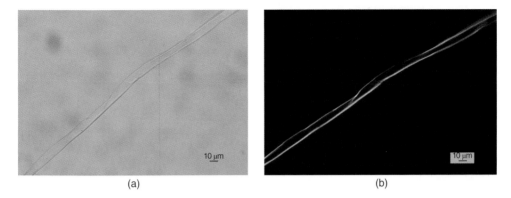

(a)   (b)

Figure 5.25 Kapok fiber under (a) transmitted light and (b) between crossed polars.

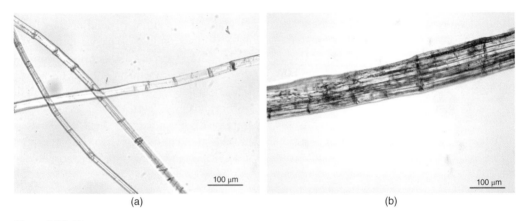

(a)   (b)

Figure 5.26 Flax.

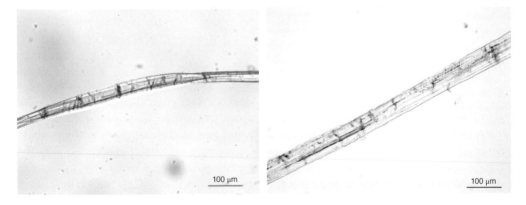

Figure 5.27 Hemp.

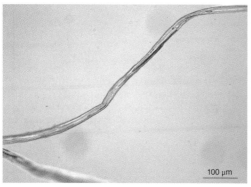 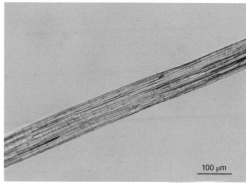

Figure 5.28 Jute.

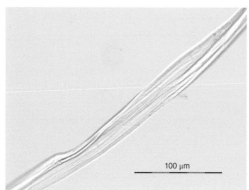 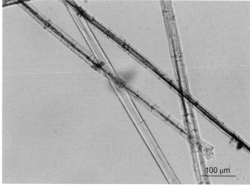

Figure 5.29 Ramie.

The cellular material in a plant is typically oriented in a particular direction (S or Z) during plant growth and this directionality can be used as a diagnostic aid to identification. This direction can be visualized through a drying twist test or microscopically with the aid of polarized light microscopy (PLM). If a bundle of fibers can be reduced to a few or a single ultimate, the fiber can be tested by the *drying twist method*. After immersing the fiber in water, it is held over a heat source and while drying the fiber will rotate in either a clockwise or counterclockwise direction (Figure 5.30). This movement in the drying process is indicative of the direction of growth, either S or Z twist. The twist direction can be used to differentiate bast fibers into two groups: those with a clockwise or counterclockwise twist or growth pattern (Table 5.1).

The direction of twist or growth can also be differentiated with PLM using the *Herzog test*. The Herzog method can reveal differences in the color of fibers under PLM with the addition of a full wave plate that correspond to the fiber's natural twist (SWGMAT 2004). A natural fiber with an S twist will appear yellow-orange under polarized light with the addition of a single wave plate when the fiber is oriented at the extinction position under crossed poles, and blue when oriented 90° off. For Z twist fibers this will be the opposite and the fibers oriented at their extinction position will appear blue and then yellow-orange when rotated 90° (Haugan and Holst 2013). Fibers should be oriented as close to their extinction position as possible rather than at a 45° angle to the polarizer or analyzer as there is some variation in natural fibers (Figure 5.31).

Table 5.1 Characteristics useful for differentiating among natural fibers

Fiber type	Turns clockwise as it dries (S twist fibers)	Turns counterclockwise as it dries (Z twist fibers)	Irregular	Herzog test at 0/270° extinction°	Characteristics of note Morphology
Cotton			Alternating	Multiple colors	Twists or convolutions
Flax	X			Blue	Expanded Transverse nodes, thick walls, small regular lumen
Hemp		X		Orange	Irregular diameter, numerous markings across bundle
Jute		X		Orange	Transverse joints bend, irregular lumen, and walls
Ramie	X			Blue	Thick walls, long ultimates, irregular lumen
Kapok*	X		X	Blue and orange	Hollow tubes with bends
Abaca		X		Orange	Spiral elements and stegmata
Sisal		X		Yellow-orange	Spiral elements at ends, undulation along edge of bundle
Coir*	X		Indecisive		Round silica stegmata along length of ultimates and in rows

* These fibers can also express a variable or no twist in the drying twist test.

  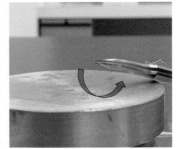

Figure 5.30 Drying twist test: as the above fiber dries, the tip starts to rotate in a counterclockwise direction.

Leaf Fibers While some fibers are processed down to the individual ultimates, the majority of leaf fibers remain in bundles able to be twisted into rough sack cloth and cordage. Identification of sisal plant fibers often relies on the presence of spiral elements found along the edges or within a fiber bundle; however, abaca fibers may also contain spiral elements.

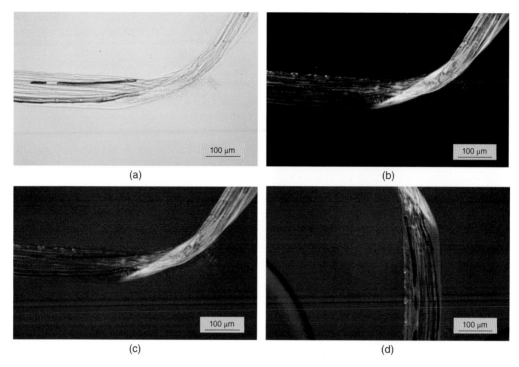

Figure 5.31 Sisal at 200×: (a) transmitted light PLM microscope, (b) crossed polars, (c) crossed polars with full wave plate inserted, Herzog colors will appear orange, and (d) undercrossed polars with full wave plate inserted, Herzog colors will appear blue.

Abaca can be differentiated by the presence of characteristic silica cells found longitudinally along the length of the bundle (see Figure 5.32). These cells appear rectangular with a circular depression along one side. The silica cells may be lost during processing so if they are absent, *Billinghame's test* (see Appendix 5.A) can be used to differentiate abaca from sisal (see Figure 5.33). Billinghame's test produces a color change in the fibers after cleaning, boiling, and soaking in a series of chemicals (Perry et al. 1975). As this is a semi-destructive test, it is not often used in forensic casework where microscopical analyses may be able to easily differentiate two fiber samples non-destructively.

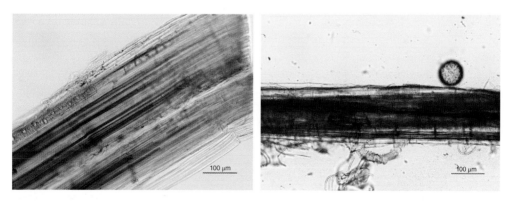

Figure 5.32 Leaf fibers: abaca (manilla) fiber with crystalline stegmata and spiral elements.

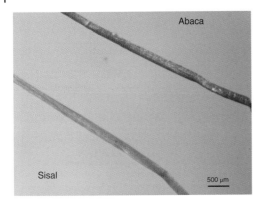

Figure 5.33 Color change in abaca and sisal after Billinghame's test.

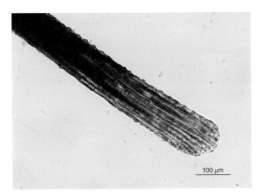

Figure 5.34 Fruit fiber: coir.

Fruit fibers, like coir fibers (Figure 5.34), are coarse short fibers that remain in distinct bundles with silica stegmata regularly spaced in rows along the fiber length (Perry et al. 1975). These fibers are typically used for ropes and mats as well as stuffing material and brushes as they are not soft and flexible enough for use in clothing textiles.

Animal fibers are wool, guard hairs, and underfur hairs as well as silk. Wool fibers are typically more elastic, and have a reduced medulla, higher water retention, and greater heat retention ability than other mammalian hairs. Processing wool and animal hairs into fibers prepared for use in textiles may modify the outer cuticle from mechanical damage and/or dyeing, potentially limiting an analysis to examination of the features present in the cortex and medulla.

Hair fibers are able to be classified to mammalian order, family, and potentially genus or species by their morphological structure and microscopic characteristics, particularly the cuticle patterns, pigment patterns within the cortex of the hair fiber, and the different medullary structures visible with transmitted light microscopy (Figure 5.35). Imaging by scanning electron microscopy (SEM) is very useful for capturing high-resolution images of cuticle pattern; however, SEM does not capture the internal microstructure or its variation along the length of a hair fiber that is often useful for identification (see Figure 5.36 above). Regional guides of mammalian hair are useful for comparison of images and descriptions to unknown hair fibers (Moore et al. 1974; Teerink 2003; Brunner and Coman 1974; Perry et al. 1975; Appleyard 1978). Human hairs can be microscopically discriminated from non-human hairs by hair morphology, pigment patterns, and medullary index

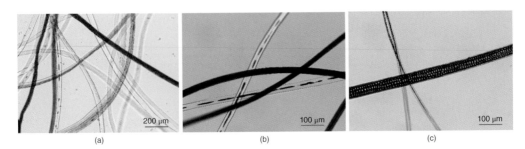

Figure 5.35 Animal hairs as textile fibers (transmitted light microscopy): (a) romney wool, (b) alpaca, (c) angora rabbit.

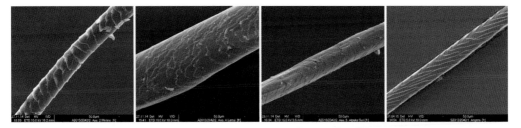

Figure 5.36 SEM images: merino wool, llama, alpaca, and angora rabbit. Source: Courtesy of ETHG fiber type information system.

(Kshirsagar et al. 2009; Deedrick and Koch 2004a,b; Ogle and Fox 1998). Additional reference material from commercial fur animals and from different species and breeds of wool producers is essential to have on hand in order to study the morphological differences along the length of animal hair fibers and wool, the varying scale patterns, and medullary structures. By creating reference slides of known hairs often found in textiles, a new examiner can compare hairs taken directly from an animal pelt with potentially altered hair or wool collected from a worn or damaged textile.

Silk fibers are typically lustrous, translucent white (before dyeing) with a triangular cross-section, though some less processed silk fibers may still have some of the sericin that glues raw silk filaments together. Silk may be differentiated as wild or cultivated. Wild silk may or may not have the gum removed, has a light tan color, and is almost rectangular in cross-section (Perry et al. 1975). Tussah silk is a type of wild silk and has a rough, uneven appearance (Perry et al. 1975). Duppioni silk is produced when two silkworms spin their cocoons together producing entangled fibers and irregular yarn similar to Tussah silk but white in color and more easily dyed (Perry et al. 1975). Silk fibers have some variation along their length and may appear as two strands fused together as shown in Figure 5.13.

Manufactured Fibers Man-made fibers generally appear more uniform in morphology than natural fibers though natural silk can be hard to differentiate from manufactured at first glance.

Some useful properties to note among the major man-made fiber types are detailed in Table 5.2 and Figures 5.16–5.23.

5.3.4 Comparison

The microscopic characteristics, optical properties, and chemical composition of a fiber are all taken into account when conducting a fiber comparison. The next sections in this chapter describe the major features, instrumentation, and exam flow with special focus on the physical characteristics of a fiber (e.g. color, diameter, cross-sectional shape, delustrants) using a comparison microscope, the optical properties (e.g. sign of elongation, dichroism, refractive indices or relative refractive index, birefringence, fluorescence) using PLM and fluorescence microscopy, and the chemical composition of fibers using FTIR. As color is one of the primary characteristics that helps an examiner differentiate fibers, the methods used to discriminate among fibers by color are discussed further in the sections describing microscopical comparisons, and the spectra produced with microspectrophotometry (MSP) and Raman spectroscopy. Comparisons of dyes can be carried out chemically with thin-layer chromatography (TLC), high performance liquid chromatography (HPLC), and/or Raman spectroscopy. All non-destructive testing should be performed prior to any destructive testing or, if the sample is large enough, a small portion of the fiber can be tested with semi-destructive tests such as FTIR (destructive to a fiber's morphology) or destructive

Table 5.2 Fiber properties useful to differentiate among manufactured fiber types

Fiber type	n‖	n⊥	Sign of elongation	Birefringence	Shape or description?
Acetate	1.474–1.485	1.473–1.480	+	0.002–0.005	Irregular/serrated longitudinally, and trilobal
Acrylic	1.510–1.520	1.512–1.252	−	−0.001 to −0.005	Dogbone, round, or acorn cross-section
Aramid: Kevlar (K) Nomex (N)	K: 2.05–2.35 N: 1.8–1.9	K: 1.641–1.646 N: 1.664–1.68	+	K: 0.2–0.72 N: 0.12–0.23	Zipper-like line visible in center
Elastomer	1.561	1.56	+	0.001	Typically, opaque and highly elastic, large diameter
Modacrylic	1.528–1.535	1.523–1.533	±	0.002–0.005	Dogbone to near-round cross-section
Nylon	1.568–1.583	1.515–1.526	+	0.049–0.063	Numerous cross-sectional shapes
PET	1.66–1.73	1.52–1.55	+	0.160–0.170	Circular to lobed cross-section, hollow, and polygonal
PP PE	PP: 1.520–1.53 PE: 1.568–1.574	PP: 1.491–1.496 PE: 1.518–1.522	+	0.028–0.034 0.5–0.52	Typically round cross-section. If colored, look for pigment particles within the polymer as these fibers cannot be dyed, also look for draw marks
Rayon	1.541–1.549	1.520–1.521	+	0.02–0.039	Serrated to near-round cross-section
Triacetate	1.469–1.472	1.468–1.472	±	0–0.001	Irregular to round cross-section
Glass	1.47–1.57	same	−	Isotropic	Uniform diameter, clear

PET, polyethylene terephthalate; PP, polypropylene; PE, polyethylene.
Source: Refractive index data are compiled from: Stoeffler (1996), the European Textile and Hair Group Fibre Type Information System, DuPont & Company (1961), Smalldon (1973), and the AATCC Test Method 20A-20018, Fiber Analysis: Quantitative, 2010.

tests such as solubility or melting point. Documentation of the tests and results from each method used should support conclusions that the fibers are consistent in the properties analyzed or are dissimilar.

5.4 Microscopical Analysis

In forensic casework, a variety of microscopes is necessary for fiber analyses.

Microscopy is the basis for all further examination of fibers. It is a highly discriminating technique and allows for identification and discrimination of the physical characteristics (morphological features) of natural and manufactured fibers. It also allows for determination of the different optical characteristics that will be discussed in more detail later.

Prior to all microscopic examinations, the microscope must be checked to establish that it is set up correctly. This step is essential to ensure the results obtained from your microscopic examinations are reliable.

Routine adjustment of all brightfield microscopes for Köhler illumination (see Chapter 3) is necessary, as is color balancing for comparison microscopes. Based on the type of microscope and individual laboratory policy, other calibration and performance checks (e.g. stage centration and eyepiece scale calibration) will be needed and should be carried out on a regular basis.

Generally, fibers and fiber fragments are observed in longitudinal view, but examination of cross-sectioned material may be required to gain additional information that may be of value for establishing manufacturer features. Optical cross-sectioning by raising and lowering the microscope stage to estimate the shape may provide enough information for a determination of the cross-sectional shape. However, physical cross-sectioning of a fiber can provide additional information (e.g. reveal the inner fiber structure, depth of penetration/distribution of delustrants, dyes, pigments) (see Figure 5.37).

5.4.1 Stereomicroscopy

A stereomicroscope allows three-dimensional viewing of objects with the ability to search for fibers on an item of evidence or in a debris collection under the microscope because of the variable working distance at a range of low order magnifications. To set up a stereomicroscope, one first places a specimen within the field of view at the lowest magnification, then focuses on the object while focusing the eyepiece to your own vision. If this is done properly, then objects will remain in focus as the magnification changes.

A fiber examination routinely involves an examination of tape lifts collected from the surface of a questioned item, debris collections, and smaller items of evidence that can be examined under a stereomicroscope. Features such as a fiber's length, its outer shape, and some production characteristics can be detected with this type of microscopy. Color and color distribution play an important role in the ability of an examiner to detect differences or similarities at low magnification. If searching for fibers of a particular color or size, fibers that show notable differences to the known sample can be eliminated from further examination at this stage. Fibers that show no differences or a representative sample of all fiber types and colors should be mounted on glass microscope slides with a suitable mounting media to allow for examination of fiber properties in more detail with the aid of higher magnification microscopes. The choice of mounting media will differ between laboratories but should allow for visualization of a variety of fibers of varied refractive indices. The

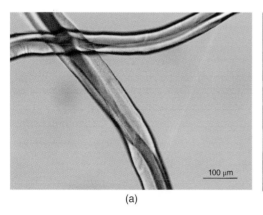

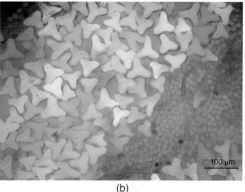

(a)   (b)

Figure 5.37 Trilobal fiber morphology (a) longitudinal view and (b) in cross-section.

fibers being compared should be mounted in the same medium. Extreme care must be taken to prevent loss or contamination during the process of collection from items of evidence and during the preparation of the fibers on glass microscope slides.

5.4.2 Brightfield Microscopy

Brightfield microscopy involves transmitting light through a sample and observing the characteristics visible under a range of magnifications. This type of microscopic examination of textile fibers provides a non-destructive means to better describe the morphological features and helps to distinguish between different fiber types and manufacture.

Natural fibers can be distinguished and identified primarily by their morphological features. Man-made fibers also offer a wide range of different morphological features (e.g. diameter, cross-sectional shape, delustrant particles, channels, or voids, inclusions, pigments) which enable the examiner to distinguish between them. Besides morphological features, the type of coloration (e.g. print and type of print, spin dye, fiber dye, yarn, or fabric dye) can be determined with the help of a brightfield microscope. Some of this information can be obtained under a stereomicroscope but other details will only be visible at a higher magnification.

5.4.3 Polarized Light Microscopy

PLM allows a fiber's optical properties (e.g. pleochroism, sign of elongation, refractive indices, birefringence, and retardation) to be studied and is useful for identifying fiber types. PLM is used to determine if a material is isotropic (not visible when analyzer and polarizer are crossed) or anisotropic (visible when analyzer and polarizer are crossed). Fiberglass is an example of an isotropic fiber, as fiberglass has the same optical properties in all directions and will not be visible when placed between a crossed analyzer and polarizer. Other fiber types are anisotropic and have

two different refractive indices 90° apart, noted as $n_\parallel$ (parallel) and $n_\perp$ (perpendicular).

With natural fibers PLM can be used to differentiate some morphological features more clearly (e.g. crossover marks in silk), and to distinguish mercerized cotton from untreated cotton. The Herzog test may also be used to indicate the S or Z twist of the ultimates in natural fibers (see Table 5.1) but this test can be difficult to interpret and not many forensic fiber examiners rely on the Herzog test when identifying natural fiber types.

For manufactured fibers, the polymer type is determinable from the optical characteristics. PLM can be used to determine the refractive index of a fiber both in parallel ($\parallel$) and perpendicular ($\perp$) directions relative to the fiber length, or to make a determination of relative refractive index (i.e. greater or less than the mounting medium) in either or both directions. In plane polarized light, the Becke line is observed moving in or out of a fiber while the stage is lowered. The Becke line moves toward the material of higher refractive index, either the fiber or the mounting medium. An authenticated collection of fiber types is necessary for learning how to differentiate the material by refractive index. Additionally, a table listing the optical properties of generic fiber types may be consulted. For confirmation and more specific classification into fiber subtypes, other methods would be employed, such as FTIR, melting point, or solubility testing.

For determining fiber type, a glass microscope slide containing the fiber sample is placed on a microscope stage with an analyzer and polarizer inserted in the light path at right angles. In this way light is blocked under the crossed polars to the oculars. By placing a fiber in the path between the two polars the fiber interferes with the rays of light and the resulting interference colors within a fiber provide information about the sign of elongation. If the fiber appears gray under crossed polars, then adding a full wave plate can help to determine the sign of elongation. If the fiber appears blue, then it was in the low positive range prior to the addition of one full order on the Michel–Lévy chart. However, if the fiber appears orange, then the sign of elongation was on the negative side of the gray region on the Michel–Lévy chart. Additionally, the interference colors can give an indication if the fiber is a low order or moderate to high order by how bright or pale they are relative to the Michel–Lévy chart. A quartz wedge or Berek compensator are especially useful for the analysis of moderate to higher order interference colors and to find the extinction point when determining a fiber's birefringence. More detailed information can be found in Section 5.7 and Table 5.2. The examination between crossed polars can assist in identifying a fiber's type but care should be taken since very fine and very thick diameters or heavily dyed fibers may cause difficulties.

PLM also offers the possibility to observe if dichroism is present in a fiber or not (De Wael and Lepot 2011, 2012; De Wael and Driessche 2011a,b; De Wael 2012). When a fiber in plane polarized light appears to be one color when oriented horizontally in the field of view but appears a different color or shade when oriented vertically then the light is being differentially absorbed based on orientation and the fiber is dichroic.

In combination with a hot stage, PLM may help with further classification as the softening range and melting point of a fiber can be determined more easily if carried out under polarized light.

5.4.4 Fluorescence Microscopy

Fluorescence microscopy involves exposing fibers to specific wavelengths of light where some of that light may be absorbed and re-emitted as fluorescence at a longer wavelength. A range of broadband excitation and barrier filters is typically used to assess the potential fluorescence in the ultraviolet (UV), violet, blue, and green regions of light.

During a fiber examination, whether or not a fiber fluoresces under excitation is noted, with a focus on the color and intensity of the fluorescence. Care should be taken to not focus too long on any one spot along a fiber as photobleaching and quenching can happen. This is the loss or reduction of fluorescing capability that can affect both the analysis and any replication of the fiber examination, which is often necessary for confirmation of results. A fiber's ability to fluorescence may vary along the length of a fiber or among the fibers making up the textile material due to artifacts or post-production treatment. It is therefore necessary to choose fibers from both the warp and weft of a textile as well as from among the differently colored fibers making up a textile material to make sure that all potential variations are detected. Handheld UV lights may provide an early indicator if such variation exists within a textile material. Fluorescence may arise from the fiber type, additives, or treatments (e.g. dye, washing powder, optical brighteners). Fibers being examined for fluorescence should be mounted in a non-fluorescing medium.

5.4.5 Comparison Microscopy

A comparison microscope is an absolute necessity in forensic fiber examinations as it allows direct comparison of two fiber samples at the same time. A comparison microscope is two compound microscopes joined by an optical bridge that allows examiners to place glass microscope slides on the stage of each microscope to view questioned and known fibers in a side-by-side field of view. Each side is minimally a brightfield microscope but may be equipped with polarizing and/or fluorescence capabilities. These microscopes are equipped with a range of higher magnifications, generally ranging from 40× to 500×, allowing examiners to differentiate fibers based on close inspection of color, diameter, shape, inclusions, and other microscopic characteristics.

If fibers are found to be similar by the first stage of analysis, then additional testing follows, though the order may vary depending on laboratory equipment and examiner preference. Some examiners conduct the majority of their examination with a comparison microscope, and then use other microscopes and equipment to further test the fibers, while others primarily work on a PLM and move to a comparison microscope once a small subset of fibers has been identified as needing additional testing. Not all comparison microscopes are equipped with fluorescence capabilities; however, such testing should be done and the results compared.

5.4.6 Scanning Electron Microscopy

SEM allows information about the fiber form or surface structure to be obtained by focusing a very fine beam of electrons on a fiber sample. From the interaction of the electrons with the fiber's molecular composition a pseudo three-dimensional image is produced that captures the features present in the fiber at much higher magnifications than light microscopy.

SEM is useful for fine morphological characterization of fiber surfaces. For a detailed examination of wool or hair scales it is an especially useful technique, but as it is a surface technique, it does not capture an image of the internal microstructure, which may be more definitive for species identification of hair fibers. Besides the fine detailed examination of fiber surface characteristics, SEM has the potential to be able to detect debris on the surface of a fiber and capture an image of the fiber cross-sectional shape (Roux 1999; Stoney and Stoney 2012). In cases where fabric damage is being examined, the fiber edges may show specific characteristics that are consistent with cuts (knife, scissor) or tears (Pelton 1995). Scanning electron microscopy with energy dispersive X-ray spectroscopy (SEM/EDX) may also be used for the identification of pigments and delustrants (additives applied as flame

retardants), or the elemental composition of glass fibers (Lynch 1981).

5.5 Instrumental Analysis

In addition to the previously described microscopical methods (here and in Chapter 3) other techniques may be of further assistance in identifying or discriminating fibers and are often used in forensic fiber examinations. The use of the different methods depends on their availability in the market and on the specific equipment within each laboratory. At a minimum, comparison microscopy, PLM, and fluorescent light microscopy should be conducted for a comparison of fiber samples with an additional method to analyze the color or dye of a fiber such as MSP (Palenik et al. 2015; Walbridge-Jones 2009) or HPLC, and FTIR to confirm the fiber type initially determined by PLM.

5.5.1 Microspectrophotmetry: UV-Visible

MSP offers additional discriminating power beyond comparison microscopy for color. MSP is an instrumental technique that is used to measure the absorbance, transmission, or emission of the wavelengths of light that interact with colored fibers. While our eyes are very sensitive to small color differences, environmental factors and lighting conditions can affect color perception. Color differences are easier to detect when comparing large samples of uniformly dyed fibers and often more difficult to distinguish when dealing with individual fibers that may have variable dye uptake. *Metamerism* is an aspect of color that must be addressed when comparing colored fibers. Under different light conditions and different orientations of a fiber under polarized light, differently colored fibers can appear similar. Metameric pairs may appear to be the same visually but can be differentiated with the use of MSP. Fibers are colored by dyes or pigments, and our eyes perceive the color by how light is absorbed and reflected. MSP offers a method to measure the interaction of light with the fiber sample in either transmittance or absorbance.

MSP can be used to graphically compare the spectra produced from fiber samples exposed to a range of wavelengths. The range of wavelengths covers ~ 380–800 nm in the visible range and ~190–380 nm into the UV range for those instruments capable of extending into the UV range. Differences in dye components (e.g. optical brighteners) may not be detected if spectroscopy is restricted to the visible range (Macrae et al. 1979). If extending into the UV region, it is critical that the microscope be equipped with mirrored or quartz objectives, the sample be mounted on quartz slides with coverslips, and the mounting medium be non-UV absorbing. The resulting graphical representation, or spectrum, plots wavelength on the x axis versus the intensity of light absorbed, transmitted, or reflected on the y axis.

5.5.2 Fourier Transform Infrared Spectroscopy

FTIR spectroscopy is an important technique to confirm the fiber type for synthetic fibers and to identify subgroups. Typically, fiber type is initially determined with PLM. For synthetic fibers, additional information can be obtained with IR spectroscopy regarding the subclass of a fiber as the chemical composition is more specifically identified by spectral analysis (e.g. whether a nylon fiber is type 6 or 6.6). For natural fibers, PLM is sufficient for identifying fiber type as fiber morphology provides more specific information for differentiating these fibers than chemical composition (i.e. different plant fibers come up as cellulose when tested by IR and wool/hair fibers as protein).

With IR analysis, samples are exposed to IR radiation and based on the chemical composition of the fibers some of that radiation is absorbed. A graphical representation, or spectrum, is produced that plots the wavelengths or frequency of infrared radiation on the x axis versus the intensity of radiation absorbed or transmitted on the y axis. Specific chemical component information on dyes and other additives may also be present within the spectra as minor peaks and can be useful when comparing a sample against a known reference.

Spectra may be obtained by a variety of IR techniques, using either transmittance or reflectance (Peets et al., 2019), on potassium bromide (KBr) plates or a diamond compression cell. In general, the wavelength range for analysis will be from 4000 to 600 cm^{-1}; however, this depends on the detector and the method used.

Preparations should be carried out under a stereomicroscope to avoid losing small fiber fragments. The same fibers should be examined throughout the analytical process to ensure sample variation does not impact a conclusion. Individual fibers that have consistent properties throughout the non-destructive portion of an examination protocol are then be tested further with semi-destructive techniques such as FTIR. The fibers may need to be removed from their previous mounting medium and cleaned with a solvent (e.g. xylene) to remove any oil or mounting media adhering to the fiber prior to being flattened. Flattening round or uneven fibers reduces scattering and produces better quality spectra for identifying peaks and conducting library searches. It should be noted that the degree of flattening may affect the spectra and interference fringes may occur if flattened too much (Tungol et al. 1993; Bartick et al. 1994). A compression cell (medium or high pressure) can be used to flatten fibers or hold elastomeric fibers under compression. Fibers can be flattened with a roller or by applying pressure from a flat surface such as the side of a razor blade. The surface of a razor blade may also add texture to a flattened fiber surface, which can be useful for polymers that continue to refract light during analysis, thus improving spectral quality.

FTIR spectroscopy is a technique that allows a fiber examiner to obtain additional information about polymer composition, and the fiber's generic class and subclass. In situations where an FTIR instrument is out of service, micro-chemical testing or melting point determination may provide some backup, but such tests cannot always give sufficient information about a fiber's subtype and are not part of a typical forensic examination because of their destructive nature.

Attenuated total reflection (ATR) and micro internal reflection spectroscopy are surface sampling techniques. When using these techniques, it is important to have the sample in direct contact with the crystal. ATR attachments are readily available for IR microscopes. While ATR may offer some benefits for opaque or highly absorbing samples, carbon-filled rubber and fibers can scatter just as badly with ATR as with transmission spectroscopy.

5.5.3 Raman Spectroscopy

Raman spectroscopy is a non-destructive technique that provides data on the vibrational energy levels within a material that is complementary, and at times supplementary (e.g. dye and pigment information), to that obtained by IR and MSP. Raman spectroscopy can aid the identification and comparison of dyes contained within polymers or the identification of fiber classes and subclasses (Meleiro and Garcia-Ruiz 2016). With this technique the focus lies on the characterization of colored fibers since FTIR is still the method of choice for identifying the chemical composition of most fibers; however, Raman spectra may prove to be helpful with the identification of certain classes and subclasses of fibers, including natural fibers (e.g. cellulosics and vegetable fibers) (Coyle and Fairchild 2003; Coyle et al. 2007; Edwards et al. 1997; Keen et al. 1998; Miller and Bartick 2001). As FTIR focuses on a different aspect of the interaction of electromagnetic radiations with a material

than Raman spectroscopy, the two methods complement each other. For example, chemical bonds that are weak or inactive in FTIR may be stronger in Raman spectroscopy, and strong IR absorbers (e.g. water) are sometimes weak or not active in Raman spectroscopy. While IR detects an absorption from a permanent dipole moment within the targeted molecular system, Raman induces polarizability to produce an inelastic scattering effect. This complementary nature explains the abilities of the two methods to gather data about the polymeric properties of fibers and their colorant contents respectively.

Dyes and pigments tend to dominate Raman spectral results, but in some cases information from the fiber substrate also appears in the spectra. For the identification of dyes and pigments, the use of a reference spectral database is required. Care must be taken with interpretation of individual spectra since different dyes can provide similar spectral results. An identification depends on the availability of a reference database and the number and variety of references contained within.

A Raman instrument needs to be equipped with a microscope to provide a reflected beam path. The depth of focus and the spot size for the laser changes with the objective's magnification. A confocal microscope allows the depth of focus to diminish to about 2 µm; however, this comes with a loss of signal. The spot size obtained with a 50× objective lens is approximately 10 µm and with a 100× objective lens is approximately 1–3 µm, which offer the suitable conditions to target single fibers.

Dispersive as well as non-dispersive instruments can typically be fitted with a microscope, and this is necessary for the analysis of single fibers. With a dispersive instrument, scattered light from the sample is split into different wavenumber intervals by a diffraction grating. The sensitivity of a dispersive instrument depends on the spectral resolution, and this is dependent on the number of lines per millimeter in the diffraction grating. The dispersed light will be projected to the charge-coupled detector (CCD). With a non-dispersive instrument, the light is not separated into different wavelengths and instead a single beam is detected by the detector. For the analysis of single fibers, dispersive instruments generally provide better results in comparison to non-dispersive instruments when used in combination with a microscope (Hemmings 2018).

To reduce fluorescence an operator can change the laser wavelength (i.e., using a longer wavelength such as a source in the near-infrared range), decrease laser power, use a short exposure time, use longer exposures to quench the fluorophore, and/or adjust the focus. Longer wavelengths can reduce the effects of fluorescence but are accompanied by a decrease in signal strength and an increase in noise. Shorter wavelengths with higher intensities show an increase in signal strength and less noise but are often accompanied by increased fluorescence effects originating from the fiber. It is therefore advisable to fit the instrument with at least two different lasers, so the signal is significantly stronger than the noise.

The combination of lasers from the visible and the near-infrared (NIR) range often provide sufficient complementary information. The availability of more lasers may prove to be helpful for some examinations. Lasers in the blue, green, red, and NIR are commercially available. In the visible range, green 514 nm or green 532 nm are often used in combination with an NIR source (e.g. NIR 785 nm or 830 nm) to provide complementary information.

UV lasers are also available but as they are prone to safety issues and they currently do not play a large role in forensic fiber examinations (Thomas et al. 2005). Lasers have a limited life span and care must be taken to replace them over time.

When preparing samples for Raman spectroscopy, a low magnification microscope should be used to avoid loss or contamination. Fibers do not need to be flattened as they do

for FTIR analysis, and Raman analysis can be done on the same sample preparation that was used for FTIR. Samples can be placed on a potassium bromide plate, a metal substrate with the fiber held in place by double-sided tape, or on a diamond cell, though diamond will give a Raman signal so examiners should keep sample preparation in mind when interpreting the spectral data. Fibers prepared on a glass slide for microscopy can also be used without any additional sample preparation. However, care needs to be taken to prevent interference from glass slides or mounting media (e.g. masking of Raman signals). Quartz cover slips may help to reduce such interference since quartz is less intrusive at 785 nm than standard glass. Quartz and diamond both contribute a peak to the spectra, but these peaks are sharp and do not tend to interfere as much as a glass slide. Equipping the microscope for the confocal mode may prevent interferences from glass cover slips, mounting media, and diamond cells, etc.

5.5.4 Other Analytical Techniques (Non-routine)

There are additional analytical techniques available which can be used on occasion, though the use of any destructive techniques should only be conducted if all parties in a criminal case agree to sample destruction.

5.5.4.1 Thin-layer Chromatography

Dyed fibers often contain a mixture of colorants that are combined to achieve a given color. TLC is a method that uses a solvent to chemically separate out the components of a colorant (ASTM 2227). The ease of dye extraction and the particular extractant required will depend on the generic class of the fiber and the dye class present (Geiss 1987; Hamilton and Hamilton 1987; Home and Dudley 1981; Rendle and Wiggins 1995; Resua 1980; Laing et al. 1990). The generic class of the known and recovered fibers must be determined prior to TLC analysis in order to choose the correct extraction procedure. Dye extraction and classification schemes have been developed which generally allow single fibers to be sequentially extracted (ASTM 2227). When it is necessary to classify very pale fibers, a large sample size (e.g. multiple fibers) will be needed. Reactive dyes, which are used on cotton and wool, can cause problems for extraction.

TLC plates should be examined immediately after drying using visible and UV light. Band(s),

position(s), and colors should be noted. Plates should be documented by photography and stored in a manner that minimizes fading. Metameric coloration of fibers can be detected using the UV/visible range. If spectroscopy is restricted to the UV range, differences in dye components may be undetected. This method should only be used after all other analyses have been carried out on the fibers as it is a destructive process.

Table 5.3 Melting point determination and thermal decomposition

Man-made fibers	Material	Melting point (°C)	Thermal decomposition (°C)
Natural polymer	Cellulosic ester		
	Acetate	250–260	255–260
	Triacetate	288–300	300
	Regenerated cellulose		
	Cupro		175–205
	Lyocell		175–205
	Modal		175–205
	Rayon/viscose		175–205
Synthetic polymer	Melamine		350
	Modacrylic	190	
	Novoloid		>150
	Polyacrylnitrile		250–350
	Poly(amid imide)	400	
	Nylon 6	215–220	310–380
	Nylon 6.6	250–260	310–380
	Polyester		
	PET	250–260	283–306
	PBT	220–230	232–267
	PTT	225–230	
	Polyolefin		
	Polyethylene	115–135	328–410
	Polypropylene	160–175	
	Polyurethane, segmented		200
	Polyvinyl		180–210
Other	Ceramic	1815	2300
	Glass	1200–1300	
	Metal	1400	

PET, polyethylene terephthalate; PBT, polybutylene terephthalate; PTT, polytrimethylene terephthalate.

5.5.4.2 Pyrolysis-Gas Chromatography Mass Spectrometry and Pyrolysis-Mass Spectrometry

Pyrolysis is a destructive analytical method and therefore consideration must be given to whether or not this technique should be applied, which will depend on the sample size and the amount of material that would be consumed during analysis. Pyrolysis gas chromatography can be used to identify natural and man-made fiber types and to compare between samples (Causin et al. 2006; Roux et al. 2017; King 2016).

5.5.4.3 High-Performance Liquid Chromatography

HPLC is another technique that can separate and identify dyes from colored fibers (Goodpaster and Liszewski 2009). Different dye compositions may produce similarly colored fibers that cannot be differentiated optically, but may be able to be discriminated based on a chromatographic analysis of the dye mixture used to color the fiber. HPLC separates dyes from fibers through a micro extraction process, one that works on multiple fiber types (e.g. nylon, polyester, acrylic), dye types (acid, basic, direct, disperse, and reactive), dye mixtures, and fiber lengths, especially small fragments (Chen et al. 1997; McMaster 2007; White and Catterick 1993; White 1994; Carey et al. 2013). When dyes can be extracted, data obtained from HPLC can be used to further differentiate fibers in a forensic fiber examination and complement information obtained through microscopy and spectrophotometry. In general, HPLC is reproducible (with sufficient sample sizes), but it can be difficult to separate dyes on a single chromatographic system. Standard dyes are needed for performance testing and validation of the system prior to use.

5.5.4.4 Melting Point

In order to analyze the melting point of a fiber, a microscope must be fitted with a hot stage so an examiner can observe the changes in the fiber as the temperature is slowly raised. Prior to attempting this technique, a preliminary determination of fiber class is necessary as there are fiber types that have similar ranges of melting point temperatures. Accordingly, melting point should be considered a complementary technique to PLM and/or FTIR that may prove helpful in some fiber examinations (Grieve 1983; Hartshorne and Laing 1984; Hartshorne et al. 1991; Kisler-Rao 2015). If the general fiber type is known, then the melting point can be used to differentiate the subtype (see Table 5.3).

5.6 Microscopic Characteristics to Note in Forensic Fiber Examinations

Description of *color* may differ between two examiners but also by the same person on different days or times of day so documentation at the time of comparison is essential to moving forward with any examination and to conduct the same analysis on all the fibers in a short period of time.

Measurement of the *diameter* of the fiber must be conducted on a microscope that has first had the scale bar within the ocular calibrated against a stage micrometer.

Determining the *cross-sectional shape* may be difficult when viewed longitudinally but by moving the stage up and down one can focus on the fiber at varying levels to see how the shape changes. During training such optical cross-sectioning should be performed on samples of known cross-sectional shapes to train the eye to recognize different cross-sections when viewed longitudinally.

The presence of any additional microscopic characteristics such as delustrants, pigment, draw marks, etc. should be noted and described in notes.

5.7 Optical Properties

Fibers (other than glass) are anisotropic materials meaning that they have at least two refractive indexes. These refractive indexes can be determined in relation to a fiber's alignment with the polarizing filters in parallel (‖) or perpendicular (⊥). Refractive index can be directly measured through immersion in a series of oils of known refractive index until the fiber is no longer refracting light differently from the mounting media in that orientation or it can be estimated by a process of determining the relative refractive index. Relative refractive index uses the known refractive index of the mounting medium as its baseline and the appearance and movement of the Becke line under polarized light to determine which is higher: the fiber or the mounting medium. By increasing the working distance (moving the stage of the microscope down) the movement of the Becke line helps show which has a higher refractive index. If a fiber has the higher refractive index, then the Becke line will move toward the center of the fiber. If the mounting medium has the higher index, then the Becke line moves away from the fiber and toward the mounting medium. By noting greater than, less than, or equal to for both n-parallel and n-perpendicular in a chart or examination notes, the relationship of the fiber's refractive index to the mounting medium is documented (see Table 5.2).

Birefringence is determined by dividing the path difference by the thickness or diameter of the fiber. The path difference is determined by finding the extinction point of the fiber either by inserting a full wave plate or a compensator and comparing to the Michel–Lévy chart.

Determining the *sign of elongation* of a fiber is an important step to indicate high or low order birefringence. Using a PLM and orienting a fiber at a 45° angle in the field of view, if a fiber appears colored when placed between crossed polars then it is generally positive and a moderate or high order fiber. If it appears gray or white when the polars are crossed, then it is typically a low order fiber. A full wave plate is then inserted into a PLM to determine whether the sign of elongation is positive or negative. If the fiber appears orange when the

fiber is oriented parallel to the compensator it is negative and if blue then it is positive. Besides the fiber orientation, the color of the fiber must also be taken into account as the dye may alter the orange/blue determination. There are exceptions to this and a new fiber examiner must become very familiar with the Michel–Lévy chart as very high order fibers may appear white, yet have faint colors barely visible along the edges of the fiber.

Dichroism should be noted by turning a fiber on a rotating stage in plane polarized light to see if the color or shade of the fiber appears different based upon its orientation (De Wael and Lepot 2011, 2012; De Wael and Driessche 2011a,b; De Wael 2012).

Fluorescence should be noted by subjecting a fiber to light with difference excitation wavelengths and then noting if there is fluorescence, its color and intensity.

5.8 Chemistry

5.8.1 Solubility Testing

In the early days of forensic fiber examinations solubility tests were used to identify man-made fibers. There are several analytical schemes for fiber examination (Du Pont & Company 1961; Hall 1982; ASTM E2227-13) through which a fiber will successively be placed in different chemicals. It is recommended that tests are run under a microscope so the rate and degree of fiber solubility can be best assessed.

- Even after the introduction of more sophisticated instrumentation, there remains some information that is arguably best achieved via microchemical tests. The low cost associated with microchemical tests along with lack of equipment maintenance, fast testing times, and little sample preparation keep microchemical tests in use today. Though destructive, very small sample sizes are necessary because chemical tests are best performed under a stereomicroscope, allowing observation of any reaction which may occur.

- Reagents, acids, and/or solvents are added dropwise or via capillary action and any resulting reactions noted. Reactions include solubility observations as well as any other effect, such as color changes, effervescence (release of air bubbles), or swelling. While generally no specific chemical information is obtained, fibers with different pigments or delustrants may behave differently. Thus, differences in microchemical reactions provide visual discrimination of fiber composition.

5.9 Forensic Examination

5.9.1 Analytical Scheme

Having reviewed the methods of fiber production, the types of fibers typically found in casework, and the types of analyses used in a forensic examination, this section will discuss the role sample selection and case circumstances play in an analytical scheme. In a typical case, debris will be collected from items of evidence through picking, tape lifting, scraping, and/or vacuuming. With the collection of fibers from a scene or evidence, the analysis has already begun. Some questions must be asked early on to ensure the reliability of the process: Are you searching for all fibers that may be present or collecting a representative sample? Can you use the case information to target search for particular color(s) or fiber types for collection and analysis? These are important considerations and a fiber examiner's training should include exposure to a range of cases that incorporate these different collection methodologies.

Under low magnification, target sampling based on the known reference sample (fiber color, shape, appearance, etc.) can be useful to reduce the amount of fibers that must be further compared microscopically.

Once the fibers that are to be examined under higher magnification are preserved on glass microscope slides, comparison between known samples or between fibers from two different people or environments commences. Many laboratories have specific worksheets to document physical characteristics and optical properties assessed through a series of microscopical examinations. Once two (or more) fibers have been identified through comparison microscopy as visually corresponding in their microscopic characteristics (e.g. color, diameter, shape, delustrants) then these fibers are the focus of more detailed analysis of the optical properties (e.g. sign of elongation, refractive index, dichroism, birefringence) and a chart can help to document those examinations.

Fiber color can be one of the easiest ways to distinguish between fibers. Comparing fiber color starts with comparison microscopy and should be accompanied by analyzing the spectra produced with a UV/visible microspectrophotometer. Likewise, the fiber type is first assessed with a PLM and the chemical composition of a fiber confirmed through FTIR spectroscopy by comparing a fiber spectrum to reference library spectra and against known samples. A chart to document the physical characteristics visible with transmitted light microscopy, the optical properties studied with PLM and fluorescence microscopy, as well as additional techniques used in an analysis (MSP, FTIR, etc.) is useful in documenting fiber examinations (Table 5.4).

5.9.2 Fabric and Cordage Examinations

5.9.2.1 Fabric Damage

Fabric damage examinations necessitate a thorough familiarity with fabric construction (woven, knit, or non-woven) and the various fiber types used to make up the textile material before assessing how the damage could have occurred. Suspected areas of damage should be photographed and examined for transferred material prior to conducting any potentially destructive examinations. A fabric damage examination typically starts with documenting

Table 5.4 Example of a table used to document the physical characteristics, optical properties, and spectral comparison of a questioned fiber to a known sample.

	Questioned fiber___	Known fiber___
Comparison microscopy		
Mounting media RI	1.524	1.524
Color	Red	Red
Diameter	~25 μm	~25 μm
Cross-sectional shape	Bilobal	Bilobal
Inclusions	Some voids, delustrants	Some voids, delustrants
Polarized light microscopy		
Sign of elongation	+	+
Path difference	2750	2750
Dichroic	No	No
(Relative RI shown here) n‖	>1.524	>1.524
n⊥	>1.524	>1.524
Birefringence	0.157	0.157
	Q fiber is consistent with fibers from KN sample by PLM	
Fluorescence microscopy		
UV filter:Ex330-380/ DM400/BA435-485	None	None
V filter: Ex380-420/ DM430/BA450	Green	Green
B filter: Ex450-490/ DM500/BA515	Bright green	Bright green
G filter: Ex510-560/DM565/ BA590	Red	Red
	Q fiber is consistent with fibers from KN sample by fluorescence microscopy	
Spectroscopy		
UV-Vis Microspectrophotometry	transmission cut-off at 320 nm	transmission cut-off at 320 nm
FTIR	4 major peaks at	4 major peaks at
	~ 1730-1710,1270-1240,1100 and 725 cm^{-1};	~ 1730-1710,1270-1240,1100 and 725 cm^{-1};
	Minor peak at ~1340 cm^{-1}	Minor peak at ~1340 cm^{-1}
Spectral identification	Polyester → PET	Polyester → PET
	Q fiber is consistent with fibers from KN sample	Q fiber is consistent with fibers from KN sample
Other analyses/notes		
Conclusion	Q fiber shares similar physical characteristics, optical properties and chemical composition with fibers from KN sample and the two samples are consistent	

the location of damage, its size and shape, and if there are indications that the damaged edges of the yarns have been frayed or altered since the damage occurred (Johnson 1991). Measurements of the damage may exceed the size of a potential weapon if additional cutting or tearing occurred beyond the insertion of the implement into the fabric. A weapon may also not become fully embedded in or through a garment or the fabric may stretch, so the dimensions of the weapon should only be cautiously used when eliminating a potential implement. A fabric damage examination typically starts with a visual examination of the fabric to assess and document the fabric construction and the size and shape of the damaged area (see Figure 5.38–5.41 examples of fabric damage). Once an overview of the amount and types of damage has been completed, a stereomicroscope or other magnifying apparatus may be useful to assess the thread ends. Are the edges of the damaged area

well defined and severed in a uniform manner across several yarns, which would be consistent with a cut, or is there variation in the length of the fiber ends extending into the damaged area and fraying, such as would occur in tears?

To test whether particular weapons or actions could have produced the damage being observed, test cuts/punctures/test fires should be made in an undamaged portion of the same garment (if possible) for direct comparison of the weapon of interest to the damaged sections. This can be done by placing the garment over a suitable substrate (e.g. ballistic gel covered in plastic) and then attempting to replicate stab/cut/tear damage by inserting a weapon in a stab or puncture movement though the garment from various angles and with different degrees of pressure. These tests should be documented throughout the examination both in the examination notes and by marking the test damage area on the garment before comparing to the primary area of damage. Single-edged

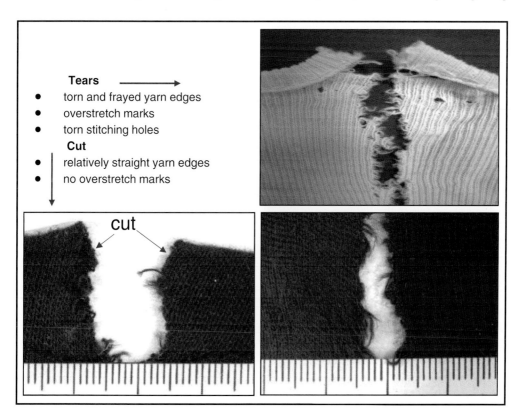

Figure 5.38 Fabric damage cut/tear differentiation.

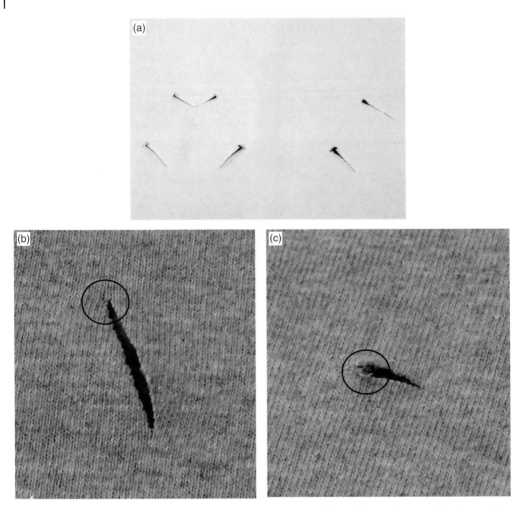

Figure 5.39 Fabric damage: a) knife stabs through folded paper shows direction changes when inserted through folded layers, b) and c) cut/tears through fabric knife blade. The expanded areas show indicators for the area where the flat side of single-edged blade inserted into the material.

blades tend to leave an expanded area or tear a V-shaped notch (see Figure 5.38) in one end of the cut mark, where the flat portion of the blade entered the fabric and can create a small flap of fabric or remnant of a knit row. The lack of this feature should not be taken to mean that the blade was double edged; however, if present it is a reliable indicator that the blade was single edged (Figure 5.39). An examiner should become familiar with the typical pattern of wear holes, hospital cuts, hesitation cuts from scissors, the effect sharp, dull, and serrated blades have on different types of fabric, and how fabric typically appears when cutting

through folded layers or edges as these patterns are often encountered in casework without having relevance to the question of damage from the alleged criminal activity. Decorative patterns may also impact an examination (Figure 5.40). During training an examiner should become familiar with the typical damage patterns that are produced by a variety of weapons in a range of fabric constructions (e.g. woven, knit, non-woven) as well as in a range of thread counts from tight to loosely woven or knit (Monahan and Harding 1990; Johnson 1991; Hearle et al. 1998; Taupin et al. 1999; Daly et al. 2009; Kemp et al. 2009; Hemmings

Figure 5.40 Fabric damage: if a decorative pattern makes it difficult to observe damage marks, the back side may be easier to characterize cut/tear features.

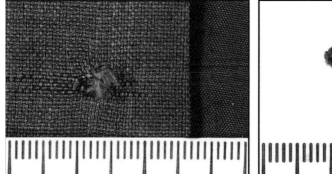

Figure 5.41 Fabric damage: (a) button torn from fabric leaving hole and (b) back of button with threads still attached to button.

2018). Further training should focus on the patterns arising when folds are present in the garment and how damage may appear to be interrupted but be due to the folds or stretches in the fabric when the damage was inflicted.

Physical fit is the strongest conclusion that can be reached in an analysis of textiles. This conclusion can only be reached when the torn areas across the warp and weft align across two separate pieces of fabric and the yarns "fit" together. In Figure 5.41, the yarns making up the woven material have torn at irregular lengths. These are often called "longs" and "shorts." When a "long" yarn is found to line up directly opposite a "short" yarn and that pattern is carried through a damaged textile (Figure 5.42), then the two pieces can be concluded to have once composition, a physical

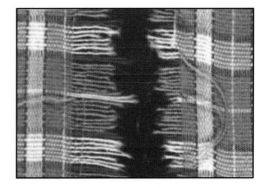

Figure 5.42 Fabric examination: "physical fit". The long and short yarns from two separate pieces of fabric align and indicate the two pieces were once joined.

fit been joined as a whole piece. If two pieces do not align but have similar color, fabric construction, and fiber cannot be made and there may be portions missing.

Thermoplastic fusions are a specific type of fabric damage that can be informative in vehicular accidents. In situations where there is a large amount of friction during an impact, the friction can cause enough heat to melt the fiber polymer and when cooled down become fused with a substrate (e.g. airbags). The fused polymer material may retain some imprint of the fabric construction or have completely lost its form. Either way, the polymer can be sampled for analysis with FTIR. Fusion marks may be found on air bags or on the outside of a vehicle at a point of impact. Such areas should be searched for fabric impressions and fused fibers.

5.9.2.2 Cordage

Cordage examinations also cover the color, construction, and composition of the cordage material similar to fabric examinations, only the construction is in the round and not flat as for most other textile materials. Cordage may be braided or twisted, have multiple plies made up of numerous fiber strands, and some have a core material that the fibers surround (see Figure 5.2). To start characterizing a piece of cordage, one describes the construction, whether it is braided or twisted, its color(s), the number of plies making up a braid or twist, and if the fibers appear to be filament length, then the number of strands in each ply are counted. If the fibers are short and easily lost when untwisted, then the fiber count is not as useful since it will vary from ply to ply and along the length.

Core materials can vary in material from non-woven fabric, paper, threads, and other fill materials. Whatever material is present should be examined and if there is the potential for a physical fit, such as with a non-woven fabric or paper core, then additional documentation is needed in case two pieces align and could have previously been joined.

5.10 Interpretation and Reporting

5.10.1 Interpretation

When assessing the significance of results in a fiber case, conclusions about potential sources of the material need to be taken into consideration but also potential activity in terms of fiber transfer and persistence. The examiner should consider when source determinations are of primary importance versus when fiber comparisons provide information more relevant to potential transfer and persistence of fibers among the people and locations involved and the different activities that could have taken place. Fiber comparisons may involve multiple questions regarding potential source materials as well as whether or not an individual may have come into contact and/or been involved in the activity or location that is under investigation. Having some background information regarding the case is essential to any interpretation of the results. Spending your time analyzing fibers collected from the scene in relation to the suspect's clothing may lose importance if it is known that individual had legitimately been at that location the day before while wearing the same clothing, thus potentially transferring fibers at that time. However, if those clothes were not worn recently and the potential for fiber transfers was focused on transfer from one environment or person to another, then the amount of fibers present gains prominence in the overall evaluation. Both the prosecution and defense positions regarding the various explanations for case activities and interactions that the scientist will be called upon to testify in regard to need to be considered during an examination and in the writing of the report. This ensures that the examiner is keeping an impartial and scientific view. Does finding a single fiber that exhibits the same microscopic characteristics, optical properties, and chemical composition as the fibers that make up a shirt found in the suspect's residence mean that the suspect committed the crime? No, it does not. It only means that shirt can be included as a possible source of the fiber found at the scene along with other textiles of similar manufacture and characteristics; however, if the textile has been significantly altered over time since its manufacture, the potential pool of "source" materials may be reduced. A forensic examiner focuses on the evidence to determine whether casework samples can be differentiated from reference materials or not and evaluates the results in relation to any background information regarding the activities of the individuals involved, known rates of transfer and persistence, and general information about fiber production and use. The total number of potential sources cannot be absolutely known, but a reference sample that cannot be discriminated must be included as a possible source of the unknown fibers. The significance of transferred fibers may increase with the number of fibers found on a person or object, along with the location that they were found in or on (e.g. external areas of clothing vs intimate clothing, under the fingernails). Situations where 50 fibers are found on the undergarments of a victim that correspond with fibers from the suspect's inner clothing in a sexual assault case have a different level of significance than finding 50 fibers on the outer clothing of an individual that correspond with fibers that make up the flock type of fabric of a vehicle in which a person recently obtained a ride. Such case-specific information gives context to the evidence and should be addressed in relation to the results of a fiber examination, so the significance is not interpreted incorrectly as overly strong or as so weak as to not be important.

5.10.2 Report Writing

Laboratory protocols may differ in how reports are written but generally reports contain a description of the items examined, the methods used in the analyses, and the limitations of those methods along with the results of analysis and some interpretation of what the results mean. Interpretation sections vary from general statements indicating a potential shared source to evaluative statements regarding transfer and persistence and references to an interpretive scale to assist the reader to understand the strengths and limitations of the analytical results.

While an expert understands their laboratory examinations, the features used as comparison criteria, and the scientific background for their conclusions, it is not sufficient to simply state the fibers are similar and can be associated. The basis for the conclusion must also be conveyed to the recipient of the report. One such explanation is as follows (single fiber for source level):

When all microscopic characteristics, optical properties, and the chemical composition of a recovered fiber are the same as in a potential source, then the possibility that the compared fibers originated from the provided reference source, or from another source comprised of fibers that exhibit the same microscopic characteristics, optical properties, and chemical composition, cannot be excluded. Accordingly, the submitted known sample material can be included as a possible source of the crime scene fiber (along with an unknown population of similar manufactured garments).

Instances where fibers are not associated through a microscopical examination does not preclude the possibility of contact. A number of factors can be considered for why no fibers were found, including fiber evidence may not have transferred, or the fibers did transfer and may have been lost prior to submission to the laboratory. Of the fibers that did transfer, they or the known comparison specimen may not be representative of the source. Accordingly, the probability of finding fibers that share characteristics sufficient to include the known as a possible source needs to be assessed in relation to the questions relevant to the case and the information available to the examiner. For example, if there is information regarding a potentially long period of time between the collection of a questioned and a known sample, or environmental conditions that could potentially alter the samples, those circumstances need to be taken into account when evaluating evidence in relation to source and activity level propositions.

Any limitations in conclusions or opinions must be stated in the report. Characteristics or observations that increase or decrease the significance of an association should also be explained. Two-way transfers, multiple transfers, and a large number of fibers transferred are all examples of circumstances that can increase the significance of the results of individual associations and should be stated in the report.

5.11 Testimony

Different jurisdictions have their own specific requirements and one must be familiar with those. An examiner should focus their testimony on explaining the methods of analysis and conclusions contained in their report, as well as clearly stating the limitations of a fiber examination based on the manufactured nature of fibers and retaining the ability to explain aspects of his or her background knowledge which influenced the final conclusions. Understanding the factors that can alter a textile over time (e.g. washing, exposure to sunlight, stains) and how that may alter the potential sample pool can be important information for a jury to know but should not be used to indicate a single potential source of an evidential fiber to the exclusion of others similarly manufactured, washed, worn, or otherwise changed over time. An expert is testifying regarding the evidence and the examinations performed and should be mindful to not change their demeanor or testimony when questioned by opposing counsel. Forensic experts should be impartial to the prosecution and defense sides, and answer the questions truthfully and in an objective manner. A new examiner can prepare by observing the testimony of other experts, reviewing transcripts with their trainer, and by participating in mock courtroom exercises. A forensic scientist serves a critical role within the legal framework, but their work is only one piece of the whole investigation. Keeping that perspective may ensure that an examiner does not become too personally involved in the results and lose scientific objectivity.

* Fibre Type Information System – FTIS

With the financial support from the Prevention of and Fight against Crime Program European Commission Directorate General

Home Affairs Home/2011/ISEC/MO/4000002384 (Z2)

ENFSI Monopoly 2011 under supervision of the ENFSI – European Textile and Hair Group "ETHG"

References

AATCC TM020-TM20-TM 20 (2018). *Test method for fiber analysis: qualitative*. Technical Manual, Analysis of Textiles: Quantitative. AATCC TM20-2013 (2018)e, *Test method for fiber analysis: qualitative*

Akulova, V., Vasiliauskiené, D., and Talaliené, D. (2002). Further insights into the persistence of transferred fibres on outdoor clothes. *Science and Justice* 42 (3): 165–171.

Appleyard, H.M. (1978). *Guide to the Identification of Animal Fibres*, 2e., Wool Industries Research Association, Leeds, U.K., 1978.

ASTM International (2012). *ASTM D276 standard test methods for identification of fibers in textiles*. West Conshohocken, PA: American Society for Testing and Materials.

ASTM International (2013) *ASTM E2227 forensic examination of non-reactive dyes in textile fibers by thin-layer chromatography.* West Conshohocken, PA: American Society for Testing and Materials.

ASTM International (2016). *ASTM D4966 standard test method for abrasion resistance of textile fabrics (martindale abrasion tester method).* West Conshohocken, PA: American Society for Testing and Materials.

ASTM International (2019a). *ASTM E2228 standard guide for microscopical examination of textile fibers.* West Conshohocken, PA: American Society for Testing and Materials.

ASTM International (2019b). *ASTM E2224 standard guide for forensic analysis of fibers by infrared spectroscopy.* West Conshohocken, PA: American Society for Testing and Materials.

ASTM International (2019c). *ASTM E2225 standard guide for forensic examination of fabrics and cordage.* West Conshohocken, PA: American Society for Testing and Materials.

Bartick, E.G., Tungol, M.W., and Reffner, J.A. (1994). A new approach to forensic analysis with infrared microscopy: internal reflection spectroscopy. *Analytica Chimica Acta* 288 (1–2): 35–42.

Bennett, S., Roux, C.P., and Robertson, J. (2010). The significance of fibre transfer and persistence – a case study. *Australian Journal of Forensic Sciences* 42 (3): 221–228.

Biermann, T.W. (2007). Blocks of colour IV: The evidential value of blue and red cotton fibres. *Science & Justice* 47 (2): 68–87.

Bologna, N.A. and Parent, S.M. (2002). Significance of fiber evidence. In: *Proceedings of American Academy of Forensic Sciences*, vol. 8, 38. Atlanta: American Academy of Forensic Sciences.

Brunner, H. and Coman, B.J. (1974). *The Identification of Mammalian Hair.* Inkata Press.

Brüschweiler, W. and Grieve, M.C. (1997). A study on the random distribution of a red acrylic target fibre. *Science and Justice* 37 (2): 85–89.

Buzzini, P. and Massonnet, G. (2015). The analysis of colored acrylic, cotton, and wool

textile fibers using micro-raman spectroscopy. Part 2: comparison with the traditional methods of fiber examination. *Journal of Forensic Sciences* 60 (3): 712–720.

Cardon, D. (2007). *Natural Dyes: Sources, Tradition, Technology and Science.* London: Archetype.

Carey, A., Rodewijk, N., Xu, X., and van der Weerd, J. (2013). Identification of dyes on single textile fibers by HPLC-DAD-MS. *Analytical Chemistry* 85 (23): 11335–11343.

Catling, D. and Grayson, J. (2004). *Identification of NATURAL FIBERS.* London: Archetype Publications.

Causin, V., Marega, C., Schiavone, S. et al. (2006). Forensic analysis of acrylic fibers by pyrolysis–gas chromatography/mass spectrometry. *Journal of Analytical and Applied Pyrolysis* 75 (1): 43–48.

Chen, X., Zhen, Z., and Shi, X. (1997). Study on determination of prohibiter azo dyes in leather and textile materials by HPLC. *Chinese Journal of Analytical Chemistry* 25: 1362–1362.

Chewning, D., Deaver, K., and Christensen, A. (2008). Persistence of fibers on ski masks during transit and processing. *Forensic Science Communications* 10 (3).

Cook, R. and Wilson, C. (1986). The significance of finding extraneous fibres in contact cases. *Forensic Science International* 32 (4): 267–273.

Coyle, T. and Fairchild, J. (2003). Raman spectroscopy of cellulosic fibres. *Forensic Science International* 136 (1): 125.

Coyle, T., Fairchild, J., Feilden, C., and Revell, D. (2007). Raman microspectroscopy and its place in forensic fibre examination – the identification of man-made cellulosic fibres. *Global Forensic Science Today* 3: 26–31.

Daly, D.J., Lee-Gorman, M.A., and Ryan, J. (2009). Distinguishing between damage to clothing as a result of normal wear and tear or as a result of deliberate damage: a sexual assault case study. *Journal of Forensic Sciences* 54 (2): 400–403.

De Wael, K. (2012). Dichroism measurements in forensic fibre examination. Part 4: Dyed acrylic and acetate fibres. *Science and Justice* 52 (2): 81–89.

De Wael, K. and Driessche, T.V. (2011a). Dichroism measurements in forensic fibre examination. Part 1: Dyed polyester fibres. *Science and Justice* 51 (2): 57–67.

De Wael, K. and Driessche, T.V. (2011b). Dichroism measurements in forensic fibre examination. Part 2: Dyed polyamide, wool and silk fibres. *Science and Justice* 51 (4): 163–172.

De Wael, K. and Lepot, L. (2011). Dichroism measurements in forensic fibre examination. Part 3: Dyed cotton and viscose fibres. *Science and Justice* 51 (4): 173–186.

De Wael, K. and Lepot, L. (2012). Dichroism measurements in forensic fibre examination. Part 5: Pigmented fibres. *Science and Justice* 52 (3): 161–167.

De Wael, K., Lepot, L., Lunstroot, K., and Gason, F. (2010). Evaluation of the shedding potential of textile materials. *Science and Justice* 50 (4): 192–194.

De Wael, K., Baes, C., Lepot, L., and Gason, F. (2011). On the frequency of occurrence of a peculiar polyester fibre type found in blue denim textiles. *Science & Justice* 51 (4): 154–162.

Deadman, H.A. and Scully, T.A. (2004). Frequency of occurrence data for textile fibers. In: *Proceedings of the American Academy of Forensic Sciences*, vol. 10, 47. Dallas: American Academy of Forensic Sciences.

Decke, U. (2000). Nochmals: Das Leitspurenkonzept. Kriminalistik 7:467–472.

Deedrick, D.W. and Koch, S.L. (2004a). Microscopy of hair part I: a practical guide and manual for human hairs. *Forensic Science Communications* 6 (1).

Deedrick, D.W. and Koch, S.L. (2004b). Microscopy of hair part II: a practical guide and manual for animal hairs. *Forensic Science Communications* 6 (3).

Du Pont & Company (1961). *Bulletin X-156: Identification of Fibers in Textile Materials*. Wilmington, Del: Technical Service Section, Textile Fibers Department, E.I. du Pont de Nemours & Company.

Edwards, H.G.M., Farwell, D.W., and Webster, D. (1997). FT Raman microscopy of untreated natural plant fibres. *Spectrochimica Acta Part A* 53: 2383–2392.

Ferreira, E.S., Hulme, A.N., McNab, H., and Quye, A. (2004). The natural constituents of historical textile dyes. *Chemical Society Reviews* 33 (6): 329–336.

Fong, W. and Inami, S.H. (1986). Results of a study to determine the probability of chance match occurrences between fibers known to be from different sources. *Journal of Forensic Sciences* 31 (1): 11859J.

Geiss, F. (1987). *Fundamentals of Thin Layer Chromatography*. Heidelberg: Huethig.

Good, I. (2001). Archaeological textiles: a review of current research. *Annual Review of Anthropology*: 209–226.

Goodpaster, J.V. and Liszewski, E.A. (2009). Forensic analysis of dyed textile fibers. *Analytical and Bioanalytical Chemistry* 394 (8).

Grieve, M.C. (1983). The use of melting point and refractive index determination to compare colourless polyester fibres. *Forensic Science International* 22 (1): 31–48.

Grieve, M.C. and Biermann, T. (1997a). The population of coloured textile fibres on outdoor surfaces. *Science and Justice* 37 (4): 231–239.

Grieve, M.C. and Biermann, T.W. (1997b). Wool fibres – transfer to vinyl and leather vehicle seats and some observations on their secondary transfer. *Science and Justice* 37 (1): 31–38.

Grieve, M., Dunlop, J., and Haddock, P. (1988). An assessment of the value of blue, red, and black cotton fibers as target fibers in forensic science investigations. *Journal of Forensic Sciences* 33 (6): 1332–1345.

Grieve, M.C., Biermann, T.W., and Davignon, M. (2001). The evidential value of black cotton fibres. *Science and Justice* 41 (4): 245–260.

Grieve, M.C., Biermann, T.W., and Davignon, M. (2003). The occurrence and individuality of orange and green cotton fibres. *Science and Justice* 43 (1): 5–22.

Grieve, M.C., Biermann, T.W., and Schaub, K. (2005). The individuality of fibres used to provide forensic evidence – not all blue polyesters are the same. *Science and Justice* 45 (1): 13–28.

Hall, D.M. (1982). *Practical Fiber Identification*. Department of Textile Engineering, Auburn University.

Hamilton, R. and Hamilton, S. (1987). *Thin Layer Chromatography*. Chichester, UK: Wiley.

Hartshorne, A.W. and Laing, D.K. (1984). The identification of polyolefin fibres by infrared spectroscopy and melting point determination. *Forensic Science International* 26 (1): 45–52.

Hartshorne, A.W., Wild, F.M., and Babb, N.L. (1991). The discrimination of cellulose di-and tri-acetate fibres by solvent tests and melting point determination. *Journal of the Forensic Science Society* 31 (4): 457–461.

Haugan, E. and Holst, B. (2013). Determining the fibrillar orientation of bast fibres with polarized light microscopy: the modified Herzog test (red plate test) explained. *Journal of Microscopy* 252 (2): 159–168.

Hearle, J.W., Lomas, B., and Cooke, W.D. (1998). *Atlas of Fibre Fracture and Damage to Textiles*. Elsevier.

Hemmings, J. (2018). Raman spectroscopy of fibres. In: *Forensic Examination of Fibres*, 3e (eds. J. Robertson, C. Roux and K.G. Wiggins). Boca-Raton, FL: CRC Press Taylor & Francis.

Home, J.M. and Dudley, R.J. (1981). Thin layer chromatography of dyes extracted from cellulosic fibers. *Forensic Science International* 17: 71–78.

Hong, S., Han, A., Kim, S. et al. (2014). Transfer of fibres on the hands of living subjects and their persistence during hand washing. *Science and Justice* 54 (6): 451–458.

Johnson, N. (1991). Physical damage to textiles. *Proceedings of Police Technology: Asia Pacific Police Technology Conference*, Canberra, Australia, November 12–14, 1991.

Jones, J. and Coyle, T. (2011). Synthetic flock fibres: a population and target fibre study. *Science and Justice* 51 (2): 68–71.

Keen, P., White, G.W., and Fredericks, P.M. (1998). Characterization of fibers by Raman microprobe spectroscopy. *Journal of Forensic Science* 43: 82–89.

Kelly, E. and Griffin, R.M. (1998). A target fibre study on seats in public houses. *Science and Justice* 38 (1): 39–44.

Kemp, S.E. et al. (2009). Forensic evidence in apparel fabrics due to stab events. *Forensic Science International* 191 (1–3): 86–96.

King, Y. (2016). *Py-GC-MS: An Underutilized Technique for the Forensic Examination of Fibers*. Doctoral dissertation: University of Canberra.

Kisler-Rao, A. (2015). Comparison of nylon, polyester, and olefin fibers using FTIR and melting point analysis. *Journal of the American Society of Trace Evidence Examiners* 6 (1).

Krauß, W. and Hildebrand, U. (1995). Fibre persistence on garments under open-air conditions. In: *Proceedings of European Fibres Group Meeting, Linkoping (Sweden)*, 32–36.

Kshirsagar, S.V., Singh, B., and Fulari, S.P. (2009). Comparative study of human and animal hair in relation with diameter and medullary index. *Indian Journal of Forensic Medicine and Pathology* 2 (3): 105–108.

Laing, D.K. et al. (1990). Thin layer chromatography of azoic dyes extracted from cotton fibers. *Journal of the Forensic Science Society* 30: 309–315.

Lepot, L., Driessche, T.V., Lunstroot, K. et al. (2015). Fibre persistence on immersed garment – Influence of knitted recipient fabrics. *Science & Justice* 55 (4): 248–253.

Lepot, L., Vanden Driessche, T., Lunstroot, K. et al. (2017). Extraneous fibre traces brought by river water – a case study. *Science and Justice* 57 (1): 53–57.

Lowrie, C.N. and Jackson, G. (1994). Secondary transfer of fibres. *Forensic Science International* 64 (2–3): 73–82.

Lynch, B. (1981). Investigation of single fibres by X-ray diffraction in forensic ananlysis. *X-Ray Spectroscopy* 10: 196–197.

Macrae, R., Dudley, R.J., and Smalldon, K.W. (1979). The characterization of dyestuffs on wool fibers with special reference to microspectrophotometry. *Journal of Forensic Science* 24 (1): 117–129.

Masson, J. (ed.) (1995). *Acrylic Fiber Technology and Applications*. CRC Press.

McIntyre, J.E. (ed.) (2005). *Synthetic Fibres: Nylon, Polyester, Acrylic, Polyolefin*. Boca Raton, FL: CRC Press.

McMaster, M. (2007). *HPLC: A Practical user's Guide*, 2e. Hoboken.: Wiley.

Meleiro, P.P. and García-Ruiz, C. (2016). Spectroscopic techniques for the forensic analysis of textile fibers. *Applied Spectroscopy Reviews* 51 (4): 278–301.

Miller, J.V. and Bartick, E.G. (2001). Forensic analysis of single fibers by Raman spectroscopy. *Applied Spectroscopy* 55: 1729–1732.

Monahan, D.L. and Harding, H.W.J. (1990). Damage to clothing – cuts and tears. *Journal of Forensic Science* 35 (4): 901–912.

Moore, T.D., Spence, L.E., and Dugnolle, C.E. (1974). *Identification of the Dorsal Guard Hairs of Some Mammals of Wyoming* (No. 14). Wyoming Game and Fish Department.

Mueller, W.F. (1962). The origins of the basic inventions underlying Du Pont's major product and process innovations, 1920 to 1950. In: *The Rate and Direction of Inventive Activity: Economic and Social Factors*, 323–358. Princeton University Press.

Neubert-Kirfel, D. (2000). Das Leitspurkonzept [bei Faserspuren]: Der Dialog mit den stummen Zeugen der Tat. *Kriminalistik* 54 (6): 398–404.

Ogle, R.R. Jr., and Fox, M.J. (1998). *Atlas of Human Hair: Microscopic Characteristics*. CRC Press.

Palenik, C.S., Beckert, J.C., and Palenik, S. (2015). Microspectrophotometry of fibers: advances in analysis and interpretation. In: *NIJ Report 2012-DN-BX–K040*. Washington DC: National Institute of Justice.

Palmer, R. (1998). The retention and recovery of transferred fibers following the washing of recipient clothing. *Journal of Forensic Sciences* 43 (3): 502–504.

Palmer, R. (2016). *The Evaluation of Fibre Evidence in the Investigation of Serious Crime*. University of Lausanne.

Palmer, R. and Banks, M. (2005). The secondary transfer of fibres from head hair. *Science and Justice* 45 (3): 123–128.

Palmer, R. and Burch, H.J. (2009). The population, transfer and persistence of fibres on the skin of living subjects. *Science and Justice* 49 (4): 259–264.

Palmer, R. and Chinherende, V. (1996). A target fibre study using car and cinema seats as recipient items. *Journal of Forensic Sciences* 41 (5): 802–803.

Palmer, R. and Oliver, S. (2004). The population of coloured fibres in human head hair. *Science and Justice* 44 (2): 83–88.

Palmer, R. and Polwarth, G. (2011). The persistence of fibres on skin in an outdoor deposition crime scene scenario. *Science and Justice* 51 (4): 187–189.

Palmer, R., Hutchinson, W., and Fryer, V. (2009). The discrimination of (non-denim) blue cotton. *Science and Justice* 49 (1): 12–18.

Palmer, R., Sheridan, K., Puckett, J. et al. (2017). An investigation into secondary transfer – the transfer of textile fibres to seats. *Forensic Science International* 278: 334–337.

Peets, P., Kaupmees, K., Vahur, S. et al. Reflectance FT-IR spectroscopy as a viable option for textile fiber identification. *Herit Sci* **7**, 93 (2019). https://doi.org/10.1186/s40494-019-0337-z.

Pelton, W.R. (1995). Distinguishing the cause of textile fibre damage using the scanning electron microscope (SEM). *Journal of Forensic Science* 40: 874–882.

Perry, D.R., Appleyard, H.M., Cartridge, G. et al. (1975). *Identification of Textile Materials*, 7e. Textile Institute.

Pounds, C.A. and Smalldon, K.W. (1975a). The transfer of fibres between clothing materials during simulated contacts and their persistence during wear. part I: Fibre transference. *Journal of the Forensic Science Society* 15 (3): 17–27.

Pounds, C.A. and Smalldon, K.W. (1975b). The transfer of fibres between clothing materials during simulated contacts and their persistence during wear. Part II: Fiber persistence. *Journal of the Forensic Science Society* 15 (3): 29–37.

Pounds, C.A. and Smalldon, K.W. (1975c). Transfer of fibers between clothing materials during simulated contacts and their persistence during wear. Part III: A preliminary investigation of mechanisms involved. *Journal of the Forensic Science Society* 15 (3): 197–207.

Rendle, D.F. and Wiggins, K.G. (1995). Forensic analysis of textile fiber dyes. *Review of Progress in Coloration* 25: 29–34.

Resua, R. (1980). A semi-micro technique for the extraction and comparison of dyes in textile fibers. *Journal of Forensic Sciences* 25: 168–173.

Roux, C. (1999). Scanning electron microscopy and elemental analysis. In: *Forensic Examination of Fibres* (eds. J. Robertson and M. Grieve), 239–250. Taylor & Francis.

Roux, C. and Margot, P. (1997). An attempt to assess the relevance of textile fibres recovered from car seats. *Science and Justice* 37 (4): 225–230.

Roux, C., Langdon, S., Waight, D., and Robertson, J. (1999). The transfer and persistence of automotive carpet fibres on shoe soles. *Science and Justice* 39 (4): 239–251.

Roux, C., Morison, R., and Maynard, P. (2017). Other instrumental approaches to fibre examination. In: *Forensic Examination of Fibres*, 309–344. CRC Press.

Salter, M.T. and Cook, R. (1996). Transfer of fibres to head hair, their persistence and retrieval. *Forensic Science International* 81 (2–3): 211–221.

Scientific Working Group for Materials Analysis (SWGMAT), and USA (2004). Forensic fiber examiner training program. *Forensic Science Communications* 7 (2) https://archives.fbi .gov/archives/about-us/lab/forensic-science-communications/fsc/april2005.

Slot, A., van der Weerd, J., Roos, M. et al. (2017). Tracers as invisible evidence – the transfer and persistence of flock fibres during a car exchange. *Forensic Science International* 275: 178–186.

Smalldon, K.W. (1973). The identification of acrylic fibers by polymer composition as determined by infared spectroscopy and physical characteristics. *Journal of Forensic Science* 18 (1): 69–81.

Smith, J.K. and Hounshell, D.A. (1985). Wallace H. Carothers and fundamental research at Du Pont. *Science* 229 (4712): 436–442.

Stoeffler, S.F. (1996). A flowchart system for the identification of common synthetic fibers by polarized light microscopy. *Journal of Forensic Science* 41 (2): 297–299.

Stoney, D.A. and Stoney, P.L. (2012). Use of scanning electron microscopy/energy dispersive spectroscopy (SEM/EDS) methods for the analysis of small particles adhering to carpet fiber surfaces as a means to test associations of trace evidence in a way that is independent of manufactured characteristics. In: *NIJ Grant 2010-DN-BX-K244*. Washington, DC: National Institute of Justice.

Szewcow, R., Robertson, J., and Roux, C.P. (2011). The influence of front-loading and top-loading washing machines on the persistence, redistribution and secondary transfer of textile fibres during laundering. *Australian Journal of Forensic Sciences* 43 (4): 263–273.

Taupin, J.M., Adolf, F.P., and Robertson, J.A. (1999). Examination of damage to textiles. In: *Forensic Examination of Fibres*, vol. 2, 65–88.

Teerink, B.J. (2003). *Hair of West European Mammals: Atlas and Identification Key*. Cambridge University Press.

Thomas, J., Buzzini, P., Massonnet, G. et al. (2005). Raman spectroscopy and the forensic analysis of black/grey and blue cotton fibres. Part 1. Investigation of the effects of varying laser wavelength. *Forensic Science International* 152: 189–197.

Tungol, M.W., Bartick, E.G., and Montaser, A. (1993). Forensic analysis of acrylic copolymer fibers by infrared microscopy. *Applied Spectroscopy* 47 (10): 1655–1658.

Vanden Berghe, I., Gleba, M., and Mannering, U. (2009). Towards the identification of dyestuffs in Early Iron Age Scandinavian peat bog textiles. *Journal of Archaeological Science* 36 (9): 1910–1921.

Viswanathan, A. (2010). Wallace carothers: more than the inventor of nylon and neoprene. *World Patent Information* 32 (4): 300–305.

Walbridge-Jones, S. (2009). Microspectrophotometry for textile fiber color measurement. In: *Identification of Textile Fibers*, 165–180. Woodhead Publishing.

Watt, R., Roux, C., and Robertson, J. (2005). The population of coloured textile fibres in domestic washing machines. *Science and Justice* 45 (2): 75–83.

Wheeler, B. and Wilson, L.J. (2011). *Practical Forensic Microscopy: A Laboratory Manual*. Wiley.

White, P.C. (1994). Coloured evidence application of HPLC in the forensic examination of dyes. *Chromatography and Analysis* 33: 9–11.

White, P.C. and Catterick, T. (1993). Characterization of acidic dyes using Euclidean distance measurements of variables derived from high-performance liquid chromatography–visible multi-wavelength detection data. *Analyst* 118 (7): 791–799.

Wiggins, K., Drummond, P., and Champod, T.H. (2004). A study in relation to the random distribution of four fibre types on clothing (incorporating a review of previous target fibre studies). *Science and Justice* 44 (3): 141–148.

Yesil, Y. and Sabir, E.C. (2011). Color matching in two color melange fiber blends by Stearns-Noechel model. *Journal of Textile & Apparel/Tekstil ve Konfeksiyon* 21 (3): 236–243.

5.A Appendix

Billinghame's test to distinguish between abaca and sisal (adapted from Perry et al. 1975, and Wheeler and Wilson 2011) (Figure 5.A1).

1) Wash fibers with 95% ethanol to remove any surface oils then allow the sample to dry.
2) Boil in 5% nitric acid for 5–10 minutes.
3) Wash with water and immerse in cold 0.25 N sodium hypochlorite (commercial bleach can be substituted) for 10 minutes.
4) Remove sample and allow fibers to dry.
5) Note the color of the fibers: Abaca will be stained an orange color while sisal and other leaf fibers take on a pale yellow color.

Graff C stain for differentiating cotton from wood cellulose.[1]

1) Place fibers on a glass microscope slide.
2) Add a small amount of stain.
3) View with transmitted light microscopy. Yellow indicates high lignin content such as wood pulp and jute. Blue indicates highly purified pulp including wood processed for paper. Red indicates an absence of lignin including cotton and the bast fibers except for jute.

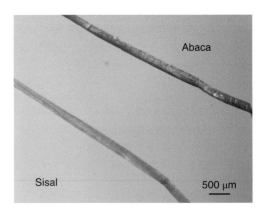

Figure 5.A1

---

1 Modified from http://cameo.mfa.org/wiki/Graff_%22C%22_stain.

6

Interpretation of Glass Evidence

James Curran[1], Tacha Hicks[2], and Tatiana Trejos[3]

[1] Department of Statistics, The University of Auckland, Auckland, New Zealand
[2] Faculty of Law, Criminal Justice and Public Administration, School of Criminal Justice and Fondation pour la formation continue UNIL-EPFL, University of Lausanne, Lausanne, Switzerland
[3] Department of Forensic and Investigative Science, West Virginia University, Morgantown, West Virginia, USA

6.1 Introduction to Glass Examination

Glass is a valuable evidential material: ubiquitous, transferable, persistent, measurable, and discriminating. Glass is part of our daily lives and plays an essential role in the construction of buildings, automobiles, electronics, and household and industrial objects. Because glass is fragile, it is likely to break and transfer during criminal incidents. Yet, its presence in the general population is fortuitous (Curran et al. 2000; Caddy 2001). Moreover, the transfer mechanisms are predictable to some extent, and glass shards persist long enough to be recovered from crime scenes and individuals of interest. Finally, the forensic community has developed consensus-based standards that yield a high degree of discrimination among different sources of glass and relatively low error rates (ASTM 2012, 2016, 2017).

The forensic examination of glass can provide information regarding the reconstruction of events, the type of glass involved in the case, and source commonality between a known and a questioned fragment.

Some of the questions of interests in glass cases are: What type of glass was transferred within the crime scene? Did the questioned glass originate from the same broken source submitted as the comparison sample? How rare are the measured properties of glass given a particular context? Who could have – or have not – broken a window? How did the events happen? Where did it happen?

For instance, in hit-and-run cases, the identification of glass on the victim and surrounding area can guide investigators to search for potential suspect vehicles (i.e. cars with damage to a headlamp, windshield, or side window). The recovery of glass fragments from a suspect's clothing can contribute to link the individual to the crime scene and in some circumstances the amount and size of fragments could help reveal relative seating locations in the vehicle during the impact.

In violent crimes, the recovery of glass can provide useful clues about how events evolved and how evidence was transferred. Did the suspect break in or was the window broken from inside? Was the victim hit with a bottle, a lamp, a decorative vase? Is the contact lens from the victim or could it belong to the perpetrator? What was the direction of the bullet when it broke through the window? Could the recovered glass from the individual of interest

Handbook of Trace Evidence Analysis, First Edition. Edited by Vincent J. Desiderio, Chris E. Taylor, and Niamh Nic Daéid.

originate from the broken window? If so, what is the weight of such evidence? In any of these cases, the association of glass recovered from the crime scene can help establish relevant links between individuals and objects of interest. In this chapter, we will describe the main aspects of glass composition, manufacture, aftermarket distribution, transfer and persistence, and the scope of analytical methods used for its examination. This foundational knowledge is essential for making informed decisions during the pre-assessment of a case, the collection and sampling of fragments at the scene, and the overall interpretation of glass evidence.

6.1.1 Composition, Manufacture, and Distribution

The forensic analysis of glass has been extensively discussed in the scientific literature (Curran et al. 2000; Caddy 2001; Koons et al. 2002; Almirall and Trejos 2006, 2015), therefore, rather than providing a comprehensive review, the following discussion aims to briefly illustrate how modern manufacturing processes impart the glass features that are relevant in a forensic investigation.

Glass is an amorphous solid formed by an asymmetric arrangement of a mixture of atoms. The relative formulation of glass defines its optical properties such as refractive index (RI), reflection, transmittance, and absorption of light. These properties relate to the mechanical, thermal, and physical characteristics of the end product.

Due to significant differences in production, glass can be classified by its chemical composition as soda-lime containers (jars, bottles), soda lime sheet glass (windows), leaded glass (houseware, decorative glass), and borosilicate glass (cookware and industrial) (Koons et al. 2002; Almirall and Trejos 2015; Ryland 1986). The most common types of glass found in cases are architectural, vehicular, and container glass, therefore we will focus on the main two modern methods of manufacture of flat glass and containers.

In a typical float glass manufacturing plant, large silos store the main ingredients of glass: sand (silicon dioxide), limestone (calcium oxide and magnesium oxide), and trona (sodium carbonate). These raw materials are mixed and slowly homogenized at high temperatures. For several hours the molten mixture is heated in large tanks with thick walls to allow gas to bubble up and out. The hot mix is then poured onto the liquid tin and will "float" on top of the denser tin, creating a flat surface. As the glass exits the tin pool, it begins to cool at controlled rates until solid glass is formed. The glass moves into the cooling conveyor as one long continuous sheet that cools gradually and stretches to the desired thickness. The glass is then cut into 10–12 ft slabs, packed and shipped to distributors.

The major constituent of glass, silicon dioxide, is responsible for forming the building network of the glass structure. The silicon-oxygen atoms are known as network formers because they solidify without crystallizing when cooled at a controlled rate. Other components, such as sodium, calcium, and magnesium, are known as fluxes or modifiers, which make the structures more complex so that it is more difficult for the atoms to rearrange and crystallize. Flux chemicals soften the glass and make it easier to melt (Caddy 2001). Many other components are added to the formulation of glass, such as secondary formers (aluminum, zirconium, titanium), decolorants, which improve transparency (iron, chromium, selenium, arsenic, manganese), refining agents, which prevent the retention of gas bubbles in the glass (arsenic, calcium), and stabilizers, which provide chemical resistance (calcium, magnesium, lead, strontium, barium, zinc). Also, recycled broken glass – known as cullet – is reused in manufacturing plants to decrease production costs.

The main formulation of bottle glass also contains silica, soda ash, and limestone, but the relative amounts of Mg, Ca, and Fe differ significantly from sheet glass (Ryland 1986). Additional materials can be added to produce desired colors and recycled glass is used on a larger scale. In the manufacture of container glass, the molten liquid pours out of the furnace, where precise portions of the mix are fed into a container-forming machine and into a blow mold with a cavity of the shape of the bottle or jar. The equipment blows compressed air, stretching the glass toward the wall of the frame and making the container hollow. After the containers leave the forming machine, they enter an annealing lehr where they are cooled at controlled rates. As the bottles exit the lehr, they are sprayed with a coating of a lubricant to move them smoothly to the final packaging area.

Regardless of the common main ingredients of glass, significant formula variations exist among products. In addition, the glass industry continuously innovates to create products with a higher degree of functionality. More resistant glass in mobile phones, ultra-clear glass for self-driving vehicles, self-cleaning glass, and E-glass are just a few examples of current trends.

The increased demand for glass has led to market globalization. As a result, it is anticipated that modern glass installed in buildings and vehicles could be manufactured anywhere in the world. For example, in 2016, the US flat glass demand included sources of glass from approximately 23 plants in the United States, 70 in Asia, 43 in Europe, and 12 in South America and the Middle East (www.statista .com).

The value of glass as evidence not only depends on understanding how glass is made and how its properties vary as a result of its production history, but also on understanding the distribution process of glass after manufacture. Ultimately, this expert knowledge is crucial to assess the significance of glass within the context of a particular crime. For instance, let us consider for a moment just the market of float glass, which accounts for two-thirds of the glass used in construction and automobiles, the two prevalent types of glass found in crime scenes. In 2018, there were approximately 500 manufacturing plants worldwide producing 52 million tons of glass per year. The US demand for flat glass is projected to be 795 million square feet in 2020 (Statista 2018).

It is known that the elemental composition of glass will vary significantly between manufacturing sites and within a single plant over short periods (Koons et al. 2002; Almirall and Trejos 2006, 2015; Trejos et al. 2013a). Even the most sensitive glass examination methods, however, cannot distinguish glass produced in the same plant within 2 weeks to 1 month apart. Therefore, as with any other mass-produced material, the forensic comparison of glass fragments cannot definitively establish that the items came from a single source.

Assuming an average production of 2500 tons of flat glass per week, there may be groups of approximately 5000–10 000 tons of glass that could not be distinguished by current analytical methods. That is a lot of windows or bottles! Nonetheless, this overwhelming large number becomes relatively insignificant when is placed within the proper context, considering the annual average global production of glass (52 million tons) in addition to the glass already in existence in the population.

These numbers are not meant to be exhaustive, but just illustrative of the complex universe of glass that surrounds us and how our knowledge of manufacture and distribution of glass is crucial to assess the rarity of observed properties in a questioned glass. The variety of glass and its physicochemical properties are a result of its composition, manufacture, distribution, and temporal history. As a result, it is not impossible that two pieces of glass with different manufacturing histories would share similar physicochemical properties, but the probability is very low when we deal with a glass of "forensic interest." Particularly because for a glass to be considered as a potential source of evidence, it has to be broken and its transfer to the object or person of interest should be plausible.

Given all the factors that play a role in the final optical and chemical properties of glass, the unpredicted final destiny of a glass piece, and the fragmentation trajectories and fate during a breaking event, it is reasonable to hypothesize that the odds of a random match of two "broken glasses" originating from different sources are very low. Comparison of casework samples from different databases have shown empirical low random match probabilities rates – 0.1% to 2% – depending on the analytical protocol used for examination and comparison criteria (Weis et al. 2011; Dorn et al. 2015; Ryland 2011; Trejos et al. 2013b; Corzo et al. 2018; Hoffman et al. 2018).

6.1.2 Forensic Examination Protocols

The most common method of recovery of glass at the crime scene and in the laboratory are handpicking (if fragments are visible with the naked eye), lifting the fragment with sharp tweezers, scrapping, tape lifting, and shaking (only at the laboratory). Stereoscopes and light sources can help with the visualization of fragments. Figure 6.1 illustrates some of these methods. A typical forensic examination of glass consists of the evaluation of physical features, followed by RI measurements and elemental analysis. Figure 6.2 summarizes a common analytical protocol for the forensic analysis of glass and the type of data generated in each step. If a significant difference is found at any stage of the examination, the comparison samples are considered to originate from different sources and no further analysis is required to demonstrate the exclusion. On the other hand, if no significant differences are observed during the whole examination, it is possible that the samples originate from the same source. Since glass is a mass-produced material, these associations are not individualizing. The assessment of the significance of such associations depends on many factors, including the combined discrimination power of the examination methods. The discrimination potential of a technique depends on

the assessment of several sources of variability (instrumental, within a single window or bottle, within production lots in a single line, between different sources produced at various sites). The larger the between-sources variability in comparison to the rest of the causes of variability, the more discriminating the method is. The scientific validity of glass evidence relies on a vast number of studies that have investigated these factors, along with the analytical performance of the assays. Current ASTM glass standard test methods are based on a broad consensus process that involves the assessment of the robustness, accuracy, repeatability, and reproducibility of the methods within an extensive community of users. Scientific working groups have also contributed to the validation of current protocols. We describe the main capabilities and limitations of conventional methods used in glass examinations to provide a framework of their impact on the overall interpretation of the evidence.

6.1.3 Refractive Index

The RI is the most common optical property measured during the forensic examination of glass. The RI describes how fast light propagates through a glass. The chemical composition and thermal history of a glass influences its RI. Since RI directly relates to the transparency of glass, the manufacturers control the glass formulation and monitor its consistency throughout production.

As a result, relatively low intra-source variability of RI within a window or bottle has been reported in the literature. For example, typical variation in RI across a pane of sheet glass ranges from 2×10^{-5} to 2×10^{-4} (Koons and Buscaglia 2001; Trimpe and Sammarco 2017) and is slightly higher for container glass (5×10^{-5} to 3×10^{-4}) (Locke and Underhill 1985; Suzuki et al. 2000). More substantial variations can be observed on tempered glass and between shards of glass coming from the surface of the fragment versus the inner bulk

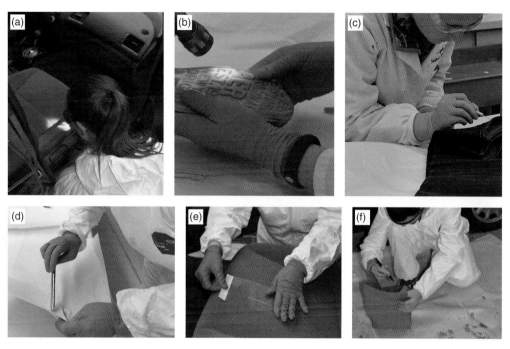

Figure 6.1 Example of methods for the recovery of glass shards using (a) and (b) light sources, (c) tweezers, (d) scraping with spatula, (e) tape lifting, and (f) handpicking.

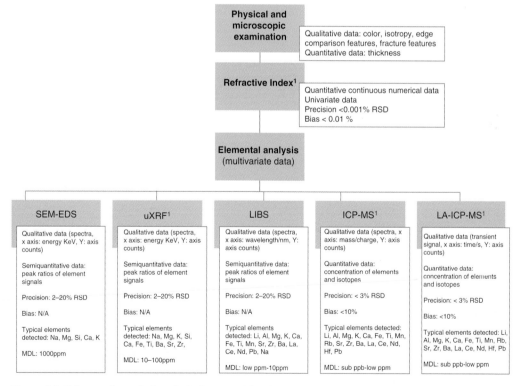

Figure 6.2 Scheme of a typical analytical protocol for the forensic examination of glass fragments and information about the type of data generated in each step. [1]Existing ASTM standard test method.

areas. Special sampling procedures should be considered in such circumstances (Bennett et al. 2003; Newton et al. 2005; Newton and Buckleton 2008; Newton 2011; Insana and Buzzini 2017).

Inter-source variability has been evaluated among different sources and within a single plant over time (Montero 2002; Koons et al. 1991). The measurement of RI is considered an effective screening method that is very useful to detect differences among potential sources of glass. However, the association of two pieces of glass by RI only is not considered highly discriminating. Further examination with elemental methods is required to reduce false positives (type I errors).

This optical property is often measured in crime laboratories by automated oil immersion refractometry with phase contrast microscopy. This method measures the match temperature at which the RI of the glass is the same as the RI of the oil where the glass is immersed. The immersion oils are calibrated with certified reference glasses with known RI. The method produces quantitative dimensionless measurements. The RI of glass can be measured with high precision, i.e. repeatability of 1.5×10^{-5} to 2.5×10^{-5} and inter-laboratory reproducibility of 3.8×10^{-5} to 5.0×10^{-5} and low bias ($<1.4 \times 10^{-2}\%$) (Alamilla et al. 2013; ASTM 2019; European Network of Forensic Science Institutes 2016).

An international standardized test method is available for the forensic comparison of glass (ASTM 2019). The reader can find detailed descriptions of the fundamentals, procedures, and recommendations for RI measurements in Curran et al. (2000), Koons et al. (2002), Almirall and Trejos (2015), and ASTM (2019).

6.1.4 Refractive Index Annealing

The term "annealing" refers to a process for cooling glass in a controlled manner through a predetermined temperature gradient. This allows the surface and interior to cool uniformly, relieving internal stress. This

process is commonly used in the manufacture of glass.

At a laboratory level, annealing is carried out on a small scale to release internal stress in the glass and modify its RI. The known and questioned glass fragments are placed in individual cavities inside a small furnace with controlled temperature programs. Both the known and the questioned shards are simultaneously heated to the annealing temperature, and then the temperature is slowly decreased until the glass is formed again. The RI is measured before and after the process and the extent of change in RI is used to enhance source classification, particularly for tempered glass (Curran et al. 2000; Koons et al. 2002; Newton et al. 2005; Newton 2011; Locke et al. 1982; Locke and Hayes 1984; Marcouiller 1990; Zadora and Wilk 2009).

6.1.5 Elemental Analysis of Glass

Elemental analysis is the most informative and discriminating step in glass comparisons. The forensic application of elemental profiles of glass was first reported in 1973 when Coleman and Goode (1973) used neutron activation (NAA) to distinguish glass originating from different sources. Since then, the forensic community has been continuously adjusting to novel technology to modernize and streamline the analytical process and improve the selectivity, sensitivity, precision, and accuracy of the measurements.

Since the most informative elements in glass comparisons are those present at minor and trace levels, the analytical method should ideally offer good analytical sensitivity, selectivity, and precision. From a large number of techniques capable of elemental analysis, the ones that have found practical application in crime laboratories are scanning electron microscope-energy dispersive spectroscopy (SEM-EDS), micro-X-ray fluorescence (µ-XRF), inductively coupled plasma optical emission spectrometry (ICP-OES), inductively coupled plasma mass spectrometry

(ICP-MS), laser ablation inductively coupled plasma mass spectrometry (LA-ICP-MS), and laser-induced breakdown spectroscopy (LIBS). Of these methods, the scientific validity of μ-XRF and ICP-MS methods is supported by consensus-based international standard methods (ASTM 2012, 2016, 2017).

6.1.5.1 SEM-EDS

SEM-EDS is readily available to forensic laboratories for the analysis of glass and other matrices such as gunshot residues, soils, metals, and paints. The advantages of SEM-EDS are that it is minimally destructive of the sample, can analyze tiny fragments (<100 μm), and sample preparation is relatively easy. However, the main drawback of SEM-EDS is its lack of sensitivity. SEM-EDS detection limits are typically in the order of 0.1% (1000 ppm), and as a result only major elements can be measured in glass, i.e. Na, Mg, Si, Ca, and K, while the most discriminating trace elements remain undetected. This drawback limits its discrimination potential and its applicability in forensic comparisons of glass. Figure 6.3 shows a schematic of a typical SEM-EDS system and compares its detection capabilities versus μ-XRF.

Moreover, SEM-EDS is a surface technique, and therefore the analysis does not allow for representative information of the bulk composition of the glass. SEM-EDS also suffers from poor precision because variation in fragment orientation, shape, and thickness affect the measurements and makes quantitative analysis very challenging. The test is relatively time-consuming with typical acquisition times in the order of 20 minutes per replicate; however, the samples can be run unattended.

SEM-EDS can show some additional discrimination to RI (Reeve et al. 1976) and has proven to be useful when the fragments are too small to measure by other means, for example in cases of glass debris on a bullet. However, SEM-EDS is not generally recommended for glass comparisons due to the limitations described above.

6.1.5.2 Micro-X-Ray Fluorescence

μ-XRF uses the same detection system as SEM-EDS but the excitation source is an X-ray rather than an electron beam. The X-ray is more energetic and therefore penetrates deeper into the glass, allowing for bulk analysis and yielding better detection limits (10–50 ppm, depending on the element, beam collimator size, and detector type). As a result, μ-XRF can detect major, minor, and trace elements, including discriminating elements such as Ti, Ba, Fe, Sr, and Zr. It can also identify elements that are added to some modern formulations such as Ce and Er (ASTM 2017; Ryland 2011; Ernst et al. 2014) (see Figure 6.3).

Other advantages of μ-XRF are that it can measure relatively small fragments (100–300 μm), is not destructive, and allows both qualitative and semiquantitative analysis. Limitations of μ-XRF are that the shape and size of the glass shards can affect precision and accuracy, therefore sample preparation must include exposure of a flat surface to the incident X-ray beam and matching of size and shape between known and questioned specimens. The precision of μ-XRF measurements can range between 2% and >20% depending on the element of interest and its concentration in the sample.

6.1.5.3 ICP Methods

The introduction of inductively coupled plasma methods (ICP-OES and ICP-MS) to the analytical market revolutionized the elemental analysis industry. It is therefore not surprising that forensic scientists devoted efforts to develop and validate their application to glass analysis. ICP methods are advantageous for glass comparisons for many reasons, including their ability to determine a wide range of elements, long linear response ranges, high selectivity, low detection limits for many elements of interest, and ability to enable quantitative measurements with excellent precision and bias, provide simultaneous multi-element analysis with high-sample throughput, and ease of automation. These methods can reach

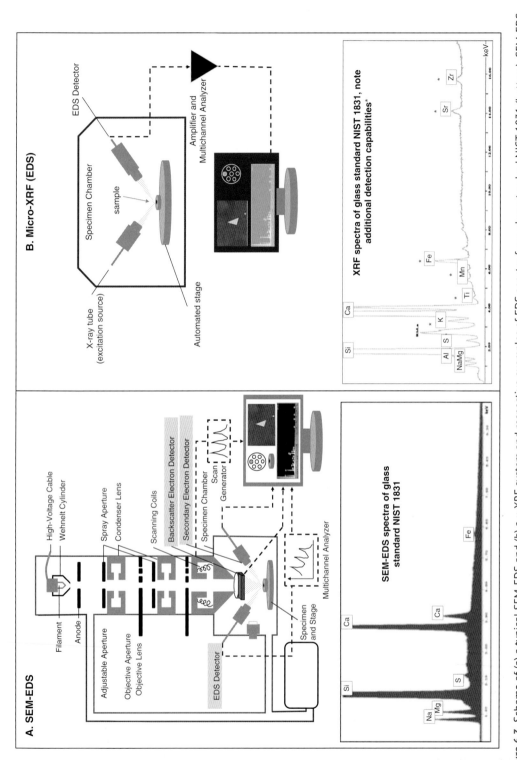

Figure 6.3 Scheme of (a) a typical SEM-EDS and (b) a μ-XRF system and respective examples of EDS spectra for a glass standard NIST 1831 (bottom). SEM-EDS detects major elements, while μ-XRF detects trace and minor elements for the same glass.

sub-ppm to ppb limits of detection with the precision of the measurements typically better than 3% RSD. ICP-MS is at least one order of magnitude more sensitive than ICP-OES, and as a result it requires a smaller amount of sample for analysis (Koons et al. 1988; Duckworth et al. 2000, 2002).

However, the drawbacks of the ICP methods are that the sample preparation is time-consuming and cumbersome as it requires the digestion of the glass into a solution and the use of hazardous reagents such as hydrofluoric acid. Moreover, the procedure is destructive of the sample and needs at least 2 mg of glass, which is not always available in casework. One limitation of the ICP methods, which initially slowed down its inclusion in crime laboratories, was the acquisition costs and need for highly trained personnel. Nonetheless, with technology advances, the instruments have become less expensive and more professionals are now trained in and exposed to these techniques, making it more accessible. With the advancement of laser ablation methods, the forensic community found a perfect opportunity to simplify the elemental analysis of glass evidence further. LA-ICP-MS is now considered the "gold standard" for glass examinations as it maintains all the advantages of ICP-MS methods while eliminating their main drawbacks: sample consumption, low speed, and complexity of analysis (ASTM 2019; Latkoczy et al. 2005; Berends-Montero et al. 2006).

LA-ICP-MS utilizes a laser beam of only 50–100 μm in diameter to mechanically remove nanoparticles from the glass fragment that are later atomized and ionized in the plasma and analyzed in the mass spectrometer. Figure 6.4 illustrates a typical configuration for LA-ICP-MS and ICP-MS. By using laser ablation instead of digestion of glass, the amount of sample needed for analysis is reduced from 2–8 mg to just 0.4–2 μg per replicate and thus this method is suitable for the study of irregularly shaped fragments as small as 0.1 × 0.4 mm. The method is minimally destructive, leaving the glass fragment almost intact after analysis (ASTM 2016).

Moreover, the analysis of glass by LA-ICP-MS does not require any sample preparation and analysis takes about 2 minutes per sample, at least 10 times faster than μ-XRF and ICP-MS assays. As a result of its valuable characteristics, LA-ICP-MS has been adopted by a large number of forensic laboratories worldwide. Several studies have identified the most informative and relevant elements for the comparison of glass fragments by ICP-MS methods (see Figure 6.1).

6.1.5.4 LIBS

Recently, LIBS has gaining interest within the forensic community (Bridge et al. 2006; Naes et al. 2008; El-Deftar et al. 2014; Gerhard et al. 2014; Rinke-Kneapler and Sigman 2014; Gupta et al. 2017). The configuration of LIBS is very similar to LA-ICP-MS, with the main difference being the detection system. LIBS detect emission of light from species that are excited in the micro-plasma, while LA-ICP-MS transports the nanoparticles that are ejected from the interaction of the laser beam with the material to an ICP-MS for further ionization and detection by mass to charge ratio. LIBS uses a short laser pulse to create a micro-plasma and excite species on the sample. When the excited electrons return into natural ground states, they emit light with discrete spectral peaks that are simultaneously detected by a spectrograph (see Figure 6.4). LIBS retains most of the advantages of LA-ICP-MS with additional simplicity, low cost, and high-speed measurements that can reduce the overall analysis time in half compared to LA-ICP-MS. The method, however, is slightly less precise and sensitive than LA-ICP-MS, with detection limits in the low-ppm range and precision in the order of 2–10% RSD. Studies have shown that the performance of LIBS lies between LA-ICP-MS and μ-XRF methods. LIBS is a promising method for glass analysis, but it is still in the process of reaching consensus validation and standardization.

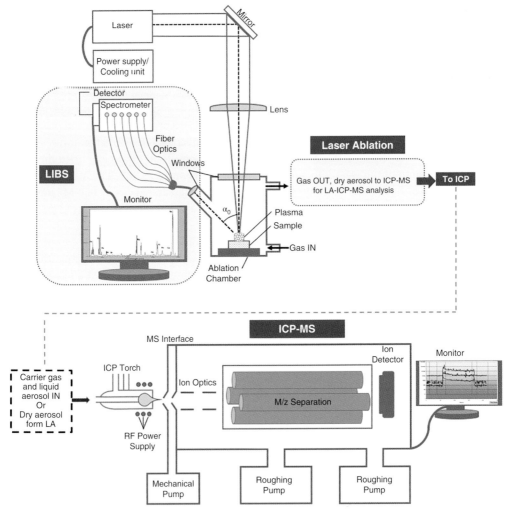

Figure 6.4 Scheme of a typical LIBS and laser ablation system attached to an ICP-MS. Note that LIBS and laser ablation can use the same laser head, optics, and ablation chamber but in LIBS the emission of light is captured by fiber optics separated in a spectrograph according to their wavelength and detected. Laser ablation removes the ablated particles from the ablation chamber and transports them to an ICP-MS (LA-ICP-MS). An ICP-MS can be also operated alone in solution mode (bottom).

6.1.6 Comparison of Discrimination Capabilities of the Methods of Analysis

The assessment of the discrimination capabilities of analytical methods for glass comparisons relies on empirically based scientific foundations. The discrimination has been typically assessed by evaluating the relative percentage of correct exclusions that are observed in a dataset of samples known to originate from different sources.

Depending on the study, these sources include (i) glass known to originate from different manufacturing sites, (ii) different makes/models/years, (iii) the same manufacturing plant at different time intervals, (iv) known samples from casework, or (v) a combination of the above. These studies have been conducted on container, architectural, and vehicle glass for datasets ranging from 40 to a few thousands of samples (Trejos et al. 2013a,b;

Weis et al. 2011; Dorn et al. 2015; Corzo et al. 2018; Hoffman et al. 2018).

The discrimination figures provided below are relative to the sample size under study and the composition of the dataset and are cited just as a general and relative indication of the utility of the methods, rather than absolute figures. Moreover, the accuracy of the methods has been assessed by taking into account not only false exclusion rates but also false association rates from datasets of samples known to originate from the same source.

RI provides useful discrimination of glass objects. However, the discrimination of glass by RI is somewhat limited (3–10% random match probability) and therefore RI analysis is often combined with elemental analysis to increase the value of the evidence (Ryland 2011; Koons and Buscaglia 2001; Locke and Hayes 1984; Garvin and Koons 2011).

The discrimination potential of μ-XRF was first documented in 1976 by Reeve et al. (1976) and Dudley et al. (1980). Both studies independently demonstrated the ability of μ-XRF to distinguish between 97.5% and 98% of fragments originating from different sources.

In 1991, Koons et al. (1991) evaluated the relative discrimination capabilities of RI, XRF, and ICP-OES to differentiate fragments sampled from 81 different tempered glasses and reported enhanced discrimination of XRF and ICP-OES when combined with optical measurements. Similar enhancement in discrimination of μ-XRF was published in 2011 by Ryland (2011) for a set of sheet glass with very similar RIs, where random match probabilities were lower than 2%.

In 2008, Naes et al. (2008) reported discrimination capabilities of μ-XRF comparable to those attained with LIBS and slightly lower than LA-ICP-MS for a set of 40 automotive glasses indistinguishable by RI. In 2013, the NIJ-funded Elemental Analysis Working Group compared the analytical performance of μ-XRF, ICP-MS, and LA-ICP-MS for the analysis of glass fragments manufactured in the same plant at short time intervals (Trejos

et al. 2013a). The studies show that these methods are suitable for discrimination of glass samples originating from different plants and glass manufactured in the same plant a few weeks to 1 month apart. Although the ability of these methods to detect temporal variations in a plant cannot be generalized, they provide valuable insight into the methods' potential.

Discrimination studies for ICP-MS have reported between-factories variability of elemental profiles for manufacturing plants in the United States, Europe, and Australia. Likewise, several authors have reported within-factory variability at different time intervals representing over 300 glass fragments collected from single plants over periods of 53 months at different time intervals, including approximately 100 samples collected every 15 minutes for 24 hours. Discrimination capabilities better than 99.8% have been consistently reported, from glass originating from different sources, with experimental random match probabilities in the order of 0.1–0.2% (Weis et al. 2011; Dorn et al. 2015; Corzo et al. 2018).

With the standardization of analytical methods and the established scientific foundation of glass examinations, current challenges are focused on the proper interpretation of the weight of the evidence, which is the main focus of this chapter and will be discussed in detail in the following sections.

6.2 Introduction to the Interpretation of Glass Evidence

Glass examiners are often asked to answer questions such as "Does the glass recovered from the POI come from the crime scene window?" or "Did this person break that window?" Such questions generally relate to an unobserved set of events and therefore the answers are inherently probabilistic or statistical in nature. We can never definitively state the source of any recovered trace because we cannot rule out the possibility that it may have come from another source. More importantly, the court does not (or should not) require the examiner to make such a statement.

Modern glass interpretation is statistical in its nature. The use of statistics recognizes the uncertainty in the questions being asked as well as the fundamental variability exhibited in measurements taken on glass from the same source and glass from different sources. The use of statistics in the interpretation of glass evidence has a very long history starting (primarily) with papers from Evett (1977) and Lindley (1977), and continuing through to the present day. Glass is considered to be the field of evidence interpretation which makes the most use of statistics outside of DNA (Curran 2003), although there have been recent advances in other forensic disciplines such as voice comparison, fingerprints, and anthropology.[1] The way in which glassd evidence is statistically evaluated is a forerunner of many ideas applied to other evidential material (Aitken and Taroni 2004). It is therefore not surprising to find that glass is the field, after DNA, where one can find the most publications showing how probabilities and statistics can help the forensic scientist to establish what are the needs in the case, which examinations should be performed, and how to assess the forensic results obtained in the case.

Glass is a very common type of trace evidence: in New Zealand, for example, in 2015/2016, approximately 7% of all physical evidence casework involved glass but this has been as high as 14% in recent years (A.W.N. Newton, personal communication). The most common scenario where glass evidence may arise in the United States is in hit-and-run cases. Outside of the United States, the most common scenario where glass evidence may arise is when a window is broken in order to gain entry to a building or vehicle. In this section, we will assume that a window in a house or commercial premises has been

broken for illustrative purposes. However, the methodology can be used in any investigation involving broken glass, such as a hit-and-run, an assault or even a laboratory accident.[2] If a window is broken, tiny fragments of glass may be transferred to a person's clothing, footwear, and headgear. If there are suspicious circumstances, the crime scene examiner will take a sample from the broken window: this sample can be referred to as the control sample, the reference, the known, the source, the bulk, or the crime sample (Aitken and Taroni 2004). If the police arrest a POI, then outer clothing, footwear. and headgear may be seized in order to search for glass fragments (Curran et al. 2000) and a case opened. The clothing will be examined for fragments if the case pre-assessment[3] indicates that useful evidence is likely to be obtained. The fragments recovered from the POI's clothing or person are referred to as unknown, questioned, transferred, recovered, or POI fragments. In this chapter we will use the terms source and recovered fragments. We will first show how the case can be pre-assessed (formally or not). Then we will discuss how to sample the evidence depending on the case, then look at how examination results can be interpreted, and finally examine how to evaluate the strength of evidence using both a two-stage, or match/non-match, approach and a continuous approach which has no matching step.

In the work ahead we will interchangeably refer to the glass examiner, the (forensic) scientist, or the expert. We make no distinction between these roles in this work even though they might have a narrower definition in reality.

6.2.1 Formulation of Working Propositions and Case Pre-assessment

Case pre-assessment involves the collection of all relevant information, setting and discussion

---

1 Forensic anthropology is statistically sophisticated but mostly frequentist in nature.

2 The model used for interpretation will differ, however, depending on where the material is found.
3 We discuss the concept of case pre-assessment in Section 6.2.1.

of the propositions, identifying the factors necessary to evaluate the evidence, discussing the search strategy (Curran et al. 2000), and estimation of the overall value of a case. The parties involved may then decide whether to proceed and expend further resources on the case.

In this section we will consider a simple example case in order to highlight issues and ideas of interest.

Suppose that a witness sees a male in his late teens break a window pane in the rear door of a house with some sort of tool and attempt to enter. The witness shouts and scares off the breaker before he enters the premises. The witness proceeds to call the police and report the attempted break in. Half an hour later, Mr. S is arrested in the vicinity of the crime scene. He denies any involvement. His outer clothing, headgear, and footwear are seized and securely packaged to prevent accidental contamination and/or evidence tampering. In additional, a sample of glass from the broken window is collected and stored in secured packaging.

In order to pre-assess (and assess) the case, the expert needs to evaluate the scientific evidence with respect to at least two propositions. The importance of establishing these working propositions cannot be overstated: this is a very critical stage and is probably the most difficult stage of evidence interpretation (Evett et al. 2000).

Cook et al. (2008), Evett and Weir (1998), and Aitken and Taroni (2004) posited three key principles to help the forensic scientist build these propositions:

1. The scientist must interpret results in the light of the case circumstances. Of course, not all information will be relevant. Examples of forensically relevant information are the timing, the extent of breaking, or if the defendant is engaged in (non-criminal) activities that involve glass. An example of irrelevant information would be that the person fits the description given by a witness. Scientists only need to know the information that has an impact on the value of the evidence.

2. The scientist must consider the results given *two mutually exclusive* propositions generally representing the viewpoints of both parties. The phrase *mutually exclusive* means that only one of these propositions can be true at any one time. It may be constructive for you to think of these as the propositions proposed by prosecution and the defense respectively, although this may not be the case in reality. It should be noted that these propositions do not need to be *collectively exhaustive*, meaning that they need not cover every single possible reason for the presence of glass.

3. The job of the scientist is to address the question of the probability of the evidence given each of the propositions. We emphasis the order of this statement because it highlights the fact that the scientist is in the courtroom to talk about the value, or significance, of the evidence with respect to the propositions and nothing else. It is the *jury* who must address questions such as "What is the probability of the proposition given the evidence?"

Cook et al. (2008) proposed a hierarchy of the different kinds of propositions: Level I, or source level, Level II, or the activity level, and Level III, or the offence level. It should be clear that the forensic scientist will require an increasing amount of information as one ascends the levels of the hierarchy in order to make substantive statements. It is sometimes said that the Court addresses questions at the offence level. This is true, as it is the Court that addresses the probability of the propositions, but this is true regardless of the level in the hierarchy. It will always be the Court that addresses the propositions. The Court will usually wish to address questions at the offence level. It may do this with assistance from the forensic scientist, who may be able to consider the evidence at given source, or activity, or offence level propositions. We note again that scientists assess the results given the propositions and not the propositions themselves. The scientists need to specify which results they are expertly qualified to evaluate in order to determine the appropriate level of the propositions. That is, one should add value using specialized knowledge when rising in the hierarchy (i.e. brings knowledge that is required, but not readily available to the court). Rising in the hierarchy, as previously mentioned, also involves having the necessary information in the actual case.

One can say, as a general guiding principle, that source level propositions are sufficient when there is a large abundance of material and that its relevance to the crime does not need specialized knowledge. Consider, for example, a hit-and-run case. Source level propositions would be sufficient in this case if the police find a large amount of glass at the scene, and if this glass appears to be there because of the crime. Source level propositions are adequate in cases where there is no risk that the Court will misinterpret them in the context of the alleged activities in the case (European Network of Forensic Science Institutes 2016).

Factors such as the presence of background glass, transfer, and persistence all have an impact on the value of the results in the context of glass recovered from clothing. The number of glass fragments and where they were recovered are important pieces of information in this case. One needs forensic knowledge in order to assess these factors. The European Network of Forensic Science Institutes (ENFSI) guidelines state (European Network of Forensic Science Institutes 2016) that "Activity level propositions should be used when expert knowledge is required to consider factors such as transfer mechanisms, persistence and background levels of the material which could have an impact on the understanding of scientific findings relative to the alleged activities. This is particularly important for trace materials such as microtraces (fibres, glass, gunshot residues, other particles) and small quantities of DNA, drugs or explosives."

In the ensuing text we give examples of propositions that could be used depending on the results that one should evaluate. Indeed,

one must be able to assess all the results given those propositions to ensure that propositions are well formulated. One must therefore specify these results. We will also give examples of relevant case information because case information is also essential for this task.

6.2.2 Evaluation of Results Given Source Level Propositions

Case information: On Sunday 25 June 2017, at 4:25 p.m., a car struck three pedestrians and left the scene without stopping. A witness called the police immediately, and they arrived a few minutes later. Large pieces of glass (typical of headlights) were collected in the middle of the road next to the victims. There is no contest to the fact that this glass is present in relation to the accident. That is, no-one disputes that the glass comes from the headlights of the car that hit the pedestrians.

Twenty minutes later, a person of interest, Mr. S, was arrested. He said he had nothing to do with the accident and that he had not driven down the road where the accident occurred for more than a month. He indicated that he had a small parking incident the day before and had hit a pillar.

The glass recovered from the scene and glass collected from the broken headlight on Mr. S's car was analyzed and compared. The recovered and source glass fragments had similar characteristics. To assess the results (RI, elemental analysis) one can consider the following propositions:

– The glass recovered from the crime scene came from Mr. S's car.
– The glass recovered from the crime scene came from an unknown car.

You will note that these propositions are mutually exclusive. That is, one or the other of the propositions is true, but they cannot both be true at the same time. They are also exhaustive in the case, but not in general. Indeed, in the context of the case we know from the information that a car was involved, it is taken as a given that the glass is relevant to the crime, thus we did not consider that the glass could come from a truck, or a bus, or some other source.

Note also how the propositions at this level consider the value of the analytical results. These propositions do not incorporate any information regarding the number of glass fragments or where they were found. This is not problematic as it would not be misleading. No specialized knowledge is needed to rise in the hierarchy.

6.2.3 Evaluation of Results Given Activity Level Propositions

Case information: On 22 May 2017, in Pully, Switzerland, a break-in occurred at a villa located at Chemin du Fau Blanc 20. An neighbor saw a man smash a window at the rear of the villa with some kind of tool. The man climbed through the window. He exited the villa shortly through the same window and ran off down the street. The neighbor immediately contacted the police, who attended the scene. The police collected fragments of glass from the broken window and stored them in secure packaging for analysis. Two hours later, the police arrested Mr. S and collected his sweater. Mr. S said that he had never been in the house located at Chemin du Fau Blanc 20, nor did he have anything to do with the incident. When asked, he said that he had not broken any glass recently nor was he aware of having been near broken glass in the last past week.

Nine glass fragments were recovered on his sweater. They were compared to the broken glass window based on RI and elemental composition. Neither technique revealed any significant difference[4] between the scene source and the recovered fragments.

One might consider the following propositions when assessing the value of the results

(nine glass fragments recovered on the sweater, RI, elemental analysis):

- Mr. S broke the window.
- Mr. S had nothing to do with the incident.

Note how the propositions at this level consider the value of the analytical results, the number of glass fragments, and where they were found. These propositions let the forensic scientist incorporate factors such as background, transfer, and persistence into the interpretation. Comprehension and consideration of all of these phenomena requires expert forensic knowledge. One can also note that contrary to source level propositions, activity level propositions can be formulated even before we have information regarding the results. Indeed, one can assess any result given those propositions: no glass, glass that is different, glass that is not differentiable, or even multiple sources of glass.

6.2.4 A Note on the Use of "Contact" or Pseudo-Activity Level Propositions

It might be tempting to formulate propositions such as:

- Mr. S was in recent contact with glass.
- Mr. S was not in recent contact with glass.

when there is little information on how the window was broken, but a large number of glass fragments were recovered. Such propositions have been referred to in the literature as pseudo-activity level propositions (Evett et al. 2000) because they give the impression that they consider factors such as transfer of background, when this in fact is not the case. The main problem with the term *contact* is that the term is vague and that it is very difficult to assign probabilities when we are vague. What do we mean by *contact* or *recent contact*? How would we describe this *contact* if we were to simulate the case? What is the probability of the results given there was *recent contact*? If this probability is always one, then maybe this is an explanation and not a proposition.

---

4 We use this phrase to simplify the exposition rather than suggest wording that might be used in a statement to the Court.

Contact also causes problems when attempting to formulate a mutually exclusive alternative proposition. That is, if we simply add the term *not* to the first proposition, then again we are being vague and thus it is very difficult to assign probabilities. To assess the results in a logical and balanced way given activity level propositions, quite logically, we need propositions that are about the activities of the person (e.g. breaking). In conclusion, if *contact* is not defined in sufficient detail, then it best is to avoid using this term altogether.

6.2.5 Evaluation of Results Given Offence Level Propositions

Evaluation of results obtained on glass are rarely assessed given offence level propositions because in most cases the added value lies in considering phenomenon such as transfer or fortuitous presence of glass on clothing. When assessing results given offence level propositions, one can take into account the relevance of the trace (i.e. how probable it is that the trace is from the offender or not), the probability that the material came from the suspect if he is the offender, the number of offenders, and the presence of the material for reasons unconnected to the crime.

Imagine the following case, which is similar to the case first described, but where one cannot infer that the relevance of the glass fragments is one.

On Sunday 25 June 2017, at 4 : 25 p.m., a car struck three pedestrians and left the scene without stopping. A witness called the police immediately, and they arrived a few minutes later. The police collected scattered pieces of glass from the road. However, in contrast to our previous example, in this case it is not obvious that the glass recovered from the scene is related to the accident.

Twenty minutes later a person of interest, Mr. S, was arrested at his place of employment. Mr. S is an automotive body repair specialist and had recently worked on several damaged cars. He said he had nothing to do with the accident. The police seized three of the cars that had physical damage, including broken headlights, from the body shop.

Glass fragments were taken from each of the cars, analyzed, and compared to the glass recovered from the scene. Glass fragments from one of the damaged cars had similar[5] characteristics to the glass recovered from the scene. One can consider the following propositions to assess the results (three damaged cars, glass scattered over the road, RI, elemental analysis):

– Mr. S is the offender.
– Mr. S has nothing to do with the accident.

The scientist, having specialized expert knowledge in interpretation, can help the court by explaining, or demonstrating, the influence of the different factors (e.g. relevance) on the value of the evidence.

It must be remembered that the higher the scientist goes in the hierarchy, then the more useful the evidence will be, providing, of course, that the scientist provides knowledge that is required, but not readily available to the court. Countering this increase in evidential value is an increased requirement for expertise and an increased need for background information. It may be a difficult task, but when expert forensic knowledge is required, we believe that the best person to help address the appropriate level of the propositions is the forensic glass examiner. This is especially true for activity level propositions when the background level of glass as well as the transfer and persistence of glass have an impact on the evaluation of forensic results.

The glass examiner can pre-assess the case either informally or formally (Cook et al. 2008) once the propositions have been established. An informal case assessment will consist of thinking about what we would expect to find if the propositions were true. For example, would we find matching[6] and/or

---

5 Again, we use this term for ease of exposition.
6 We use these terms very loosely to mean glass fragments with similar physical characteristics to the

non-matching[6] glass, how many fragments would we expect given each proposition? Formal pre-assessment (Cook et al. 2008) using the likelihood ratio (LR) approach consists of assessing six different probabilities using published data and/or personal knowledge, before even looking at the evidence. For example, consider a case where the clothing of a person suspected of breaking a window is going to be searched for glass. In this example, these probabilities could be:

1. The probability of finding no matching glass fragments if the POI is the person who broke the window.
2. The probability of finding a few (1–2) matching glass fragments if the POI is the person who broke the window.
3. The probability of finding many (≥3) matching glass fragments if the POI is the person who broke the window.
4. The probability of finding no matching glass fragments if the POI had nothing to do with the incident.
5. The probability of finding few (1–2) matching glass fragments if the POI had nothing to do with the incident.
6. The probability of finding many (≥3) matching glass fragments if the POI had nothing to do with the incident.

These probabilities are not always easy to assign because of the lack of information and the variability of the different factors. Sensitivity analysis (Evett and Weir 1998; Hicks 2003) with, for example, Bayesian Networks (Taroni et al. 2014) can be used to estimate the influence of the lack of information. Once the propositions have been established and the case pre-assessed, a discussion between the forensic scientist and the client should take place in order to discuss the case and its possible value. We use the word *client* to refer to the party who has retained the services of the forensic scientist or forensic

laboratory. This may be the police, a lawyer or law firm, the defendant themselves, or the court in those jurisdictions where forensic scientists are retained independently of either party. If expectations regarding the number of fragments to be found given that the person has broken the window have been quantified, then one might search the items taken from the POI for glass and only evaluate two of the six probabilities above. For example, if we search the POI's clothing and recover six fragments, then we would pre-assess the case using only probabilities (3) and (6). This would give the client more value for little additional cost.

6.2.6 Evaluation of Results Given Source Level Propositions

Source level propositions address, as the name suggests, questions of common source. Propositions at the source level are used to help the court determine whether the recovered fragments come from the broken material or from a different source. Such determinations are made with respect to some analytical characteristics of the source material. Glass may be characterized by shape, color, density, RI, or elemental concentration. Modern forensic laboratories use either RI or elemental concentration, or occasionally both. RI is strongly correlated with density, with the former being easier to determine. Forensic laboratories who do glass casework often have a GRIM3 or GRIM2 instrument made by Foster and Freeman. Other popular instruments include Laboratory Imaging's Lucia RI[7] and CRAIC Technologies' rIQ.[8] These instruments use the standard oil immersion/temperature variation technique (Ojena and De Forest 1972) and can determine RI within a source with a standard 2×10^{-5}. Elemental concentration may be determined by a variety of instruments, such as SEM-EDS, μ-XRF, ICP-MS/ICP-AES, LA-ICP-MS, or LIBS. Many laboratories use

---

glass found at the scene. This state may, or may not, be formalized by some statistical match-step.

7 https://www.forensic.cz/en/products/lucia_ri.
8 http://www.microspectra.com/products/riq.

laser ablation units in conjunction with their ICP instruments (e.g. LA-ICP-MS). This has the advantage of allowing rapid measurements to be taken in an effectively non-destructive manner, as opposed to acid digestion methods which are time consuming and destroy the recovered items. The ability to remeasure evidence can be useful in retrials.

The evaluation can take place in one or two stages. A two-stage approach consists of a match step that precedes the evaluation step. If the recovered fragments are deemed to not match the source (according to whatever criteria are employed) then the evidence is said to support exclusion and evaluation does not proceed. The overwhelming majority of researchers engaged in statistical interpretation of forensic evidence believe that the Bayesian approach to evaluating the strength of evidence is both very useful and logical. This approach is not new. Richard Price posthumously published the Reverand Thomas Bayes' theorem in 1763 (Bayes 1763), and in more modern times Alan Turing and Jack Good (1950) used Bayes' Theorem to specifically evaluate the strength of evidence. Ian Evett introduced the glass problem to renowned statistician Dennis Lindley in the late 1970s, which resulted in a publication (Lindley 1977) with a Bayesian solution and a raft of ensuing journal articles, books, and conference presentations, in both glass and many other forensic disciplines.

Let E denote the evidence, H_p and H_d be the propositions under consideration, and I the background information we have on the case (e.g. breaking method, time elapsed, and so on). The odds form of Bayes' Theorem states:

$$\underbrace{\frac{\Pr(H_p \mid E, I)}{\Pr(H_d \mid E, I)}}_{\text{posterior odds}} = \underbrace{\frac{\Pr(E \mid H_p, I)}{\Pr(E \mid H_d, I)}}_{\text{likelihood ratio}} \times \underbrace{\frac{\Pr(H_p \mid I)}{\Pr(H_d \mid I)}}_{\text{prior odds}}$$

(6.1)

The odds form of Bayes' Theorem lends itself to a very simple method for updating prior belief. We may rewrite (6.1) as:

$$\text{posterior odds} = \text{likelihood ratio}$$
$$\times \text{prior odds} \quad (6.2)$$

This formulation is convenient because it separates the probabilities relating to the evidence from those relating to the propositions. As mentioned earlier, the former usually concerns the forensic scientist and the latter the Court. The Bayesian approach can be applied in one or two steps, that is, at the comparison stage (Lindley 1977; Evett 1986) or after comparison. The so-called continuous likelihood ratio approach (one step), by comparison, is more complex but more efficient than the two-stage approach. However, it is useful to begin with the two-stage approach (Evett and Buckleton 1990) in order to understand the Bayesian thinking.

6.2.7 The Two-Stage Approach

Let us take our example where a window was broken, and say that, after case pre-assessment, the decision was made to search for glass on Mr. S's jacket and that six fragments were recovered. The RIs of each of those six fragments were measured, as well as the RIs for a selection of fragments from the window broken at the crime scene.

6.2.7.1 Interpretation Based on RI Measurements

The first stage of the two-stage approach consists of determining if the measurements made on the two samples are different or not. This may be done in a variety of different ways and will change depending on jurisdiction.

The least formal, and perhaps most subjective, way is to plot both the source and recovered RI measurements along a horizontal RI axis with vertical separation between the two samples. The recovered fragments are declared to match if they are within the range (between the minimum and maximum) of the source measurements, or "reasonably close." The phrase "reasonably close" is too vague to be repeatable even though it may be based heavily on the examiner's expertise, and therefore should be regarded as unacceptable.

All other match steps (that we know of) are statistically oriented, that is, they try in some way to take account of the variability that we might expect to see within a source of glass.

The graphical method described above includes an informal application of a range test. In this context, recovered fragments whose RI is within the range of the source measurements are deemed matches, and those that fall outside this range are deemed non-matches. If there are no matching fragments in the recovered sample, then evaluation does not proceed. Range tests, although objective in the sense that they are repeatable and based on transparent criteria, are generally not advisable because the sample range is a very poorly behaved statistic as it is highly susceptible to outliers. This means that tests based on the range will often have poor type I or type II error rates, or in statistical terminology poor size and poor power.

Type I and Type II Errors, Size, and Power

A statistical hypothesis test is said to have a *type I error rate* of α if the probability of rejecting the null hypothesis when it is true is α. The *size* of this test is said to be α.

We realize we have not formally defined the term *null hypothesis* in this chapter. It suffices to think of the null hypothesis as a mathematical formalization of the idea of "no difference" or perhaps "no departure from expectation." In the context of glass interpretation, the null hypothesis is that the two samples (source and recovered) come from sources with the same, but unknown, mean. There is considerable debate as to whether the Court has any interest in this hypothesis.

A statistical hypothesis test is said to have a *type II error rate* of β if the probability of failing to reject the null hypothesis when it is false is β. The *power* of this test is said to be $1 - \beta$. Putting these definitions

---

in less formal terms: the type I error rate, or size, is the chance you will form an incorrect conclusion when the two sources are the same, and the type II error rate is the chance you will form an incorrect conclusion when the two sources are different. They are sometimes referred to as the *false exclusion rate* or *false negative rate*, and the *false inclusion rate* or *false positive rate*, for obvious reasons.

2σ and 3σ tests represent a statistical advance over straight range tests. There are a number of variants. Their details are given, and their strengths and weaknesses are evaluated, in Garvin and Koons (2011). We describe here the most common variant. We assume that the forensic scientist has determined the RI of n fragments of glass from the scene source. We denote these measurements $x_1, x_2, \ldots, x_n$. The 3σ test proceeds by calculating the 3σ match interval given by

$$\bar{x} \pm 3 \times s_x$$

where $\bar{x}$ is the sample mean of the source measurements, i.e.

$$\bar{x} = \frac{1}{n} \sum_{i=1}^{n} x_i$$

and s_x is the sample standard deviation of the source measurements, i.e.

$$s_x = \sqrt{\frac{1}{n-1} \sum_{i=1}^{n} (x_i - \bar{x})^2}.$$

The RI measurements on the recovered fragments, denoted $y_1, y_2, \ldots, y_m$ are compared sequentially to the 3σ match interval. Any measurement that falls within the interval is deemed a match, and interval that falls outside the interval is deemed a non-match. A 2σ match step is conducted in the same way with the only difference being that the match interval is narrower ($\bar{x} \pm 2s_x$). The effect of increasing the width interval decreases the false exclusion rate when the two samples have the same source and increases the false inclusion rate when two samples are from different sources. This trade-off between size and power is inherent in all hypothesis tests.

The match steps described thus far are sequential in nature, that is, the recovered fragments are compared to the source interval one at a time. This practice reflects the common forensic idea that we cannot assume that all the recovered fragments come from the same source. One might consider an example case where glass is recovered from a POI's shirt and from their footwear. There would significant merit in the a priori belief that the glass from the footwear originated from container glass (broken bottles) whereas glass from the shirt may have originated from the scene window. However, sequential comparison is not a zero-cost procedure, in that one increases the chance of falsely excluding at one least recovered fragment with every comparison that is performed. This is known as the problem of multiple comparisons in statistics.

An alternative is to group the recovered fragments. Several grouping algorithms have been proposed (Evett and Lambert 1982; Curran 1996; Triggs et al. 1997). The main point is not so much how RI measurements are grouped but that they are grouped at all. Treating the recovered fragments as having come from a single source, when, for example, the fragments have been recovered from the same item and have properties that are comparable, keeps the type I error rate of the procedure at α and increases the power of the test. This is because the test simply has more information to work with, and therefore confers more certainty to the result.

Multiple Comparisons

If a set of k independent pairwise comparisons are performed using a statistical hypothesis test with size α then the probability that at least one of these tests results in a false exclusion is under certain assumptions given by

$$1 - (1 - \alpha)^k.$$

This probability is approximately equal to $k\alpha$ for $k \leq 10$. For example, if $\alpha = 0.01$ and $k = 1$, then the probability of making one false exclusion is $\alpha = 0.01$. However, if $k = 5$, then this probability jumps to $0.04900995 \approx 0.05$.

There are a number of statistical treatments designed to deal with the problem of multiple comparisons. These range from the simple Bonferroni correction (Bonferroni 1936) to the much more statistically complex false discovery rate (FDR) of Benjamini and Hochberg (1995). The Bonferroni correction is conservative in that it reduces the type I error rate, but it increases the type II error rate. The FDR is regarded as less conservative, but is unlikely to have much effect with the number of recovered fragments that are normally present in casework. Pawluk-Kołc et al. (2006) considered the application of the FDR to glass evidence.

A traditional statistical test for the difference in two population means with unknown variances is Student's t-test. Evett (1977,1978) proposed the use of Student's t-test for comparing the mean RIs of recovered and source samples. Walsh and Buckleton (1996) suggested that Welch's modification of Student's t-test was perhaps more appropriate as it allows unequal variances in the two populations. This relaxation is quite useful, as it has been shown that measurements on recovered fragments present a standard deviation larger (often 50% larger) than measurements made on a large sample of a window (Newton 2011). Both variants of the tests require measurements to be grouped before testing.

Assuming the RI measurements of the recovered fragments have been grouped, and that the significance level (α) has been chosen, then one can proceed with the test. The significance level is simultaneously the value at which the scientist decides to act as if the null hypothesis is false, and a specification of the "acceptable type I error rate." For example, assume we have a case which involves 20 fragments and that a significance level of 0.05 (or 5%) has been chosen. If the test statistic for the pooled *t*-test (given below) exceeds approximately 2.1 (in magnitude), then the forensic scientist would *reject the null hypothesis* and effectively decide that the scene source and recovered samples originated from different sources. In making such a decision the forensic scientist accepts, assuming that samples truly originate from the same source, that (on average) this decision will be incorrect approximately 5% of the time because of random chance alone. The choice of significant level is *utterly arbitrary*. There is a commonly held misconception in science that α should always be 0.05.

The choice of this value supposedly comes from the father of modern statistics, R.A. Fisher, who wrote "… it is convenient to draw the line at about the level at which we can say: *Either there is something in the treatment, or a coincidence has occurred such as does not occur more than once in twenty trials* … If one in twenty does not seem high enough odds, we may, if we prefer it, draw the line at one in fifty (the 2 per cent point), or one in a hundred (the 1 per cent point). Personally, the writer prefers to set a low standard of significance at the 5 per cent point, and ignore entirely all results which fail to reach this level. A scientific fact should be regarded as experimentally established only if a properly designed experiment rarely fails to give this level of significance (Fisher 1926)." However, Fisher himself argued vociferously against the rigid applications of such thresholds in science (see Fisher (1956), for example).

The choice of α = 0.01 is common in forensic science. Some researchers justify this choice in terms of the feeling that α = 0.05 is simply too high. Others appeal to Blakestone's formulation "… it is better that ten guilty persons escape, than that one innocent party suffer" (Blakestone and Browne 1897). However, this seems misguided because decreasing α increases β, the probability of false inclusion. We wish to emphasize again here that the choice of α is arbitrary, and that there is always a trade-off between minimizing false inclusions and the ability of a test to detect differences.

6.2.7.2 Student's *t*-Test

There are two variants of Student's *t*-test for the difference in population means: the pooled or standard two-sample *t*-test and Welch's modification to the two-sample *t*-test. We briefly describe these tests in this section. The hypotheses under consideration in both variants are:

$$H_0 : \mu_x - \mu_y = 0$$

where H_0 is the null hypothesis, H_1 is the alternative hypothesis, and μ_x and μ_y are the true (but unknown) means of the sources from which the scene and recovered samples originated. We use our information about our samples, and some distributional assumptions about the behavior of the test statistic under the assumption that H_0 is true, to make an inferential statement about H_0. We make such inferences by calculating a test statistic and then calculating an associated P value. The P value tells us the probability of observing a test statistic as large, or larger (in magnitude), *under the assumption that H_0 is true*. A essential point of difference between this approach and the Bayesian approach is that there is no explicit consideration of the behavior of the test statistic with respect to the alternative hypothesis, H_1.

The pooled *t*-test test statistic is

$$T_0 = \frac{\bar{x} - \bar{y}}{\sqrt{\frac{1}{n} + \frac{1}{m}}\sqrt{\frac{(n-1)s_x^2 + (m-1)s_y^2}{n+m-2}}}$$

and the Welch *t*-test test statistic is

$$W_0 = \frac{\bar{x} - \bar{y}}{\sqrt{\frac{s_x^2}{n} + \frac{s_y^2}{m}}}$$

A P value is obtained for these statistics by calculating $2(1 - \Pr(T < |T_0|))$ or $2(1 - \Pr(W < |W_0|))$, where T and W are random variables from a Student's t distribution with degrees of freedom given by

$$df_T = n + m - 2 \text{ and } df_W$$

$$= \frac{\left(\frac{s_x^2}{n} + \frac{s_y^2}{m}\right)^2}{\frac{s_x^4}{n^2(n-1)} + \frac{s_y^4}{m^2(m-1)}}, \text{ respectively.}$$

If the P value is greater than α, then the recovered fragments are deemed to match. If the P value is less than α, then the hypothesis of a common source is rejected, that is, the samples are said to be statistically different. Both P values consider the absolute value ($|T_0|$ and $|W_0|$, respectively) of the test statistic because we are interested only in whether the sources are different, and not in whether one source has a higher (or lower) mean than the other.

Let us assume that, as in our example, all recovered fragments are grouped and that there has been only one source of broken glass. If the fragments do not match, then the likelihood ratio given source level propositions is zero (i.e. $LR = 0$). If the fragments do match, then the LR is:

$$LR = \frac{1}{f} \tag{6.3}$$

where f is the frequency of the mean of the recovered fragments in the relevant population. We deliberately leave the definition of what constitutes the relevant population vague at this point.

Example: Comparing RI Measurements As an example we will take casework data (Courtesy of the Forensic Science Service, FSS London Laboratory Glass Workshop, January 2003) from fragments recovered on a jacket and on a hat. The RI measurements are shown in Table 6.1 and the summary statistics for the data in Table 6.1 are shown in Table 6.2.

We can see from Table 6.2 that the range of measurements from the crime scene source is 1.51825–1.51828. Therefore, if we use the range test, four fragments recovered from the hat and three recovered from the jacket match the control window.

Table 6.1 Refractive index measurements from an example case.

Window	Hat	Jacket
1.518 25	1.518 20	1.518 19
1.518 26	1.518 24	1.518 21
1.518 26	1.518 26	1.518 24
1.518 27	1.518 26	1.518 26
1.518 27	1.518 27	1.518 26
1.518 28	1.518 27	1.518 27
1.518 28		

Table 6.2 Summary statistics from an example case.

Statistic	Window	Hat	Jacket
N	7	6	6
Minimum	1.518 25	1.518 20	1.518 19
Maximum	1.518 28	1.518 27	1.518 27
Mean	1.518 27	1.518 25	1.518 24
Standard deviation	1.113×10^{-5}	2.683×10^{-5}	3.189×10^{-5}

The range test is shown graphically in Figure 6.5. The 3σ rule yields an interval of $1.51827 \pm 3 \times 1.11270 \times 10^{-5} = [1.51823, 1.51830]$. This interval, shown in Figure 6.6, is wider than the range test interval, and includes an additional fragment from both the hat and the jacket samples.

If the fragments are grouped in one group and then compared using the standard pooled t-test, then the P values using Student's t-test are 0.14 and 0.04 for the hat and the jacket, respectively. If we use the Welch test, which seems prudent given the increased variation in each of the recovered samples, the P values are 0.19 and 0.07. We have not subjected you, the reader, to all the computational details of calculating these values. They can be calculated very simply using the T.TEST function in Microsoft Excel with two-tails and TYPE=2 for the standard t-test or TYPE=3 for the Welch t-test. Alternatively, you can use the t.test

Figure 6.5 Using the range test to determine matching fragments. The five fragments colored red are deemed different from the known source, or non-matching.

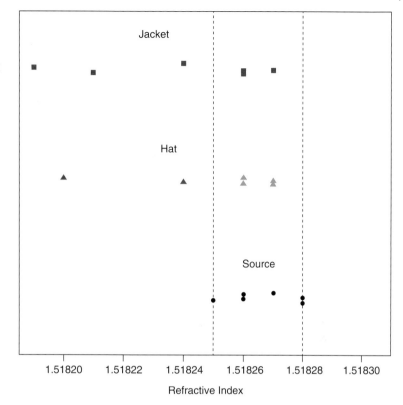

Figure 6.6 Using the 3σ test to determine matching fragments. The three fragments colored red are deemed different from the known source, or non-matching.

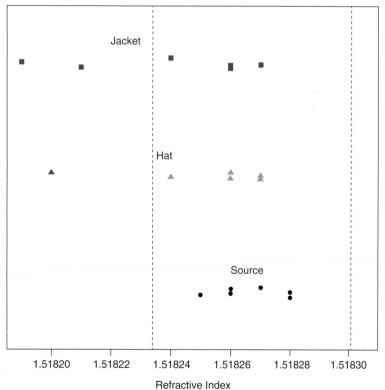

function in the statistical R programming language (R Core Team 2016), with `var.equal` set to `TRUE` or `FALSE` depending on whether you want the standard *t*-test or the Welch *t*-test.

We present here results using significance levels of 0.05 and 0.01 to illustrate the effect of choosing α.

If we choose a significance level of 0.05, then we would fail to reject the null hypothesis using the Welch test, that is, we would say that we were unable to determine any statistically significant difference between these samples on the basis of their means, and that the observed differences can be explained by random measurement error alone. However, if we use Student's *t*-test, we would reject the null hypothesis for the jacket, that is, we would conclude that the fragments recovered from the jacket appear to have a different average RI than those from the scene source and therefore *do not match* the scene source. We note here that we find ourselves in a position where the *P* value is "very close" to the rejection boundary of 0.05, that is, a small change in the recovered or scene samples might push the *P* value to 0.051, say, and therefore lead to a different conclusion. One of us (Curran) has asked forensic practitioners what they do in this situation (especially with respect to elemental analysis). Some advocate remeasuring the evidence. Such a practice should be frowned upon because it is essentially evidence tampering and it renders your statistical inference invalid.

If we choose a significance level of 0.01, then we would fail to reject the null hypothesis using either test, that is, we would say that we were unable to determine any statistically significant difference between these samples on the basis of their means, and that the observed differences can be explained by random measurement error alone. Therefore, using the Student's *t*-test or the Welch test with a significance level of 0.01, we would conclude that the recovered fragments *match* the scene source. Assuming that we proceed with this set of conclusions, then we find that they are in slight contrast to the results

we obtained from the range test (Figure 6.5) and the 3σ tests (Figure 6.6). One should reasonably ask which set of test conclusions we should use. Taking into account the higher variability in the recovered sample, and the fact that all the fragments were found on the same garment, we would, from an expert point of view, be inclined to take the results of the *t*-tests. If one accounts only for results that support the prosecution's proposition (i.e. the glass cannot be distinguished from the known source), then, given source level propositions, this result does not change the value of the evidence. This is a procedure that would be unbalanced. Indeed, one should also take into account the non-matching glass. If we do so in this case, where we have two different sources of recovered glass, then the value must be divided by two (Evett 1987). If there are N sources, and only one source that is indistinguishable, then the value is divided by N in order to take into account the glass fragments that are distinguishable (Triggs and Buckleton 2003). The choice of the test will therefore impact the value of the results. This is also true when we assess our results given activity level propositions.

The results of the tests are shown graphically in Figure 6.7. The dashed lines represent the means of each of the samples. If any pair of intervals overlap, then we would fail to reject the null hypothesis at the 0.01 level of significance. The interval widths change depending on which pair of means is under consideration when using the Welch *t*-test. They should, in theory, change for the standard pooled *t*-test as well. We have used a slightly different method to calculate the interval widths so that they are constant for each comparison. As noted, they should actually change, but they do not change as much as the Welch intervals.

To estimate the occurrence, the expert then will search the relevant database. Examples and formulae for this procedure can easily be found in Curran et al. (2000). The means, standard deviation, and critical value of the *t* distribution (using the Welch degrees of

Figure 6.7 Using the two-sample *t*-test to determine matching fragments. In this figure, it is the overlap of the intervals, determined from the means and standard deviations, that are important. If two intervals overlap, then the samples are deemed to match. It can be seen here that all of the intervals (either standard or Welch) for the jacket and hat match the scene window.

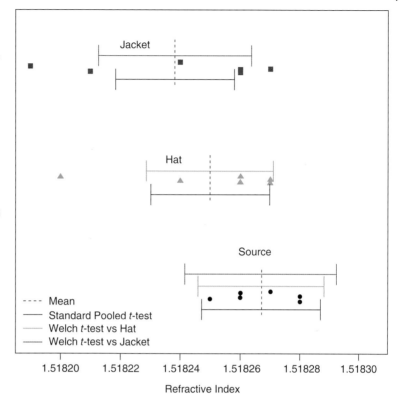

freedom) are used along with the appropriate formula in Curran et al. (2000) to give a *match window*. This can then be used to determine the occurrence. In our example case, using a significance level of 0.99 gives us a match window of 1.51821 to 1.51829. Using this window with the Lambert et al. survey (Lambert et al. 1995) yields a relative frequency of 2%. The corresponding *LR* would be 50. The corresponding *LR*, when we use the same match window and numerical integration with the New Zealand glass data from the R package `dafs` (Curran and Chang 2012), is in the order of 80. These figures clearly differ, but have the same order of magnitude.

6.2.7.3 Interpretation Based on Elemental Analysis Measurements

Modern methods of glass production are extraordinarily well-controlled. Window glass can be manufactured to have very precise optical properties. This is especially true,

and necessary, in the case of vehicle glass, as changes in the optical properties of the glass can interfere with the view of the vehicle operator. Koons and Buscaglia (2001) noted a narrowing of the RI distribution in glass recovered in FBI casework in 2001. Reeve et al. (1976) reported, in a very much earlier publication, that they could discriminate between sources of glass using SEM-EDS. As noted earlier, laboratories performing elemental analysis typically use SEM-EDS, μ-XRF, or LA-ICP-MS. An ICP-MS with a laser ablation unit is probably the gold-standard in the field, offering rapid, accurate, and precise determination of elemental concentrations. ASTM standards exist for μ-XRF (ASTM 2017), ICP-MS (ASTM 2012) and LA-ICP-MS (ASTM 2016). The ASTM E2927-16 and ASTM E2926-17 standards arose from considerable research effort that the Elemental Analysis Working Group put into designing and running inter-laboratory trials to evaluate the performance characteristics of μ-XRF, ICP-MS, LA-ICP-MS, and LIBS. The results of these exercises are described in Trejos et al. (2013a,b) and Ernst et al. (2014).

6.2.7.4 Match Steps for Elemental Analysis

ASTM standards E2330-12 and ASTM 2E926-17 describe match steps for μ-XRF and LA-ICP-MS, respectively. They essentially both offer variants of the 3σ rule, with adaptions for the multivariate case. We describe the match step from E2926-17 here, retaining the original section numbers.

> *10.1.1 For the Known source fragments, using a minimum of 3 measurements, calculate the mean for each element.*
>
> *10.1.2 Calculate the standard deviation for each element. This is the Measured SD.*
>
> *10.1.3 Calculate a value equal to 3% of the mean for each element. This is the Minimum SD.*
>
> *10.1.4 Calculate a match interval for each element with a lower limit equal to the mean minus 4 times the SD (Measured or Minimum, whichever is greater) and an upper limit equal to the mean plus 4 times the SD (Measured or Minimum, whichever is greater).*
>
> *10.1.5 For each Recovered fragment, using a minimum of 3 measurements, calculate the mean concentration for each element.*
>
> *10.1.6 For each element, compare the mean concentration in the Recovered fragment to the match interval for the corresponding element from the Known fragments.*
>
> *10.1.7 If the mean concentration of one (or more) element(s) in the Recovered fragment falls outside the match interval for the corresponding element in the Known fragments, the element(s) does not "match" and the glass samples are considered distinguishable.*

We can put this match step in traditional statistical notation. Let the measurements made on the source/control fragments be denoted x_{ij}

where i is the fragment and j is the element. Similarly, let y_{ij} denote the recovered measurements.

10.1.1

$$\bar{x}_{\bullet j} = \frac{1}{n_c} \sum_{i=1}^{i=n} x_{ij}, n \geq 3, j = 1, \dots, p$$

Note: Each measurement is averaged over at least three replicate measurements.[9]

10.1.2/3

$$s_{\bullet j} = \max\left[0.03\bar{x}_{\bullet j}, \sqrt{\frac{1}{n-1} \sum_{i=1}^{i=n} (x_{ij} - \bar{x}_{\bullet j})^2}\right]$$

10.1.4

$$m_j = \bar{x}_{\bullet j} \pm 4s_{\bullet j}$$

10.1.5 The recovered measurements are only averaged over the replicate measurements, so they remain as y_{ij}.

10.1.6/7

If

$$y_{ij} \notin [\bar{x}_{\bullet j} - 4s_{\bullet j}, \bar{x}_{\bullet j} + 4s_{\bullet j}]$$
$$\text{for } \textbf{any } j = 1, \dots, p$$

then the *fragment* is distinguishable.

10.1.6/7

By negation if

$$y_{ij} \in [\bar{x}_{\bullet j} - 4s_{\bullet j}, \bar{x}_{\bullet j} + 4s_{\bullet j}] \forall j = 1, \dots, p$$

then the *fragment* is indistinguishable.

There are some points of interest in this match step. First, we note that the match step proceeds element by element. This practice carries with it the inherent problem of multiple comparisons. This is addressed by using a 4σ interval rather than a 3σ interval. Similarly, each recovered fragment is compared sequentially. Finally, the match step contains an empirically derived rule whereby the minimum standard deviation to be used in the

---

9 The same may be true for RI measurements made using a GRIM3 instrument, where each reported RI is the average of up to four measurements corresponding to the four "cursors" that may be used on each fragment. Such averaging leads to more stable measurements of RI.

method is set to 3% of the mean concentration of the element for the control sample. Statisticians can and have taken issue with all of these points. If we step over all of these objections and note that (i) this is an inherently multivariate problem and therefore requires a multivariate solution, and (ii) grouping recovered fragments (for the same reasons we gave before) offers improved performance, then we arrive at a point where we ask why the use of a test like Hotelling's T^2 (Hotelling 1931), which is a multivariate equivalent of Student's two-sample t-test, is not part of this match step. The use of Hotelling's T^2 was suggested by Curran and Triggs (1997). This test was not practical until laser ablation became more common. This is because in order to perform Hotelling's T^2 test, the total number of fragments (both source and recovered) must be at least two more than the number of elements used for comparison. That is, if comparison is to be made on 10 elements, then we need at least 12 fragments in total. This data requirement was typically impractical before laser ablation. It should be added that forensic scientists still feel the data requirement of Hotelling's test are unreasonable and that the assumptions of the test are untenable. Hotelling's T^2 assumes that the data originate from multivariate normal distributions (MVNs) with a common variance-covariance matrix. Campbell and Curran (2009) showed how the method could be used without the assumption of multivariate normality and with less data, and provided software to do so (Curran 2017). However, this has had little uptake. This is perhaps of no consequence because it leaves interpretation mired in the "match/non-match" paradigm. Trejos et al. (2013a,b) evaluated Hotelling's T^2, using it on a sequential basis, and came to the conclusion that the 4σ method had the best performance, in terms of type I and type II error rates. It is for this reason that the ASTM standards suggest this rule.

Assuming one or more fragments match, we now find ourselves in a situation where we must determine the frequency. This is hard for evidence that may be measured on upwards of 10 or more elements. The reason it is hard is that it is very difficult to collect sufficient background information (or build a database) that will reliably estimate the occurrence in the population. One unsatisfactory approach is to say that we will never find glass in the population that matches the characteristics of the recovered sample. This is unsatisfactory for two reasons. First, we have decided via our match step that the recovered sample does indeed match the source. This means that if the glass recovered from the scene did not come from the scene source, then there is at least one source in the population that has similar (matching) characteristics to our recovered sample. Secondly, Trejos et al. (2013b) report study results that show round robin participants had difficulty, even using LA-ICMP-MS, in discriminating between glass samples made on the same line but collected 2 weeks apart. A float glass factory can produce 400–500 tonnes of glass per day. That means that there is potentially 5600–7000 tonnes of glass with the same ICP-MS characteristics. The problem gets worse with older, less precise instrumentation. Zadora and colleagues (pers. comm.) have shown 50% overlap in container glass (using SEM-EDS) collected over a 6-month period. So we do not believe that all glass is so rare in elemental space that it will never match by chance, but we do have good reason to think that than "random match probability" will be small. How small is small? Good question. A very simple, but naïve, approach is to return to our first statement: if the glass recovered from the scene did not come from the scene source, then there is at least one source in the population that has similar (matching) characteristics to our recovered sample. If we then add that crime scene source to our database of size N samples, then there is one match in $N + 1$ comparisons, that is:

$$\hat{f} = \frac{1}{N + 1} \quad \text{and so}$$

$$LR = \frac{1}{\frac{1}{N+1}} = N + 1 \approx N$$

If we have a typical size database of around $N = 700$ sources, then the *LR* is 700, that is, the evidence is 700 times more likely if it did originate from the crime scene source, than if it originated from some unknown source. This is very crude, and wastes a lot of information, but it does impart information that reflects the rarity of the evidence and it is stronger evidence than we would get from RI measurements. We can also justify this from a Bayesian estimation point of view. Let us assume, in the absence of any information, that the matching probability is completely unknown and could be any value between zero and one, that is, f is follows a *Uniform*(0, 1) distribution. Then let us consider that we observed zero matches in the N comparisons we make between our recovered measurements and the database. We can model this matching process as a binomial distribution with parameters N and f, then Bayes' Theorem lets us combine these two pieces of information (our uniform prior and our zero matches out of N comparisons) to show that f now follows a *Beta* distribution with parameters $\alpha = 1$ and $\beta = N + 1$. It is easy to show that this distribution has mean

$$\mathrm{E}[f] = \frac{1}{N + 2}$$

which is very close to our previous estimator of $1/(N + 1)$. The choice of uniform prior is non-sensical and perhaps a prior such as a *Beta*(α, 1) where α is very small might be more desirable. Another attractive potential solution is offered by Aitken and Lucy (2004), which we will discuss with respect to a continuous approach to glass interpretation.

6.2.7.5 Disadvantages of the Two-Stage Approach

The two-stage approach suffers from several drawbacks. First it assumes that if the fragments come from the broken window, then they would match with probability 1. There is, however, a possibility that certain fragments would not match the crime scene sample, for example because of the float manufacturing process and/or sampling procedures (Walsh

and Buckleton 1996). Another disadvantage of the two-stage approach is the significance test and what former Forensic Science Service scientist Ken Smalldon labeled the "fall-off-the cliff effect." Imagine a situation where we are employing a two-stage approach with a 0.01 significance level. Imagine further that the P value from the case is 0.009. In this situation the samples would be declared to not match. However, if the P value changed by 0.002 to 0.011, then the samples would be declared to match. Such a reversal would be difficult to justify to the court and would certainly trouble the forensic scientist if multiple matching fragments, with a rare RI close to the window, had been recovered in that case. Hypothesis testing fails to incorporate relevant evidence such as the relative frequency of the glass and the number of glass fragments that have been recovered. It does not answer either the question "How much does this evidence increase the likelihood that the recovered come from the source?" but rather "What is the probability of a match if I carry out this procedure?" (Robertson et al. 2016). This is why we advocate the use of a continuous approach.

6.2.8 The Continuous Approach

Abandoning a match/not match approach (Lindley 1977) is one of the great advances in interpretation. It enables the forensic scientist to assign different values to a "good" or "close" match and a to "poor" match. Furthermore, there is no fall-off-the cliff effect, and it allows the scientist to weigh all the evidence in one process rather than in a step-by-step fashion. Moreover, it is less prone to be influenced by departure from normality (Bennett et al. 2003; Curran 2003) than significance testing is. The approach is described in several texts, for example Curran et al. (2000) and Aitken and Taroni (2004), and has been applied to different evidence types (e.g. inks, speaker recognition, fingerprints). To distinguish the likelihood ratio applied for the assessment of evidence and for assessing the value of a comparison, we will use LR for the global assessment of glass evidence and LR_{cont} for the assessment of the value of a comparison. The LR_{cont} is one factor that appears, as we will see, in the global LR.

6.2.8.1 Interpretation Based on RI Measurements

Walsh and Buckleton (1996) presented the details of a burglary case in which a pharmacy window was broken to gain entrance to the premises. Two POIs were apprehended 90 minutes later and their outer clothing, head gear, and footwear were taken as per usual procedure. The confiscated clothing was searched and fragments were recovered from the clothing of both POIs. The fragments were compared to the broken window using RI measurements. The measurements are shown in Table 6.3.

The t-test results are shown in Table 6.4. The samples did not match using a standard pooled t-test. The fragments from the second POI barely matched using Welch's modification of the t-test. This latter result is more likely due to a small sample size and widely disparate standard deviations, as evidenced by the low degrees of freedom, than the similarity of the results. These results, however, seemed contrary in the face of the case information. First,

Table 6.3 Refractive index measurements from an example case.

Source	POI 1	POI 2
1.519 50	1.519 40	1.519 44
1.519 52	1.519 46	1.519 49
1.519 53	1.519 47	1.519 50
1.519 56	1.519 48	
1.519 57	1.519 50	
1.519 59	1.519 52	
1.519 60	1.519 52	
1.519 60	1.519 53	
1.519 62	1.519 56	
1.519 64	1.519 57	
	1.519 57	

a large number of glass fragments were recovered from POI 1. Multiple studies have shown that, with the exception of people who handle window glass for a living, such as glaziers (Jackson et al. 2013), finding a large number of glass fragments on the upper clothing is rare. Second, there was good evidence, using fluorescence spectrometry (Lloyd 1981), to suggest that some of these fragments recovered from each of the POI's clothing originated from a float surface. This too is a rare event for individuals unassociated with criminal activity. A majority of the RI measurements of the recovered fragments were close to those of the scene source. Finally, paint flakes which were "indistinguishable"[10] from the crime scene window frame had also been found on one of the POIs. Thus, despite the results of the t-test, the evidence supported the proposition that the POIs were at the crime scene when the window was broken. This situation may be considered an example of Lindley's paradox. Lindley's paradox is a counter-intuitive situation in statistics in which the Bayesian and frequentist approaches to a hypothesis testing problem give opposite results for certain choices of the prior distribution. The problem of the disagreement between the two approaches was discussed in Harold Jeffreys' textbook (Jeffreys 1939). It became known as Lindley's paradox after Dennis Lindley (1957) called the disagreement a paradox in a 1957 paper (Lindley's n.d.). In this situation we phrase the paradox as:

- The data give rise to a very small P value under the null hypothesis of coming from the same source

but

- the results are still more likely if they had come from the same source than if they had come from different sources.

---

10 We do note the irony of using such terms in a chapter on the statistical interpretation of glass. Let it suffice to say that the color of the recovered fragments was very similar to that used on the scene window frame, and that the layers present in the recovered paint flakes were also present in the scene frame.

Table 6.4 Match results from an example case.

Comparison	Test	*t* statistic	*df*	*P* value
Source–POI 1	Standard	3.06	19	0.006 50
Source–POI 1	Welch	3.08	18.97	0.006 20
Source–POI 2	Standard	3.38	11	0.006 19
Source–POI 2	Welch	4.10	4.74	0.010 42

Lindley's original glass paper (Lindley 1977) did not include a match step, but this solution had little uptake. Walsh and Buckleton (1996) suggested to a modified version of Lindley's original which dispensed with some assumptions of normality and factored in the expectation of increased variation in the recovered measurements (Newton 2011). Walsh and Buckleton (1996) proposed the following continuous *LR*:

$$LR_{\text{cont}} = \frac{f(\bar{x} - \bar{y} \mid s_X, s_Y)}{\hat{g}(\bar{y})} \qquad (6.4)$$

where $\hat{g}(\overline{Y})$ is the probability density for float glass computed at the mean of the recovered sample. This value may be obtained from a kernel density estimate. $f(\bar{x} - \bar{y} \mid s_x, s_y)$ is the value of the probability density for the difference of the two sample means. This is approximated by an unscaled *t* distribution using Welch's modification to Student's *t*-test. Aitken (1995) also showed that the assumption of normality could be dropped and the numerator of the likelihood ratio replaced by a univariate kernel density estimate.

The code below can be used with R Core Team (2016) and the dafs package (Curran and Chang 2012) to calculate LR_{cont} for each of the recovered samples. The code assumes that measurements for the three samples are stored in vectors called `ctrl`, `rec1` and `rec2`:

```
means = c(mean(ctrl), mean(rec1), mean(rec2))
sds = c(sd(ctrl), sd(rec1), sd(rec2))
n = c(10, 11, 3)
names(means) = names(sds) = names(n) = c("ctrl","rec1","rec2")
## Make a a function out of the KDE for the denominator
## using the NZ data from the dafs package
library(dafs)
data(nzglass.df)
ghat = approxfun(density(nzglass.df$ri))

## Calculate the numerator
tStat = t.test(ctrl, rec1)$statistic
degF = t.test(ctrl, rec1)$parameter
num = dt(tStat, df = degF) * (1/sqrt(sds["ctrl"]^2/n["ctrl"] +
    sds["rec1"]^2/n["rec1"]))

## Calculate the denominator
denom = ghat(means["rec1"])

## Calculate the LR
LRCont1 = num/denom
LRCont1
```

```
## Calculate the numerator
tStat = t.test(ctrl, rec2)$statistic
degF = t.test(ctrl, rec2)$parameter
num = dt(tStat, df = degF) * (1/sqrt(sds["ctrl"]^2/n["ctrl"] +
    sds["rec2"]^2/n["rec2"]))

## Calculate the denominator
denom = ghat(means["rec2"])

## Calculate the LR
LRCont2 = num/denom
LRCont2
```

This code returns continuous *LR*s of 2.99 for POI 1 and 1.88 for POI 2. These are small values, but still reflect the positive weight of the evidence.

6.2.8.2 Interpretation Based on Elemental Analysis Measurements

Curran (1996) and Curran and Triggs (1997) suggested a multivariate analogue to Eq. (6.4) based on Hotelling's T^2. However, this result was mostly ignored by the elemental community, who at that time were content to make statements regarding their ability to discriminate or not discriminate between sources of glass. Aitken and Lucy (2004), prompted by interactions with Polish forensic scientist and researcher Grzegorz Zadora, returned to this problem in early 2002. They initially extended the univariate solution proposed by Lindley (1977) to the multivariate situation. However, being aware of the dissatisfaction in the elemental community with assumptions of multivariate normality, they also proposed a method based on multivariate kernel density estimation. The results of their initial work were published in Aitken and Lucy (2004) and extended in Aitken et al. (2006) to allow for multiple sources of variation (within fragments, within samples, and between samples). Aitken et al. (2006, 2007) also showed how the use of graphical models (which can be regarded as a broader class of structures incorporating Bayesian networks) could be used to deal with the problems arising from the

(relatively) high dimensional nature of the problem. Aitken and Lucy's work has been explored extensively in the field of glass problems by Zadora, culminating in the publication of a book (Zadora et al. 2014), which although not limited to glass, does primarily use glass as an exemplar. Zadora et al. (2014) provide free software with their book, and David Lucy – now sadly deceased – wrote an R package called comparison (Lucy 2013). Curran or Zadora may resume the maintenance of this package.

It would be nice to say that this is a problem with a solution. However, we do believe that further work is required. Forensic scientists who use LA-ICP-MS instrumentation may consider up to 17 trace elements. This number of elements puts severe strain on the ability of databases to inform the model. For example, unless some effort is made to factorize the *LR*s involved, using a method like that detailed in Aitken et al. (2006, 2007), then the Aitken–Lucy model requires, for example, estimation of variance–covariance matrices which contain $17 \times 16 \div 2 = 136$ unique terms. To estimate these values well requires a significantly sized database. Employing the Aitken–Lucy model naïvely on data sets with large numbers of elements (variables) is not advised. The model requires extensive data analysis and fine tuning.

Zadora et al. (2014) are exponents of calibration using the empirical cross entropy (ECE) methods suggested by Ramos (2013) and Ramos et al. (2013). Lucy's comparison package contains a function called calc.ece which allows the empirical cross entropy to be calculated for a set of *LR*s. Ramos et al.'s motivation springs from a desire to make sure that the given *LR*s are not misleading. That is, a desirable property of any system that computes *LR*s is that the computed *LR*s do not give strong support to the incorrect proposition. This procedure of calibration is described in Ramos (2013) and we believe it is a useful tool to for researchers who develop models for *LR* computation.

Franco-Pedroso et al. (2016) used ECE to show that the Aitken and Lucy (2004) kernel density approach overestimates the between-source density function in some areas of the feature space for datasets where sources are grouped in several clusters. They propose, as an alternative, representing the between-source distribution as a Gaussian mixture model. Technically, a kernel density estimate (KDE) (using a Gaussian kernel) is a special case of a Gaussian mixture model, where the number of components in the mixture is equal to the number of observations in the data set. KDEs, however, impose a constraint that all the components of the mixture have equal variance. The method proposed by Franco-Pedroso et al., however, relaxes this constraint and works by assuming fewer components in the mixture model. There is an analogy that may be drawn here with grouping of fragments, namely that some strength is drawn from the factor that the observations (in the database) have been grouped together in some way and therefore provide more information about the quantities of interest. This method seems promising and warrants more attention.

van Es et al. (2017) also proposed a calibration method, but used calibration in perhaps the more traditional sense of adjusting an instrument so that it returns more accurate and precise measurements. The van Es et al. (2017) calibration procedure, crudely, takes an *LR* calculated on the original variables,

converts it into a score, and then computes the *LR* based on the scores. Therefore, the authors label this method a post-hoc calibration method. The method, as described, attempts to constrain the *LR* to a specific range defined by a minimum and a maximum. These values may be determined with the empirical lower and upper bound LR method described in Vergeer et al. (2016). van Es et al. (2017) used the ECE to show that their method is both well-calibrated and has good discrimination power. They go on to state that, at least for glass, they could not achieve the same performance using the Gaussian mixture model of Franco-Pedroso et al. (2016). Again this is a method that warrants more attention.

One can certainly envision estimators for the *LR* which are misspecified and so may have these properties. Model misspecification, in the statistical sense, means models which assume that the data follow distribution f, when in fact the data follow distribution g. Model misspecification is essentially unavoidable, but we can attempt to minimize the harm incurred. It is almost certain that any model we care to choose for elemental measurements is not the "true" model. Therefore, we are certainly proponents of the examination of performance of any method that purports to calculate the weight of evidence to make sure it is simultaneously helpful (in terms of having good discrimination) and that is it not misleading. It is not clear which of the alternatives explored above is the best. However, we believe this area, especially in the comparatively data-rich field of forensic glass analysis, could withstand more research. Two recent publications (Corzo et al. 2018; Hoffman et al. 2018) have started to address this shortfall.

6.2.8.3 Evaluation of Results Given Activity Level Propositions

Important forensic results such as the number of glass fragments, where they have been recovered (e.g. hair, garments, shoes), and information such as the method of breaking are taken into account when helping to address activity level propositions. As mentioned earlier, unless there is no doubt that the glass is relevant to the offence, we think that experts should always try to assess their results given activity level propositions because the higher in the hierarchy we go the greater the value added by the evidence. These results have to be taken into account for the Court to address the Offence level. We ask you, the reader, who is best placed to evaluate these results (i.e. number of glass fragments, where they were recovered) if it is not the forensic scientist?

6.2.8.4 Example 1: One Group, One Control

Consider a case where only one window was broken. A POI Mr. S was apprehended in connection with the window breaking. Mr. S denied the breaking and proffered no other information to the arresting officers. His outer clothing, headgear and footwear were confiscated. One of these clothing items was a fleece jacket. The forensic scientists recovered a number of fragments from the fleece jacket and subsequently, through some method, made the assumption that all the recovered fragments came from a single source and therefore could be grouped. The method of grouping is not important at this level of discussion. After case pre-assessment the following propositions were chosen:

– -Mr. S is the person who broke the window.
– -Mr. S had nothing to do with the incident.

Two questions must be answered in order to evaluate the weight of the evidence, *E*. These are:

1. What is the probability of the evidence given that the prosecution proposition is correct and given the background information?
2. What is the probability of the evidence given that the defense proposition is correct and given the background information?

The background information is a key element in both cases in that if this information changes, then probabilities must be reassessed.

These two probabilities form the numerator and denominator of the likelihood ratio.

$$LR = \frac{\Pr(E \mid H_p, I)}{\Pr(E \mid H_d, I)} \qquad (6.5)$$

If we consider the denominator first, then the question, phrased in more detail, might be:

2. What is the probability that one would find a single group of *m* matching fragments on the surface of the fleece jacket if Mr. S has not broken the window at the scene, given what is known about the incident and Mr. S?

Recall that the information that we have on the POI's activities is provisional and that it may change. Regardless of what we know about Mr. S, it is inarguable that he has come to the attention of the police in connection with a breaking offence. Casework clothing surveys, which we shall discuss in a later section, are surveys of people who have also come to police notice in such a way. Thus, it is believed that this kind of survey is the most relevant in this case. If Mr. S had said that he worked in a glass recycling center, then the most relevant survey would have been surveys carried out on persons working in glass recycling centers. However, in this particular case, he has given no explanation. If, using this information, we rephrase our question it becomes:

2. If we examine the fleece jacket of a man who has come to the attention of the police on suspicion of a breaking offence, yet he is unconnected with the offence, then what is the probability that one would find a single group of *m* fragments which matches the scene source in that particular case?

Casework clothing surveys distinguish between groups of glass that match the casework crime scene samples and those that do not. If we assume that the matching glass did come from the incident investigated, then the non-matching glass can be considered as the background.

Let P_g be the probability of finding *g* groups of glass on an individual. Let S_j be the probability that a particular group of glass consists of *j* fragments. Let *f* denote the probability of observing the matching analytical characteristics given that the fragments are present as background and that they do not come from the control source. This probability can be assigned using the proportion of glass (from one source) recovered on fleeces that match the RI of the recovered glass. If we take a continuous approach, then LR_{cont} will be used in place of f. Evett and Buckleton (1990) make two assumptions:

A1: There is no association between the number of groups of glass found on a person's clothing and the size of these groups.

A2: There is no association between the frequency of a given RI on clothing with either the number or the size of the group.

It is unlikely that either of these assumptions is exactly true, but it is believed that they are correct at least as any first-order approximation (Curran et al. 2000; Evett and Buckleton 1990). These two assumptions make the process of estimating the denominator of the *LR* feasible, and in turn answer our question, "What is the probability that one would find a single group of *m* fragments which matches the scene source in that particular case on a person unconnected with the crime?" This is

$$\Pr(E \mid H_d, I) = P_1 \cdot S_m \cdot f \qquad (6.6)$$

if we are taking a two-stage approach, or

$$\Pr(E \mid H_d, I) = P_1 \cdot S_m \cdot 1/LR_{cont} \qquad (6.7)$$

if we are taking a continuous approach.

Assigning the numerator is slightly more complex as we have to allow for at least two possible explanations. In reality there are $m + 1$ explanations, which allow for the partitioning of the recovered fragments into two classes: those that have been transferred from the scene window and those which were there beforehand (Curran et al. 2000). However, consideration of all of these explanations becomes unwieldy and does not illuminate the case any further. We consider the explanations relating to the end cases of the range. That is:

1. either the group of fragments was transferred from the scene window, and Mr. S had no glass on him beforehand
2. or no glass was transferred from the window and/or recovered, but Mr. S had already one group of glass on his fleece.

If we invoke the assumptions A1 and A2, and furthermore let T_m denote the probability *m* glass fragments would be recovered from Mr. S's fleece (given H_p and *I*), then the nominator is:

$$\Pr(E \mid H_p, I) = T_0 \cdot P_1 \cdot S_m \cdot f + T_m \cdot P_0 \qquad (6.8)$$

Both the numerator and denominator have been defined. Now that we have defined the numerator and denominator terms, we can calculate the LR:

$$LR = \frac{\Pr(E \mid H_p, I)}{\Pr(E \mid H_d, I)} = T_0 + \frac{P_0 \cdot T_m}{P_1 \cdot S_m \cdot f} \qquad (6.9)$$

If we are using the continuous approach to glass comparison, then this becomes

$$LR = T_0 + \frac{P_0 \cdot T_m}{P_1 \cdot S_m} \cdot LR_{cont} \qquad (6.10)$$

There are infinite variations around this scenario (Curran et al. 2000; Aitken and Taroni 2004), but this example shows how probabilities can help the forensic scientist to assess the value of glass. This framework allows all factors that are intuitively important to be taken into account and it helps preventing fallacies.

6.2.9 Assigning Background and Transfer Probabilities

The example given in the previous section involved a number of probability terms which must be assigned in order to assess the value of the glass evidence given activity level propositions. These are the *P* terms, the *S* terms, and the *T* terms. The *P* and *S* terms relate to the number of groups of glass, and their associated sizes, that one might expect to find on an individual. The T terms relate to the amount of glass that one might expect to recover if glass was transferred from the scene window and it persisted.

In general, clothing surveys enable one to assign the P and S terms. Two types of clothing surveys have been performed: some on general populations (Jackson et al. 2013; Pearson and May 1971; McQuillan and Edgar 1992; Hoefler et al. n.d.; Lau et al. 1997; Petterd et al. 1999; Roux and Kirk 2001; Coulson et al. 2001; Nic Daéid et al. 2009) and some on individuals associated with criminal activity (Lambert et al. 1995; Coulson et al. 2001; Harrison et al. 1985). The expert will use either a "general" survey or a "crime" survey depending on the case and on the defense proposition. For example, when the POI does not have any explanation for the presence of glass on his/her clothing, then the surveys on POIs' clothing may be used. If the recovered glass has been found on a victim, then general clothing surveys may be more relevant. Surveys have shown that more glass is recovered as background on persons suspected of breaking offences than on the general population. It is important to consider the population of interest when choosing the relevant survey as well as where and how the fragments have been searched for and on which garment. For instance, if the fragments have been recovered from the pockets of a person who is the victim of a crime, then a survey of a general population (Pearson and May 1971) where the scientists looked for fragments on pockets and turn-ups should be used. If the fragments were recovered from the outer the surfaces of the clothing of a POI, then surveys on POI populations (e.g. from casework) should be used (Hicks 2003; Lambert et al. 1995; Coulson et al. 2001). There are also surveys which look at the question of background glass on shoes (Lau et al. 1997; Harrison et al. 1985; DeHaan and Davis 1977) or in hair (Jackson et al. 2013; McQuillan and McCrossan 1987). Curran et al. (2000) have a comprehensive section on background surveys. This section, however, was published nearly 17 years ago, and therefore is now incomplete in that it only refers to studies published prior to 2000. Curran et al. (2000) also cite research reports from the now defunct Forensic Science Service and its predecessors. Many of these reports are no longer available or require a complex permissions process from the UK government to be accessed. This unfortunately diminishes the value of information in those reports, but opens the door for some of the experiments to be repeated.

One reference not available at the time of the Curran et al. (2000) survey is the work done by Coulson et al. (2001). We regard this work as very important. This study is a combination of survey data and statistical modeling of the P and S terms and should be regarded as an essential contribution to this subject.

It has been argued that theoretically, depending on the proposition chosen, different values of the P and S terms should be used (Buckleton and Hicks, pers. commun.; Hicks 2003) in the numerator and the denominator of the LR. That is, we might consider the idea that under the assumption that the proposition *Mr. S has nothing to do with the incident* is true, Mr. S might just be considered a member of the general public. Therefore, the probability of finding a single group of fragments of size m should be estimated using survey information from studies involving general population. Alternatively, under the assumption the proposition *Mr. S broke the window* is true, Mr. S might be regarded as being associated with crime, and therefore crime surveys should be used. This is an area of research that has not had much attention and that should be explored. It is unclear what the net effect on the value of the results will be. All we can say is that the expressions for the LR will be more complex as they cannot be simplified through cancelation.

The T terms are referred to as transfer probabilities even though they refer to the probability of recovering a given number of fragments if the person broke the window, and that they incorporate three distinct processes.

These processes are the initial transfer, the persistence, and the recovery. It has been argued that they depend on too many factors and are too difficult to assess. Transfer is a stochastic phenomenon. However, it is essential that transfer probabilities be assigned. Substantial research effort has been used filling in the gaps in our knowledge. Curran et al. (2000) and Bottrell (2009) both contain reviews which are somewhat dated. Experiments have been carried out to identify parameters involved in the initial transfer (Nelson and Revell 1967; Pounds and Smalldon 1978; Luce and Buckle 1991; Locke and Unikowski 1991, 1992; Locke and Scranage 1992; Allen et al. 1998a). Hicks et al. (2005) and Wong (2007) studied transfer when firearms were used. Irwin (2011) studied the breaking of containers. Most recently Cooper (2013) investigated secondary transfer and persistence of glass. Many researchers have studied transfer (Pounds and Smalldon 1978; Luce and Buckle 1991) and persistence of glass recovered on garments (Hoefler et al. n.d.; Pounds and Smalldon 1977; Brewster and Thorpe 1985; Hicks et al. 1996; Allen and Scranage 1998; Allen et al. 1998b,c,d).

The modular nature of the transfer, persistence, and recovery processes makes them amenable to modeling using Bayesian networks. Curran et al. (1998) used graphical models (a super class of Bayesian networks) to do just this. The software described in Curran et al. (1998) was recoded as an R package, `tfer` (Curran and Huang 2012), and then David Banks added an R `shiny` (Chang et al. 2017) interface. The shiny app is hosted on http://tfer.docker.stat.auckland .ac.nz. Transfer is a stochastic phenomenon, therefore we suggest that the forensic scientist assigns different probabilities depending on the case information available before searching the garments (when pre-assessing the case). For example, the information may be lacking regarding the distance between the breaker and the window. In such a case, a simulation can be performed with different distances. This will allow a sensitivity analysis

to be performed and show how the lack of information regarding transfer probabilities influences the overall value of glass evidence in that particular case. We also encourage the development of knowledge-based systems such as CAGE (Computerised Assistance for Glass Evidence). CAGE was developed in the 1990s by John Buckleton, Richard Pinchin, and Ian Evett. These systems not only guide experts when assigning the value of their results, but also enable storage of knowledge on an essential area of expertise (i.e. transfer, persistence, and recovery probabilities).

6.3 Concluding Remarks

We have presented a summary of the methodology for glass analysis and interpretation in this chapter. We have not covered material regarding the literature on fragmentation and other physical phenomena, nor the extensive literature on instrumentation or methodology for the quantification of glass evidence. Such topics are described well elsewhere (Curran et al. 2000; Almirall and Trejos 2015; Bottrell 2009). We have described the Bayesian approaches to glass evidence. The frequentist approach, should one want to follow it, is simply the first part of the two-stage approach described in Section 6.2.7, that is, the match step. Curran (2013) described the variation of practice that still exists within the field of forensic glass interpretation. The Bayesian approach has gained some foothold in the discipline, but the vast majority of practitioners are still content to exist within the match/no-match paradigm, despite the criticism of this by the National Academy of Sciences (National Research Council 2009) and the President's Council of Advisors on Science and Technology (PCAST 2016; Morrison et al. 2017) reports.

The Bayesian approach may not be a panacea, but it does provide a very good framework for forensic thinking and for the evaluation of evidence. It has been argued that because glass characteristics change a lot, then one should not attempt to estimate its frequency of occurrence. The same argument was made with respect to bullet lead (National Research Council 2004), and unfortunately seems to have become a template argument for not constructing trace evidence databases. There seems to be a belief that DNA databases are immune to such problems, when in fact this is patently untrue. Equally there is a school of thought that we should not bother with transfer or background probabilities because they are hard to assess. Proponents of such arguments believe that the solution is to analyze the glass with more discriminating techniques so that the glass would become "unique" like DNA. There are many articles (Champod 2000; Kaye 2009, 2010; Cole 2009) arguing that claims of uniqueness are not only ridiculous, but unnecessary. Furthermore, the question before the Court is inherently probabilistic no matter what level of discrimination a technique may provide. Assessing the strength of the match is only one part of the process. As we have seen, this information is essential to help address questions relative to activity level propositions, and to assess all our results (the analytical characteristics and the number of glass fragments, as well as where they were recovered). Statistical tools enable us to deal with the uncertainty inherent in these questions and those uncertainties will remain regardless of whether we can determine a "match" between two samples of glass with 100% accuracy.

References

Aitken, C.G.G. (1995). *Statistics and the Evaluation of Evidence for Forensic Scientists*. Chichester, England: Wiley.

Aitken, C.G.G. and Lucy, D. (2004). Evaluation of trace evidence in the form of multivariate data. *Journal of the Royal Statistical Society: Series C (Applied Statistics)* 53: 109–122.

Aitken, C.G.G. and Taroni, F. (2004). *Statistics and the Evaluation of Evidence for Forensic Scientists*. Chichester, England: Wiley.

Aitken, C.G.G., Lucy, D., Zadora, G., and Curran, J.M. (2006). Evaluation of transfer evidence for three-level multivariate data with the use of graphical models. *Computational Statistics and Data Analysis* 50: 2571–2588.

Aitken, C.G.G., Zadora, G., and Lucy, D. (2007). A two-level model for evidence evaluation. *Journal of Forensic Sciences* 52: 412–419.

Alamilla, F., Calcerrada, M., Garcia-Ruiz, C., and Torre, M. (2013). Validation of an analytical method for the refractive index measurement of glass fragments. Application to a hit-and-run incident. *Analytical Methods* 5: 1178–1184.

Allen, T.J. and Scranage, J.K. (1998). The transfer of glass. Part 1: Transfer of glass to individuals at different distances. *Forensic Science International* 93: 167–174.

Allen, T.J., Locke, J., and Scranage, J.K. (1998a). Breaking of flat glass. Part 4: Size and distribution of fragments from vehicle windscreens. *Forensic Science International* 93: 209–218.

Allen, T.J., Hoefler, K., and Rose, S.J. (1998b). The transfer of glass. Part 2: A study of the transfer of glass to a person by various methods. *Forensic Science International* 93: 175–193.

Allen, T.J., Hoefler, K., and Rose, S.J. (1998c). The transfer of glass. Part 3: The transfer of glass from a contaminated person to another uncontaminated person during a ride in a car. *Forensic Science International* 93: 195–200.

Allen, T.J., Cox, A.R., Barton, S. et al. (1998d). The transfer of glass. Part 4: The transfer of glass fragments from the surface of an item to the person carrying it. *Forensic Science International* 93: 201–208.

Almirall, J.R. and Trejos, T. (2006). Advances in forensic analysis of glass fragments with a focus on refractive index and elemental analysis. *Forensic Science Review* 18: 74–96.

Almirall, J.R. and Trejos, T. (2015). Analysis of glass evidence. In: *Forensic Chemistry* (ed. J.A. Siegel), 228–272. Wiley.

ASTM E1967-19 (2019). *Standard test method for the automated determination of refractive index of glass samples using the oil immersion method and a phase contrast microscope*. West Conshohocken, PA: ASTM International.

ASTM E2330-12 (2012). *Standard test method for determination of concentrations of elements in glass samples using inductively coupled plasma mass spectrometry (ICP-MS) for forensic comparisons*, vol. 14.02. West Conshohocken, PA: ASTM International.

ASTM E2926-17 (2017). *Standard test method for forensic comparison of glass using micro X-ray fluorescence (μ-XRF) spectrometry*. vol. 14.02. West Conshohocken, PA: ASTM International.

ASTM E2927-16 (2016). *Standard test method for determination of trace elements in soda-lime glass samples using laser ablation inductively coupled plasma mass spectrometry for forensic comparisons*, vol. 14.02. West Conshohocken, PA: ASTM International.

Bayes, T. (1763). An essay towards solving a problem in the doctrine of chance. *Philosophical Transactions Royal Society of London* 53: 370–418.

Benjamini, Y. and Hochberg, Y. (1995). Controlling the false discovery rate: a practical and powerful approach to multiple testing. *Journal of the Royal Statistical Society: Series B: Methodological* 57: 289–300.

Bennett, R.L., Kim, N.D., Curran, J.M. et al. (2003). Spatial variation of refractive index in a pane of float glass. *Science and Justice* 43: 71–76.

Berends-Montero, S., Wiarda, W., de Joode, P., and van der Peijl, G. (2006). Forensic analysis of float glass using laser ablation inductively coupled plasma mass spectrometry (LA-ICP-MS): validation of a method. *Journal of Analytical Atomic Spectrometry* 21: 1185–1193.

Blakestone, W. and Browne, W.H. (1897). *Commentaries on the Laws of England in One Volume Together with a Copious Glossary of Writers Referred to, and a Chart of Descent of English Sovereigns*. Great Britain: West Publishing Company.

Bonferroni, C.E. (1936). *Teoria statistica delle classi e calcolo delle probabilità*. Pubblicazioni del R Istituto Superiore di Scienze Economiche e Commerciali di Firenze 8: 3–62.

Bottrell, M.C. (2009). Forensic glass comparison: background information used in data interpretation. *Forensic Science Communications* 11.

Brewster, F. and Thorpe, J.W. (1985). The retention of glass particles on woven fabrics. *Journal of Forensic Sciences* 30: 798–805.

Bridge, C.M., Powell, J., Steele, K.L. et al. (2006). Characterization of automobile float glass with laser-induced breakdown spectroscopy and laser ablation inductively coupled plasma mass spectrometry. *Applied Spectroscopy* 60: 1181–1187.

Caddy, B. (2001). *Forensic Examination of Glass and Paint: Analysis and Interpretation*. New York, NY: Taylor & Francis.

Campbell, G.P. and Curran, J.M. (2009). The interpretation of elemental composition measurements from forensic glass evidence III. *Science and Justice* 49: 2–7.

Champod, C. (2000). Identification/individualization: overview and meaning. In: *Encyclopedia of Forensic Science* (eds. J.A. Siegel, P.J. Saukko and G.C. Knupfer), 1077–1083. London, UK: Academic Press.

Chang, W., Cheng, J., Allaire, J.J. et al. (2017). shiny: web application framework for r. https://cran.r-project.org/package=shiny (accessed 10 March 2020).

Cole, S.A. (2009). Forensics without uniqueness, conclusions without individualization: the new epistemology of forensic identification. *Law, Probability and Risk* 8: 233–255.

Coleman, R.F. and Goode, G.C. (1973). Comparison of glass fragments by neutron activation analysis. *Journal of Radioanalytical Chemistry* 15: 367–388.

Cook, R., Evett, I.W., Jackson, G. et al. (2008). A hierarchy of propositions: deciding which level to address in casework. *Science and Justice* 38: 231–239.

Cooper, G. (2013). The indirect transfer of glass fragments to a jacket and their subsequent persistence. *Science and Justice* 53: 166–170.

Corzo, R., Hoffman, T., Weis, P. et al. (2018). The use of LA-ICP-MS databases to calculate likelihood ratios for the forensic analysis of glass evidence. *Talanta* 186: 655–661.

Coulson, S.A., Buckleton, J.S., Gummer, A.B., and Triggs, C.M. (2001). Glass on clothing and shoes of members of the general population and people suspected of breaking crimes. *Science and Justice* 41: 39–48.

Curran, J.M. (1996). Forensic applications of bayesian inference to glass evidence. PhD thesis, Department of Statistics. University of Auckland.

Curran, J.M. (2003). The statistical interpretation of forensic glass evidence. *International Statistical Review* 71: 497–520.

Curran, J.M. (2013). Is forensic science the last bastion of resistance against statistics? *Science and Justice* 53: 251–252. https://doi.org/10.1016/j.scijus.2013.07.001.

Curran, J.M. (2017). Hotelling: hotelling's T-squared test and variants. https://cran.r-project.org/package=Hotelling (accessed 10 March 2020).

Curran, J.M. and Chang, D. (2012). dafs: data analysis for forensic scientists. https://cran.r-project.org/package=dafs (accessed 10 March 2020).

Curran, J.M. and Huang, T.Y. (2012). tfer: forensic glass transfer probabilities. https://cran.r-project.org/package=tfer (accessed 10 March 2020).

Curran, J.M. and Triggs, C.M. (1997). The interpretation of elemental composition measurements from forensic glass evidence: II. *Science and Justice* 37: 245–249.

Curran, J.M., Triggs, C.M., Buckleton, J.S. et al. (1998). Assessing transfer probabilities in a Bayesian interpretation of forensic glass evidence. *Science and Justice* 38: 15–21.

Curran, J.M., Hicks, T.N., Buckleton, J.S. et al. (2000). *Forensic Interpretation of Glass Evidence*. Boca Raton, FL: CRC Press.

DeHaan, J.D. and Davis, R.J. (1977). A survey of men's footwear. *Journal of Forensic Sciences* 17: 185–271.

Dorn, H., Ruddell, D.E., Heydon, A., and Burton, B.D. (2015). Discrimination of float glass by LA-ICP-MS: assessment of exclusion criteria using casework samples. *Canadian Society of Forensic Science Journal* 48: 85–96.

Duckworth, D.C., Bayne, C.K., Morton, S.J., and Almirall, J.R. (2000). Analysis of variance in forensic glass analysis by ICP-MS: variance within the method. *Journal of Analytical Atomic Spectrometry* 15: 821–828.

Duckworth, D.C., Morton, S.J., Bayne, C.K. et al. (2002). Forensic glass analysis by ICP-MS: a multi-element assessment of discriminating power via analysis of variance and pairwise comparisons. *Journal of Analytical Atomic Spectrometry* 17: 662–668.

Dudley, R.J., Howden, C.R., Taylor, T.J., and Smalldon, K.W. (1980). The discrimination and classification of small fragments of window and non-window glasses using energy-dispersive X-ray fluorescence spectrometry. *X-Ray Spectrometry* 9: 119–122.

El-Deftar, M.M., Speers, N., Eggins, S. et al. (2014). Assessment and forensic application of laser-induced breakdown spectroscopy (LIBS) for the discrimination of Australian window glass. *Forensic Science International* 241: 46–54.

Ernst, T., Berman, T., Buscaglia, J. et al. (2014). Signal-to-noise ratios in forensic glass analysis by micro X-ray fluorescence spectrometry. *X-Ray Spectrometry* 43: 13–21.

van Es, A., Wiarda, W., Hordijk, M. et al. (2017). Implementation and assessment of a likelihood ratio approach for the evaluation of LA-ICP-MS evidence in forensic glass analysis. *Science and Justice* 57: 181–192.

European Network of Forensic Science Institutes (2016). ENFSI guidelines for evaluative reporting in forensic science. Available at: http://enfsi.eu/wp-content/uploads/2016/09/m1_guideline.pdf (accessed 10 March 2020).

Evett, I.W. (1977). The interpretation of refractive index measurements. *Forensic Science International* 9: 209–217.

Evett, I.W. (1978). The interpretation of refractive index measurements II. *Forensic Science International* 12: 37–47.

Evett, I.W. (1986). A Bayesian approach to the problem of interpreting glass evidence in forensic science casework. *Journal of the Forensic Science Society* 26: 3–18.

Evett, I.W. (1987). On meaningful questions: a two-trace transfer problem. *Journal of the Forensic Science Society* 27: 375–381.

Evett, I.W. and Buckleton, J. (1990). The interpretation of glass evidence – a practical approach. *Journal of the Forensic Science Society* 30: 215–223.

Evett, I.W. and Lambert, J.A. (1982). The interpretation of refractive index measurements III. *Forensic Science International* 20: 237–245.

Evett, I.W. and Weir, B.S. (1998). *Interpreting DNA Evidence—Statistical Genetics for Forensic Scientists*. Sunderland, MA: Sinauer Associates Inc.

Evett, I.W., Jackson, G., and Lambert, J.A. (2000). More on the hierarchy of propositions: exploring the distinction between explanations and propositions. *Science and Justice* 40: 3–10.

Fisher, R.A. (1926). The arrangement of field experiments. *Journal of the Ministry of Agriculture Great Britain* 33: 503–513.

Fisher, R.A. (1956). *Statistical Methods and Scientific Inference*. New York, NY: Hafner.

Franco-Pedroso, J., Ramos, D., and Gonzalez-Rodriguez, J. (2016). Gaussian mixture models of between-source variation for likelihood ratio computation from multivariate data. *PLoS One* 11: 1–25.

Garvin, E.J. and Koons, R.D. (2011). Evaluation of match criteria used for the comparison of refractive index of glass fragments. *Journal of Forensic Sciences* 56: 491–500.

Gerhard, C., Hermann, J., Mercadier, L. et al. (2014). Quantitative analyses of glass via laser-induced breakdown spectroscopy in argon. *Spectrochimica Acta Part B: Atomic Spectroscopy* 101: 32–45.

Good, I.J. (1950). *Probability and the Weighing of Evidence*. London, England: Griffen.

Gupta, A., Curran, J.M., Coulson, S., and Triggs, C.M. (2017). Comparison of intra-day and inter-day variation in LIBS spectra. *Forensic Chemistry* 3: 36–40.

Harrison, P.H., Lambert, J.A., and Zoro, J.A. (1985). A survey of glass fragments recovered from clothing of persons suspected of involvement in crime. *Forensic Science International* 27: 171–187.

Hicks, T.N. (2003). De l'interprétation des fragments de verre en criminalistique. PhD thesis. Université de Lausanne.

Hicks, T., Vanina, R., and Margot, P. (1996). Transfer and persistence of glass fragments on garments. *Science and Justice* 36: 101–108.

Hicks, T., Schütz, F., Curran, J.M., and Triggs, C.M. (2005). A model for estimating the number of glass fragments transferred when breaking a pane: experiments with firearms and hammer. *Science and Justice* 45: 65–74.

Hoefler, K., Hermann, P., Hansen, C. (1994). A Study on the Persistence of Glass Fragments on Clothing after Breaking a Window. The 12th Australian & New Zealand International Symposium on the Forensic Sciences, Auckland, New Zealand.

Hoffman, T., Corzo, R., Weis, P. et al. (2018). An inter-laboratory evaluation of LA-ICP-MS analysis of glass and the use of a database for the interpretation of glass evidence. *Forensic Chemistry* 11: 65–76.

Hotelling, H. (1931). The generalization of student's ratio. *Annals of Mathematical Statistics* 2: 360–378.

Insana, J. and Buzzini, P. (2017). The differences between RI measurements of the external surface and bulk area of container glass.

Journal of the American Society of Trace Evidence Examination 7: 41–50.

Irwin, M. (2011). Transfer of glass fragments when bottles and drinking glasses are broken. *Science and Justice* 51: 16–18.

Jackson, F., Maynard, P., Cavanagh-Steer, K. et al. (2013). A survey of glass found on the headwear and head hair of a random population vs. people working with glass. *Forensic Science International* 226: 125–131.

Jeffreys, H. (1939). *Theory of Probability*. Oxford, United Kingdom: Oxford University Press.

Kaye, D.H. (2009). Identification, individualization and uniqueness: what's the difference? *Law, Probability and Risk* 8: 85–94.

Kaye, D.H. (2010). Probability, individualization, and uniqueness in forensic science evidence: listening to the academies. *Brooklyn Law Review* 75: 1164–1185.

Koons, R.D. and Buscaglia, J. (2001). Distribution of refractive index values in sheet glasses. *Forensic Science Communications* 3 https://www.fbi.gov/about-us/lab/forensic-science-communications/fsc/jan2001/koons.htm.

Koons, R.D., Fiedler, C., and Rawalt, R. (1988). Classification and discrimination of sheet and container glasses by inductively coupled plasma-atomic emission spectrometry and pattern recognition. *Journal of Forensic Sciences* 33: 49–67.

Koons, R.D., Peters, C.A., and Rebbert, P.S. (1991). Comparison of refractive index, energy dispersive X-ray fluorescence and inductively coupled plasma atomic emission spectrometry for forensic characterization of sheet glass fragments. *Journal of Analytical Atomic Spectrometry* 6: 451–456.

Koons, R.D., Buscaglia, J., Bottrell, M.C., and Miller, E.T. (2002). Forensic glass comparisons. In: *Forensic Science Handbook*, 2e (ed. R. Saferstein). Upper Saddle River, NJ: Prentice Hall.

Lambert, J.A., Satterthwaite, M.J., and Harrison, P.H. (1995). A survey of glass fragments recovered from clothing of persons suspected of involvement in crime. *Science and Justice* 35: 273–281.

Latkoczy, C., Becker, S., Dücking, M. et al. (2005). Development and evaluation of a standard method for the quantitative determination of elements in float glass samples by LA-ICP-MS. *Journal of Forensic Sciences* 50: 1–15.

Lau, L., Beveridge, A.D., Callowhill, B.C. et al. (1997). The frequency of occurrence of paint and glass on the clothing of high school students. *Canadian Society of Forensic Science Journal* 30: 233–240.

Lindley, D.V. (1957). A statistical paradox. *Biometrika* 44: 187–192.

Lindley, D.V. (1977). A problem in forensic science. *Biometrika* 64: 207–213.

Lindley's paradox (n.d.). https://en.wikipedia.org/wiki/Lindley%27s_paradox (accessed 10 March 2020).

Lloyd, J. (1981). Fluorescence spectrometry in the identification and discrimination of float and other surfaces on window glasses. *Journal of Forensic Sciences* 26: 325–342.

Locke, J. and Hayes, C.A. (1984). Refractive index variations across glass objects and the influence of annealing. *Forensic Science International* 26: 147–157.

Locke, J. and Scranage, J.K. (1992). Breaking of flat glass. Part 3: Surface particles from windows. *Forensic Science International* 57: 73–80.

Locke, J. and Underhill, M. (1985). Automatic refractive index measurement of glass particles. *Forensic Science International* 27: 247–260.

Locke, J. and Unikowski, J.A. (1991). Breaking of flat glass. Part 1: Size and distribution of particles from plain glass windows. *Forensic Science International* 51: 251–262.

Locke, J. and Unikowski, J.A. (1992). Breaking of flat glass. Part 2: Effect of pane parameters on particle distribution. *Forensic Science International* 56: 95–106.

Locke, J., Sanger, D.G., and Roopnarine, G. (1982). The identification of toughened glass by annealing. *Forensic Science International* 20: 295–301.

Luce, R.J.W. and Buckle, J.L. (1991). Study on the backward fragmentation of window glass and the transfer of glass fragments to individual's clothing. *Canadian Society of Forensic Science Journal* 24: 79–89.

Lucy, D. (2013). Comparison: multivariate likelihood ratio calculation and evaluation. https://cran.r-project.org/package=Hotelling (accessed 10 March 2020).

Marcouiller, J.M. (1990). A revised glass annealing method to distinguish glass types. *Journal of Forensic Sciences* 35: 554–559.

McQuillan, J. and Edgar, K. (1992). A survey of the distribution of glass on clothing. *Journal of the Forensic Science Society* 32: 333–348.

McQuillan, J. and McCrossan, S. (1987). *The Frequency of Occurrence of Glass Fragments in Head Hair Samples – a Pilot Investigation.* Belfast: Northern Ireland Forensic Science Laboratory.

Montero, S. (2002). Trace elemental analysis of glass by inductively coupled plasma-mass spectrometry (ICP-MS) and laser ablation-inductively coupled plasma-mass spectrometry (LA-ICP-MS). PhD thesis. Florida International University.

Morrison, G.S., Kaye, D.H., Balding, D.J. et al. (2017). A comment on the PCAST report: skip the "match/non-match" stage. *Forensic Science International* 272: e7–e9.

Naes, B.E., Umpierrez, S., Ryland, S. et al. (2008). A comparison of laser ablation inductively coupled plasma mass spectrometry, micro X-ray fluorescence spectroscopy, and laser induced breakdown spectroscopy for the discrimination of automotive glass. *Spectrochimica Acta Part B: Atomic Spectroscopy* 63: 1145–1150.

National Research Council (2004). *Forensic Analysis: Weighing Bullet Lead Evidence.* Washington, DC: The National Academies Press https://www.nap.edu/catalog/10924/forensic-analysis-weighing-bullet-lead-evidence.

National Research Council (2009). *Strengthening Forensic Science in the United States: A Path Forward.* Washington, DC: The National Academies Press.

Nelson, D.F. and Revell, B.C. (1967). Backward fragmentation from breaking glass. *Journal of the Forensic Science Society* 7: 58–61.

Newton, A.W.N. (2011). An investigation into the variability of the refractive index of glass. Part II: The effect of debris contamination. *Forensic Science International* 204: 182–185.

Newton, A.W.N. and Buckleton, J.S. (2008). An investigation into the relationship between edge counts and the variability of the refractive index of glass. *Forensic Science International* 177: 24–31.

Newton, A.W.N., Kitto, L., and Buckleton, J.S. (2005). A study of the performance and utility of annealing in forensic glass analysis. *Forensic Science International* 155: 119–125.

Nic Daéid, N.S., McColl, D., and Ballany, J. (2009). The level of random background glass recovered from fleece jackets of individuals who worked in law enforcement or related professions. *Forensic Science International* 191: 19–23.

Ojena, S.M. and De Forest, P.R. (1972). Precise refractive index determination by the immersion method, using phase contrast microscopy and the Mettler hot stage. *Journal of the Forensic Science Society* 12: 315–329.

Pawluk-Kołc, M., Zięba-Palus, J., and Parczewski, A. (2006). Application of false discovery rate procedure to pairwise comparisons of refractive index of glass fragments. *Forensic Science International* 160: 53–58.

PCAST (2016). Forensic science in criminal courts: ensuring scientific validity of feature-comparison methods. Available at: https://obamawhitehouse.archives.gov/sites/default/files/microsites/ostp/PCAST/pcast_forensic_science_report_final.pdf (accessed 10 March 2020).

Pearson, E.F. and May, R.W. (1971). Glass and paint fragments found in men's outer clothing – report of a survey. *Journal of Forensic Sciences* 16: 283–300.

Petterd, C.I., Hamshere, J., Stewart, S. et al. (1999). Glass particles in the clothing of members of the public in south-eastern Australia – a survey. *Forensic Science International* 103: 193–198.

Pounds, C.A. and Smalldon, K.W. (1977). *The Efficiency of Searching for Glass on Clothing and the Persistence of Glass on Clothing and Shoes*. Forensic Science Service Report.

Pounds, C.A. and Smalldon, K.W. (1978). The distribution of glass fragments in front of a broken window and the transfer of fragments to individuals standing nearby. *Journal of the Forensic Science Society* 18: 197–203.

R Core Team (2016). R: a language and environment for statistical computing. https://www.r-project.org (accessed 10 March 2020).

Ramos, D. (2013). Reliable support: measuring calibration of likelihood ratios. *Forensic Science International* 230: 156–169.

Ramos, D., Gonzalez-Rodriguez, J., Zadora, G., and Aitken, C.G.G. (2013). Information-theoretical assessment of the performance of likelihood ratio computation methods. *Journal of Forensic Sciences* 58: 1503–1518.

Reeve, V., Mathiesen, J., and Fong, W. (1976). Elemental analysis by energy dispersive X-ray: a significant factor in the forensic analysis of glass. *Journal of Forensic Sciences* 21: 291–306.

Rinke-Kneapler, C.N. and Sigman, M.E. (2014). Applications of laser spectroscopy in forensic science. *Laser Spectroscopy for Sensing*: 461–495.

Robertson, B., Vignaux, G.A., and Berger, C.H. (2016). *Interpreting Evidence: Evaluating Forensic Science in the Courtroom*, 2e. Chichester, West Sussex/Hoboken, NJ: Wiley.

Roux, C. and Kirk, R. (2001). Glass particles in footwear of member of the public in south-eastern Australia – a survey. *Forensic Science International* 116: 149–156.

Ryland, S.G. (1986). Sheet or container? Forensic glass comparisons with an emphasis on source classification. *Journal of Forensic Sciences* 31: 1314–1329.

Ryland, S.G. (2011). Discrimination of flat (sheet) glass specimens having similar refractive indices using micro X-ray fluorescence spectrometry. *Journal of the American Society of Trace Evidence Examiners* 2: 2–12.

Statista (2018). Savaete, Glass industry: statistics and facts. Statista 2018 Report. https://www.statista.com/topics/4108/glass/.

Suzuki, Y., Sugita, R., Suzuki, S., and Marumo, Y. (2000). Forensic discrimination of bottle glass by refractive index measurement and analysis of trace elements with ICP-MS. *Analytical Sciences* 16: 1195–1198.

Taroni, F., Biedermann, A., Bozza, S. et al. (2014). *Bayesian Networks for Probabilistic Inference and Decision Analysis in Forensic Science*. Chichester, England: Wiley.

Trejos, T., Koons, R.D., Becker, S. et al. (2013a). Cross-validation and evaluation of the performance of methods for the elemental analysis of forensic glass by μ-XRF, ICP-MS, and LA-ICP-MS. *Analytical and Bioanalytical Chemistry* 405: 5393–5409.

Trejos, T., Koons, R.D., Weis, P. et al. (2013b). Forensic analysis of glass by μ-XRF, SN-ICP-MS, LA-ICP-MS and LA-ICP-OES: evaluation of the performance of different criteria for comparing elemental composition. *Journal of Analytical Atomic Spectrometry* 28: 1270–1282.

Triggs, C.M. and Buckleton, J.S. (2003). The two trace transfer problem re-examined. *Science and Justice* 43: 127–134.

Triggs, C.M., Curran, J.M., Buckleton, J.S., and Kevan, A.J. (1997). The grouping problem in forensic glass analysis: a divisive approach. *Forensic Science International* 85 https://doi.org/10.1016/S0379-0738(96)02037-3.

Trimpe, M. and Sammarco, J. (2017). Variability of RI and thickness of tempered glass throughout an automotive window. *Journal of the American Society of Trace Evidence Examination* 7: 35–40.

Vergeer, P., van Es, A., de Jongh, A. et al. (2016). Numerical likelihood ratios outputted by LR systems are often based on extrapolation: when to stop extrapolating? *Science and Justice* 56: 482–491.

Walsh, K.A.J. and Buckleton, J.S. (1996). A practical example on the interpretation of glass evidence. *Science and Justice* 36: 213–218.

Weis, P., Dücking, M., Watzke, P. et al. (2011). Establishing a match criterion in forensic comparison analysis of float glass using laser ablation inductively coupled plasma mass spectrometry. *Journal of Analytical Atomic Spectrometry* 26: 1273.

Wong, S.C.K. (2007). The effects of projectile properties on glass backscatter: a statistical analysis. MSc thesis. University of Auckland.

Zadora, G. and Wilk, D. (2009). Evaluation of evidence value of refractive index measured before and after annealing of container and float glass fragments. *Problems Forensic Science* 80: 481–486.

Zadora, G., Martyna, A., Ramos, D., and Aitken, C.G.G. (eds.) (2014). *Statistical Analysis in Forensic Science: Evidential Value of Multivariate Physicochemical Data.* Chichester, England: Wiley.

7

Interpreting Trace Evidence

Patrick Buzzini[1] and James M. Curran[2]

[1] *Department of Forensic Science, Sam Houston State University, Huntsville, TX, USA*
[2] *Department of Statistics, University of Auckland, Auckland, New Zealand*

7.1   What is Evidence Interpretation?

Interpreting evidence is an intellectual process that encompasses the evaluation of the significance and the uncertainties of many pieces of information recovered in a particular case. These may include the spatial, temporal, morphological, and compositional properties, and the number or quantities of recovered vestiges left behind as a result of some activities. In the context of forensic analyses of (trace) materials, these traces left behind typically consist of a variety of fragments, debris, particles, residues, stains, volatile compounds, or altered objects. Interpreting evidence involves the use of inferential steps that can help establish some kinds of interrelationships or associations between individuals (i.e. victims, suspects, perpetrators), objects (e.g. crime weapons, vehicles, garments), and places (i.e. crime scenes). Buzzini et al. (2019) discuss the terms *associative traces* and *interrogatable traces* to distinguish the concept of the adjective trace used to define size, type, nature, state of materials, or the way they are produced from the concept of trace as a noun that defines

instead the way in which traces are recognized, utilized, and contribute to the understanding of an event.

When is evidence interpretation carried out? Initially, one may consider the typical case where a trace evidence examiner cannot analytically differentiate questioned specimens and reference samples,[1] and seeks to understand the evidential value of this observation. It is important to emphasize that evidence interpretation is not only confined to the analytical results obtained during laboratory testing. It is also not limited to the ability to gather features from unknown specimens, for example interpreting an image of particles through a microscope. It is not limited to comparing matching features that lead to a decision of distinguishability between two compared sets (e.g. the visual comparison of microspectrophotometry

---

1 The distinction between specimens and samples described by Margot (2014) is adopted here. Samples are portions that have been consciously selected to be representative of a whole. They typically inform about the intra-source variation of some properties of a given suspected source. On the other hand, specimens can also be regarded as portions of a whole but without any guarantee or information that they are representative of the whole.

[MSP] or Fourier transform infrared spectroscopy [FTIR] spectra). Evidence interpretation may be carried out before any laboratory testing. A judgment of the relevancy of particles recovered from a crime scene is an important form of interpretation since it implies the evaluation of their connection to the investigated event. This consideration also applies to objects seized during the investigation and then sent to the laboratory (e.g. garments). Interpretation steps can also be carried out in cases where the scientist has all seized items available and must then prioritize which specimens, samples, and examinations will be most informative for the case at hand (i.e. triaging). This undertaking is known as case assessment or case pre-assessment (Cook et al. 1998a; Association of Forensic Science Providers 2009). Interpretation is also necessary in cases where a suspect is not available yet. Here, unknown specimens have the potential to provide clues and as a result develop investigative leads by inferring a potential source such as a particular end use, product, manufacturer or geographical location (Palenik 1979, 2007). From this perspective, trace evidence can also contribute to the inference of case linkages.

In this chapter, evidence interpretation is regarded as the assessment of the contribution of scientific findings such as observations, measurements, and analyses toward questions of interest or propositions (as defined in Section 7.3.2) set in the light of the context of the case. The context of the case is therefore an essential component to be considered in order to understand the evidential weight of any findings resulting from trace materials analyses.

The majority of trace evidence assessments occur at the level of laboratory examinations and consists primarily of the identification of unknown specimens and their comparison to reference samples. Although the current chapter mainly reflects this practice, the enormous potential of trace evidence beyond mere comparative examinations is briefly discussed.

7.2 A Process of Uncertainties

In a legal matter, scientific evidence does not present itself as a proof of absolute certainty. In order to be offered as evidence, the traces, or vestiges, left behind and/or taken during a given activity under investigation undergo an evolutionary process that starts typically from their generation at the crime scene and ends with their presentation in reports and ultimately in court. If it is true that evidence has the purpose of decreasing uncertainties in so far as the occurrence or causes of an event, then it is also true that other uncertainties arise at every level within this process. These traces are generated during a single event, at a particular time, in a single location, and in a non-premeditated manner. The conditions under which the interactions, transfers, alterations, or persistence of these traces or remnants occur are not controlled. This lack of control is the main and initial source of uncertainty in this process. Forensic scientists do not have any control over these remnants or traces, which can be considered an *imperfect record* (De Forest 2001). Different studies regarding the transfer and persistence of various types of trace evidence by means of simulated contacts exist and show how the number of recovered particles varies even under controlled conditions. This variation is documented in many pioneering studies such as those by Pounds and Smalldon (1975a,b,c) on fiber transfer and persistence, and those by Nelson and Revell (1967) on glass transfer. The phenomenon is demonstrated in more recent studies from Roux et al. (1996), Monard (2007), Lepot et al. (2015), and Lepot and Vanden Driessche (2015) for fibers and Hicks et al. (1996), Irwin (2011), and Cooper (2013) involving glass fragments, as well as Grima et al. (2014) and French and Morgan (2015) for gunshot residue, and Buzzini et al. (2005) on tool and architectural paint. Readers who are interested in more information about transfer and persistence studies may consider the comprehensive review by McDermott (2009).

Traces are searched for, recovered, and collected some time after the event. The outcome of this process depends on the ability of the crime scene investigators and on the efficiency of the available collection methods. The utility of traces has to be recognized during crime scene investigation and also in the laboratory. Their relevancy or potential connection to the case needs to be evaluated. This process also constitutes a source of uncertainty, particularly in trace evidence, where traces need to be isolated from a background noise of the surrounding environment following an understanding of their deposition during the investigated event as opposed to being transferred during pre- or post-events. Once regarded as connected or possibly connected to the case, these traces assume a status of *indicia*, also conceptually denoted as clue materials (Osterburg 1968), physical signs (De Forest et al. 2015), material clues (Buzzini and Yu 2017) or physical clues (Buzzini et al. 2019). Evett (1993), Stoney (1994), and Evett et al. (1998) discuss the relevancy in cases of bloodstains left at the scene, and the possibility that they were actually left by the offender. Biedermann and Taroni (2011) expand on these discussions with cases involving potential trace transfer from the victim or scene to the offender. Uncertainties are also inevitable during the process of evidence collection. In particular, the uncertainty related to the efficiency of a given collection method will have an impact on recovery, in addition to the influence of the variables affecting the quantity and quality of the traces after their transfer and persistence.

The critical decision about which collected specimens will be examined and which methods will be applied in the particular case must also be made. Forensic laboratory examinations are essentially comparative: they imply the comparison of designated features deemed to be selective. For the identification of unknowns, the properties observed or measured within a specimen are compared to those of similar materials within a given database or to actual reference samples from a dedicated reference collection. The examiner will observe similarities and dissimilarities in order to evaluate whether or not a differentiation can be ascertained between two (or more) compared sets of features. It is important to note that the process of comparative examinations typically stops at the point where dissimilarities between the compared sets are observed or, on the contrary, it continues toward the end of an analytical sequence previously tested to maximize its discriminating potential. However, the comparison process is not always straightforward. For example, it can often be difficult to reach a conclusion about a so-called "match"[2] when comparing sets of MSP spectra. Spectral intra-source variation is one of the main factors which an examiner must cope with during this type of examination. Intra-source variation is an important source of uncertainty in many instances. Another typical example is the microscopical comparison of human hair, where the forensic scientist studies the range of variation of the relevant features within the questioned hairs (if more than one and under the assumption that they belong to the same individual) and assesses whether the observed range would overlap the range of variation for the features of the reference hair samples.

Analytical methods (i.e. laboratory instruments) have inherent characteristic sources of uncertainties and errors related to their ability to detect and correctly identify features of interest, to discriminate and produce repeatable and reproducible data, and to evaluate associations of some kind. Wallace (2010), for example, describes methods for calculating measurement uncertainties of laboratory analytical results.

---

2 The term "match" is used here to express the inability of an examiner to differentiate two (or more) sets of compared data. It does not imply any inference or decision of source attribution between the two compared sets. Moreover, the term "match" is a one-word convenient expression to summarize the above-mentioned concept. However, it is considered as a colloquialism rather than appropriate scientific terminology.

Once all the analytical results have been obtained, the forensic scientist must address the question of the analysis request. In other words, he or she needs to assess the significance of the results in order to address questions regarding the identification of unknown specimens, the source of the recovered indicia, the presence of traces as a result of suspected activities, or the occurrence of certain events and their time sequence (i.e. reconstruction). Addressing these types of questions requires the evaluation of all of these related uncertainties.

Given that all of these phases and aspects pertaining to the physical evidence process cannot be achieved with an absolute proof of certainty, it is not expected that forensic scientists will embrace a "yes or no" or *deterministic* approach. Instead, physical evidence often offers values which lie between two extremes. The value of physical evidence, its weight, must be evaluated based on a *degree of certainty* or *uncertainty*. This approach rather follows a *probabilistic* reasoning.

The reasoning and operating tools that allow for measurements of uncertainties are statistical methods and probability. Although the importance of the role and use of probabilistic and statistical approaches has been emphasized in the 2009 National Academy of Science's (NAS) report (National Research Council 2009) and more recently in the President's Council of Advisors on Science and Technology (PCAST) report (PCAST 2016), early pioneers in criminalistics advocated these approaches to purport their significance. In the United States, for example, Kirk (1953) pointed out that in a court of law it is often not recognized that all identification is purely a matter of probability. In his classical article, *The Ontogeny of Criminalistics*, Kirk also indicated that, "While it may be both correct and useful, too much room still exists for honest disagreement between witnesses. Much of this problem would be avoided if systematic study were devoted to the development of sound probability considerations applied to evidence

interpretation and also to the areas in which statistical analysis could properly contribute to correct evaluations (Kirk 1963a)." In a later article, Kirk and Kingston (1964) suggested abandoning the idea of absolute certainty in favor of statistics, which offers the most valuable approach to determine the degree of confidence to be assigned to a particular belief.

In Europe, Locard, in his 70-page chapter on the methodology of scientific evidence, suggests that the essential problem of the methodology addresses the question, "What is the nature of certainty and what is its degree?" He advocates that scientific evidence provides a certainty in measurable degrees and that the number expressing the chance of error is never zero, but can often provide chances of error tending toward zero (Locard 1920). He describes the distinction between *mathematical certainty* and *physical certainty*, this latter term denoting uncertainty.

Statistics may be defined as the science of collecting, analyzing, and interpreting data, with the goal of acquiring understanding about a problem or question of interest from them. However, statistics is also concerned with reasoning under uncertainty. This intellectual endeavor is intrinsic in a forensic science setting. Probability is typically defined as the measurement of uncertainty or the study of randomness. The probability of an event expresses the proportion of times that a given event would occur in many repeated trials of a random phenomenon where the outcome is uncertain among a total number of possible outcomes. This concept describes the occurrence of an event of interest in a very long series of repetitions where its probability of occurrence implies a long-term or long run relative frequency.[3] This definition of probability is

---

3 When repeating an experiment multiple times, the probability of the random event corresponds to the relative frequency of occurrence of the outcome of that particular experiment. In this setting, the number of individuals or objects in a category is denoted *frequency* for that category and the *relative frequency* is the number of individuals or objects divided by the total sample size.

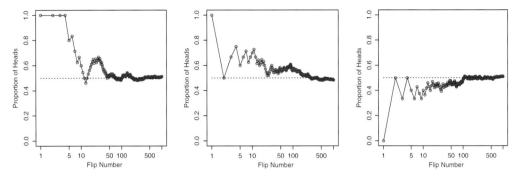

Figure 7.1 Graphs for three long run repetitions trials ($N = 1000$) for the coin toss experiment. The three experiments exhibit different outcomes of observing a head face when a small number of flips are considered and they tend to converge to the expected probability of 0.5 when the number of repetitions increases.

commonly known as the *frequentist definition*. A typical illustration is the well-known coin toss experiment. The question of interest regards the probability of observing a head. Assuming a fair coin, there are two possible outcomes: heads or tails. Figure 7.1 shows three trials of 1000 repetitions each. Each of the three experiments exhibits different trends when a small number of flips is considered, but tend to converge at a probability of 0.5 when, in the long run, the number of trials or repetitions is increased.

However, this is not the only definition or view of probability. Another school of thought regards probability as a *degree of belief* of the occurrence of a certain event. This is known as the *Bayesian definition*. The Bayesian approach assumes that all probabilities are *conditional*, meaning that the assignment of a probability for the occurrence of an event is based on some available information. This concept applies to the example of the coin toss too: the probability of 0.5 of observing a head depends not only on your knowledge of coins, but also the assumption that the coin is a fair one. This shows that the process of allowing the probabilities to be conditioned on the circumstances of the case is not unique to the Bayesian philosophy, but perhaps it does fit more naturally with the fundamental Bayesian definition of probability.

Bayes' Theorem, at its simplest, is a mathematical formula that allows for the update of current beliefs about the occurrence of an event when new information is acquired. It allows assessment questions such as, "What are the chances with regards to the degree of belief in A, assuming that the degree of belief of B is high?" or, "How does the degree of belief in A change, if the degree of belief in B is lowered? (Taroni et al. 2014)."

Both approaches rely on the laws of probability and available information (including assumptions). One of the major distinctions between the two approaches is the input of the data of interest. Berger et al. (2011a) emphasize the distinction between the two approaches in the following terms: the frequentist approach uses *aleatory probabilities*, whereas the Bayesian approach utilizes *epistemic probabilities*. Aleatory probabilities are those gathered from experiments such as the coin toss, card games, or throwing dice, whereas uncertainty is based solely on the randomness of the conditions of the experiment. On the other hand, in epistemic probabilities, uncertainty is based on the limitations of available information. Aleatory probabilities are also known as "objective," while epistemic probabilities are called "subjective." The former do not depend on human or expert judgment, while the latter do.

7.3 Factors Affecting Evidence Interpretation

In this chapter, it is mainly considered that traces recovered from a given case require comparative laboratory examinations. The following factors affect the interpretation of the analytical findings:

1. the context of the case
2. the questions put to the forensic scientist
3. the extent, reliability, and validity of collected analytical information
4. the degree of *similarity* between compared sets.

7.3.1 The Context of the Case

Understanding the interactions that may occur between transferred traces and the surrounding environment is of upmost importance. It should be the duty of the forensic scientist to evaluate, inquire, or discuss whether some unknown particles originate from part of the environment where they have been recovered or if they may have been transferred during the suspected activity, even if they may been deposited afterwards (i.e. contamination). Although this type of determination is not systematically straightforward, or even possible in every case, it is clear that it depends on the context of the case. This evaluation is related to the concept of relevancy discussed in Section 7.2.

Prosecution and defense strategies both play an important role in weighing trace evidence. An example of the impact of the defense strategy is discussed in Section 7.4. The position of the prosecutor or the investigators may be clear from the beginning. However, the position of the defense may be unknown until advocacy during trial. Suspects are not usually required to offer statements and even when they might be required to do so, they may change their statements, sometimes more than once. The experienced forensic scientist, with available information in hand, might consider several alternative scenarios and in so doing address questions such as, "Would I expect my observations, if this alternative hypothesis is true?" Postulating alternative hypotheses requires knowledge about the circumstances of the case and would be beneficial to circumvent expert unpreparedness during cross-examination with respect to challenging questions about evidence interpretation.

The context of the case also dictates the population of potential sources (including the putative sources) in cases where the question of interest is about a common source between two compared sets. A pertinent question for consideration is whether or not the recovered traces should be evaluated in an open set or a closed set. This concept was discussed in detail by Kwan (1977). The open set considers a population at large. Typical examples include all individuals on Earth or all garments of certain type and color on Earth, even any vehicle of a given color from a large undefined geographical area. In contrast, a closed set confines the number of potential individuals or objects susceptible to be the source of the recovered traces in a restricted and definite group. For example, Robertson (1999) describes the classic example of a road accident involving a vehicle with two occupants. Neither of these occupants admits to being the driver. A tuft of hair is recovered from a specific location of the windshield. Based on dissimilarities between the hair features of the two individuals, in such a case the recovered hair specimens clearly were not shed by one of the two occupants and could then be attributed to the second one based on microscopical comparisons. Haag and Haag (2011) utilize the expression of *limited universe* to refer to a closed set in the context of shooting reconstructions. For example, trajectories may be explained by deposits of materials such as paint or wood debris transferred on traveling bullets from the surrounding environment during their impact. Conversely, lead or copper residues can be shed from bullets to a given surface at the shooting scene. In such a case, the potential sources of such substances are restricted to the specific context of the shooting scene being investigated. This type of scenario clearly shows that it may be more appropriate to consider only paint, wood, or other involved materials that are characteristic of the environment where the investigated shooting transpired.

The history of the seized items must also be considered in light of the circumstances of the case. Here, the term "history" does not refer to the critical concept and practice of chain of custody. Nehse (2011) discussed a case involving an attempted assault where the victim claimed that her offender grabbed her from behind. A suspect was identified straight-away and subsequently arrested. His garments, along with those belonging to the victim, were seized. Fibers were recovered from the victim's garments which could not be differentiated from the reference fibers collected from the suspect's garments. Also, fibers were recovered from the suspect's garments; they could not be differentiated from the reference fibers collected from the victim's garments, suggesting a cross-transfer. However, assuming that appropriate packaging and collection operations were conducted, discrepancies between the location of the recovered fibers and the *expected* location of fibers following the victim's account were found. Further consideration of the case circumstances in conjunction with knowledge regarding the seized garments poses a different interpretative perspective. Indeed, the suspect was brought to the police station in a patrol car. Later, the victim was transported to the same station for her depositions, in the very same vehicle. To make matters worse, she sat down in the same chair for her interview as the suspect sat in during his interrogation. Their garments were seized afterwards. As a consequence, it is not possible to evaluate if the presence of the fibers can be explained by the victim's account or by the exposure of the garments to the same surfaces prior to their collection. Note how knowledge about the case circumstances would prevent a misinterpretation of the evidential value.

However, measures against the risks of context biases or confirmation biases among others need to be taken. Some laboratories have implemented protocols to filter the relevant case information that is needed to the forensic scientist to address the tasks at hand. More development in this area is foreseen within the operations of forensic laboratories in the years to come.

7.3.2 The Questions Directed to the Forensic Scientist and Hypothesis Formulation

A formal statement usually accompanies trace materials analysis requests when seized items collected at crime scenes are submitted to a laboratory for testing. Typical questions include, "Do Q and K share a common source?" or "Do the submitted items bear relevant trace evidence?" It is important to reiterate that the contributions of trace evidence should not be confined to this limited framework of questions. The popular Wayne Williams case is an excellent example which highlights the multi-faceted, contributory nature of trace evidence. A peculiarity in this case was the fact that a conviction was achieved primarily with evidence from textile fibers and dog hairs. On the night of 22 May 1981, police patrolling at the Chattahoochee River in Atlanta, Georgia, heard an abrupt splash near a bridge and noticed a young African-American male driving away from that area. When they approached him, he identified himself as Wayne Williams, a music promoter and freelance photographer (Durden Smith 2007). Initially they did not detain him, but tracked him down again when a dead body was found in the river a couple of days later. Hair and fibers in this case produced useful information as evaluative evidence (i.e. comparative examinations between questioned and reference fiber sets) as well as in the form of investigative leads. Indeed, fiber and dog hair evidence was utilized to (i) help investigators link the bodies recovered from the river,

(ii) produce investigative leads by means of sourcing the manufacturer of the main synthetic fibers involved in this case, and (iii) obtain statistical estimates of the rarity of the recovered fibers in the population by means of manufacturer inquiries.

Yellowish-green nylon fibers as well as violet acetate fibers were recovered from earlier victims' clothing and bodies. These bodies had been found between 1979 and 1981, prior to Williams' arrest. The recovered yellowish-green fibers were very coarse and had an unusual lobed cross-sectional shape. Dog hairs were also found. Based on these findings, police searched Williams' home and found a throw rug from Williams' bed and a green carpet, and discovered that Williams had a dog. The fibers recovered from many victims' bodies were indistinguishable from the carpet in Williams' bedroom.

A manufacturer inquiry determined that the Wellman Corporation produced the yellowish-green nylon fibers during a single year, 1971. Sales records showed that the carpet was manufactured in relatively small amounts and for only a short period of time. Other uncommon fiber types were recovered and compared to the rayon/nylon carpet in Williams' 1970 station wagon or the undyed man-made fibers with black adhesive particles from the trunk liners in two other vehicles that Williams had access to in 1979 and 1980 (Deadman 1984). Williams was charged with the murders of two young African-American boys. However, as shown in Figure 7.2, a combination of fiber types recovered from victims who were missing or had been murdered in the Atlanta area from 1979 and 1981 proved indistinguishable from textiles seized from Williams' property.

The questions of interest may be provided by the court, the investigators, and perhaps the forensic scientist. These may later be distilled into questions which science may allow us to address. Framing the questions of interest is a prerogative of the scientific method (Gauch 2003). Hence, hypotheses are generated in order to be scientifically tested. Generally, hypotheses are generated by direct observation or erstwhile observations (i.e. past experience), first-hand personal knowledge, belief, guess, or even intuition (i.e. Peirce's abductive form of reasoning). In casework, it is often true that the default position is to accept the question in the analysis request as a hypothesis to be tested or question to be answered.

Cook et al. (1998b) developed a framework to formally articulate questions of interest into hypotheses. The term "proposition" is preferred to express statements submitted to formal logical evaluation (Evett et al. 2000a). Their framework is known as the *hierarchy of propositions* and distinguishes hypotheses in three broad categories: *source level* (level I), *activity level* (level II), and *offence level* (level III). Source level propositions are at the bottom level of the hierarchy[4] and address questions about the source of the recovered traces. Activity level propositions aim to explain the *presence* (or absence) of traces with regards to the occurrence of particular activities. The quantity and the location of recovery of the traces are of utmost interest. For example, level II propositions qualify a specific contact between two surfaces or a particular way to explain the spatial relocation of some particles of interest. Consideration of activity level propositions requires more circumstantial information about the case than source level propositions. Aspects regarding transfer, persistence, and efficiency of recovery are included in the evaluation at the activity level. Finally, offense level propositions are concerned with the crime or felony under investigation. Thus, they are outside of the competence of the forensic scientist and they are responsibility of the trier-of-fact, attorneys, and investigators. The hierarchy

---

4 A *subsource* level is also used in the context of DNA interpretation to define propositions in cases where a DNA profile is obtained without identifying the originating biological material (i.e. trace DNA). In the context of trace materials analyses this level is not evoked because the characterization of the recovered unknown particles is a pre-condition to address at least questions about source attributions.

NAME OF VICTIM	VIOLET AND GREEN BEDSPREAD WILLIAMS BEDROOM	GREEN CARPET WILLIAMS BEDROOM	DOG HAIRS WILLIAM'S DOG	YELLOW BLANKET WILLIAMS BEDROOM	BLUE RAYON FIBERS DEBRIS FROM WILLIAMS HOME	TRUNK LINER 1978 PLYMOUTH	CARPET 1979 FORD	CARPET 1970 CHEVROLET	ADDITIONAL ITEMS FROM WILLIAMS'S HOME. AUTOMOBILES OR PERSON
Alfred Evans	X	X	X			X			
Eric Middlebrooks	X		X				X		YELLOW NYLON — FORD TRUNK LINER
Charles Stephens	X	X	X		X				YELLOW NYLON — WHITE POLYESTER — BACKROOM CARPET — FORD TRUNK LINER
Lubie Geter	X	X	X					X	KITCHEN CARPET
Terry Pue	X	X	X						WHITE POLYESTER — BACKROOM CARPET
Patrick Baltazar	X	X	X	X				X	YELLOW NYLON — WHITE POLYESTER — HEAD HAIR — GLOVE — JACKET PIGMENTED POLYPROPYLENE
Joseph Bell	X			X					
Larry Rogers	X	X	X	X				X	YELLOW NYLON — PORCH BEDSPREAD
John Porter	X	X	X	X	X			X	PORCH BEDSPREAD
Jimmy Payne	X	X	X	X	X			X	BLUE THROW RUG
William Barrett	X	X	X	X	X			X	GLOVE
Nathaniel Cater	X	X	X	X					BACKROOM CARPET — YELLOW. GREEN SYNTHETIC

Figure 7.2 Table summarizing the fibers from Wayne Williams's property that were found indistinguishable from the fibers recovered from victims who were missing or had been murdered in the Atlanta area from 1979 and 1981. In addition to the significance associated to the traditional comparisons between questioned specimens and reference samples obtained from Williams' environment, it is important to note just how impactful these findings were in linking the victims even before any consideration of known sources. This latter aspect highlights the potential of trace evidence to address investigative needs. Source: Deadman HA 1984, FBI Law Enforcement Bulletin.

of propositions is useful to identify the most appropriate level of questions of interest according to the available information about the circumstances of the case. It is also helpful to confine the expertise to the appropriate level of competency. For example, a forensic scientist limited to comparative examinations between questioned specimens and reference samples may not be in a position to comment about the plausibility of the occurrence of a particular contact without considering appropriate parameters such as transfer and persistence in the context of the case. Framing propositions is not always trivial. Hicks et al. (2015) suggest that it is problematic to include observations in the propositions themselves and the consecutive implication that the evaluation of such observations is left to the stakeholders of justice. It is clearly problematic if the interpretive tasks belonging to the forensic scientist are left to non-scientists in cases where scientific expertise is needed.

If the forensic scientist has an opportunity to discuss the case file and identify the needs of the submitter, then a judgment of relevancy leads to the development of pertinent questions for the case. Indeed, the definition of the scientific problems in a case is critical in order to identify the most useful questions which need to be addressed.

7.3.3 Extent of Collected Analytical Information, Reliability, and Validity

Inferences from insufficient or unreliable data cannot be drawn. As stated by Neumann (2013), all forensic examinations are by nature aimed at investigating and minimizing the uncertainty related to traces resulting from wrongdoings. An important step toward minimizing uncertainty entails the ability to collect as much information as possible from the recovered specimens and reference samples during laboratory examinations.

Section 7.3 discussed the fact that major sources of uncertainty in the process of physical evidence are due to the quality and quantity of indicia left behind. Both quality and quantity of recovered traces clearly affect the extent to which analytical information can be obtained, particularly for types of materials that are usually analyzed following an analytical sequence. Less information can be derived from a transferred paint smear as opposed to a four-layer multilayered fragment. Less information can be obtained from a single hair as opposed to a strand of five or more hair specimens in light of appreciating the intra-source variation of macroscopical and microscopical characteristics. The analysis of degraded specimens may clearly be less informative than that of similar objects in pristine conditions.

Another limiting factor to the collection of analytical information stems from whether the analyzed object is a recovered specimen or a reference sample. There is generally less recovered material available than reference material. For example, it is unusual to find a large number of glass fragments on someone even if they have broken a window. However, it is extremely easy to take as much glass as needed from the scene source. In some circumstances some of the features of interest that are usually measured may prove challenging to detect utilizing a given analytical method. A common example is the difficulty in obtaining informative microspectrophotometric data from pale fibers at low dye concentrations. Analytical methods are chosen to detect, observe, and exploit relevant features, which in turn provide measurements for comparative examinations. Intra-source and inter-sources variations are factors that affect the interpretation of the findings. While these sources of variations are clearly related to the studied objects and their detected properties, this section only considers the ability of the chosen analytical techniques to capture and describe them. This ability qualifies the validity and reliability of the chosen analytical methods as a precondition to properly interpret findings (Gott and

Duggan 2003). Although practical criteria such as non-destructivity, simplicity, rapidity, and time-effectiveness affect the choice of a particular method (or an analytical sequence), other fundamental criteria utilized as indicators of the reliability of an adopted analytical method are taken into account, namely sensitivity, precision, accuracy, and selectivity. While sensitivity, precision, and accuracy are factors that are well-defined in analytical chemistry, and science in general (e.g. Skoog et al. 1994), selectivity may assume a specific meaning in the context of forensic science examinations. In analytical chemistry, selectivity refers to the extent to which a method can determine particular analytes in mixtures or matrices without interferences from other components (Vessman et al. 2001). This terminology also differs from the classical definitions of sensitivity and specificity adopted, for example, in diagnostic medical tests that refer to true positive rate and true negative rate, respectively, while attempting to detect a given disease. In forensic science, it is appropriate to use the term "selectivity" to express the degree of variability of detected features within a population of interest. Kwan (1977) uses the term *distinguishability*. With respect to the attributes of an analytical method, selectivity also refers to the ability of a technique to detect the features of interest and, in particular, their degree of variability in order to separate, distinguish, or identify a group of objects or individuals. This is known as *discrimination* or *discriminating power* (e.g. Smalldon and Moffat 1973). Total separation is known as specificity and occurs when the method or protocol detects attributes which lead to the distinction of one object or individual at the exclusion of all the others within a group or population. The discriminating power has been an object of multiple studies involving different types of materials to typically evaluate and compare analytical methods. For example, Grieve et al. (1988) tested the discriminating capabilities of comparison microscopy, fluorescence microscopy, and visible MSP on blue, red, and black cottons. Similar studies were carried out by Cassista and Peters (1997), Grieve et al. (2001, 2003, 2005), Wiggins et al. (2005), Biermann (2007), Palmer et al. (2009), and Buzzini and Massonnet (2015). For paint, studies dedicated to testing the discriminating power of various analytical methods have been tested, for example by Gothard (1976), Ryland and Kopec (1979), Massonnet (1996), and Edmondstone et al. (2004) on automotive paints, by Tippett et al. (1968), May and Porter (1975), Laing et al. (1982), Muehlethaler et al. (2011), and Wright et al. (2011, 2013) on architectural paints, and by Buzzini and Massonnet (2004), Govaert and Bernard (2004), and Muehlethaler et al. (2014) on spray paints. For glass, discrimination studies have been carried out, for example by Andrasko and Maehly (1978), Koons et al. (1988), Pitts and Kratochvil (1991), Trejos et al. (2003), Bridge et al. (2007), Naes et al. (2008), and Trejos et al. (2013). Goodpaster et al. (2007, 2009) and Mehltretter et al. (2011a,b) have investigated various techniques for the discrimination of electrical tapes.

The discriminating power does not inform about the evidential value in the specific case; it justifies the use of the adopted protocol so that an examination maximizes the chances to differentiate compared sets when these indeed exhibit different detectable features.

7.3.4 The Degree of Similarity Between Compared Sets

Through comparisons between unknown specimens and reference samples, forensic scientists ponder concordances and discordances between selected features of interest. In colloquial terms, this step expresses the confidence of an examiner to declare a match. However, inevitably issues which affect evidence interpretation arise.

The comparison process implies a continuum of possibilities that range between two extreme situations: the observation of differences only and the observation of concordances only. In most cases, a given number of concordances are observed along with a given number of discordances during comparative evaluations. This would correspond, in the Bayesian approach (Section 7.5), to a value of the numerator of the likelihood ratio (LR) at the source level lower than 1. That is, the presence of discordances introduces (further) uncertainty into the comparison process. The forensic scientist has to explain the observed discordances considering aspects like the limitations of the adopted methodology, intra-source variations of the properties detected within both the set of recovered specimens and the obtained reference samples, the representativeness of the reference samples, and the potential influence of some background noise (e.g. infrared spectra potentially presenting infrared absorption bands from the surface where an unknown paint transfer is detected) or contaminations. Verbal scales that attempt to address this continuum have been constructed. They are known in the trace evidence community as terminology keys for associative evidence and define different levels of "associations" (Section 7.6.5). One of the major criteria historically used to qualify a given association type is the consideration of similarities of *all* or *some* (or the dissimilarities) of the measured physical properties and/or chemical composition.

Furthermore, the process of comparison depends on expert (or subjective) judgment in different material analysis subdisciplines. Typical examples are comparison microscopy (e.g. human hair) and comparisons of spectroscopic data (e.g. MSP of fibers). While expertise (as a combination of knowledge, skills, abilities, and experience) is valuable and will always play a critical role in forensic examinations, an approach based on the collection of numbers (i.e. numerical or quantitative variables) would be more robust in order to support expert judgment during the comparison process, particularly in cases where uncertainties are preponderant and the expert is confronted with a high volume of data. For example, in glass examination, the Student's *t*-test and, in particular, its modified version known as Welch test are utilized to statistically compare refractive index data. The use of the T^2 Hoteling test has also been suggested to compare multivariate glass elemental data (Curran et al. 2000). To this end, Taroni et al. (2016) have discussed the concept of P values used in traditional null hypothesis significance testing and addressed the question of whether such an approach should be abandoned in forensic science applications. With regards to typical high-dimensional data encountered in casework, Morgan et al. (2007), among others, have shown the usefulness of chemometrics and in their particular case the use of principal component analysis (PCA) and linear discriminant analysis (LDA) to distinguish MSP spectra of various types of fibers.

7.4 Some Interpretive Issues: The Example of the Birmingham Six Bombing Case

On 21 November 1975, two bombing devices exploded in two pubs in the city of Birmingham in the UK. A third device failed to detonate. Twenty-one people were killed and 182 were injured (Richards and Cannon 2014). Six men were accused and four of them were forced to sign confessions. These men were later acquitted, at retrial, of all charges and received financial compensation for wrongful conviction and imprisonment. Investigators were convinced that the culprit was the Irish Republican Army (IRA) since the six men were Irish citizens and, on the evening of the bombings, they were all traveling by train to attend the funeral of an IRA member. When police stopped them, they did not divulge the real reason for their travel and as a result their previous statements were used against them.

Dr. Frank Skuse, a forensic scientist with the Home Office North-West Forensic Laboratory in Chorley, Lancashire, was assigned to test the suspects for explosive residue. He swabbed the hands and fingernails of five of the six suspects and carried out the Griess test, the classic chemical chromophoric test that detects the presence of organic nitrite (NO_2^-) compounds. Dr. Skuse documented a positive result when he observed a red-pink coloration as he exposed the collected specimens to the Griess reagent and solution of sodium hydroxide, as opposed to the lack of any coloration by exposing the specimens to the Griess reagent only. The Griess test showed negative results on three suspects, Richard McIlkenny, Gerry Hunter, and Johnny Walker. Positive results were observed on the right hands of two suspects, Billy Power and Paddy Hill.[5]

During his testimony, Dr. Skuse declared he was "quite happy" that the two positive Griess test results confirmed contact with commercial explosives (Mullin 1997). When asked what "quite happy" meant, the expert answered "99% certain." In summary, the expert concluded that he was "99% certain that the suspects had been in contact with nitroglycerin, a common explosive used to make bombs.[6]"

The fallacies and issues involved in this conclusion are identified at different levels:

1. Prosecutor's fallacy or transposing the conditional.
2. Inappropriate level of propositions.
3. Misconception of the 99% uncertainty.
4. Non consideration of (possible) defense arguments.

---

5 As reported by Mullin (1997), confirmatory testing using thin layer chromatography and gas chromatography/mass spectrometry gave a negative result.

6 It is not intention of the authors to offer a critical review of the case itself or to focus on the choice of appropriate analytical methods to typically address the limited value of presumptive testing without consideration of confirmatory testing. For the purpose of this chapter only the fallacious arguments of the expert's conclusion are discussed in the light of the factors that affect evidence interpretation on a general basis.

7.4.1 Prosecutor's Fallacy or the Transposed Conditional

The expert in the Birmingham Six case expressed a 99% probability that the suspects handled nitroglycerin, following the observation of the positive results. This is a typical example of what is known as a prosecutor's fallacy. If his task in this case consisted of detecting explosive particles only, then the reach of his statement should be of the order of expressing uncertainty regarding the observation of a positive result, and not about the claim that the suspects handled nitroglycerin. The expert is not in a position to comment on the plausibility of the suspects handling explosives based on the Griess test data only. Let E denote the event "the test gives a positive result" and H the event "the suspects handled nitroglycerin," Dr. Skuse expressed $p(H|E) = 0.99$. The vertical bar denotes that the probability given is conditional and that the event(s) to the right of the bar is assumed to have occurred or to be true. It is important to note that the conditioning event may only be assumed true for the sake of evaluating the probability in question. An example might be, "What do you think the probability is of finding a person over 2 m tall IF you assume that person is an adult female?" In this example the probability is conditional on the assumption that the person in question is an adult female. Returning to the case example, Dr. Skuse should have assessed $p(E|H)$, the probability of a test giving a positive result IF we assume the defendants handled nitroglycerin.

The prosecutor's fallacy occurs when someone transposes the conditional, that is, (unintentionally) claims (or implies) that $p(E|H)$ is the same as $p(H|E)$ (Robertson et al. 2016). This concept evokes Sherlock Holmes' statement: "Insensibly one begins to twist facts to suit theories, instead of theories to suit facts" (Doyle 1887). The expression *transposing the conditional* comes from the fact that the terms E and H have switched position around the conditioning symbol of the

probability of interest. Evett (1995) offers the following example to demonstrate the fallacy: The probability that an animal has four legs if it is a cow is one does not mean the same thing, as the probability that an animal is a cow if it has four legs is one. Evett also offers examples of statements that show the subtle difference between the fallacy and the correct conclusion respectively: "The probability that the stain has come from some other person is 1 in 1000" [as opposed to] "the probability that the stain would be type X if it had come from some other person is 1 in 1000."

Thompson and Schumann (1987) discuss a case where a bloodstain left at the scene by the perpetrator could not be differentiated from the biological reference of a suspect. They indicated that the profile was found in only one person in 1000 in the population of interest. The fallacy took the form: "There is 0.1% of chance that the defendant would have this set of features if he were innocent, and therefore there is 99.9% of chance that he is guilty." This statement can be expressed as $p(H_1|E) = 1 - p(E|H_2)$, where H_1 is the event "the defendant is guilty," H_2 is the event "the defendant is innocent," and E is the event "the defendant has the observed set of features."

The boundaries that an expert needs to respect can also be viewed in terms of *probabilities of causes* and *probabilities of effects*. French mathematicians Darboux, Appel, and Poincaré raised this notion during the famous Dreyfus case in the late nineteenth century, where Alphonse Bertillon, the father of anthropometry, offered a flawed and fallacious testimony during his handwriting examination in that case (Taroni et al. 1998). Scientific evidence, laboratory results, or, more generally, observations are the effects of events or activities. Their presence or source can be explained by one or more causes. In the Birmingham Six case, the probability that the suspects handled nitroglycerin depends on factors that go beyond the probability of observing a positive result from a given test.

Even if irrelevant in this particular case, it is worth mentioning another fallacy that can result from the misuse of statistical arguments: the defense attorney's fallacy. In a case such as the one involving the bloodstain whose profile has an occurrence of 0.1% in the population, a defense counsel may conclude that "in a population of 500 000 individuals, a blood type with an occurrence of 0.1% would be found in about 500 people. This implies, according to the argument, that the suspect is one of 500 individuals in the population who might have committed the crime." In this argument, the defense counsel fails to consider that the vast majority of individuals in the population with this feature are not suspects in the case at hand. Otherwise expressed, not all of these possible 500 individuals have a priori to be a plausible suspect in this particular case. This argument sheds light on the fact that scientific evidence narrows down considerably the pool of individuals who could have committed the crime, but fails to exclude the very individual on which suspicion has already focused (Thompson and Schumann 1987). Imwinkelried (2004) suggested this argument as a possible strategy for attacking scientific evidence.

7.4.2 Inappropriate Level of Propositions

Considering the concept of hierarchy of propositions discussed above, a conclusion stating a contact or exposure to a substance such as nitroglycerin is described according to an activity level or level II of the hierarchy. This implies consideration of factors that go beyond the mere application of any analytical method and transcends the source of the detected particles. Indeed, the presence of the detected particles, in terms of location and quantity, must be evaluated with respect to this particular level. The forensic scientist should consider questions such as, "Is the presence of the detected residues attributed to the handling of explosives?" This question requires assessment of factors including the transfer and persistence of such particles as well as the ability and efficiency to recover them. At the activity level, the expert should ask, "Assuming that the particles are nitroglycerin, are the suspects susceptible being exposed to an environment with nitroglycerin, without having necessarily handled it?" Without a specific explanation or proposition, typically from the part of the defendant, the presence of these particles may be the result of an aleatory presence. With respect to the source level, or first level of the hierarchy of proposition, a possible question of interest may be, "Do the residues recovered on the hands of the suspects share a common origin with those recovered from the scenes?" This question is irrelevant in this particular case. Clearly the Griess test alone, or any other analytical technique, cannot address these questions. The form of statement that can be advanced by Dr. Skuse, based on his testing, is akin to, "The residues recovered on the hands of the suspects are nitroglycerin." Alternatively, this is a statement of an *identification* of unknown specimens. Kirk (1963a) describes *identification* as a narrowing-down process of placing an object in a restricted class. In this context, the detection of some unknown particles is performed and the study of their properties aims to label them and consequently place them in a category of substances with similar physical and/or chemical properties.

7.4.3 Misconception of the 99%

Dr. Skuse's conclusion would have been misleading even if he had stated that he was "99% certain that the particles are nitroglycerin, based on the results of the Griess test," instead of being "99% certain that the suspects handled nitroglycerin." Note that the former conclusion has been revised in consideration of the appropriate level of proposition that can be assigned on the basis of the use of the Griess test only. Let us ignore for a moment the prosecutor's fallacy in light of the following considerations.

Being "99% certain that the particles are nitroglycerin" may imply from the part of the expert that he believes that there is 99% probability that the particles are nitroglycerin. That is, if one swabs hands from 100 individuals *known* to have been in contact with nitroglycerin and test them with the Griess test, a positive observation is expected 99 times. This is the true positives rate (TPR) (or sensitivity as in medical diagnostic applications, for example). On the other hand, in one occasion an expected coloration is not observed, which is 1% and corresponds to the false negatives rate (FNR).

However, the crucial question in this case is whether or not the Griess test is specific to nitroglycerin. This is not the case. The Griess test detects nitrites, which although present in nitroglycerin, can also be present in many substances lawfully present in our environment such as plastic materials or food preservatives. One of the first uses of this test was the detection of nitrites in water samples. Clearly, Dr. Skuse did not take into account alternative substances. By analogy to the estimation of the rate of true positives and false negatives, a sample of 100 individuals *known to not* have been in contact with nitroglycerin should be tested using the Griess test. The occurrences of a positive coloration would permit to estimate the false positives rate (FPR). The estimated true positive rate of 99% is not informative without simultaneously considering the FPR.

Dennis et al. (2016) used an approach that could formally address this problem. They implemented discrete comparison likelihood ratios and score-based likelihood ratio calculations for pairwise comparisons of intact smokeless powders.

The way of estimating TPR and FPR described above allows for obtaining general information about the ability of this particular test. The example above assumed that individuals randomly selected were from a general population. However, such an approach should encapsulate the context of the case at hand. The next section will elaborate further on this

concept and discuss how in casework, such as in the Birmingham case, it is critical to consider alternative propositions and, when possible, the strategy of the defense in order to explain the obtained scientific findings.

7.4.4 Non-consideration of Plausible Defense Arguments

Dr. Skuse ignored any possible alternative explanations on the part of suspects Power and Hill when they were found to be Griess test positive. The expert should consider alternative substances that can produce a positive result with the Griess test and evaluate what may be applicable to the case at hand. Conversations with the investigators in the case could be helpful to identify such alternative substances. The claims of the defendants must also be considered because they affect the outcome and significance of these findings. Consider the typical case where the suspects deny exposure to nitroglycerin but are not able to offer any explanation about these particles, in the sense that they do not admit or recollect having been exposed to any particular substance. The proposition that "the residues detected on the suspects' hands are not nitroglycerin" is considered as an alternative to the statement that "the residues detected on the suspects' hands are nitroglycerin." At this point, the expert, unaware, already has estimated the chances of a positive coloration if the residues detected on the suspects' hands are nitroglycerin, which is 0.99. However, he has omitted the chances of a positive coloration if the residues detected on the suspects' hands are *not* nitroglycerin, which is the rate of false positives mentioned in the previous section. Without any specification from the part of the suspects or from the background information about the case, estimations could be obtained from a survey in a general population. What would be the probability that a randomly chosen individual from the general population would exhibit positive coloration if the Griess test were performed? The lower the occurrence of a positive coloration, the higher the value of the Griess test toward the proposition of the residues resulting in nitroglycerin.

Consider, instead, that the suspects in addition to denying exposure to nitroglycerin indicate that they were playing cards (nitrocellulose-coated plastic materials) and smoking cigarettes during their travel on the train to Heyshman. In this case, the expert should evaluate how plausible it is that a positive coloration would result from the residues of these substances. A population survey involving individuals playing cards and smoking cigarettes should be selected. Indeed, researchers at the Home Office Forensic Science Laboratory in Aldermaston, UK, conducted a study in 1986 on a group of people who played cards for two hours. The researchers swabbed their hands and applied the Griess test. All swabs produced positive results. Also, when a number of playing cards from different manufacturers were tested, all but one brand proved positive (Connor 1987).[7] In light of these results as well as the consideration of the case context, it can be concluded that the Griess test is not capable of discriminating the two considered propositions and, therefore, the scientific evidence based on this particular test is inconclusive.

7.5 The Bayesian Approach

The Bayesian approach has been proposed as a logical framework for reasoning under uncertainty and weighing the strength of scientific evidence for several decades. It is a reasoning tool that allows revising or reassigning a probability or a belief of a given event when new information becomes available. It is appealing

for forensic science problems because (i) it favors the integration of scientific evidence into an existing context (e.g. crime under investigation), (ii) it addresses simultaneously opposing positions such as those within an adversarial system, and (iii) it separates and defines the specific contribution of the forensic scientist from those of other involved parties.

The forensic science literature abounds on this topic and includes the pioneering works of Finkelstein and Fairley (1970), Lindley (1977), Aitken (1987), and Evett (1990). In addition, various textbooks cover the topic relevant to the forensic scientist involved in trace material analyses (Aitken and Stoney 1991; Lucy 2005; Taroni et al. 2014; Zadora et al. 2014; Robertson et al. 2016). Particularly detailed descriptions and examples are provided by Champod and Taroni (1999) for textile fibers, by Curran et al. (2000) for glass, and by Willis et al. (2001) for paint evidence. The NAS report (NRC 2009) states that, "publications such as Evett et al., Aitken and Taroni, and Evett provide the essential building blocks for the proper assessment and communication of forensic findings."

Assume an event under investigation such as a crime. The prosecutor will have a theory about that event. The defense will have an opposing theory, although this may be unknown until trial or may change multiple times during the investigation. The Bayesian approach, as applied to evidence interpretation, recognizes the existence of these two opposing positions and aims at weighing the value of the scientific findings in consideration of the two. As Jackson describes (Jackson 2000), this process can be regarded as an analog of the scales of justice, whose pans represent the positions of the two sides, typically those of the prosecutor and the defense, respectively. These pans carry different weights consisting of different evidence that both parties collect. Scientific evidence is regarded as a weight to be placed in one, both, or neither of these two pans. The impact of the evidence depends on the weight that is added to a given pan, but

---

7 Such studies were also conducted on soaps and detergents (like those used by Dr. Skuse to clean the porcelain bowls used for the testing on the suspects' hands), meat pies that suspect Hill might have consumed at the Crewe station, nitrocellulose lacquers, and aerosol spray (Mullin 1997).

also on the initial position of the pans. It is inappropriate to assume that the two pans are equally balanced before the contribution of scientific evidence. Two propositions are typically formalized as follows:

H_1: Proposition expressing the position of the prosecutor or first party.

H_2: Proposition expressing the position of the defense or opposing party.

Note that the two competing propositions are mutually exclusive and are formed according to the appropriate level of the *hierarchy of propositions*. Mathematically, the Bayesian approach is expressed as follows:

$$\underbrace{\frac{p(H_1|I)}{p(H_2|I)}}_{} \times \underbrace{\frac{p(E|H_1,I)}{p(E|H_2,I)}}_{} = \underbrace{\frac{p(H_1|E,I)}{p(H_2|E,I)}}_{}$$

Prior odds	Likelihood ratio	Posterior odds
Assessed by stakeholders of justice (e.g., attorneys, police, jury)	Assessed by the forensic scientist	Assessed by stakeholders of justice (e.g., attorneys, police, jury)

In the formula, E denotes the scientific findings and I describes the knowledge about the relevant circumstances of the case at hand. Note that the likelihood ratio is the forensic scientist's domain of competence. Therefore, the likelihood ratio approach rather than the Bayesian approach is preferred, if one is only concerned with the physical evidence aspects of the case. The likelihood ratio is defined as the probability of obtaining certain results given that the proposition H_1 is true, divided by the probability of obtaining the same results given that the proposition H_2 is true. The likelihood ratio can assume values in a continuum between zero and infinity. If the likelihood ratio is greater than one (LR > 1), the evidence supports H_1, if the likelihood ratio is equal to 1, then the evidence supports neither H_1 nor H_2 (i.e., inconclusive), and if the likelihood ratio is less than one (LR < 1), the evidence supports H_2. The likelihood ratio may be expressed by a verbal equivalent following a scale of conclusions if the service requestor or the trier-of-fact may not appreciate a numerical

form (Section 7.6.6). The *posterior odds* express the updated beliefs or uncertainties about the two competing positions, meaning the *prior odds* after consideration of the scientific findings.

Evett (1991) has enunciated the following three principles for evidence interpretation:

1. To assess the strength of scientific evidence it is necessary to consider (at least) two propositions for its occurrence.
2. The evidence is evaluated by assessing its probability under each of the competing propositions.
3. The strength of the evidence in relation to one of the propositions is the probability of the evidence given that explanation, divided by the probability of the evidence given the alternative explanation.

These principles – more recently renamed *principles of forensic science evaluation* – have matured following intellectual developments and practice in the field of scientific evidence interpretation (Evett et al. 2000a,b; ENFSI 2015):

1. Interpretation of scientific findings is carried out within a framework of circumstances. The interpretation depends on the structure and content of the framework.
2. Interpretation is only meaningful when two or more competing propositions are addressed.
3. The role of the forensic practitioner is to consider the probability of the findings given the propositions that are addressed, and not the probability of the propositions.

More recently, these principles have been readdressed in terms of balance, logic, robustness, and transparency as requirements to be met to properly interpret evidence (Association of Forensic Science Providers 2009; ENFSI 2015).

Although this chapter mainly focuses on comparative examinations between unknown specimens and reference samples in order to address questions about their source, it must be emphasized that likelihood ratio models allow for more complex questions such as those at the activity and offense levels. The model can include estimates of additional probabilities such as those of transfer, persistence, background noise, and relevancy. Bayesian networks can be useful when the level of complexity increases and the expert needs to evaluate different variables simultaneously. There have been noteworthy developments in the last 15 years with regard to the application of Bayes nets in forensic science (Taroni et al. 2014; Zadora et al. 2014). Bayesian networks are graphical models that provide a means to structure the dependencies between variables in a complex problem. They are used to represent variables in a problem graphically, their associated probabilities and, most importantly, their dependencies. They are constructed by means of (i) nodes that represent the random variables (discrete or continuous) as well as the considered hypotheses, (ii) arrows connecting the nodes, which represent the dependencies between the variables and the hypotheses, and (iii) marginal and conditional probabilities for nodes, which are organized in probability tables that sum up to 1 (or probability density functions that integrate to 1). Bayesian networks have shown great potential to carry out the simultaneous interpretation of different types of evidence (Juchli et al. 2012).

7.6 Implications of Expert Conclusions from Comparative Examinations: An Example with Fiber Evidence

In this section, different types of historically used expert conclusions are discussed in consideration primarily of the reasoning and interpretation steps that lead to a particular statement. The focus of this section is not the wording of a given conclusion or statement, although some terminology requires some comments. The conclusions stated below are not necessarily confined to written reports, but they could be part of presentations of interpretations in court. The term "conclusion" is preferred here instead of "opinion" because, as discussed below, not all conclusions are necessarily opinions. It should be stated that there is no perfect way to offer expert conclusions. As discussed in Section 7.2, a conclusion offers answers about uncertain events and follows an approach that bears uncertainties. Conveying these uncertainties is not straightforward, particularly in the field of the analysis of mass-produced materials or natural substances widely occurring in a given environment.

Different criteria should be considered when offering a conclusion, namely does it:

- correctly address the case question(s), the analysis request, or the problem at hand
- express the appropriate evidential strength
- properly identify and convey uncertainties
- effectively communicate to the intended audience.

Also, according to standard ASTM E 620-18, the report should contain the logic and reasoning of the expert by which each of the opinions and conclusions were reached (ASTM 2018). Howes et al. (2014) discuss the aspects of the readability of expert reports from non-scientists.

Consider a hypothetical scenario where a dead body of a young woman is recovered in the woods. Crime scene investigators apply adhesive tape to her body. A large number of orange viscose fibers are recovered. During the investigation, a suspect is identified and, in his environment, an orange throw of an expensive brand made of viscose is seized. Investigators transmit the seized items to the laboratory and request comparisons of the two sets of fibers in order to determine if they may share a common origin. Comparative examinations with the appropriate methodology are performed and the forensic scientist cannot differentiate the two sets of fibers at the end of the apposite analytical sequence.

7.6.1 Conclusion 1: Factual Reporting

> I found that the questioned specimens and the known samples were microscopically and analytically indistinguishable.

This statement does not involve any interpretive evaluation on the part of the forensic scientist. The forensic scientist reports results of observations and particularly his or her inability to note differences that would allow differentiating the two compared sets. This conclusion may be adopted in cases where the forensic scientist does not have access to any relevant information about the case circumstances. However, its impact on the case may be weak, misunderstood, or misleading if the interpretation of these findings is passively left to stakeholders such as attorneys or the fact-finder.

7.6.2 Conclusion 2: Consistent with, Cannot Be Excluded, and Reasonable Degree of Certainty

> The questioned fibers are consistent with having originated from the seized throw. Based on a reasonable degree of scientific certainty, a common origin cannot be excluded.

This statement does not offer any interpretive evaluation from the part of the forensic scientist. This type of statement could be recycled any time that the forensic scientist cannot distinguish between compared sets. In this case, the unwilling examiner seems to adopt an unbalanced approach in the sense that he or she fails to explain to what extent a common origin is *inconsistent with* or *could be excluded* despite the analytical non-differentiation.

Some authors advocate that one should use the magic words "based on a reasonable degree of [scientific] certainty or probability" in a written report (Babitsky and Mangraviti 2004). This is only advisable if and when it is possible to scientifically determine and articulate the meaning of *reasonable*, particularly in the context of the case. This possibility is not regarded with optimism, however.

7.6.3 Conclusion 3: High Discriminating Procedure

> The results in this case are highly probative: in fact, I have used a very discriminating analytical sequence. The analytical procedure has been tested on a set of 1000 samples from different origins (499 500 pairwise comparisons). Only five pairs resulted to be indistinguishable. This means that it is highly improbable that two samples coming from different origins cannot be analytically distinguished.

This statement does not consider the case at hand and provides average statistical data given the adopted protocol. It comments on the capabilities offered by the analytical instrumentation to discriminate samples of different origin (i.e. discriminating power). Discriminating power, which depends on the test criteria as applied to a population, is insensitive to the rarity (or commonness) of the features observed in the particular case, and only gives "an average probability" of finding a match when using the adopted test criteria (Stoney 1991a). This approach is useful to justify the choice of the analytical techniques used. In order to contribute to express evidential value, the starting point should not be the analytical protocol itself, but the considered population, which should be representative and applicable to the case under investigation.

7.6.4 Conclusion 4: Rarity Assessment of the Suspected Source

> The results in this case are highly probative: in fact, the seized throw is a very uncommon item. After inquiry from manufacturers, it was determined that this particular model was imported from Asia in 2003 only and it is no longer manufactured. Furthermore, only 500 throws of this particular model were sold in this country. Therefore, it is extremely rare to randomly observe another item like the one seized in this case.

Manufacturers' inquiries are valuable methods to estimate the rarity of occurrence of an object within a given population. Temporal and geographical data can be obtained. Evett et al. (1998) discuss an example involving footwear evidence. While it is possible to gather manufacturing information directly from a trace left at the scene (i.e. brand, maybe model and size), in the fiber example in this section the expert may be tempted to incur in the fallacy of focusing on manufacturing information from the item seized from the suspect instead (suspected source). If this is the case, the statement above cannot be regarded as valid, unless there exists no other textiles of different manufacturing specifications (i.e. brand, models, yarn construction or fabric structure) that bear fibers with similar properties. In other words, is it plausible to encounter orange viscose fibers with the observed features (such as morphology, color, fluorescence properties, and dye composition) from brands of textiles other than the one seized from the suspect? If yes, then a rarity assessment should be made based on the features observed within the questioned fibers only disregarding the focus on the suspected source. Stoney (1984) explains this aspect in detail. A more appropriate statement would be:

The results in this case are highly probative: in fact, the characteristics observed from the questioned fibers are very uncommon. This is because the combination of the observed type (viscose), color (orange), and observed properties is very rarely encountered in the relevant population, and thus the probability of observing similar items by chance is extremely low.

This statement implies that the forensic scientist is in a position to evaluate the rarity (or commonness) of the occurrence of the recovered questioned specimens, fiber evidence in the instance of this particular case. This conclusion may be based on the fact

that he or she seldom observes the properties gathered from the questioned fibers, and therefore such features are deemed to be unusual. Besides this expert judgment, the scientist may have available data from local (i.e. representative) surveys such as the population studies carried out by Fong and Inami (1986), Grieve and Dunlop (1992), Roux and Margot (1997), and Grieve and Biermann (1997a).

7.6.5 Conclusion 5: "Association Key" Verbal Scale

This is a type II association. The recovered and the reference fibers are consistent in all measured physical and chemical properties, and share unusual characteristics that would not be expected to be found in the population of this evidence type.

This conclusion is one of the options that the expert can choose from among different statements in Table 7.1. The chosen statement is the one that better describes the observations made about similarities and dissimilarities during comparative examinations as well as the judgment of the unusual or common occurrence of the observed features in the population.

The use of a verbal scale is valuable to better describe the continuum of possible evidential strengths following observations during comparative examinations. Footwear examiners have been using an analogous scale (SWGTREAD 2013). By accompanying the scale with the conclusion statement, the reader is not provided with a conclusion in isolation and is in a position to better appreciate where the evidential weight resides, with respect to the extreme options of common source[8] and elimination.[9]

8 The term "positive identification" is reported here. According to the literature (e.g. Kirk 1963a; Inman and Rudin 2001) the term "identification" is not appropriate to describe a decisional inference of common source between two compared sets.
9 It is important to note that a conclusion of elimination, in the sense that the compared items do

Table 7.1 Association key verbal scale. Source: Courtesy of Bommarito 2009.

Type I association	A positive identification; an association in which items share individual characteristics that show with reasonable scientific certainty that the items were once from the same source.
Type II association	An association in which items are consistent in all measured physical properties or chemical properties and share unusual characteristic(s) that are unexpected in the population of this evidence type.
Type III association	An association in which items are consistent in all measured physical properties or chemical properties and could have originated from the same source. Because similar items have been manufactured or could exist in nature and could be indistinguishable from the submitted evidence, an individual source cannot be determined.
Type IV association	An association in which items are consistent in all measured physical properties and chemical properties so could have originated from the same source. This sample type is commonly encountered in our environment and may have limited associative value.
Type V association	An association in which some minor variation exists between the known and questioned items that could be due to factors such as sample heterogeneity, contamination of the sample(s), or the quality of the sample. The items may be associated, but other sources exist with the same level of association.
Inconclusive	No conclusion can be reached regarding the association between the items.
Elimination	The items are dissimilar in physical properties or chemical composition and did not originate from the same source.

Previous versions of verbal scales have been suggested in the case of hair evidence. Gaudette (1999) describes the "symmetric spectrum of conclusions" reported in Table 7.2. He defines a positive conclusion as one drawn from finding similarities between a questioned hair and a known sample, and a negative conclusion as one arising from a finding of dissimilarity. This means – or induces one to think – that every time that a hair examiner cannot distinguish questioned hairs from reference hair samples, a conclusion of common origin can be stated. This practice is clearly inadequate.

Another variant of a statement within a verbal scale may take the following form:

> The recovered fibers very probably come from the seized throw. Therefore, in my opinion, it is highly probable that the seized throw came to contact with the victim.

The scale in this case could include expressions such as "very probably," "probably," "slightly probably" between the extreme conclusions of common source, different source, and inconclusive. Questioned documents examiners have adopted an analogous scale where the gradations of conclusions express the degree of confidence of the examiner to conclude the authorship of a given writing (ASTM 2008).

In the statement above, the forensic scientist commits the prosecutor's fallacy in both sentences, in the sense that he or she offers a conclusion about the *cause* instead of the *effects* (see Section 7.4.1 above). Moreover, the second sentence comments on the plausibility of a "contact" between the seized object (i.e. the throw) and the victim. As described in Section 7.3.2, the forensic scientist should not entwine the levels of source (first sentence) and activity (second sentence). Addressing a contact implies articulation of two concepts. First, the forensic scientist should qualify the alleged contact in light of the context of the case. The notion of "contact between two

---

not originate from a common source, may imply a decision based on a *risky* assumption of homogeneity of the properties detected within the unknown specimens and/or within those resulting from proper sampling of known reference samples.

Table 7.2 Symmetric spectrum of conclusions for hair comparisons Source: Reproduced with permission of Taylor & Francis.

Strong positive	The questioned hairs originated from the same person as the known sample.
Normal positive	The questioned hairs are consistent with having originated from the same person as the known sample.
Inconclusive	No conclusion can be given as to whether the questioned and known hairs have a common origin.
Normal negative	The questioned hairs are not consistent with having originated from the same person as the known sample.
Strong negative	The questioned hairs could not have originated from the same person as the known sample.

surfaces" is just too superficial to address specific interactions between individuals, objects, and/or places. Also, alternative scenarios involving a particular contact (or more) should be considered (e.g. consideration of the claims of the defendant, if possible). Second, the expert should consider parameters such as transfer, persistence, efficiency of the recovery method, and casual presence to evaluate the plausibility of a particular contact.

7.6.6 Conclusion 6: Likelihood Ratio Verbal Scale

> Fiber evidence in this case offers a moderately strong support to the proposition that the two compared fiber sets share a common origin rather than the proposition that they are from a different source. A survey consisting of a population study conducted in the relevant population allowed estimation of the probability of observing orange viscose by chance in the population of interest to be of the order of 1 in 1000. The fiber evidence is 1000 times more probable if the two items share a common origin than if they do not.

As described in Section 7.5, the forensic scientist reports her expectations of observing her findings considering two distinct, mutually exclusive, and clearly articulated propositions. The first proposition states that the two compared fiber sets share a common origin (H_1) and the second one that the two compared fiber

sets share a different origin (H_2). In this case, the examiner has not observed differences allowing for the analytical differentiation of the compared sets, resulting in the estimation of the numerator of the likelihood ratio close to one. Indeed, if it is true that two compared fiber sets share a common origin (H_1), then there are very high expectations to observe findings that do not allow differentiation of the two compared fiber sets (E). On the other hand, with regards to the denominator of the likelihood ratio (i.e. considering H_2 to be true), the expert is tasked to estimate the chances of observing the features detected from the questioned fibers in the population of interest by chance. At the source level, the only parameter which must be estimated is the rarity of occurrence of the observed features in the population of interest, meaning orange viscose in this case. The expert provides an estimation of a chance out of 1000. The likelihood ratio is thus calculated to be 1000. As in the previous section, a verbal scale is utilized to understand the value of 1000 in the continuum expressing the strength of the evidence. The verbal scale for likelihood ratios translates a number into a verbal equivalent and expresses the support that the obtained findings bear toward a proposition versus its alternative. The numerical form is the key point of this approach. An example of verbal scale is reported in Table 7.3.

Recurring questions about the likelihood ratio become challenging as the forensic scientist develops a given value of the

Table 7.3 Example of likelihood ratio scale.

LR value	Verbal equivalent
1 000 000 and above	Extremely strong support for H_1 rather than H_2
10 000–1 000 000	Very strong support for H_1 rather than H_2
1000–10 000	Strong support for H_1 rather than H_2
100–1000	Moderately strong support for H_1 rather than H_2
10–100	Moderate support for H_1 rather than H_2
1–10	Weak support for H_1 rather than H_2
1	Inconclusive
1–0.1	Weak support for H_2 rather than H_1
0.1–0.01	Moderate support for H_2 rather than H_1
0.01–0.001	Moderately strong support for H_2 rather than H_1
0.001–0.0001	Strong support for H_2 rather than H_1
0.0001–0.000 001	Very strong support for H_2 rather than H_1
0.000 001 and below	Extremely strong support for H_2 rather than H_1

Source: Adapted from ENFSI (2015) and Hicks et al. (2016).

likelihood ratio or the estimation of the various parameters for its calculation. Faigman et al. (2011) claim that there is no objective or scientific basis for the verbal scale. They contend that no work has been done to assess whether the various expressions are understood similarly, or at all, by lay persons or scientists, if any given qualifier in the scale represents the same significance within or between disciplines, and if each discipline is capable of having the precision to enable the use of a certain number of conclusions rather than others. They also state that the likelihood ratio takes no account of any difference in the confidence to be attached to the numerator and the denominator. Berger et al. (2011a,b) indicate that the qualifiers (weak, moderate,

strong, etc.) are not set in stone and more research in this sense is needed. However, they point out that it is inevitable that any set of verbal statements must be related to ranges of the likelihood ratio values. Faigman et al. (2011) also discuss the aspect that the verbal scale in many disciplines conceals the subjective nature of the opinion and this may lead to the adoption of different qualifiers from the part of different forensic scientists concluding on the same issue. Martire et al. (2013, 2014), Mullen et al. (2014), and Martire and Watkins (2015) caution about the risks of misinforming the trier-of-fact when using a verbal scale.

When available, data can be acquired from available surveys, population studies (such as those described in Section 7.6.4) or dedicated databases. However, major critics to this approach contend that data from surveys do not provide accurate figures, data are not universally applicable, their trends change over time, they are not representative of the population of interest, and the collection of representative and up-to-date data is time-consuming. Vooijs et al. (2015) discuss four case scenarios involving fiber evidence where different likelihood ratios at the source level are derived; they address the difficulties related to the numerical evaluation of fiber evidence and the reliance of the approach on different assumptions.

It is important to emphasize that these figures are estimations based on sample sets aiming to describe a larger population. For example, data collected during casework (e.g. from questioned items of various types of evidence) could provide reasonable estimations. A key – and not trivial – aspect is to demonstrate how data are representative of the population of interest. Independent surveys could be carried out for this purpose. Personal probability assignments based on a body of knowledge that should be available for auditing and disclosure (that are not arbitrary or speculative) could also be made (Evett and Buckleton 1989; Taroni et al. 2001; ENFSI 2015). Of course, this approach is not immune to disagreement between different forensic scientists and this is why it is critical to document and properly articulate the choice of a given estimate. While temporal variation reflects the changes in society and it is hard for the forensic scientist to keep up with various trends, it is quite surprising to identify geographical variation as a limitation to this approach. The forensic scientist called to interpret her findings in the context of a case occurring in a given geographical area should be familiar with the possible trends in her jurisdiction. It may not be relevant for an expert to be concerned with trends of other jurisdictions. Champod et al. (2004) discuss different types of databases and offer guidelines to determine which ones should be used in particular situations.

Note that these considerations apply to the conclusions offered in Sections 7.6.4 and 7.6.5. In Section 7.6.5 particularly (i.e. Table 7.1), the forensic scientist shall be competent in articulating what "unusual characteristics" and "commonly encountered in our environment" mean in order to justify her conclusion. While the likelihood ratio approach favors the consideration of an estimated number, preferably based on an observational study, Table 7.1 leaves this aspect in the hands of the expert.

The likelihood ratio approach and the rarity assessment in Section 7.6.4 show similarities in the following situations:

1. A correspondence is observed between the compared sets without some differences or high intra-source variation. If this is the case, due to some to high disagreement, then the numerator of the likelihood ratio is lower than one. This would not reflect the estimated frequency of occurrence itself.

2. Only one group of relevant particles (compared to the reference samples) is recovered on a surface of interest: if n groups of particles of relevant size are recovered on a given surface, then the likelihood ratio value is divided by the n number of groups. Evett (1987) and then Triggs and Buckleton (2003), Aitken and Taroni (2004), and

Gittelson et al. (2013) addressed the issue of recovering more than one (non-matching) bloodstain from the scene. This logic applies to the fiber example in this section and to any other trace materials as well.

3. There is no qualified alternative proposition at the source level other than the negation of the proposition on common source between the compared sets. If the defendant is able to point out an alternative source that cannot be analytically differentiated from the putative one, then rarity assessment data is not informative. The likelihood ratio would be estimated as one since the denominator becomes one too.

Another pertinent question surrounds the correlation between a given likelihood ratio value and the strength that it purports to express. In the present example, is a likelihood ratio of approximately 1000 considered to be strong evidence? There are two approaches to address this question (Royall 1997). The first consists of an analogy with a simple experiment such as a coin toss.[10] This may be amenable to explain the likelihood ratio approach to a jury, for example. Suppose that Chris and Vinny use a coin to make a bet. Chris flips the coin and after five tosses the same outcome occurs, let us say heads. Vinny starts wondering about the fairness of the coin (clearly, in this trivial example, Vinny does not dare ask Chris to show him the two faces of the coin). Therefore, Vinny envisions the two propositions "the coin is fair" and "the coin is unfair." If the coin is flipped five times and all five times the outcome is head, would you attribute this outcome to be mere chance or would you start questioning the fairness of the coin? If five successive heads are observed, the likelihood ratio in support of the proposition that "the coin is unfair" over the proposition that "the coin is fair" is $1/(\frac{1}{2})^5$ or

---

10 I would like to thank my former professor, Prof. Christophe Champod, from the School of Criminal Sciences of the University of Lausanne, Switzerland, for sharing this example. PB.

2^5 or 32. Although possible, is it fair to say that one would not expect to observe five heads in a row using a fair coin? A likelihood ratio of 1000, like in the present example, would be (approximately) equivalent to tossing the coin 10 times and observing heads all 10 times (as $2^{10} = 1024 \approx 1000$).

The second approach considers the effect of the likelihood ratio on the prior odds, namely the difference between the prior odds and the posterior odds. Suppose that a suspect is apprehended. A given type of trace is recovered at the scene and after laboratory examination it cannot be differentiated from some appropriate reference material seized from the suspect. The frequency of occurrence of the observed features in the relative population is estimated to 5%. For the sake of simplicity, assume that this finding leads to a calculation of the likelihood ratio to be 20. Suppose that the investigator in charge does not have compelling evidence against the suspect at this point and thus is not entirely sure about his involvement in the case.[11] Let's translate this uncertainty as a *prior probability* of 0.20. What is the impact of the likelihood ratio on the initial belief of the investigator? The odds form of Bayes' Theorem[12] is applied:

$$\frac{0.2}{0.8} \times \frac{1}{0.05} = 5$$

The *posterior probability* expressing the belief of the investigator is updated from 0.2 to about 0.83 (or $p = 5/(5+1)$). This change is due to the effect of the likelihood ratio.

---

11 The investigator is interested in the involvement of the suspect, which corresponds to an offence level type of proposition in the hierarchy of propositions, while the likelihood ratio in this example refers to a source level. For the sake of simplicity, we omit elaboration to fix this discrepancy.

12 The odds form of a probability p_1 is $p_1/(1 - p_1)$, therefore the *prior odds* (left term) are 0.2/(1 – 0.2). The likelihood ratio, in the middle, is 1/0.05 or 20. The multiplicative effect of the likelihood ratio modifies, or updates, the *prior odds* to 5. This expresses the *posterior odds* and they are said to be *5 to 1 in favor* of the involvement of the suspect. This corresponds to a *posterior probability* $p_2 = 5/(5 + 1)$ or p_2 calculated to about 83%.

Consider instead that the investigator has some conflicting evidence against the suspect. A *prior probability* of 0.50 is assigned to the investigator's uncertainty. In this case the *posterior probability* ends up being about 0.95 using a likelihood ratio of 20. Finally, assume that the investigator already has some other evidence that makes him believe that the suspect is involved in the case. This new belief is assigned a *prior probability* of 0.90. The *posterior probability* is about 0.99 in this case. In reality, assignments of prior probabilities are not made numerically, at least they are not formalized. Investigators, attorneys, judges, and jury members do not quantify their beliefs by assigning particular probabilities. From a forensic science perspective, this is not important since the expert is concerned only with the likelihood ratio and not the prior odds. If an expert offers an opinion describing a posterior probability (prosecutor's fallacy), she should integrate the prior odds (i.e. other evidence than the one that she offers). In current practice, prior probabilities are implicitly regarded to be 0.50, which is not necessarily the case in light of other evidence and information collected during an investigation that the forensic scientist is seldom aware of. This concept is verbally captured in another form, a conclusion statement described by Robertson et al. (2016), that is:

> Whatever the odds in favor of [proposition of interest] based on other evidence (which I have not heard), my evidence makes them X times higher.

where X is the estimated value of the likelihood ratio.

Quoting Evett (1995), it is not possible for a scientist, following the Bayesian paradigm, to say, "I am satisfied that this tool made this mark" unless he assumes a prior probability, quantifies the evidence, and assumes a threshold posterior probability at which he becomes virtually certain about a hypothesis. Developments in the area of decision theory have enabled an understanding about the facets of the reasoning about the *leap of faith* – as described by Stoney (1991b) – that forensic scientists make to reach a conclusion of a common source between questioned specimens and reference samples. Biedermann et al. (2008) describes the role of the utility/loss function as a necessary step to meet the threshold and make a decision. The utility/loss function weights the losses and the gains inherent to the decision consequences that the forensic scientist faces.

7.7 Conclusion

Interpreting evidence is without any doubt one of the most, if not the most, complex tasks for the forensic scientist. It is not trivial to identify, address, evaluate, and join uncertainties encountered during the entire physical evidence process or even part of it.

The main *desideratum* of this chapter was to emphasize the importance of identifying the following:

1. The appropriate questions relevant to the case where trace evidence may play an impactful role.
2. Major interpretive fallacies and how to avoid them.
3. Uncertainties related to the generation, recognition, collection, examination, and evaluation of trace materials.
4. The necessity to evaluate scientific findings within the context of the case at hand.

Probability is considered to be the standard for measuring uncertainty (Lindley 2006). The understanding and use of both statistical and probabilistic methods is, therefore, critical in order to address problems in forensic science. There are two main uses for statistics in forensic science in fundamental research and development (including data analysis) and in evidence interpretation. Trace evidence interpretation, as we have discussed in this chapter, relies on a solid foundational

understanding of probabilistic reasoning and statistical models which can be built using a combination of expert knowledge and data collected from experiments and surveys. The nature and complexity of the majority of findings collected during forensic investigations as well as the nature of the uncertainties that surround trace evidence problems can very seldom be solved by means of the basic knowledge received during typical introductory statistics courses offered by traditional forensic science and natural science curricula. We speculate that the statistics requirements in many of these programs are no more than the statistics requirement of any science degree. That is, students receive some elementary training in basic data analysis techniques such as hypothesis testing, regression, and maybe basic multivariate analysis. The skills that students learn in such courses is essential for basic laboratory research, and hence for much forensic research. It appears that what is lacking in many curricula is specialist instruction in the statistical interpretation of evidence. It is recommended that forensic science education curricula should include modules on statistical interpretation of trace evidence. We feel it is vital that a forensic scientist also understands Bayes' Theorem, at least in its odds form, and how this relates to the role of the forensic scientist in court. As noted earlier, the likelihood ratio allows the logical updating of any belief a juror might hold about the propositions put before them to a revised belief after seeing the expert assessment of the evidence. The likelihood ratio is the link between prior belief and posterior belief.

We state again, it is vital that an expert in trace evidence understands the probabilistic nature of their task and how to reflect statistical uncertainty in their reasoning. However, it is also vital that he or she possesses at least enough statistical skill to defend the models used for evidence evaluation, or to recognize when it is necessary to defer to someone with superior domain knowledge (of statistics and the evidence type). A viable, and by no means novel, solution for the forensic scientist is to establish strong collaborations with statisticians. Kirk and Kingston (1964) encouraged this endeavor while highlighting the misunderstanding of statistics on the part of criminalists during their time. They also pointed out that statisticians do not necessarily understand the types of problems inherent to criminalistics. In short, even today there exist enormous opportunities to initiate conversations and collaborations between forensic scientists and statisticians in order to address the various problems encountered in trace evidence.

The questions received by the forensic scientist (i.e. analysis requests) tend to define his/her role within the criminal justice system. To what extent is trace evidence expertise required in a given case? That is, can one expect more than confining forensic scientists to identifying unknowns, conducting comparative examinations, and addressing questions on the source provenance of some recovered particles? The involvement of the forensic scientist in addressing questions beyond mere comparative examinations was brought up very early in the historical development of criminalistics:

> It is possible to identify all types of textile fiber with exactness, through a variety of methods that include microscopy, chemical testing, X-ray diffraction, and pyrolysis-gas chromatography. However, the probabilistic value of a fiber transfer between two sets of clothing, as in a crime, is still a matter of controversy, even though such transfers constitute one of the more valuable types of evidence.
>
> (Kirk 1963b)

Clearly, this statement applies to many other types of trace materials as well. It also leads us to think about the nature of traces as valued physical remnants left behind, and more specifically as *products of a particular activity*. Every forensic scientist ought to mention Locard's postulate (usually in the reduced and inaccurate form of *every contact leaves a trace*) when called to describe his or her specific discipline. Maybe incongruously, in practice, it is seldom the case that a trace specialist assists the trier or fact, or the investigators with aspects pertaining to activities that involve, for example, evaluations of transfer phenomena. Should the most pertinent questions focus more on activities rather than sources, then who would be the most qualified individuals to evaluate aspects such as the presence or quantity of recovered particles in a given case? With respect to evidence interpretation, it is expected that the forensic scientist will play a more proactive role in offering such assistance.

It is the hope of the authors that this chapter might offer guidance about questions and aspects which the forensic scientist concerned with (trace) material analyses needs to consider when attempting to understand the significance of his/her scientific findings.

Acknowledgments

The authors are very grateful to Dr. Sheila Willis, former Director General of the Irish Forensic Science Ireland National Laboratory, for commenting the manuscript and offering much appreciated feedback for improvements.

References

Aitken, C.G.G. (1987). Attempting to measure the value of evidence. *The Professional Statistician* 6: 8–15.

Aitken, C.G.G. and Stoney, D.A. (eds.) (1991). *The Use of Statistics in Forensic Science*. New York, London: Ellis Horwood.

Aitken, C. and Taroni, F. (2004). *Statistics and the Evaluation of Evidence for Forensic Scientists*, 2e. Chichester: Wiley.

Andrasko, J. and Maehly, A.C. (1978). The discrimination between samples of window glass by combining physical and chemical techniques. *Journal of Forensic Sciences* 23: 250–262.

Association of Forensic Science Providers (2009). Standards for the formulation of evaluative forensic science expert opinion. *Science & Justice* 49: 161–164.

ASTM E1658-08 (2008). *Standard terminology for expressing conclusions of forensic document examiners*. West Conshohocken, PA: ASTM International. www.astm.org.

ASTM E620-18 (2018). *Standard practice for reporting opinions of scientific or technical experts*. West Conshohocken, PA: ASTM International. www.astm.org.

Babitsky, S. and Mangraviti, J.J. (2004). *Writing and Defending Your Expert Report – The Step-by-Step Guide with Models*. Falmouth, MA: SEAK, Inc.

Berger, C.E.H., Buckleton, J., Champod, C. et al. (2011a). Evidence evaluation: a response to the court of appeal judgment in R v T. *Science & Justice* 51: 43–49.

Berger, C.E.H., Buckleton, J., Champod, C. et al. (2011b). Response to Faigman et al. *Science & Justice* 51: 215.

Biedermann, A. and Taroni, F. (2011). Evidential relevance in scene to offender transfer cases: development and analysis of a likelihood ratio for offence level propositions. *Law, Probability, & Risk* 10: 277–301.

Biedermann, A., Bozza, S., and Taroni, F. (2008). Decision theoretic properties of forensic identification: underlying logic and argumentative implications. *Forensic Science International* 177: 120–132.

Biermann, T.W. (2007). Block of colour IV: the evidential value of blue and red cotton fibres. *Science & Justice* 47: 68–87.

Bommarito, C. (2009). A likely misguided attempt at changing the way we write associative reports that could have far reaching Impact on how our message is misunderstood. *Trace Evidence Symposium*, Clearwater, FL, August 3–7, 2009.

Bridge, C.M., Powell, J., Steele, K.L., and Sigman, M.E. (2007). Forensic comparative glass analysis by laser-induced breakdown spectroscopy. *Spectrochimica Acta Part B* 62: 1419–1425.

Buzzini, P. and Massonnet, G. (2004). A market study of green spray paints by Fourier transform infrared (FTIR) and Raman spectroscopy. *Science & Justice* 44: 123–131.

Buzzini, P. and Massonnet, G. (2015). The discrimination of colored acrylic, cotton, and wool textile fibers using micro-Raman spectroscopy. Part 2: Comparison with the traditional methods of fiber examination. *Journal of Forensic Sciences* 60: 712–720.

Buzzini, P. and Yu, J.C.-C. (2017). General principles and techniques of trace evidence collection (ch. 7). In: *Forensic Evidence Management: From Scene to Courtroom* (eds. A. Mozayani and C. Parish-Fisher), 75–98. Boca Raton, FL: Taylor & Francis, CRC Press.

Buzzini, P., Massonnet, G., Birrer, S. et al. (2005). Survey of crowbar and household paints in burglary cases – population studies, transfer and interpretation. *Forensic Science International* 152: 221–234.

Buzzini, P., Kammrath, B.W., and De Forest, P. (2019). Trace evidence? The term trace from adjective to noun. *WIREs Forensic Science*: e1342. https://doi.org/10.1002/wfs2.1342.

Cassista, A. and Peters, A.D. (1997). Survey of red, green and blue cotton fibres. *Canadian Society of Forensic Science Journal* 4: 225–231.

Champod, C. and Taroni, F. (1999). The Bayesian approach (ch. 13.3). In: *Forensic Examination of Fibres*, 2e (eds. J. Robertson and M. Grieve), 379–398. Boca Raton, FL: Taylor & Francis, CRC Press.

Champod, C., Evett, I.W., and Jackson, G. (2004). Establishing the most appropriate databases for addressing source level propositions. *Science & Justice* 44: 153–164.

Connor, S. (1987). The science that changed a Minister's mind. *New Scientist* 29: 24.

Cook, R., Evett, I.W., Jackson, G. et al. (1998a). A model for case assessment and interpretation. *Science & Justice* 38: 151–156.

Cook, R., Evett, I.W., Jackson, G. et al. (1998b). A hierarchy of propositions: deciding which level to address in casework. *Science & Justice* 38: 231–239.

Cooper, G. (2013). The indirect transfer of glass fragments to a jacket and their subsequent persistence. *Science & Justice* 53: 166–170.

Curran, J.M., Hicks, T.N., and Buckleton, J. (2000). *Forensic Interpretation of Glass Evidence*. Boca Raton, FL: CRC Press.

De Forest, P.R. (2001). What is trace evidence? (ch. 1). In: *Forensic Examination of Glass and Paint – Analysis and Interpretation* (ed. B. Caddy). London, Philadelphia: Taylor & Francis.

De Forest, P., Bucht, R., Buzzini, P., et al. (2015). The making of the criminalistics maestro: On the knowledge, skills, and abilities to oversee and coordinate the work on non-routine and complex cases. *Proceedings of the 67th Meeting of the American Academy of Forensic Sciences*, Orlando, FL, February 16–20, 2015.

Deadman, H.A. (1984). Fiber evidence and the Wayne Williams trial. *FBI Law Enforcement Bulletin*. US Department of Justice, Washington, DC, May 53: 10–19.

Dennis, D.-M.K., Williams, M.R., and Sigman, M.E. (2016). Assessing the evidential value of smokeless powder comparisons. *Forensic Science International* 259: 179–187.

Doyle, A.C. (1887). *A Study in Scarlet*. Part 1, ch. 3. London: Ward Lock & Co.

Durden Smith, J. (2007). *100 Most Infamous Criminals*. New York, NY: Metro Books.

Edmondstone, G., Hellman, J., Legate, K. et al. (2004). An assessment of the evidential value of automotive paint comparisons. *Canadian Society of Forensic Science Journal* 37: 147–153.

ENFSI (2015). Guideline for evaluative reporting in forensic science. In: *Strengthening the Evaluation of Forensic Results across Europe (STEOFRAE)*. European Network of Forensic Sciences Institutes. Avaiable at: http://enfsi.eu/wp-content/uploads/2016/09/m1_guideline.pdf.

Evett, I.W. (1987). On meaningful questions: a two-trace transfer problem. *Journal of the Forensic Science Society* 27: 375–381.

Evett, I.W. (1990). The theory of interpreting scientific transfer evidence. In: *Forensic Science Progress*, vol. 4 (eds. A. Maehly and R.L. Williams), 141–179. Berlin: Springer Verlag.

Evett, I.W. (1991). Interpretation: a personal odyssey. In: *The Use of Statistics in Forensic Science* (eds. A. CGG and D.A. Stoney), 9–22. New York, London: Ellis Horwood.

Evett, I.W. (1993). Establishing the evidential value of a small quantity of material found at a crime scene. *Journal of the Forensic Science Society* 33: 83–86.

Evett, I. (1995). Avoiding the transposed conditional. *Science & Justice* 35: 127–131.

Evett, I.W. and Buckleton, J.S. (1989). Some aspects of the Bayesian approach to evidence evaluation. *Journal of the Forensic Science Society* 29: 317–324.

Evett, I.W., Lambert, J.A., and Buckleton, J.S. (1998). A Bayesian approach to interpreting footwear marks in forensic casework. *Science & Justice* 38: 241–247.

Evett, I.W., Jackson, G., and Lambert, J.A. (2000a). More on the hierarchy of propositions: exploring the distinction between explanations and propositions. *Science & Justice* 40: 3–10.

Evett, I.W., Jackson, G., Lambert, J.A., and McCrossan, S. (2000b). The impact of the principles of evidence interpretation on the structure and content of statements. *Science & Justice* 40: 233–239.

Faigman, D., Jamieson, A., Noziglia, C. et al. (2011). Response to Aitken et al. on R v T. *Science & Justice* 51: 213–214.

Finkelstein, M.O. and Fairley, W.B. (1970). A Bayesian approach to identification evidence. *Harvard Law Review* 83: 489–517.

Fong, W. and Inami, H. (1986). Results of a study to determine the probability of chance match occurrences between fibres known to be from different sources. *Journal of Forensic Sciences* 31: 65–72.

French, J. and Morgan, R. (2015). An experimental investigation of the indirect transfer and deposition of gunshot residue: further studies carried out with SEM-EDX analysis. *Forensic Science International* 247: 14–17.

Gauch, H.G. (2003). *Scientific Method in Practice.* New York, NY: Cambridge University Press.

Gaudette, B. (1999). Evidential value of hair examination (ch. 7). In: *Forensic Examination of Hair*, Forensic Science Series (ed. J. Robertson), 243–260. London, Philadelphia, PA: Taylor & Francis.

Gittelson, S., Biedermann, A., Bozza, S., and Taroni, F. (2013). Modeling the forensic two-trace problem with Bayesian networks. *Artificial Intelligence and Law* 21: 221–252.

Goodpaster, J.V., Sturdevant, A.B., Andrews, K.L., and Brun-Conti, L. (2007). Identification and comparison of electrical tapes using instrumental and statistical techniques: I. Microscopic surface texture and elemental composition. *Journal of Forensic Sciences* 52: 610–629.

Goodpaster, J.V., Sturdevant, A.B., Andrews, K.L. et al. (2009). Identification and comparison of electrical tapes using instrumental and statistical techniques: II. Organic composition of the tape backing and adhesive. *Journal of Forensic Sciences* 54: 328–338.

Gothard, J.A. (1976). Evaluation of automobile paint flakes as evidence. *Journal of Forensic Sciences* 21: 636–641.

Gott, R. and Duggan, S. (2003). *Understanding and Using Scientific Evidence – How to Critically Evaluate Data.* Thousand Oaks, CA: SAGE Publications.

Govaert, F. and Bernard, M. (2004). Discriminating red spray paints by optical microscopy, Fourier transform infrared spectroscopy and X-ray fluorescence. *Forensic Science International* 140: 61–70.

Grieve, M.C. and Biermann, T. (1997a). The population of coloured textile fibres on

outdoor surfaces. *Science & Justice* 37: 231–239.

Grieve, M.C. and Biermann, T.W. (1997b). Wool fibres – Transfer to vinyl and leather vehicle seats and some observations on their secondary transfer. *Science and Justice – Journal of the Forensic Science Society* 37(1): 3138.

Grieve, M.C. and Dunlop, J. (1992). A practical aspect of the Bayesian interpretation of fibre evidence. *Journal of the Forensic Science Society* 32: 169–175.

Grieve, M., Dunlop, J., and Haddock, P. (1988). An assessment of the value of blue, red, and black cotton fibers as target fibers in forensic science investigations. *Journal of Forensic Sciences* 33: 1332–1344.

Grieve, M.C., Biermann, T.W., and Davignon, M. (2001). The evidential value of black cotton fibres. *Science & Justice* 41: 245–260.

Grieve, M.C., Biermann, T.W., and Davignon, M. (2003). The occurrence and individuality of orange and green cotton fibers. *Science & Justice* 43: 5–22.

Grieve, M.C., Biermann, T.W., and Schaub, K. (2005). The individuality of fibres used to provide forensic evidence – not all polyesters are the same. *Science & Justice* 45: 13–28.

Grima, M., Hanson, R., and Tidy, H. (2014). An assessment of firework particle persistence on the hands and related police force practices in relation to GSR evidence. *Forensic Science International* 239: 19–26.

Haag, M.G. and Haag, L.C. (2011). *Shooting Incident Reconstruction*, 2e. San Diego, CA, Oxford: Elsevier, Academic Press.

Hicks, T., Vanina, R., and Margot, P. (1996). Transfer and persistence of glass fragments on garments. *Science & Justice* 36: 101–107.

Hicks, T., Biedermann, A., De Koeijer, J.A. et al. (2015). The importance of distinguishing information from evidence/observations when formulating propositions. *Science & Justice* 55: 520–525.

Hicks, T., Buckleton, J.S., Bright, J.-A., and Taylor, D. (2016). A framework for interpreting evidence (ch. 2). In: *Forensic DNA*

Evidence Interpretation, 2e (eds. J.S. Buckleton, J.-A. Bright and D. Taylor), 37–86. Boca Raton, FL: CRC Press, Taylor & Francis.

Howes, L.M., Kirkbride, P.K., Kelty, S.F., and Julian, R. (2014). The readability of expert reports for non-scientist report-users: reports of forensic comparison of glass. *Forensic Science International* 236: 54–66.

Imwinkelried, E.J. (2004). *The Methods of Attacking Scientific Evidence*, 4e. LexisNexis Group, Newark, NJ: Matthew Bender & Co Inc.

Inman, K. and Rudin, N. (2001). *Principles and Practice of Criminalistics – The Profession of Forensic Science*. Boca Raton, FL: CRC Press.

Irwin, M. (2011). Transfer of glass fragments when bottles and drinking glasses are broken. *Science & Justice* 51: 16–18.

Jackson, G. (2000). The scientist and the scales of justice. *Science & Justice* 40: 81–85.

Juchli, P., Biedermann, A., and Taroni, F. (2012). Graphical probabilistic analysis of the combination of items of evidence. *Law, Probability, & Risk* 11: 51–84.

Kirk, P. (1953). *Crime Investigation: Physical Evidence and the Police Laboratory*. New York, NY: Interscience Publishers Inc.

Kirk, P.L. (1963a). The ontogeny of criminalistics. *The Journal of Criminal Law, Criminology, and Police Science* 54: 235–238.

Kirk, P.L. (1963b). Criminalistics. *Science* 140: 376–370.

Kirk, P.L. and Kingston, C.R. (1964). Evidence evaluation and problems in general criminalistics. *Journal of Forensic Sciences* 9: 434–444.

Koons, R.D., Fiedler, C., and Rawalt, R.C. (1988). Classification and discrimination of sheet and container glasses by inductively coupled plasma-atomic emission spectrometry and pattern recognition. *Journal of Forensic Sciences* 33: 49–67.

Kwan, Q.Y. (1977). Inference of identity of source. PhD dissertation. University of California, Berkeley, CA.

Laing, D.K., Dudley, R.J., Home, J.M., and Isaacs, M.D.J. (1982). The discrimination of small fragments of household gloss paint by microspectrophotometry. *Forensic Science International* 20: 191–200.

Lepot, L. and Vanden Driessche, T. (2015). Fibre persistence on immersed garment – influence of water flow and stay in running water. *Science & Justice* 55: 431–436.

Lepot, L., Vanden Driessche, T., Lunstroot, K. et al. (2015). Fibre persistence on immersed garment – influence of knitted recipient fabrics. *Science & Justice* 55: 248–253.

Lindley, D.V. (1977). A problem in forensic science. *Biometrika* 64: 207–213.

Lindley, D.V. (2006). *Understanding Uncertainty*. Chichester: Wiley.

Locard, E. (1920). *L'enquête criminelle et les méthodes scientifiques*. Paris: Ernest Flammarion Editeur.

Lucy, D. (2005). *Introduction to Statistics for Forensic Scientists*. Chichester: Wiley.

Margot, P. (2014). Traçologie: la trace, vecteur fondamental de la police scientifique. *Revue internationale de criminologie et de police technique et scientifique* LXVII: 72–97.

Martire, K.A. and Watkins, I. (2015). Perception problems of the verbal scale: a reanalysis and application of a membership function approach. *Science & Justice* 55: 264–273.

Martire, K.A., Kemp, R.I., and Newell, B.R. (2013). The psychology of interpreting expert evaluative opinions. *Australian Journal of Forensic Sciences* 45: 305–314.

Martire, K.A., Kemp, R.I., Sayle, M., and Newell, B.R. (2014). On the interpretation of likelihood ratios in forensic science evidence: presentation formats and the weak evidence effect. *Forensic Science International* 240: 61–68.

Massonnet G (1996) Les peintures automobiles en criminalistique. PhD dissertation, University of Lausanne, Lausanne.

May, R.W. and Porter, J. (1975). An evaluation of common methods of paint analysis. *Journal of the Forensic Science Society* 15: 137–146.

McDermott, S.D. (2009). Trace Evidence: Transfer, Persistence, and Value. In: *Wiley Encyclopedia of Forensic Science*, vol. 5 (eds. A.

Jamieson and A. Moenssens), 2534–2540. Chichester, UK: Wiley.

Mehltretter, A.H., Bradley, M.J., and Wright, D.M. (2011a). Analysis and discrimination of electrical tapes: part II. Adhesives. *Journal of Forensic Sciences* 56: 82–94.

Mehltretter, A.H., Bradley, M.J., and Wright, D.M. (2011b). Analysis and discrimination of electrical tapes: Part II. Backings. *Journal of Forensic Sciences* 56: 1493–1504.

Monard, F. (2007). Étude des mécanismes de transfert des fibres en sciences forensiques. PhD dissertation. University of Lausanne, Lausanne, Switzerland.

Morgan S.L., Bartick, E.G. (2007). Discrimination of forensic analytical chemical data using multivariate statistics (ch. 13). In: *Forensic Analysis on the Cutting Edge – New Methods for Trace Evidence Analysis* (ed. R.D. Blackledge), 333–374. Hoboken, NJ: Wiley.

Muehlethaler, C., Massonnet, G., and Esseiva, P. (2011). The application of chemometrics on infrared and Raman spectra as a tool for the forensic analysis of paints. *Forensic Science International* 209: 173–182.

Muehlethaler, C., Massonnet, G., and Esseiva, P. (2014). Discrimination and classification of FTIR spectra of red, blue and green spray paints using a multivariate statistical approach. *Forensic Science International* 244: 170–178.

Mullen, C., Spence, D., Moxey, L., and Jamieson, A. (2014). Perception problems of the verbal scale. *Science & Justice* 54: 154–158.

Mullin, C. (1997). *Error of Judgment – The Truth about the Birmingham Bombings*. Revised edition. Vale, Guernsey: The Guernsey Press Ltd.

Naes, B.E., Umpierrez, S., Ryland, S. et al. (2008). A comparison of laser ablation inductively coupled plasma mass spectrometry, micro X-ray fluorescence spectroscopy, and laser induced breakdown spectroscopy for the discrimination of automotive glass. *Spectrochimica Acta, Part B* 63: 1145–1150.

National Research Council Committee on Identifying the Needs of the Forensic Sciences Community (2009). *Strengthening Forensic Science in the United States: A Path Forward*. Washington, DC.: National Academies Press.

Nehse K. (2011). Report writing in the EU from the perspective of the European Fibres Group. *Trace Evidence Symposium*, Kansas City, MO. http://projects.nfstc.org/trace/2011/presentations/Nehse-Report-Writing-EU.pdf (accessed 01 March 2016).

Nelson, D.F. and Revell, B.C. (1967). Backward fragmentation from breaking glass. *Journal of the Forensic Science Society* 7: 58–61.

Neumann, C. (2013). Statistics and probabilities as a means to support fingerprint examination (ch. 15). In: *Lee and Gaensslen's Advances in Fingerprint Technology*, 3e (ed. R. Ramotowski), 419–465. Taylor & Francis, Boca Raton, FL: CRC Press.

Osterburg, J.W. (1968). *The Crime Laboratory: Case Studies of Scientific Criminal Investigation*. Bloomington: Indiana University Press.

Palenik, S.J. (1979). The determination of geographical origin of dust samples. In: *The Particle Atlas*, 2e (eds. W.C. McCrone, J.G. Delly and S.J. Palenik), 1347–1361. Ann Arbor, MI: Ann Arbor Science Publishers.

Palenik, S.J. (2007). The use of microscopic evidence to develop investigative leads in criminal investigations. *The Microscope* 55: 35.

Palmer, R., Hutchinson, W., and Fryer, V. (2009). The discrimination of (non-denim) blue cotton. *Science & Justice* 49: 12–18.

PCAST (2016) Forensic science in criminal courts: ensuring scientific validity of feature-comparison methods. Executive Office of the President's Council of Advisors on Science and Technology, Washington, DC.

Pitts, S.J. and Kratochvil, B. (1991). Statistical discrimination of flat glass fragments by instrumental neutron activation analysis methods for forensic science applications. *Journal of Forensic Sciences* 36: 122–137.

Pounds, C.A. and Smalldon, K.W. (1975a). The transfer of fibres between clothing materials during simulated contacts and their persistence during wear. Part 1: Fibre transference. *Journal of the Forensic Science Society* 15: 17–27.

Pounds, C.A. and Smalldon, K.W. (1975b). The transfer of fibres between clothing materials during simulated contacts and their persistence during wear. Part 1: Fibre persistence. *Journal of the Forensic Science Society* 15: 29–37.

Pounds, C.A. and Smalldon, K.W. (1975c). The transfer of fibres between clothing materials during simulated contacts and their persistence during wear. Part 3: A preliminary investigation of the mechanisms involved. *Journal of the Forensic Science Society* 15: 17–27.

Richards, A. and Cannon, M. (2014). Birmingham pub bombings: the 28 numbers that add up to a cover-up, say campaigners. *Birmingham Mail* (19 November) www .birminghammail.co.uk/news/birmingham-pub-bombings-28-numbers-8097369 (accessed 14 July 2019).

Robertson, J. (1999). Forensic and microscopic examination of human hair (ch. 2). In: *Forensic Examination of Hair*, Forensic Science Series (ed. J. Robertson), 79–155. London, Philadelphia, PA: Taylor & Francis.

Robertson, B., Vignaux, G.A., and Berger, C.E.H. (2016). *Interpreting Evidence – Evaluating Forensic Science in the Courtroom*, 2e. Chichester: Wiley.

Roux, C. and Margot, P. (1997). The population of textile fibres on car seats. *Science & Justice* 37: 25–30.

Roux, C., Chable, J., and Margot, P. (1996). Fibre transfer experiments onto car seats. *Science & Justice* 36: 143–152.

Royall, R. (1997). *Statistical Evidence – A Likelihood Paradigm*. London, New York: Chapman & Hall, CRC.

Ryland, S.G. and Kopec, R.J. (1979). The evidential value of automobile paint chips. *Journal of Forensic Sciences* 24: 140–147.

Scientific Working Group for Shoeprint and Tire Tread Evidence (SWGTREAD) (2013). Range of conclusions standard for footwear and tire impression examinations (03/2013). https://

www.nist.gov/sites/default/files/documents/ 2016/10/26/swgtread_10_range_of_ conclusions_standard_for_footwear_and_ tire_impression_examinations_201303.pdf (accessed 14 July 2019).

Skoog, D.A., West, D.M., and Holler, F.J. (1994). *Analytical Chemistry – An Introduction*. Philadelphia, PA: Saunders College Publishing, Harcourt Brace College Publishers.

Smalldon, K. and Moffat, A. (1973). The calculation of discriminating power for a series of correlated attributes. *Journal of the Forensic Science Society* 13: 291–295.

Stoney, D.A. (1984). Evaluation of associative evidence: choosing the relevant question. *Journal of the Forensic Science Society* 24: 473–482.

Stoney, D.A. (1991a). Transfer evidence (ch. 4). In: *The Use of Statistics in Forensic Science* (eds. C.G.G. Aitken and D.A. Stoney), 107–138. New York, London: Ellis Horwood.

Stoney, D.A. (1991b). What made us ever think that we could individualize using statistics? *Journal of the Forensic Science Society* 31: 197–199.

Stoney, D. (1994). Relaxation of the assumption of relevance and an application to one-trace and two-trace problems. *Journal of the Forensic Science Society* 34: 17–21.

Taroni, F., Champod, C., and Margot, P. (1998). Forerunners of Bayesianism in early forensic science. *Jurimetrics* 38: 183–200.

Taroni, F., Aitken, C.G.G., and Garbolino, P. (2001). De Finetti's subjectivism, the assessment of probabilities and the evaluation of evidence: a commentary for forensic scientists. *Science & Justice* 41: 145–150.

Taroni, F., Biedermann, A., Bozza, S. et al. (2014). *Bayesian Networks for Probabilistic Inference and Decision Analysis in Forensic Science*, 2e. Chichester: Wiley.

Taroni, F., Bierdermann, A., and Bozza, S. (2016). Statistical hypothesis testing and common misinterpretations: should we abandon p-value in forensic science applications. *Forensic Science International* 259: e32–e36.

Thompson, W.C. and Schumann, E.L. (1987). Interpretation of statistical evidence in criminal trials. *Law and Human Behavior* 11: 167–187.

Tippett, C.F., Emerson, V.J., Fereday, M.J. et al. (1968). The evidential value of the comparison of paint flakes from sources other than vehicles. *Journal of the Forensic Science Society* 8: 61–65.

Trejos, T., Montero, S., and Almirall, J.R. (2003). Analysis and comparison of glass fragments by laser ablation inductively coupled plasma mass spectrometry (LA-ICP-MS) and ICP-MS. *Analytical and Bioanalytical Chemistry* 376: 1255–1264.

Trejos, T., Koons, R., Weis, P. et al. (2013). Forensic analysis of glass by μ-XRF, SN-ICP-MS, LA-ICP-MS and LA-ICP-OES: evaluation of the performance of different criteria for comparing elemental composition. *Journal of Analytical Atomic Spectrometry* 28: 1270–1282.

Triggs, C.M. and Buckleton, J.S. (2003). The two trace transfer problem re-examined. *Science & Justice* 43: 127–134.

Vessman, J., Stefan, R.I., Van Staden, J.F. et al. (2001). *Selectivity in analytical chemistry (IUPAC Recommendations 2001). Pure and Applied Chemistry* 73: 1381–1386.

Vooijs, C., Vergeer, P., and Van der Weerd, J. (2015). Towards source level evaluation of the evidential value of fibre examinations. *Forensic Science International* 250: 57–67.

Wallace, J. (2010). The methods for calculating the uncertainty of measurements. *Science & Justice* 50: 182–186.

Wiggins, K., Holness, J.-A., and March, B.M. (2005). The importance of thin layer chromatography and UV microspectro-photometry in the analysis of reactive dyes released from wool and cotton fibers. *Journal of Forensic Sciences* 50: 364–368.

Willis, S., McCullough, J., and McDermott, S. (2001). The interpretation of paint evidence (ch. 12). In: *Forensic Examination of Glass and Paint, Analysis and Interpretation* (ed. B. Caddy), 273–287. Taylor & Francis, CRC Press: Boca Raton, FL.

Wright, D.M., Bradley, M.J., and Hobbs Mehltretter, A. (2011). Analysis and discrimination of architectural paint samples via a population study. *Forensic Science International* 209: 86–95.

Wright, D.M., Bradley, M.J., and Hobbs Mehltretter, A. (2013). Analysis and discrimination of single-layer white architectural paint samples. *Journal of Forensic Sciences* 58: 358–364.

Zadora, G., Martyna, A., Ramos, D., and Aitken, C. (2014). *Statistical Analysis in Forensic Science – Evidential Value of Multivariate Physicochemical Data*. Chichester: Wiley.

Index

Handbook of Trace Evidence Analysis, First Edition. Edited by Vincent J. Desiderio, Chris E. Taylor, and Niamh Nic Daéid.
© 2021 John Wiley & Sons Ltd. Published 2021 by John Wiley & Sons Ltd.